ALL · IN · ONE

CISM®

Certified Information Security Manager

EXAM GUIDE

Second Edition

ALL ■ IN ■ ONE

CISM®

Certified Information Security Manager

EXAM GUIDE

Second Edition

Peter H. Gregory

New York   Chicago   San Francisco
Athens   London   Madrid   Mexico City
Milan   New Delhi   Singapore   Sydney   Toronto

Library of Congress Control Number: 2022944276

ISBN   978-1-264-26831-3
MHID   1-264-26831-9

Sponsoring Editor	**Technical Editor**	**Production Supervisor**
Wendy Rinaldi	Jay Burke	Thomas Somers
Editorial Supervisor	**Copy Editor**	**Composition**
Patty Mon	Lisa Theobald	KnowledgeWorks Global Ltd.
Project Manager	**Proofreaders**	**Illustration**
Nitesh Sharma,	Lisa McCoy, Richard Camp	KnowledgeWorks Global Ltd.
KnowledgeWorks Global Ltd.	**Indexer**	**Art Director, Cover**
Acquisitions Coordinator	Ted Laux	Jeff Weeks
Caitlin Cromley-Linn		

To Rebekah, the love of my life.

ABOUT THE AUTHOR

Peter H. Gregory, CISM, CISA, CRISC, CDPSE, CISSP, CIPM, DRCE, CCSK, is a 30-year career technologist and a security leader in a regional telecommunications company. He has been developing and managing information security management programs since 2002 and has been leading the development and testing of secure IT environments since 1990. Peter has also spent many years as a software engineer and architect, systems engineer, network engineer, and security engineer.

Peter is the author of more than 50 books about information security and technology, including *Solaris Security, CIPM Certified Information Privacy Manager All-in-One Exam Guide,* and *CISA Certified Information Systems Auditor All-in-One Exam Guide.* He has spoken at numerous industry conferences, including RSA, Interop, (ISC)² Security Congress, ISACA CACS, SecureWorld Expo, West Coast Security Forum, IP3, Source Conference, Society for Information Management, the Washington Technology Industry Association, and InfraGard. Interviews of Peter appear in *SC Magazine, U.S. News & World Report, CNET News, SearchSecurity, Information Security Magazine, CIO, The Seattle Times,* and *Forbes.*

Peter serves on advisory boards for cybersecurity education programs at the University of Washington and the University of South Florida. He was the lead instructor for nine years in the University of Washington certificate program in applied cybersecurity, a former board member of the Washington State chapter of InfraGard, and a founding member of the Pacific CISO Forum. He is a 2008 graduate of the FBI Citizens' Academy and a member of the FBI Citizens' Academy Alumni Association. Peter is an executive member of the CyberEdBoard and the Forbes Technology Council.

Peter resides with his family in Washington state and can be found online at www.peterhgregory.com.

About the Technical Editor

Jay Burke, CISSP, CISM, RBLP-T, is a highly accomplished information security professional with more than 20 years of operational and executive experience across a variety of industries.

Jay has worked with customers of different sizes and types to build, enhance, and manage best-in-class cybersecurity programs. As an executive-level security professional, he has led detailed maturity assessments and facilitated executive workshops to assist CISOs in maturing their cybersecurity programs. His practical experience includes engagements addressing strategic consulting, project management, regulatory compliance (Sarbanes–Oxley, PCI, NERC CIP, HIPAA, SOC 1 and SOC 2), and cybersecurity program development leveraging ISO 27001/2, NIST 800-53, Cloud Security Alliance CCM, Shared Assessments SIG, and Unified Compliance Framework.

Jay currently serves as the strategic service manager for Tenable, helping customers gain visibility of cyber risk by leveraging the Tenable Cyber Exposure platform while also providing the executive suite and board of directors with insight to focus on the issues that matter most and make better strategic decisions. Additionally, Jay is a partner at Sage Advisory, LLC, which helps young professionals find their voice in the workplace and supports the SMB market in the cybersecurity space.

Disclaimer

None of the information in this book reflects the security posture or practices of any current or former employer or client.

CONTENTS AT A GLANCE

Part I   Information Security Governance

Chapter 1   Enterprise Governance 3

Chapter 2   Information Security Strategy 37

Part II   Information Security Risk Management

Chapter 3   Information Security Risk Assessment 101

Chapter 4   Information Security Risk Response 165

Part III   Information Security Risk Management

Chapter 5   Information Security Program Development 191

Chapter 6   Information Security Program Management 241

Part IV   Incident Management

Chapter 7   Incident Management Readiness 405

Chapter 8   Incident Management Operations 499

Part V   Appendix and Glossary

Appendix   About the Online Content 531

               Glossary 535

               Index 577

CONTENTS

Acknowledgments   xix
Introduction   xxi

Part I   Information Security Governance

Chapter 1   Enterprise Governance   3

Introduction to Information Security Governance   4
   Reason for Security Governance   6
   Security Governance Activities and Results   7
   Business Alignment   8
Organizational Culture   9
   Acceptable Use Policy   10
   Ethics   10
Legal, Regulatory, and Contractual Requirements   11
Organizational Structure, Roles, and Responsibilities   12
   Organizational Roles   13
   Board of Directors   16
   Executive Management   18
   Security Steering Committee   19
   Business Process and Business Asset Owners   20
   Custodial Responsibilities   21
   Chief Information Security Officer   21
   Chief Privacy Officer   23
   Chief Compliance Officer   23
   Software Development   23
   Data Management   24
   Network Management   24
   Systems Management   25
   IT Operations   25
   Governance, Risk, and Compliance   26
   Business Resilience   27
   Security Operations   27
   Security Audit   28
   Service Desk   28
   Quality Assurance   28
   Other Roles   28
   General Staff   29
   Monitoring Responsibilities   29

Chapter Review   30
    Notes   31
    Questions   32
    Answers   34

Chapter 2   Information Security Strategy   37
    Information Security Strategy Development   38
        Strategy Objectives   38
        Strategy Participants   39
        Strategy Resources   40
        Strategy Development   55
        Strategy Constraints   68
    Information Governance Frameworks and Standards   72
        Business Model for Information Security   73
        The Zachman Framework   81
        The Open Group Architecture Framework   83
        ISO/IEC 27001   83
        NIST Cybersecurity Framework   85
        NIST Risk Management Framework   87
    Strategic Planning   88
        Roadmap Development   89
        Developing a Business Case   89
    Chapter Review   91
        Notes   93
        Questions   94
        Answers   97

Part II   Information Security Risk Management

Chapter 3   Information Security Risk Assessment   101
    Emerging Risk and Threat Landscape   102
        The Importance of Risk Management   102
        Outcomes of Risk Management   103
        Risk Objectives   103
        Risk Management Technologies   104
        Implementing a Risk Management Program   105
        The Risk Management Life Cycle   115
    Vulnerability and Control Deficiency Analysis   127
    Risk Assessment and Analysis   129
        Threat Identification   129
        Risk Identification   136
        Risk Likelihood and Impact   137
        Risk Analysis Techniques and Considerations   139
        Risk Management and Business Continuity Planning   145
        The Risk Register   146
        Integration of Risk Management into Other Processes   150

Chapter Review 157
  Notes 159
  Questions 160
  Answers 162

Chapter 4 Information Security Risk Response 165

Risk Treatment / Risk Response Options 166
  Risk Mitigation 167
  Risk Transfer 168
  Risk Avoidance 169
  Risk Acceptance 170
  Evaluating Risk Response Options 171
  Costs and Benefits 172
  Residual Risk 173
  Iterative Risk Treatment 173
  Risk Appetite, Capacity, and Tolerance 174
  Legal and Regulatory Considerations 175
  The Risk Register 177
Risk and Control Ownership 178
  Risk Ownership 178
  Control Ownership 179
Risk Monitoring and Reporting 180
  Key Risk Indicators 180
  Training and Awareness 181
  Risk Documentation 182
Chapter Review 182
  Notes 183
  Questions 184
  Answers 186

Part III Information Security Risk Management

Chapter 5 Information Security Program Development 191

Information Security Program Resources 192
  Trends 192
  Outcomes 193
  Charter 194
  Scope 195
  Information Security Processes 195
  Information Security Technologies 196
Information Asset Identification and Classification 199
  Asset Identification and Valuation 199
  Asset Classification 202
  Asset Valuation 209

Industry Standards and Frameworks for Information Security 210
    Control Frameworks 210
    Information Security Management Frameworks 218
    Information Security Architecture 218
Information Security Policies, Procedures, and Guidelines 220
    Policy Development 220
    Standards 223
    Guidelines 223
    Requirements 223
    Processes and Procedures 224
Information Security Program Metrics 225
    Types of Metrics 227
    Audiences 231
    The Security Balanced Scorecard 232
Chapter Review 233
    Notes 236
    Questions 237
    Answers 239

Chapter 6   **Information Security Program Management** 241

Information Security Control Design and Selection 242
    Control Classification 242
    Control Objectives 245
    General Computing Controls 246
    Controls: Build Versus Buy 247
    Control Frameworks 248
Information Security Control Implementation and Integrations ... 272
    Controls Development 272
    Control Implementation 275
    Security and Control Operations 275
Information Security Control Testing and Evaluation 321
    Control Monitoring 322
    Control Reviews and Audits 322
Information Security Awareness and Training 339
    Security Awareness Training Objectives 339
    Creating or Selecting Content
      for Security Awareness Training 340
    Security Awareness Training Audiences 340
    Awareness Training Communications 343
Management of External Services 344
    Benefits of Outsourcing 345
    Risks of Outsourcing 345
    Identifying Third Parties 348
    Cloud Service Providers 350
    TPRM Life Cycle 351

Risk Tiering and Vendor Classification 354
Assessing Third Parties 356
Proactive Issue Remediation 360
Responsive Issue Remediation 362
Security Incidents 362
Information Security Program Communications and Reporting . . . 363
Security Operations 363
Risk Management 363
Internal Partnerships 364
External Partnerships 370
Compliance Management 373
Security Awareness Training 375
Technical Architecture 376
Personnel Management 376
Project and Program Management 382
Budget 382
IT Service Management 383
Service Desk 384
Incident Management 384
Problem Management 385
Change Management 386
Configuration Management 388
Release Management 389
Service-Level Management 391
Financial Management 391
Capacity Management 392
Service Continuity Management 393
Availability Management 393
Asset Management 394
Continuous Improvement 394
Chapter Review 394
Notes 396
Questions 397
Answers 400

Part IV Incident Management

Chapter 7 Incident Management Readiness 405
Incident Response Plan 406
Security Incident Response Overview 408
Incident Response Plan Development 411
Business Impact Analysis 417
Inventory of Key Processes and Systems 417
Statements of Impact 419
Criticality Analysis 420
Determine Maximum Tolerable Downtime 422

Determine Maximum Tolerable Outage 422
Establish Key Recovery Targets 423
Business Continuity Plan (BCP) 426
Business Continuity Planning 427
Disaster Recovery Plan (DRP) 455
Disaster Response Teams' Roles and Responsibilities 456
Recovery Objectives 457
Incident Classification/Categorization 473
Incident Management Training, Testing, and Evaluation 475
Security Incident Response Training 475
Business Continuity and Disaster Response Training 476
Testing Security Incident Response Plans 477
Testing Business Continuity and Disaster Recovery Plans . . . 478
Evaluating Business Continuity Planning 484
Evaluating Disaster Recovery Planning 488
Evaluating Security Incident Response 492
Chapter Review 493
Notes 494
Questions 494
Answers 497

Chapter 8   Incident Management Operations 499
Incident Management Tools and Techniques 502
Incident Response Roles and Responsibilities 502
Incident Response Tools and Techniques 503
Incident Investigation and Evaluation 507
Incident Detection 507
Incident Initiation 509
Incident Analysis 509
Incident Containment Methods 513
Incident Response Communications 515
Crisis Management and Communications 515
Communications in the Incident Response Plan 516
Incident Response Metrics and Reporting 517
Incident Eradication, and Recovery 519
Incident Eradication 520
Incident Recovery 520
Incident Remediation 521
Post-incident Review Practices 522
Closure 522
Post-incident Review 522
Chapter Review 523
Notes 524
Questions 524
Answers 527

Part V   Appendix and Glossary

Appendix   About the Online Content   531

System Requirements   531
Your Total Seminars Training Hub Account   531
    Privacy Notice   531
Single User License Terms and Conditions   531
TotalTester Online   533
Technical Support   533

Glossary   535

Index   577

Figure Credits

Figure 2-1 Courtesy Xhienne: SWOT pt.svg, CC BY-SA 2.5, https://commons.wikimedia.org/w/index.php?curid=2838770.

Figure 2-2 Adapted from the Business Model for Information Security, ISACA.

Figure 2-3 Adapted from the University of Southern California Marshall School of Business Institute for Critical Information Infrastructure Protection, USA.

Figure 2-5 Courtesy The Open Group.

Figure 2-7 Courtesy *High Tech Security Solutions* magazine.

Figure 3-1 Source: National Institute for Standards and Technology.

Figure 6-8 Courtesy Bluefoxicy at en.wikipedia.org.

Figure 7-4 Source: NASA.

Figure 7-6 Courtesy Gustavo Basso.

Figure 7-7 Courtesy John Crowley at en.wikipedia.org.

ACKNOWLEDGMENTS

I am immensely grateful to Wendy Rinaldi for affirming the need to have this book published on a tighter than usual timeline. My readers, including current and future information security managers, deserve nothing less.

Heartfelt thanks to Wendy Rinaldi and Caitlin Cromley-Linn for proficiently managing and coordinating this project, facilitating rapid turnaround, and equipping us with the information and guidance we needed to produce the manuscript.

Many thanks to Patty Mon, Nitesh Sharma, and Thomas Somers for managing the editorial and production ends of the project, and to Lisa Theobald for copy editing the book and further improving readability. I appreciate KnowledgeWorks Global Ltd. for expertly laying out the final manuscript pages. Also, thanks to Rick Camp and Lisa McCoy for expert proofreading and Ted Laux for indexing. Like stage performers, they make hard work look easy, and I appreciate their skills.

I would like to thank my former consulting colleague, Jay Burke, who took on the task of tech reviewing the entire manuscript. Jay carefully and thoughtfully scrutinized the entire draft manuscript and made scores of valuable suggestions that have improved the book's quality and value for readers. Thanks also to two BCDR colleagues: Charlein Barni, for reviewing Chapter 7, and Michael Kenney, who confirmed some concepts. Finally, thanks to Ben Everett, a reader who informed me of a couple of typos or ambiguities in the first edition.

Many thanks to my literary agent, Carole Jelen, for her diligent assistance during this and other projects. Sincere thanks to Rebecca Steele, my business manager and publicist, for her long-term vision and keeping me on track.

This is the 52nd book manuscript I have written since I started writing in 1998. I'm grateful for those who initially brought me into the publishing business, particularly Liz Suto (author of *Informix Online Performance Tuning,* and my first official gig as a tech editor) and Greg Doench (executive editor at Prentice-Hall Publishers), and so many more along the way, including Melody Layne, Mark Taub, Rev Mengle, Sebastian Nokes, Greg Croy, Katie Feltman, Katie Mohr, Lindsey Lefevere, Josh Freel, Amy Fandrei, Amy Gray, Tim Green, Steve Helba, and many others. Thank you, all of you, for the splendid opportunity that has enabled me to help so many readers.

I have difficulty putting into words my gratitude for my wife and love of my life, Rebekah, for tolerating my frequent absences (in the home office) while I developed the manuscript. This project could not have been completed without her loyal and unfailing support and encouragement.

INTRODUCTION

The dizzying pace of information systems innovation has made vast expanses of information available to organizations and the public. Design flaws and technical vulnerabilities often bring unintended consequences, usually in the form of information theft and disclosure. Attacks from nation-states and cybercriminal organizations are increasing dramatically. The result is a patchwork of laws, regulations, and standards such as Sarbanes–Oxley, GDPR, CCPA, Gramm–Leach-Bliley, HIPAA, PCI DSS, PIPEDA, NERC CIP, CMMC, and scores of U.S. state laws requiring public disclosure of security breaches involving private information. The relatively new Cybersecurity & Infrastructure Security Agency (CISA) has become a prominent voice in the United States, and executive orders require organizations to improve defenses and disclose breaches. As a result of these laws and regulatory agencies, organizations are required or incentivized to build or improve their information security programs to avoid security breaches, penalties, sanctions, lawsuits, and embarrassing news headlines.

These developments continue to drive demand for information security professionals and information security leaders. These highly sought-after professionals play a crucial role in developing better information security programs that reduce risk and improve confidence in effective systems and data protection.

The Certified Information Security Manager (CISM) certification, established in 2002, has become the leading certification for information security management. Demand for the CISM certification has grown so much that the once-per-year certification exam was changed to twice per year in 2005 and is now offered continually. In 2005, the CISM certification was accredited by the American National Standards Institute (ANSI) under the international standard ISO/IEC 17024:2012 and is also one of the few certifications formally approved by the U.S. Department of Defense in its Information Assurance Technical category (DoD 8570.01-M). In 2018 and again in 2020, CISM was awarded the Best Professional Certification by SC Media. There are now more than 50,000 professionals with the certification, and the worldwide average salary for CISM holders is more than US$149,000.

Founded in 1969 as the Electronic Data Processing Auditors Association (EDPAA), ISACA is a solid and lasting professional organization. Its first certification, Certified Information Systems Auditor (CISA), was established in 1978.

Purpose of This Book

Let's get the obvious out of the way: This is a comprehensive study guide for the security management professional who needs a serious reference for individual or group-led study for the Certified Information Security Manager (CISM) certification. The content in this book contains the technical information that CISM candidates are required to know.

This book is one source of information to help you prepare for the CISM exam, but it should not be thought of as the ultimate collection of all the knowledge and experience that ISACA expects qualified CISM candidates to possess. No single publication covers all of this information.

This book is also a reference for aspiring and practicing IT security managers, security leaders, and CISOs. The content required to pass the CISM exam is the same content that practicing security managers must be familiar with in their day-to-day work. This book is a definitive CISM exam study guide as well as a desk reference for those who have already earned their CISM certification.

This book is also invaluable for information security professionals who are not in leadership positions today. You will gain considerable insight into today's information security management challenges. This book is also helpful for IT and business management professionals working with information security leaders who need to understand what they are doing and why.

This is an excellent guide for anyone exploring a security management career. The study chapters explain the relevant technologies, techniques, and processes used to manage a modern information security program. This is useful if you are wondering what the security management profession is all about.

How to Use This Book

This book covers everything you'll need to know for ISACA's CISM certification examination. Each chapter covers specific objectives and details for the exam, as ISACA defines in its job practice areas. The chapters and their sections correspond precisely to the CISM job practice that ISACA updates from time to time, most recently in mid-2022.

Each chapter has several components designed to effectively communicate the information you'll need for the exam.

- The **topics** covered in each chapter are listed in the first section to help map out your study.

- **Tips** in each chapter offer great information about how the concepts you're reading about apply in a place I like to call "the real world." Often, they may give you more information on a topic covered in the text.

- **Exam Tips** are included to highlight areas you need to focus on for the exam. They won't give you any exam answers, but they help you know about important topics you may see on the test.

- **Notes** may be included in a chapter as well. These bits of information are relevant to the discussion and point out extra information.

- Fifteen **practice questions** at the end of each chapter are designed to enable you to attempt some exam questions on the topics covered in the domain.

- Access to an **online question bank** is available from TotalTester Online, customizable practice exam software with 300 practice exam questions.

- A **glossary** contains about 650 terms used in the information security management profession.

About This Second Edition

ISACA has historically recalibrated the contents of its certifications every five years. I learned that ISACA would update the CISM job practice (the basis for the exam and the requirements to earn the certification) in early 2022, effective in mid-2022. To ensure that this information is up to date, Wendy Rinaldi and I developed a plan for the second edition as quickly as possible; this book is the result of that effort.

The new CISM job practice information was made available in March 2022. We began work at that time to update the second edition manuscript. This has been updated to reflect all of the changes in the CISM job practice and changes in information security and information technology since the first edition was published.

Information Security vs. Cybersecurity

In our profession, the term "information security" is giving way to "cybersecurity." Both terms are used in this book, and generally they can be considered equal in meaning. The fact that the certification, Certified *Information Security* Manager, contains those core words means that the phrase "information security" isn't quite gone yet. Indeed, ISACA will eventually have to grapple with the brand recognition of CISM and deal with the possibility that this moniker may be seen as antiquated because of those two words. Will CISM someday be known as CCM?

Changes to the CISM Job Practice

For the 2022 CISM job practice, ISACA reformatted how the practice areas are described. Previously, each job practice had a set of Knowledge Statements and Task Statements. In the 2022 model, each job practice consists of two major categories with three to six subtopic areas each. This is followed by 37 Supporting Tasks for CISM that are not specifically associated with the four domains. Table 1 illustrates each previous and current CISM job practice and its corresponding chapters in this book, along with the structure of the new job practice and coverage in this book.

As is typical for each new job practice and revision of this *CISM Certified Information Security Manager All-in-One Exam Guide,* I performed a gap analysis to understand what subject matter was added to the new job practice and what was eliminated. My conclusion: ISACA made no significant additions or changes to the CISM 2022 job practice besides numerous structural changes and changes in the weighting between domains.

Several topics are new or expanded from the first edition, including the following:

- The distinction between control frameworks, program management frameworks, risk management frameworks, and architecture frameworks (with examples of each)
- Mention and discussion of a published information security framework that is older than most living people in the world
- New challenges in obtaining cyber-insurance policies
- Bow-tie risk analysis

CISM Certified Information Security Manager All-in-One Exam Guide

xxiv

2016 CISM Job Practice			2022 CISM Job Practice			All-in-One Coverage
1. Information Security Governance	24%		1. Information Security Governance	17%		
			A. Enterprise Governance			Chapter 1
			B. Information Security Strategy			Chapter 2
2. Information Risk Management	30%		2. Information Security Risk Management	20%		
			A. Information Security Risk Assessment			Chapter 3
			B. Information Security Risk Response			Chapter 4
3. Information Security Program Development and Management	27%		3. Information Security Program	33%		
			A. Information Security Program Development			Chapter 5
			B. Information Security Program Management			Chapter 6
4. Information Security Incident Management	19%		4. Incident Management	30%		
			A. Incident Management Readiness			Chapter 7
			B. Incident Management Operations			Chapter 8

Table 1 Previous and Current CISM Job Practices and Corresponding Chapters

- Control architecture, implementation, and operation
- Controlled unclassified information (CUI)
- Crisis communications and crisis management
- Crosswalks
- Cybersecurity maturity model certification (CMMC)
- Data debt
- Data governance
- Distributed workforce
- Endpoint detection and response (EDR)
- European ETSI standards

- Extended detection and response (XDR)
- Foreign Corrupt Practices Act (FCPA)
- Groupthink
- Information governance
- Integrated risk management (IRM)
- MITRE ATT&CK framework
- Network traffic analysis (NTA)
- NIST SP 800-171 and SP 800-172
- Passwordless authentication
- Personnel classification
- Reference architectures
- Functional and nonfunctional requirements
- Risk and control ownership
- Security orchestration, automation, and response (SOAR)
- Software as a service (SaaS) disaster recovery
- SaaS security incident response
- Technical debt
- Threat intelligence platform (TIP)
- Three lines of defense
- Workforce transformation, remote work, and hybrid work models
- Zero-trust network architecture
- Addition of about 70 new entries and several cross-references to the glossary (and a few deprecated entries such as SAS-70, SET, and S-HTTP removed)

By the time we completed this book, even more new developments, technologies, techniques, and breaches provided additional insight and the promise of still more changes. Like the surface of Saturn's moon, Io, our profession is ever-changing. The technology boneyard is filled with vendors, products, protocols, techniques, and methodologies that once held great promise, later replaced with better things. This underscores the need for security leaders (and IT, audit, and risk professionals) to stay current by reading up on current events, new technologies, and techniques. Some last-minute changes that may not be fully reflected in the manuscript include the following:

- ISO/IEC 27001:2013 was replaced by ISO/IEC 27001:2022 in early 2022.
- ISO/IEC 27002:2013 is scheduled to be replaced by ISO/IEC 27002:2022 in late 2022.
- A new U.S. national law on privacy may have been enacted.
- Additional U.S. presidential Executive Orders on the topic of cybersecurity may have been issued.

Becoming a CISM Professional

To become a CISM professional, you must pay the exam fee, pass the exam, prove that you have the necessary education and experience, and agree to uphold ethics and standards. To keep your CISM certification, you must take at least 20 continuing education hours each year (120 hours in three years) and pay annual maintenance fees. This life cycle is depicted in Figure 1.

The following list outlines the primary requirements for becoming certified:

- **Experience** A CISM candidate must submit verifiable evidence of at least five years of professional work experience in information security management. Experience must be verified and gained within the ten years preceding the application date for certification or within five years from passing the exam. Experience waivers are available for as many as two years.

- **Ethics** . Candidates must commit to adhering to ISACA's Code of Professional Ethics, which guides the personal and professional conduct of those certified.

- **Exam** Candidates must receive a passing score on the CISM exam. A passing score is valid for up to five years, after which the passing score is void. A CISM candidate who passes the exam has a maximum of five years to apply for CISM certification; candidates who pass the exam but fail to act after five years must retake the exam if they want to become CISM certified.

- **Education** Those who are certified must adhere to the CISM Continuing Professional Education Policy, which requires a minimum of 20 continuing professional education (CPE) hours each year, with a total requirement of 120 CPEs over each three-year certification period.

- **Application** After successfully passing the exam, meeting the experience requirements, and reading through the Code of Professional Ethics and Standards, a candidate is ready to apply for certification. An application must be received within five years of passing the exam.

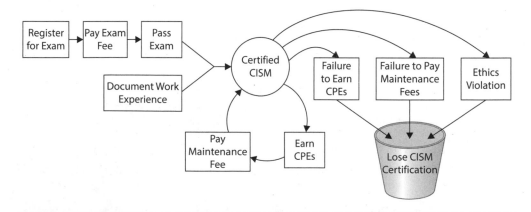

Figure 1 The CISM certification life cycle (Source: Peter Gregory)

Experience Requirements

To qualify for CISM certification, you must have completed the equivalent of five years of total work experience in information security management. Additional details on the minimum certification requirements, substitution options, and various examples are discussed next.

 NOTE Although it is not recommended, a CISM candidate can take the exam before completing any work experience directly related to information security management. As long as the candidate passes the exam and the work experience requirements are filled within five years of the exam date and ten years from the application for certification, the candidate is eligible for certification.

Direct Work Experience

You must have a minimum of five years of work experience in the field of information security management. This is equivalent to roughly 10,000 actual work hours, which must be related to three or more of the CISM job practice areas, as follows:

- **Information security governance**   Establish and/or maintain an information security governance framework and supporting processes to ensure that the information security strategy is aligned with organizational goals and objectives.
- **Information security risk management**   Manage information risk to an acceptable level based on risk appetite to meet organizational goals and objectives.
- **Information security program**   Develop and maintain an information security program that identifies, manages, and protects the organization's assets while aligning to information security strategy and business goals, thereby supporting an effective security posture.
- **Incident management**   Plan, establish, and manage the capability to detect, investigate, respond to, and recover from information security and disaster incidents to minimize business impact.

All work experience must be completed within the ten-year period before completing the certification application or within five years from the date of initially passing the CISM exam. You will need to complete a separate Verification of Work Experience form for each segment of experience.

Substitution of Experience

Up to two years of direct work experience can be substituted with the following to meet the five-year experience requirement. Only one waiver is permitted.

Two Years

- Certified Information Systems Auditor (CISA) in good standing
- Certified Information Systems Security Professional (CISSP) in good standing

- MBA or master's degree in information security or a related field; transcripts or a letter confirming degree status must be sent from the university attended to obtain the experience waiver

One Year

- Bachelor's degree in information security or a related field
- Skill-based or general security certification
- One full year of information systems management experience

Here is an example of a CISM candidate whose experience and education are considered for CISM certification: A candidate graduated in 2002 with a bachelor's degree in computer science. They spent five years working for a software company managing IT, and in January 2015, they began managing information security. In January 2017, they took some time off work for personal reasons. In 2019, they earned their Security+ certification and rejoined the workforce in December 2019, working as a risk manager for a public company in its enterprise risk management department. The candidate passed the CISM exam in June 2022 and applied for CISM certification in September 2022. Do they have all of the experience required? What evidence will they need to submit?

- **Skills-based certification**   The candidate obtained their Security+ certification, which equates to a one-year experience substitution.
- **Two years of direct experience**   They can count their two full years of information security management experience in 2015 and 2016.
- **One-year substitution**   They cannot take into account one year of IT management experience completed between January 2002 to January 2007, because it was not completed within ten years of their application.
- **One-year direct experience**   The candidate would want to utilize their new risk manager experience for work experience.

The candidate would need to send the following with their application to prove the experience requirements are met:

- Verification of Work Experience forms filled out and signed by their supervisors (or any superior) at the software company and the public company, verifying both the security management and non–security management work conducted
- Transcripts or letters confirming degree status sent from the university

---

 TIP   Read the CISM certification qualifications on the ISACA web site. ISACA changes the qualification rules from time to time, and I want you to have the most up-to-date information available.

ISACA Code of Professional Ethics

Becoming a CISM professional means adhering to the ISACA Code of Professional Ethics, a formal document outlining what you will do to ensure the utmost integrity in a way that best supports and represents the profession. Specifically, the ISACA code of ethics requires ISACA members and certification holders to do the following:

- Support the implementation of, and encourage compliance with, appropriate standards and procedures for the effective governance and management of enterprise information systems and technology, including audit, control, security, and risk management.

- Perform their duties with objectivity, due diligence, and professional care, in accordance with professional standards.

- Serve in the interest of stakeholders in a lawful manner, while maintaining high standards of conduct and character and not discrediting their profession or the association.

- Maintain the privacy and confidentiality of information obtained in the course of their activities unless disclosure is required by legal authority. Such information shall not be used for personal benefit or released to inappropriate parties.

- Maintain competency in their respective fields and agree to undertake only those activities they can reasonably expect to complete with the necessary skills, knowledge, and competence.

- Inform appropriate parties of the results of work performed, including the disclosure of all significant facts known to them that, if not disclosed, may distort the reporting of the results.

- Support the professional education of stakeholders in enhancing their understanding of the governance and management of enterprise information systems and technology, including audit, control, security, and risk management.

Failure to comply with this Code of Professional Ethics can result in an investigation into a member's or certification holder's conduct and, ultimately, disciplinary measures, including the forfeiture of hard-won certification(s).

You can find the full text and terms of enforcement of the ISACA Code of Ethics at www.isaca.org/ethics.

The Certification Exam

The certification is offered throughout the year in several examination windows. You have several ways to register; however, I highly recommend planning and registering early regardless of your chosen method.

In 2022, as I write, the schedule of exam fees in U.S. dollars is

- CISM application fee: $50
- Regular registration: $575 member/$760 nonmember

As I write this, we're emerging from the global COVID-19 pandemic. During the pandemic, ISACA and other certification bodies adapted and developed remotely proctored exams that permitted test-takers to sit for a certification exam from their residence. I have observed that ISACA has returned to tests administered at testing centers while continuing to offer remotely proctored exams for those who prefer remote testing. I'll discuss both options in this section.

 NOTE Pay close attention to information on ISACA's web site regarding testing logistics and locations.

Once your registration is complete, you will immediately receive an e-mail acknowledging this. Next, you will need to schedule your certification exam. The ISACA web site will direct you to the certification registration page, where you will select a date, time, and (optionally) location to take your exam. When you confirm the date, time, and location for your exam, you will receive a confirmation via e-mail. You will need the confirmation letter to enter the test location—make sure to keep it unmarked and in a safe place until test time.

Onsite Testing Center

When you arrive at the test site, you will be required to sign in, and you may be required to sign an agreement. Also, you will be asked to turn in your smartphone, wallet or purse, and other personal items for safekeeping. The exam proctor will read aloud the rules you must follow while taking the exam. These rules will address matters such as breaks, drinking water, and snacks. While you take the exam, you will be supervised by the proctor, who may monitor you and your fellow test-takers by video surveillance in the test center to ensure that no one can cheat.

Remote Proctored Testing

If you have registered for a remote proctored exam, you must meet all of the technical requirements. ISACA has published the "Remote Proctoring Guide" that includes all of the necessary technical requirements and describes the step-by-step procedures for taking the exam.

A remote proctored exam means you'll be taking the exam on your own computer in your residence or other location. You'll be in live contact with an exam proctor, and your webcam will be turned on throughout the exam so that the proctor can observe while you take the exam to ensure you are not cheating through the use of reference materials (books or online). You will also be required to use your webcam to show the entire room to your proctor, to demonstrate that you do not have reference materials or information anywhere in view.

To be eligible for a remote proctored exam, you must have a supported version of Windows or macOS, a current Google Chrome or other Chromium (such as Brave, SRware Iron) browser, a webcam with at least 640×480 resolution, a microphone, and a stable broadband Internet connection. You must be able to install the PSI Secure Browser and modify firewalls and other administrative tasks on the day of the exam (this requires administrative privileges on the computer you are using, which might be a problem if you are using a company-issued computer).

You'll be required to log in to your My ISACA account when your exam is scheduled. Next, you'll navigate to your certifications, find the exam you have scheduled, and launch the exam. You'll be directed to perform several tasks, including installing the secure browser and closing several other programs on your computer, such as other web browsers and programs such as Adobe Reader, Word, Excel, and any others that could include reference material.

You are not permitted to speak or perform gestures during the exam. In short, you cannot be seen to perform any action that may be an indication of aid by an accomplice.

You'll be required to verify your ID by holding it near your webcam so that the proctor can see it to confirm that you, not someone else, are taking the exam. You will also be required to use your webcam to show the entire room to your proctor.

After completing all steps, the proctor will release the exam and you may begin.

Exam Questions

Each registrant has four hours to take the exam, with 150 multiple-choice questions representing the four job practice areas. Each question has four answer choices; you must select only one best answer. You can skip questions and return to them later, and you can also flag questions you want to review later if time permits. While you are taking your exam, the time remaining will appear on the screen.

When you have completed the exam, you'll be directed to close the exam. At that time, the exam will display your pass or fail status, reminding you that your score and passing status are subject to review. You will be scored for each job practice area and then provided one final score. All scores are scaled. Scores range from 200 to 800; a final score of 450 is required to pass.

Exam questions are derived from a job practice analysis study conducted by ISACA. The selected areas represent tasks performed in a CISM's day-to-day activities and the background knowledge required to develop and manage an information security program. You can find more detailed descriptions of the task and knowledge statements at www.isaca.org/credentialing/cism/cism-exam-content-outline.

Exam Coverage

The CISM exam is quite broad in its scope. It covers four job practice areas, as shown in Table 2.

Domain	CISM Job Practice Area	Percentage of Exam
1	Information security governance	17%
2	Information security risk management	20%
3	Information security program	33%
4	Incident management	30%

Table 2 CISM Exam Practice Areas

Independent committees have been developed to determine the best questions, review exam results, and statistically analyze the results for continuous improvement. Should you come across a horrifically difficult or strange question, do not panic. This question may have been written for another purpose. A few questions on the exam are included for research and analysis purposes and will not be counted against your score. The exam contains no indications in this regard, so do your best to answer every question.

Preparing for the Exam

The CISM certification requires that CISM candidates possess much knowledge and experience. You need to map out a long-term study strategy to pass the exam. The following sections offer some tips to help guide you to, through, and beyond exam day.

Before the Exam

Consider the following list of tips on tasks and resources for exam preparation. They are listed in sequential order.

- **Read the candidate's guide**   For information on the certification exam and requirements for the current year, go to www.isaca.org/credentialing/exam-candidate-guides and select the guide in your language of choice.

- **Register**   If you can, register early for any cost savings and solidify your commitment to moving forward with this professional achievement.

- **Schedule your exam**   Find a location, date, and time, and then commit.

- **Become familiar with the CISM job practice areas**   The job practice areas serve as the basis for the exam and requirements. Beginning with the 2022 exam, the job practice areas have changed. Ensure that your study materials align with the current list at www.isaca.org/credentialing/cism.

- **Download and study the ISACA Glossary**   It's important for you to be familiar with ISACA's vocabulary, which you can download from www.isaca.org/resources/glossary.

- **Know your best learning methods**   Everyone has preferred learning styles, whether self-study, a study group, an instructor-led course, or a boot camp. Try to set up a study program that leverages your strengths.

- **Self-assess**   Run through practice exam questions available for download (see the appendix for more information). ISACA may offer a free online CISM self-assessment.

- **Iterative study**   Depending on your work experience in information security management, I suggest you plan your study program to take at least two months but as long as six months. During this time, periodically take practice exams and note your areas of strength and weakness. Once you have identified your weak areas, focus on those areas weekly by rereading the related sections in this book, retaking practice exams, and noting your progress.

- **Avoid cramming** We've all seen the books on the shelves with titles that involve last-minute cramming. The Internet reveals various web sites that teach individuals how to cram for exams. Research sites claim that exam cramming can lead to susceptibility to colds and flu, sleep disruptions, overeating, and digestive problems. One thing is certain: many people find that good, steady study habits result in less stress and greater clarity and focus during the exam. Because of the complexity of this exam, I highly recommend the long-term, steady-study option. Study the job practice areas thoroughly. There are many study options. If time permits, investigate the many resources available to you.

- **Find a study group** Many ISACA chapters and other organizations have formed specific study groups or offer less expensive exam review courses. Contact your local chapter to see whether these options are available to you. In addition, be sure to keep your eye on the ISACA web site. And use your local network to find out whether there are other local study groups and helpful resources.

- **Confirmation letter** Recheck your confirmation letter. Do not write on it or lose it. Put it in a safe place and note on your calendar when you will need to arrive at the site. Confirm that the location is the one you selected and is nearby.

- **Logistics check** Check the candidate guide and your confirmation letter for the exact time you are required to report to the test site (or log in from home if you registered for a remote proctored exam). A few days before the exam, check the site—become familiar with the location and tricks to getting there. If you are taking public transportation, be sure to look at the schedule for the day of the exam: if your CISM exam is on a Saturday, public transportation schedules may differ from weekday schedules. If you are driving, know the route and where to park your vehicle.

- **Pack** The night before, place your confirmation letter and a photo ID in a safe place, ready to go. Your ID must be a current, government-issued photo ID that matches the name on the confirmation letter and must not be handwritten. Examples of acceptable forms of ID are passports, driver's licenses, state IDs, green cards, and national IDs. Leave behind food, drinks, laptops, cell phones, and other electronic devices, because they are not permitted at the test site. For information on what can and cannot be brought to the exam site, see the CISM exam candidate guide at www.isaca.org/credentialing/cism.

- **Notification decision** Decide whether you want your test results e-mailed to you. You will have the opportunity to consent to e-mail notification of the exam results. If you are fully paid (zero balance on exam fee) and have agreed to the e-mail notification, you should receive a one-time e-mail approximately eight weeks from the exam date with the results.

- **Sleep** Make sure you get a good night's sleep before the exam. Research suggests that you avoid caffeine at least four hours before bedtime. Keep a notepad and pen next to the bed to capture late-night thoughts that might keep you awake, eliminate as much noise and light as possible, and keep your room a suitable temperature for sleeping. In the morning, rise early so as not to rush and subject yourself to additional stress.

Day of the Exam

On the day of the exam, follow these tips:

- **Arrive early**   Check the Bulletin of Information and your confirmation letter for the exact time you are required to report to the test site. The confirmation letter and the candidate guide explain that you must be at the test site *no later* than approximately 30 minutes *before* testing time. The examiner will begin reading the exam instructions at this time, and any latecomers will be disqualified from taking the test and will *not* receive a refund of fees.

- **Observe test center rules**   There may be rules about taking breaks. This will be discussed by the examiner, along with exam instructions. If you need something during the exam and are unsure about the rules, be sure to ask first. For information on conduct during the exam, see the ISACA Exam Candidate Information Guide at www.isaca.org/credentialing/exam-candidate-guides.

- **Answer all exam questions**   Read questions carefully, but do not try to overanalyze. Remember to select the *best* solution based upon the CISM Job Practice and ISACA's vocabulary. There may be several reasonable answers, but one is *better* than the others. If you aren't sure about an answer, mark the question, so that after working through all the questions, you can return to any marked questions (and others) to read them and consider them more carefully. Above all, don't try to overanalyze questions, and do trust your instincts. Do not try to rush through the exam; there is plenty of time to take as much as a few minutes for each question. But at the same time, do watch the clock so that you don't find yourself going so slowly that you won't be able to answer every question thoughtfully.

- **Note your exam result**   When you have completed the exam, you should see your pass/fail result. Your results may not be in large, blinking text; you may need to read the fine print to get your preliminary results. If you passed, congratulations! If you did not pass, observe any remarks about your status; you will be able to retake the exam—you'll find information about this on the ISACA web site.

If You Do Not Pass

Don't lose heart if you do not pass your exam on the first attempt. Instead, remember that failure is a stepping stone to success. Thoughtfully take stock and determine your improvement areas. Be honest about areas where you need to learn more. Then reread the chapters or sections and return to this book's practice exams. If you participated in a study group or training, contact your study group coach or class instructor if you believe you may get advice about how to study up on the topics you need to master. Take at least several weeks to study those topics, refresh yourself on other topics, and then give it another go. Success is granted to those who are persistent and determined.

After the Exam

A few weeks from the exam date, you will receive your exam results by e-mail or postal mail. Each job practice area score will be noted in addition to the final score. All scores are scaled. Should you receive a passing score, you will also receive the application for certification.

Those unsuccessful in passing will also be notified. These individuals will want to closely look at the job practice area scores to determine areas for further study. They may retake the exam as often as needed on future exam dates, as long as they have registered and paid the applicable fees. Regardless of pass or fail, exam results will not be disclosed via telephone, fax, or e-mail (except for the consented e-mail notification).

NOTE   You are not permitted to display the CISM moniker until you have completed certification. Passing the exam is *not* sufficient to use the CISM anywhere, including e-mail, résumés, correspondence, or social media.

Applying for CISM Certification

You must submit evidence of a passing score and related work experience to apply for certification. Remember that you have five years to apply for CISM certification after you receive a passing exam score. After this time, you will need to retake the exam before you can apply. In addition, all work experience submitted must have occurred within ten years of your new certification application.

To complete the application process, you need to submit the following information:

- **CISM application**   Note the exam ID number in your exam results letter, list the information security management experience and any experience substitutions, and identify which CISM job practice area (or areas) your experience pertains to.

- **Verification of Work Experience forms**   These must be filled out and signed by your immediate supervisor or a person of higher rank in the organization to verify your work experience noted on the application. You must fill out a complete set of Verification of Work Experience forms for each separate employer.

After you've submitted the application, you will wait approximately eight weeks for processing. Then, if your application is approved, you will receive an e-mail notification, followed by a package in the postal mail containing your letter of certification, certificate, and a copy of the Continuing Professional Education Policy. You can then proudly display your certificate and use the "CISM" designation on your résumé, e-mail, social media profiles, and business cards.

NOTE   You are permitted to use the CISM moniker *only* after receiving your certification letter from ISACA.

Retaining Your CISM Certification

There is more to becoming a CISM professional than passing an exam, submitting an application, and receiving a paper certificate. Becoming a CISM professional is an ongoing and continuous lifestyle. Those with CISM certification agree to abide by the code of ethics, meet ongoing education requirements, and pay annual certification maintenance fees. Let's take a closer look at the education requirements and explain the costs of retaining certification.

Continuing Education

The goal of professional continuing education requirements is to ensure that individuals maintain CISM-related knowledge to help them successfully develop and manage security management programs. To maintain CISM certification, individuals must obtain 120 continuing education hours within three years, with a minimum requirement of 20 hours per year. Each CPE hour accounts for 50 minutes of active participation in educational activities.

What Counts as a Valid CPE Credit?

For training and activities to be utilized for CPEs, they must involve technical or managerial training directly applicable to information security and information security management. The following activities have been approved by the CISM certification committee and can count toward your CPE requirements:

- ISACA professional education activities and meetings
- ISACA members can take *Information Systems Control Journal* CPE quizzes online or participate in monthly webcasts, earning CPEs after passing a quiz
- Non-ISACA professional education activities and meetings
- Self-study courses
- Vendor sales or marketing presentations (10-hour annual limit)
- Teaching, lecturing, or presenting on subjects related to job practice areas
- Publication of articles and books related to the profession
- Exam question development and review for any ISACA certification
- Passing related professional examinations
- Participation in ISACA boards or committees (20-hour annual limit per ISACA certification)
- Contributions to the information security management profession (10-hour annual limit)
- Mentoring (10-hour annual limit)

For more information on acceptable CPE credit, see the Continuing Professional Education Policy at www.isaca.org/credentialing/how-to-earn-cpe/#cpe-policy.

Tracking and Submitting CPEs

Not only are you required to submit a CPE tracking form for the annual renewal process, but you also should keep detailed records for each activity. Records associated with each activity should include the following:

- Name of attendee
- Name of sponsoring organization
- Activity title
- Activity description
- Activity date
- Number of CPE hours awarded

It is best to track all CPE information in a single file or worksheet. ISACA has developed a tracking form for your use in the Continuing Professional Education Policy. To make it easy on yourself, consider keeping all related records such as receipts, brochures, and certificates in the same place. Documentation should be retained throughout the three-year certification period and for at least one additional year afterward. Evidence retention is essential, as you may someday be audited. If this happens, you will be required to submit all paperwork. So why not be prepared?

For new CISMs, the annual and three-year certification period begins on January 1 of the year following certification. You are not required to report CPE hours for the first partial year after your certification; however, the hours earned from the time of certification to December 31 can be utilized in the first certification reporting period the following year. Therefore, should you get certified in January, you will have until the following January to accumulate CPEs. You will not have to report them until you report the totals for the following year, in October or November. This is known as the *renewal period*. You will receive an e-mail directing you to the web site to enter CPEs earned over the year. Alternatively, the renewal will be mailed to you, and then CPEs can be recorded on the hard-copy invoice and sent with your maintenance fee payment. CPEs and maintenance fees must be received by January 15 to retain certification.

Notification of compliance from the certification department is sent after all the information has been received and processed. If ISACA has questions about your submitted information, you will be contacted directly.

Sample CPE Records

Table 3 contains an example of CPE records.

Name   John Jacob

Certification Number   67895787

Certification Period   1/1/2023 to 12/31/2023

Activity Title/Sponsor	Activity Description	Date	CPE Hours	Support Docs Included?
ISACA presentation/lunch	PCI compliance	2/12/2023	1	Yes (receipt)
ISACA presentation/lunch	Security in SDLC	3/12/2023	1	Yes (receipt)
Regional Conference, RIMS	Compliance, risk	1/15–17/2023	6	Yes (CPE receipt)
BrightFly webinar	Governance, risk, & compliance	2/16/2023	3	Yes (confirmation e-mail)
ISACA board meeting	Chapter board meeting	4/9/2023	2	Yes (meeting minutes)
Presented at ISSA meeting	Risk management presentation	6/21/2023	1	Yes (meeting notice)
Published an article in XYZ	Journal article on SOX ITGCs	4/12/2023	4	Yes (article)
Vendor presentation	Learned about GRC tool capability	5/12/2023	2	Yes
Employer-offered training	Change management course	3/26/2023	7	Yes (certificate of course completion)

Table 3   Sample CPE Records

CPE Maintenance Fees

To remain CISM certified, you must pay CPE maintenance fees each year. These annual fees are (as of 2022) $45 for members and $85 for nonmembers. The fees do not include ISACA membership and local chapter dues (neither is required to maintain your CISM certification). More information is available from www.isaca.org/credentialing/cism/maintain-cism-certification.

Revocation of Certification

A CISM-certified individual may have his or her certification revoked for the following reasons:

- Failure to complete the minimum number of CPEs during the period
- Failure to document and provide evidence of CPEs in an audit

- Failure to submit payment for maintenance fees
- Failure to comply with the Code of Professional Ethics, which can result in investigation and ultimately lead to revocation of certification

If you have received a revocation notice, contact the ISACA Certification Department at https://support.isaca.org/ for more information.

Living the CISM Lifestyle

Being a CISM-certified individual involves much more than passing the exam, participating in continuous learning, and paying the annual maintenance fees. There are numerous opportunities to get involved in local, national, and global activities and events to help you grow professionally and meet other risk management professionals.

Find a Local Chapter

ISACA has more than 200 chapters in about 100 countries around the world. Chances are there is a chapter near you. I attended many ISACA chapter meetings and other events in Seattle when I lived there, where engaging speakers spoke on new topics, and I met many like-minded security and audit professionals over the years.

Local chapters rely entirely on volunteers, and there is room for you to help in some way. Some chapters have various programs, events, study groups, and other activities that enrich participants professionally. Most of my ISACA experiences happen in my local chapter.

Attend ISACA Events

ISACA puts on fantastic in-person conferences with world-class keynote speakers, expert presentations, vendor demonstrations and exhibits, a bookstore, and opportunities to meet other security, risk, and audit professionals. I find ISACA conferences enriching to the point of being overwhelming. With so many learning and networking opportunities, I have found myself nearly exhausted at the end of an ISACA conference.

Join the Online Community

ISACA has an online community known as Engage, in which participants can discuss any topic related to security, risk, audit, privacy, and IT management. You can read and participate in online discussions, ask questions, help others with their questions, and make new professional connections. You can join Engage at https://engage.isaca.org/.

Pay It Forward Through Mentorship

If you are at the point in your career where you qualify for and have a reasonable prospect of passing the CISM exam, chances are you have had a mentor or two earlier, and maybe you have one now. As you grow in your professional stature, others will look to you as a potential mentor. Perhaps someone will ask if you would consider mentoring him or her.

The world needs more, and better, information security professionals and leaders. Mentoring is a great way to "pay it forward" by helping others get into the profession and grow professionally. Mentoring will enrich your life as well.

Volunteer

As a nonprofit organization, ISACA relies upon volunteers to enrich its programs and events. There are many ways to help, and one or more of these volunteer opportunities may suit you:

- **Speak at an ISACA event** Whether you make a keynote address or host a session on a specific topic, speaking at an ISACA event is a mountaintop experience. You can share your knowledge and expertise on a particular topic with attendees, but you'll learn some things too.

- **Serve as a chapter board member** Local chapters don't run by themselves; they rely on volunteers—working professionals who want to improve the lot of other professionals in the local community. Board members can serve in various ways, from financial management to membership to events.

- **Start or help a CISM study group** Whether part of a local chapter or a chapter at large, consider starting or helping a group of professionals who want to learn the details of the CISM job practice. I am a proponent of study groups because study group participants make the best students: they take the initiative to take on a big challenge to advance their careers.

- **Write an article** ISACA has online and paper-based publications that feature articles on various subjects, including current developments in security, privacy, risk, and IT management from many perspectives. If you have specialized knowledge on some topic, other ISACA members can benefit from this knowledge if you write about it.

- **Participate in a credential working group** ISACA works hard to ensure that its many certifications remain relevant and up to date. Experts worldwide in many industries give of their time to ensure that ISACA certifications remain the best in the world. ISACA conducts online and in-person working groups to update certification job practices, write certification exam questions, and publish updated study guides and practice exams. I contributed to the first CRISC certification working group in 2013 when ISACA initially developed the CRISC certification exam; I met many like-minded professionals, some of whom I am still in regular and meaningful contact with.

- **Participate in ISACA CommunITy Day** ISACA organizes a global effort of local volunteering to make the world a better, safer place for everyone. Learn about the next CommunITy day at https://engage.isaca.org/communityday/.

- **Write certification exam questions** ISACA needs experienced subject matter experts willing to write new certification exam questions. ISACA has a rigorous, high-quality process for exam questions that includes training. You could even be invited to an in-person exam item writing workshop. You can find out more about how this works at www.isaca.org/credentialing/write-an-exam-question.

Please take a minute to reflect upon the quality and richness of the ISACA organization and its many world-class certifications, publications, and events. These are all fueled by volunteers who made ISACA into what it is today. Only through your contribution of time and expertise will ISACA continue in its excellence for future security, risk, privacy, and IT professionals. And one last thing you can only experience on your own: volunteering helps others and enriches you. Will you consider leaving your mark and making ISACA better than you found it? For more information about these and many other volunteer opportunities, visit www.isaca.org/why-isaca/participate-and-volunteer.

Continue to Grow Professionally

Continual improvement is a mindset and lifestyle built into IT service management and information security, and it's even a formal requirement in ISO/IEC 27001! I suggest you periodically take stock of your career status and aspirations, be honest with yourself, and determine what mountain you will climb next. If needed, find a mentor who can guide you and give you solid advice.

Although this may not immediately make sense to you, know this: helping others, whether through any of the volunteer opportunities listed here, or in other ways, will enrich you personally and professionally. I'm not talking about feathers in your cap or juicy items in your résumé, but rather the growth in character and wisdom that results from helping and serving others, particularly when you initiated the helping and serving.

Professional growth means different things to different people. Whether it's a better job title, more money, a better (or bigger, or smaller) employer, a different team, more responsibility, or more certifications, embarking on long-term career planning will pay dividends. Take control of your career and your career path. This is yours to own and shape as you will.

Summary

Becoming and being a CISM professional is a lifestyle, not just a one-time event. It takes motivation, skill, good judgment, persistence, and proficiency to be a strong and effective leader in information security management. The CISM certification was designed to help you navigate the security management world more easily and confidently.

Each CISM job practice area is discussed in detail in the following chapters, and additional reference material is presented. Not only is this information helpful for those of you who are studying before taking the exam, but it is also meant to serve as a resource throughout your career as an information security management professional.

PART I

Information Security Governance

■ **Chapter 1**   Enterprise Governance
■ **Chapter 2**   Information Security Strategy

Enterprise Governance

In this chapter, you will learn about
- Organizational culture
- Types of legal and regulatory requirements
- Organization structure, roles, and responsibilities
- Ethics and codes of conduct

This chapter covers Certified Information Security Manager (CISM) job practice 1, "Information Security Governance," part A, "Enterprise Governance." The entire Information Security Governance domain represents 17 percent of the CISM examination.

Supporting Tasks in the CISM job practice that align with the Information Security Governance / Enterprise Governance domain include:

4. Integrate information security governance into corporate governance.
8. Define, communicate, and monitor information security responsibilities throughout the organization and lines of authority.
21. Identify legal, regulatory, organizational, and other applicable compliance requirements.

Governance is a process whereby senior management exerts strategic control over business functions through policies, objectives, delegation of authority, and monitoring. Governance is management's oversight of all other business processes to ensure that business processes effectively meet the organization's business vision and objectives.

Organizations usually establish governance through steering committees responsible for setting long-term business strategy and making changes to ensure that business processes continue to support business strategy and the organization's overall needs. This is accomplished through the development and enforcement of documented policies, standards, procedures, and requirements. Various reporting metrics provide feedback to business leaders on organizational performance and the results of their decisions.

Introduction to Information Security Governance

Information security governance typically focuses on several key processes, which include personnel management, sourcing, risk management, configuration management, change management, access management, vulnerability management, incident management, and business continuity planning. Another key component is establishing an effective organizational structure and clear statements of roles and responsibilities. An effective governance program will use a balanced scorecard, metrics, or other means to monitor these and other key processes. Security processes will be changed to remain effective and support ongoing business needs through continuous improvement.

Information security is a business issue, and organizations that are not yet adequately protecting their information have a business problem. The reason for this is almost always a lack of understanding and commitment by boards of directors and senior executives. For many, information security is only a technology problem at the tactical level. Recent events have brought the issue of information security to the forefront for many organizations. Information security leaders are challenged with how to organize, manage, and communicate about information security and the business impacts successfully because of a lack of awareness or cybersecurity savviness among the organization's executive leadership and board of directors.

To be successful, information security must also be a people issue. When people at each level in the organization—from boards of directors to individual contributors—understand the importance and impact of information security and their own roles and responsibilities, the organization will be in a position of reduced risk. This reduction in risk or identification of potential security events results in fewer incidents that, when they do occur, will have a lower impact on the organization's ongoing reputation and operations.

Information security governance is a set of established activities that helps management understand the state of the organization's security program, its current risks, and its direct activities. A goal of the security program is to continue to contribute toward the fulfillment of the security strategy, which itself will continue to align with the business and the business objectives. Whether the organization has a board of directors, council members, commissioners, or some other top-level governing body, governance begins with establishing top-level strategic objectives translated into actions, policies, processes, procedures, and other activities downward through each level in the organization.

An organization must also have an effective IT governance program for information security governance to succeed. IT is the enabler and force multiplier that facilitates business processes that fulfill organization objectives. Without effective IT governance, information security governance will not be able to reach its full potential. The result may be that the proverbial IT bus will travel safely but to the wrong destination. This is depicted in Figure 1-1.

While the CISM certification is not directly tied to IT governance, this implicit dependence of security governance on IT governance cannot be understated. IT and security professionals specializing in IT governance itself may be interested in the ISACA's Certified in the Governance of Enterprise IT (CGEIT) and the Certified in Risk and Information Systems Control (CRISC) certifications, which specialize in this domain.

Figure 1-1
Vision flows
downward in
an organization.

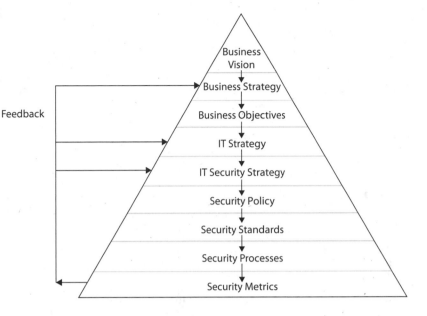

While IT governance and information security governance may be separate, in many organizations, these governance activities will closely resemble each other, and in practice, each affects the other. Both may also resemble other instances of governance in the organization. Many issues will span IT and security governance bodies, and some individuals will participate actively in both areas, further helping to "cross-pollinate" vital issues. Some organizations may integrate IT and information security governance into a single set of participants, activities, and business records. The most important thing is that organizations figure out how to establish effective governance programs for achieving desired and documented business outcomes.

The purpose of security governance is to align the organization's security program with the needs of the business. *Information security governance* refers to a collection of top-down activities intended to control the security of the organization (and security-related activities in every part of the organization) from a strategic perspective to ensure that information security supports the business. Following are some of the artifacts and actions that flow out of healthy security governance:

- **Objectives**   These desired capabilities or end states are ideally expressed in achievable, measurable terms.
- **Strategy**   This is a plan to achieve one or more objectives.
- **Policy**   At its minimum, security policy should directly reflect the mission, objectives, and goals of the overall organization.
- **Priorities**   The priorities in the security program should flow directly from the organization's mission, objectives, and goals. Whatever is most important to the organization should also be essential to information security.

- **Standards**   The technologies, protocols, and practices used by IT should align with the organization's needs. On their own, standards help drive a consistent approach to solving business challenges; the choice of standards should facilitate solutions that meet the organization's needs in a cost-effective and secure manner.

- **Processes**   These formalized descriptions of repeated business activities include instructions to applicable personnel. Processes include one or more procedures and definitions of business records and other facts that help workers understand how things are supposed to be done.

- **Controls**   These are formal descriptions of critical activities to ensure desired outcomes

- **Program and project management**   The organization's IT and security programs and projects should be organized and performed in a consistent manner that reflects business priorities and supports the business.

- **Metrics/reporting**   This includes the formal measurement of processes and controls so that management understands and can measure them.

To the greatest possible extent, security governance in an organization should be practiced the same way it performs IT governance and corporate governance. Security governance should mimic corporate and/or IT governance processes, or security governance may be integrated into corporate or IT governance processes.

While security governance contains the elements just described, strategic planning is also a key governance component. Strategy development is discussed in the next section.

Reason for Security Governance

Organizations in most industry sectors and at all levels of government are increasingly dependent on their information systems. This has progressed to the point at which organizations—including those whose products or services are not information related—are entirely dependent on the integrity and availability of their information systems to continue business operations. The dependency on information systems can have either a positive or a severe negative impact on an organization's upstream and downstream customer base as well as the supply chain as a whole. It is imperative that you, as an information security professional, understand both the appetite and the priority of the business concerning confidentiality, integrity, and availability (CIA). All three of these should be considered when building out the security governance structure, but the type of information used by the business will drive the priority given to confidentiality, integrity, and availability. Information security governance, then, is needed to ensure that security-related incidents do not threaten critical systems and their support of the ongoing viability of the organization.

Information security professionals know that IT assets that are Internet accessible would be compromised in mere minutes of being placed online without adequate safeguards. Further, many, if not all, IT assets thought to be behind the protection of firewalls and other control points may also be easily accessed and compromised. The tools, processes, and controls needed to protect these assets are as complex as the information systems they are designed to protect. Without effective top-down management of the security controls and processes protecting IT assets, management will not be informed or in control of these protective measures. The consequences of failure can impair, cripple, and/or embarrass the organization's core operations.

Security Governance Activities and Results

Within an effective security governance program, an organization's senior management team will ensure that information systems necessary to support business operations will be adequately protected. These are some of the activities required to protect the organization:

- **Risk management**   Management will ensure that risk assessments are performed to identify risks in information systems and supported processes. Follow-up actions will be carried out to reduce the risk of system failure and compromise.

- **Process improvement**   Management will ensure that key changes will be made to business processes that will result in security improvements.

- **Event identification**   Management will put technologies and processes in place to ensure that security events and incidents will be identified as quickly as possible.

- **Incident response**   Management will put incident response procedures into place to help avoid incidents, reduce the impact and probability of incidents, and improve response to incidents to minimize their impact on the organization.

- **Improved compliance**   Management will identify all applicable laws, regulations, and standards and carry out activities to confirm that the organization can attain and maintain compliance.

- **Business continuity and disaster recovery planning**   Management will define objectives and allocate resources to develop business continuity and disaster recovery plans.

- **Metrics**   Management will establish processes to measure key security events such as incidents, policy changes and violations, audits, and training.

- **Resource management**   The allocation of workforce, budget, and other resources to meet security objectives is monitored by management.

- **Improved IT governance**   An effective security governance program will result in better strategic decisions in the IT organization that keep risks at an acceptably low level.

These and other governance activities are carried out through scripted interactions among key business and IT executives at regular intervals. Meetings will include a discussion of the impact of regulatory changes, alignment with business objectives, effectiveness of measurements, recent incidents, recent audits, and risk assessments. Other discussions may include changes to the business, recent business results, and any anticipated business events such as mergers or acquisitions.

There are two key results of an effective security governance program:

- **Increased trust**   Customers, suppliers, and partners will trust the organization to a greater degree when they see that security is managed effectively.
- **Improved reputation**   The business community, including customers, investors, and regulators, will hold the organization in higher regard.

Business Alignment

An organization's information security program needs to fit into the rest of the organization. This means that the program needs to understand and align with the organization's highest-level guiding principles, including the following:

- **Mission**   Why does the organization exist? Who does it serve and through what products and services?
- **Goals and objectives**   What goals does the organization hope to achieve, and when does it want to accomplish them?
- **Strategy**   What activities need to occur to fulfill the organization's goals and objectives?

To be business aligned, people in the security program should be aware of several characteristics of the organization, including the following:

- **Culture**   Organizational culture includes how personnel in the organization work, think, and relate to one another.
- **Asset value**   Assets are information the organization uses to operate. They often consist of intellectual property such as designs, source code, production costs, pricing, sensitive information related to personnel and customers, information-processing infrastructure, and service functions.
- **Risk tolerance**   Risk tolerance for the organization's information security program needs to align with the organization's overall tolerance for risk.
- **Legal obligations**   What external laws and regulations govern what the organization does and how it operates? These laws and regulations include the Gramm-Leach-Bliley Act (GLBA), Payment Card Industry Data Security Standard (PCI DSS), European General Data Protection Regulation (GDPR), the California Consumer Privacy Act (CCPA), the Health Insurance Portability and Accountability Act (HIPAA), and the North American Electric Reliability Corporation (NERC) standard. Also, contractual obligations with other parties often shape the organization's behaviors and practices.
- **Market conditions**   How competitive is the marketplace in which the organization operates? What strengths and weaknesses does the organization have in comparison with its competitors? How does the organization want its security differentiated from its competitors?

Security as Business Prevention

The information security profession is still plagued by the reputation of "being the department of 'no'" or as the "department of business prevention." This stems from overzealous security managers who were more risk-averse than the business itself and did not understand the organization's need to grow, expand, and establish new products and services. The result of this reputation is the still-present tendency for IT and other parts of the business to avoid involvement with security professionals out of fear that their participation will hamper their efforts.

This can lead to *shadow IT* (where individuals and groups bypass corporate IT and procure their own computing services), which in many cases puts the organization at a greater risk of data leakage. Most people within a business want to do the right thing and complete their job activities. They do not intentionally set out to expose sensitive data; many employees are just trying to complete their assigned duties. For example, a person in the new accounts department receives an e-mail from the external marketing team listing all newly signed-up accounts and fails to recognize that the file contains sensitive cardholder data and is being shared over a public connection.

Goals and Objectives

An organization's goals and objectives specify the activities intended to support the organization's overall strategy. Goals and objectives are typically statements in the form of imperatives that describe the development or improvement of business capabilities. For instance, goals and objectives may be related to increases in capacity, improvements in quality, or the development of entirely new capabilities. Goals and objectives further the organization's mission, helping it to continue to attract new customers or constituents, increase market share, and increase revenue and/or profitability.

Risk Appetite and Risk Tolerance

Each organization has a particular appetite for risk, although few have documented that appetite. ISACA defines risk appetite as the level of risk that an organization is willing to accept while pursuing its mission, strategy, and objectives before taking action to treat the risk. This topic is discussed fully in Chapter 4.

Organizational Culture

Organizational culture is the term that describes how people within an organization treat one another and how they get things done. Many organizations establish a set of values that defines the norms of professional behavior. Terms such as *respect, collaboration,* and *teamwork* are often used in these values. Some organizations publish formal value statements and print them for display in lobbies, offices, and conference rooms.

The way an organization's leaders treat one another and the rest of the organization's employees sets an example for behavioral norms. Often, these norms reflect those formal values, but sometimes they may differ. One could say that an organization's stated culture and its actual culture may vary a little or a lot. The degree of alignment itself is a reflection of an organization's culture.

Every organization also has a risk culture, which affects how the organization deals with risk and how it treats risk over time. This culture is developed from several sources. First, it can come from the organization's leadership, based on their business and management philosophies, attitudes, education, and experience. It can also come from the organization's governance. Remember that governance essentially comprises the rules and regulations imposed on the organization by either external entities (in the form of laws, for example) or internally by the organization itself. As discussed, risk tolerance and risk appetite support the organizational risk culture.

Acceptable Use Policy

An *acceptable use policy (AUP)* is a formal policy statement that defines permitted activities and forbidden activities in an organization. An AUP is typically cybersecurity-centric and broadly states how IT can be used to support the organization. For instance, an AUP may stipulate that only organization-owned computers may be used to conduct business and only organization-approved applications, service providers, and vendors may be used. An AUP will also define acceptable and forbidden uses for company information, including trade secrets, intellectual property, and information about employees and customers.

Many organizations require their personnel to acknowledge, in writing, their intended compliance to the AUP, usually in addition to several other important policies such as harassment and ethics policies. Requiring workers to acknowledge policies emphasizes the policies' importance, and it also protects the organization by preventing misbehaving employees from later claiming, "I didn't know about that policy!"

Often, an acceptable use policy serves as the body of security policy that is applicable to all of an organization's workers. A more specific security policy that defines acceptable uses for access control, encryption, and other measures is generally intended for information workers designing, implementing, and operating information systems. Security policy is discussed fully in Chapter 5.

Ethics

Most organizations, particularly professional ones, have requirements for a code of conduct or professional ethics. This is especially true in the cybersecurity and risk management professions. These codes of ethics regulate the behavior of professionals and ensure that those professionals maintain high standards of conduct. Most industry-recognized professional certifications also require adherence to a code of ethics, and ISACA is no exception.

ISACA's Code of Professional Ethics is available at www.isaca.org/credentialing/code-of-professional-ethics and is imposed upon all organizational members and certification holders.

If a professional bound to uphold those ethical standards fails to do so, ISACA implements procedures for filing a complaint. The ISACA Code of Professional Ethics includes provisions for the following (paraphrased here):

1. Supporting and complying with standards and procedures for governance and management of information systems and technology

2. Performing duties professionally, with due diligence and care, as required by professional standards

3. Conducting activities in a lawful manner and maintaining the high standards of conduct and character required by the profession and ISACA

4. Ensuring privacy and confidentiality of sensitive information obtained in the course of professional duties

5. Maintaining competency in the professional field

6. Full disclosure and impartiality regarding results of work performed to ensure that the results of that work are not distorted

7. Supporting professional education in the areas of governance and management of enterprise information systems and technology, to include auditing, controls, security, and risk management

Many organizations have a formal, written policy called a code of ethics or a code of conduct. Such a policy defines acceptable professional behavior across many areas of business dealings, including relationships with customers, regulators, and public officials on topics such as financial dealings, kickbacks, bribes, and personal favors. The U.S. Foreign Corrupt Practices Act of 1977 (FCPA) prohibits individuals and organizations from bribing foreign government officials. Other countries have similar laws, such as the United Kingdom Bribery Act of 2010.

The resulting behavioral standard for information security professionals, then, is a synthesis of association codes of ethics such as the ISACA Code of Professional Ethics, an employer's code of conduct, applicable laws, as well as each professional's worldview that may include concepts of good versus evil, right versus wrong, and other moral standards.

Legal, Regulatory, and Contractual Requirements

Governance imposed by entities external to the organization usually takes the form of laws, regulations, professional standards and requirements, and so on. Laws and regulations may be in place to impose governance, or a company may formally accept professional standards. Sometimes, however, governance is also imposed as part of contractual requirements between organizations. Including governance requirements in contracts, even if an organization would otherwise not be required to meet those requirements, makes them legally enforceable. In any event, organizations are required to fulfill obligations imposed by these external governance sources.

Additionally, laws, regulations, and other governance sources sometimes conflict with or supplement each other. One regulation may require a specific level of protection for sensitive data, and another law or regulation may require additional layers of protection based on the characteristics of the data, the organization, or the industry. For example, privacy data and healthcare data are often regulated by multiple sources of governance, and the organization must implement internal policies and procedures to fulfill the requirements of all governance imposed on it. Even in the case of industry standards, organizations must fulfill the requirements imposed on them if they have agreed to do so through contract or by virtue of their industry. Organizations aren't legally required to comply with the PCI DSS standard, for example, but if they process credit card transactions, they are required to abide by the standard or face censure from credit card companies or banishment from processing transactions.

Compliance with legal and regulatory requirements is a critical factor in most organizations, and many of these requirements also impose information security and risk management requirements—so information security and risk management are often dictated, to a degree, by governance. Many laws and regulations, such as the Sarbanes-Oxley Act, GLBA, and HIPAA, require a formalized information security program, safeguards to protect sensitive information, and requirements for the retention of records.

In addition to laws and regulations, legal agreements between business entities can also include numerous stipulations regarding information management, protection, usage, and retention. When establishing and maintaining business rules, security and privacy policies, data classification policies, and data retention schedules, information security and governance leaders must consider these additional requirements.

Management must identify and resolve conflicts that sometimes arise when mapping out all of these requirements. For example, a regulation may require that certain business records be retained for at least seven years, while a legal agreement may limit the storage of pertinent business records to a maximum of five years. This is not simply an IT issue: business leaders from both entities must reconcile these conflicting requirements so that both parties will be compliant with applicable laws and meet their respective business needs.

Organizational Structure, Roles, and Responsibilities

How the business is organized can help drive how it deals with cybersecurity. Most companies are managed from a functional perspective; in other words, departments and other hierarchical structures are established to take care of specific functions that contribute to business goals and objectives. For example, a production-driven business may have a manufacturing or production department, an engineering department, a research and development department, and an assembly line. Additional departments may also cover support functions such as marketing, accounting and finance, public relations, and so on. On the other hand, a hospital will be organized according to its specific functions, such as the emergency department, surgery, neurology, radiology, and so on. Businesses in other markets or areas will be organized differently as well. In any case, the organization of the business is structured as its mission and business purposes dictate. Certain functions are found in any business, such as information technology, information security, privacy, and legal compliance. Each functional area has a primary mission and function, but an important thing to consider is that all different organizational structures, from lower-level work sections to higher-level departments and divisions, have responsibilities regarding cybersecurity.

Each unit, whether in the lower levels of the business hierarchy or at the highest levels, should be aware of, and responsible for, its impact on information protection and cybersecurity at its level. This innate responsibility originates from the well-known phrase, "information security is everyone's responsibility." Beyond an awareness of how a worker handles files on a laptop with tools such as e-mail and cloud storage, "information security is everyone's responsibility" covers everything, including the following:

- Designing and operating a business process
- Acquiring, integrating, and operating on-premises or cloud-based application software
- Designing, managing, and using file shares for the storage of unstructured data
- Developing organization policy, including acceptable use policy, to shape the use of information and information systems
- Setting examples of appropriate ethics and behavior, especially by executives and leaders

Organizational Roles

Information security governance is most effective when every person in the organization knows what is expected of them. Better organizations develop formal roles and responsibilities so that personnel will have a clearer idea of their part in all matters related to the protection of systems, information, and even themselves.

In organizational structure and behavior, a *role* describes expected activities that employees are obliged to perform as part of their employment. Roles are typically associated with a *job title* or *position title,* a label assigned to each person that designates his or her place in the organization. Organizations strive to adhere to standard position titles so that other people in the organization, upon knowing someone's position title, will have at least a general idea of each person's role in the organization.

Typical roles include the following:

- IT auditor
- Systems engineer
- Accounts receivable manager
- Individual contributor

Often a position title also includes a person's *rank*, which denotes a person's seniority, placement within a command-and-control hierarchy, span of control, or any combination. Typical ranks include the following, in order of increasing seniority:

- Supervisor
- Manager
- Senior manager
- Director
- Senior director
- Executive director
- Vice president
- Senior vice president
- Executive vice president
- President
- Chief executive officer
- Member, board of directors
- Advisor, board of directors
- Chairman, board of directors

Note that this should not be considered a complete listing of ranks. Larger organizations also include the modifiers *assistant* (as in assistant director), *general* (general manager), *managing* (managing director), and *first* (first vice president).

A *responsibility* is a statement of activities that a person is expected to perform. Like roles, responsibilities are typically documented in position descriptions and job descriptions. Typical responsibilities include the following:

- Perform monthly corporate expense reconciliation
- Troubleshoot network faults and develop solutions
- Audit user account terminations and produce exception reports

In addition to specific responsibilities associated with individual position titles, organizations typically also include general responsibilities in all position titles. Examples include the following:

- Understand and conform to information security policy, harassment policy, and other policies
- Understand and conform to the code of ethics and behavior

In the context of information security, an organization assigns roles and responsibilities to individuals and groups to meet the organization's security strategy and objectives.

RACI Charts

Many organizations utilize RACI (Responsible, Accountable, Consulted, Informed) charts to denote key responsibilities in business processes, projects, tasks, and other activities. A RACI chart assigns levels of responsibility to individuals and groups. The development of a RACI chart helps personnel determine roles for various business activities. A typical RACI chart follows.

Activity	Responsible	Accountable	Consulted	Informed
Request User Account	End user	End-user manager	IT service desk End-user manager	Asset owner Security team
Approve User Account	Asset owner	Chief operating officer (COO)	End-user manager Security team	End user Internal audit IT service desk
Provision User Account	IT service desk	IT service manager	Asset owner	End user End-user manager Security team
Audit User Account	Internal auditor	Internal audit manager	Asset owner	IT service desk IT service manager End-user manager

The same RACI chart can also be depicted in this second example:

Activity	End User	Manager	IT Service Desk	IT Service Manager	Asset Owner	COO	Internal Audit	Audit Manager	Security Team
Request User Account	R	A	I		I				I
Approve User Account	I	C	I	I	R	A	I		C
Provision User Account	I	I	R	A	C				I
Audit User Account		I	I	I	C		R	A	I

This RACI chart specifies the roles carried out by several parties in the user account access request process.

(continued)

The four roles in a RACI chart are defined as follows:

- **Responsible**   The person or group that performs the actual work or task.
- **Accountable**   The person who is ultimately answerable for complete, accurate, and timely execution of the work. Often this is a person who manages those in the Responsible role.
- **Consulted**   One or more people or groups consulted for their opinions, experience, or insight. People in the Consulted role may be a subject-matter expert for the work or task, or an owner, steward, or custodian of an asset associated with the work or task. Communication with the Consulted role is two-way.
- **Informed**   One or more people or groups informed by those in other roles. Depending on the process or task, people in the Informed role may be told of an activity before, during, or after its completion. Communication with the Informed role is one-way.

When assigning roles to individuals and groups in a RACI chart, several aspects must be considered, including the following:

- **Skills**   Some or all individuals in a team assignment, as well as specifically named individuals, need to have the skills, training, and competence to carry out tasks as required.
- **Segregation of duties**   Critical tasks, such as the user account provisioning RACI chart depicted earlier, must be free of segregation of duties conflicts. This means that two or more individuals or groups must be required to carry out a critical task. In this example, the requestor, approver, and provisioner cannot be the same person or group.
- **Conflict of interest**   Critical tasks must not be assigned to individuals or groups when such assignments will create conflicts of interest. For example, a user who is an approver cannot approve a request for their own access. In this case, a different person must approve the request while avoiding a segregation of duties conflict.

Two variations of the RACI model include PARIS (Participant, Accountable, Review Required, Input Required, Sign-off Required), and PACSI (Perform, Accountable, Control, Suggest, Informed).

Board of Directors

An organization's board of directors oversees activities in the organization. Depending on the type of organization, board members may be elected by shareholders or constituents, or they may be appointed. This role can be either paid or voluntary in nature.

Activities performed by the board of directors, as well as directors' authority, are usually defined by a constitution, bylaws, or external regulation. The board is typically accountable to the organization's owners or, in the case of a government body, to the electorate.

In many cases, board members have *fiduciary duty*. This means they are accountable to shareholders or constituents to act in the organization's best interests with no appearance of impropriety, conflict of interest, or ill-gotten profit resulting from their actions.

In nongovernment organizations (NGOs), the board of directors is responsible for appointing a chief executive officer (CEO) and possibly other executives. The CEO, then, is accountable to the board of directors and carries out the board's directives.

Board members may also be selected for any of the following reasons:

- **Investor representation**   One or more board members may be appointed by significant investors to give them control over the strategy and direction of the organization.

- **Business experience**   Board members bring outside business management experience, which helps them develop successful business strategies for the organization.

- **Access to resources**   Board members bring business connections, including additional investors, business partners, suppliers, or customers.

Often, one or more board members will have business finance experience to bring financial management oversight to the organization. In the case of U.S. public companies, the Sarbanes-Oxley Act requires board members to form an audit committee; one or more audit committee members are required to have financial management experience. External financial audits and internal audit activities are often accountable directly to the audit committee to oversee the organization's financial management activities. As the issue of information security and privacy becomes more prevalent in discussions at the executive level, some organizations have added a board member who is technically savvy or have formed an additional committee, often referred to as the technology risk committee. The U.S. Securities and Exchange Commission (SEC) has proposed amendments that would require public companies to disclose whether any of their board members have cybersecurity expertise.

Boards of directors are generally expected to require that the CEO and other executives implement a corporate *governance* function to ensure that executive management has an appropriate level of visibility and control over the organization's operations. Executives are accountable to the board of directors to demonstrate that they effectively carry out the board's strategies.

Many, if not most, organizations are highly dependent upon IT for their daily operations. As a result, information security is an important topic for boards of directors. Today's standard of due care for corporate boards requires that they include information security considerations in the strategies they develop and the oversight they exert on the organization. Most boards of directors now include subcommittees that focus on risk and information security.

In its publication "Cyber-Risk Oversight 2020," the National Association of Corporate Directors (NACD) has developed five principles regarding the importance of information security:

- Principle 1: Directors need to understand and approach cybersecurity as a strategic, enterprise risk—not just as an IT risk.
- Principle 2: Directors should understand the legal implications of cyber risks as they relate to their company's specific circumstances.
- Principle 3: Boards should have adequate access to cybersecurity expertise, and discussions about cyber-risk management should be given regular and adequate time on board meeting agendas.
- Principle 4: Directors should set the expectation that management will establish an enterprise-wide cyber-risk management framework with adequate staffing and budget.
- Principle 5: Board-management discussions about cyber risk should include identification and quantification of financial exposure to cyber risks and which risks to accept, mitigate, or transfer, such as through insurance, as well as specific plans associated with each approach.

This and other resources are available at www.nacdonline.org.

Executive Management

Executive management is responsible for carrying out directives issued by the board of directors. Information security management includes ensuring that sufficient organizational resources are devoted to implementing a security program and developing and maintaining security controls to protect critical assets.

Executive management must ensure that priorities are balanced. In the case of IT and information security, these functions are usually tightly coupled but sometimes in conflict. IT's primary mission is to develop and operate business-enabling capabilities through the use of information systems, while information security's mission includes risk management, security, privacy, and compliance. Executive management must ensure that these two sometimes-conflicting missions are successful.

Typical IT- and security-related executive position titles include the following:

- **Chief information officer (CIO)** This is the topmost leader in a larger IT organization.
- **Chief technical officer (CTO)** This position is usually responsible for an organization's overall technology strategy. Depending upon the organization's purpose, the CTO may be separate from IT.
- **Chief information security officer (CISO)** This position is responsible for all aspects of data-related security. This usually includes incident management, disaster recovery, vulnerability management, and compliance. This role is typically separate from IT.

To ensure the success of the organization's information security program, executive management should be involved in three key areas:

- **Ratify corporate security policy**   Security policies developed by the information security function should be visibly ratified or endorsed by executive management. This may take different forms, such as formal, minuted ratification in a governance meeting; a statement of the need for compliance along with a signature within the body of the security policy document; a separate memorandum to all personnel; or other visible communication to the organization's rank and file that stresses the importance of, and need for compliance to, the organization's information security policy.

- **Leadership by example**   With regard to information security policy, executive management should lead by example and not exhibit behavior suggesting they are "above" security policy—or other policies. Executives should not be seen to enjoy special privileges of the nature that suggest that one or more security policies do not apply to them. Instead, their behavior should visibly support security policies that all personnel are expected to comply with.

- **Ultimate responsibility**   Executives are ultimately responsible for all actions carried out by the personnel who report to them. Executives are also ultimately responsible for all outcomes related to organizations to which operations have been outsourced.

Security Steering Committee

Many organizations form a security steering committee consisting of stakeholders from many (if not all) of the organization's business units, departments, functions, and principal locations. A steering committee may have a variety of responsibilities, including the following:

- **Risk treatment deliberation and recommendation**   The committee may discuss relevant risks, discuss potential avenues of risk treatment, and develop recommendations for said risk treatment for ratification by executive management.

- **Discussion and coordination of IT and security projects**   Committee members may discuss various IT and security projects to resolve resource or scheduling conflicts. They may also discuss potential conflicts between multiple projects and initiatives and work out solutions.

- **Review of recent risk assessments**   The committee may discuss recent risk assessments to develop a common understanding of their results, and they may discuss remediation of findings.

- **Discussion of new laws, regulations, and requirements**   The committee may discuss new laws, regulations, and requirements that may impose changes in the organization's operations. Committee members can develop high-level strategies that their respective business units or departments can further build out.

- **Review of recent security incidents**   Steering committee members can discuss recent security incidents and their root causes. Often this can result in changes in processes, procedures, or technologies to reduce the risk and impact of future incidents.

Reading between the lines, the primary mission of a security steering committee is to identify and resolve conflicts and to maximize the effectiveness of the security program, as balanced among other business initiatives and priorities.

Business Process and Business Asset Owners

Business process and business asset owners are typically nontechnical personnel in management positions within an organization. Although they may not be technology experts, their business processes are often enhanced by IT in business applications and other capabilities in many organizations.

Remembering that IT and information security serve the organization and not the other way around, business process and business asset owners are accountable for making business decisions that sometimes impact the use of IT, the organization's security posture, or both. A simple example is a decision on whether an individual employee should have access to specific information. While IT or security may have direct control over which personnel have access to what assets, the best decision to make is a business decision by the manager responsible for the process or business asset.

The responsibilities of business process and business asset owners include the following:

- **Access grants**   Asset owners decide whether individuals or groups should be given access to the asset and the level and type of access. Example access types include combinations of read-only, read-write, create, and delete.

- **Access revocation**   Asset owners should also decide when individuals or groups no longer require access to an asset, signaling the need to revoke that access.

- **Access reviews**   Asset owners should periodically review access lists to determine whether each person and group should continue to have access. Access reviews may also include access activity reviews to determine whether people who have not accessed assets still require access.

- **Configuration**   Asset owners determine the configuration needed for assets and applications, ensuring their proper function and support of applications and business processes.

- **Function definition**   In the case of business applications and services, asset owners determine which functions will be available, how they will work, and how they will support business processes. Typically, this definition is constrained by functional limitations within an application, service, or product.

- **Process definition**   Process owners determine the sequence, steps, roles, and actions carried out in their business processes.

- **Physical location**   Asset owners determine the physical location of their assets. Factors influencing choices of location include physical security, proximity to other assets, proximity to relevant personnel, and data protection and privacy laws.

Business and asset owners are often nontechnical personnel, so it may be necessary to translate business needs into technical standards and specifications.

Custodial Responsibilities

In many organizations, asset owners are not involved in the day-to-day activities related to managing their assets, particularly when those assets are information systems and the data stored within them. Instead, somebody (or several people) in the IT organization acts as a proxy for asset owners and makes access grants and other decisions on their behalf. While this is a common practice, it is often carried too far, resulting in the asset owner being virtually uninvolved and uninformed. Instead, asset owners should be aware of, and periodically review, activities carried out by people, groups, and departments making decisions on their behalf.

In a typical arrangement, people in IT make access decisions on behalf of asset owners. Unless there is a close partnership between these IT personnel and the asset owners, IT personnel often do not adequately understand the business nature of assets or the implications when certain people are given access to them. Often, far too many personnel have access to assets, usually with higher privileges than necessary.

Chief Information Security Officer

The CISO is the highest-ranking security person in an organization. A CISO will develop business-aligned security strategies that support current and future business initiatives and will be responsible for developing and operating the organization's information risk program, developing and implementing security policies, developing and implementing security incident response, and perhaps developing operational security functions.

The CISO reports to the COO or the CEO in some organizations. In other organizations, the CISO may report to the CIO, chief legal counsel, or another person in the organization.

Other similar titles with similar responsibilities include the following:

- **Chief security officer (CSO)** This position generally has the responsibilities of a CISO, plus responsibilities for non-information assets such as business equipment and work centers. A CSO often is responsible for workplace safety.

- **Chief information risk officer (CIRO)** Generally, this represents a change of approach to the CISO position, from protection-based to risk-based.

- **Chief risk officer (CRO)** This position is responsible for all aspects of risk, including information, business, compliance, and market risk. This role is separate from IT. Note that some organizations have a chief revenue officer (also CRO); ensure that you understand how the organization structures its leadership roles.

Many organizations do not have a CISO but instead have a director or manager of information security who reports to someone further down in the organization chart.

An organization may not have a CISO for several reasons, but, in general, the organization does not consider information security as a strategic function. In some cases, an organization lacks a CISO because other C-level executives feel that a CISO would hinder business development and agility. Regardless of the reason, not having a CISO will hamper the visibility and importance of information security and often results in information security being a tactical function concerned with primary defenses such as firewalls, antivirus, and other tools. In such situations, responsibility for strategy-level information security implicitly lies with some other executive, such as the CIO. This situation often results in the absence of a security program and the organization's general lack of priority for and awareness of relevant risks, threats, and vulnerabilities.

The one arena where a CISO may not be required is in small to medium-sized organizations where a full-time strategic leader may not be cost effective. It is advisable to contract with a virtual CISO (vCISO) to assist with strategy and planning. When organizations do not require or cannot afford a full-time person, this approach enables the organization to benefit from the knowledge of a seasoned security professional to assist in driving the information security program forward. This book's technical editor and I have served organizations in this capacity for several years.

Rank Sets Tone and Gives Power

A glance at the title of the highest-ranking information security position in a large organization reveals much about executive management's opinion of information security. Executive attitudes about security are reflected in the security manager's title and may resemble the following:

- **Security manager**   Information security is tactical and often viewed as consisting only of antivirus software and firewalls. The security manager has no visibility into the development of business objectives. Executives consider security as unimportant and based on technology only.

- **Security director**   Information security is essential and has moderate decision-making capability but little influence on the business. A director-level person in a larger organization may have little visibility of overall business strategies and little or no access to executive management or the board of directors.

- **Vice president**   Information security is strategic but does not influence business strategy and objectives. The vice president will have access to executive management and possibly the board of directors.

- **CISO/CIRO/CRO/CSO/vCISO**   Information security is strategic, and business objectives are developed with full consideration for risk. The C-level security person has free access to executive management and the board of directors.

Chief Privacy Officer

Typically, some organizations that manage large amounts of sensitive data on customers will employ a chief privacy officer (CPO), sometimes known as a data protection officer (DPO). In some organizations, a CPO is required by applicable regulations such as GDPR. In contrast, others have a CPO because they store massive amounts of personally identifiable information (PII).

The roles of a CPO typically include the safeguarding of PII and ensuring that the organization does not misuse PII at its disposal. Because many organizations with a CPO also have a CISO, the CPO's duties mainly involve oversight of the organization's proper handling and use of PII, leaving information protection to the CISO.

The CPO is sometimes seen as a customer advocate, and often this is the role of the CPO, particularly when regulations require a privacy officer.

Chief Compliance Officer

Some organizations, particularly those subject to several sources of regulations, will employ a chief compliance officer (CCO). This role typically includes oversight over policy and organization functions that come into scope for regulations and standards. A CCO generally is a high-level position and a peer of the CIO, CISO, and CPO.

Software Development

Positions in software development are involved in the design, development, and testing of software applications.

- **Systems architect**   This position is usually responsible for the overall information systems architecture in the organization. This may or may not include overall data architecture and interfaces to external organizations.

- **Systems analyst**   A systems analyst is involved with the design of applications, including changes in an application's original design. This position may develop technical requirements, program design, and software test plans. If organizations license applications developed by other companies, systems analysts design interfaces for those applications.

- **Software engineer/developer**   This position develops application software. Depending upon their level of experience, people in this position may also design programs or applications. Developers often create custom interfaces, application customizations, and custom reports in organizations that utilize purchased application software.

- **Software tester**   This position tests changes in programs made by software engineers/developers.

While the trend of outsourcing applications has resulted in organizations infrequently developing their applications from scratch, software development roles persist in organizations. Developers are needed to create customized modules within software platforms and integrations and integration tools to connect applications and databases. Still, most organizations have fewer developers today than they did a decade or two ago.

Data Management

Positions related to data management are responsible for developing and implementing database designs and maintaining databases. These positions are concerned with data within applications and data flows between applications.

- **Data manager**   This position is responsible for data architecture and management in larger organizations.
- **Database architect**   This person develops logical and physical designs of data models for applications. With sufficient experience, this person may also design an organization's overall data architecture.
- **Big data architect**   This position develops data models and data analytics for large, complex data sets.
- **Database administrator (DBA)**   This position builds and maintains databases designed by the database architect and databases that are included as part of purchased applications. The DBA monitors databases, tunes them for performance and efficiency, and troubleshoots problems.
- **Database analyst**   This person performs tasks that are junior to the database administrator, carrying out routine data maintenance and monitoring tasks.
- **Data scientist**   This position applies scientific methods, builds processes, and implements systems to extract knowledge or insights from data.

 EXAM TIP   The roles of data manager, database architect, big data architect, database administrator, database analyst, and data scientist are distinct from data owners. Don't confuse them on the exam. The former are IT department roles for managing data models and data technology, whereas the latter (data owner) governs the business use of and access to data in information systems.

Network Management

Positions in network management are responsible for designing, building, monitoring, and maintaining voice and data communications networks, including connections to outside business partners and the Internet.

- **Network architect**   This position designs data and voice networks and designs changes and upgrades to networks to meet new organization objectives.
- **Network engineer**   This person implements, configures, and maintains network devices such as routers, switches, firewalls, and gateways.

- **Network administrator**   This position performs routine tasks in the network, such as making configuration changes and monitoring event logs.
- **Telecom engineer**   Those serving in this role work with telecommunications technologies such as telecom services, data circuits, phone systems, conferencing systems, and voicemail systems.

Systems Management

Positions in systems management are responsible for the architecture, design, building, and maintenance of servers and operating systems. This may include desktop operating systems as well. Personnel in these positions also design and manage virtualized environments and microsegmentation.

- **Systems architect**   This position is responsible for the overall architecture of systems (usually servers) in terms of the internal architecture of a system and the relationship between systems. This person is generally responsible for designing services such as authentication, e-mail, and time synchronization.
- **Systems engineer**   This person is responsible for designing, building, and maintaining servers and server operating systems.
- **Storage engineer**   This position is responsible for designing, building, and maintaining storage subsystems.
- **Systems administrator**   This administrator is responsible for performing maintenance and configuration operations on systems.

IT Operations

Positions in operations are responsible for day-to-day operational tasks that may include networks, servers, databases, and applications.

- **Operations manager**   This position is responsible for overall operations carried out by others. Responsibilities include establishing operations and shift schedules.
- **Operations analyst**   This person may be responsible for developing operational procedures; examining the health of networks, systems, and databases; setting and monitoring the operations schedule; and maintaining operations records.
- **Controls analyst**   This analyst monitors batch jobs, data entry work, and other tasks to make sure they are operating correctly.
- **Systems operator**   This position is responsible for monitoring systems and networks, performing backup tasks, running batch jobs, printing reports, and performing other operational tasks.
- **Media manager**   This position is responsible for maintaining and tracking the use and whereabouts of backup volumes and other media.

> ### Cloud Business Titles
>
> An organization's migration to the cloud is often emphasized with a certain amount of fanfare. To highlight this transformation, many organizations add the word "cloud" in some of their job titles to indicate leadership and staff expertise. Here are a few examples:
>
> - Cloud systems architect
> - Cloud database administrator
> - Cloud operations manager
> - Cloud security architect
>
> When cloud development and operations are more common, the word "cloud" may eventually disappear from these and other job titles.

Governance, Risk, and Compliance

Positions in governance, risk, and compliance (GRC) are responsible for a wide range of activities within a security organization.

- **Risk manager**   This person is responsible for performing risk assessments and maintaining the risk register.
- **Policy manager**   This position is responsible for maintaining security and privacy policy documents and related information. This person works closely with the risk manager, identifying risks that may identify the need for new and updated policy.
- **Controls manager**   This position is responsible for maintaining security controls, advising control owners on responsibilities and expectations, and assessing controls for effectiveness.
- **Third-party risk management**   This position is responsible for assessing new and existing vendors and service providers, identifying and reporting on risks, and developing mitigation strategies.
- **Information governance**   This position is responsible for data classification policy and serves as a governance function to manage the organization's use of information.
- **Security awareness training**   This person is responsible for developing and delivering content of various types to enable the workforce to understand their information security and privacy responsibilities.

Business Resilience

Personnel in positions related to business resilience are responsible for various activities that ensure the organization can continue operations despite disruptive events.

- **Crisis communications**   This position is responsible for developing and executing communications plans to keep employees, customers, regulators, and shareholders informed of business emergencies and disruptive events. This responsibility may lie with corporate communications, or it could be separate.
- **Crisis management**   These positions are responsible for developing and executing plans to manage business emergencies when they occur.
- **Business continuity planning**   These positions are responsible for conducting business impact analysis and criticality analysis and for developing and testing business continuity plans.
- **Disaster recovery planning**   These positions are responsible for developing and testing procedures that ensure information systems' continued operation and recovery when disruptive events occur.

Security Operations

Positions in security operations are responsible for designing, building, and monitoring security systems and security controls to ensure information systems' confidentiality, integrity, and availability.

- **Security architect**   This person is responsible for designing technical security controls, systems, and solutions in contexts such as authentication, audit logging, intrusion detection systems (IDSs), intrusion prevention systems, access control, antimalware, and firewalls.
- **Security engineer**   This position is responsible for designing, building, and maintaining security services and systems designed by the security architect.
- **Security analyst**   This position is responsible for examining logs from firewalls and IDSs and audit logs from systems and applications. This person may also be responsible for issuing security advisories to others in IT.
- **Forensics analyst**   This position is responsible for conducting forensic investigations on information systems to identify the presence and effect of malware, misbehavior of employees, and actions taken by intruders.
- **Penetration tester**   This position is responsible for using tools to identify vulnerabilities in information systems and advising system owners to develop mitigation strategies. Most organizations outsource this function to outside firms that perform penetration tests on a periodic (usually annual) basis.
- **Access administrator**   This position is responsible for accepting approved requests for user access management changes and performing the necessary changes at the network, system, database, or application level. Often, this position consists of personnel in network and systems management functions; only in larger organizations is user account management performed in security or even in a separate user access department.

Security Audit

Positions in security audit are responsible for examining process design and verifying the effectiveness of security controls.

- **Security audit manager**   This position is responsible for audit operations and scheduling and managing audits.
- **Security auditor**   This position is responsible for performing internal audits of IT controls to ensure that they are operated properly.

 CAUTION   Security audit positions need to be carefully placed in the organization so that people in this role can be objective and independent from the departments, processes, and systems they audit. Often, this function is known as *internal audit*.

Service Desk

Positions at the service desk are responsible for providing frontline support services to IT and IT customers.

- **Service desk manager**   This position serves as a liaison between end users and the IT service desk department.
- **Service desk analyst**   This person is responsible for providing frontline user support services to personnel in the organization. This is sometimes known as a help-desk analyst.
- **Technical support analyst**   This position is responsible for providing technical support services to other IT personnel and IT customers.

Quality Assurance

Positions in quality assurance are responsible for evaluating IT systems and processes to confirm their accuracy and effectiveness.

- **QA manager**   This position is responsible for facilitating quality improvement activities throughout the IT organization.
- **QC manager**   This position is responsible for testing IT systems and applications to confirm whether they are free of defects.

Other Roles

Other roles in IT and security organizations include the following:

- **Vendor manager**   This person is responsible for maintaining business relationships with external vendors, measuring their performance, and handling business issues.

- **Business analyst**   This position is responsible for performing tasks supporting numerous functions in IT, information security, and privacy organizations.

- **Project manager**   This position is responsible for creating project plans and managing IT and security projects.

- **Finance manager**   This person is responsible for financial planning and budget management for IT.

General Staff

The rank and file in an organization may or may not have explicit information security responsibilities, as determined by executive management's understanding of the broad capabilities of information systems and the personnel who use them.

Typically, general staff security-related responsibilities include the following:

- Understanding and complying with organization security policy

- Acceptable use of organization assets, including information systems and information

- Proper judgment, including proper responses to people who request information or request that staff members perform specific functions (the primary impetus for this is the phenomenon of social engineering and its use as an attack vector)

- Reporting of security-related matters and incidents to management

Better organizations have standard language in job descriptions that specify general responsibilities for protecting assets.

> ### The Workforce Includes Contractors and Temps
> When pondering the topic of security- and privacy-related responsibilities in an organization, you must not overlook contractors, temps, and other similar positions. To the extent that these other workers have access to information and information systems, the organization needs to ensure that these persons are equally responsible for complying with security policy and other policies. All workers should be required to complete security awareness training and acknowledge their conformance to policy in writing.

Monitoring Responsibilities

The practice of monitoring responsibilities helps an organization confirm that the correct jobs are being carried out in the right way. There is no single approach, but several activities provide information to management, including the following:

- **Controls and internal audit**   Developing one or more controls around specific responsibilities gives management greater control over key activities. An internal audit of controls provides an objective analysis of control effectiveness.

- **Metrics and reporting**   Developing metrics for repeated activities helps management better understand work output.

- **Work measurement**   This is a more structured activity used to measure repeated tasks carefully to help management better understand the volume of work performed.

- **Performance evaluation**   This is a traditional qualitative method used to evaluate employee performance.

- **360 feedback**   Soliciting structured feedback from peers, subordinates, and management helps subjects and management better understand characteristics related to specific responsibilities.

- **Position benchmarking**   This technique is used by organizations that want to compare job titles and people holding them with those in other organizations. There is no direct monitoring of responsibilities. Instead, benchmarking helps an organization determine whether they have the right positions and are staffed by competent and qualified personnel. This may be useful for organizations that are troubleshooting employee performance.

Chapter Review

Information security governance is the top-down management and control of security and risk management in an organization. Governance is usually undertaken through a steering committee that consists of executives from throughout the organization. The steering committee is responsible for setting overall strategic direction and policy, ensuring that security strategy aligns with the organization's IT and business strategy and objectives. The directives of the steering committee are carried out through projects and tasks that steer the security organization toward strategic objectives. The steering committee can monitor progress through metrics and a balanced scorecard.

For an information security program to be successful, it must align with the business and its overall mission, goals and objectives, and strategy. The security program must consider the organization's notion of asset value, culture, risk tolerance/appetite, legal obligations, and market conditions. A successful and aligned security program does not lead the organization but enables and supports it to carry out its mission and pursue its goals.

Security governance is accomplished using the same means as IT governance: it begins with board-level involvement that sets the tone for risk appetite and is carried out through the chief information security officer, who develops security and privacy policies, as well as strategic security programs, including software assurance, change management, vendor management, configuration management, incident management, vulnerability management, security awareness training, and identity and access management.

Security governance is used to establish roles and responsibilities for security-related activities throughout all layers of the organization, from the board of directors to individual staff. Roles and responsibilities are defined in job descriptions, policy and process documents, and RACI charts.

The board of directors in the defined team is responsible for overseeing all activities in an organization. Boards select and manage a chief executive officer responsible for developing a governance function to manage assets, budgets, personnel, processes, and risk.

The security steering committee is responsible for security strategic planning. The security steering committee will develop and approve security policies and appoint managers to develop and maintain processes, procedures, and standards, all of which should align with one another and with the organization's overall mission, strategy, goals, and objectives.

The CISO develops business-aligned security strategies that support the organization's overall mission and goals and is responsible for the organization's overall security program, including policy development, risk management, and perhaps some operational activities such as vulnerability management, incident management, access management, and security awareness training. In some organizations, the topmost security executive has the title of chief security officer or chief information risk officer.

The chief privacy officer is responsible for the protection and proper use of sensitive personal information (often referred to as personally identifiable information). The CPO's information protection responsibilities are sometimes shared with the CISO, who has overall information protection responsibilities. The chief compliance officer is responsible for a broad range of compliance tracking and reporting.

Virtually all other roles in IT have security responsibilities, including software development and integration, data management, network management, systems management, operations, service desk, internal audit, and all staff members.

Notes

- The addition of information security as part of fiduciary duty by board members and executives is an important and growing trend in business today.

- Security executives and the board of directors are responsible for implementing a security governance model encompassing information security strategy and mandates. As a result, the industry is seeing a shift from a passive to a more active board with regard to cybersecurity issues.

- A security program should align with the organization's overall mission, goals, strategy, and objectives. This means that the CISO and others should be aware of, and involved in, strategic initiatives and the execution of the organization's strategic goals.

- Risk appetite is generally expressed in qualitative terms such as "very low tolerance for risk" and "no tolerance for risk." Different activities in an organization will have different risk appetites.

- An organization's definitions of roles and responsibilities may or may not be in sync with its culture of accountability. For instance, an organization may have clear descriptions of responsibilities documented in policy and process documents and yet rarely hold individuals accountable when preventable security events occur.

- Ideally, an organization's board of directors will be aware of information security risks and may direct that the organization enact safeguards to protect itself. However, in many organizations, the board of directors is still uninvolved in information security matters; in these cases, it is still possible to have a successful risk-based information security program, provided senior executives support it.

- While security steering committees are not required, organizations may find it helpful to implement single-level or multilevel security steering groups as a cross-functional vehicle for discovering security risks and disseminating security organization.

- Information security is the responsibility of every person in an organization; however, the means for assigning and monitoring security responsibilities to individuals and groups varies widely.

Questions

1. An organization is subject to healthcare regulations that govern individual health data protection requirements. Which of the following describes this type of governance?

    A. External

    B. Internal

    C. Regulatory

    D. Professional

2. Your company handles credit card transaction processing as part of its business processes. Which of the following best describes the source and type of governance it may incur because of these business processes?

    A. Internal, policies and procedures

    B. External, industry standards

    C. External, laws and regulations

    D. Internal, industry standards

3. Which the following describes why the organization exists?

    A. Organizational mission statement

    B. Organizational strategy

    C. External governance

    D. Organizational policy

4. All of the following factors influence an organization's culture *except* which one?

    A. Published values

    B. Policies

    C. Leadership behavior

    D. Behavioral norms

5. Which of the following roles is responsible for control assurance?

   A. Business leader

   B. Information security

   C. Control owner

   D. Internal audit

6. Security governance is most concerned with:

   A. Security policy

   B. IT policy

   C. Security strategy

   D. Security executive compensation

7. The purpose of a RACI chart is:

   A. Determine who is responsible for security governance

   B. Map the culture to a controls framework

   C. Document the roles of persons or positions

   D. Define the checks and balances in IT governance

8. While gathering and examining various security-related business records, the security manager has determined that the organization has no security incident log. What conclusion can the security manager make from this?

   A. The organization does not have security incident detection capabilities.

   B. The organization has not yet experienced a security incident.

   C. The organization is recording security incidents in its risk register.

   D. The organization has effective preventive and detective controls.

9. The entity that is ultimately responsible for security governance is:

   A. Chief information officer

   B. Chief information security officer

   C. Board of directors

   D. Chief risk officer

10. A business asset owner is responsible for all of the following *except*:

   A. Periodically reviewing and approving continued access to the asset

   B. Physical protection of the asset

   C. Approving or denying individual access requests

   D. Physical location of the asset

11. Which of the following people is/are responsible for ensuring that PII is not used improperly?

    A. Chief privacy officer

    B. Data governance manager

    C. Asset owner

    D. All employees

12. An information security manager documents all of the data retention requirements associated with a specific set of business records. The manager should consider all of the following sources of requirements *except*:

    A. Data governance requirements

    B. Stipulations in legal contracts

    C. Applicable laws

    D. Non-applicable laws

13. A new employee in an organization is reviewing organization documents to begin learning about the organization's culture and operations. One document describes situations where an employee must report gifts and favors from vendor organizations. Which of the following documents is the employee likely reading?

    A. Acceptable use policy

    B. Employee handbook

    C. Privacy policy

    D. Code of conduct

14. An acceptable use policy is likely to contain all of the following *except*:

    A. Rules regarding the use of personally owned assets

    B. Permitted uses of corporate assets

    C. Data retention requirements

    D. Protection of sensitive information

15. The best definition of governance is:

    A. Corporate policies and procedures

    B. Management control of business functions

    C. Regular reporting of metrics and key performance indicators (KPIs)

    D. Formal roles and responsibilities documented in a RACI chart

Answers

1. **A.** Laws and regulations are a form of external governance.

2. **B.** This describes an external source of governance in the form of industry standards, specifically the Payment Card Industry Data Security Standard (PCI DSS).

3. A. The organization develops the organizational mission statement to describe its overall mission, which is its very reason for existence.

4. B. Of the available choices, an organization's policies are the least likely to influence an organization's culture.

5. D. Internal audit is responsible for control assurance, meaning a periodic examination of a control's design, implementation, and records (if any), to determine whether the control's design and effectiveness are sound.

6. C. Security governance is the mechanism through which security strategy is established, controlled, and monitored. Long-term and other strategic decisions are made in the context of security governance.

7. C. The purpose of a RACI chart is to document the activities of a program, process, or procedure and the roles of various individuals or positions, whether each is accountable, responsible, consulted, or informed.

8. A. An organization that does not have a security incident log probably lacks the capability to detect and respond to an incident. It is unreasonable to assume that the organization has had no security incidents, since minor incidents occur regularly. Claiming that the organization has effective controls is unreasonable, as it is understood that incidents occur even when effective controls are in place (because not all types of incidents can reasonably be prevented).

9. C. The organization's board of directors is ultimately responsible for security governance.

10. B. A business asset owner is typically not responsible for physically protecting the asset. Instead, asset protection would be the responsibility of the chief security officer or the chief information security officer.

11. A. The chief privacy officer is responsible for establishing business rules, policies, and controls to ensure that PII is not used improperly.

12. D. It is not necessary for the information security manager to consider laws that are not applicable to the situation. All of the other answers are relevant and must be considered.

13. D. An organization's code of conduct policy generally defines business ethics rules, including receiving and offering gifts and favors to others.

14. C. An acceptable use policy (AUP) is likely to contain statements about the use of corporate assets, personally owned assets, and information protection. Data retention requirements are not likely to be included.

15. B. Governance is best defined as management's control over business functions throughout an organization.

Information Security Strategy

In this chapter, you will learn about

- Business alignment
- Security strategy development
- Security governance activities
- Information security strategy development
- Resources needed to develop and execute a security strategy
- Obstacles to strategy development and execution

This chapter covers Certified Information Security Manager (CISM) job practice 1, "Information Security Governance," part B, "Information Security Strategy." The entire Information Security Governance domain represents 17 percent of the CISM examination.

Supporting Tasks in the CISM job practice that align with the Information Security Governance / Information Security Strategy domain include:

1. Identify internal and external influences to the organization that impact the information security strategy.

2. Establish and/or maintain an information security strategy in alignment with organizational goals and objectives.

3. Establish and/or maintain an information security governance framework.

6. Develop business cases to support investments in information security.

7. Gain ongoing commitment from senior leadership and other stakeholders to support the successful implementation of the information security strategy.

If for no other reason than cyber threats are ever-changing and increasingly dangerous, all organizations need to reassess their information security programs and develop strategies for key improvements.

Information Security Strategy Development

Among business, technology, and security professionals, there are many different ideas about what exactly a strategy should entail and which techniques are best used to develop it, as well as general confusion on the topic. While a specific strategy itself may be complex, the concept of a *strategy* is quite simple: it can be defined as *the plan to achieve an objective.*

The effort to build a strategy requires more than saying those six words. Again, however, the idea is not complicated. The concept is this: Understand where you are now and where you want to be. The strategy is the path you have outlined, communicated, and documented that the organization will follow to get from where you are (*current state*) to where you want to be (*strategic objective*).

This chapter explores strategy development in detail.

Strategy Objectives

A *strategy* is the plan to achieve an objective. The *objective* (or objectives) is the desired future state of the organization's security posture and level of risk.

There are, in addition, objectives *of* a strategy. These objectives are as follows:

- **Business alignment**   The desired future state, and the strategy to get there, must be in alignment with the organization and *its* strategy and objectives.

- **Risk appetite alignment**   An organization's information security program implicitly drives an organization toward a specific level of risk, which may or may not align with the organization's true level of risk appetite.

- **Effective risk management**   A security program must include a risk management policy, processes, and procedures. Without effective risk management, decisions are made blindly without regard to their consequences or level of risk.

- **Value delivery**   The desired future state of a security program should include a focus on continual improvement and increasing efficiency. No organization has unlimited funds for security; instead, organizations need to reduce risk at the lowest reasonable cost.

- **Resource optimization**   Similar to value delivery, strategic goals should efficiently utilize available resources. Among other things, this means having only the necessary staff and tools to meet strategic objectives.

- **Performance measurement**   Although it is important for strategic objectives to be SMART (specific, measurable, achievable, relevant, and time-related), the ongoing security and security-related business operations should themselves be measurable, giving management an opportunity to drive continual improvement.

- **Assurance process integration**   Organizations typically operate one or more separate assurance processes in silos that are not integrated. An effective strategy would work to break down these silos and consolidate assurance processes, reducing hidden risks.

All of these should be developed in a way that makes them measurable. These components were made to fit together in this way.

The Criticality of Business Alignment

The need for an organization's information security program to be business aligned cannot be overstated. The lack of business alignment could be considered a program's greatest failing if not corrected.

It is critical for an information security program to be aligned in terms of support for the organization's overall goals and to utilize existing mechanisms such as corporate governance, established business communication protocols, and policy enforcement. However, if and where dysfunction exists in the organization in terms of culture (for instance, a casual attitude or checkbox approach toward security or privacy), the program may position itself deliberately out of phase with the organization to alter the culture and bring it to a better place. In another example, rather than be satisfied with what may be low organizational maturity, security program leaders may influence process maturity by example through the enactment of higher-maturity processes and procedures.

As change agents, security leaders need to understand where alignment is beneficial and where influence is essential. Here's an example of the criticality of business alignment: the information security program in a software as a service (SaaS) company needs to be fully involved in the software and systems development life cycle in the company's SaaS products to ensure that the products are free of exploitable vulnerabilities that could wreak havoc via a security incident.

Strategy Participants

An information security leader needs to involve a number of key stakeholders and others in developing a strategy that is business aligned and that has a reasonable chance to succeed. The most important resources for the development of an information security program strategy are the opinions, observations, and analytical abilities of a number of key personnel in the organization, including the following:

- **Board of directors**   With explicit responsibility for establishing risk appetite, board members should have a clear understanding of the level of risk they desire for the organization. That said, few boards may have formally established a specific risk appetite, but, certainly, one or more of them will have an opinion on the matter.

- **Executive management**   As the personnel responsible for corporate governance, executives' decisions impart their attitudes about risk, whether implicit or explicit, subconscious or spoken aloud.

- **Security leader**   An experienced security leader needs to be an effective communicator and must be able to sell the strategy to business leaders. It's not enough to know information security inside and out; if the security leader cannot develop and sell a strategy to those who control resources (executives and board members), the strategy has little chance of succeeding.

- **Security team**   Members of the security team must be able to collaborate with one another and with others in the organization to contribute to the development of strategy details. Security team members must be familiar with their specialties in information security, must recognize essential improvement areas, and must articulate them to the security leaders and other leaders.

- **Business leaders**   The security leader must collaborate with business leaders in the organization to understand their business models, strategies, goals, objectives, and operations. Without this knowledge, the security strategy may not align well with the organization.

- **Rank and file**   Many individual contributors will have key knowledge and valuable insight that will enable the security leader (and team) to craft an effective strategy for the program. The security leader's challenge is to identify those individuals and collaborate with them to understand their perspectives on information security.

- **Outside experts**   An effective security leader has a network of experienced, trusted professionals to consult with on large or small matters concerning strategy development. Even the most accomplished leaders have mentors who can provide guidance and feedback on professional matters.

Strategy Resources

Before a strategy can be developed, it is first necessary to understand everything that is in place currently. A strategy describes how goals and objectives are to be met. Without knowing the starting place of a journey, it is not possible to chart a course to the journey's destination. Before future security capabilities can be mapped out, it's necessary to understand an organization's current state and capabilities. The differences can be seen as a gap that needs to be filled, whether that means employing tools, technologies, skills, policies, or practices.

More than simply defining point A in a journey to point B, existing resources also paint a picture of an organization's current capabilities, including behaviors, skills, and practices, and how they contribute to the organization's current security posture.

Two types of inputs must be considered: those that will influence the development of strategic objectives, and those that define the current state of the security program and protective controls. The following inputs must be considered before objectives are developed:

- Risk assessments
- Threat assessments

When suitable risk and threat assessments have been completed, the security strategist can then develop strategic objectives, or, if they have been created already, validate that the established strategic objectives will satisfactorily address risks and threats identified in those assessments.

Next, security strategists can examine several other inputs that help them understand the workings of the current security program, including the following:

- Risk assessments
- Threat assessments
- Policy
- Standards
- Guidelines
- Processes and procedures
- Architecture
- Controls
- Skills
- Metrics
- Assets

- Risk register
- Vulnerability assessments
- Insurance
- Critical data
- Business impact analysis
- Security incident log
- Outsourced services
- Audits
- Culture
- Maturity
- Risk appetite

These focus areas are described in the following sections.

Risk Assessments

A strategist should choose to have a risk assessment performed to reveal risks present in the organization. This helps the strategist understand threat scenarios and their estimated impact and frequency of occurrence. The results of a risk assessment give the strategist valuable information on the types of resources required to bring risks down to acceptable levels. This is vital for developing and validating strategic objectives.

Any historical record of risk assessments may give the strategist a better idea of the maturity of the organization's security program, as well as an indication of whether risks in the past had been mitigated. If older risk assessments indicate significant risks that are still present in newer risk assessments, or if risk assessments are performed only for compliance purposes and not for making actual improvements in the organization's security posture, you could wonder whether the organization places much credence in those risk assessments.

Risk assessments should drive the actual creation of strategic objectives. Otherwise, there is a danger that strategic objectives may not include changes to an organization's security program and the protective measures needed to reduce significant risks.

The strategist should also request corporate risk assessments to feed into the strategy; many times, IT risk assessments are technology focused. By reviewing and using the corporate risk assessment, the strategist can better align the security strategy with the organization's business objectives.

Threat Assessments

Strategists should have a threat assessment performed so that they can better understand relevant threats. This assessment provides the strategist with information about the types of threats most likely to have an impact on the organization, regardless of the effectiveness of controls.

Performing a threat assessment provides an additional perspective on risk. This is because a threat assessment focuses on external threats and threat scenarios, regardless of the presence or effectiveness of preventive or detective controls. While vulnerabilities may change frequently, threats are considered to be constant. Because of this, security policies need to reflect threats that have been identified.

A threat assessment is an essential element of strategy development. Without a threat assessment, there is a possibility that strategic objectives may fail to address important threats. This would result in a security strategy that will not adequately protect the organization.

A history of threat assessments gives the strategist insight into the maturity of the organization's security program: an absence of threat assessments may be an indication of low maturity or scarce resources. Details in threat assessment records may reveal remediation trends if key threats are not appearing repeatedly, which would indicate that they have not been mitigated.

Policy

An organization's security policy, as well as its practices in relation to its policy, may say a great deal about its desired current state. Security policy can be thought of as an organization's internal laws and regulations with regard to the protection of important assets (as well as personnel safety). Examination of current security policy can reveal a lot about what behaviors are required in the organization.

The following are a few aspects of security policy:

- **Breadth of coverage**   What subject areas are covered by the policy? Does it include expected computer and mobile device usage behavior? Are other topics such as vulnerability management, third-party risk, or software development included in security policy?

- **Relevance**   Does the policy include content on new technologies and practices?

- **Policy communication**   How well is policy communicated to the user community, with what frequency, and with what level of understanding by the workforce?

- **Workforce transformation**   Does the policy address matters related to the shift to remote work in many organizations? Topics may include remote access and VPN, home networks, physical security, travel, and the applicability of employment laws when employees decide to relocate to another city, state, or country.

- **Policy strictness**   Does the policy broadly prohibit certain behaviors such as the occasional personal use of corporate e-mail or limit or prohibit the use of external USB data storage devices?

- **Accountability and consequences**   Does the policy specify expectations for adherence to policy or the consequences of willingly violating policy? For instance, do policy violations include the prospect of suspension or termination of employment?

- **Compliance**   It is important to understand the degree to which the organization is in compliance with its policy, including the margin of compliance. Does the organization's security policy reflect good practices, and does the organization meet most or all of them? Or does its policy appear to be more of a vision statement of how things could be in the future?

- **Last management review**   It is important to know when an organization's security was last updated, reviewed, and approved by management. This speaks to more than just the organization's policy but also to how active its security program has been in the recent past.

Standards

An organization's security standards describe, in detail, the methods, techniques, technologies, specifications, brands, and configurations to be used throughout the organization. As with security policy, it is important to understand the organization's standards, including the breadth of coverage, strictness, compliance, and last review and update. These all tell the security manager the extent to which an organization's security standards are used—if at all.

In addition to the aforementioned characteristics, it is important to know how the organization's standards were developed and how good they are. For instance, are there device-hardening standards, and are they aligned to or derived from industry-recognized standards such as those from the Center for Internet Security (CIS), National Institute for Standards and Technology (NIST), European Union Agency for Cybersecurity (ENISA), Defense Information Systems Agency Security Technical Implementation Guides (DISA STIG), or another standardization body?

Similarly, it is important to know whether standards are highly detailed (configuration item by configuration item) or whether they are principle-based. If they are the latter, engineers may exercise potentially wide latitude when implementing these standards. You should understand that highly detailed standards are not necessarily better than principle-based standards; it depends on the nature of the organization, its risk tolerance, and its maturity.

Guidelines

While an organization's guidelines are not "the law" per se, the presence of guidelines may signal higher than average organizational maturity. Many organizations don't go beyond creating policies and standards, so the presence of proper guidelines means that the organization may have (or had in the past) sufficient resources or prioritization to make documenting guidance on policies important enough to do.

According to their very nature, guidelines are typically written for personnel who need a little extra guidance on how to adhere to policies.

Like other types of security program documents, guidelines should be reviewed and updated regularly. Because guidelines bridge rarely changing policy with often-changing technologies and practices, a strategist examining guidelines should find them being changed frequently—or they may be found to be irrelevant. But that, too, is possibly evidence of an attempt to improve maturity or communications (or both) but with the absence of long-term commitment.

Processes and Procedures

An organization's processes and procedures may speak volumes about its level of discipline, consistency, risk tolerance, and maturity with regard to its security program, plus IT and the business in general. Like other types of documents discussed in this section, the relevance, accuracy, and thoroughness of process and procedure documents are indicators of the organization's maturity and commitment to a solid security program.

Relying on process documentation is not sufficient; strategists need to examine more than process and procedure documents. Additionally, they must interview personnel, examine business records, and observe processes in action to ensure that they are being carried out as designed.

Further evidence of process and procedure effectiveness can be found in risk assessments and audits. Those topics are discussed later in this section.

Architecture

An organization's architecture—its documentation of systems, networks, data flows, and other aspects of its environment—gives the security strategist a lot of useful information about how the organization has implemented its information systems.

Although it's good to look for and examine network diagrams, system diagrams, data flow diagrams, and so forth, it's nearly as valuable to find good and consistent designs even if they aren't documented anywhere. I'd rather see an organization's infrastructure as modern, effective, and consistent versus a collection of outdated diagrams or, worse yet, inconsistent uses of technologies and techniques throughout an organization. Whether or not architecture diagrams exist is a concern that is similar to that regarding policies, standards, guidelines, and other artifacts.

Equally important here is whether the architecture of technology effectively supports the organization. Does the organization's technology, and the way that the technology has been implemented, adequately support the organization's goals, objectives, and operations? Like so many other aspects of information security and IT, alignment with the business and its goals and objectives is critical and cannot be disregarded. Making key changes in this regard may need to be part of an overall strategy.

Another aspect of architecture is known as *technical debt*. This term represents two characteristics of an organization's infrastructure:

- **Poor design**   Lack of an overall design, or a poor design, causes subsequent additions and changes to the environment to be made in a less than optimal manner, further degrading the environment in terms of performance, resilience, or simplicity.

- **Outdated and unsupported components** In this instance, major hardware or software components of the environment have exceeded their service life, are no longer supported by their manufacturers, or have subcomponents that cannot be easily replaced.

The concept of technical debt is a metaphor for financial debt in two aspects: First, "interest payments" come in the form of additional effort every time the environment requires attention. Next, "retiring the debt" requires major architectural changes and/or replacement of many components.

Technical debt is accumulated when organizations lack personnel capable of creating good architectural designs and also when an organization fails to upgrade end-of-life components.

Data debt is a phenomenon similar to technical debt. The data models in an organization saddled with data debt are no longer business aligned. Often, new business needs result in a further fracturing of once cohesive, enterprise-wide data models into an increasing number of silos.

Controls

The presence of controls—and the control framework—speaks volumes about the organization's security program. Controls, however, may exist only on paper and not in practice. It is useful to read about the organization's controls, but on paper alone, they offer little information about whether the controls are actually being implemented. It's even more important to know whether they are effective.

When examining control documentation, the strategist should look for details such as control owners, the purpose and scope of controls, related process and procedure documents, and other metadata that will help the strategist understand their purpose.

Next, the strategist should look for artifacts or interview personnel to determine whether specific controls are in place. Again, the presence of documentation alone may not indicate whether controls are actually being implemented or whether documentation is just more shelfware. Interviewing personnel and observing controls in action is a better way to see whether controls are in place.

Internal and external audits, discussed later in the "Audits" section, are another way to understand control effectiveness.

A strategist will want to understand whether the controls in place are part of a control framework such as COBIT, ISO/IEC 27002, NIST SP 800-53, NIST SP 800-171, HIPAA, or PCI DSS. But more than that, the strategist should know whether all controls in the control framework are implemented—or have some been omitted? The reason for omission may vary from irrelevance to irresponsible avoidance.

Finally, the strategist should look for additional controls that have been implemented. This may be a sign of regulatory requirements or the result of an effective risk management program, where identified risks compelled management to enact additional controls to mitigate risk.

Skills

An inventory of skills provides the strategist with an idea of what staff members are able to accomplish. This is useful on a few levels:

- **Tenure**   This includes how many years of different types of experience a staff member may have.

- **Behavioral**   This includes leadership, management, coordination, and logistics.

- **Disciplines**   This includes fields such as systems engineering, network engineering, controls development, audit, risk management, and risk analysis.

- **Technologies**   This includes skills with specific technologies such as Palo Alto Networks firewalls, CentOS operating systems, LogRhythm, and AppScan.

Understanding skills at all of these levels helps the strategist understand the types of work that the current staff is able to perform, where minor skills gaps exist, and where the strategist may recommend adding staff through hiring, contracting, or professional services.

A key consideration for a strategist is the potential for a major shift in technologies. Suppose, for example, that the organization has been using products from a particular vendor for many years, but because of a change in leadership and a good deal offered by a different vendor, the decision was made to migrate to the other vendor's products. Without fully understanding the skills and capabilities of the team, the organization leadership can create significant risks resulting from the lack of skills required to manage the new products effectively. This could lead to outages, departure of key resources, increased costs associated with consulting, and a loss of trust from the end-user community. A good way to validate whether the organization has stayed on top of such an issue is to see whether a *skills matrix* exists. If so, when was the last time it was reviewed, updated, and approved?

Metrics

Metrics indicate the state of an information security program over time. Proper metrics help personnel see how effectively the security program is protecting the organization; this is a key consideration for the people developing long-term strategies.

If metrics are properly established, they'll serve as a guide for the long-term effectiveness of security controls. This helps the strategist understand what works well and where improvement opportunities may be. The strategist can then design end states with more certainty and confidence than if metrics didn't exist.

When examining metrics, a strategist needs to understand the audience. For example, were security metrics developed for internal security operations' use only, or were the metrics developed for consumption by other audiences, such as internal users, senior management, or the board of directors? Next, the strategist will want to look for evidence that metrics were delivered to these audiences and whether metrics were ever used as a reason for making tactical or strategic changes in the security program.

Metrics are discussed fully in Chapter 5.

Assets

It is often said among information security professionals, "You cannot protect what you cannot find." This refers to assets in an organization—namely, servers, network devices, end-user workstations, and mobile devices—but also application software and software tools. Because many security incidents involve the exploitation of a vulnerability (usually with malware), organizations must have effective vulnerability management programs in place. The life-cycle process in a vulnerability management program is as follows:

1. Identify the environment to be scanned.

2. Scan assets for vulnerabilities.

3. Identify and categorize vulnerabilities.

4. Remediate vulnerabilities (often through applying security patches but sometimes through configuration changes or increased monitoring and alerting).

Depending on an organization's tools and methods, typically, only known identified assets are scanned. Unknown or unidentified assets may or may not get scanned, but even if they do, they might get lost in the process later. Intruders are familiar with this, and they use this to their advantage: by performing scans of their own, they can identify unpatched systems and use them as a beachhead from which to infiltrate the organization.

Further, some organizations have a practice of avoiding scanning some assets (and sometimes even entire subnets), either because the security team knows that some assets are poorly managed (skewing otherwise favorable metrics) or because some assets behave badly or even malfunction when scanned. Such practices indicate subpar asset management and the potential for considerable risk to the business.

Risk Register

A risk register, also known as a risk ledger, can offer the strategist a great deal of insight into risk management and risk analysis activities in the organization. Depending on the detail available in the risk register a strategist may be able to discern the following:

- Scope, frequency, quality, and maturity of risk assessments

- Presence or absence of risk treatment

- Security incidents

A risk register is the business record reflecting the history and findings from risk assessments, threat assessments, vulnerability assessments, security incidents, and other activities. Its content reflects the types of activities occurring in the information security program and the significant results of those activities.

The lack of a risk register would indicate that the organization's security management program is not taking a risk-based approach. Instead, the organization may be compliance-based or, worse yet, asset-based or ad hoc. These approaches are signs of lower maturity, where the organization's security personnel are mainly reactive and do little planning.

The strategist should also inquire as to the existence of a corporate or enterprise risk register that would be a part of an overall enterprise risk management (ERM) program. Further, if a risk register exists, the strategist should determine whether any formal or informal communication exists between those who manage the ERM risk register and those who manage the cyber-risk register.

Vulnerability Assessments

Strategists may choose to have a vulnerability assessment performed so that they may better understand the current security posture of the organization's technology infrastructure. The vulnerability assessment may target network devices, appliances, operating systems, subsystems such as web servers and database management systems, and applications—or any suitable combination thereof.

The results of a vulnerability assessment will tell the strategist several things about the organization, including the following:

- **Operational maturity** The consistency of vulnerabilities among targets will reveal whether the organization has configuration standards or automated tools for managing the configuration across targets. When a vulnerability assessment finds variations in vulnerabilities among similar systems, the strategist may assume that the organization is not using automated tools to distribute patches to its systems but instead appears to be installing patches in an ad hoc manner. On the other hand, when the vulnerability assessment shows consistency in vulnerabilities among similar systems, this is an indication of greater operational maturity and possibly the presence and use of automated tools for system management.

- **Security maturity** The range of vulnerabilities among targets will reveal the maturity of the organization's vulnerability management program. If the presence or absence of security patches is inconsistent or if numerous older vulnerabilities are found, this may indicate that vulnerability management is given a low priority or insufficient resources. When a vulnerability assessment identifies large numbers of vulnerabilities—particularly "high" and "critical" vulnerabilities dating back many months or longer—this is an indication that the organization is not placing emphasis on basic security hygiene.

Insurance

The security strategist may want to know whether the organization has cybersecurity insurance or any general insurance policy that covers some types of cyber events and incidents. As important as having cyber insurance is, equally important is the reason the organization purchased it. A strategist will want to explore possible reasons.

- **Compliance** The organization may have purchased a cyber-insurance policy to be compliant with a law, regulation, or standard.

- **Customer requirement** The organization may have a cyber-insurance policy because a key customer required it.

- **Prior incidents**   Perhaps the organization has a cyber-insurance policy because a costly incident occurred in the past. Similarly, a company known to the organization's management may have suffered an incident, prompting the organization to purchase cyber insurance in case a similar event could happen to them.

- **Risk treatment**   The organization may have purchased cyber insurance because risks were identified that the organization chose to have transferred to another organization.

It is vitally important to understand the terms of any cyber-insurance policy. While the amounts of benefits are important, the most important aspects of a cyber-insurance policy are its terms and conditions. Many organizations have been known to purchase cyber insurance only to find out later that they receive little or no relief from it because of one or more exclusions. Cyber-insurance policies vary quite a lot, and many require policyholder organizations to have many policies, controls, and capabilities in place. Interestingly enough, organizations that have the required components in their security programs are much less likely to experience significant security incidents—but risk reduction is the whole point of developing an information security strategy and using cyber insurance. This is similar to automobile insurance, homeowners' insurance, and renters' insurance: it is important to read and fully understand insurance policies in detail.

Here are a few key questions to consider with regard to a cyber-insurance policy:

- **Ransomware**   Under what conditions will a cyber-insurance policy pay a ransom?

- **Third-party breach**   Will cyber insurance cover losses if a breach occurs at a third-party service provider?

- **Proactive support**   What assistance does the insurance company provide prior to any incident, and is the organization required to accept this assistance as a condition of the policy?

- **Incident reporting and assistance**   What notification does the insurance policy require in order to provide assistance? Does the insurance company select a forensics investigator?

Insurance companies are becoming increasingly adept at identifying the risk factors associated with security breaches, resulting in policies requiring that certain safeguards be put into place to reduce the risk of a security breach. Security leaders need to understand the details of their cyber-insurance policies and determine whether the organization meets all requirements.

Critical Data

Most organizations do not have an accurate notion regarding the location and use of their critical data. Organizations usually use key business applications that store and process critical data, but in most organizations, copies of parts of their critical data also reside in many other places, including internal file servers, sanctioned data storage services such as Box and Dropbox, and unsanctioned data storage services and cloud-based applications.

Though this section is not about the cloud and cloud services, the existence and ease of use of cloud services make it easy for individuals and groups in an organization to upload critical data to these services. The fact that many cloud-based services offer low-cost and zero-cost services encourages this phenomenon all the more. This has given rise to the colloquial phrase "bring your own app" (BYOA) to describe this growing problem. Most organizations have lost sight of all the locations and uses of their critical data, whether sanctioned or not.

The strategist should seek to understand the extent to which the organization's data in the cloud is a part of an overall architecture, including the use of cloud regions that are employed for resilience purposes. This will help the strategist better understand whether the organization has a data governance function and a data management strategy.

Another component of critical data is the bring-your-own-device (BYOD) phenomenon, which results in sensitive business information residing on personally owned devices, outside of the organization's direct control. The ubiquity and openness of IT services make it all but impossible for organizations to prevent staff members from using personally owned devices as part of their work.

The cloud, BYOA, and BYOD underscore the lack of visibility and control over critical and sensitive data. Understanding this is important for strategists when determining the current state of security, which, as stated, is required if a viable strategy is to be developed to take the organization to a desired future state. This is one of many categories where a strategist will be unable to gather all desired facts about the state of security and where experience and judgment are required to discern the state of data management.

Business Impact Analysis

A business impact analysis (BIA) is used to identify an organization's business processes, the interdependencies between processes, the resources required for process operation, and the impact on the organization if any business process is incapacitated for a time.

A BIA is a cornerstone of a business continuity and disaster recovery (BCDR) program, because the BIA indicates which business processes and underlying resources are most vital to the organization. The most critical processes receive the most attention during the development of disaster recovery and business continuity plans.

The BIA is also useful for information security professionals aside from business continuity purposes. Again, the BIA indicates the most critical processes (and underlying resources such as information systems and other IT infrastructure), giving the security strategist a better idea of which business processes and systems warrant the greatest protection.

The presence of a BIA provides a strong indication of the organization's maturity through its intention to protect its most critical processes from disaster scenarios. Correspondingly, the absence of a BIA suggests that the organization does not consider BCDR as having strategic importance.

Security Incident Log

A security incident log provides a history of security incidents in the organization. Depending on the information that is captured in the incident log, the strategist may be able to discern the maturity of the organization's information security program, especially its incident response program. For instance, a highly mature organization will perform a post-mortem analysis on significant incidents and direct changes with regard to people, processes, and technology to reduce the probability, impact, or scope of similar incidents in the future.

Like other business records and activities, the strategist needs to understand the reason for the existence of the security incident log. Is it intended for compliance purposes (in which case the incident log may be sparsely populated, and there may be an absence of corrective actions), or does the organization really want to use the log information to learn from and even anticipate security incidents? These are the deeper questions that the security strategist needs to discover and know.

A sparsely populated incident log may be an indication of several things, including the following:

- **Lack of/deficient SIEM**   A *security information and event management* (SIEM) is a system that collects log data from servers, endpoints, network devices such as firewalls, and other sources such as antivirus consoles. It correlates this log data and produces security alerts when actionable security-related activities are taking place. An organization without a SIEM may have little way of knowing whether security incidents such as break-ins are occurring. Similarly, an organization with a SIEM that is not well maintained may also have many blind spots and may be unaware of incidents occurring in its environment.

- **Training**   Personnel may not be trained in the recognition of security incidents. Security incidents may be occurring but unrecognized, resulting in incidents with greater impact and the loss of learning opportunities.

Outsourced Services

Most organizations outsource a good portion of their IT systems and services. Unlike earlier eras when organizations had their own data centers and when most or all applications were running in-house (aka on-premises), today, the model has almost completely flipped: organizations are moving the bulk of their business applications to cloud-based infrastructure as a service (IaaS), platform as a service (PaaS), and software as a service (SaaS) environments.

The degree to which any particular organization has outsourced its business applications to the cloud is not a concerning matter. Instead, what's important is the amount of due care exercised in the process of outsourcing.

The practice of determining and managing risks associated with outsourcing is called *third-party risk*. In lawyer-speak, these external organizations are called third parties (and the organizations *they* outsource to are called *fourth parties*).

The third-party risk practices that the strategists are looking for include the following:

- **Up-front due diligence**   This is an assessment of risk performed on a service provider prior to the organization electing to use the service. This initial risk assessment gives the organization an opportunity to enforce security-related terms and conditions on the service provider in the legal agreement. An up-front risk assessment may include one or more of the following:
    - **Relationship risk assessment**   The organization analyzes the strategic importance of the service provider in terms of contract value and service criticality.

- **Inherent risk assessment**   This is an analysis of the service provider's financial health and geopolitical risk.

- **Control risk assessment**   This is an analysis of the controls that the organization would like the service provider to use to protect the organization's data.

- **Site visit**   The organization may elect to visit one or more of the service provider's processing sites and perhaps corporate offices.

- **Risk tiering**   This is the practice of establishing tiers of service provider risk. Each service provider, based on the nature of services provided to the organization, is assigned a risk level, or *tier*. The due diligence activities performed for each tier are commensurate with the risk level. For example, service providers at the highest risk tier may be issued a lengthy questionnaire annually, and they may be required to undergo annual penetration tests, as well as an onsite visit to confirm the presence of key controls. Service providers at a middle tier of risk may be issued a shorter questionnaire annually, and service providers at the lowest tier may be issued a brief questionnaire annually. Responses to questions answered unsatisfactorily will also vary according to risk tier. For top-tier services providers, this may involve a detailed mitigation plan; at lower tiers, there is less concern.

- **Ongoing due diligence**   Throughout the duration of a service provider relationship, the organization will periodically assess each service provider to ensure that risks discovered at the start of the relationship have not significantly changed. An organization will carry out a number of activities, as outlined for up-front due diligence.

It's Turtles All the Way Down

"Turtles all the way down" refers to an idea that the flat earth rests on the back of a giant turtle, which itself rests on the back of an even larger turtle, which rests on a still larger turtle, and so on, forever. This is a mythological way of explaining *infinite regress*. Third-party risk management can be likened to the epistemological stack of world turtles, in that each organization obtains goods and services from other organizations, those organizations depend on others, and so on, with no apparent end. All organizations are at least partly dependent upon others for goods or services essential for delivering goods or services to their customers.

So where does it all end? Depending upon the industry and the criticality of individual goods or services, third-party risk management generally vets critical vendors and determines whether those vendors have effective third-party risk management programs.

After all, we're all in this together.

Audits

Internal and external audits can tell the strategist quite a bit about the state of the organization's security program. A careful examination of audit findings can potentially provide significant details on control effectiveness, vulnerabilities, disaster preparedness, or other aspects of the program—depending on the objectives of those audits.

When examining audit results, a security strategist needs to understand several things.

- **Objective**   The objective or purpose of the audit tells the reader why the audit took place. This often provides additional insight into why certain people, processes, or technologies were examined while others were apparently omitted. For example, was an audit performed because it is required by regulation or another requirement, or was it performed voluntarily as another means of organization improvement?

- **Scope**   The scope of an audit tells the reader which technologies, business processes, business locations, or other aspects of the organization were examined.

- **Qualifications of auditors**   An audit is only as effective as its auditors are skilled and experienced in performing audits, as well as their familiarity with the things being audited. An IT auditor with little operational IT experience is not going to be as effective and as insightful as an IT auditor with a background in some aspect of IT engineering or operations.

- **Audit methodologies**   It is important for the reader to understand the audit methodologies used in any particular audit. For instance, did the auditor interview personnel, examine systems and records, observe personnel performing their tasks, or perform tasks of their own? Equally important are sampling methodologies, including how samples are selected and who performs the selection.

The security strategist needs to consider the bigger picture: mainly, is the organization using audit results to drive improvements in the organization, or are audit reports merely shelfware shown to regulators on their annual visit?

Culture

The culture of an organization can tell the strategist a lot about the state of security. Many people mistakenly believe that information security is all about technology. While technology is part of security, the most important aspect of information security is people. No amount of technology can adequately compensate for a person's wrong attitude and understanding about protecting an organization's information assets. People are absolutely key.

A strategist will want to explore a few aspects of an organization's culture, including the following:

- **Leadership**   It is important to understand the actions of executive management, mainly to see whether they abide by company policies and lead by example. A classic example is a "no personal devices for company business" organizational policy, yet the CEO connects his personal iPad to corporate e-mail.

- **Accountability**   The strategist will look for evidence that the organization enforces company policies and requires employees to be accountable for violations. Equally important is the observation of outcomes of bad decisions—are decision-makers held accountable?

- **Empowerment**   Organizations are sometimes measured by employee empowerment: whether employees are implicitly given the go-ahead to act and "ask for forgiveness" if something goes wrong, versus organizations that do not empower employees, requiring them to "ask for permission" before acting. This is not so much about good versus bad policy, but more about understanding how the organization behaves. Also important is the organization's behavior when things go wrong. Does the organization seek to punish the person or people responsible for the mistakes or learn from its mistakes—or is it somewhere in between?

- **Security awareness buy-in**   Even today, people seem to lack much common sense regarding Internet safety and seem willing to click anything arriving in their inboxes. While this may seem a discouraging point of view, many organizations do an inadequate job of informing their personnel about the various risks associated with Internet and computer usage. A strategist should investigate the organization's security awareness program to determine how engaging the program is, how rigorous any training is, whether workers take security awareness seriously, and whether there are rewards for good behavior and penalties for risky behavior. The other aspects in this section—leadership, accountability, and empowerment—are all related to security awareness, because they help the strategist understand whether executives lead by example, whether empowered personnel make good decisions that impact security, and whether personnel are accountable for their actions.

These and other aspects of an organization's culture help the strategist better understand the organization's present state.

Maturity

The characteristics of a security management program discussed in this section all contribute to the overall maturity of the organization's program. Although the maturity level of the program doesn't tell the strategist everything they need to know about the program, the strategist's observations of the overall program will provide a "thumb in the air" feeling for its overall maturity.

The strategist will probably find that the maturity levels of various aspects of the organization's security program vary widely. For instance, the organization may have mature asset management and vulnerability management programs but be lacking in other areas such as internal audit and security awareness.

The levels of maturity are discussed in greater detail in the next section. Maturity also plays a part during a gap assessment, also discussed in the next section.

Risk Appetite

Every organization has a risk appetite, although most have not formally documented it. A security strategist needs to understand business leaders' implicit and explicit risk appetite, which is manifested in many ways:

- The nature of top executives' support for information security
- Whether adequate resources are available to manage identified risks
- Whether the organization has a documented risk appetite and, if so, is it followed
- Whether information security is a part of, or aligns to, the organization's overall strategy and objectives
- Whether risk treatment decisions portray an overall consistent approach to risk

Risk appetite can be summed up this way: *does anyone really care?*

Strategy Development

After performing risk and threat assessments and carefully reviewing the state of the security program through the examination of artifacts, the strategist can develop strategic objectives. Generally speaking, strategic objectives will fall into one of these categories:

- Improvements in protective controls
- Improvements in incident visibility
- Improvements in incident response
- Reductions in risk, including compliance risk
- Reductions in cost
- Increased resiliency of key business systems

These categories all contribute to strategic improvements in an organization's security program. Depending on the current and desired future state of security, objectives may represent large projects or groups of projects implemented over several years to develop broad new capabilities, or they may be smaller projects focused on improving existing capabilities.

Following are examples of broad, sweeping objectives for developing new security capabilities:

- Define and implement a SIEM to provide visibility into security and operational events.
- Define and implement a security incident response program.
- Define and implement a security awareness learning program.

Examples of objectives for improving existing capabilities include the following:

- Integrate vulnerability management and integrated risk management (IRM) systems.
- Link security awareness and access management programs so that staff members must successfully complete security awareness training to retain their system access.

Once one or more objectives have been identified, the security strategist will undertake several activities that are required to meet the objectives. These activities are explained in the remainder of this section.

The strategist must consider many inputs before developing objectives and strategies to achieve them. These inputs serve a critical purpose: to help the strategist understand the organization's current state. The journey to developing and achieving a strategy is not possible without understanding the journey's starting point, which are discussed in the previous section, "Strategy Resources."

Gap Assessment

To implement a security strategy and accomplish objectives, security professionals often spend too much time focusing on the end goal and not enough time on the starting point. Without sufficient knowledge of the starting point, accomplishing objectives will be more difficult, and achieving success will be less certain.

A gap assessment should focus on several aspects of a security program, including one or more of the following:

- **Business alignment**   The most important aspect of an organization's information security program is whether it is suitably aligned with the business. This concept of alignment is mentioned throughout this chapter.
- **Existing/previous strategy**   Understanding prior strategies can reveal much about the security program in the past. Several aspects of prior strategies to consider include the following:
  - Was the prior strategy actually a strategy, or was it an objective, a roadmap, or something else?
  - Was the strategy achievable?
  - Was the strategy achieved, or was reasonable progress made?
  - Was the strategy business aligned?
  - Was the strategy measurable?
  - Were sufficient resources made available to achieve the strategy?
- **Security program charter**   The organization may have a charter that defines a strategy, roles and responsibilities, objectives, or other matters.
- **Security policy**   Existing security policy needs to be carefully studied to understand alignment between security policy and the strategy. The security manager should review security policy enforcement as well as exceptions and related incidents.

- **Security standards** Existing security standards should be examined to understand what emphasis has been placed on proven and consistent methods for hardening systems. The security manager will want to look at the approach. Are security standards a set of principles only, or do they include configuration details?

- **Security procedures** This includes security procedures, as well as IT and other business procedures that have security subject matter or implications.

- **Security guidelines** While security guidelines are considered optional, it is important to understand what they say about implementing security policies and procedures. Content in security guidelines may provide important clues on organizational culture and its views about policy.

- **Security controls** Although it is necessary to review control objectives and control narratives, it is equally important to understand control effectiveness and how well controls support existing objectives.

- **Risk assessments** Available risk assessments may provide insight into risks observed in the organization. This would provide a valuable risk-based perspective on the state of the organization in the recent—or not so recent—past.

- **Internal and external audit results** Audit reports are generally seen as an in-depth view of the effectiveness of internal controls in the organization. A security manager needs to understand how to read the audit report—as well as be able to read between the lines—to understand specific audit methodologies used to examine controls and report on them. Note that for some audits, auditors are examining specific controls, whether or not they actually exist in the organization. Understanding the scope of an audit is also important, as it may, in some cases, be quite narrow and not provide a broad view of control risk.

- **Security metrics** Examining security metrics over time should give a security manager some important information. Not only can certain details of the security program be evaluated, but the bigger picture is also important: the metrics that the organization chose to measure. If metrics have been in place long enough, there may be trends that can be observed.

- **Risk register** An organization's risk register can provide insight into the issues that are considered important security issues. Depending on the details available in the risk register, a security manager may be able to discern the various activities and methods in place to capture content for the register.

- **Risk treatment decision records** When available, risk treatment records reveal what issues warranted attention, discussion, and decisions. Coupled with the risk register, information here can provide a record of issues tackled by the organization's risk management process.

- **Security incident program** This includes program objectives, processes, procedures, records, tools, and practices. Further, the presence of playbooks indicates a desire to respond quickly and effectively when an incident occurs.

- **Security incident records**   The record of security incidents can reveal a lot about the capabilities and attitudes in the security program. A sparse record might indicate gaps in capabilities or skills. A rich record is probably an indication of a more mature program and personnel intent on identifying issues so that improvements can be made.

- **Third-party risk**   Vendor risk, also known as third-party risk, is a near-universal problem for organizations, given the trend in outsourcing line-of-business applications and the use of cloud-based services. Here, the security manager needs to understand the degree of attention the organization places on third-party risk, including the completeness of business records, the frequency of risk and control assessments, the history of site visits, and the organization's practice of following up on risk issues discovered in key third parties.

- **Business continuity and disaster recovery program**   The presence of business continuity planning (BCP) and/or disaster recovery planning (DRP) activities is a good indication (although not a certain one) that the organization cares enough about its long-term viability that it wants to minimize the impact of natural and manmade disasters. A security manager needs to understand whether BCP/DRP records and procedures are up-to-date and to what extent the organization elects to train its personnel and conduct tests of its plans.

- **Security awareness training program**   A security awareness training and communications program says a lot about an organization—namely, the extent to which the organization acknowledges that people are a critical aspect to the success of a program and its ability to protect itself from harm. The variety and frequency of messaging techniques used are important aspects of a security awareness program, but they are not as important as the program's alignment with the organization.

- **IT and security projects**   Business records for recent projects speak volumes about the organization's value and emphasis on security. The security manager will want to look through the list of project participants to see whether security personnel are included. Equally important is the presence (or absence) of security requirements—if requirements are part of bigger projects.

When examining all of this and other information about an organization's security program, the security strategist should bring the right measure of skepticism, because although there is much to know about information that is found, the absence of information may speak volumes as well. Here are some considerations:

- **Absence of evidence is not evidence of absence**   This time-honored quote applies to artifacts in any security program. For instance, a sparse or nonexistent security incident log may be an indication of several things: the organization may not have the required visibility to know when an incident has taken place, the organization's staff may not be trained in the recognition of incidents, or the organization may be watching only for "black swan" events and are missing the routine incidents.

- **Freshness, usefulness, and window dressing**   When it comes to policy, process, and procedure documentation, it is important for strategists to determine whether documents are created for appearances only (in which case they may be well-kept secrets, except by their owners) or whether they are widely known and utilized. A look at these documents' revision histories tells you part of the story, while interviewing the right personnel completes the picture by revealing how well their existence is known and whether they are really used.

- **Scope, turf, and politics**   In larger organizations, the security manager needs to understand current and historical practices with regard to roles and responsibilities for security and security-related activities. For example, records for a global security program may instead reflect only what is occurring in the Americas, even though nothing found in documentation supports this.

- **Reading between the lines**   Depending upon the organization's culture and the ethics of current or prior security personnel, records may not accurately reflect what's really happening in the security program. Records may be incomplete as a result of overemphasis, underemphasis, distortions, or simply "looking the other way" when situations arise.

- **Off-the-books institutional knowledge (aka "tribal knowledge")**   For various reasons, certain activities and proceedings in a security program may not be documented. For example, certain incidents may conveniently *not* be present in the incident log—otherwise, external auditors might catch the scent and go on a foxhunt, causing all manner of unpleasantries.

- **Regulatory requirements**   When examining each aspect of a security program, the security manager needs to understand one thing: Is the activity being undertaken because it is required by regulations (with hell and fury from regulators if absent) or because the organization is managing risk and attempting to reduce the probability and/or impact of potential threats?

When performing a gap assessment, a strategist is examining the present condition of processes, technologies, and people. But, by definition, a gap assessment is the study of the difference between the present condition of something and the desired future state. A common approach to determining the future state is to determine the current maturity of a process or technology and compare that to the desired maturity level. Continue reading the next section for a discussion on maturity levels.

Strengths, Weaknesses, Opportunities, and Threats Analysis

Strengths, weaknesses, opportunities, and threats (SWOT) analysis is a tool used in support of strategy planning. SWOT involves introspective analysis, where the strategist asks four questions about the object of study:

- **Strengths**   What characteristics of the business give it an advantage over others?
- **Weaknesses**   What characteristics of the business put it at a disadvantage?

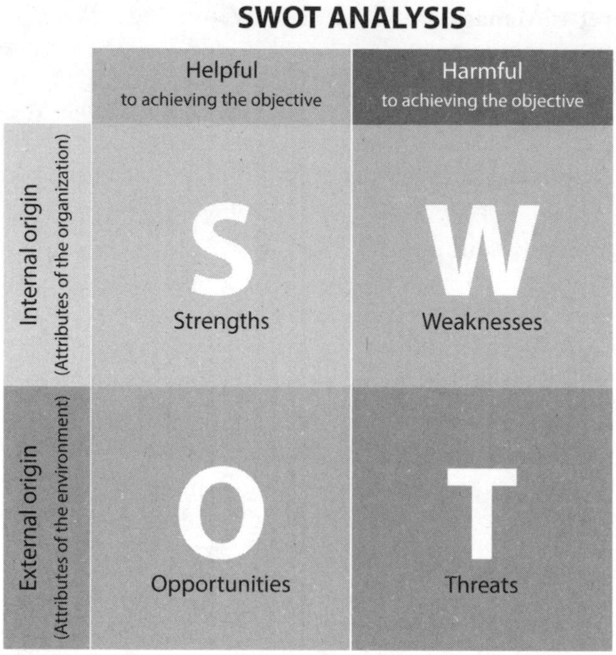

Figure 2-1
A SWOT matrix with its four components (Courtesy of Xhienne)

SWOT ANALYSIS

- **Opportunities**   What elements in the environment could the business use to its advantage?
- **Threats**   What elements in the environment threaten to harm the business?

SWOT analysis uses a matrix, which is shown in Figure 2-1.

Capability Maturity Models

The Software Engineering Institute (SEI) at Carnegie Mellon University accomplished a great deal with its development of the Capability Maturity Model Integration for Development (CMMI-DEV). Capability maturity models are useful tools for understanding the maturity level of a process. Maturity models in other technology disciplines have also been developed, such as the Systems Security Engineering Capability Maturity Model (SSE-CMM).

The CMMI-DEV uses five levels of maturity to describe the formality of a process:

- **Level 1: Initial**   This represents a process that is ad hoc, inconsistent, unmeasured, and unrepeatable.
- **Level 2: Repeatable**   This represents a process that is performed consistently and with the same outcome. It may or may not be well-documented.
- **Level 3: Defined**   This represents a process that is well-defined and well-documented.

- **Level 4: Managed** This represents a quantitatively measured process with one or more metrics.
- **Level 5: Optimizing** This represents a measured process that is under continuous improvement.

Not all security strategists are familiar with maturity models. Strategists unaccustomed to capability maturity models need to understand two important characteristics of maturity models and how they are used:

- *Level 5 is not the ultimate objective.* Most organizations' average maturity level targets range from 2.5 to 3.5. There are few organizations whose mission justifies level 5 maturity. The cost of developing a level 5 process or control is often prohibitive and out of alignment with risks.
- *Each control or process may have its own maturity level.* It is neither common nor prudent to assign a single maturity level target for all controls and processes. Instead, organizations with skilled strategists can determine the appropriate level of maturity for each control and process. They need not all be the same. Instead, it is more appropriate to use a threat-based or risk-based model to determine an appropriate level of maturity for each control and process. Some will be 2, some will be 3, some will be 4, and a few may even be 5.

The common use of capability maturity models is the determination of the current maturity of a process, together with analysis, to determine the desired maturity level process by process and technology by technology. The maturity level should be in alignment with the organization's risk appetite.

Policy Development

The execution of a security strategy may result in additions or improvements in its security-related capabilities. These additions or improvements may require that one or more security policies be updated to reflect the new or improved capabilities.

While security policies are designed to be durable and not tied to specific technologies, significant changes in technologies may put security policy at odds with them. Here is an example:

> *The Fast Car Company recently implemented its first security incident and event monitoring system that produces alerts whenever actionable security events occur. Prior to implementing the SIEM, IT and security personnel would examine security logs every day to see whether any security events had occurred in the past 24 hours.*

> *Before implementing the SIEM, Fast Car Company's security policy stated that appropriate personnel were required to examine security logs daily and log any actions taken. Now that the company has a SIEM, IT and security personnel no longer need to examine logs. The company's policy needs to be changed so that 1) personnel are required to respond to security alerts and 2) personnel are required to examine the SIEM's configuration periodically so that it will produce alerts for relevant events.*

Security policies are supposed to align with current capabilities and are not a vision statement describing future capabilities. This is the case whether policies are addressing the use of technologies or business processes. It's generally considered unwise to develop a security policy that requires an activity that the organization is incapable of performing.

Industries generally consider security policies as being out-of-date if they are not examined and updated annually. This is not saying that security policies are required to be updated annually, but they should be examined and approved annually and updated as needed.

It is a common practice to structure the organization's security policy using one or more relevant standards or frameworks, though this is not generally required for most industries. Common standards and frameworks used in this way include

- NIST SP 800-53
- NIST SP 800-171 and NIST SP 800-172
- ISO/IEC 27001 and ISO/IEC 27002
- COBIT (formerly, Control Objectives for Information and Related Technologies)
- HIPAA/HITECH (Health Insurance Portability and Accountability Act/Health Information Technology for Economic and Clinical Health)
- PCI DSS (Payment Card Industry Data Security Standard)
- CIS CSC (Center for Internet Security Critical Security Controls)

Because security frameworks are moderately to highly technical, some organizations develop a shorter information security policy focused on Internet hygiene and data protection for all of its workers (often called an *acceptable-use policy*) and a separate technical security policy for its technology workers who design, implement, and manage information systems and applications. This pragmatic approach helps to avoid, for instance, nontechnical office workers trying to understand and comply with cryptography and access management policy; with such unintelligible content, workers are more likely to "tune out" the security policy in its entirety and not benefit from the relevant parts of policy that really matter, such as recognizing phishing scams.

The goal of a good security policy is to define the "rules of the road" for an organization's employees. Policies should be clear, concise, and applicable to the organization. The policies should be developed in a collaborative manner to ensure that appropriate information is delivered to the appropriate audience. Additionally, if policies are written without the involvement or buy-in of the different stakeholders, an organization risks deploying policies that it cannot adhere to or that will cause significant investment to comply with.

Controls Development

When an organization executes or updates a security strategy, this often means that the organization has made changes to its security-related capabilities. This, in turn, may necessitate changes to one or more aspects of existing controls, as well as the development of new controls and the retirement of controls that are no longer necessary.

Controls are generally changed as a result of a risk assessment, where some unacceptable risk was identified and a decision made to implement a control to ensure better outcomes. Quite possibly, a risk assessment may have compelled the organization to make some changes in the form of security projects that were part of a strategy. When these projects are executed and completed, controls related to the processes or technologies involved need to be changed accordingly. Here are some of the possible outcomes:

- **Changes to control narrative**   Changes to processes, procedures, or technologies will undoubtedly impact control narratives, which often describe controls in detail. Project deliverables will include these changes.

- **Changes to scope**   Changes in processes, procedures, or technologies may require that the scope of one or more controls be changed. For instance, if an organization replicates sensitive data to another data center as part of a business continuity strategy, the scope of controls related to the protection of sensitive data may need to be expanded to include the additional data center.

- **Changes in control testing**   New or different processes, procedures, or technologies will often mean that the procedures for testing a control will have changed. One of the project deliverables will be updates to control testing procedures. For example, the implementation of a new single sign-on (SSO) tool will require new instructions for control testing so that internal auditors and others will know what steps to perform to view information related to access controls.

- **Entirely new control**   Sometimes a new or changed security capability provides an opportunity (or possibly a mandate) to create a new control. For instance, the acquisition of a new identity and access management auditing tool brings an entirely new capability, that of auditing various aspects of user accounts, roles, and accesses. Prior to the tool, performing the work manually was infeasible, so there was no control. And this absence may have been documented in a risk assessment, which gave way to the project that enables this capability. When the new capability is finally implemented, a new control is developed to ensure the user audits are regularly performed.

Selecting a Control Framework

Organizations seeking to raise their security maturity often start by selecting a control framework. Organizations often spend an excessive amount of time selecting a control framework, typically struggling to decide between CIS CSC, ISO/IEC 27002, COBIT, NIST SP 800-53, and NIST SP 800-171. An organization lacking a control framework typically spends too much time stuck at this point, arguing the finer points of each control framework without realizing that there is not a great deal of difference between them. This is like a person accustomed to walking everywhere shopping for an automobile and getting hung up on two-door versus four-door or gas-powered versus diesel or hybrid, all the while ignoring the fact that any of these choices is going to result in a significant shift in safety or travel time. Instead, an organization should select a control framework that best aligns with its industry, and then tailor controls to align with the business.

Standards Development

An organization executing a security strategy may find that one or more of its standards are impacted or that new standards need to be developed.

While policies define *what* is to be done, standards define *how* policies are to be carried out. For instance, a policy may stipulate that strong passwords are to be used for end-user authentication. A password standard, then, would be more specific by defining the length, complexity, and other characteristics of a strong password.

Where policies are designed to be durable and long-lasting, they do so at the expense of being somewhat unspecific. Standards take on the burden of being more specific, but they also change more frequently, because they are closer to the technology and are concerned with the details of the implementation of policy.

Standards need to be developed carefully, for several reasons:

- They must properly reflect the intent of one or more corresponding policies.
- They have to be able to be successfully implemented.
- They need to be unambiguous.
- Their directives need to be able to be automated, where large numbers of systems, endpoints, devices, or people are involved, leading to consistency and uniformity.

Several types of standards are in use, including the following:

- **Protocol standards**   Examples include TLS 1.2 for web server session encryption, AES-256 for encryption at rest, 802.11ac for wireless networking, and SAML 2.0 for authentication.
- **Vendor standards**   For example, tablet computers are to be Apple iPad and iPad Pro, perhaps with specific model numbers.
- **Configuration standards**   For instance, a server-hardening standard would specify all of the security-related settings to be implemented for each type of server operating system in use.
- **Programming language standards**   Examples include C++, Java, and Python. Organizations that do not establish and assert programming language standards may find themselves with programs written in dozens of different languages, which may drive up the cost of maintaining them.
- **Methodology standards**   Examples include the use of Factor Analysis of Information Risk (FAIR) risk analysis techniques; Operationally Critical Threat, Asset, and Vulnerability Evaluation (OCTAVE) for security assessments; and SMART for the development of strategic objectives.
- **Control frameworks**   These include NIST SP 800-53, NIST SP 800-171, PCI DSS, HIPAA, COBIT, and ISO/IEC 27002.

Because technologies change so rapidly, standards are often reviewed and updated more frequently than policies. New security strategies are not the only reason that standards are reviewed and updated; other reasons include the release of new versions of hardware and software, new techniques for data protection, and the acquisition of new network devices and applications.

Here is a good illustration of the relationship of policies and standards: A policy statement would read, "All users must obey the speed limit." Standards would be enacted based on local conditions and indicated with speed limit signs. The key is that all users are aware that they must obey the policy (the speed limit).

Processes and Procedures

Processes and procedures describe the steps to be followed when carrying out functions and tasks. They exist so that these activities may be performed more consistently, in the right sequence, and in the right way.

Implementation of a security strategy means that new things will be done, some things will be done differently, and other things will no longer be done. All of these have a direct impact on processes and procedures.

Often, the purpose of a new security strategy is the increase in maturity of security-related technologies and activities in an organization. And because many organizations' security maturity levels are low, often this means that many important tasks are poorly documented or not documented at all. The desired increase in maturity may compel an organization to identify undocumented processes and procedures and assign staff to document them. An organization in such a state may also consider developing document management procedures and standards so that there is consistency among all processes, procedures, and their written documents, as well as consistent development and review.

Roles and Responsibilities

The implementation of a new security strategy often impacts the way people work. When the strategy involves changes in technologies or processes (as they usually do), this may, in turn, impact the roles and responsibilities for security personnel, IT workers, and perhaps other staff. Where business processes are added or changed, this often means that changes need to be made to the roles and responsibilities of personnel.

In organizations without documented roles and responsibilities, this is an opportunity to document them. This can be done in a number of different ways, including the following:

- Job descriptions
- Department charter documents
- Department policy documents
- Roles and responsibility sections of process documents

Training and Awareness

Execution of a new security strategy often has a broad reach, impacting technology as well as policies, standards, processes, and procedures. The result of this is new information, in many forms and for several audiences, including the following:

- General security awareness
- New and updated processes and procedures
- New and updated technologies

Each of these may necessitate additions or updates to training content.

Recent studies indicate that more than 90 percent of breaches begin with phishing attacks. Arguably, security awareness training is one of the most important defenses available for an organization, given that with even the best spam filters, some phishing attacks do successfully penetrate even the best defenses. The next line of defense is the sound judgment on the part of every worker with an e-mail account. Organizations implementing new security strategies often do so to improve their defenses; it makes sense, then, to include a review and perhaps an upgrade in security awareness training for all personnel. Some of the new features available in security awareness training include the following:

- **Engaging multimedia content** Rather than just displaying text on a screen, using audio and video content, including playback of computer sessions, will better hold viewers' attention, ensuring they will retain content.

- **Opportunities to learn and practice skills** Better training programs, even online varieties, provide opportunities to practice skills such as creating strong passwords, spotting phishing messages, and understanding how to recognize other threats.

- **Quizzes at the end of each topic** Short quizzes throughout training sessions hold a viewer's interest and keep them engaged. Better training programs don't let a participant proceed until previous learning has been proven.

- **Live exercises** Real-world exercises such as phishing testing campaigns and other social-engineering drills help organization workers learn how to recognize attacks and use the appropriate techniques to respond to them.

- **Built-in acknowledgment of organization security policy** Online and in-person awareness training can incorporate acknowledgment of security policy. This helps raise awareness of corporate security policy and its content and drives home the point that all staff members are expected to comply with it.

- **A permanent record of quiz scores and completion** Modern learning management systems (LMSs) keep a permanent record of test and quiz scores. This helps to reinforce the notion that an employer is holding staff members responsible for complying with policy.

When new technologies are introduced into the organization, individuals and even entire teams may often need to be trained so that they will better understand how to operate and maintain the new programs and products. Unfortunately, many organizations skimp on training, and this can result in organizations underutilizing new products or not using them correctly.

Establishing Communications and Reporting

Effective communications and reporting are critical elements of a successful security program. Because success depends mainly on people, in the absence of effective communications, they won't have the required information to make good security-related decisions. Without regard for information security, the results of decisions may include harmful incidents.

These are common forms of communications and reporting that are related to information security:

- **Board of directors meetings**   Discussions of strategies, objectives, risks, incidents, and industry developments keep board members informed about security in the organization and elsewhere.

- **Governance and steering committee meetings**   Discussions of security strategies, objectives, assessments, risks, incidents, and developments guide decision-makers as they discuss strategies, objectives, projects, and operations.

- **Security awareness**   Periodic communications to all personnel help keep them informed on changes in security policy and standards, good security practices, and risks they may encounter, such as phishing and social engineering attacks. New hires often get a healthy dose of security-related information that includes current security policies and practices, acceptable use, security tools, and where to go for help.

- **Security advisories**   Communications on potential threats helps keep affected personnel aware of developments that may require them to take steps to protect the organization from harm.

- **Security incidents**   Communications internally as well as with external parties during an incident keep incident responders and other parties informed. Organizations typically develop security incident plans and playbooks in advance, which include business rules on internal communications as well as with outside parties, including customers, regulators, and law enforcement.

- **Metrics**   Key metrics are reported upward in an organization, keeping management, executives, and board members informed as to the effectiveness and progress in the organization's security program.

When building or expanding a security program, it's best to utilize existing communications channels and add relevant security content to those channels, as opposed to building new, parallel channels. An effective security program makes the best use of existing processes, channels, and methods in an organization.

Obtaining Management Commitment

The execution of a security strategy requires management commitment. Without that commitment, the security strategist will be unable to obtain funding and other resources to implement the strategy.

Getting management commitment is not always straightforward. Often, executives and board members are unaware of their fiduciary responsibilities as well as the potency of modern threats. Many organizations mistakenly believe they are unlikely targets of hackers and cyber-criminal organizations because they are small or uninteresting. Further, the common perception of executives and senior managers is that information security is a tactical problem solved with "firewalls and antivirus software" and that information security is in no way related to business issues and business strategy.

A security strategist facing a situation where top management lacks a strategic understanding of security will need to embark on efforts to inform top management on one or more aspects of modern information security management. When success is elusive, it may be necessary to bring in outside experts to convince executives that their security manager is not attempting to build a kingdom, but instead is just trying to build a basic program to keep the organization out of trouble. As part of developing an effective communication approach, the security strategist should not use fear, uncertainty, and doubt (FUD) in an attempt to move the leadership team toward adopting the strategy. The better approach, as noted in this section, is to relate it to the leadership team in business terms and as opportunities to improve business functions.

Strategy Constraints

While the development of a new security strategy may bring hope and optimism to the security team, there is no guarantee that changes in an organization can be implemented without friction and even opposition. Instead, the security manager should anticipate many constraints and obstacles and be prepared to maneuver around, over, or through them.

No security manager plans to fail. However, the failure to anticipate obstacles and constraints may result in the failure to execute even the best strategy. The presence of an excellent strategy, even with executive support, does not mean that obstacles and constraints will simply get out of the way. Instead, obstacles and constraints represent the realities of human behavior, as well as structural and operational realities that may present challenges to the security manager and the organization as a whole. There is apt meaning to the phrase "the devil's in the details."

Typical constraints, obstacles, and other issues are discussed in this section.

Basic Resistance to Change

It is our basic human nature to be suspicious of change, particularly when we as individuals have no control over it and have no say about it. Change is bad, or so we tend to think. For this reason, organizations need to consider methods of involving management and staff members in anticipated changes, such as town-hall meetings, surveys, and cross-functional committees. Organizations are cautioned to ensure that these efforts are not merely window dressing but serious efforts on management's part to understand staff points of view.

Normalcy Bias

People at all levels can suffer from *normalcy bias,* a pattern of thinking in which people believe that because a disaster or breach has never occurred, it will never occur. Normalcy bias manifests itself in many situations, the common theme being a general lack of personal and corporate preparedness for disastrous events. This may be part of the reason that organizations do not take information security seriously—they have never had a breach before. Experienced information security professionals understand that an organization claiming to have not suffered from security breaches in the past may simply be unaware of them because of a lack of visibility into events in their environment. A common saying in the information security profession is, "There are two types of organizations: those that have been breached and those that do not yet realize they have been breached."

Culture

Organizational culture, according to the Business Dictionary (www.businessdictionary .com), is the collection of values and behaviors that "contribute to the unique social and psychological environment of an organization." In other words, it's the way that people think and act in an organization and how people feel as employees.

Aspects of organizational culture that are important for the security strategist to understand include the following:

- **Strong culture** The culture reflects and aligns with stated organizational values. Personnel understand and support organizational goals and objectives and need little prodding to figure out how to be productive and provide value to the organization and its constituents.

- **Weak culture** The culture is not well-aligned with the organization. As a result, management must spend more time managing employees who are not motivated and feel micromanaged.

- **Culture of fear** Workers are distrustful of management who act as tyrants, resulting in pervasive feelings of fear and doubt.

- **Healthy culture** Workers and management value and respect each other, have a strong sense of accountability, and cooperate to be successful and accomplish organizational goals and objectives.

One might consider organizational culture as the collective consciousness of all workers, regardless of rank. The security strategist should not expect to change the culture significantly but should instead work with the culture when developing and executing the information security strategy.

Organizational Structure

The security strategist must understand the organization's command-and-control structure, which is often reflected by the organizational chart. However, there may be an undocumented aspect to the org chart, which is actually more important: who is responsible for what activities, functions, and assets. In other words, security strategists must understand "who owns what turf" and develop collaborative relationships with those individuals and groups to implement a successful strategy. As with other considerations in a security strategy, alignment with written and unwritten organizational structures is the key to success.

Staff Capabilities

A security strategy generally represents the introduction of new capabilities, as well as changes or upgrades to existing capabilities. A strategy cannot be expected to succeed if the new or changed capabilities do not align with what staff members are able to do.

A gap analysis to understand the present state of the organization's security program (discussed earlier in this chapter) needs to include staff knowledge, skills, and capabilities. Where gaps are found, the strategy needs to include training or other activities to impart the necessary skills and language to staff.

This is not limited to technical workers who design, build, and manage information systems and applications. To the extent that all staff members are impacted by some change introduced by the strategy, those staff members need to be informed or trained so that they, too, will be successful.

For example, an organization that needs to improve its ability to protect sensitive data includes the development of a data protection program in its strategy. The strategy for data protection includes the development of a data classification scheme with data-handling policies and procedures for data at each classification level and in each use case. This is a high-impact endeavor that will require that many, if not all, workers in the organization be trained in data classification and handling procedures. If new security systems are in place that augment manual tasks, personnel will need to be trained in the use of these tools as well.

When an organization lacks staff with specific knowledge of security techniques or tools, organizations may look to external resources to augment internal staff. The security strategist needs to consider the costs and availability of these resources. Consultants and contracts in many skill areas are difficult to find; even larger firms may have backlogs of several months as a result.

Budget and Cost

A security strategy is a statement of changes to take place in the organization to improve its ability to protect critical or sensitive information and systems. These changes will have hard and soft associated costs that represent expenditures for hardware, software, and cloud services, as well as consultants, contractors, and the cost of existing workers' time.

The security strategist must determine, with a high degree of precision, all of the hard and soft costs associated with each element of a strategy. Often, executive management will want to see alternative approaches; for example, if additional labor is required, the security strategist may want to determine the costs of hiring additional personnel versus the retention of consultants or contractors.

Every organization has a core business to run, with budgeted costs for all associated activities. A security strategy almost always represents added costs, which must also be funded. While it is possible to obtain out-of-budget money for unbudgeted activities, it is usually necessary to create security strategy initiatives and attempt to get those activities budgeted in future fiscal cycles. For initiatives in future budget cycles, the security strategist needs to determine the price increases that may occur that will impact the strategy. A key project that will cost $100,000 this year may cost $105,000 to $110,000 a year from now and be even more expensive in future years.

Time

As security strategies take shape, each initiative will have its own project plan with associated timelines for executing various tasks. Realistic project planning is needed so that everyone will know when project and strategy milestones will be completed. Project and strategy timelines need to take into account all business circumstances, including peak periods and holiday production freezes (where IT systems are maintained in a more stable state), external events such as regulatory audits, and other significant events that may impact schedules.

Time constraints may also involve legal and regulatory obligations, discussed next.

Legal and Regulatory Obligations

An organization may include items in its strategy that may represent business capabilities that are required to exist for legal or regulatory reasons. For example, a public company may be compelled to complete a key identity and access management project before its next public audit cycle begins to ensure a favorable audit outcome. In another example, an organization may be undertaking the implementation of an intrusion prevention system (IPS) to meet a contractual obligation with a customer that has a hard deadline. In a final example, an organization may be implementing a web application firewall (WAF) in order to maintain its PCI DSS compliance.

These examples suggest that legal and regulatory obligations often have time components. New laws and contracts require organizations to have specific capabilities in place by established deadlines. For organizations that have failed to meet a deadline, the obligation still exists, and its completion has a greater sense of urgency.

Legal and regulatory requirements often have international considerations. What is legal and required in one country may be forbidden in another. For instance, an international organization may have, as a part of its strategy, key improvements in its pre-employment and post-employment background checks. The organization needs to understand that some countries, such as the United States, are quite permissive with background checks, while other countries, such as France, do not permit background checks for most positions. In another example, a security project that is improving its endpoint protection capabilities with cloud-based web proxy filters will find that users' Internet access activities may not be observed or logged in some countries.

Acceptable Risk

A security strategist who develops an information security policy needs to be familiar with the organization's current risk appetite or threshold for acceptable risk.

Risk is, by its nature, difficult to quantify. Most organizations, then, have a cultural "feel" for risk appetite that may or may not be documented. The security strategist must be familiar with the organization's risk appetite, in whatever formal or informal sense, and keenly understand two important aspects of the strategy:

- **Its alignment with risk appetite**   Initiatives in the security strategy need to align with executive management's risk appetite. For example, implementation of a data loss prevention (DLP) system together with restricting the use of USB-attached external storage may help to protect data, but this may be viewed as excessive in some organizations. A common mistake made by security strategists is the incorporation into strategies of new capabilities that may not be urgently needed. This can happen, especially if a strategy is developed without soliciting input from key stakeholders in the organization.

- **Its impact on risk appetite**   Specific initiatives within the security strategy may, by design, "push the envelope." A typical organization's security strategy probably contains initiatives to improve security capabilities that better align capabilities with risk appetite. But because many organizations are deficient in their security practices, the perception is that the organization is becoming less tolerant of risk, when in fact it's just trying to get its practices into alignment with its risk tolerance. The appearance of lowering risk appetite may be more of a "catchup."

The Obstacle of Organizational Inertia

Every organization has a finite capacity to undergo change. This is a fact that is often overlooked by overly ambitious security strategists who want to accomplish a great deal in too short a time. I have coined the term "organizational inertia" to represent an analogy to Newton's laws of motion: an object either remains at rest or continues to move at a constant velocity, unless acted upon by a force. In an organization, this means that things will be done in the same way until a change is exerted upon the organization to change what is done or how things are done.

The nature of organizational inertia, or its resistance to change, is threefold:

- **Operational people performing change**   For an organization to make major changes, some of the people making the change are the same people who perform the work. Because business processes undergoing change must continue operation, changes must be enacted slowly and carefully so that operational and quality levels are not adversely affected.

- **Learning curve**   Any time there is a significant change to a system or process, affected personnel need to learn the new systems, processes, or procedures. This involves a learning curve and possibly training that will take them offline for hours or even days.

- **Human resistance to change**   Left alone, people have a tendency to want to do things the same way, even if new and better ways are developed. People, particularly when they have no influence, tend to resist change, which makes adoption take longer.

Information Governance Frameworks and Standards

It is not necessary for organizations to develop governance models from scratch: plenty of mature models are available to adapt to individual organization needs. Like other types of models, organizations are expected to consider tailoring a standard framework to align with the organization and its business model, practices, and culture.

Security professionals often confuse governance frameworks with control frameworks. While the two are related, they are distinct and different from each other. *Governance frameworks* involve activities to ensure that executives are in control of the organization and that they are adequately informed. *Control frameworks* involve IT, security, and privacy controls, the detailed statements describing desired outcomes that are examined for proper design and effectiveness.

NOTE In ISACA's CISM study guide, the section on information governance describes various forms of information *security* governance while ignoring information governance entirely. Both will be covered in this section.

Several security governance frameworks are in use today, including the following:

- Business Model for Information Security
- Zachman Framework
- The Open Group Architecture Framework (TOGAF)
- ISO/IEC 27001
- NIST Risk Management Framework

Governance framework models help organizations establish visibility and control of key operations without having to start from scratch. This is not to say that an organization must conform strictly to a chosen framework; instead, a selected framework should be used as a starting point. By taking into account the business objectives, strategy, and culture, an organization can tailor the models to support the business.

Business Model for Information Security

Developed by ISACA in 2009, the Business Model for Information Security (BMIS) is a guide for business-aligned, risk-based security governance. The use of BMIS helps security leadership ensure that the organization's security program continues to address emerging threats, developing regulations, and changing business needs. BMIS is a three-dimensional, three-sided pyramid, depicted in Figure 2-2.

Figure 2-2
The BMIS model (Adapted from *The Business Model for Information Security*, ISACA)

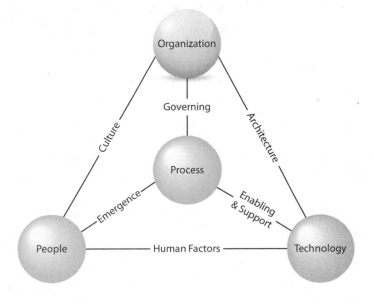

BMIS Elements and Dynamic Interconnections

The BMIS model includes the three traditional elements found in IT, which are people, process, and technology, and adds a fourth element, organization. The elements are connected by dynamic interconnections (DIs), which are culture, governing, architecture, emergence, enabling and support, and human factors. The elements and DIs are described in more detail in the following sections.

NOTE BMIS is described fully in the document, *The Business Model for Information Security,* from ISACA, available at www.isaca.org/bmis.

NOTE The BMIS is derived from the Systemic Security Management framework developed by the University of Southern California (USC) Marshall School of Business in 2006.

Organization The organization element in the BMIS model makes the model unique. Most other models focus on people, process, technology, or other aspects of an organization, without considering the organization itself. BMIS defines the organization as "a network of people interacting, using processes to channel this interaction." This is not unlike the executive management perspective that views the organization as a set of elements that act together to accomplish strategic objectives. The organization includes not only the permanent staff but also temporary workers, contractors, consultants, and third-party organizations that also play roles in helping the organization achieve its objectives.

Organizations are formally structured through organization charts, command-and-control hierarchy, policies, processes, and procedures. But organizations also have an informal, undocumented structure, which can be viewed like additional synapses that connect people or groups across the organization in ways not intended, but that nonetheless help the organization achieve its objectives. This is often seen in distributed organizations, where expediency and pragmatism often rule over policy and process, particularly in locations farther away from corporate headquarters.

People The people element in the BMIS model represents all of the people in an organization, whether full-time employees or temporary workers, contractors, or consultants. Further, as an organization outsources its operations to other organizations, the people in those organizations are also part of this element in BMIS. Like the other elements in the BMIS model, people cannot be studied by themselves but instead must be considered alongside the other elements of process, technology, and organization.

Process The process element in the BMIS model represents the formal structure of all defined activities in the organization, which together help the organization achieve its strategic objectives. Process defines practices and procedures that describe how activities are to be carried out.

ISACA's Risk IT framework defines an *effective process* as a reliable and repetitive collection of activities and controls to perform a certain task. Processes take input from one or more sources (including other processes), manipulate the input, utilize resources according to the policies, and produce output (including output to other processes). Processes should have clear business reasons for existing, accountable owners, clear roles and responsibilities around the execution of each key activity, and the means to undertake and measure performance. Individual processes have the attribute of *maturity*, which qualitatively describes how well the process is designed, as well as how it is measured and improved over time.

Technology   The technology element in the BMIS model represents all of the systems, applications, and tools used by practitioners in an organization. Technology is a powerful enabler of an organization's processes and of its strategic objectives, although unless tamed with process and by people, technology by itself can accomplish little for an organization. As the BMIS model illustrates, technology in an organization does not run by itself. Instead, people and processes are critical to any successful use of technology. Technology can be viewed as a process enabler and as a force multiplier, helping the organization accomplish more work in less time, for less cost, and with greater accuracy.

Culture   The culture DI connects the organization and people elements. Culture as part of a governance model makes BMIS unique, as most other models do not consider culture with strategic importance. BMIS defines *culture* as "a pattern of behaviors, beliefs, assumptions, attitudes, and ways of doing things."

Culture is the catalyst that drives behavior, with as much or more influence than formal directives such as policies and standards. Culture determines the degree to which personnel strive to conform to security policy and contribute to the protection of critical assets, or the degree to which they behave contrary to policy and put critical assets in jeopardy. An organization's culture is considered one of the most critical factors in the success or failure of an information security program. By its nature, culture cannot be legislated or controlled directly; instead, it reflects the attitudes, habits, and customs adopted by the people in the organization.

The civil culture of the community in which the organization resides plays a large role in shaping the organization's culture. For this reason, establishing a single culture in an organization with many regional or global locations is not feasible.

Of utmost importance to the security strategist is the development of a productive security culture. Like other aspects of organizational culture, the desired security culture cannot simply be legislated through policy but must be carefully curated and grown. Steps to create a favorable security culture include the following:

- Involve personnel in discussions about the protection of critical assets.
- Executive leadership must lead by example and follow all policies.
- Include security responsibilities in all job descriptions.
- Include security factors in employees' compensation—for example, merit increases and bonuses.

- Link the protection of critical assets to the long-term success of the organization.

- Integrate messages related to the protection of assets, and other aspects of the information security program, into existing communications such as newsletters.

- Incorporate "secure by design" into key business processes so that security is part of the organization's routine activities.

- Reward and recognize desired behavior; similarly, admonish undesired behavior privately.

Changing an organization's security culture cannot be accomplished overnight, and it cannot be forced. Instead, every individual needs to understand consistent messaging that reiterates the importance of sound security practices. For individuals and teams who don't "get it," the organization must be willing to take remedial action, not unlike that which would be undertaken when other undesired behavior is witnessed. Individuals who are teachable need to be coached on desired behavior. Those who prove to be unteachable may be dealt with in other ways, including training, reassignment, discipline, and termination.

Governing   The governing DI connects the organization and process elements. Per the definition from ISACA, "governance is the set of responsibilities and practices exercised by the board and executive management with the goal of providing strategic direction, ensuring that objectives are achieved, ascertaining that risks are managed appropriately and verifying that the enterprise's resources are used responsibly." This means that processes are influenced, or even controlled, by the organization's mission, strategic objectives, and other factors. In other words, the organization's processes must support the organization's mission and strategic objectives. When they don't, governance is used to change them until they are. When the governing DI fails, processes no longer align with organization objectives and take on a life of their own.

These tools are used by management to exert control over the development and operation of business processes, ensuring desired outcomes:

- Policies
- Standards
- Guidelines
- Process documentation
- Resource allocation
- Compliance

Communications is vital in the governing DI. Information flows down from management in the form of directives to influence change in business processes.

Architecture   The architecture DI connects the organization and technology elements. The purpose of the DI between organization and technology signifies the need for the use of technology to be planned, orderly, and purposeful. The definition of *architecture*, according to ISO/IEC 42010, "Systems and software engineering — Architecture description," is the fundamental concepts or properties of a system in its environment embodied in its elements, in its relationships, and in the principles of its design and evolution. The practice of architecture ensures the following:

- **Alignment**   Applications and infrastructure will support the organization's mission and objectives.

- **Consistency**   Similar or even identical practices and solutions will be employed throughout the IT environment.

- **Efficiency**   The IT organization as well as its environment can be built and operated more efficiently, mainly through consistent designs and practices.

- **Low cost**   With a more consistent approach, acquisition and support costs can be reduced through economy of scale and less waste.

- **Resilience**   Purposeful architectures and designs with greater resilience can be realized.

- **Flexibility**   Architectures must have the desired degree of flexibility to accommodate changing business needs and external factors such as regulations and market conditions.

- **Scalability**   Sound architectures are not rigid in their size but can be made larger or smaller to accommodate various business needs, such as growth in revenue, various size branch offices, and larger data sets.

- **Security**   With the development of security policies, standards, and guidelines, the principle of "secure by design" is more certain in future applications and systems.

Emergence   The emergence DI connects the people and process elements. The purpose of the emergence DI is to bring focus to the way people perform their work. Emergence is seen as the arising of new opportunities for organizations, new processes, new practices, and new ways of doing things. Emergence can be a result of people learning how to do things better, faster, more accurately, or with less effort.

Emergence can be a two-edged sword. The creativity and ingenuity of people can lead to better ways of doing things, but, on the other hand, this can lead to inconsistent results, including errors or lapses in product or service quality. Organizations that want to reduce work output deviation caused by emergence have a few potential remedies:

- **Increase automation**   Removing some of the human factors from a process through automation can yield more consistent outcomes. However, automation does not ensure correct outcomes; it only improves efficiency.

- **Enact controls**   Putting key controls in place can help management focus on factors responsible for outcome deviation. This can lead to process improvements later.

- **Increase process maturity**   Changing a business process can increase the maturity of the process. Examples include adding key measurements or producing richer log data so that a process can be better understood and improved over time.

Organizations need to understand which activities can benefit from automation and which require human judgment that cannot be programmed into a computer. This sometimes involves human factors, because there may be times when people prefer to interact with a person versus a machine, even if the machine is faster or more accurate. Automation does not always equal improvement for all parties concerned.

Enabling and Support   The enabling and support DI connects the process and technology elements. The purpose of this DI is the enablement and support of business processes by technology. Put another way, business processes are faster and more accurate with IT than they would be if they were performed manually.

In an appropriate relationship between business processes and technology, the structure of business processes determines how technology will support them. Unfortunately, many organizations compromise their business processes by having capabilities in poorly selected or poorly designed technology determine how business processes operate. Although it is not feasible for technology to support every whim and nuance in a business process, many organizations take the other extreme by selecting technology that does not align with their business processes or the organization's mission and objectives and changing their processes to match capabilities provided by technology. This level of compromise is detrimental to the organization.

A part of the disconnect between business processes and the technologies that do not fully support them is that technology experts often do not sufficiently understand the business processes they support, and business owners and users do not sufficiently understand the technologies supporting them. To paint with a broad brush, technology people and businesspeople think differently about technology and business and often find it difficult to understand each other enough to make technology's support of business processes as successful as they could be.

The tool that is used to fill this gap is the requirements document. Often developed at the onset of a major project (and often a minor one), business people endeavor to develop charts listing required and desired functionality for new technologies to improve their chances of selecting and implementing a technology that will support their business processes.

Human Factors   The human factors DI connects the people and technology elements. The purpose of this DI is the interaction between people and information systems. This is an extensively studied and researched topic, sometimes known as *human–computer interaction* (HCI). The elements of information systems that people interact with are often known as *user interfaces* (UIs); considerable research is devoted to the improvement of UIs to make software and systems easier to use and more intuitive.

From an information security perspective, information systems need to implement security requirements in ways that do not impede users' interaction wherever possible. Where users have choices to make while interacting with a system, security features and functions need to be easy to use and intuitive. Further, users should not be able to easily circumvent security controls put in place to protect systems and data. Finally, systems should be designed so that they cannot be abused or that their use permits abuse of other assets.

Many considerations need to be included in the design of information systems (both hardware and software):

- **Consistency**   Operating an information system should resemble other commonly used systems. For instance, keyboard arrangement should be consistent with other products in use.

- **Typing and data entry**   Entering text should be straightforward and simple. The method for entering data should be commensurate with the interface. For instance, a small touchscreen keyboard would be a poor choice for entering large amounts of data (such as sentences and paragraphs). Further, pointing methods should be easy to use and intuitive.

- **Display and readability**   Users should be able to read text and images easily.

- **Error recovery**   Users should be able to repeat a step when they have recognized that they have made an error.

- **Sound**   Sounds as part of interaction should be adjustable and loud enough to be heard. The system should not emit prolonged loud noise, such as banks of cooling fans, if users are expected to work in proximity without hearing protection.

- **Voice and biometric recognition**   Technologics used to recognize voice commands and various types of biometrics should be easy to use and accurate as well.

- **Ergonomics**   Whether portable or stationary, devices should be easy to use without inducing strain or requiring contortions.

- **Environment**   Information systems should be designed to operate in a variety of environments where they would typically be used. For instance, ruggedized laptops for use at construction sites should withstand dust, dirt, water, and sunlight, while small portable devices should be water-resistant and not break when dropped.

Using BMIS

Organizations employ BMIS to help them better understand how their people, processes, and technologies help to protect the overall organization. BMIS helps the strategist understand the holistic relationships between various aspects (the *elements*) in the organization and the factors that influence them (the *dynamic interconnections*).

The structure of BMIS itself is a key factor in its success. Equally important, however, is the ability for holistic thinking rather than detailed thinking. It is vital to understand that BMIS shows how everything is connected to everything else. A change introduced at any element or DI will affect other elements and DIs and will most likely affect the adjacent elements and DIs the most. Considering, again, the structure of BMIS, refer to Figure 2-2.

When a security analyst or strategist is pondering an incident, problem, or situation, they identify the element or DI in the BMIS that corresponds to the subject of the matter. Next, they identify the adjacent elements or DIs and think about the relationships: these represent aspects in the organization that would be related or affected.

Examining one element, noting the DI connecting it to another element, helps identify the nature of the connecting factor. Examples are covered next, which should make these concepts clearer.

Example 1: Adverse Effects of a Policy Change   A security manager wants to enact a new policy regarding the use of personally owned mobile devices for corporate use, including e-mail. Policy is a part of the governing DI, and the adjacent elements are organization and process. The organization element here means that a new policy affects the organization in some way by altering how it does things. The process element means that one or more processes or procedures may be affected.

But what if the new mobile device policy adversely affects other processes? One would then follow the DIs from process and see where they lead and how they lead. First, the emergence DI connects to people. In the case of this policy, emergence includes ways in which people follow—or don't follow—the process. Next, following the enabling and support DI to technology, this could indicate how other technologies may be affected by the policy change.

Example 2: Examining Causes for Process Weakness   An organization hired a security consulting company to perform security scans of its internal network. The consulting company found numerous instances of servers being several months behind in their security patches. The organization uses a vulnerability scanning tool and is wondering why patches are so far behind.

Thinking that technology is the problem, the investigator examines the scanning tool to see whether it is operating properly. This would be the technology element. The tool is seen to be operating correctly and is running up-to-date software. The investigator next examines the BMIS model to see what DIs are connected to technology.

First, the architecture DI is examined. This prompts the investigator to think about whether the scanning tool is able to reach all systems in the network. The investigator confirms that it is.

Next, the human factors DI is examined. The investigator contacts the engineer who runs the scanning tool and asks to observe the engineer's use of the tool. The investigator is wondering whether the engineer understands how to use the tool properly (there has been a history of problems because the scanning tool is not easy to use). The engineer is using the scanning tool correctly, so the investigator needs to keep looking.

Finally, the enabling and support DI is examined. This prompts the investigator to ponder whether any business processes related to the use of the scanning tool might be a factor. When interviewing engineers, the investigator discovers that several new networks in the organization are not included in the scanner's configuration.

By using the BMIS tool to understand how people, processes, and technologies relate to one another, the investigator was able to determine the cause of the problem: the failure of a network change process to notify security personnel caused those security personnel to *not* configure the scanning tool to include them. Thus, for some time, security scans did not identify vulnerabilities present in systems in the new network segments. The security consulting company's scans included all of the organization's networks, including those that the organization did not scan itself.

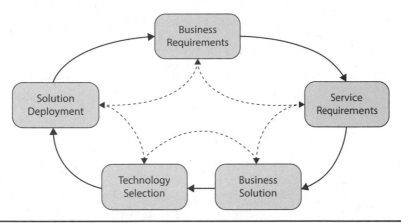

Figure 2-3 BMIS enabling and support life cycle (Adapted from The University of Southern California, Marshall School of Business, Institute for Critical Information Infrastructure Protection, USA)

The BMIS model for enabling and support is a life cycle, as opposed to a do-it-once approach, as depicted in Figure 2-3.

The Zachman Framework

The Zachman Framework for Enterprise Architecture, established in the late 1980s, continues to be the dominant enterprise architecture standard today. Zachman likens IT enterprise architecture to the construction and maintenance of an office building: at a high (abstract, not the number of floors) level, the office building performs functions such as containing office space. At increasing levels of detail in the building, one encounters various trades (steel, concrete, drywall, electrical, plumbing, telephone, fire control, elevators, and so on), each with its own specifications, standards, regulations, construction and maintenance methods, and so on.

In the Zachman Framework model, IT systems and environments are described at a high, functional level and then, in increasing detail, encompass systems, databases, applications, networks, and so on. The Zachman Framework is illustrated in Table 2-1.

Although the framework enables an organization to peer into cross-sections of an IT environment that supports business processes, it does not convey the relationships between IT systems. Data flow diagrams are used instead to depict information flows.

Data flow diagrams (DFDs) are frequently used to illustrate the flow of information between IT applications. Like the Zachman model, a DFD can begin as a high-level diagram, where the labels of information flows are expressed in business terms. Written specifications about each flow can accompany the DFD; these specifications would describe the flow in increasing levels of detail, all the way to field lengths and communication protocol settings.

Similar to Zachman, DFDs help nontechnical business executives understand the various IT applications and the relationships between them. Figure 2-4 shows a typical DFD.

	Data	Functional (Application)	Network (Technology)	People (Organization)	Time	Strategy
Scope	List of data sets important in the business	List of business processes	List of business locations	List of organizations	List of events	List of business goals and strategy
Enterprise Model	Conceptual data/object model	Business process model	Business logistics	Workflow	Master schedule	Business plan
Systems Model	Logical data model	System architecture	Detailed system architecture	Human interface architecture	Processing structure	Business rule model
Technology Model	Physical data/class model	Technology design	Technology architecture	Presentation architecture	Control structure	Rule design
Detailed Representation	Data definition	Program	Network architecture	Security architecture	Time definition	Rule speculation
Function Enterprise	Usable data	Working function	Usable network	Functioning organization	Implemented schedule	Working strategy

Table 2-1   The Zachman Framework Shows IT Systems in Increasing Levels of Detail

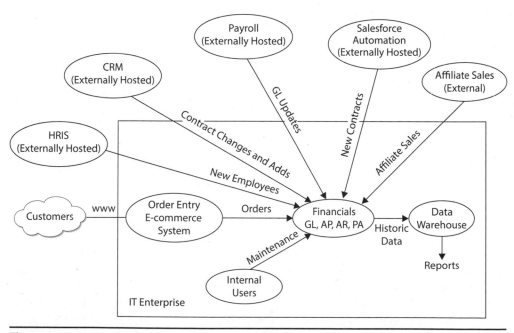

Figure 2-4   A typical DFD shows the relationship between IT applications.

The Open Group Architecture Framework

The Open Group Architecture Framework (TOGAF) is a life-cycle enterprise architecture framework used for designing, planning, implementing, and governing an enterprise technology architecture. TOGAF could be considered a high-level approach for designing enterprise infrastructure.

The phases used in TOGAF are as follows:

- Preliminary
- Architecture vision
- Business architecture
- Information systems architecture
- Technology architecture
- Opportunities and solutions
- Migration planning
- Implementation governance
- Architecture change management
- Requirements management

TOGAF is a business-driven, life-cycle management framework for enterprise architecture overall, and it certainly can be used for information security architecture as well. Figure 2-5 depicts TOGAF visually.

 NOTE You can find information on TOGAF at https://togaf.info or www.opengroup.org/subjectareas/enterprise/togaf/.

ISO/IEC 27001

ISO/IEC 27001, "Information technology — Security techniques — Information security management systems — Requirements," is an international standard for information security and risk management. This standard contains a requirements section that outlines a properly functioning information security management system (ISMS), as well as a comprehensive control framework.

ISO/IEC 27001 is divided into two sections: requirements and controls. The requirements section describes required activities found in effective ISMSs. The controls section contains a baseline set of controls that serve as a starting point for an organization. The standard is updated periodically; as of this writing, the latest version, ISO/IEC 27001:2013, was released in 2013. ISO has published two corrigendums and one amendment to the 2013 standard.

Figure 2-5
TOGAF
components
(courtesy The
Open Group)

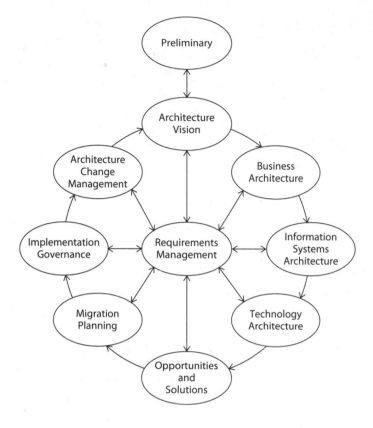

The requirements in ISO/IEC 27001 are described in these seven sections:

- Context of the organization
- Leadership
- Planning
- Support
- Operation
- Performance evaluation
- Improvement

ISO/IEC 27001 contains an appendix containing 14 categories of controls:

- Information security policies
- Organization of information security
- Human resource security
- Asset management

- Access control
- Cryptography
- Physical and environmental security
- Operations security
- Communications security
- System acquisition, development, and maintenance
- Supplier relationships
- Information security incident management
- Information security aspects of business continuity management
- Compliance

NOTE   Many readers of ISO/IEC 27001 gloss over the core of the standard, the seven sections of requirements for managing an ISMS, and instead focus on the appendix with its list of controls. The controls in the appendix are there for the reader's convenience and are fully explained in the companion standard, ISO/IEC 27002.

Although ISO/IEC 27001 is a highly respected governance framework, its adoption has been modest, partly because the standard costs about US$125 per single user copy. Unlike NIST and ENISA standards, which are free of charge, ISO/IEC 27001 is unlikely to be purchased by students or professionals who want to learn more about it. Despite this, ISO/IEC 27001 is growing in popularity in organizations throughout the world.

NOTE   ISO/IEC 27001:2013 is available from www.iso.org/standard/54534.html (registration and payment required).

NIST Cybersecurity Framework

The NIST Cybersecurity Framework (NIST CSF) was published in 2014 as a response to President Barak Obama's Executive Order 13636, Improving Critical Infrastructure Cybersecurity. The order reads, "[D]irected NIST to work with stakeholders to develop a voluntary framework—based on existing standards, guidelines, and practices—for reducing cyber risks to critical infrastructure" (NIST, 2018). Though required for implementation within the U.S. government, the CSF is voluntary guidance for private, commercial, and other organizations. It is heavily integrated into the latest version of the NIST Risk Management Framework (RMF) (version 2, as of December 2018) and is essentially a catalog of cybersecurity activities. These activities describe desired outcomes from performing these activities. As of the writing of this book, the current version of the CSF is 1.1, released in April 2018.

The NIST CSF is made up of three main components: the core, implementation tiers, and profiles. The core is broken down into five functions, each including categories of cybersecurity outcomes and informative references that provide guidance to standards and practices that illustrate methods to achieve the stated outcomes within each category. The implementation tiers provide context on how well an organization understands its cybersecurity risk and the processes in place to manage that risk. Finally, the profiles assist an organization in defining the outcomes it desires to achieve from the framework categories.

NIST CSF Highlights

The CSF consists of five activities or functions, further divided into 23 categories and 108 subcategories. Each of these is also matrixed with five informative references—CIS, COBIT 2019, ISA 62443-2-1:2009, ISO/IEC 27001:2013, and NIST SP 800-53 Rev. 5—although, obviously, the emphasis throughout is on the NIST control catalog. All of this together is referred to as the "CSF core." The mapping to CIS CSC, COBIT 2019, ISA 62443, ISO/IEC 27001, and NIST SP 800-53 alone makes the CSF a valuable reference tool.

The five functions are

- **Identify** Develop an understanding of the business context and resources that support critical operations to enable the organization to identify and prioritize cybersecurity risks that can impact operations.

- **Protect** Implement appropriate safeguards to minimize the operational impact of a potential cybersecurity event.

- **Detect** Implement capabilities to detect suspicious and malicious activities.

- **Respond** Implement capabilities to respond to cybersecurity events properly.

- **Recover** Maintain plans and activities to enable timely restoration of capabilities or services that might be impaired after a cybersecurity event.

Four tiers are intended to describe an organization's cybersecurity program capabilities in support of organizational goals and objectives. It is important to highlight that the tiers do not represent maturity levels or how well capabilities are executed. The tiers are meant to describe and support decision-making about how to manage cybersecurity risk and prioritization of resources. Here is a summary of the tiers:

- **Partial** Cybersecurity programs may not be formalized, and risks are managed in an ad hoc or reactive manner. There is limited awareness of cybersecurity risk across the organization.

- **Risk Informed** Cybersecurity program activities are approved by management and linked to organizational risk concerns and business objectives. However, cybersecurity considerations in business programs may not be consistent at all levels in the organization.

- **Repeatable**   Cybersecurity program activities are formally approved and supported by policy. Cybersecurity program capabilities are regularly reviewed and updated based on risk management processes and changes in business objectives.

- **Adaptive**   There is a consistent organization-wide approach to managing cybersecurity risk through formal policies, standards, and procedures. Cybersecurity program capabilities are routinely updated based on previous and current cybersecurity events, lessons learned, and predictive indicators. The organization strives to adapt proactively to changing threat landscapes.

Note that the text of the CSF claims that these tiers are not maturity levels, but upon reading the tier descriptions, it is difficult to come to any other conclusion.

For implementation in the private sector, the CSF can be customized into profiles. A *profile* is a particular customization of the CSF core for an organization or sector; it is based on the organization's or sector's unique requirements. NIST publishes profiles for a variety of industry sectors, such as the manufacturing and petroleum industries.

NIST Risk Management Framework

NIST Special Publication (SP) 800-37, "Risk Management Framework for Information Systems and Organizations," is a risk management governance model that provides a means for executives and organization ownership to manage the organization's information security program properly. The RMF comprises seven steps that ensure that organizations can successfully execute their risk management programs:

- Prepare
- Categorize
- Select
- Implement
- Assess
- Authorize
- Monitor

The RMF is visually depicted in Figure 2-6.

Will the Real Information Governance Please Stand Up?

As noted earlier in this chapter, ISACA apparently mislabeled information security governance as simply "information governance," and then proceeded to ignore the real practice of information governance. I will briefly describe information governance here.

(continued)

Information governance (IG) comprises a set of activities that provides management with visibility and control over an organization's acquisition and use of information. Indeed, the full information life cycle falls under the control of IG. Activities found in IG include

- Data architecture and design
- Data classification and handling
- Data usage and control
- Data retention
- Data destruction
- Records management
- Electronic discovery
- Records retention

Access management, while not directly related to IG, is closely related, as access management controls which individuals, systems, and entities have access to specific data sets.

These topics are discussed fully in Chapter 5.

Figure 2-6
The NIST Risk Management Framework

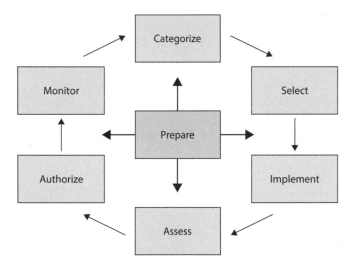

Strategic Planning

In strategic planning, one or more persons develop the steps and resources required to achieve a desired end state. In the context of information security, strategic planning should include the steps and resources required for principal functions of the information security program to adequately protect the organization's information assets and to continue doing so despite changes in threats, defensive techniques, technologies, and even the organization's overall strategic objectives.

In the "Strategy Resources" section earlier in this chapter, I discuss the inputs that help a security leader gain a comprehensive understanding of the current state of an information security program. In some cases, those inputs are also the resources required to make the necessary changes to the program to bring it closer to its desired end state. Additional resources may be required, either to help the security leader better understand the program's current state or to develop or improve components that will be a part of the new end state.

Unless only minor improvements are needed in an organization's information security program, it is likely that several individual steps are required to transform the program from its current state to the desired end state. The security leader is likely to develop a roadmap that defines and describes those steps. The leader may need to develop one or more business case statements to obtain the necessary resources to execute the roadmap. Both are described here.

Roadmap Development

Once strategic objectives, risk and threat assessments, and gap analyses have been completed, the security strategist can begin to develop roadmaps to accomplish each objective. A *roadmap* is a list of steps required to achieve a strategic objective. "Roadmap" is an appropriate metaphor, because it represents a journey that, in the details, may not always appear to be contributing to the objective. But in a well-designed roadmap, each objective, milestone, initiative, and project gets the organization closer to the objective.

A roadmap is just a set of plans, but the term is often used to describe the steps that an organization needs to take to undertake a long-term, complex, and strategic objective. Often a roadmap can be thought of as a series of projects—some running sequentially, others concurrently—that an organization uses to transform its processes and technology to achieve the objective.

Figure 2-7 depicts a roadmap for an 18-month identity and access management project.

Developing a Business Case

Many organizations require the development of a business case prior to approving expenditures on significant security initiatives. A *business case* is a written statement that describes the initiative and describes its business benefits.

In big-picture strategic planning for an information security program, the security leader may develop a single business case for the entire long-range plan, or they may develop a business case for each component. If a leader takes the latter approach, each business case should show how each respective component contributes to the whole.

The typical elements found in a business case include the following:

- **Problem statement** This is a description of the business condition or situation that the initiative is designed to solve. The condition may be a matter of compliance, a finding in a risk assessment, or a capability required by a customer, partner, supplier, or regulator.

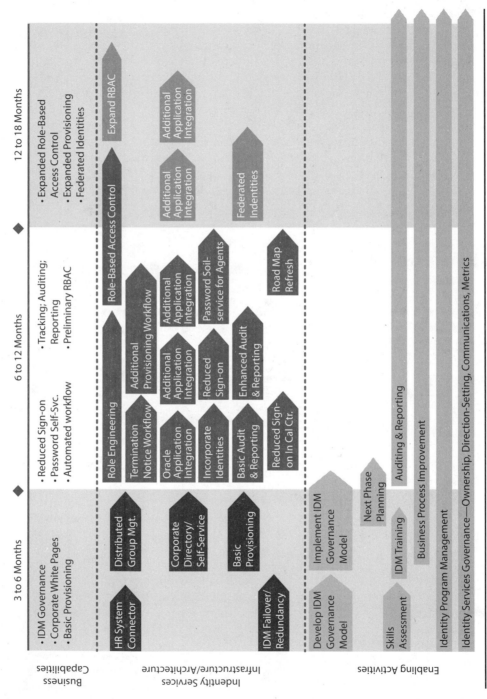

Figure 2-7 Sample roadmap for identity and access management initiative (Courtesy of *High Tech Security Solutions Magazine*)

- **Current state** This is a description of the existing conditions related to the initiative.

- **Desired state** This describes the future state of the relevant systems, processes, or staff.

- **Success criteria** These are the defined items that the program will be measured against.

- **Requirements** This is a list of required characteristics and components of the solution that will remedy the current state and bring about the desired future state.

- **Approach** This describes the proposed steps that will result in the desired future state. This section may include alternative approaches that were considered, with reasons why they were not selected. If the initiative requires the purchase of products or professional services, business cases may include proposals from vendors. Alternatively, the business case may include a request for proposal (RFP) or a request for information (RFI) that will be sent to selected vendors for additional information.

- **Plan** This includes costs, timelines, milestones, vendors, and staff associated with the initiative.

Mature organizations utilize an executive steering committee that evaluates business cases for proposed initiatives and makes go/no-go decisions for initiatives. Business cases are often presented to a steering committee in the form of an interactive discussion, providing business leaders with the opportunity to ask questions and propose alternative approaches.

Business cases should include the following characteristics:

- **Alignment with the organization** The business case should align with the organization's goals and objectives, risk appetite, and culture.

- **Statements in business terms** Problem statements, current state, and future state descriptions should all be expressed in business terms.

Chapter Review

A strategy is a plan to achieve a defined set of objectives to enable the vision of the organization to be successfully achieved. Objectives are the desired future states in an organization and, in the context of information security, in the organization's information security program. A strategy should be business aligned, and it should deliver value, optimize resources, and be measurable.

To be successful, an information security program must align with the business and its overall mission, goals and objectives, and strategy. The security program must take into account the organization's notion of asset value, culture, risk tolerance/appetite, legal obligations, and market conditions. A successful and aligned security program does not lead the organization but enables and supports it as it carries out its mission and pursues its goals.

Many resources are needed for the development of a strategy, including several types of information that reveal the current state of the organization, such as risk assessments, vulnerability assessments, threat assessments, business impact analysis, metrics, risk register, and incident log. Several other inputs are required that define the structure of the security program, including policy, standards, guidelines, processes and procedures, architecture, controls, staff skills, insurance, and outsourced services. It is critical that the security leader understand the culture of the security team, the IT department, and the entire organization.

To develop a strategy, the security strategist must first understand the organization's present state and then define one or more desired future states. A gap analysis helps the strategist understand missing capabilities. The development of a roadmap defines the steps to develop missing capabilities and augment existing capabilities so that the strategy will be realized.

The security strategist may choose to use the SWOT (strengths, weaknesses, opportunities, and threats) analysis model in support of strategy planning. The strategist may also employ capability maturity models such as CMMI-DEV to help determine appropriate future states of key security processes.

Strategy development should begin with developing or updating security policy and controls. A security leader may choose to align the structure of security policy and controls to one of several standards, such as COBIT, NIST SP 800-53, NIST SP 800-171, ISO/IEC 27002, HIPAA/HITECH, PCI DSS, or CIS CSC. Next, standards should be developed or updated, roles and responsibilities established, and personnel trained.

Commitment from organizational executives and owners is essential if the strategy is to succeed. Business leaders provide the necessary resources that enable the security leader to execute the strategy; leaders lead by example and set the tone for the level of importance of information security and privacy.

A security strategist must be aware of potential obstacles to achieving strategic objectives, including culture, organizational structure, existing staff capabilities, budgets, time, and legal and regulatory obligations. Security leaders should be aware of the phenomenon of normalcy bias and be able to recognize it. A business-aligned strategy should take these obstacles into account and minimize them if the strategy is to be approved and achieved.

Strategy development may include understanding and establishing desired risk levels. This may be expressed in qualitative or quantitative terms, depending upon an organization's maturity.

The Business Model for Information Security (BMIS), developed by ISACA, is a guide for business-aligned, risk-based security governance. The model consists of four elements: organization, people, process, and technology. It consists of six dynamic interconnections (DIs): culture (connecting organization and people elements), governing (connecting organization and process elements), architecture (connecting organization and technology elements), emergence (connecting people and process elements), enabling and support (connecting process and technology elements), human factors (connecting people and technology elements). BMIS helps the strategist understand the dynamics between the four elements and how they may be manifested. The key takeaway from BMIS is that everything is connected to everything else.

Security architecture represents the implementation of the overall strategy as well as the details that define the role of technology and asset protection. The Open Group Architecture Framework (TOGAF) and the Zachman Framework are two architecture models that can be used to build a security architecture.

ISO/IEC 27001 is a renowned standard for the development and management of an information security management system (ISMS). The NIST Cybersecurity Framework (CSF) is a taxonomy for assessing security capabilities and maturity; it maps high-level outcomes to several control frameworks. The NIST risk management framework (RMF), described in NIST SP 800-37, provides a model for the risk management life cycle, which is considered essential for organizations to identify and manage cyber risks purposefully.

In strategic planning, one or more persons develop the steps and resources required to achieve a desired end state. In the context of information security, strategic planning should include the steps and resources required for principal functions of the information security program to protect the organization's information assets adequately, and to continue doing so despite changes in threats, defensive techniques, technologies, and even the organization's overall strategic objectives.

A roadmap is the list of steps required to achieve strategic objectives. Where a significant amount of change is warranted, a roadmap may consist of a series of projects.

Often it is necessary to build a business case so that executive management will agree to support and fund a strategy. A business case typically includes a problem statement, followed by a description of the current state, the desired future state, requirements, an approach, and a plan to achieve the strategy. Often a business case is reviewed by a business or IT steering committee consisting of business stakeholders.

Notes

- A security program should align with the organization's overall mission, goals, and objectives. This means that the security leader and others should be aware of, and involved in, strategic initiatives and the execution of the organization's strategic goals.

- Security leaders developing an information security strategy in an organization without a program will need to rely on their past experiences, anecdotal accounts of practices, and policies in the organization. By taking on the Listen, Learn, Observe, Act (LOLA) approach, a security leader can gain solid insights into an organization that will greatly increase the chances of aligning the security strategy with the business.

- While it is important for the security strategist to understand the present state of the organization when developing a strategic roadmap, the strategist must proceed despite knowing that there can never be a sufficient level of understanding. Besides, if even the most thorough snapshot has been taken, the organization is slowly (or perhaps quickly) changing. Execution of a strategic plan aims to accelerate changes in certain aspects of an organization that are already slowly changing.

- Security strategists should be mindful of each organization's tolerance for change within a given period of time. Although much progress may be warranted, a limited amount of change can be reasonably implemented within a set time period.

- A security strategist must anticipate obstacles and constraints affecting the achievement of strategic objectives and consider refining those objectives so that they can be realized.

- The business model for information security is useful for understanding the qualitative relationships among various aspects of an organization, as well as the types of activities that relate to these aspects.

- Many organizations ruminate over the selection of a control framework. Instead, the organization should select a framework and then make adjustments to the framework's controls to suit the business. A control framework should generally be considered a starting point, not a rigid and unchanging list of controls—except in cases where regulations stipulate that controls may not be changed.

- Capability maturity models are useful tools for understanding the maturity level of a process and developing desired future states. The maturity of processes in the organization will vary; it is appropriate for some processes to have high maturity and acceptable for others to have lower maturity. The right question to ask about each separate process is this: what is the appropriate level of maturity for this process?

- Each organization has its own practice for the development of business cases for the presentation, discussion, and approval of strategic initiatives.

Questions

1. What are the elements of the Business Model for Information Security (BMIS)?

   A. Culture, governing, architecture, emergence, enabling and support, human factors

   B. People, process, technology

   C. Organization, people, process, technology

   D. Financial, customer, internal processes, innovation, and learning

2. The best definition of a strategy is:

   A. The objective to achieve a plan

   B. The plan to achieve an objective

   C. The plan to achieve business alignment

   D. The plan to reduce risk

3. As part of understanding the organization's current state, a security strategist is examining the organization's security policy. What does the policy tell the strategist?

   A. The level of management commitment to security

   B. The compliance level of the organization

    C. The maturity level of the organization

    D. None of these

4. A security strategist has examined several business processes and has found that their individual maturity levels range from Repeatable to Optimizing. What is the best future state for these business processes?

    A. All processes should be changed to Repeatable.

    B. All processes should be changed to Optimizing.

    C. There is insufficient information to determine the desired end states of these processes.

    D. Processes that are Repeatable should be changed to Defined.

5. A security strategist is seeking to improve the security program in an organization with a strong but casual culture. What is the best approach here?

    A. Conduct focus groups to discuss possible avenues of approach.

    B. Enact new detective controls to identify personnel who are violating policy.

    C. Implement security awareness training that emphasizes new required behavior.

    D. Lock users out of their accounts until they agree to be compliant.

6. A security strategist recently joined a retail organization that operates with slim profit margins and has discovered that the organization lacks several important security capabilities. What is the best strategy here?

    A. Insist that management support an aggressive program to improve the program quickly.

    B. Develop a risk ledger that highlights all identified risks.

    C. Recommend that the biggest risks be avoided.

    D. Develop a risk-based strategy that implements changes slowly over an extended period of time.

7. Security governance is most concerned with:

    A. Security policy

    B. IT policy

    C. Security strategy

    D. Security executive compensation

8. What relationship should exist between an ERM risk register and a cyber-risk register?

    A. Cyber risks should influence ERM risks.

    B. ERM risks should influence cyber risks.

    C. ERM and cyber-risk registers should link bidirectionally.

    D. ERM and cyber risks should not be related.

9. The primary factor related to the selection of a control framework is:

    A. Industry vertical

    B. Current process maturity level

    C. Size of the organization

    D. Compliance level

10. As part of understanding the organization's current state, a security strategist is examining the organization's security standards. What do the standards tell the strategist?

    A. The level of management commitment to security

    B. The compliance level of the organization

    C. The maturity level of the organization

    D. None of these

11. While gathering and examining various security-related business records, the security manager has determined that the organization has no security incident log. What conclusion can the security manager make from this?

    A. The organization does not have security incident detection capabilities.

    B. The organization has not yet experienced a security incident.

    C. The organization is recording security incidents in its risk register.

    D. The organization has effective preventive and detective controls.

12. A security strategist has examined a business process and has determined that personnel who perform the process do so consistently, but there is no written process document. The maturity level of this process is:

    A. Initial

    B. Repeatable

    C. Defined

    D. Managed

13. A security strategist has discovered that IT does not control the usage and acquisition of software on endpoints. What can the strategist conclude?

    A. There is no EDR on endpoints.

    B. There is no XDR on endpoints.

    C. IT lacks an application whitelisting capability.

    D. Acceptable-use policy does not address unauthorized software.

14. In an organization using PCI DSS as its control framework, the conclusion of a recent risk assessment stipulates that additional controls not present in PCI DSS but present in ISO/IEC 27001 should be enacted. What is the best course of action in this situation?

    A. Adopt ISO/IEC 27001 as the new control framework.

    B. Retain PCI DSS as the control framework and update process documentation.

    C. Add the required controls to the existing control framework.

    D. Adopt NIST 800-53 as the new control framework.

15. What is the purpose of a gap analysis in the context of strategy development?

    A. A gap analysis identifies key process and system improvement needs.

    B. A gap analysis identifies vulnerable systems.

    C. A gap analysis identifies ambiguous policies.

    D. A gap analysis helps to identify ineffective controls.

Answers

1. **C.** The elements of BMIS are organization, people, process, and technology. The dynamic interconnections (DIs) are culture, governing, architecture, emergence, enabling and support, and human factors.

2. **B.** A strategy is the plan to achieve an objective. An objective is the "what" that an organization wants to achieve, and a strategy is the "how" the objective will be achieved.

3. **D.** By itself, security policy offers little information about an organization's security practices. An organization's policy is only a collection of statements; without examining business processes and business records and interviewing personnel, a security professional cannot develop any conclusions about an organization's security practices.

4. **C.** No rules specify that the maturity levels of different processes need to be the same or at different values relative to one another. In this example, each process may already be at an appropriate level, based on risk appetite, risk levels, and other considerations.

5. **A.** Organizational culture is powerful; it reflects how people think and work. In this example, there is no mention that the strong culture is bad, only that it is casual. Punishing people for their behavior may cause employees to resent the organization, revolt against the organization, or leave the organization. The best approach here is to work toward understanding the culture and to work with people in the organization to figure out how a culture of security can be introduced successfully.

6. **D.** A security strategist needs to understand an organization's capacity to spend its way to lower risk. It is unlikely that an organization with low profit margins will agree to an aggressive and expensive improvement plan. Developing a risk register that depicts these risks may be a helpful tool for communicating risk, but a register doesn't provide a way to change anything. Similarly, recommending risk avoidance may mean discontinuing the very operations that bring in revenue.

7. **C.** Security governance is the mechanism through which security strategy is established, controlled, and monitored. Long-term and other strategic decisions are made in the context of security governance.

8. **C.** The ERM and cyber-risk registers should influence one another. For instance, chronic risks in the cyber-risk register should compel the creation of a new entry in the ERM risk register.

9. **A.** The most important factor influencing a decision of selecting a control framework is the industry vertical. For example, a healthcare organization would likely select HIPAA as its primary control framework, whereas a retail organization may select PCI DSS.

10. **C.** The presence of security standards indicates an organization with a higher level of maturity than that of an organization that lacks them.

11. **A.** An organization that does not have a security incident log probably lacks the capability to detect and respond to an incident. It is not reasonable to assume that the organization has had no security incidents, since minor incidents occur with regularity. Claiming that the organization has effective controls is unreasonable, as it is understood that incidents occur even when effective controls are in place (because not all types of incidents can reasonably be prevented).

12. **B.** A process that is performed consistently but is undocumented is generally considered to be Repeatable.

13. **C.** The absence of application whitelisting is the best available answer. It can also be said that end users are probably local administrators, a setting required for most software programs to be installed on an endpoint.

14. **C.** An organization that needs to implement new controls should do so within its existing control framework. It is not necessary to adopt an entirely new control framework when a few controls need to be added.

15. **A.** In the context of strategy development, a gap analysis identifies the areas in systems, processes, policies, and controls that are in need of improvement. The gap analysis identifies the gaps between the present state of these areas and the desired future state, enabling the strategist to develop plans to close each gap.

PART II

Information Security Risk Management

■ **Chapter 3**   Information Security Risk Assessment
■ **Chapter 4**   Information Security Risk Response

Information Security Risk Assessment

In this chapter, you will learn about

- Benefits and outcomes of an information risk management program
- Developing a risk management strategy
- Risk assessment and risk management standards and frameworks
- The risk management life-cycle process
- Vulnerability and threat analysis
- Integrating risk management into an organization's practices and culture
- The components of a risk assessment: asset value, vulnerabilities, threats, and probability and impact of occurrence
- Qualitative and quantitative risk analysis
- The risk register
- Risk management in other business processes

This chapter covers Certified Information Security Manager (CISM) Domain 2, "Information Security Risk Management," part A, "Information Security Risk Assessment." The entire Information Security Risk Management domain represents 20 percent of the CISM examination.

Supporting Tasks in the CISM job practice that align with the Information Security Risk Management / Information Security Risk Assessment domain include:

22. Participate in and/or oversee the risk identification, risk assessment, and risk treatment process.

23. Participate in and/or oversee the vulnerability assessment and threat analysis process.

26. Facilitate the integration of information risk management into business and IT processes.

Information security risk management is the practice of balancing business opportunities with potential information security–related losses or negative impacts to business operations. Information security risk management is largely a qualitative effort, because it is difficult to know the probability and costs of significant loss events. Still, several methods for measuring risk have been established that help organizations better understand risks and how they can be handled. These methods include qualitative and quantitative techniques used to contribute to business decisions.

Emerging Risk and Threat Landscape

Risk management is the fundamental undertaking for any organization that desires to be reasonably aware of risks that, if not identified or monitored, could result in unexpected losses or loss of life, and even threaten the survival of the organization. The purpose of risk management is to identify credible threats and determine the best ways to deal with those threats. Organizations using effective risk management processes experience fewer security incidents; any incidents that do occur have lower impact, in part because the organization is better prepared to deal with them.

The Importance of Risk Management

Risk management is the cornerstone of any good information security program. Risk management represents time-proven methods and techniques used to identify risks, understand their probability of occurrence and potential impact on the organization, make decisions about those risks based on established decision criteria, and measure key attributes of security and risk for long-term trending and reporting to executive management.

Risk management provides key information that enables the security manager to prioritize scarce resources to result in the greatest possible risk reduction. Without risk management techniques, security managers would be making prioritization decisions based on gut feelings or other arbitrary means.

Though risk management may seem like a very complex and overwhelming subject, we as humans practice risk management every day. For example, suppose you are driving to work, and you know that the interstate is the fastest route, except not at this time of the day. Also, you know there are more wrecks during this time. What do you do? You use risk management techniques to help you make a risk-based decision and take a different route. There is no guarantee that you will arrive early at work or that you won't get into a car accident or get a speeding ticket, but the chances of any of these are much lower by taking this route, so you have reduced the risk of arriving late (or worse).

The effectiveness of a risk management program is largely dependent on two factors: support from executive management and an organization's culture with respect to security awareness and accountability. Additionally, an effective risk management program can serve as a catalyst for making subtle but strategic changes to an organization's culture.

No two risk management programs are alike; instead, each is uniquely different, based on several factors:

- Culture
- Mission, objectives, and goals

- Management structure
- Management support
- Industry sector
- Market conditions
- Applicable laws, regulations, and other legal obligations
- Stated or unstated risk tolerance
- Financial health
- Operating locations

Outcomes of Risk Management

An organization that implements an effective risk management program will have heightened awareness about the business use of technology and how that technology can impact the business. The greatest benefit that an organization will derive is a lower probability of security incidents; for incidents that do occur, the organization will be better prepared, and the impact of the incident will be reduced.

An organization with the risk management program will develop a culture of risk-aware planning, thinking, and decision-making. Executives in the organization will be fully aware of information risk, resulting in a more realistic view of the risks associated with the use of information technology (IT) and the Internet. Executives and other decision-makers will begin to develop an instinct for the risk levels of different kinds of business activities.

Risk Objectives

A vital part of strategy development is the determination of desired risk levels. One of the inputs to strategy development is the understanding of the current level of risk, and the desired future state may also have an associated level of risk.

It is quite difficult to quantify risk, even for the most mature organizations. Getting risk to a reasonable "high/medium/low" is simpler, though less straightforward, and difficult to do consistently across an organization. In specific instances, the costs of individual controls can be known, and the costs of theoretical losses can be estimated, but doing this across an entire risk-control framework is tedious, yet uncertain, because the probabilities of occurrence for threat events amounts to little more than guesswork. Spending too much time analyzing risks brings diminishing returns.

Still, in a general sense, a key part of a security strategy may well be the reduction of risk (it could also be cost reduction or compliance improvement). When this is the case, the strategist will need to employ a method for determining before-and-after risk levels that are reasonable and credible. For the sake of consistency, a better approach would be the use of a methodology—however specific or general—that fits with other strategies and discussions involving risk.

Risk Management Technologies

Throughout the risk management process, an organization will identify specific risks and will often choose to mitigate those risks with specific process and technology solutions. The categories and types of solutions include the following:

- Access governance systems
- Access management systems
- Advanced antimalware software (often touted as a replacement for antivirus)
- Antivirus software
- Cloud access security brokers (CASBs)
- Data loss prevention (DLP) systems
- Dynamic application security testing tools (DASTs)
- External monitoring and threat intelligence services
- File activity monitoring systems (FAMs)
- File integrity monitoring systems (FIMs)
- Firewalls (including so-called next-generation firewalls)
- Forensics tools
- Integrated risk management (IRM) systems, formerly known as governance, risk, and compliance (GRC) systems
- Intrusion detection systems (IDSs)
- Intrusion prevention systems (IPSs)
- Network access controls (NACs)
- Phishing assessment tools
- Privileged access management systems (PAMs)
- Public key infrastructure (PKI)
- Security information and event management (SIEM) system
- Security orchestration, automation, and response (SOAR) systems
- Single sign-on (SSO) systems
- Static application security testing (SAST) tools
- Spam filters
- Third-party risk management (TPRM) systems
- Threat intelligence platform (TIP)
- Unified threat management (UTM) systems
- User behavior analytics (UBA) systems

- Virtual private network (VPN) systems
- Vulnerability scanning tools
- Web application scanning tools
- Web content filtering
- Wireless access controls

Organizations without effective risk management programs often acquire many of these capabilities but do so without first identifying specific, relevant risks to their organizations. Instead, they are purchasing these solutions for other reasons, often based on the following:

- Salespeople who claim their solutions will solve the organization's security risks (without actually knowing what the specific risks are)
- Security managers in other organizations who purchase the same or similar solutions (again, in the presence or absence of sound risk management)
- Articles in trade publications that explain the merits of security solutions

 NOTE   The organization's security solutions portfolio should be based on supporting the business objectives and should have defined success criteria, business requirements, and technical requirements prior to the purchase of specific technologies.

Implementing a Risk Management Program

The implementation of a risk management program is not a straightforward undertaking. There are several risk management frameworks to choose from, and they share common principles, including the concept of risk management being a life-cycle process, periodic assessment, and continuous improvement.

Both internal and external factors will influence what risk management framework should be adopted and how it will be implemented. Applying a risk management framework in an organization requires a keen understanding of the organization's mission, objectives, strategies, cultures, practices, structure, financial condition, risk appetite, and level of executive management support. External factors that will influence the selection and implementation of a risk management framework include market and economic conditions, applicable regulations, geographical operations, customer base/type, and the social and political climates. Specific frameworks are discussed later in this section.

Once a framework has been selected, the security manager can then start to develop a sound risk management strategy. Security managers will need to perform one or more gap analyses to understand the organization's current state so that they can develop adequate plans to define, document, and highlight the desired future state. Because no security manager has a complete repertoire of knowledge and skill, many outside resources are available to supplement their knowledge and/or provide direct assistance.

NOTE Enterprise risk management (ERM) and information risk management share concepts and techniques and often work together. They deal mainly with different subject matter, however.

Risk Management Strategy

The objectives of a risk management strategy are to identify all credible risks and to reduce them to a level that is acceptable to the organization. The acceptable level of risk is generally related to these factors:

- Executive management's risk appetite
- The organization's ability to absorb losses, as well as its ability to build defenses
- Regulatory and legal requirements

As the organization establishes its acceptable level of risk (also known as *risk tolerance*), this will drive the implementation and refinement of controls. Then, over time, risk assessments and risk treatment will drive adjustments to its controls. This is because controls are the primary means for mitigating risks by ensuring desired outcomes, whatever they may be.

For organizations with other instances or pockets of risk management, it is important that the strategist consider merging these functions, or at least aligning them so that they are more consistent with one another. For organizations with enterprise risk management (ERM) functions, this may represent an opportunity to feed information risk into the ERM system so that its overall depiction of all business risk will include information risk.

It should be noted that in many small to midsize organizations, risk management programs originate from the IT group. This can be an opportunity for the IT team and security manager to increase the awareness and visibility of issues that could have a negative impact on the organization. An added benefit is the fostering of relationships with business leaders and moving away from the view of IT and security being seen as the "no" group and instead of being viewed as a business enabler.

Several internal and external factors will govern the implementation of risk management objectives, including the following:

- Culture
- Organizational maturity
- Management structure
- Management support
- Market conditions
- Regulatory and legal requirements

Possibly the most important factor that will enable or constrain security managers as they develop a risk management strategy is the development of key relationships throughout the organization. When a security manager develops and implements a risk management strategy, he or she is acting as a change agent in the organization. The security manager is subtly but intentionally driving key changes in the organization through changes in people, processes, and technologies. This role as a security catalyst is an ongoing journey that will become a way of life as the organization becomes a risk-aware culture.

Risk Communication   Risk management cannot be a secret business function; instead, it must be introduced to the organization's key stakeholders in a way that helps them understand the role of risk management in the organization. Stakeholders need to understand how the risk management program will work and the role they will play in it being an effective program in helping to achieve business objectives. An important factor in the process is helping stakeholders understand the impact that the risk management program will have on their relationships with one another, on their autonomy, and on the organization's well being and health, including that of their own jobs.

Successful information security risk management requires that the channels of communication be open at all times and operate in all directions. Successful information risk programs operate through transparency so that all stakeholders understand what is happening in the program and why. Certainly, there are some matters of information security that need to be kept confidential, but generally speaking, information about risks should be readily available to all board members, executives, stakeholders, and risk owners.

Risk Awareness   Risk awareness activities help make business leaders, stakeholders, and other personnel aware of the organization's information risk management program. Similar to security awareness programs, the goal of risk awareness is to ensure that business leaders and decision-makers recognize that all business decisions have a risk component and that many decisions have implications on information risk. Further, they need to be aware of the presence of a formal information risk management program, which includes a process and techniques for making risk-aware decisions.

There is some overlap in the content and audience of security awareness and risk awareness programs. Primarily, security awareness applies to an entire organization, whereas risk awareness encompasses senior personnel who are involved in the risk management process. Also, the methods for communicating this information in these two programs are the same. Ideally, security awareness and risk awareness programs are developed side-by-side, ensuring that all audiences receive useful and actionable information when needed.

Risk Consulting   Security managers often play the role of security and risk consultant in their organizations. As they develop trusted relationships throughout the business, security managers are regarded as technology risk experts who are available to consult with on a wide variety of issues. Though these mini-consulting engagements may seem like ad hoc activities, security managers should treat them as formal service requests, even in the absence of a service request system or formal capability. This includes being mindful of responsiveness and service levels. Here are some of the key attributes that make a good information risk consultant:

- Ability to listen to business leaders and rephrase the key concepts or information back to the business leaders to gain confirmation of what was heard
- Ability to assess the information and how it may impact a process or business unit, and to identify other areas in the business that may be affected by the issue
- Have a good understanding of the business, not just the technology supporting the business

Risk Management Frameworks

When building an information risk management program, the security manager needs to develop processes and procedures, roles and responsibilities, and templates for business records. This can be a lengthy and laborious undertaking that lacks assurance of success. Instead of building a program from scratch, security managers can refer to the multitude of high-quality risk management frameworks, including the following:

- ISO/IEC 27001, "Information technology — Security techniques — Information security management systems — Requirements," especially requirements 4 through 10, which describe the structure of an entire information security management system (ISMS), including risk management
- ISO/IEC 27005, "Information Technology — Security Techniques — Information security risk management"
- ISO/IEC 31010, "Risk management — Risk assessment techniques"
- NIST Special Publication 800-37, "Guide for Applying the Risk Management Framework to Federal Information Systems: A Security Life Cycle Approach"
- NIST SP 800-39, "Managing Information Security Risk"
- COBIT 2019 (Control Objectives for Information and Related Technology) framework
- Risk IT framework
- RIMS Risk Maturity Model

Risk managers can take two main approaches when considering existing frameworks: use a single framework that has the best alignment with the organization's practices, or use elements from one or more frameworks to build the organization's risk management program. As noted earlier in the chapter, several considerations influence the decision.

Framework Components   Risk management frameworks have a common core of components, including the following:

- Program scope
- Information risk objectives

- Information risk policy
- Risk appetite/tolerance
- Roles and responsibilities
- Risk management life-cycle process
- Risk management documentation
- Management review

Security managers in regulated industries need to understand legal and regulatory requirements so that they can select a framework and build a program that includes all the required activities and characteristics. If an ERM program is already in place within the organization, the security manager should consult with the ERM team to understand how elements from one or more frameworks will support and share information with one another.

Integration into the Environment   To be efficient and effective, the organization's information risk management program needs to fit neatly and easily into the organization's existing policies, processes, and systems. The information risk management program should complement existing structures instead of building separate structures. The principle at work here is one of utilizing existing structures and minimizing impact to the organization. A new or improved information risk management program will already be disruptive to an organization in need of such a program—there is no point in making the componentry of a program disruptive as well.

For instance, a security manager should consider acquiring risk management modules in an existing IRM platform used to manage policies and external vendors, as opposed to purchasing a separate IRM platform for managing risk—even if a new, separate platform might do a better job. In another example, the security manager should consider supplementing an existing security awareness program platform with material about information risk, as opposed to building or acquiring a completely separate security awareness system that deals only with information risk management.

Any risk management program needs to integrate easily into the organization's existing culture. To the greatest extent possible, a new or improved risk management program should leverage current thinking, vocabulary, customs, and practices to fit seamlessly into the organization. However, if the organization's culture needs minor adjustments with regard to information risk and information security, the new risk management program should be "eased into" the culture as opposed to being haphazardly imposed upon the organization.

Risk Management Context

When designing and establishing an information risk management program, the information security manager needs to understand the business context in which the program will exist. This includes the scope of the information risk management program along with the entire business environment in which the program will operate, including the organization's policies, processes, practices, and culture. The information security manager, together with executive management, must define the boundaries within which the risk management program will operate, which may include the following:

- Business units, lines of business, locations/regions
- Participants and stakeholders in the information risk management program
- Roles and responsibilities for participants and stakeholders
- Risk appetite/tolerance

Internal Environments   While designing an information risk program, the security manager must understand many key aspects of the organization's internal environment. If a security manager fails to consider these issues, the program may be less effective or may fail altogether. Key aspects include the following:

- Organization mission, goals, and objectives
- Existing business strategies, including major initiatives and projects in flight
- Financial health and access to capital
- Existing risk practices
- Organizational maturity
- Formal and informal communication protocols/relationships
- Culture

External Environments   It is critical that the security manager and executive management understand the entities that affect the risk environment outside the organization. Although the external environment is not within the scope of an organization's risk management program, many aspects of the external environment must be well understood by the organization to ensure that it and its risk management program are successful. These aspects include the following:

- Market conditions
- Economic conditions
- Applicable laws and regulations
- Social and political environments
- External stakeholders, including regulators, business partners, suppliers, and customers
- External threats and threat actors
- Geopolitical factors

By being aware of these external factors, the organization can better understand their potential influences on the organization, which in turn may influence various aspects of the risk management program, including considerations when making risk decisions and overall risk tolerance.

The Three Levels of Risk Management

Modern risk management encounters a broad assortment of issues, ranging from corporate culture to misconfiguration of individual servers. Conceptually, these issues are handled in the same way, with risk identification, analysis, treatment, and closure, but the personnel involved will often vary, and the deliberations will sound quite different.

Risk management is best divided into three tiers:

- **Enterprise-level risks**   Risks at this level are generally associated with organization culture and management's adequate support of cybersecurity capabilities. Risks at this level are conceptual in nature and often are reported to a board of directors. The practice of risk management at this level is known as *enterprise risk management*, or ERM. An organization's ERM will often include not only cybersecurity risk, but also risks related to competition, market share, economic, workforce matters, and more.

- **Process-level risks**   Risks at this level are usually associated with the effectiveness of business processes, typically those that affect cybersecurity posture. Issues at this level typically involve security policies, standards, process design, workflow, and workload.

- **Asset-level risks**   Risks at this level are associated with individual systems or small groups of systems. Generally, asset-level risks involve configuration and small-scale architecture. Analysis is focused on technical vulnerabilities and threats, and remediation is usually tactical.

As depicted in Figure 3-1, these three levels of risk management may be managed by a single group or multiple groups. Though the subject matter varies between levels, the basic principles of risk identification, risk analysis, and risk treatment apply to all.

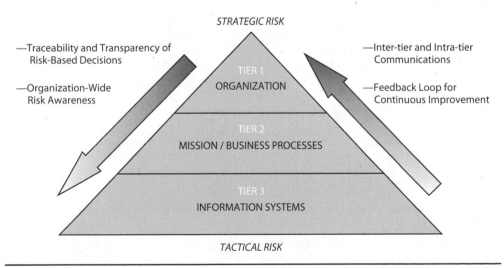

Figure 3-1   Multitier risk management in NIST SP 800-39 (Source: National Institute for Standards and Technology)

Risks at one tier sometimes inform adjacent tiers. For instance, a surge in asset-level risks may indicate defects in process-level risks, or even a shift in workforce priorities. Similarly, the presence of multiple process-level risks may be an indication of macro issues that should be addressed at the enterprise level.

Gap Analysis

As security managers design the organization's information risk management program, they envision the desired end state, which is often based on one or more information risk frameworks, as discussed earlier in this section. But when it comes to developing actual plans for implementing components of the program, the security manager must understand the current state of the program, even if there is no formal program at all. To do this, the security manager should conduct a gap analysis to determine which characteristics of the current state can remain, which aspects should be discarded, which should be replaced, and which should be added.

For example, suppose a security manager examines an organization's existing change control process. She finds only a log of changes and e-mail attachments containing management approvals for changes. Her gap analysis reveals the lack of a change request procedure, change advisory board (CAB) calls, and roles and responsibilities. The existing business record is usable but needs additional fields and annotations. With this information, the security manager can now undertake (or direct) the work required to implement change control process improvements. Or suppose a security manager identifies that the current risk audit is conducted annually with no input from the business and process leaders. The information is kept by the internal audit team and updated by the chief executive officer (CEO). In this case, a gap analysis would identify several opportunities for improvement within the program through the involvement of senior leaders.

External Support

Setting up a new information risk management program involves a great deal of knowledge and details. Even the most experienced information security managers may find themselves lacking in a few areas. For instance, a new security manager may have worked previously in an organization without an existing risk management program, or the security manager may have worked in a different industry sector in the past. Or perhaps the organization may use tools, technologies, or processes that are unfamiliar to the security manager. Fortunately, a wealth of information is available to security managers, which will help to supplement their existing knowledge and skills so that they can proceed with building and running an information risk management program with more confidence and with better assurances of positive outcomes.

Here are some of these information sources:

- **Consultants** Many large and numerous small security professional services firms are equipped to provide professional advice on the establishment of a security strategy, and they can do the actual work of designing and implementing a risk management program. Sometimes, executive management needs affirmation from outside experts on the need for, and the ways to implement and operate, an information security program.

- **Security round tables**   Many areas have informal security round tables whose members include chief information security officers (CISOs) and security managers. These local networks of information risk security professionals are invaluable for networking and advice.

- **Organization chapters**   Several professional organizations have local chapters, where security professionals can congregate and learn from one another and from event speakers, including the following:

  - Cloud Security Alliance (CSA)

  - Information Systems Security Association (ISSA)

  - InfraGard

  - International Information Systems Security Certification Consortium, (ISC)²

  - International Association of Privacy Professionals (IAPP)

  - ISACA

  - Society for Information Management (SIM)

  - Society of Information Risk Analysts (SIRA)

- **Published information risk management practices**   Several organizations, such as the following, publish standards and/or articles describing risk management practices, techniques, and case studies:

  - (ISC)²

  - ISACA

  - SANS Institute

- **Sources for security industry news**   Many organizations publish articles and white papers on various information security and risk management topics, including the following:

  - *CIO* magazine

  - *CSO* magazine

  - Dark Reading

  - Information Security Media Group (ISMG)

  - *Infosecurity Magazine*

  - ISACA

  - (ISC)²

  - SANS Institute

  - *SC Magazine*

  - TechTarget

- **Reports from research organizations** Several organizations conduct research and publish reports on many security-related topics:
  - Ernst & Young (EY)
  - Ponemon Institute
  - PricewaterhouseCoopers (PwC)
  - Symantec
  - Verizon Business
- **Advisory services** Several advisory firms, including the following, publish articles, studies, and advice for security and risk managers:
  - Forrester
  - Frost Sullivan
  - Gartner
  - IDC
  - Ovum
- **Training** Education and training courses tailored for established security and risk professionals are available from many universities, community colleges, and vocational schools, as well as ISACA, (ISC)², and SANS.
- **Books** Some of the titles listed in *The Cybersecurity Canon* are focused on risk management and go deeper into the topic than is needed for the CISM certification. Originally curated by Palo Alto Networks, *The Cybersecurity Canon* is now managed by Ohio State University (https://icdt.osu.edu/about-cybersecurity-canon).
- **Conferences** Regional, national, and international conferences on security and risk management attract large numbers of security and risk professionals and include speakers, workshops, and training. Like other events listed here, these conferences provide numerous professional networking opportunities. Conferences include the following:
  - Black Hat
  - Defcon
  - Evanta (hosts several conferences)
  - Gartner Security & Risk Management Summit
  - ISACA Conference
  - ISSA (hosts several conferences)
  - RSA
  - SecureWorld Expo
  - Security Advisor Alliance Summit

- **Intelligence services**   Several organizations publish advisories on threat actors, threats, and vulnerabilities. Some are designed to be human-readable, while others are designed as machine-readable and intended to be fed into an organization's SIEM or TIP. A word of caution: Many organizations are promoting and selling threat intelligence services today. The security manager should fully vet the services and the specific value they will add to the organization.

The Risk Management Life Cycle

Like other life-cycle processes, risk management is a cyclical, iterative activity that is used to acquire, analyze, and treat risks. This book focuses on information risk, but overall, the life cycle for information risk is functionally similar to that for other forms of risk: a new risk is introduced into the process, the risk is studied, and a decision is made about its outcome. Like other life-cycle processes, risk management is formally defined in policy and process documents that define scope, roles and responsibilities, workflow, business rules, and business records.

Several frameworks and standards from U.S. and international sources define the full life-cycle process. Security managers are generally free to adopt any of these standards, use a blend of different standards, or develop a custom framework.

Information risk management relies upon risk assessments that consider valid threats against the organization's assets, considering any present vulnerabilities. Several standards and models for risk assessments can be used. The results of risk assessments are placed into a risk register, which is the official business record containing current and historic information risk threats.

Risk treatment decisions about risks are made after weighing various risk treatment options. These decisions are typically made by a business owner associated with the affected business activity.

The Risk Management Process

The risk management process consists of a set of structured activities that enable an organization to manage risks systematically. Like other business processes, risk management processes vary somewhat from one organization to the next, but generally, they consist of the following activities:

- **Scope definition**   The organization defines the scope of the risk management process itself. Typically, scope definitions include geographical or business unit parameters. Scope definition is not part of the iterative portion of the risk management process, although scope may be redefined from time to time.

- **Asset identification and valuation**   The organization uses various means to discover and track its information and information system assets. A classification scheme may be used to identify risk and criticality levels. Asset valuation is a key part of asset management processes, and the value of assets is appropriated for use in the risk management processes. Asset valuation is described in detail in Chapter 5.

- **Risk appetite**   Developed outside of the risk management life-cycle process, risk appetite is an expression of the level of risk that an organization is willing to accept. A risk appetite that is related to information risk is typically expressed in qualitative means; however, organizations in financial services industries often express risk in quantitative terms.

- **Risk identification**   In this first step in the iterative risk management process, the organization identifies a risk that comes from one of several sources, including the following:

  - **Risk assessment**   This includes an overall risk assessment or a focused risk assessment.

  - **Vulnerability assessment**   This may be one of several activities, including a security scan, a penetration test, or a source code scan.

  - **Threat advisory**   This is an advisory from a product vendor, threat intelligence feed, or news story.

  - **Risk analysis**   This is an analysis of risk that is focused on some other matter that may uncover additional risks requiring attention.

- **Risk analysis**   In the second step in a typical risk management process, the risk is analyzed to determine several characteristics, including the following:

  - **Probability of event occurrence**   The risk analyst studies event scenarios and calculates the likelihood that an event associated with the risk will occur. This is typically expressed in the number of likely events per year.

  - **Impact of event occurrence**   The risk analyst studies different event scenarios and determines the impact of each. This may be expressed in quantitative terms (dollars or other currency) or qualitative terms (high/medium/low or a numeric scale of 1 to 5 or of 1 to 10).

  - **Mitigation**   The risk analyst studies different available methods for mitigating the risk. Depending upon the type of risk, there are many techniques, including changing a process or procedure, training staff, changing architecture or configuration, or applying a security patch.

  - **Recommendation**   After studying a risk, the risk analyst may develop a recommended course of action to address the risk. This reflects the fact that the individual performing risk analysis is often not the risk decision-maker.

- **Risk treatment**   In the last step in a typical risk management process, an individual decision-maker or committee makes a decision about a specific risk. The basic options for risk treatment are as follows:

  - **Accept**   The organization elects to take no action related to the risk.

  - **Mitigate**   The organization chooses to mitigate the risk, which can take the form of some action that serves to reduce the probability of a risk event or reduce the impact of a risk event. The actual steps taken may include business process changes, configuration changes, the enactment of a new control, or staff training.

- **Transfer** The practice of transferring risk is typically achieved through an insurance policy, although other forms are available, including contract assignment.

- **Avoid** The organization chooses to discontinue the activity associated with the risk. This choice is typically selected for an outdated business activity that is no longer profitable or for a business activity that was not formally approved in the first place.

- **Risk communication** This takes many forms, including formal communications within risk management processes and procedures, as well as information communications among risk managers and decision-makers.

In addition to business processes, a risk management process has business records associated with it. The *risk register,* sometimes known as a risk ledger, is the primary business record in most risk management programs that lists risks that have been identified. Typically, a risk register contains many items, including a description of the risk, the level and type of risk, and information about risk treatment decisions. The risk register is discussed in detail later in this chapter.

Figure 3-2 shows the elements of a typical risk management life cycle.

Risk Management Methodologies

Several established methodologies are available for organizations that want to manage risk using a formal standard. Organizations select one of these standards for a variety of reasons: they may be required to use a specific standard to address regulatory or contractual terms, or they may feel that a specific standard better aligns with their overall information risk program or the business as a whole.

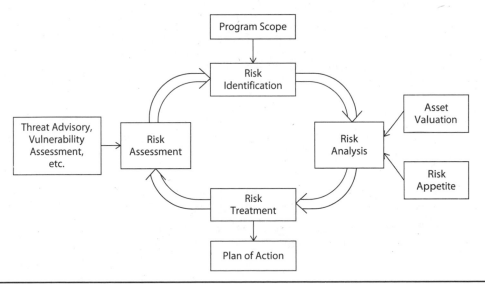

Figure 3-2 The risk management life cycle

NIST Standards　The National Institute for Standards and Technology (NIST) develops standards for information security and other subject matter. NIST Special Publication (SP) 800-30, "Guide for Conducting Risk Assessments," is a detailed, high-quality standard that describes the steps used for conducting risk assessments. NIST SP 800-39, "Managing Information Security Risk: Organization, Mission, and Information, System View," describes the overall risk management process.

NIST SP 800-39　The methodology described in this publication consists of multilevel risk management, at the information systems level, at the mission/business process level, and at the overall organization level. Communications up and down these levels ensure that risks are communicated upward for overall awareness, while risk awareness and risk decisions are communicated downward for overall awareness. Figure 3-1 depicts this approach.

The tiers of risk management are described in NIST SP 800-39 in this way:

- **Tier 1: Organization view**　This level focuses on the role of governance, the activities performed by the risk executive, and the development of risk management and investment strategies.

- **Tier 2: Mission/business process view**　This level is all about enterprise architecture, enterprise security architecture, and ensuring that business processes are risk-aware.

- **Tier 3: Information systems view**　This level concentrates on more tactical things such as system configuration and hardening specifications, vulnerability management, and the detailed steps in the systems development life cycle.

Other concepts discussed in this publication include trust, the trustworthiness of systems, and organizational culture.

The overall risk management process defined by NIST SP 800-39 consists of several steps:

- **Step 1: Risk framing**　This consists of the assumptions, scope, tolerances, constraints, and priorities—in other words, the business context that is considered prior to later steps taking place.

- **Step 2: Risk assessment**　This is the actual risk assessment, where threats and vulnerabilities are identified and assessed to determine levels and types of risk.

- **Step 3: Risk response**　This is the process of analyzing each risk and developing strategies for reducing it, through appropriate risk treatment for each identified risk. Risk treatment options are *accept, mitigate, avoid,* and *transfer*. This step is defined in more detail in NIST SP 800-30, described later in this section.

- **Step 4: Risk monitoring**　This is the process of performing periodic and ongoing evaluation of identified risks to see whether conditions and risks are changing.

NIST SP 800-30   This publication describes in greater detail a standard methodology for conducting a risk assessment. The techniques in this document are quite structured and essentially involve setting up a number of worksheets where threats and vulnerabilities are recorded, along with the probability of occurrence and impact if they occur.

In this standard, the steps for conducting a risk assessment are as follows:

- **Step 1: Prepare for assessment**   The organization determines the purpose of the risk assessment. Primarily, it is important to know the purpose of the results of the risk assessment and the decisions that will be made as a result of the risk assessment. Next, the scope of the assessment must be determined and known. This may take many forms, including geographic and business unit boundaries, as well as the range of threat scenarios that are to be included. Also, any assumptions and constraints pertaining to the assessment should be identified. Further, the sources of threat, vulnerability, and impact information must be identified. (NIST SP 800-30 includes exemplary lists of threats, vulnerabilities, and impacts in its appendixes.)

- **Step 2: Conduct assessment**   The organization performs the actual risk assessment. This consists of several tasks.

  A. **Identify threat sources and events**   The organization identifies a list of threat sources and events that will be considered in the assessment. The standard includes the following sources of threat information. Organizations are advised to supplement these sources with other information as needed.

    - Table D-1: Threat source inputs
    - Table D-2: Threat sources
    - Table D-3: Adversary capabilities
    - Table D-4: Adversary intent
    - Table D-5: Adversary targeting
    - Table D-6: Nonadversary threat effects
    - Table E-1: Threat events
    - Table E-2: Adversarial threat events
    - Table E-3: Nonadversarial threat events
    - Table E-4: Relevance of threat events

  B. **Identify vulnerabilities and predisposing conditions**   The organization examines its environment (people, processes, and technology) to determine what vulnerabilities exist that could result in a greater likelihood that threat events may occur. The standard includes the following sources of vulnerability and predisposing condition information that can be used in a risk assessment. Like the catalog of threats, organizations are advised to supplement these lists with additional vulnerabilities as needed.

    - Table F-1: Input—vulnerability and predisposing conditions
    - Table F-2: Vulnerability severity assessment scale

- Table F-4: Predisposing conditions
- Table F-5: Pervasiveness of predisposing conditions

C. **Determine likelihood of occurrence**   The organization determines the probability that each threat scenario identified earlier will occur. The following tables guide the risk manager in scoring each threat:

- Table G-1: Inputs—determination of likelihood
- Table G-2: Assessment scale—likelihood of threat event initiation
- Table G-3: Assessment scale—likelihood of threat event occurrence
- Table G-4: Assessment scale—likelihood of threat event resulting in adverse impact
- Table G-5: Assessment scale—overall likelihood

D. **Determine magnitude of impact**   In this phase, the risk manager determines the impact of each type of threat event on the organization. These tables guide the risk manager in this effort:

- Table H-1: Input—determination of impact
- Table H-2: Examples of adverse impacts
- Table H-3: Assessment scale—impact of threat events
- Table H-4: Identification of adverse impacts

E. **Determine risk**   The organization determines the level of risk for each threat event. These tables aid the risk manager in this effort:

- Table I-1: Inputs—risk
- Table I-2: Assessment scale—level of risk (combination of likelihood and impact)
- Table I-3: Assessment scale—level of risk
- Table I-4: Column descriptions for adversarial risk table
- Table I-5: Template for adversarial risk table to be completed by risk manager
- Table I-6: Column descriptions for nonadversarial risk table
- Table I-7: Template for nonadversarial risk table to be completed by risk manager

- **Step 3: Communicate results**   When the risk assessment has been completed, the results are communicated to decision-makers and stakeholders in the organization. The purpose of communicating risk assessment results is to ensure that the organization's decision-makers make decisions that include considerations for known risks. Risk assessment results can be communicated in several ways, including the following:

  - Publishing to a central location
  - Briefings

- Distributing via e-mail
- Distributing hard copies
- **Step 4: Maintain assessment**   After a risk assessment has been completed, the organization will maintain the assessment by monitoring risk factors identified in the risk assessment. This enables the organization to maintain a view of relevant risks that incorporates changes in the business environment since the risk assessment was completed. NIST SP 800-137, "Information Security Continuous Monitoring (ISCM) for Federal Information Systems and Organizations," provides guidance on the ongoing monitoring of information systems, operations, and risks.

NIST SP 800-30 is available at https://csrc.nist.gov/publications/sp.

ISO/IEC 27005   This international standard defines a structured approach to risk assessments and risk management. The methodology outlined in this standard is summarized here:

- **Step 1: Establish context**   Before a risk assessment can be performed, a number of parameters need to be established, including the following:
  - **Scope of the risk assessment**   This includes which portions of an organization are to be included, based on business unit, service, line, geography, organization structure, or other means.
  - **Purpose of the risk assessment**   Reasons include legal or due diligence or support of an ISMS, business continuity plan, vulnerability management plan, or incident response plan.
  - **Risk evaluation criteria**   Determine the means through which risks will be examined and scored.
  - **Impact criteria**   Determine how the impact of identified risks will be described and scored.
  - **Risk acceptance criteria**   Specify the method that the organization will use to determine risk acceptance.
  - **Logistical plan**   This includes which personnel will perform the risk assessment, which personnel in the organization need to provide information such as control evidence, and what supporting facilities are required, such as office space.
- **Step 2: Risk assessment**   The risk assessment is performed.
  - **Asset identification**   Risk analysts identify assets, along with their value and criticality.
  - **Threat identification**   Risk analysts identify relevant and credible threats that have the potential to harm assets, along with their likelihood of occurrence. There are many types of threats, both naturally occurring and human-caused, and they could be accidental or deliberate. Note that some threats may affect more than one asset. ISO/IEC 27005 contains a list of threat types, as does NIST SP 800-30 (in Table D-2) described earlier in this section. Note that a risk analyst may identify additional threats.

PART II

- **Control identification** Risk analysts identify existing and planned controls. Those controls that already exist should be examined to see whether they are effective. The criteria for examining a control includes whether it reduces the likelihood or impact of a threat event. The results of this examination will conclude whether the control is effective, ineffective, or unnecessary. Finally, when identifying threats, the risk analyst may determine that a new control is warranted.

- **Vulnerability identification** Vulnerabilities that can be exploited by threat events that cause harm to an asset are identified. Remember that a vulnerability does not cause harm, but its presence may enable a threat event to harm an asset. ISO/IEC 27005 contains a list of vulnerabilities. Note that a risk analyst may need to identify additional vulnerabilities.

- **Consequences identification** The risk analyst will identify consequences that would occur for each identified threat against each asset. Consequences may be the loss of confidentiality, integrity, or availability of any asset, as well as a loss of human safety. Depending on the nature of the asset, consequences may take many forms, including service interruption or degradation, reduction in service quality, loss of business, reputation damage, or monetary penalties including fines. Note that consequences may be a primary result or a secondary result of the realization of a specific threat. For example, the theft of sensitive financial information may have little or no operational impact in the short term, but legal proceedings over the long term could result in financial penalties, unexpected costs, and loss of business.

- **Step 3: Risk evaluation** Levels of risk are determined according to the risk evaluation and risk acceptance criteria established in step 1. The output of risk evaluation is a list of risks, with their associated threats, vulnerabilities, and consequences.

- **Step 4: Risk treatment** Decision-makers in the organization will select one of four risk treatment options for each risk identified in step 3. Decision-makers weigh the costs and benefits associated with each of these four options and decide the best course of action for the organization.

These four options are not mutually exclusive; sometimes, a combination of risk treatment options is the best option for an organization. For instance, if a business application is found to accept weak passwords, the chosen risk treatment may be a combination of security awareness training (mitigation) and acceptance (the organization elected not to modify the application as this would have been too expensive). Further, some treatments can address more than one risk. For example, security awareness training may reduce several risks associated with end-user computing and behavior.

Because some forms of risk treatment (mainly, risk reduction and risk transfer) may require an extended period of time to be completed, risk managers usually track ongoing risk treatment activities to completion.

- **Risk reduction (aka risk mitigation)**   The organization alters something in information technology (such as security configuration, application source code, or data), business processes and procedures, or personnel (such as training).

   In many cases, an organization will choose to update an existing control or enact a new control so that the risk reduction may be more effectively monitored over time. The cost of updating or creating a control, as well as the impact on ongoing operational costs of the control, will need to be weighed alongside the value of the asset being protected, as well as the consequences associated with the risk being treated. A risk manager remembers that a control can reduce many risks, and potentially for several assets, so the risk manager will need to consider the benefit of risk reduction in more complex terms.

   Chapter 6 includes a comprehensive discussion on the types of controls.

- **Risk retention (aka risk acceptance)**   The organization chooses to accept the risk and decides not to change anything. Do note that risks should not be accepted in perpetuity, but instead should be periodically reviewed.

- **Risk avoidance**   The organization decides to discontinue the activity associated with the risk. For example, suppose an organization assesses the risks related to the acceptance of credit card data for payments and decides to change the system so that credit card data is sent instead directly to a payment processor so that the organization will no longer be accepting that data.

- **Risk transfer**   The organization transfers risk to another party. The common forms of risk transfer are insurance and outsourcing security monitoring to a third party. When an organization transfers risk to another party, there will usually be residual risk that is more difficult to treat. For example, while an organization may have had reduced costs from a breach because of cyber insurance, the organization may still suffer reputational damage in the form of reduced goodwill.

- **Step 5: Risk communication**   All parties involved in information risk—the CISO (or other top-ranking information security official), risk managers, business decision-makers, and other stakeholders—need channels of communication throughout the entire risk management and risk treatment life cycle. Examples of risk communication include the following:

  - Announcements and discussions of upcoming risk assessments
  - Collection of risk information during risk assessments (and at other times)
  - Proceedings and results from completed risk assessments
  - Discussions of risk tolerance
  - Proceedings from risk treatment discussions and risk treatment decisions and plans
  - Educational information about security and risk
  - Updates on the organization's mission and strategic objectives
  - Communication about security incidents to affected parties and stakeholders

- **Step 6: Risk monitoring and review**   Organizations are not static, and neither is risk. The value of assets, impacts, threats, vulnerabilities, and likelihood of occurrence should be periodically monitored and reviewed so that the organization's view of risk continues to be relevant and accurate. Monitoring should include the following:

  - Discovery of new, changed, and retired assets

  - Changes in business processes and practices

  - Changes in technology architecture

  - New threats that have not been assessed

  - New vulnerabilities that were previously unknown

  - Changes in threat event probability and consequences

  - Security incidents that may alter the organization's understanding of threats, vulnerabilities, and risks

  - Changes in market and other business conditions

  - Changes in applicable laws and regulations

ISO/IEC 27005 may be purchased from www.iso.org.

Factor Analysis of Information Risk   Factor Analysis of Information Risk (FAIR) is an analysis method that helps a risk manager understand the factors that contribute to risk, as well as the probability of threat occurrence and an estimation of loss. FAIR is used to help a risk manager understand the probability of a given threat event and the losses that may occur.

In the FAIR methodology, there are six types of loss:

- **Productivity**   Lost productivity caused by the incident

- **Response**   The cost expended in incident response

- **Replacement**   The expense required to rebuild or replace an asset

- **Fines and judgments**   All forms of legal costs resulting from the incident

- **Competitive advantage**   Loss of business to other organizations

- **Reputation**   Loss of goodwill and future business

FAIR also focuses on the concept of asset value and liability. For example, a customer list is an asset because the organization can reach its customers to solicit new business; however, the customer list is also a liability because of the impact on the organization if the customer list is obtained by an unauthorized person.

FAIR guides a risk manager through an analysis of threat agents and the different ways in which a threat agent acts upon an asset:

- **Access**   Reading data without authorization

- **Misuse**   Using an asset differently from intended usage

- **Disclose**   Sharing data with other unauthorized parties
- **Modify**   Modifying assets
- **Deny use**   Preventing legitimate subjects from accessing assets

FAIR is claimed to be complementary to risk management methodologies such as NIST SP 800-30 and ISO/IEC 27005. You can obtain information about FAIR at www .fairinstitute.org.

ISACA's Risk IT Framework   ISACA developed the Risk IT Framework to align with its COBIT framework. While COBIT is used to manage other aspects of business infrastructure and risk, the Risk IT Framework is explicitly used to enable organizations to identify and manage IT risk. The framework is broken down into three major process areas: Risk Governance (RG), Risk Evaluation (RE), and Risk Response (RR).

The RE processes in the framework cover not only assessment, but overlap with the risk identification areas. In RE processes, business impact is framed and described and risk scenarios are developed. Risks are assessed and analyzed as well as presented to the organization's management. The RE processes are divided into three areas (numbered RE1–RE3).

Collect Data (RE1)   The data collection process aligns with some of the risk identification processes previously described. During this process, risk management personnel develop a model for data collection, which provides for standardized data formats, measurements, and common data definitions. Data is collected on the various aspects of the organization and risk scenarios, including the business's operating environment, risk factors, threat sources and events, vulnerability data, and asset data. Data is also collected on the effectiveness of existing controls in the organization.

Analyze Risk (RE2)   In this part of the framework, the organization begins to assess and analyze risk. First, it defines the risk analysis scope. The scope determines how broad and deep the risk analysis efforts will be, what areas the risk analysis will cover, and which assets will be examined for risk. To complete this part of the process, you'll need to consider all the documentation assembled up to this point: risk scenarios, asset inventories, breakdowns of business processes, prioritization of assets, and so on. This will help frame the risk analysis as well as determine scope.

During this step, IT risk is also estimated. This involves determining likelihood and impact values associated with the developed risk scenarios. In addition, it involves consideration of existing controls and how effective they are as currently installed and functioning. Likelihood and impact values are considered after existing controls are considered.

Although risk response is the subject of Chapter 4, the identification and consideration of possible risk response options are also part of this step of the process. The person assessing the risk may recommend several different response options, based on the identified risk. What risk options an organization will use is determined later in the process and typically with the input and approval of senior management. Risk response options should be recommended that reduce risk to an acceptable level directly based on the risk appetite and tolerance of the organization. Finally, knowledgeable peers should review risk analyses to verify that the analysis process is sound and to validate the results.

PART II

Maintain Risk Profile (RE3)   A *risk profile* is a collection of detailed data on identified IT risks. Risk profiles can cover a single system or asset but are also often seen as describing risks on an organization-wide basis. During this risk evaluation step, a comprehensive document of identified risks and their characteristics, such as details regarding impact, likelihood, and contributing factors, is developed and maintained throughout the asset or system's life cycle. Remember that system or asset risk profiles are usually rolled up into a more comprehensive risk document that covers systems, assets, and business processes across the entire organization.

IT assets are also mapped to the business and organizational processes they support during this step; this helps translate IT risk to corresponding business risk and enables management to see how the organization would be affected if IT risk were realized on specific assets. It also enables the organization to develop criticality estimates of IT resources from a business perspective. It's worth noting that this is similar to the same process followed during a business impact assessment (BIA). The key to understanding how IT risk affects business operations at this point is in understanding how the capabilities of IT are provided to the business processes in question and how critical IT is to a particular business process or operation. Maintaining a risk profile also means monitoring and updating risk scenarios and analysis as conditions and risk factors change. This involves keeping the risk register up to date as well. Finally, the organization should develop key risk indicators (KRIs) during this step, specifically focusing on IT resources. While key risk indicators are discussed in Chapter 5, for now, you should know that they enable the organization to monitor changes in risk for given scenarios and to modify its risk profiles as these indicators change. Table 3-1 summarizes some of the different risk assessment methodologies available.

 EXAM TIP   Because this is an ISACA-sponsored exam, you should understand risk assessment terms and processes from the perspective of the ISACA framework more so than any other. The ISACA Risk IT Framework directly aligns with ISO/IEC standards as well.

Methodology	Sponsor	Notes
NIST SP 800-30, "Guide for Conducting Risk Assessments"	NIST	Part of the NIST Risk Management Framework
OCTAVE (OCTAVE, OCTAVE-S, and OCTAVE Allegro)	Software Engineering Institute, Carnegie Mellon University	Uses workgroups, is suited for any organization, and does not require extensive risk management experience or knowledge
ISO/IEC	ISO/IEC	Prescribes methods and processes for developing assessment programs as well as describes more than 30 different means to assess risk factors and elements
The ISACA Risk IT Framework	ISACA	Risk assessments covered in the Risk Evaluation (RE) phase

Table 3-1   Summary of Available Risk Assessment Methods and Frameworks

Vulnerability and Control Deficiency Analysis

The identification of vulnerabilities is an essential part of any risk assessment. A *vulnerability* is any weakness in a system that permits an attacker to compromise a target process or system successfully.

In the security industry, the key terms involved with risk assessments are often misunderstood and misused. These terms are distinguished from one another in this way: a vulnerability is a weakness in a system that could permit an attack to occur. A vulnerability is not the attack vector or technique—this is known as a *threat*.

Vulnerabilities usually take one of these forms:

- **Configuration fault**   A system, program, or component may have one or more incorrectly set configuration settings that could provide an attacker with opportunities to compromise a system. For example, the authentication settings on a system may enable an attacker to employ a brute-force password-guessing attack that will not be stopped by target user accounts being automatically locked out after a small number of unsuccessful login attempts.

- **Design fault**   The relationship between components of a system may be arranged in such a way that makes it easier for an attacker to compromise a target system. For instance, an organization may have placed a database server in its DMZ network instead of in its internal network, making it easier for an attacker to identify and attack.

- **Known unpatched weakness**   A system may have one or more vulnerabilities for which security patches are available but not yet installed. For example, a secure communications protocol may have a flaw in the way that an encrypted session is established, which could permit an attacker to easily take over an established communications session. There may be a security patch available for the security flaw, but until the security patch is installed, the flaw exists and may be exploited by any individual who understands the vulnerability and available techniques to exploit it.

    Sometimes, known weaknesses are made public through a disclosure by the system's manufacturer or a responsible third party. Even if a patch is unavailable, other avenues may be available to mitigate the vulnerability, such as a configuration change in the target system.

- **Undisclosed unpatched weakness**   A system may have unpublicized vulnerabilities that are known only to the system's manufacturer. Until an organization using one of these systems learns of the vulnerability via a security bulletin or a news article, the organization can do little to defend itself, short of employing essential security techniques such as system hardening, network hardening, and secure coding.

- **Undiscovered weakness** Security managers have long accepted the fact that all kinds of information systems have security vulnerabilities that are yet to be discovered, disclosed, and mitigated. New techniques for attacking systems are constantly being developed, and some of these techniques can exploit weaknesses no one knew to look for. As new techniques have been discovered that involve examining active memory for snippets of sensitive information, system and tool designers can design defense techniques for detecting and even blocking attacks. For example, techniques were developed that would permit an attacker to harvest credit card numbers from PCI-compliant point-of-sale software programs. Soon, effective attacks were developed that enabled cybercriminal organizations to steal tens of millions of credit card numbers from global retail companies.

Vulnerabilities exist everywhere—in software programs, database management systems, operating systems, virtualization platforms, business processes, encryption algorithms, and personnel. As a rule, security managers should consider that every component of every type in every system has both known and unknown vulnerabilities, some of which, if exploited, could result in painful and expensive consequences for the organization. Table 3-2 lists the places where vulnerabilities may exist, with techniques that can be used to discover at least some of them.

Table 3-2 Vulnerabilities and Detection Techniques	**Vulnerability Context**	**Detection Technique**
	Network device	Vulnerability scanning Penetration testing Code analysis Network architecture review
	Operating system	Vulnerability scanning Penetration testing System architecture review
	Database management system	Vulnerability scanning Penetration testing
	Software application	Vulnerability scanning Penetration testing Dynamic application scanning Static code scanning Application architecture review
	Physical security	Reviews of physical security controls Social engineering assessments Physical penetration testing
	Business process	Process review Internal audit Control self-assessment
	Personnel	Social engineering assessments Competency assessments Phishing assessments (continual)

Third-Party Vulnerability Identification

Most organizations outsource at least a portion of their software development and IT operations to third parties. Mainly this occurs through the use of cloud-based applications and services such as SaaS applications, PaaS, and IaaS environments. Many organizations have the misconception that third parties take care of all security concerns in their services. As a result, they fail to thoroughly understand the security responsibility model for each outsourced service and fail to understand which portions of security are their responsibility and which are managed by the outsourced service.

Regardless of whether security responsibilities for any given aspect of operations are the burden of the organization or the outsourcing organization, vulnerabilities need to be identified and managed. For aspects of security that are the responsibility of the organization, the organization needs to employ normal means for identifying and managing them. For aspects of security that are the responsibility of the outsourced organization, that organization needs to identify and manage vulnerabilities; in many cases, the outsourced organization will make these activities available to their customers upon request.

Further discussion on the risks identified with third parties appears in Chapter 6.

Risk Assessment and Analysis

A *risk assessment* is intended to discover and identify threats that, if realized, could result in some unwanted event or incident. Two principal portions of a risk assessment are vulnerability identification and analysis (discussed in the preceding section) and threat identification and analysis, discussed next.

Threat Identification

The identification of threats is a key step in a risk assessment. A *threat* is defined as an event that, if realized, would bring harm to an asset and, thus, to the organization.

In the security industry, the key terms involved with risk assessments are often misunderstood and misused. These terms are distinguished from one another in this way: a threat is the actual action that would cause harm, not the person or group (generically known as an actor or threat actor) associated with it. A threat is also not a weakness that may permit a threat to occur; that is known as a *vulnerability*, discussed earlier in this chapter.

Threats are typically classified as external or internal, as intentional or unintentional, and as human-made or natural. The origin of many threats is outside the control of the organization but not necessarily out of their awareness. A good security manager can develop a list of threats that are likely (more or less) to occur to any given asset.

When performing a risk assessment, the security manager needs to develop a complete list of threats for use in the risk assessment. Because it's not always possible for a security manager to memorize all possible threats, the security manager may turn to one or more well-known sources of threats, including the following:

- ISO/IEC 27005, Appendix C, "Examples of Typical Threats"
- NIST SP 800-30, Appendix E, "Threat Events"

Upon capturing threat events from one or both of these sources, the security manager may identify a few additional threats not found in these lists. These additional threats may be specific to the organization's location, business model, or other factors.

A security manager will typically remove a few of the threats from the list that do not apply to the organization. For instance, an organization located far inland is not going to be affected by tsunamis, so this threat source can be eliminated. Similarly, in an organization located in an area not affected by tornados, volcanos, or earthquakes, these threat sources can be removed.

Internal Threats

Internal threats originate within the organization and are most often associated with employees of the organization. Quite possibly, internal employees may be the intentional actors behind these threats.

Security managers need to understand the nature of internal threats and the interaction between personnel and information systems. A wide range of events can take place that constitute threats, including the following:

- Well-meaning personnel making errors in judgment
- Well-meaning personnel making errors in haste
- Well-meaning personnel making errors because of insufficient knowledge or training
- Well-meaning personnel being tricked into doing something harmful
- Disgruntled personnel being purposefully negligent
- Disgruntled personnel deliberately bringing harm to an asset
- Threat actor acting on behalf of a foreign government or company posing as internal employee to exfiltrate information
- A trusted individual in a trusted third-party organization doing any of these

After understanding all the ways that something can go wrong, security managers may sometimes wonder if things can ever proceed as planned!

An important concept for a security manager to understand is this: while employees are at the top of a short list of potential threat actors, employees are the same actors who need to be given broad access to sensitive data to do their jobs and for the organization to function. Though there have been marginal improvements in technologies such as data loss prevention (DLP), employers have no choice but to trust employees by giving them access to virtually all of the organization's information, with the hope that they will not accidentally or deliberately abuse those privileges with potential to cause the organization great harm.

Examples of employees "going rogue" include the following:

- A network manager in San Francisco locks all other network personnel out of the network on the claim that no others are competent enough to manage it.
- A securities trader at a U.K.–based brokerage firm bankrupts the firm through a series of large unauthorized trades.

- A systems administrator at an intelligence agency acquires and leaks thousands of classified documents to the media.

- A Chinese national pleads guilty to conspiracy to commit economic espionage. Despite the employee's agreements to protect the company's intellectual property, the employee admits that he stole a trade secret from his employer, transferred it to a memory card, and attempted to take it to the People's Republic of China for the benefit of the Chinese government.

A significant factor in employees going rogue is an access control policy that results in individual employees having access to more information than is prudent. That said, increasing the granularity of access controls is known to be time-consuming and costly, and it increases the friction of doing business; few organizations tolerate this despite identified risks.

Access controls are only one of several areas of concern. Table 3-3 contains human-made threats that may be included in an organization's risk assessment.

Leak data via e-mail
Leak data via upload to unauthorized system
Leak data via external USB storage device or medium
Leak information face-to-face with unauthorized person
Perform a programming error
Misconfigure a system or device
Shut down an application, system, or device
Error perpetrated by any internal staff
Phishing attack
Social engineering attack
Share login credential with another person
Install or run unauthorized software program
Copy sensitive data to unauthorized device or system
Destroy or remove sensitive or critical information
Retrieve discarded, recycled, or shredded information
Conduct security scan
Conduct denial-of-service attack
Conduct physical attack on systems or facilities
Conduct credential-guessing attack
Eavesdrop on a sensitive communication
Impersonate another individual
Obtain sensitive information through illicit means

Table 3-3 Internal and External Human-Made Threats (*continued*)

Cause data integrity loss through any action
Intercept network traffic
Obtain sensitive information through programmatic data leakage
Perform reconnaissance as part of an attack campaign
Conduct a social engineering attack
Power anomaly or failure
Communications failure
Heating, venting, or air-conditioning failure
Degradation of electronic media
Fire
Smoke damage
Fire retardant damage
Flood due to water main break or drainage failure
Vandalism
Demonstrations/protests/picketing
Terrorist attack
Electromagnetic pulse
Explosion
Bombing

Table 3-3 Internal and External Human-Made Threats

It may be useful to build a short list of threat actors (the people or groups that would initiate a threat event), but remember that these are not the threats themselves. Building such a list may help the security manager identify additional threat events that may not be on the list.

Table 3-4 contains a list of internal and external natural threats.

External Threats

Like internal threats, threats that originate outside of the organization can include both deliberate and accidental actions. External threats can also be human-made or associated with naturally occurring events.

The security manager performing a risk assessment needs to understand the full range of threat actors, along with their motivations. This is particularly important for organizations where specific types of threat actors or motivations are more common. For example, certain industries such as aerospace and weapons manufacturers attract industrial espionage and intelligence agencies, and certain industries attract hacktivists.

Forest fire or range fire
Smoke damage from forest fire or range fire
River flood
Landslide
Avalanche
Tornado
Hurricane
Wind storm
Hailstorm
Earthquake
Tsunami
Lightning
Epidemic
Explosion of naturally occurring substances
Solar storm

Table 3-4   Internal and External Natural Threats

Table 3-5 contains a list of external threat actors, and Table 3-6 lists the motivations behind these actors.

 NOTE   External threat actors often become trusted insiders as employees, contractors, consultants, or service providers, transitioning to an internal threat.

Former employees
Current and former consultants
Current and former contractors
Competitors
Hacktivists
Personnel in current and former third-party service organizations, vendors, and suppliers
Government intelligence agencies (foreign and domestic)
Criminal organizations (including individuals)
Terrorist groups (including individuals)
Activist groups (including individuals)
Armed forces (including individuals)

Table 3-5   External Threat Actors

Competitive advantage
Economic espionage
Monetary gain
Political gain
Intelligence
Revenge
Shaming
Ego
Curiosity
Unintentional errors

Table 3-6 Threat Actor Motivations

In a risk assessment, it is essential to identify all threats that have a reasonable likelihood of occurrence. Those threats that are unlikely because of geographical and other conditions are usually excluded. For example, hurricanes can be excluded for locations far from oceans, and volcanoes can be excluded from locations where no volcanoes exist. Threats such as meteorites and space debris are rarely included in risk assessments because of the minute chance of occurrence.

Advanced Persistent Threats

An advanced persistent threat (APT), whether an individual or a cybercrime organization, is known for using techniques that indicate resourcefulness, patience, and resolve. Rather than employing a "hit-and-run" or "smash-and-grab" operation, an APT will patiently perform reconnaissance on a target and use tools to infiltrate the target and build a long-term presence there.

APT is defined by NIST SP 800-39 as follows:

> An APT is an adversary that possesses sophisticated levels of expertise and significant resources which allow it to create opportunities to achieve its objectives using multiple attack vectors (e.g., cyber, physical, and deception). These objectives typically include establishing and extending footholds within the IT infrastructure of the targeted organizations for purposes of exfiltrating information, undermining or impeding critical aspects of a mission, program or organization; or positioning itself to carry out these objectives in the future. The advanced persistent threat: (i) pursues its objectives repeatedly over an extended period of time; (ii) adapts to defenders' efforts to resist it; (iii) is determined to maintain the level of interaction needed to execute its objectives.

The term "APT" was developed in the early 2000s to describe a new kind of adversary that worked slowly but effectively to compromise a target organization. Prior to APTs, threat actors were unsophisticated and conducted operations that ran for short periods of time, a few days at most. But as more organizations put more valuable information assets online, threat actors became craftier and more resourceful; they resorted to longer-term campaigns to study a target for long periods of time before attacking it, and once an attack began, it would carry on for months or longer. APTs would compromise multiple systems inside the target organization and use a variety of stealthy techniques to establish and maintain a presence using as many compromised targets as possible. Once an APT was discovered (if it was *ever* discovered), the security manager would clean up the compromised target, often not knowing that the APT had compromised many other targets, with not all of the compromises using the same technique.

This cat-and-mouse game could continue for months, or even years, with the adversary continuing to compromise targets and study the organization's systems—all the while searching for specific targets—while the security manager and others would continually chase the adversary around like the carnival game of "whack a mole."

NOTE   The term "APT" is not used often nowadays, although its definition is largely unchanged. APTs were discussed more often when these techniques were new. But today, the techniques used by a multitude of cybercriminal organizations, along with hundreds if not thousands of talented, individual threat actors, resemble the APTs of a dozen years ago. Today APTs are not novel but routine.

Emerging Threats

The theater in which cyberwarfare takes place today is constantly changing and evolving. Several forces are at work, as explained in Table 3-7, that continually "push the envelope" in the areas of attack techniques as well as defense techniques.

Emerging threats will always represent the cutting edge of attack techniques and will be difficult to detect and/or remediate when they are first discovered. For this reason, emerging threats should be viewed as a phenomenon of new techniques, rather than as a fixed set of techniques. Often, the latest attack techniques are difficult to detect because they fall outside the span of techniques that security professionals expect to observe from time to time. Security managers need to understand that, although defensive technologies

Phenomenon	Response
Emerging technologies, including bring your own device (BYOD), bring your own application (BYOA), cloud computing, virtualization, and Internet of Things (IoT)	New targets of opportunity, many of which are poorly guarded when first implemented
Improved technologies (faster processing time)	More rapid compromise of cryptosystems
Improved technologies (faster network speeds)	More rapid exfiltration of larger data sets; easier transport of rainbow tables used to crack hash tables
Improved antimalware controls	Attack innovation—techniques evaded antimalware controls

Table 3-7   The Cascade of Emerging Threats

continuously improve to help prevent and/or detect attacks of increasing sophistication, attack techniques will continuously improve in their ability to evade detection by even the most sophisticated defense techniques.

Threat Forecasting Data Is Sparse

One of the biggest problems with information risk management is the lack of reliable data on the probability of many types of threats. Although the probability of some natural threats can sometimes be obtained from local disaster response agencies, the probabilities of most other threats are notoriously difficult to predict.

The difficulty in predicting security events sits in stark contrast to volumes of available data related to automobile and airplane accidents and human life expectancy. In these cases, insurance companies have been accumulating statistics on these events for decades, and the variables (for instance, tobacco and alcohol use) are well known. On the topic of cyber-related risk, there is a general lack of reliable data, and the factors that influence risk are not yet well known from a statistical perspective. For this reason, risk analysis still relies on educated guesses for the probabilities of most events. But given the recent surge in the popularity of cyber insurance, the availability and quality of cyberattack risk factors may soon be better understood.

Risk Identification

During risk identification, various scenarios are studied for each asset to identify which risks pose the greatest potential for realization. Several considerations are applied in the identification of each risk, including the following:

- **Threats**   All realistic threat scenarios are examined for each asset to determine which are most likely to occur.

- **Threat actors**   The risk manager must understand the variety of threat actors and know which ones are more motivated to target the organization and for what reasons. This further illuminates the likelihood that a given threat scenario will occur.

- **Vulnerabilities**   For all assets, business processes, and staff members being examined, vulnerabilities need to be identified. Then various threat scenarios are examined to determine which ones are more likely as a result of corresponding vulnerabilities.

- **Asset value**   The value of each asset is an important factor to include in risk analysis. As described earlier, assets may be valued in several ways. For instance, a customer database may have a modest recovery cost if it is damaged or destroyed; however, if that same customer database is stolen and sold on the black market, the value of the data may be much higher to cybercriminals, and the resulting costs to the organization to mitigate the harm done to customers may be higher still. Other ways to examine asset value is through the revenue derived from the asset's existence or use.

- **Impact**   The risk manager examines vulnerabilities, threats (with threat actors), and asset value and estimates the impact of the different threat scenarios. Impact is considered separately from asset value, because some threat scenarios have minimal correlation with asset value but are instead related to reputation damage. Breaches of privacy data can result in high mitigation costs and reduced business. Breaches of hospital data can threaten patient care. Breaches in almost any IoT context can result in extensive service interruptions and life safety issues.

Qualitative and quantitative risk analysis techniques help to distinguish higher risks from lower risks. These techniques are discussed later in this section. Risks above a certain level are often transferred to a risk register, where they will be processed through risk treatment.

Risk Likelihood and Impact

During risk analysis in a risk assessment, the risk manager will perform some simple calculations to stratify all of the risks that have been identified. These calculations generally resemble one or more of the following:

$$\text{Risk} = \text{threats} \times \text{vulnerabilities}$$
$$\text{Risk} = \text{threats} \times \text{vulnerabilities} \times \text{asset value}$$
$$\text{Risk} = \text{threats} \times \text{vulnerabilities} \times \text{probabilities}$$

ISO/IEC Guide 73, "Risk management – Vocabulary," defines risk as "the combination of the probability of an event and its consequence." This is an excellent way to understand risk in simple, nonnumeric terms.

Likelihood

In risk assessments, likelihood is an important dimension that helps a risk manager understand several aspects related to the unfolding of a threat event. The likelihood of a serious security incident has less to do with technical details and more to do with the thought process of an adversary. Considerations related to likelihood include the following:

- **Hygiene**   This is related to an organization's security operations practices, including vulnerability management, patch management, and system hardening. Organizations that do a poor job in these areas are more likely to suffer incidents simply because they are making it easier for adversaries to break into systems.

- **Visibility**   This is related to the organization's standing, including how large and visible the organization is, and how much the attacker's prestige will increase after successfully compromising the target.

- **Velocity**   This factor is related to the timing of various threat scenarios and whether there is any warning or foreknowledge.

- **Motivation**   It is important to consider various types of adversaries to better understand the factors that motivate them to attack the organization: it could be about money, reputation, or rivalry, for example.

- **Skill** For various threat scenarios, what skill level is required to attack the organization successfully? If attackers require a higher skill level to infiltrate an organization's system, this doesn't mean that an attack is less likely; other considerations such as motivation come into play as well.

Impact

In the context of information security, an *impact* is the actual or expected result of some action, such as a threat or disaster. During a risk assessment, impact is perhaps the most important attribute for a risk manager to understand in a threat scenario. A risk assessment can describe all types of threat scenarios, the reasons behind them, and how they can be minimized. If the risk manager fails to understand the impact of these scenarios, he or she cannot determine the level of importance imposed by one threat factor versus another, in terms of the urgency to mitigate the risk.

A wide range of possible impact scenarios include the following:

- Direct cash losses
- Reputation damage
- Loss of business—decrease in sales
- Drop in share price—less access to capital
- Reduction in market share
- Diminished operational efficiency (higher internal costs)
- Civil liability
- Legal liability
- Compliance liability (fines, censures, and so on)
- Interruption of business operations

Some of these impact scenarios are easier to analyze in qualitative terms than others, and the magnitude of most of these is difficult to quantify except in specific threat scenarios.

One of the main tools in the business continuity and disaster planning world, the business impact analysis (BIA), is highly useful for information security managers. A BIA can be conducted as part of a risk assessment or separate from it. A BIA differs from a risk assessment in this way: A risk assessment is used to identify risks and, perhaps, suggested remedies. A BIA is used to identify the most critical business processes, together with their supporting IT systems and dependencies on other processes or systems.

The value that a BIA brings to a risk assessment is the understanding of which business processes and IT systems are the most important to the organization. The BIA helps the information security manager understand which processes are the most critical and, therefore, which warrant the most strident protection, all other considerations being equal. Business impact analysis is described in detail in Chapter 7.

In qualitative risk analysis, where probability and impact are rated on simple numeric scales, a risk matrix is sometimes used to portray levels of risk based on probability and impact. The risk matrix in Figure 3-3 depicts qualitative risk.

Figure 3-3
Qualitative
risk matrix

Probability		Consequences		
Likely	Medium Risk	High Risk	Extreme Risk
Unlikely	Low Risk	Medium Risk	High Risk
Highly Unlikely	Insignificant Risk	Low Risk	Medium Risk
	Slightly Harmful	**Harmful**	**Extremely Harmful**

Consequences

Risk Analysis Techniques and Considerations

In a risk assessment, the security manager examines assets, together with associated vulnerabilities and likely threat scenarios. This detailed examination, or *risk analysis,* considers many dimensions of an asset, including the following:

- Asset value
- Threat scenarios
- Threat probabilities
- Relevant vulnerabilities
- Existing controls and their effectiveness
- Impact

Risk analysis can also consider business criticality, if a BIA is available.

Various risk analysis techniques are discussed in the remainder of this section.

Gathering Information

A security manager needs to gather a considerable amount of information to ensure that that the risk analysis and the risk assessment are valuable and complete. Several sources are available, including the following:

- Interviews with process owners
- Interviews with application developers
- Interviews with security personnel
- Interviews with external security experts
- Security incident records

- Analysis of incidents that have occurred in other organizations
- Prior risk assessments (caution is advised, however, to stop the propagation of errors from one assessment to the next)

Qualitative Risk Analysis

Most risk analysis begins with *qualitative* risk analysis, a rating technique that does not seek to identify exact (or even approximate) asset value or impact or the exact probability of occurrence. Risk items are expressed in levels such as high, medium, and low. The purpose of qualitative risk analysis is to understand each risk relative to other risks, so that higher risks can be distinguished from lower risks. This system enables the organization to focus on risks that are more critical, based on impact in qualitative terms.

Semiquantitative Risk Analysis

In semiquantitative risk analysis, the probability of occurrence and impact can be expressed as a numeric value in the range 1 to 5 (where 5 is the highest probability), for example. Then, for each asset and for each threat, risk can be calculated as probability × impact.

For example, suppose an organization has identified two risk scenarios. The first is a risk of data theft from a customer database; the impact is scored as a 5 (highest), and probability is scored as a 4 (highly likely). The risk is scored as 5 × 4 = 20. The second is a risk of theft of application source code; the impact is scored as a 2 (low), and probability is scored as a 2 (less likely). This risk is scored as 2 × 2 = 4. This system helps the security manager understand that the data theft risk is a larger risk (scored as 20) compared to the source code theft risk (scored as 4). These risk scores do not imply that the larger risk is five times as likely to occur, nor do they imply that protecting against the larger risk is five times as expensive. The scores are used to determine only that one risk is larger than another.

 NOTE Some security managers consider this a qualitative risk analysis, because the results are no more accurate in terms of costs and probabilities than those obtained using the qualitative technique.

Quantitative Risk Analysis

In *quantitative* risk analysis, risk managers attempt to determine the actual costs and probabilities of events. This technique provides more specific information to executives about the actual costs that they can expect to incur in various security event scenarios.

There are two aspects of quantitative risk analysis that prove to be a continuing challenge:

- **Event probability** It is difficult to come up with even an order-of-magnitude estimate on the probability of nearly every event scenario. Even with better information coming from industry sources, the probability of high-impact incidents is dependent upon many factors, some of which are difficult to quantify.

- **Event cost** It is difficult to put an exact cost on any given security incident scenario. Security incidents are complex events that involve many parties and have unpredictable short- and long-term outcomes. Despite improving information from research organizations on the cost of breaches, these are still rough estimates and may not take into account all aspects of cost.

Because of these challenges, quantitative risk analysis should be regarded as an effort to develop estimates, not exact figures. In part, this is because risk analysis is a measure of events that *may* occur, not a measure of events that *do* occur.

Standard quantitative risk analysis involves the development of several figures:

- **Asset value (AV)** The value of the asset is usually (but not necessarily) the asset's replacement value. Depending on the type of asset, different values may need to be considered.

- **Exposure factor (EF)** The financial loss that results from the realization of a threat is expressed as a percentage of the asset's total value. Most threats do not completely eliminate the asset's value; instead, they reduce its value. For example, if an organization's $120,000 server is rendered unbootable because of malware, the server will still have salvage value, even if that is only 10 percent of the asset's actual value. In this case, the EF would be 90 percent. Note that different threats have different impacts on EF, because the realization of different threats will cause varying amounts of damage to assets.

- **Single loss expectancy (SLE)** This value represents the financial loss when a threat scenario occurs one time. SLE is defined as AV × EF. Note that different threats have a varied impact on EF, so those threats will also have the same multiplicative effect on SLE.

- **Annualized rate of occurrence (ARO)** This is an estimate of the number of times that a threat will occur per year. If the probability of the threat is 1 in 50 (one occurrence every 50 years), ARO is expressed as 0.02. However, if the threat is estimated to occur four times per year, then ARO is 4.0. Like EF and SLE, ARO will vary by threat.

- **Annualized loss expectancy (ALE)** This is the expected annualized loss of asset value due to threat realization. ALE is defined as SLE × ARO.

ALE is based upon the verifiable values AV, EF, and SLE, but because ARO is only an estimate, ALE is only as good as ARO. Depending upon the value of the asset, the risk manager may need to take extra care to develop the best possible estimate for ARO, based upon whatever data is available. Sources for estimates include the following:

- History of event losses in the organization
- History of similar losses in other organizations
- History of dissimilar losses
- Best estimates based on available data

When performing a quantitative risk analysis for a given asset, risk managers can add up the ALEs for all threats. The sum of all ALEs is the annualized loss expectancy for the total array of threats. A particularly high sum of ALEs would mean that a given asset is confronted with a lot of significant threats that are more likely to occur. But in terms of risk treatment, ALEs are better off left as separate and associated with their respective threats.

OCTAVE

Operationally Critical Threat, Asset, and Vulnerability Evaluation (OCTAVE) is a risk analysis approach developed by Carnegie Mellon University. The latest version, OCTAVE Allegro, is used to assess information security risks so that an organization can obtain meaningful results from a risk assessment.

The OCTAVE Allegro methodology uses eight steps:

- **Step 1: Establish risk measurement criteria**   The organization identifies the most important impact areas. The impact areas in the model are reputation/customer confidence, financial, productivity, safety and health, fines/legal penalties, and other. For example, reputation may be the most important impact area for one organization, while privacy or safety may be the most important for other organizations.

- **Step 2: Develop an information asset profile**   The organization identifies its in-scope information assets and develops a profile for each asset that describe its features, qualities, characteristics, and value.

- **Step 3: Identify information asset containers**   The organization identifies all the internal and external information systems that store, process, and transmit in-scope assets. Note that many of these systems may be operated by third-party organizations.

- **Step 4: Identify areas of concern**   The organization identifies threats that, if realized, could cause harm to information assets. Typically, this is identified in a brainstorming activity.

- **Step 5: Identify threat scenarios**   This is a continuation of step 4, where threat scenarios are expanded upon (and unlikely ones eliminated). A threat tree may be developed that first identifies actors and basic scenarios and then is expanded to include more details.

- **Step 6: Identify risks**   A continuation of step 5, the consequences of each threat scenario are identified.

- **Step 7: Analyze risks**   This simple quantitative measurement is used to score each threat scenario based on risk criteria developed in step 1. The output is a ranked list of risks.

- **Step 8: Select mitigation approach**   A continuation of step 7, the risks with higher scores are analyzed to determine methods available for risk reduction.

The OCTAVE Allegro methodology includes worksheets for each of these steps, making it easy for a person or team to perform a risk analysis based on this technique. Further information about OCTAVE Allegro is available at www.cert.org/resilience/products-services/octave/.

Bow-Tie Analysis

A *bow-tie analysis* uses diagrams to analyze and explain relationships between various risk elements, from causes (threats) to events and then to impacts (consequences). It is similar to both the fault-tree analysis and the event-tree analysis (discussed next). It looks at the various causes of a risk event (fault tree) and analyzes the consequences of the event (event tree). The difference, however, is that the bow-tie analysis looks at the intervening characteristics of the events and causes, such as the path by which the cause leads to the event and then the consequences. Figure 3-4 illustrates a bow-tie diagram. In this figure, the adverse event is shown as the center of the bow tie, with potential causes on the left and possible consequences on the right.

Other Risk Analysis Methodologies

Additional risk analysis methodologies provide more complex approaches that may have usefulness for certain organizations or in selected risk situations:

- **Delphi method** Questionnaires are distributed to a panel of experts in two or more rounds. A facilitator will anonymize the responses and distribute them to the experts. The objective is for the experts to converge on the most important risks and mitigation strategies.

- **Bayesian analysis** This technique uses data distribution and statistical inference to determine risk probability values, checklists, scenario analysis, and business impact analysis.

- **Fault-tree analysis (FTA)** This logical modeling technique is used to diagram all the consequences for a given event scenario. FTA begins with a specific scenario and proceeds forward in time with all possible consequences. A large "tree" diagram can result that depicts many different chains of events.

- **Event-tree analysis (ETA)** Derived from the fault-tree analysis method, ETA is a logic-modeling technique for analysis of success and failure outcomes given a specific event scenario, in this case a threat scenario.

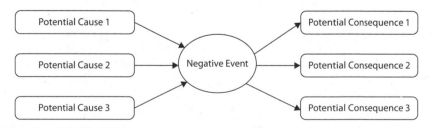

Figure 3-4   An example of a bow-tie analysis diagram

- **Monte Carlo analysis**   Derived from Monte Carlo computational algorithms, this analysis begins with a given system with inputs, where the inputs are constrained to minimum, likely, and maximum values. Running the simulation provides some insight into actual likely scenarios.

Risk Evaluation and Ranking

Upon completion of a risk assessment, when all risks have been identified and scored, the security manager, together with others in the organization, will begin to analyze the results and begin to develop a strategy going forward.

Risks can be evaluated singly, but the organization will better benefit from an analysis of all the risks together. Many risks are interrelated, and the right combination of mitigation strategies can result in many risks having been adequately treated.

The results of a risk assessment should be analyzed in several different ways, including the following:

- Looking at all risks by business unit or service line
- Looking at all risks by asset type
- Looking at all risks by activity type
- Looking at all risks by type of consequence

Because no two organizations (or their risk assessment results) are alike, this type of analysis is likely to identify themes of risk treatment that may have broad implications across many risks. For example, an organization may have several tactical risks, all associated with access management and vulnerability management. Rather than treating individual tactical risks, a better approach may be to improve or reorganize the access or vulnerability management programs from the top down, resulting in many identified risks being mitigated in a programmatic fashion. Organizations need to consider not just the details in a risk assessment, but the big picture.

Another type of risk to look for is a risk with a low probability of occurrence and high impact. This is typically the type of risk treated by transfer. Risk transfer most often comes in the form of cyber-risk insurance but also in security monitoring when it includes indemnification.

Risk Ownership

When considering the results of a risk assessment, the organization needs to assign individual risks to individual people, typically middle- to upper-management business leaders. These leaders, who should also have ownership of controls that operate within their span of control, have budget, staff, and other resources used in daily business operations. These are the risk owners, and, to the extent that there is a formal policy or statement on risk tolerance or risk appetite, they should be the people making risk treatment decisions for risks in their domain. To the extent that these individuals are accountable for operations in their part of the organization, they should also be responsible for risk decisions, including risk treatment, in their operational areas. A simple concept to approach risk ownership is that if nobody owns the risk, then nobody is accountable for managing the risk, which will lead to a great probability of the risk becoming an active issue with negative impacts on the business, along with the possible identification of a scapegoat who will be blamed if an event occurs. The scapegoat is usually the person responsible for information security.

Risk Treatment

In risk treatment, management makes a choice regarding the disposition of each identified risk. Management can choose to accept the risk, mitigate the risk, transfer it to another organization, or avoid the activity altogether. Risk treatment is described in detail in Chapter 4.

Controls

A common outcome of risk treatment, when mitigation is chosen, is the enactment of controls. Put another way, when an organization identifies a risk in a risk assessment, the organization may decide to develop (or improve) a control that will mitigate the risk that was found. Controls are measures put in place to ensure a desired outcome. Controls can come in the form of procedures, or they can be implemented directly in a system.

Suppose an organization realized that its procedures for terminating access for departing employees were resulting in a lot of user accounts not being deactivated. The existing control was a simple, open-loop procedure, whereby analysts were instructed to deactivate user accounts. Often they were deactivating user accounts too late or not at all. To reduce this risk, the organization modified the procedure (updated the control) by introducing a step in which a second person would verify all account terminations on a daily basis.

There are many categories and types of controls, as well as standard control frameworks. These are discussed in great detail in Chapter 6.

Risk Management and Business Continuity Planning

These two disciplines, risk management and business continuity planning, are focused on identifying risks that may adversely impact the organization's operations. Risk management and business continuity planning have several common characteristics and goals:

- Both seek to discover risks and develop remedies for events that threaten business operations and the ongoing viability of an organization.
- Both rely on risk assessments to identify risks that will require mitigation.
- Both can rely on the results of a business impact analysis to better understand the criticality of business processes and the interdependency of processes and assets.

Risk management identifies threats that, if unchecked, could unfold into disaster scenarios. Many of the threat scenarios in a risk assessment are disaster situations used in business continuity planning.

Business continuity planning is described in detail in Chapter 7.

The Risk Register

A risk register is a business record that contains information about business risks and information about their origin, potential impact, affected assets, probability of occurrence, and treatment. A risk register is the central business record in an organization's risk management program. Together with other records, the risk register serves as the focal point of evidence that an organization is at least attempting to manage risk. Other records include evidence of risk treatment decisions and approvals, tracking of projects linked to risks, and risk assessments and other activities that contribute content to the risk register.

A risk register can be stored in a spreadsheet, database, or within a governance, risk, and compliance tool used to manage risk and other activities in the security program. Table 3-8 shows the columns in a typical risk register.

Item	Description
Entry number	A unique numeric value identifying the entry, which can be in the form of a date, such as 20220127a (for January 27, 2022)
Status	Current status of the entry: Open, Assigned, or Closed
Date entered	The date the risk register entry was created
Entered by	The person who created the risk register entry
Source	The activity or event that compelled someone to create this entry, which may include a risk assessment, a vulnerability assessment, a security incident, threat intelligence, or an external party
Incident number	Reference to an incident record, if applicable
Title	Short title describing the risk entry
Description	Description of the risk
Threat description	Description of the potential threat activity
Threat actor	Description of the type of threat actor, such as worker, former worker, supplier, vendor, or partner, cybercriminal, or nation-state
Vulnerability description	Description of one or more vulnerabilities that increases the probability or impact of threat realization
Third-party organization	Name of the third-party organization where the risk is present, if applicable
Third-party classification	Classification level of the third-party organization, if applicable
Business impact	Business language description of the impact of threat realization
Technical impact	Technical language description of the impact of threat realization, if applicable
Asset	The specific asset, asset group, or asset class affected by the risk
Asset owner	The owner of the affected asset
Risk owner	The owner of the risk
Control group	A reference to the affected control group, if applicable
Control	A reference to the affected control, if applicable

Table 3-8 Sample Risk Register Data Structure (*continued*)

Item	Description
Process	A reference to the affected process, if applicable
Untreated probability of occurrence	An estimate of the probability of occurrence of the threat event associated with the risk, usually expressed as high, medium, or low or on a numeric scale such as 1 to 5
Untreated impact of occurrence	An estimate of the impact of occurrence of the threat event associated with the risk, usually expressed as high, medium, or low or on a numeric scale such as 1 to 5
Untreated risk score	An overall risk score that is generally a product of probability, impact, and asset value
Treated probability of occurrence	An estimate of the probability of occurrence of the threat event associated with the risk, after risk treatment, usually expressed as high, medium, or low or on a numeric scale such as 1 to 5
Treated impact of occurrence	An estimate of the impact of occurrence of the threat event associated with the risk, after risk treatment, usually expressed as high, medium, or low or on a numeric scale such as 1 to 5
Treated risk score	An overall risk score that is generally a product of probability, impact, and asset value, after risk treatment
Estimated cost of risk treatment	An estimated cost of risk treatment, expressed in dollars or the local currency
Estimated level of effort of risk treatment	An estimated level of effort of risk treatment, expressed as high, medium, or low or on a numeric scale such as 1 to 5 or as an estimate of a range of man-hours: • Less than 1 hour • Less than 10 hours • Less than 100 hours • Less than 1,000 hours • Less than 10,000 hours
Risk treatment	The chosen method of risk treatment: accept, mitigate, transfer, or avoid
Risk treatment approver	The person or body that approved the risk treatment method
Risk treatment approval date	The date that the risk treatment method was approved
Risk treatment owner	The person responsible for carrying out risk treatment
Risk treatment description	A description of the risk treatment
Risk treatment planned completion	Date when risk treatment is expected to be completed
Actual cost of risk treatment	The actual cost of risk treatment, which would be known when risk treatment has been completed, expressed in dollars or the local currency
Actual level of effort of risk treatment	The actual level of effort of risk treatment, which would be known when risk treatment has been completed, expressed in man-hours
Risk treatment closure date	Date when risk treatment is actually completed
Next review date	Date when the risk will be reviewed again (usually applies to accepted risk)

Table 3-8   Sample Risk Register Data Structure

Sources of Information for the Risk Register

Awareness of risks can come from many places and through a variety of events. The information in Table 3-8 provides some hints about the potential sources of information that would lead to the creation of a risk register entry, which include the following:

- **Risk assessment**   A prime source for risk register entries, a risk assessment identifies risks in the organization's staff (such as excessive workload, competency, and training issues), business processes, and technology.

- **Vulnerability assessment**   The high-level results of a vulnerability assessment (or penetration test, code review, social engineering assessment, and so on) may indicate overarching problems in staff, business processes, or technology at a strategic level.

- **Internal audit**   Internal audits and other internal control self-assessments can identify problems in staff, business processes, or technology.

- **Security incident**   The occurrence of a security incident may reveal the presence of one or more risks that require attention. Note that a security incident in another organization may highlight risks in one's own organization.

- **Threat intelligence**   Formal and informal subscriptions or data feeds on threat intelligence may reveal risks that warrant attention.

- **Industry development**   Changes in the organization's industry sector, such as new business activities and techniques, may reveal or magnify risks that require attention.

- **New laws and regulations**   The passage of new laws, regulations, and applicable standards and private legal obligations may reveal the presence of risks that require attention. Also, note that compliance risk (the possibility that regulators or others may impose fines or sanctions on the organization) may well be included in one or more risk register entries, if the organization has identified such risks.

- **Consultants**   A visit by, or conversation with, an expert security consultant may reveal risks that were previously unknown. The consultant, who may be an auditor or assessor or may be working in the organization on a project, may or may not be expecting to find risks that the organization's security manager would want to be aware of.

Strategic vs. Tactical Risks

When managing the contents of the risk register, an organization may establish business rules related to the types of content that may be included in the risk register. An important distinction is the matter of strategic versus tactical: strategic risks certainly belong in a risk register, but tactical risks often do not.

For instance, an organization that performs vulnerability scans or application scans would not put all of the contents of the vulnerability scan in the risk register. In even modest-sized organizations, there can be hundreds or thousands of entries in a vulnerability scan that warrant attention (and occasionally immediate action). But these are considered tactical because they are associated with individual assets. However, if, in the course of conducting vulnerability scans, the security manager discovers that there are systemic problems with recurring vulnerabilities, this phenomenon may warrant an entry in the risk register. For example, there may be recurring instances of servers that are not being patched or a problem that results in patches being removed. This could be part of a larger problem that incurs significant risk to the organization, deserving of an entry in the risk register.

Risks identified in third parties in the organization's third-party risk management program should be included in the risk register.

Risk Analysis Contribution

Note that Table 3-8 includes ratings for mitigated probability, impact, and risk, as well as a description of risk treatment with associated cost and level of effort. The information in those fields should represent the result of more detailed risk analysis for each entry in the risk register.

For example, a security manager may have discovered that the organization's software development team continues to produce code containing numerous security defects. The security manager would analyze the situation and consider many different potential remedies, each with its own costs, levels of effort, and impact on risk. The security manager may then consider the following:

- Secure development training
- An incentive program that rewards developers who produce the fewest security defects
- Code scanning tools present in each developer's integrated development environment (IDE)
- Code scanning tools in the organization's software build system
- Periodic application penetration tests performed by a qualified external party
- Web application firewall appliances
- Web application firewall in the organization's content delivery network (CDN) service

In the course of analyzing this situation, the security manager will probably confer with people in various parts of the organization to discuss these and other potential solutions. Depending on the practices and processes that are in place in the organization, the security manager may unilaterally select a decision or bring the array of choices to a security steering committee for discussion. In this example, the security manager may select two or more methods to mitigate the risk. In this case, the security manager may decide to have developers undergo secure development training and also implement a web application firewall.

Ultimately, the ratings in the risk register, as well as the risk mitigation description, will reflect the mitigation technique that is selected.

Residual Risk

Risk treatment rarely eliminates all risk; instead, risk treatment will reduce the probability and/or the impact of a specific threat. The leftover, or residual, risk should be entered into the risk register for its own round of risk treatment. Depending upon the nature of the original risk, an individual risk may undergo two or more cycles of risk treatment, until finally, the residual risk is accepted and the risk matter closed.

Integration of Risk Management into Other Processes

The risk management life-cycle process is not the only place where risk analysis and risk management are performed in an organization. The concept of risk should be integrated into several other IT and business processes in an organization. This section describes the incorporation of security and risk into several processes, including the following:

- Architecture
- Software development
- Change management
- Configuration management
- Incident and problem management
- Physical security
- Information risk and enterprise risk management
- Human resource management
- Project management

Architecture

IT architects and solution architects create macro- and micro-level designs for networks, systems, applications, integrations, and other technology components. These activities should be reviewed by security subject matter experts such as security architects to ensure that the work of IT and solution architects do not introduce new, undesired risk to the organization.

Software Development

Developers, in the creation and maintenance of software programs, sometimes introduce software defects (commonly known as *bugs*) in their programs, resulting in unexpected behavior. This unexpected behavior may include calculation errors or errors in the way that information is displayed, read from storage, or written to storage. Sometimes, these defects can be exploited by a user or attacker to trick the software program into performing unexpected or unwanted activities.

Unless software developers are specifically aware of the security implications of the use of specific functions and calculations, they may unknowingly introduce benign to serious security defects in their programs. Some of these defects may be easily discovered with scanning programs or other techniques, while others may remain undiscovered for years. Often, a researcher will find security defects associated with a particular coding technique that is present in many programs; this can result in many organizations discovering for the first time that their programs have a particular exploitable defect.

Without specific software development experience, a security manager in a smaller organization may not have specific knowledge of the pitfalls associated with the use of the programming language in that organization. Oftentimes, an outside security expert with experience in software development and insecure coding is needed to assist such an organization in discovering any weaknesses in its coding practices. In a larger organization, assistance may be provided by one or more internal security experts who are familiar with the languages used in development.

In addition to secure coding, organizations need to introduce several security-related steps into their software development process:

- **Threat modeling**   These techniques are implemented during the design phase to anticipate potential threats and incorporate design features to block them.

- **Coding standards**   These standards specify allowed and disallowed coding techniques, including those more likely to introduce security defects and other defects.

- **Code reviews**   Performed by peers, code reviews are part of the program development and maintenance process. A peer is more likely to find defects and security problems than the developer who wrote the code.

- **Code scanning**   This is performed in the developer's IDE or executed separately in the developers' central software build environments.

- **Application scanning**   This is performed on web applications to discover exploitable defects.

- **Application penetration testing**   Testing is performed periodically by internal personnel or by qualified security advisory firms.

The concept of *security by design* is used to incorporate security and risk into every level of product development, from inception to development, testing, implementation, maintenance, and operations. Organizations that incorporate security by design into their development and business processes are less likely to suffer from security incidents than those that do not. They are also less likely to undergo frequent security changes caused by unexpected security incidents.

NOTE   Security managers need to understand the root causes of developers introducing security defects into their software. Most university computer science programs, where many if not most software developers receive their formal education, do not include the concepts of secure programming in their curricula. Many universities do not even offer secure development as an elective course. Instead, developers encounter this subject matter in their jobs, and because secure development was not part of their formal education, the concepts and principles behind secure development are often rejected. We are continuing to churn out new developers from universities who have little or no exposure to security.

Change Management

Change management is the IT function used to control changes made to an IT environment. The purpose of change management is to reduce the likelihood that proposed changes will introduce unexpected risks, which could lead to unplanned outages and security incidents.

A basic change management process begins with a formal *request for change,* which includes several specific pieces of information:

- Description of the change
- Reason for the change
- Who will perform the change
- When will the change be performed
- A procedure for making the change
- A procedure for verifying the change
- A back-out procedure in case the change cannot be verified
- Security impact of the change and also of not implementing the change
- Privacy impact
- Dependencies
- Defined change windows

A group of individuals from IT and across the business (a change review board or change control board) can meet periodically to discuss new change requests. After the requestor describes the change, including the elements listed previously, others on the change review board will have an opportunity to ask questions or voice concerns related to the change. In many organizations, one or more security personnel are permanent members of the change review board and will have a voice in the discussion about each change to ensure that security and privacy issues are properly identified, discussed, and managed.

Security professionals overall are maligned by the few who frequently seek to block proposed changes and other activities on account of the risks that may be introduced. Generally, this creates a challenge, where change review boards need to incorporate security concerns and ensure that security managers are included in all discussions. Also, security managers need to be pragmatic and understand that there is no advancement of business without risk.

Configuration Management

Configuration management is the IT function by which the configuration of components in an IT environment is independently recorded. Configuration management is usually supported by the automated tools used to inventory and control system configurations, but sometimes manual means are used. A configuration management database (CMDB) is the repository for this information.

Configuration management can be thought of as the creation of a historical record of the configuration of devices and systems. This historical record can sometimes be useful during troubleshooting, in support of investigations, as personnel need to understand in detail any changes in configuration that may have occurred in a system that could account for an incident or problem.

Security and risk considerations in configuration management are as follows:

- Protection of configuration management data from unauthorized access
- Inclusion of security-related information in configuration management data

Looking into the content itself in configuration management, this brings to mind the fact that organizations need to develop server, endpoint, and network device–hardening standards to make them more resilient to attack. Once an organization develops a hardening standard, it is implemented in some manner, such as a golden server or endpoint image, which should also be managed and protected, whether contained in the CMDB or not.

IT and information security need to be aware of the phenomenon of *configuration drift,* where the configuration of a component or system slowly diverges from its initial or intended state. Configuration drift often occurs in organizations that lack automation for applying configurations to systems.

Incident and Problem Management

The IT service management companion activities, incident management and problem management, are important activities for IT organizations. *Incident management* is the IT function that is used to analyze service outages, service slowdowns, service errors, security incidents, and software bugs, as well as to restore the agreed-on service as soon as possible. *Problem management* is the IT function used to analyze chronic and recurring incidents to discover their root cause and prevent further occurrences.

Incident management and problem management need to include the disciplines of security and risk. There are four primary security- and risk-related considerations in incident management.

Security or Risk Component Associated with an Incident   IT personnel analyzing an incident or a problem need to understand the security nature of the incident or problem, including whether the incident or problem has an impact on security. For instance, a malfunctioning firewall may be allowing traffic to pass through a control point that should not be permitted. Further, many security incidents are first recognized as simple malfunctions or outages and recognized later as symptoms of an attack. For example, users complaining of slow or unresponsive servers may be experiencing the effects of a distributed denial-of-service (DDoS) attack on the organization's servers, which, incidentally, may be a diversionary tactic to an actual attack occurring elsewhere in the organization. In the context of problem management, a server suffering from availability or performance issues may have been compromised and altered by an attacker.

Security or Risk Implication Associated with Actions to Restore Service   IT personnel analyzing an incident and working to restore service need to understand the security and risk impacts that their analysis and corrective actions have on IT systems and associated information. For example, rebooting a security server in an attempt to remedy a situation may result in a temporary loss of visibility and/or protection from events.

Security or Risk Implications Associated with Root-Cause Analysis   *Root-cause analysis* is defined as the analysis of a problem to identify its underlying origin instead of merely its symptoms and factors. IT personnel analyzing a problem must be aware of the security and risk considerations while performing root-cause analysis. IT personnel need the skills to recognize the security and risk implications of symptoms and origins. For example, a problem with server availability was traced to some file system permissions that were set improperly; those file system permission changes affected the ability of users to directly access sensitive data that should be accessed only by an application.

Security or Risk Implications Associated with Corrective Action   IT personnel analyzing a problem must be aware of the security and risk implications of changes being considered within business processes and technology. For instance, an application malfunction that is corrected by elevating its service account to the privileged (administrative) level may solve the underlying access permission error, but it creates significant risks as well.

Physical Security

Physical security is mainly concerned with the development and management of controls to protect physical assets, workplaces, and personnel. There is significant intersection between information security and physical security: information security relies upon physical security controls for the protection of information processing and communications equipment. While some of this equipment resides in data centers, some also resides in workplaces where an organization's personnel also work. These common controls make workplace safety a close relative to information security.

Changes in physical security technologies such as video surveillance and building access control systems are bringing information and physical security closer together than they have ever been before. In most organizations, however, information security and physical security are still managed separately. In these cases, because they share many technologies, assets, and overall objectives of protecting the organization from harm, information and physical security personnel can form partnerships.

Information and physical security functions can be integrated together in a number of ways, including the following:

- Ensuring that organization-wide risk and threat assessments cover both areas adequately
- Ensuring that business continuity and disaster recovery planning adequately covers both concerns

- Ensuring that information and physical security risks exist on a common risk register and are managed in a common risk management and risk treatment process

- Ensuring that information systems with high availability requirements are located in facilities with high availability as part of their design

- Ensuring that IP-based physical security assets and systems are incorporated into the organization's overall technology and security architecture, with adequate protection based on risk

- Incorporating physical facilities into the organization's information and asset classification program so that facilities and work centers can also be rated and adequately protected based on classification and risk

- Incorporating physical facility access into the organization's identity and access management program

- Ensuring that supervisory control and data acquisition (SCADA) and industrial control systems (ICSs) are supporting, monitoring, and controlling the environmental systems that support information technology such as heating, ventilation, and air-conditioning (HVAC) and that physical access control systems are monitored in a common monitoring platform

Information Risk and ERM

Larger organizations, more mature organizations, and organizations in financial services industries often have an enterprise risk management (ERM) function. Typical ERM programs are developed to identify and manage business-specific risks, and they frequently use a life-cycle process similar (if not identical) to the information risk processes described in this book.

Organizations with ERM and information risk functions have an opportunity to combine or leverage these functions. For example, information risk issues that are placed in the information risk register can also be entered into the ERM risk register. Further, organizations with both functions could decide to use a common risk register for all business and information risks. Often, this makes sense, because information risk is just one form of business risk, and organizations that blend these risks in a register will have a more complete view of all business risks, regardless of the context. For organizations that do not combine their risk registers, there are still opportunities for synergy, including having some personnel involved in both risk processes so that there are people in the organization who have a complete picture of all of its risks.

Human Resource Management

The entire life-cycle process of human resource management (HRM or HR, and increasingly called human capital management, or HCM) is involved in the acquisition, onboarding, care, and termination of permanent, temporary, and contingency workers in an organization. Many aspects of HRM are risk related, as well as related to information security.

PART II

An organization's workers are tasked with the acquisition and management of critical and sensitive information. Thus, there are several practices in HR that contribute to the support of information protection, including the following:

- **Background checks**   Prior to hiring an individual, an organization uses various means to verify the background of a candidate and to ensure that the person is free of a criminal history and other undesired matters.

- **Legal agreements**   An organization will generally direct new employees to agree to and sign legal documents, including nondisclosure and noncompete agreements, as well as agreements concerning compliance with security and other organization policies.

- **Training**   HR organizations are typically responsible for delivering training of all kinds to its workers, including but not limited to security awareness training. This helps workers in the organization better understand the organization's security policy, the importance of information and asset protection, and practices in place for information protection.

- **Development and management of roles**   HR organizations typically create and maintain job descriptions, which should include security-related responsibilities, and a hierarchy of positions in the organization.

- **Management of the human resource information system (HRIS)**   Most HR organizations today utilize an HRIS for all official records concerning its workers. Many HRIS systems today are integrated with an organization's identity and access management (IAM) system: when an employee is hired, transferred, or terminated, a data feed from the HRIS to the IAM platform ensures that access management information and systems are kept up to date. This makes it all the more important that HRIS systems have accurate information in them.

Bring Back the Contractors

A 1996 class-action lawsuit against Microsoft charged that Microsoft employed thousands of contractors who were treated like employees but forbidden from participating in Microsoft's employee stock purchase plan (ESPP). This created a chilling effect on companies' use of contractors. In many cases, HR departments wanted nothing to do with contractors, and this rift continues to this day. The result: many organizations struggle with the flagging integrity of access management and other processes that depend upon accurate records related to contractors and other temporary workers.

Centralized, controlled records of contractors benefits information security functions such as access management through being a reliable business record of the temporary workers in an organization. Modern HRIS systems are able to neatly segregate full-time employees from temporary workers, so that organizations can avoid the blurry situation that brought about the Microsoft class-action lawsuit.

Project Management

Whether a centralized project management office is utilized or project managers are scattered throughout an organization, security and risk are essential elements of program management and project planning. There are several ways in which security and risk should be incorporated into projects, including the following:

- Risk analyses should be performed at the onset of a project to identify potential risks in the proposed finished project or program. This gives organizations an opportunity to refine project/program objectives, architecture, and requirements.

- The impact of a project or program on the organization's security, compliance, and privacy must be established prior to any procurement, development, or implementation.

- Security requirements need to be included in any activity where requirements are developed. Like other requirements, security requirements must be verifiable.

- Security should be included as a part of approval gates if they are used in projects.

Chapter Review

Risk management is the core of an organization's information security program. By using risk management techniques to identify risks and understand the probability of their occurrence and impact upon the organization, risk managers can help the organization prioritize scarce resources to reduce risk effectively. The proper application of risk management helps an organization reduce the frequency and impact of security incidents through improved resilience and preparation.

When implementing a risk management program, the organization must consider several characteristics, including its risk tolerance, management structure, executive management support, culture, and any regulatory and legal obligations.

A risk management program should include several avenues of communication so that business leaders and stakeholders understand the program and how it is integrated into the organization. The program should be transparent with regard to its procedures and practices.

When building or improving a risk management program, security managers may select one of several industry frameworks, such as ISO/IEC 27001, ISO/IEC 27005, ISO/IEC 31010, NIST SP 800-37, NIST SP 800-39, COBIT, Risk IT, RIMS, and FAIR. These and other frameworks offer similar components, including scope, objectives, policy, risk tolerance, roles and responsibilities, the risk management life-cycle process, and management review. To the greatest reasonable extent, a risk management program should be integrated into the business to avoid disruption to the organization while minimizing risk.

When planning a risk management program, the security manager and executive leadership need to understand—and to some extent, define—the context of the program. This includes the program's scope, participants and stakeholders, and risk tolerance.

The security manager must consider many aspects of the organization's internal environment, as well as external environments such as market and economic conditions, external stakeholders, customers, and external threats. The security manager may need to perform gap analyses to better understand the current state as compared to the desired future state of the program. Security managers can fill gaps in knowledge and experience through networking with other security and risk professionals, training, periodicals, and conferences.

The risk management life cycle consists of a set of activities that enable the discovery and management of risks. The steps in the process include scope definition, asset identification and valuation, risk identification, risk analysis, risk treatment, and risk communication. Periodic risk assessments and other means contribute to continued risk identification.

A key step in risk analysis is the identification of vulnerabilities, or weaknesses, in people, business processes, or technology.

Another key step in risk analysis is the identification and analysis of internal and external threats. Risk management standards such as NIST SP 800-37 contain comprehensive lists of credible threats. Security managers need to recognize that emerging threats often need to be considered in a risk assessment, and some may not yet be included in current standards. Further, there are sometimes threats specific to an industry sector.

After risks are identified, the amount of risk present can be calculated using input from threats, threat actors, vulnerabilities, asset value, and impact. In most cases, risk is calculated in a qualitative way, primarily because it is difficult to know the precise (or even an approximate) probability of threat occurrence and somewhat difficult to know the financial impact of a threat.

In quantitative risk analysis, key values are asset value, exposure factor, single loss expectancy, annualized rate of occurrence, and annualized loss expectancy.

Industry-standard techniques are available for performing risk analysis, including OCTAVE Allegro, bow-tie analysis, Delphi method, Bayesian analysis, event-tree analysis, fault-tree analysis, and Monte Carlo analysis.

Risks identified in a risk assessment or risk analysis need to be evaluated, ranked, categorized, and assigned to a risk owner. Often, an organization will enact a control to address a risk.

Risk management and business continuity planning have several common components and linkages. Both are concerned with business resilience and survival, and both utilize business impact analysis to better understand the organization's most critical processes.

The risk register is the central business record in a risk management program. A risk register is a catalog of all current and historical risks, along with many pieces of metadata describing each risk in detail. A risk register may be stored in a spreadsheet, in a database, or in a governance, risk, and compliance tool's risk management module.

Security and risk management are incorporated into many other business activities, including but not limited to software development, change management, configuration management, incident and problem management, physical security, enterprise risk management, and human resource management.

Notes

- Like other activities in information security, measuring the benefits of an information risk management program can be difficult, mainly because it is difficult to identify security events that did not occur because of the program.

- Understanding and changing aspects of an organization's culture is one of the most important success factors and also one of the most difficult. Culture is the collective way that people in the organization think and work. It is documented everywhere and nowhere.

- Selecting a risk management and risk assessment framework is among the least important decisions in the development of a risk management program. Nevertheless, organizations often get as hung up on choosing management and assessment frameworks as they do on choosing a control framework. Consensus on framework selection is vital for long-term success.

- The need to minimize the impact of the risk management business process cannot be overstated. Where possible, utilize existing governance, management, control, and communications structures already present in the organization. The impact on decisions made in the risk management program may be significant; the process itself need not be.

- External factors such as market conditions, competition, and the sentiment of clients or customers are as important as internal factors such as access to capital and culture. Organizations in some industry sectors may have an opportunity to make security a competitive differentiator, in which case it will be more important to establish effective security management and risk management programs. Customers and competitors will notice.

- Security managers, when their knowledge or skills fall short on any topic, underestimate the value of networking and soliciting advice from industry peers. Many security professionals are willing to help, and plenty of events provide networking opportunities to meet them.

- In a risk assessment, while listing credible threat events, first obtain the list of threats from a standard such as NIST SP 800-30, and then add other threats that may be relevant for the asset, organization, or geographic location.

- The term "advanced persistent threats" was developed when such threats were novel. They no longer are new. Although use of the term has diminished, this type of threat has become commonplace.

- Identifying all reasonable vulnerabilities during a risk assessment is not as easy as identifying threats. You must know more about the asset or process being examined.

- In qualitative risk assessments, it's easy to become focused on the risk scores for various risks. Remember that risk scores are the result of basic calculations based on very coarse threat and vulnerability ratings. Risk ratings should serve only to distinguish very high risks from very low ones—and even then, these are just rough approximations.

- Most organizations that are establishing a risk management program for the first time can use spreadsheets for key business records such as the risk register and the security incident log. As organizations become more mature, they can acquire a governance, risk, and compliance platform that includes risk management modules.

Questions

1. A risk manager is planning a first-ever risk assessment in an organization. What is the best approach for ensuring success?

   A. Interview personnel separately so that their responses can be compared.

   B. Select a framework that matches the organization's control framework.

   C. Work with executive management to determine the correct scope.

   D. Do not inform executive management until the risk assessment has been completed.

2. A security manager has completed a vulnerability scan and has identified numerous vulnerabilities in production servers. What is the best course of action?

   A. Notify the production servers' asset owners.

   B. Conduct a formal investigation.

   C. Place a single entry into the risk register.

   D. Put individual vulnerability entries into the risk register.

3. The concept of security tasks in the context of a SaaS or IaaS environment is depicted in a:

   A. Discretionary control model

   B. Mandatory control model

   C. Monte Carlo risk model

   D. Shared responsibility model

4. A security manager is developing a vision for the future state of a risk management program. Before she can develop the plan to achieve the vision, she must perform a:

   A. Gap analysis

   B. Risk analysis

   C. Risk assessment

   D. Threat assessment

5. All of the following are techniques to identify risks *except*:

   A. Penetration tests

   B. Threat modeling

   C. Vulnerability assessment

   D. Risk treatment

6. The main advantage of NIST standards versus ISO standards is:

   A. NIST standards are considered global standards.

   B. NIST standards are not copyrighted.

   C. NIST standards are available without cost.

   D. NIST standards cost less to implement.

7. Which of the following statements is true about compliance risk?

   A. Compliance risk can be tolerated when fines cost less than controls.

   B. Compliance risk is just another risk that needs to be understood.

   C. Compliance risk can never be tolerated.

   D. Compliance risk can be tolerated when it is optional.

8. Misconfigured firewalls, missing antivirus, and lack of staff training are examples of:

   A. Risks

   B. Threats

   C. Vulnerabilities

   D. Threat actors

9. A phishing attack, network scan, and social engineering are examples of:

   A. Risks

   B. Threats

   C. Vulnerabilities

   D. Threat actors

10. A security manager has been directed by executive management *not* to document a specific risk in the risk register. This course of action is known as:

   A. Burying the risk

   B. Transferring the risk

   C. Accepting the risk

   D. Ignoring the risk

11. A security manager is performing a risk assessment on a business application. The security manager has determined that security patches have not been installed for more than a year. This finding is known as a:

    A. Probability

    B. Threat

    C. Vulnerability

    D. Risk

12. A security manager is performing a risk assessment on a data center. He has determined that it is possible for unauthorized personnel to enter the data center through the loading dock door and shut off utility power to the building. This finding is known as a:

    A. Probability

    B. Threat

    C. Vulnerability

    D. Risk

13. Hacktivists, criminal organizations, and crackers are all known as:

    A. Threat actors

    B. Risks

    C. Threats

    D. Exploits

14. All of the following are core elements used in risk identification *except*:

    A. Threats

    B. Vulnerabilities

    C. Asset value

    D. Asset owner

15. What is usually the primary objective of risk management?

    A. Fewer and less severe security incidents

    B. No security incidents

    C. Improved compliance

    D. Fewer audit findings

Answers

    1. C. The best approach for success in an organization's risk management program, and during risk assessments, is to have support from executive management. Executives need to define the scope of the risk management program, whether by business unit, geography, or other means.

2. A. Most organizations do not place individual vulnerabilities into a risk register. The risk register is primarily for strategic issues, not tactical issues such as individual vulnerabilities. However, if the vulnerability scan report was an indication of a broken process or broken technology, then that matter of brokenness may qualify as a valid risk register entry.

3. D. The shared responsibility model, sometimes known as a shared responsibility matrix, depicts the operational model for SaaS and IaaS providers where client organizations have some security responsibilities (such as end user access control) and service provider organizations have some security responsibilities (such as physical access control).

4. A. The risk manager must perform a gap analysis to understand the difference between the current state of the risk management program and its desired future state. Once the gap analysis is completed, it will become clear what steps must be performed to achieve that desired future state.

5. D. Risk treatment is not a tool to identify risks. It is the process of making a decision about what to do with an identified risk.

6. C. One of the main advantages of NIST standards is that they are available free of charge. ISO standards are relatively expensive, ranging from US$100 to $200 for single user copies.

7. B. In most cases, compliance risk is just another risk that needs to be understood. This includes the understanding of potential fines and other sanctions in relation to the costs required to reach a state of compliance. In some cases, being out of compliance can also result in reputation damage as well as larger sanctions if the organization suffers from a security breach because of the noncompliant state.

8. C. These are all vulnerabilities, or weaknesses that could potentially be exploited by a threat.

9. B. These are all threats, which could be more easily carried out if targets are vulnerable.

10. D. The refusal of an organization to formally consider a risk is known as ignoring the risk. This is not a formal method of risk treatment because of the absence of deliberation and decision-making. It is not a wise business practice to keep some risk matters "off the books."

11. C. The absence of security patches on a system is considered a vulnerability, which is defined as a weakness in a system that could permit an attack to occur.

12. B. Any undesired action that could harm an asset is known as a threat.

13. A. These are all threat actors, or persons/entities that may carry out threats against targets if sufficiently motivated.

14. **D.** The identity of an asset owner does not factor into the risk identification process. Although knowing the asset owner is important in subsequent phases of the risk management process, it is not relevant in identifying the risk. The factors relevant to risk identification are threats, threat actors, vulnerabilities, asset value, and impact.

15. **A.** The most common objective of a risk management program is the reduction in the number and severity of security incidents.

Information Security Risk Response

In this chapter, you will learn about
- Risk response options and considerations
- Responding to risk via risk treatment
- Ownership of risks, risk treatment, and controls
- Monitoring and reporting on risk
- Key risk indicators

This chapter covers Certified Information Security Manager (CISM) Domain 2, "Information Security Risk Management," part B, "Information Security Risk Response." The Entire Information Security Risk Management domain represents 20 percent of the CISM examination.

Supporting Tasks in the CISM job practice that align with the Information Security Risk Management / Information Security Risk Response domain include:

9. Compile and present reports to key stakeholders on the activities, trends, and overall effectiveness of the information security program.

22. Participate in and/or oversee the risk identification, risk assessment, and risk treatment process.

24. Identify, recommend, or implement appropriate risk treatment and response options to manage risk to acceptable levels based on organizational risk appetite.

25. Determine whether information security controls are appropriate and effectively manage risk to an acceptable level.

27. Monitor for internal and external factors that may require reassessment of risk.

28. Report on information security risk, including noncompliance and changes in information risk, to key stakeholders to facilitate the risk management decision-making process.

Risk response is the entirety of actions undertaken once the organization becomes aware of a risk. The risk management life cycle specifies that when a risk is identified, it is first analyzed (covered in Chapter 3). Next, a business decision, known as risk treatment, determines what the organization will do about an identified risk. Each risk is assigned an owner who participates in risk treatment decisions. If a control must be created or modified to mitigate the risk, management assigns an owner to the control itself. Finally, each risk is monitored and reports are created to track any changes in risk over time.

Risk Treatment / Risk Response Options

When risks to assets have been identified through qualitative or quantitative risk analysis, the organization's next step in the risk management process is to decide what to do about the identified risks. In the risk analysis, one or more potential solutions may have been examined, along with their cost to implement and their impact on risk. In risk treatment, a decision about whether to proceed with any of the proposed solutions (or others) is needed.

In a general sense, risk treatment represents the actions that the organization undertakes to reduce risk to an acceptable level. More specifically, for each risk identified in a risk assessment, an organization can take four actions:

- Risk mitigation
- Risk transfer
- Risk avoidance
- Risk acceptance

These four actions are explained in more detail in the following sections.

The decision to ignore a *known* risk is different from an organization ignoring an *unknown* risk, which is usually a result of a risk assessment or risk analysis that is not properly scoped or sufficiently thorough to identify all relevant risks. The best solution for these "unknown unknowns" is to have an external, competent firm perform an organization's risk assessment every few years, or have the firm examine the organization's risk assessment thoroughly to discover opportunities for improvement, including expanding the span of threats, threat actors, and vulnerabilities so that there are fewer or no unknown risks. Now that we know the options for risk responses, we should consider the impact of those responses.

One impact of risk treatment is that it pits available resources against the need to reduce risk. In an enterprise environment, not all risks can be mitigated or eliminated, because there are not enough resources to treat them all. Instead, a strategy for choosing the best combination of solutions that will reduce risk by the greatest possible margin is needed. For this reason, risk treatment is often more effective when all the risks and solutions are considered together, instead of each one separately. Then they can be compared and prioritized.

When risk treatment is performed at the enterprise level, risk analysts and technology architects can devise ways to bring about the greatest possible reduction in risk. This can be achieved through the implementation of solutions that will reduce many risks for many assets at once. For example, a firewall can reduce risks from many threats on many assets; this will be more effective than individual solutions for each asset.

The Most Important Aspect of Risk Treatment

The aspect of risk treatment of utmost importance to the ongoing success of an organization's security management program is *who* makes the risk treatment decisions:

- **Security manager** This person may be the most knowledgeable about risk, but this is not the best choice. A security manager who makes risk treatment decisions runs the risk of others in the organization not supporting those decisions.

- **Security steering committee** A consensus decision is often the best choice, because stakeholders and others provide input and contribute to a decision. When stakeholders have a say in risk matters, they're more likely to support decisions affecting them.

- **Owner** This may be a business process owner, business unit leader, or other senior executive whose process or system is the nexus of any particular risk.

- **Undefined** An organization that does not define who makes risk treatment decisions is, by definition, not running an effective security management program.

In many organizations, consensus decisions are made by a combination of these parties.

Risk Mitigation

Risk mitigation is one of four choices that an organization can take when confronted with a risk. *Risk mitigation,* aka risk reduction, involves the implementation of some solution that will reduce an identified risk—for example, by changing a process or procedure, changing how a security control functions, or adding a security control. In another example, the risk of advanced malware being introduced onto a server can be mitigated with advanced malware prevention software or a network-based intrusion prevention system. Either of these solutions would constitute mitigation of some of this risk on a given asset.

An organization usually makes a decision to implement some form of risk mitigation only after performing a cost analysis to determine whether the reduction of risk is worth the expenditure of risk mitigation. Sometimes, however, an asset's value is difficult to measure, or there may be a high degree of goodwill associated with the asset. For example, the value of a customer database that contains sensitive data, including bank account or credit card information, may itself be low; however, the impact of a breach of this database may be higher than its book value because of the loss of business or negative publicity that may result.

During the risk analysis phase of risk management, a risk analyst will explore one or more potential ways of mitigating risk and will document the time, effort, and cost involved for each. The development of multiple options helps inform those responsible for making risk treatment decisions.

Risk mitigation may, at times, result in a task that can be carried out in a relatively short period of time. However, risk mitigation may also involve one or more major projects that start in the future, perhaps in the next budget year or many months, quarters, or years in the future. Further, such a project may be delayed, its scope may change, or it may be canceled altogether. For this reason, the security manager needs to monitor risk mitigation activities carefully to ensure that they are completed as originally planned so that the risk mitigation is not forgotten.

Another consideration when determining the cost/benefit of mitigation is the upstream and downstream impacts of the system(s) in question on the other systems. For instance, can a threat actor use this system or platform to gain access to other systems? It can be challenging to consider all these aspects when flushing out the cost versus benefits of conducting risk mitigation activities. It is vital to keep the big picture in mind when developing a risk mitigation plan.

Risk Mitigation and Control Frameworks

Controls and risk assessments are tightly coupled in the risk management life cycle. In a typical security program, an organization selects a control framework (such as NIST SP 800-53, ISO/IEC 27002, HIPAA, NERC, CIS CSC, or PCI DSS) as a starting point. Then, as the organization conducts risk assessments, from time to time, the action taken to mitigate risk is the creation of a new control. It is important to understand that control frameworks represent a starting point, not the entire journey, in an information security program. Every organization is different, and no experienced information risk professional believes that any of the standard control frameworks will address all risks in an organization.

Risk Transfer

Risk transfer, or risk sharing, means that some or all of the risk is being transferred to some external entity, such as an insurance company, service provider, business process outsourcer (BPO), or business partner. The risk transfer option is selected when an organization does not have the operational or financial capacity to accept the risk and when risk mitigation is not the best choice.

When an organization purchases an insurance policy to protect an asset against damage or loss, the insurance company is assuming a part of the risk in exchange for payment of insurance premiums; however, the intangible losses mentioned previously would still be present. The details of a cyber-insurance policy need to be carefully examined to be sure that any specific risk is transferrable to the policy. Cyber-insurance policies typically have exclusions that limit or deny payment of benefits in certain situations.

Sharing offsite (co-location) assets and contractual obligations with other entities is one way that organizations implement risk transfer; a cloud service provider can be used within this scenario. The cloud provider may be contractually obligated to assume part of the financial impact in the event of a breach, but be aware that there is a potential loss of brand goodwill or other intangible assets that can be difficult to offload.

Risk transfer through a BPO results in the outsourcer having accountability for some risk. For instance, the outsourcing of software development will require the BPO firm to enact some controls related to a secure systems development life cycle (SDLC) and protection of intellectual property.

In another example, a risk assessment may reveal the absence of security monitoring of a critical system. Risk transfer, in this case, may involve the use of an external security services provider to perform monitoring of the critical system. Here, only part of the risk is being transferred, as the consequences of any security event that is detected (or one that is not detected) arc entirely borne by the organization.

Risk transfer typically works with only a portion of the risk; it does not reduce all of the risk. Therefore, multiple risk response options used concurrently will likely be needed.

 EXAM TIP CISM candidates need to understand that the use of a risk transfer scheme does not totally absolve an organization of its responsibilities; organizations may still retain responsibility—and more importantly, accountability—if there is loss of data, revenue, or customers. Additionally, legal liabilities may also be involved.

Risk Avoidance

In *risk avoidance,* the organization abandons the risk-inducing activity altogether, effectively taking the asset out of service or discontinuing the activity so that the risk is no longer present. In another scenario, the organization may believe that the risk of pursuing a given business activity is too great, so they may decide to avoid that particular venture.

Often, risk avoidance is selected in response to an activity that was not formally approved in the first place. For example, a risk assessment may have identified a department's use of an external service provider that represented a measurable risk to the organization. The service provider may or may not have been formally vetted in the first place. Regardless, after the risk is identified in a risk assessment (or by other means), the organization may choose to cease activities with that service provider; this is risk avoidance.

NOTE Organizations do not often back away completely from an activity because of identified risks. Generally, this avenue is taken only when the risk of loss is great and when the perceived probability of occurrence is high.

Risk Acceptance

Management may be willing to accept an identified risk as is, with no effort taken to reduce it. *Risk acceptance* is an option in which the organization finds the presence of a risk acceptable and determines that it requires no reduction or mitigation. Risk acceptance also takes place (sometimes implicitly) for residual risk, after other forms of risk treatment have been applied.

If only risk acceptance were this simple. Further analysis of risk acceptance shows that there are conditions under which an organization will elect to accept risk:

- The cost of risk mitigation is greater than the value of the asset being protected.
- The impact of compromise is low, or the value or classification of the asset is low.

Organizations may elect to establish a framework for risk acceptance, as shown in Table 4-1.

After an organization accepts a risk, instead of closing the matter for perpetuity, it should review the risk at least annually (or after a significant event that would change the conditions surrounding the accepted risk) for the following reasons:

- The value of the asset may have changed during the year.
- The value of the business activity related to the asset may have changed during the year.
- The potency of threats may have changed during the year, potentially leading to a higher risk rating.
- The cost of mitigation may have changed during the year, potentially leading to greater feasibility for risk mitigation or transfer.

Risk Level	Level Required to Accept
Low	Business process owner, plus chief information officer (CIO) or manager of information security
Medium	Business process owner, plus chief information security officer (CISO) or director of information security
High	Business unit leader, plus chief executive officer (CEO), chief operations officer (COO), or company president
Severe	Business unit leader and board of directors

Table 4-1 Framework for Risk Acceptance

As with other risk treatment activities, detailed records help the security manager better track matters such as risk assessment review.

The Fifth Option in Risk Treatment

For decades, risk management frameworks have cited the same four risk treatment options: accept, mitigate, transfer, and avoid. There is, however, a fifth option that some organizations select: ignore the risk.

Ignoring risk is a choice, although it is not considered a wise choice. Ignoring a risk means doing nothing about it—not even making a decision about it. It amounts to little more than pretending the risk does not exist. It's off the books.

Organizations without risk management programs may be implicitly ignoring all risks, or many of them at least. Organizations may also be practicing informal and maybe even reckless risk management—risk management by gut feel. Without a systematic framework for identifying risks, many are likely to go undiscovered. An implicit refusal to identify risks and treat them properly could also be considered ignoring risks.

Evaluating Risk Response Options

Risk mitigation, transfer, acceptance, and avoidance are all valid options to consider (sometimes at the same time) when attempting to reduce the level of risk. The key is to use these options together, balancing risk and reward to maximize the benefits. These benefits can be financial or some other benefit, one perhaps difficult to quantify (such as morale, partnerships, or long-term strategy).

One of the key considerations in balancing risk options is the cost and effectiveness of any response option. For example, as briefly mentioned, if the value of the asset to the organization is much lower than the security controls it would take to protect it, is risk mitigation or reduction the right option? A risk manager should also consider the effectiveness of the controls: if all possible controls that could be implemented still don't reduce the risk to an acceptable level, are they worth the effort?

Other factors that should be considered in risk response options include those inherent to the organization itself. Sometimes, organizational design and layout are factors because the ways divisions and departments are structured within the organization can affect resource allocation, the chain of command, and other aspects. Sometimes these factors have to be changed in order to implement an effective risk response. Other considerations are governance, including legal and regulatory requirements, and organizational culture.

An example of how organizational culture can affect a risk response occurs when an organization determines that it needs to pull back administrative privileges from ordinary users (end users being local administrators is very much frowned upon in the information security community). Although this action may not be expensive in terms of any required equipment or additional controls, the cost incurred is qualitative in the form of an upswell of complaints from end users. People normally do not like giving up what they already have, and administrative rights is one of those things that all users seem to believe they need. Organizational culture will definitely be an impediment to implementing this particular risk response.

In evaluating and selecting risk responses, risk managers should consider all the factors discussed so far, such as the cost of the response (and of the potential cost of not responding), organizational context and associated missions, risk tolerance, governance, and the ease of implementation.

Costs and Benefits

As organizations ponder options for risk treatment (and, in particular, risk mitigation), they generally will consider the costs of the mitigating steps and the benefits they may expect. When an organization understands the costs and benefits of risk mitigation, this helps them develop strategies that either are more cost-effective or result in greater cost avoidance.

Organizations need to understand several cost- and benefit-related considerations when weighing mitigation options:

- **Change in threat probability**   Organizations must understand how a mitigating control changes the probability of threat occurrence and what that means in terms of cost reduction and avoidance.

- **Change in threat impact**   Organizations need to understand the change in the impact of a mitigated threat in terms of an incident's reduced costs and avoided costs versus the cost of the mitigation.

- **Change in operational efficiency**   Aside from the direct cost of the mitigating control, organizations must understand the impact on the mitigating control on other operations. For instance, adding code review steps to a software development process may mean that the development organization can complete fewer fixes and enhancements in a given period of time.

- **Total cost of ownership (TCO)**   When an organization considers a mitigation plan, the best approach is to understand its total cost of ownership, which may include costs for the following:
  - Acquisition
  - Deployment and implementation
  - Recurring maintenance
  - Testing and assessment
  - Compliance monitoring and enforcement
  - Reduced throughput of controlled processes
  - Training
  - End-of-life decommissioning

While weighing costs and benefits, organizations should consider the following:

- Estimating the probability of any particular threat is difficult, particularly infrequent, high-impact events such as large-scale data thefts.

- Estimating the impact of any particular threat is difficult, especially those infrequent, high-impact events.

In other words, the precision of cost-benefit analysis is no better than estimates of event probability and impact.

An old adage in information security states that an organization would not spend $20,000 to protect a $10,000 asset. Though that may be true in some cases, there is more to consider than just the replacement (or depreciated) value of the asset. For example, loss of the asset could result in an embarrassing and costly public relations debacle, or that asset may play a key role in the organization's earning hundreds of thousands of dollars in revenue each month.

Still, the principle of proportionality is valid and is often a good starting point for making cost-conscious decisions on risk mitigation. The principle of proportionality is described in generally accepted security systems principles (GASSPs), as well as in section 2.5 of the generally accepted information security principles (GAISPs).

Residual Risk

Residual risk is the leftover risk that exists after some of the risk has been removed through mitigation or transfer. For instance, if a particular threat had a probability of 10 percent before risk treatment and 1 percent after risk treatment, the residual risk is that 1 percent. This is best illustrated by the following formula:

Original Risk – Mitigated Risk – Transferred Risk – Avoided Risk = Residual Risk

It is unusual for any form of risk treatment to eliminate risk altogether; rather, various controls are implemented or changed to remove some of the risk. Often, management implicitly accepts the leftover risk; however, it's a good idea to make that acceptance of residual risk more formal by documenting the acceptance in a risk management log or a decision log.

In addition to the risk treatment life cycle, subsequent risk assessments and other activities will identify risks that represent residual risk from earlier risk treatment activities. Over time, the nature of residual risk may change, based on changing threats, vulnerabilities, or business practices, resulting in an originally acceptable residual risk that is no longer acceptable.

Iterative Risk Treatment

Some organizations approach risk treatment and residual risk improperly. They identify a risk, employ some risk treatment, and then fail to identify or understand the residual risk; then, they close the risk matter. A better way to approach risk is to analyze the residual risk as though it were a new risk and apply risk treatment to the residual risk.

This iterative process provides organizations with an opportunity to revisit residual risk and make new risk treatment decisions about it. Ultimately, after one or more iterations, the residual risk will be accepted, and finally, the matter can be closed.

Suppose, for example, that a security manager identifies a risk in the organization's access management system, where multifactor authentication (MFA) is not used. This is considered a high risk, and the IT department implements a MFA solution. When security managers reassess the access management system, they find that MFA is required in some circumstances but not in others. A new risk is identified, at perhaps a lower level of risk than the original risk. But the organization once again has an opportunity to examine the risk and make a decision about it. It may improve the access management system by requiring MFA in more cases than before, which further reduces risk, which should be examined again for further risk treatment opportunities. Finally, the residual risk will be accepted when the organization is satisfied that the risk has been sufficiently reduced.

Here's another example. Risk analysis identifies a risk of malware attack through web sites containing malicious code (typically known as a watering hole attack). The first round of risk treatment is risk mitigation, through the introduction of a centralized web-filtering device that blocks user access to known malicious web sites. Residual risk is identified: when users are away from office locations, the web filter is not in their Internet data path, and they remain vulnerable. This new risk is treated through mitigation, this time in the form of a proxy agent installed on all workstations that direct their web traffic through a SaaS-based web-filtering service. After this second round of risk treatment, residual risk consists of user access to web sites not yet flagged as malicious. Since the organization also has advanced antimalware software on each workstation, the organization elects to accept the risk introduced through the SaaS web-filtering service that is not yet aware of some malicious web sites.

Risk Appetite, Capacity, and Tolerance

Each organization has a particular appetite for risk, although few have documented that appetite. ISACA defines *risk appetite* as "the level of risk that an organization is willing to accept while pursuing its mission, strategy, and objectives before taking action to treat the risk." Risk capacity is related to risk appetite. ISACA defines *risk capacity* as "the objective amount of loss that an organization can tolerate without its continued existence being called into question." *Risk tolerance* is the acceptable level of deviation in risk for a particular endeavor or business pursuit. In other words, risk tolerance is the amount of variation from the expected level of risk the organization is willing to put up with.

Generally, only highly risk-averse organizations such as banks, insurance companies, and public utilities will document and define risk appetite in concrete terms. Other organizations are more tolerant of risk and make individual risk decisions based on gut feeling. However, because of increased influence and mandates by customers, many organizations are finding it necessary to document and articulate the risk posture and appetite of the organization. This is an emerging trend in the marketplace but is still relatively new to many organizations.

Risk-averse organizations generally have a formal system of accountability and traceability of risk decisions back to department heads and business executives. This activity is often seen within risk management and risk treatment processes, where individual risk treatment decisions are made and one or more business executives are made accountable for their risk treatment decisions.

In a properly functioning risk management program, the CISO is rarely the person who makes a risk treatment decision and is accountable for that decision. Instead, the CISO is a facilitator for risk discussions that eventually lead to a risk treatment decision. The only time the CISO would be the accountable party would be when risk treatment decisions directly affect the risk management program itself, such as selecting an integrated risk management (IRM) tool for managing and reporting on risk.

Organizations rarely have a single risk-appetite level across the entire business; instead, different business functions and aspects of security will have varying levels of risk. For example, a mobile gaming software company may have a moderate tolerance for risk concerning the introduction of new products, a low tolerance for workplace safety risks, and no tolerance for risk for legal and compliance matters. Mature organizations will develop and publish a statement of risk appetite that expresses risk tolerance levels throughout the business.

Legal and Regulatory Considerations

Organizations in many industries are subject to regulatory and legal requirements. Many organizations are also duty-bound through legal agreements between companies. Many of these legal obligations involve the topic of data protection, data privacy, and data usage.

Risk treatment decisions must, in many cases, abide by regulatory and legal requirements, which may include the following:

- **Mandatory protective measures**   Many laws, regulations, and private legal obligations require organizations to enact a variety of specific measures to protect information. Typically, these measures are required to be in place, regardless of the reduction of actual risk in any specific organization, simply because the law or regulation says so. A good example of this is the PCI DSS, which requires any organization that stores, processes, or transmits credit card data to implement a large set of controls. The PCI DSS makes no provision for whether any particular control is actually going to reduce risk in any specific organization. Instead, all the controls are required all the time in every such organization.

- **Optional protective measures**   Some laws, regulations, and other legal obligations include a number of specific protective measures that the organization *could* choose not to implement. For example, HIPAA lists required controls and "addressable" controls. In most cases, the organization would be required to have a formal, valid business reason (such as a risk assessment and a documented risk treatment decision) why any optional measures are not implemented.

- **Mandatory risk assessments**   Some laws, regulations, and legal obligations require organizations to perform risk assessments, but many do not require that the organization take specific actions as a result of those risk assessments. For instance, the PCI DSS requires organizations to perform annual risk assessments (in requirement 12.2), but nowhere does the standard (version 3.2.1 is the current version as of the writing of this book; 4.0 has been released and becomes effective in 2024) permit an organization to opt-out of any PCI DSS control because of the absence of risk.

Another facet of concern related to laws, regulations, and other legal obligations is the concept of compliance risk. *Compliance risk* is defined as any risk associated with any general or specific consequences of not being compliant with a law, regulation, or private legal obligation. Compliance risk takes on two forms:

- An organization may be out of compliance with a specific law, regulation, or obligation because of the absence of a protective measure, whose absence could lead to a security incident that could bring fines and other sanctions from regulators or other organizations, or civil lawsuits from injured parties.

- An organization that is out of compliance with a specific law, regulation, or obligation could incur fines and other sanctions simply because of the noncompliant condition, regardless of the level of actual risk. In other words, an organization can get into trouble with regulators or other bodies simply because it is not in compliance with a specific legal requirement, regardless of the presence or absence of any actual risk.

Security managers sometimes fail to understand a business strategy in which executive management chooses to pay fines instead of bringing their organizations into compliance with a law or regulation. Fines or other sanctions may have a lesser impact on the organization than the cost and effort to be compliant. At times, security managers and other security professionals may face an ethical dilemma if their professional codes of conduct require them to obey the law versus obeying directives from management that may be contrary to the law.

Compliance Risk: The Risk Management Trump Card

Organizations that perform risk management are generally aware of the laws, regulations, and standards they are required to follow. For instance, U.S.-based banks, brokerages, and insurance companies are required to comply with the Gramm-Leach-Bliley Act (GLBA), and organizations that store, process, or transmit credit card numbers are required to comply with the PCI DSS.

GLBA, PCI DSS, and other regulations and standards often state that specific controls are required in an organization's in-scope IT systems and business processes. This brings to light the matter of compliance risk. Sometimes, the risk

(continued)

associated with a specific control (or lack of a control) may be rated as a low risk, either because the probability of a risk event is low or because the impact of the event is low. However, if a given law, regulation, or standard requires that the control be enacted anyway, the organization must consider the compliance risk in addition to the information security risk. The risk of noncompliance may result in fines or other sanctions against the organization, which may (or may not) have consequences greater than the actual risk.

The end result is that organizations often implement specific security controls because they are required by laws, regulations, or standards—not because their risk analysis would otherwise compel them to do so.

The Risk Register

A *risk register,* sometimes known as a risk ledger, is a business record that documents risks identified through risk assessments, risk analyses, and other means. It's also used to record the discovery of risks and track decisions about their disposition. The risk register or another document in the risk management process may refer to those details in some way. When properly implemented, a risk register is a concise summary record of the entire life cycle of an individual risk. The risk register is described in detail in Chapter 3 but is summarized here.

Typical elements in a risk register include these groupings and details:

- **Risk identification**   Information about the introduction of the risk into the risk register, including a unique ID designation, the date of discovery, how it was discovered, and by whom

- **Risk description**   Information about the risk itself, including relevant threats, vulnerabilities, and consequences

- **Affected assets**   Information about assets or asset groups in the organization that are affected by the risk, as well as the business owners of those assets

- **Risk score**   Information about the probability and impact of threat occurrence expressed in qualitative terms and possibly quantitative terms

- **Risk treatment analysis**   Information about the potential impact of various risk treatment options

- **Risk treatment**   Information about risk treatment approved by the organization, including the person, group, or asset owner that made the risk treatment decision; the date that the decision was made; and the person or group responsible for carrying out the risk treatment

This summary represents details that may appear in an organization's risk register. Each organization's risk management program and methods for risk treatment will govern what additional information may be included in a risk register.

Organizations that are just getting started on information risk management may opt to use a spreadsheet program for their first risk register. This is often a recommended low-cost strategy. As organizations mature, they may begin to realize that many aspects of their security program record-keeping are not scaling up with them. This compels organizations to move their risk register and other risk management records to a governance, risk, and compliance (GRC) tool. It should be noted that those risks may also leverage the enterprise risk team's tools, if such a team is in place in the organization.

Risk and Control Ownership

Information security as a discipline cannot thrive, or even survive, if it lacks the concept and the practice of ownership. In practical terms, this means that risks, controls, assets, processes, procedures, and records all have assigned owners who are formally assigned and recorded.

Risk Ownership

Depending on how the organization is structured and how the risk management strategy has been developed, risk ownership may be assigned to one or several different managers, spanning multiple functional areas. This is because the risk that affects one area likely affects other areas as well, so many different people may have responsibility for affected areas and be required to deal with and respond to risk.

Documenting Risk Ownership

Risks are identified and recorded in the risk register, and each risk should be assigned an owner. The risk owner is not necessarily the same individual who is accountable for making the risk treatment decision, nor is it the person who owns the asset(s) associated with the risk. Generally, the risk owner is the department or business unit owner where the risk resides.

For example, a risk associated with the potential leakage of customer data in a customer relationship management (CRM) system is identified on account of how the CRM is used. The risk owner will most likely be the person whose department is identified as the primary user of the CRM, often Customer Service. In this example, risk treatment may be in the form of mitigation, and someone in IT will be responsible for making changes to the CRM to mitigate the risk. The owner of the mitigation may be the leader of the IT group making the change.

The risk owner will generally want a risk treatment decision to be made, particularly in circumstances where the risk owner is uncomfortable accepting the entire risk as it is. However, the risk owner should also have a say in the risk treatment decision with regard to whether they are inclined to accept the risk or whether they want the risk reduced through mitigation, transfer, or even avoidance.

Changes in Risk

As risk managers or security managers routinely monitor risks, they should inform risk owners of any change in risk, whether the risk increases, decreases, or changes in some other way. This will help the risk owner continue to own the risk by being fully informed and aware of the nature of the risk as it changes over time. For instance, a risk associated with a limitation in password length and complexity in a business application may have been accepted years ago, but with the proliferation of attacks on systems with weak passwords, the risk manager may rate the risk as being more likely to occur, which may push the risk into a higher category that will compel the business to change its risk treatment from accept to mitigate.

Changes in Personnel

Risk or security managers need to manage risk ownership actively when personnel changes occur in an organization. When a person designated as the owner of one or more risks leaves the organization or is transferred elsewhere, the ownership of risk should remain with the position and be assigned to the replacement individual. If the position is not filled, ownership should be transferred to the next higher-up in the organization.

In such circumstances, a person may not have the same view or comfort level with the risk(s) they have inherited. Risks that a predecessor accepted in the past may seem too high for the new risk manager, who may want to perform risk treatment again in the hope that mitigation or transfer will be chosen.

Control Ownership

As defined in Chapter 6 and discussed throughout this book, a *control* is a policy, process, procedure, or other measure that is created to ensure desired outcomes or to avoid unwanted outcomes. Put another way, controls exist to mitigate risk. To ensure that controls become and remain effective, management should formally assign the responsibility of ownership to each control.

Control owners should be formally assigned to be accountable for the following activities regarding their controls:

- Any documented policies, procedures, and/or standards that define the nature of the control are periodically reviewed and updated as required.

- Any records or other artifacts created through normal control operation are correct and complete.

- The control is operating as intended.

- All personnel related to the control understand their individual roles and responsibilities, to ensure that the control operates as intended.

- The control is periodically reviewed to ensure that it continues to operate as intended.

- The appropriate personnel are notified when the control is known to have failed.

- As applicable, the operation of a control is monitored and measured, and statistics, metrics, or key performance indicators (KPIs) are recorded and kept.

- The owner represents the control in discussions with internal or external auditors or regulators and provides any requested documentation and records.

Control owners should have the authority to make decisions about the operation of their controls to ensure that these activities and outcomes can be assured.

Some controls may have multiple instantiations and, thus, multiple control owners. For instance, a control related to system authentication may apply to numerous information systems managed by multiple personnel. Each of those personnel may be considered a control owner for such a control.

Management of the framework of controls, including their scope, applicability, and ownership, generally falls upon personnel in the information security organization. Security personnel often will create a control matrix that includes these and other characteristics of each control as a way of formally tracking control information.

 NOTE Risk, asset, and control owners are not always the same person, in the same functional area, or even in the same organization. It's important that you identify these particular owners early in the assessment process and maintain careful coordination and communication between these and other relevant stakeholders within the boundaries of your authority and assessment scope. Having different types of owners can result in politically sensitive issues that revolve around resourcing, responsibility, accountability, and sometimes even blame.

Risk Monitoring and Reporting

Risk monitoring is defined as ongoing activities, including control effectiveness assessments and risk assessments, used to observe changes in risk. Security managers perform risk monitoring to report risk levels to executive management and to identify unexpected changes in risk levels.

Typical activities that contribute to risk monitoring include internal audits, control self-assessments, vulnerability assessments, and risk assessments. Because the primary audience of risk monitoring is executive management, the reporting of risk monitoring is often done using dashboards, which may be part of a GRC system's risk management function that permits drill-down when desired.

Information security managers should regularly meet with senior managers and executives to update them on key changes in the information security program and on changes to key risk indicators. When meeting with senior leaders, information security managers should understand what information leaders are looking for and convey the information in terms they will understand. Rather than describing the technical details, information security managers should describe the risks as they pertain to business impacts or business opportunities. Further, executives should be notified of key security-related and risk-related events, such as security incidents and changes in compliance risk.

Key Risk Indicators

A *key risk indicator (KRI)* is a measure of information risk and is used to reveal trends related to levels of risk of security incidents in the organization. KRIs are security metrics designed to serve as early indicators of rising or falling risk and of the rising or falling probability of various types of security incidents and events.

No standard set of KRIs is used across organizations; rather, each organization develops its own set of KRIs based on specific requirements from regulators, board members, senior executives, and other parties. KRIs are often derived from operational activities throughout the IT and business environment. On their own, those activities are often meaningless to executives and others, but when properly developed, they can serve as valuable risk signposts that help executives and others better understand information risk in the business over time.

For example, basic operational metrics in an organization's vulnerability management program provide information about vulnerabilities in the organization's business applications. These metrics by themselves are not useful to executives. But when the metrics are combined with business context, tactical and transactional activities can also be portrayed as strategic and in business terms.

Adding remediation information can transform a metric from a number of vulnerabilities identified (which is useless to executives) into a better metric, such as the time to remediate critical vulnerabilities. This, however, can be transformed still further into a KRI, such as the percentage of vulnerabilities in systems supporting revenue operations that are remediated in less than 30 days. This is a valuable risk indicator for executives, as it will help them more easily understand how quickly IT is patching critical vulnerabilities in key systems.

Several other KRIs can be developed in various operational areas, including the following:

- Number of security incidents resulting in external notifications
- Changes in attrition rates for IT workers and key business employees
- Amount of money paid out each quarter in an organization's bug bounty program
- Percentage of employees who have not completed the required security training
- Numbers of critical and high risks identified in risk assessments

The most useful KRIs serve as *leading indicators*, which communicate increases or decreases in the probability of future security incidents and events.

Training and Awareness

The majority of security incidents happen because of human error. Further analysis indicates that several factors contribute to security incidents:

- Lack of awareness of the risks associated with general computing and Internet use
- Lack of training and experience in the configuration and operation of systems and applications
- Lack of training and awareness of key business processes and procedures
- Lack of information regarding workers' responsibilities for reporting problems and incidents

A security awareness program is an essential ingredient in every organization; information on safe computing, security policy, security procedures, and workers' security-related responsibilities can be imported to all workers through training programs, messaging, and other means. Chapter 6 contains more details on establishing and managing a security awareness program.

Risk Documentation

Any business process that warrants the time and effort to execute deserves to be documented so that it can be performed consistently and correctly. An organization's risk management program should be fully documented, including the following:

- Policy and objectives, such as how risk management is run in the organization
- Roles and responsibilities, such as who is responsible for various activities
- Methods and techniques, such as how probability and impact of risks are evaluated and scored
- Locations for data storage and archives, such as where the risk register and risk treatment records reside
- Risk tolerance, such as how acceptable and unacceptable risks are defined
- Business rules regarding what is included in the risk register and why
- Risk treatment procedures and records
- Procedures and methods for the development of metrics and key risk indicators
- Communication and escalation protocols defined
- Review cycle defined to ensure that the program is in alignment with the business

Chapter Review

An information security program comprises all the activities used to identify and treat risks. At tactical and strategic levels, all activities in a program fulfill this purpose. A security program is outcomes based; when a strategy is developed, the objectives of the strategy are desired end states or outcomes. Tasks and projects carried out in the program bring the organization closer to these desired outcomes.

Risk treatment is the activity in risk management whereby the organization chooses how to handle an identified risk. The four risk treatment choices are accept, mitigate, transfer, and avoid. Risk treatment decisions should be made by the affected line-of-business owner, executive management, or security steering committee empowered by executive management. After risk treatment, the leftover risk is known as residual risk. Residual risk should be processed through the risk management process as though it were a new risk.

During risk treatment, the organization needs to consider legal and regulatory issues to ensure that risk treatment decisions and methods of risk mitigation do not themselves create compliance risk.

The costs and benefits of risk treatment should also be considered. Although, as the adage goes, it doesn't make sense to spend $20,000 to protect a $10,000 asset, the value and role of an asset need to be considered. As the adage continues, it may be a $10,000 asset, but it may also be a critical component in the earning of $1 million in revenue every month.

Risk appetite is the level of risk that an organization is willing to accept while in the pursuit of its mission, strategy, and objectives. Risk treatment and risk acceptance decisions should be assigned to and made by associated business owners and executives who are accountable for those decisions. The chief information security officer facilitates and communicates the information; only in specific instances will the CISO own a risk item.

Risk monitoring is the set of ongoing activities to detect changes in risks. Typical risk monitoring activities include risk assessments, vulnerability assessments, internal audits, and control self-assessments.

Key risk indicators are metrics used in a risk management program to communicate risk trends to executive management. KRIs help an organization understand key risks in strategic business terms. The most useful KRIs are leading indicators, which help an organization better understand the rising and lowering probabilities of security incidents.

Like a security awareness program, training and other forms of information dissemination to affected personnel are essential for the success of a risk management program. A risk awareness program helps the organization better understand the purpose of the risk management program and its part in it.

Like any formal business process, a risk management program needs to be documented. Required documentation includes policy and processes, roles and responsibilities, risk tolerance/appetite, and records such as the risk register.

Notes

- Risk tolerance/appetite is difficult to quantify, and few organizations have defined it for themselves. A lack of a formal risk tolerance statement should not be an impediment to starting or continuing a risk management program. Instead, risk decisions should be made one at a time.

- If a decision is made to accept a risk, the risk should remain on the risk register, and the matter should be considered again one to two years later. Risks that are accepted should not be accepted in perpetuity, because conditions may change in the future that could compel management to make a different decision.

- Residual risk is often swept under the rug and forgotten.

- Any risk that is not identified, documented, and treated is, by definition, accepted.

- Risk transfer is often misunderstood, primarily because accountability is not included in the risk transfer transaction.

Questions

1. A gaming software startup company does not employ penetration testing of its software. This is an example of:

   A. High tolerance of risk

   B. Noncompliance

   C. Irresponsibility

   D. Outsourcing

2. The categories of risk treatment are:

   A. Risk avoidance, risk transfer, risk mitigation, and risk acceptance

   B. Risk avoidance, risk transfer, and risk mitigation

   C. Risk avoidance, risk reduction, risk transfer, risk mitigation, and risk acceptance

   D. Risk avoidance, risk treatment, risk mitigation, and risk acceptance

3. When would it make sense to spend $50,000 to protect an asset worth $10,000?

   A. The protective measure reduces threat impact by more than 90 percent.

   B. It would never make sense to spend $50,000 to protect an asset worth $10,000.

   C. The asset was required for realization of $500,000 in monthly revenue.

   D. The protective measure reduced threat probability by more than 90 percent.

4. A security steering committee empowered to make risk treatment decisions has chosen to accept a specific risk. What is the best course of action?

   A. Refer the risk to a qualified external security audit firm.

   B. Perform additional risk analysis to identify residual risk.

   C. Reopen the risk item for reconsideration after one year.

   D. Mark the risk item as permanently closed.

5. The responsibilities of a control owner include all of the following *except*:

   A. Review the control.

   B. Audit the control.

   C. Document the control.

   D. Maintain records for the control.

6. Accountability for the outcome of accepted risk is known as:

   A. Risk acceptance

   B. Risk transfer

   C. Risk treatment

   D. Risk ownership

7. A risk committee has formally decided that a specific risk is to be mitigated through the enactment of a specific type of control. What has the committee done?

   A. Risk acceptance

   B. Risk treatment

   C. Redefined risk tolerance

   D. Redefined risk appetite

8. A risk committee has formally decided to mitigate a specific risk. Where should this decision be documented?

   A. Risk register

   B. Meeting minutes

   C. Risk charter

   D. Key risk indicator

9. A risk manager is contemplating risk treatment options for a particularly large risk that exceeds the organization's stated risk tolerance. How should risk treatment proceed?

   A. The risk should be divided into smaller risks.

   B. The risk manager is empowered to make the risk treatment decision.

   C. The risk manager should escalate the decision to executive management.

   D. The risk should be put on hold.

10. A cybersecurity leader is recording a decision to accept a particular risk. What, if anything, should the cybersecurity leader do concerning this accepted risk?

    A. Queue the accepted risk to be redeliberated in one year.

    B. Consider the risk to be accepted in perpetuity.

    C. Convert the accepted risk to a residual risk.

    D. Perform a risk analysis to confirm risk acceptance.

11. In a risk assessment, a risk manager has identified a risk that would cause considerable embarrassment to the organization if it were revealed to the workforce and the public. Executives have directed the risk manager to omit the finding from the final report. What has executive management done in this case?

    A. Delayed the risk

    B. Committed a crime

    C. Transferred the risk

    D. Ignored the risk

12. A risk manager is documenting a newly identified risk in the risk register and has identified the department head as the risk owner. The department head has instructed the risk manager to identify one of the lower level managers in the department as the risk manager. What has the department head done in this situation?

A. Abdicated his risk ownership responsibility

B. Accepted the risk

C. Delegated risk ownership to the lower level manager

D. Transferred the risk

13. The leftover risk that exists after risk mitigation has been performed is known as:

A. Residual risk

B. Open risk

C. Untreated risk

D. Accepted risk

14. A recent risk assessment has identified a data loss risk associated with the use of unapproved software. Management has directed the removal of the unapproved software as a result of the risk assessment. What risk decision has been made in this situation?

A. Risk mitigation

B. Risk avoidance

C. Risk abrogation

D. Risk reduction

15. When faced with a particularly high risk, executive management has decided to outsource the business operation associated with the risk. A legal agreement identifies that the outsourcer accepts operational risks. What becomes of the accountability associated with the risk?

A. Accountability is transferred to the outsourcer.

B. Accountability remains with executive management.

C. Accountability is reduced by the amount of the risk.

D. Accountability is transferred to the board of directors.

Answers

1. **A.** A software startup in an industry like gaming is going to be highly tolerant of risk: time to market and signing up new customers will be its primary objectives. As the organization achieves viability, other priorities such as security will be introduced.

PART II

2. A. The four categories of risk treatment are risk avoidance (the risk-producing activity is discontinued), risk transfer (risks are transferred to an external party such as an insurance company or managed services provider), risk mitigation (risks are reduced through a control or process change), and risk acceptance (management chooses to accept the risk).

3. C. Ordinarily, it would not make sense to spend $50,000 to protect an asset worth $10,000, but other considerations can make it a reasonable option, such as revenue realization or reputation damage, which can be difficult to quantify.

4. C. A risk item that has been accepted should be shelved and considered after a period of time, such as one year. This is a better option than closing the risk item permanently; in a year's time, changes in business conditions, security threats, and other considerations may compel the organization to take different action with regard to the risk.

5. B. Control owners are responsible for documenting a control, maintaining records, and reviewing the control to ensure that it is continuing to operate properly. Auditing of a control is performed by another internal or an external party.

6. D. In the case of an accepted risk, risk ownership is the assignment of accountability for the specific risk.

7. B. The risk committee has formally treated the risk through its decision to mitigate the risk.

8. A. The risk register is the best place to document a formal risk treatment decision. It may also be appropriate to publish meeting minutes and document the decision in a decision log if one exists.

9. C. If a particular risk exceeds an organization's stated risk tolerance, upper management may be required to make or approve a risk treatment decision for that risk.

10. A. Risks that are accepted should not be accepted in perpetuity, because conditions may change in the future that could compel management to make a different decision.

11. D. Ignoring the risk is the best answer to this question, but it could also be said that executive management accepted the risk. However, since the risk was not documented, there was no formal risk acceptance.

12. C. Ownership of the risk has been delegated to another person in the department. This is not necessarily inappropriate, because the other person may be more directly responsible for business operations related to the risk.

13. A. Any leftover risk that remains after risk mitigation is performed is known as residual risk. However, if the organization does not formally address residual risk, it may be considered accepted.

14. **B.** Risk avoidance is the decision made in this situation. Risk avoidance is defined as a discontinuation of the activity associated with an identified risk.

15. **B.** When transferring risk to another business entity, accountability remains with those originally accountable for the business function and the associated risk. Accountability cannot be transferred to another party.

PART III

Information Security Risk Management

■ **Chapter 5**   Information Security Program Development
■ **Chapter 6**   Information Security Program Management

Information Security Program Development

In this chapter, you will learn about
- Resources and outcomes related to information security programs
- Asset, system, data, facilities, and personnel classification
- Control and security management framework development
- Policies, standards, guidelines, procedures, and requirements
- Metrics that tell the security management and operations story

This chapter covers Certified Information Security Manager (CISM) Domain 3, "Information Security Program," part A, "Information Security Program Development." The entire Information Security Program domain represents 33 percent of the CISM examination.

Supporting Tasks in the CISM job practice that align with the Information Security Program / Information Security Program Development domain include:

5. Establish and maintain information security policies to guide the development of standards, procedures, and guidelines.

10. Evaluate and report information security metrics to key stakeholders.

11. Establish and/or maintain the information security program in alignment with the information security strategy.

12. Align the information security program with the operational objectives of other business functions.

13. Establish and maintain information security processes and resources to execute the information security program.

14. Establish, communicate, and maintain organizational information security policies, standards, guidelines, procedures, and other documentation.

20. Establish and/or maintain a process for information asset identification and classification.

Establishing and modernizing an organization's cybersecurity program is one of the most impactful activities with long-term benefits (and consequences) a security leader will undertake. Cybersecurity program improvements are implemented as a result of a strategic plan, discussed in Chapter 2. Cybersecurity program development consists of creating policies, controls, standards, requirements, guidelines, and a formal structure for security functions described in separate charters. Security leaders can choose from one of several frameworks that describe the structure of a security program. Security leaders use metrics to measure events and activities, enabling senior management to see the results of their directives.

Information Security Program Resources

Information security programs comprise a collection of activities used to identify, communicate, and address risks. The security program consists of controls, processes, and practices intended to increase the resilience of the computing environment and ensure that risks are known and handled effectively. These activities may be handled by a single individual in a smaller organization, while larger organizations will have a security leader that leads an internal team. Organizations of all sizes may have additional support from external partners as needed.

Security program models have been developed that include the primary activities needed in any organization's security program. However, because every organization is different, each security manager needs to understand their particular organization's internal workings so that their security programs can effectively align with the organization's operations, practices, and culture.

The activities in an information security program serve to operationalize the security manager's vision for effective security and risk management in the organization. Generally, a security manager's vision focuses on *how* the security program aligns with and supports the business.

Trends

Fueled by the sharp increase in the number and impact of ransomware attacks on private organizations and government agencies, cybersecurity is getting more attention in the media and boardrooms than in the past. The United States and other countries have been issuing advisories, directives, and edicts and enacting new laws and regulations requiring greater transparency of security incidents, and many are requiring that one or more board members have cybersecurity experience.

Further, the Cyber Incident Reporting for Critical Infrastructure Act of 2022 expands on Executive Order 14208 by requiring all critical infrastructure owners and operators (whether they contract with the federal government or not) to submit reports of cybersecurity incidents and ransomware payments to CISA. Also, many U.S. states have passed privacy laws, and there is a possibility of a federal law on privacy being enacted.

While more organizations recognize cybersecurity's strategic nature and enabling characteristics, more security leaders are considered "real" C-level executives. However, numerous organizations still consider cybersecurity as nonstrategic and tactical.

Security and privacy are often not a part of the initial design of new products and services, because security is still seen not as a business enabler but as an impediment. But cybersecurity is regarded as unimportant, until it is. Often, only a serious security breach will change this mindset among executives.

Outcomes

The primary outcome of a security program is the realization of its strategy, goals, and objectives, as discussed in Chapter 2. When a strategy is aligned with the business and its risk tolerance and operations, the organization's security program will act as a business enabler, allowing it to consider new business ventures while being fully aware of associated risks that can be mitigated or accepted. Like the brakes on a race car that enable it to maneuver more quickly, an effective security program helps the organization embark on new ventures, knowing that the security program acts as the organization's brakes that allow it to adjust effectively to keep it on the road.

The outcomes that should be part of any information security program include the following:

- **Strategic alignment**   The program needs to align with and work in harmony with the rest of the organization. This includes being aware of—and supporting—all new business initiatives, developing risk tolerance criteria that business leaders agree with, and working daily with business leaders to establish mutual trust. Better security programs utilize a security council or governance committee consisting of stakeholders from across the business; this helps ensure that information security activities work with the business instead of against it.

- **Risk management**   An effective security program includes an effective risk management program that identifies risks and facilitates desired outcomes through appropriate risk treatment.

- **Value delivery**   An effective information security program delivers value to the organization. This is most often achieved by aligning security activities directed toward risk reduction in the organization's most critical activities. Effectively and efficiently reducing risk to an acceptable level is another key part of value delivery.

- **Resource management**   An information security program's primary objective is risk management and risk reduction. This requires resources in the form of permanent and temporary staff, external service providers, and tools. These resources must be managed so that they are used effectively to reduce risks in alignment with the risk management program. Additionally, efficiently using resources will assist security managers in "rightsizing" the information security budget and spending. This will lead to greater confidence in the business regarding "resource requests" from the security manager.

- **Performance management**   As a security program is developed and implemented, key activities need to be measured to ensure that they are operating as planned. Security metrics are used to measure and report key activities to management.

- **Assurance process integration** An effective information security program is aligned with other assurance processes and programs in an organization, including human resources, finance, legal, audit, enterprise risk management, information technology, and operations. Further, a security program should influence these activities to protect them adequately from harm.

Charter

A *charter* is a formal, written definition of the objectives of a program, its main timelines, the sources of funding, the names of its principal leaders and managers, and the business executives sponsoring the program. In many organizations, a program charter document is approved by the CEO or other executive leader that gives authority to the person or group that runs the program. The charter also demonstrates the support from the executive leadership team.

An information security program charter gives authority to the security leader to develop and/or perform several functions, including the following:

- Develop and enforce security policy.
- Develop and implement the risk management process.
- Develop and manage security governance.
- Develop and direct the implementation and operation of controls across department or business unit boundaries.
- Develop and direct the implementation of key security processes, including vulnerability management, incident management, third-party risk, security architecture, business continuity planning, and security awareness training.

Information security in an organization of any size is a team sport. The security manager (with or without staff) does not perform security functions alone; rather, these activities involve nearly every other department, business unit, and affiliate in the organization. For this reason, the security charter must be ratified by executive management.

A security charter that designates the security manager as the person responsible for implementing the program does not give the security manager the right to dictate the program to others. As is stated numerous times in this book, a security management program may be led and guided by the security manager, but it will be effective and successful only through collaboration and consensus by stakeholders across the business. For this reason, it may be appropriate to say that a charter empowers the security manager to be a facilitator of security in the organization. Another key element that should be understood is that although the security manager is the facilitator of the program, the ultimate responsibility or ownership for protecting information is at the executive leadership and board of directors levels. The security charter gives the security leader authority to design and operate the program, but accountability is shared between the security leader and the executive leadership team and board of directors.

Scope

An early step in the creation of an information security program is the definition of its scope. Management needs to define the departments, business units, affiliates, and locations to be included in the organization's information security program. The scope of a program is essential, because it defines the boundaries and what parts of the organization are to be included and subject to information security governance and policy.

The discussion of scope is generally more relevant in larger organizations with autonomous business units or affiliates. In larger organizations, business units or affiliates may have programs of their own, which may be defined as part of a larger security program or may be entirely autonomous. If the scope of a security program is defined as "headquarters only" in an organization with autonomous business units, this does not mean there is no interaction between the headquarters security program and business unit security programs. For instance, there may be a single set of policies for all entities, but separate processes, personnel, and standards in each business unit.

There is no right or wrong way to define the relationship between two or more security programs in an organization. Rather, management needs to be aware of factors that represent similarities and differences between parts of larger organizations that will help them define the scope to result in effective security management throughout the organization. This is sometimes easier said than done, particularly in cases where the scope of security programs and IT departments differ.

Information Security Processes

Information security programs include numerous business processes that fulfill the overall mission of information and information systems protection. These processes fall into three major categories: risk and compliance, architecture, and operations.

Risk and compliance processes often include the following:

- Risk assessments and risk management
- Security policy management
- Security controls management
- Requirements development
- Compliance monitoring
- Data classification and handling
- Third-party risk management
- Contingency planning
- Access governance
- Security awareness training
- Privacy (which can also be entirely separate from information security as a standalone program)

Architecture processes often include these:

- Reference architecture development (both on-premises and cloud)
- Architecture reviews
- Technical standards

Security operations processes often include the following:

- Security event logging and monitoring
- Security incident response
- Forensics
- Vulnerability management
- Penetration testing (often outsourced as individual projects)
- Threat intelligence
- Identity and access management

The Three Lines of Defense

The *three lines of defense* is a functional model that defines three aspects of the development and operation of controls:

- **Control development**   Generally assigned to an information security or risk management function, controls are developed based on the results of risk assessments and prior audits.
- **Control operation**   Assigned to the persons and teams that operate controls, who are free to develop processes and procedures as they see fit to implement controls.
- **Control assurance**   Assigned to an independent audit function, controls are assessed or audited to determine whether they are designed and operated effectively.

These three functions are assigned to three different persons or teams that operate independently and collaborate extensively. The three lines of defense model is an implementation of separation of duties, where essential functions are divided among multiple parties so that no single party can exert excessive control or suffer from groupthink.

Information Security Technologies

Modern information security includes essential business processes such as risk and policy management, but overall, it is also heavily involved in information technology. After all, information security's mission is the protection of all things IT. To scale with the power and speed of IT, information security has its own portfolio of protective and detective technologies that include the following:

- Foundation technologies
  - TCP/IP internals
  - Operating systems internals
  - Middleware
  - Applications and tools
- Endpoint protection
  - Antimalware
  - Firewalls
  - Patch and configuration management
  - Host-based intrusion detection systems (HIDSs)
  - Mobile device management (MDM)
  - Mobile application management (MAM)
  - Secure access service edge (SASE)
- Network protection
  - Antimalware
  - Firewalls
  - Patch and configuration management
  - Intrusion detection systems (IDSs/NIDSs)
  - Intrusion prevention systems (IPSs)
  - Web content filtering
  - Cloud access security brokers (CASBs)
  - Spam and phishing filtering
  - Remote access and virtual private networks (VPNs)
- Data protection
  - Data loss prevention (DLP)
  - Backup, replication, snapshots, and vaulting
  - Removable storage monitoring and management
  - Encryption and digital signatures
  - Fingerprinting, tagging, and watermarking

- Identity and access management
  - Password vaults
  - Privileged access gateways
  - Multifactor authentication (MFA)
  - Federated identity (OAuth, FIDO Alliance, and so on)
- Event management
  - Centralized logging
  - Security information and event management (SIEM) systems
  - Threat intelligence platforms (TIPs)
  - Security orchestration, automation, and response (SOAR)
- Vulnerability management
  - Security scanning
  - Penetration testing
  - Social engineering testing
- Systems and software development
  - Dynamic application security testing (DAST)
  - Static application security testing (SAST)
  - Penetration testing
  - Code review
- Governance, risk, and compliance
  - Governance, risk, and compliance (GRC) platform
  - Integrated risk management (IRM) platform

The information security leader does not need to have expertise in all of these technologies. Further, some of these technologies are managed outside of information security, such as IT or product development. That said, information security needs to employ risk management to identify whether controls and technologies in these and other areas adequately reduce risk and to ensure that there are staff members in the organization who understand their architecture, implementation, and operation.

Keeping Up with the Joneses

Risk management and risk treatment are not the only drivers compelling an organization to implement new information security tooling. A major factor is peer pressure; many organizations adopt new security tooling for several reasons, including these:

- A salesperson claims their company's product detects or prevents (insert the latest threat here).

(continued)

- Leaders in other organizations tout their preferences for specific new technologies.
- Articles and case studies promote new security technologies.

Indeed, there is only one valid reason for adopting new security technology: risk analysis and risk treatment call for it, and the organization is unwilling to accept a related risk. All other reasons are generally invalid and the result of peer pressure, emotional decision-making, or the desire to "get their hands dirty" in the latest security tooling fad.

Information Asset Identification and Classification

Assets are the things of value that an organization protects in an information security program. They consist of tangible things, including the following:

- **Information systems hardware**   Servers, laptops, tablets, mobile devices, and network devices of various sorts
- **Software**   Operating systems, subsystems, applications, and tools—regardless of location
- **Virtual assets**   Operating system guests, containers, and so on
- **Information**   Structured databases and unstructured data
- **Facilities**   Data centers, development centers, operations centers, business offices, sales offices, retail locations, and so on
- **Personnel**   Staff, contractors, temporary workers

Asset Identification and Valuation

After security leadership has determined the scope of the security program, an initial step of program development is the identification of assets and a determination of each asset's value. In a typical organization, assets consist of information and the information systems that support and protect those information assets.

Hardware Assets

Hardware assets may include server and network hardware, user workstations, office equipment such as printers and scanners, and Wi-Fi access points. Depending on the scope of the risk assessment, assets in storage and replacement components may also be included.

Accurately identifying hardware assets can be challenging, and many organizations do a subpar job of building and maintaining inventory information. Accounting may have asset inventory in its accounting system, but this would not account for assets not in use or retired assets reverted to storage. Further, asset inventory in accounting often does not cite the business applications they support. Tools used by IT for security scans or patch management are another source of inventory information, although these are often incomplete for many reasons. Even purpose-made asset inventory systems are plagued with inaccuracies, because maintaining the data is not always a high priority.

An organization responsible for managing information and information systems must know what its assets are. More than that, IT needs to acquire and track several characteristics of every asset, including the following:

- **Identification** This includes the make, model, serial number, asset tag number, logical name, and other means for identifying the asset.
- **Value** Initially, this may signify the purchased value, but it may also include its depreciated value if an IT asset management program is associated with the organization's financial asset management program.
- **Location** The asset's location needs to be specified so that its existence may be verified in a periodic inventory.
- **Security classification** Security management programs almost always include a plan for classifying the sensitivity of information and/or information systems. Example classifications include secret, restricted, confidential, and public.
- **Asset group** IT assets may be classified into a hierarchy of asset groups. For example, servers in a data center that support a large application may be assigned to an asset group known as "*Application X* Servers."
- **Owner** This is usually the person or group responsible for the operation of the asset.
- **Custodian** Occasionally, the ownership and operations of assets will be divided into two bodies, where the owner owns them but a custodian operates or maintains them.

Because hardware assets are installed, moved, and eventually retired, it is important to verify the information in the asset inventory periodically by physically verifying the existence of the physical assets. Depending upon the value and sensitivity of systems and data, this inventory "true-up" may be performed as often as monthly or as seldom as once per year. Discrepancies in actual inventory must be investigated to verify that assets have not been moved without authorization or stolen.

Subsystem and Software Assets

Software applications such as software development tools, drawing tools, security scanning tools, and subsystems such as application servers and database management systems are all considered assets. Like physical assets, software assets have tangible value and should be periodically inventoried. Some of the purposes for inventorying software include license agreement compliance, business continuity planning, and disaster recovery planning. If an organization tracks the return on investment of information systems, then, certainly, the value of software assets makes up the whole of the assets that support or enable key business processes and activities.

Information Assets

Information assets are less tangible than hardware assets, because they are not easily observed. Information assets take many forms:

- **Customer information** Most organizations store information about people, whether employees, customers, constituents, beneficiaries, or citizens. The information may include sensitive information such as contact information and personal details, transactions, order history, and other details.

- **Intellectual property** This type of information can take the form of trade secrets, source code, product designs, policies and standards, and marketing collateral.

- **Business operations** This generally includes merger and acquisition information and other types of business processes and records not mentioned earlier.

- **Virtual assets** Most organizations are moving their business applications to the cloud, eliminating the need to purchase hardware. Organizations that use infrastructure as a service (IaaS) have virtual operating systems that are another form of information. Even though IaaS operating systems are not purchased, but rented or leased, there is nonetheless an asset perspective: they take time to build and configure and therefore have a replacement cost. The value of assets is discussed more fully later in this section.

Cloud-Based Information Assets

One significant challenge related to information assets lies in the nature of cloud services. A significant portion of an organization's information assets may be stored by other organizations in their cloud-based services. Some of these assets will be overlooked unless an organization has exceedingly good business records. The main reason for this is because of how cloud services work: It's easy to sign up for a zero-cost or low-cost service and immediately begin uploading business information to the service. Unless the organization has advanced tools such as a CASB, it will be next to impossible for an organization to know all of the cloud-based services in use.

 NOTE The nature of shadow IT (where individuals and groups bypass corporate IT and procure their own computing services) implies that not all assets can be identified. This is particularly true of cloud-based assets and virtual assets.

Virtual Assets

Virtualization technology, which enables an organization to employ multiple, separate operating systems to run on one server, is a popular practice for organizations, whether it's used on hardware servers located in their data centers or in hosting facilities. Organizations that use IaaS are also employing virtualization technology.

IaaS and virtualization make it far easier to create and manage server assets, but maintaining an accurate inventory of virtual server assets is even more challenging than it is for physical assets, and more discipline is required to track and manage virtual server assets properly. Unlike physical servers, which require that different stakeholders initiate and approve a purchase, virtual servers can be created at the click of a button, with or without additional cost to the organization and often without approval. The term *virtual sprawl*, or *virtualization sprawl*, reflects this tendency.

The creation/use of virtual servers and other virtual machines is not limited to manual techniques. Virtual machines can also be created through automatic means. A typical example of this is through a cloud services feature known as *elasticity*. Additional virtual machines can be automatically created and started during heavy workloads when more servers are needed.

Containerization is another form of virtualization where multiple software instantiations execute on a running operating system. The existence of these running instances may be a part of virtual asset inventory.

Software-defined networking (SDN), the class of technologies that facilitate the creation and management of virtual network devices, poses the same challenge to organizations. Additional devices can be created at will or by automatic means. Managing them requires more discipline and potentially greater effort.

Asset Classification

In asset classification, an organization assigns an asset to a category representing usage or risk. In an information security program, the purpose of asset classification is to determine, for each asset, its level of criticality to the organization.

Criticality can be related to information sensitivity. For instance, a customer information database that includes contact and payment information would be considered highly sensitive and could significantly impact present and future business operations in the event of compromise.

Criticality can also be related to operational dependency. For example, a database of virtual server images may be considered highly critical. If an organization's server images were to be compromised or lost, this could adversely affect its ability to continue its operations.

These and other criticality measures form the basis for information protection, system redundancy and resilience, business continuity planning, disaster recovery planning, and access management. Scarce resources in the form of information protection and resilience need to be allocated to the assets that require it the most, because it doesn't usually make sense to protect all assets to the same degree; instead, more valuable and critical assets should be more fully protected than those deemed less valuable and critical. To illustrate this point, the late McGeorge Bundy, former U.S. National Security Advisor, is known to have said, "If we guard our toothbrushes and diamonds with equal zeal, we will lose fewer toothbrushes and more diamonds."

The best approach to asset classification in most organizations is to identify and classify *information* assets first, followed by system classification. One area often overlooked or not addressed to a satisfactory level is dealing with unstructured data and data that resides outside of the organization's approved systems.

Information Classification

Information classification is a process whereby different sets and collections of data in an organization are analyzed for various types of value, criticality, integrity, and sensitivity. There are different ways to understand these characteristics. These are some examples:

- **Monetary value**   Some information may be easily monetized by intruders who steal it, such as credit card numbers, bank account numbers, gift certificates or cards, and discount or promotion codes. Loss of this type of information may cause direct financial losses.

- **Operational criticality**   This information must be available at all times, or perhaps the information is related to some factors of business resilience. Examples include virtual server images, incident response procedures, and business continuity procedures. Corruption or loss of this type of information may significantly impact ongoing business operations.

- **Accuracy or integrity**   Information in this category is required to be highly accurate. If altered, the organization could suffer significant financial or reputational harm. Examples include exchange rate tables, product or service inventory data, machine calibration data, and price lists. Corruption or loss of this type of information impacts business operations by causing incomplete or erroneous transactions.

- **Sensitivity**   Information of a sensitive nature is commonly associated with individual citizens, including personal contact information, personal financial data such as credit card and bank account numbers, and medical records.

- **Reputational value**   Another dimension of classification, denoting the potential loss of reputation should certain sensitive or critical information be lost or compromised. Information such as customers' personal information fits here.

Most organizations store information that falls into all of these categories, with degrees of importance within them. Though this may result in a complex matrix of information types and degrees of importance or value, the most successful organizations will build a fairly simple information classification scheme. For instance, an organization may develop four levels of information classification, such as the following:

- Secret
- Restricted
- Confidential
- Public

These levels of information, examples of the types of levels that fall into each category, and instructions on handling information at each level form the heart of a typical information classification program.

Most organizations depend on their personnel to understand the information classification program, including correctly classifying information and handling it properly. This is why better information classification programs have only three or four classification levels. It may be more desirable to have more classification levels, but this often results in confusion and misclassification or mishandling of sensitive and critical data.

Drilling into further detail, following are some examples of information at each of these levels of classification:

- **Secret**   Merger and acquisition plans, user and system account passwords, and encryption keys
- **Restricted**   Credit card numbers, bank account numbers, Social Security numbers, detailed financial records, detailed system configuration, and vulnerability scan reports
- **Confidential**   System documentation, end-user documentation, internal memos, and network diagrams
- **Public**   Marketing collateral, published financial reports, and press releases

The next step in information classification is the development of handling procedures that instruct users in the proper acquisition, storage, transmission, and destruction of information at every classification level. Table 5-1 shows a sample information-handling procedure matrix.

The classification and handling guidelines shown here illustrate the differences in various forms of information handling for different classification levels. The contents of Table 5-1 can serve as a starting point for a data classification and handling procedure.

Organizations that develop and implement information classification programs find that personnel will often misclassify information, either because they do not understand the nature of the sensitivity of a particular set of data or because they may believe that at a higher classification level they cannot store or transmit the information in a way they think is needed. This is a classic case of people taking shortcuts in the name of expediency, mainly when they are not aware of the possible harm that may befall the organization as a result.

The Ideal Number of Classification Levels

Would it be easier if we simply handled all information in the same way, as the most sensitive information in the organization? While this would make it easier to remember how to handle and dispose of all information, it might also be onerous, particularly if all information is handled at the level warranted for the organization's most sensitive or critical information. Encrypting everything and shredding everything would be a wasteful use of resources.

That said, it is incumbent on an organization to build a simple information classification program that is easy to understand and follow. Too many levels of classification would be as burdensome as a single level. With too many classification levels, there is a greater chance that information will be misclassified and then put at risk when handled at a too low a level. With too few levels, the organization will either have excessive resources protecting all information at a higher level or insufficient resources protecting information inadequately.

	Secret	Restricted	Confidential	Public
Example Information Types	Passwords, merger and acquisition plans and terms	Credit card numbers, bank account numbers, Social Security numbers, detailed financial records, detailed system configuration, vulnerability scan reports	System documentation, end-user documentation, internal memos, network diagrams	Brochures, press releases
Storage on Server	Must be encrypted; store only on servers labeled sensitive	Must be encrypted	Access controls required	Access controls required for update
Storage on Mobile Device	Must never be stored on a mobile device	Must be encrypted	Access controls required	No restrictions
Storage in the Cloud	Must never be stored in the cloud	Must be encrypted	Access controls required	Access controls required for update
E-mail	Must never be e-mailed	Must be encrypted	Authorized recipients only	No restrictions
Website	Must never be stored on any web server	Must be encrypted	Access controls required	No restrictions
Fax	Encrypted; manned fax only	Manned fax only; no e-mail–based fax	Manned fax only	No restrictions
Courier and Shipment	Double wrapped; signature and secure storage required	Signature and secure storage required	Signature required	No restrictions
Hard-Copy Storage	Double locked in authorized locations only	Double locked	Locked	No restrictions
Hard-Copy Distribution	Only with owner permission; must be registered	To authorized parties only, only with owner permission	To authorized parties only	No restrictions
Hard-Copy Destruction	Cross-cut shred; make specific record of destruction	Cross-cut shred	Cross-cut shred or secure waste bin	No restrictions
Soft-Copy Destruction	Erase with DoD 5220.22-M spec tool	Erase with DoD 5220.22-M spec tool	Delete and empty recycle bin	No restriction

Table 5-1 Example Information-Handling Requirements

System Classification

Once an organization is satisfied that its information classification is in order, it can embark on system classification. Like various information assets, information systems can also be classified according to various security and operational criteria. The purpose for system classification is similar to the purpose for information criteria: to identify and categorize system assets according to the classification of information stored, processed, or transmitted by them, so that an appropriate level of protection can be determined and implemented.

Once a system is classified according to the highest classification level of information stored, processed, or transmitted through it, the measures used to protect the information system may well play a role in protecting the information—or, in some cases, it will protect only the system. Both means are utilized, and both are essential.

A typical approach to system classification and protection is this: for each level of classification and each type of system, a system-hardening standard is developed that specifies the features and configuration settings to be applied to the system. These settings help make the system resistant to attack, and in some cases, the settings will help protect the information being stored, processed, or transmitted by the systems.

Some examples will help illustrate these points:

- **Database management server**   A database management server is used to store information, perhaps credit card data, at the Restricted level of classification. The system itself will be classified as Restricted, and the organization will develop system-hardening standards for the operating system and database management systems.

- **Demilitarized zone (DMZ) firewall**   A firewall protects servers located in a DMZ from threats on the Internet and protects the organization's internal assets from the DMZ if an attacker compromises an asset in the DMZ. Though the firewall does not store information, it protects information by restricting the types of traffic permitted to flow from the Internet to systems upon which the information resides. The organization will develop and implement hardening standards for the firewall.

- **Internet time server**   A server provides precise time clock data to other servers, network devices, and end-user workstations. Although the time server itself does not store, process, or transmit sensitive information, it is classified as Restricted because this server has direct access (via time protocols and possibly other protocols) to assets that are classified as Restricted. This server will be hardened according to hardening standards developed by the organization.

This final example helps to introduce the concept of zones of protection. In the architecture of typical information-processing environments, information systems directly store, process, and transmit information at various classification levels, and the systems themselves are classified accordingly. The other servers and assets in the same environment that access these servers or are accessed by them typically need to be classified at the same level.

Figure 5-1
Example network
segmentation
scheme

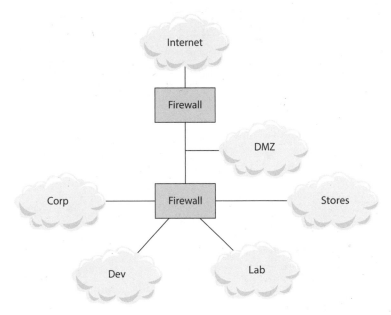

If one of these support servers were compromised by an attacker, the attacker would have direct, and perhaps unrestricted, access to one of the assets that stores, processes, or transmits sensitive or valuable data.

In a large, flat network, this logic could result in an organization classifying many or all of its systems at the same level as the highest classified system. This could require an organization to implement costly and complex protective and administrative measures for large numbers of systems. For this and other reasons, organizations often employ *network segmentation,* which divides a large, flat network into multiple zones, with firewalls and other protective measures implemented at the boundaries between these zones.

Figure 5-1 depicts a typical network segmentation scheme.

Facilities Classification

Data, asset, and systems classification can often be extended to facilities classification in larger organizations. *Facilities classification* is a method for assigning classification or risk levels to work centers and processing centers, based on their operational criticality or other risk factors. Facilities classification aims to develop more consistent security controls for facilities with similar risk levels. For instance, a processing center may have extensive video surveillance and layers of multifactor physical access controls, whereas a sales office may have minimal (if any) video surveillance and simpler access controls.

Personnel Classification

In some organizations, additional requirements are imposed on persons who have access to particularly sensitive information. Whether this information consists of trade secrets, government secrets, or other information, organizations may be required to meet specific requirements such as more thorough or frequent background investigations.

Because of the higher cost of these investigations (to continue this example), it makes more sense to establish a classification scheme for personnel in the organization. For instance, the usual classification for personnel requires a standard background investigation at the time of hire. A higher classification, required for access to specific information, may require a more rigorous background investigation at the time of hire. The highest classification may require this rigorous background investigation to be performed annually. Organizations in a situation like this may want to classify their employees to keep track of the requirements for initial and ongoing background investigations to ensure compliance with whatever applicable laws, regulations, or contracts require them.

Organizations with no legally imposed requirements for personnel classification may still have good reasons to do so. Such circumstances may include the following:

- Specific policy and standards with additional sign-off/acknowledgment as well as more robust awareness and security training
- Personnel with access to the most sensitive information (trade secrets and other intellectual property)
- Personnel with access to sensitive functions (domain administrators and personnel with other privileged system access)
- Personnel being promoted to an executive level such as vice president

Thus far, only background investigations have been mentioned as variables applied to personnel in various classification levels. Other differences in the treatment of personnel at higher security levels may include the following:

- Assigned devices may have a higher level of security protection.
- Access reviews may occur more frequently or be more rigorous.
- Authentication requirements may be more stringent (such as multifactor authentication for every login).
- A different color of badge may outwardly signify a higher security level.
- Personnel may be assigned to work in a facility (or portion thereof) with more stringent physical security controls, such as biometrics and mantraps or the presence of security guards or additional video surveillance.

Personnel Are More than a Number

I hope readers are not offended by my mention of personnel as "assets" in an organization. Certainly, people are more than just a number; they are the soul and essence of an organization, through which its culture is personified and activities of value are accomplished. People are of value and warrant protection—hence, the emphasis on workplace safety and employee assistance programs (EAPs). In some organizations, personnel will also be classified into two or more security levels—for example, to limit the number of authorized persons who can access certain classified assets.

Asset Valuation

A key part of a risk assessment is identifying the value of an asset. In the absence of an asset's value, it is more difficult to calculate risks associated with an asset, even when qualitative risk valuation is employed. Without a known valuation, the impact of loss can be more difficult to know.

Qualitative Asset Valuation

Because risk analysis is often qualitative, establishing asset valuation in qualitative terms is common in many organizations. Instead of assigning a dollar (or other currency) value to an asset, the organization can assign a value using a low-medium-high scale or a numeric scale such as 1 to 5 or 1 to 10. By using qualitative asset valuation, an organization can establish which assets have more or less value relative to others. This can be highly useful in an organization with many assets, because it can provide a view of its high-value assets without the "noise" of comingled lower valued assets.

Quantitative Asset Valuation

Many organizations opt to surpass qualitative asset valuation and assign a dollar (or other currency) valuation to their assets. This is common in larger or more mature organizations that want to understand all the costs associated with loss events.

In a typical quantitative valuation of an asset, its value may be one of the following:

- **Replacement cost**   The valuation for a hardware asset may be determined to be the cost of purchasing (and deploying) a replacement. For a database, its replacement cost may be the operational costs required to restore it from backup or the costs to recover it from its source, such as a service provider.

- **Book value**   This represents the value of an asset in the organization's financial system, typically the purchase price less depreciation.

- **Net present value (NPV)**   If the asset directly or indirectly generates revenue, this valuation method may be used.

- **Redeployment cost**   The value of a virtual machine may be determined to be the cost of setting it up again. This is typically a soft cost if it is set up by internal staff, but it could be a hard cost if another company is hired to redeploy it. Remember to include any software licensing costs.

- **Creation or reacquisition cost**   If the asset is a database, its cost may be determined to be the cost of creating it again. If the asset is intellectual property such as software source code, its valuation may be determined to be the effort for developers to re-create it.

- **Consequential financial cost**   The valuation of a database containing sensitive data may be measured in the form of financial costs that result from its theft or compromise. Though the cost of recovering that database may be relatively low, the consequences of its compromise could cost hundreds of dollars per record. This is a typical cost when measuring the full impact of a breach.

Information security managers need to carefully determine the appropriate method for setting the value of each asset. While some instances will be fairly straightforward, others will not. In many cases, an individual asset will have more than a single valuation category. For example, a credit card database may primarily be valued on its consequential cost (because of the potential fines plus remediation costs associated with consumers who may have been harmed) and also redeployment costs—although, in this case, this may be a small fraction of the total valuation.

Information security managers should document their rationales and methods of valuation, particularly for sensitive information assets whose valuations could vary widely depending on the method used. Better yet, larger and more mature organizations will have guidelines that specify methods and formulas for information asset valuation.

Industry Standards and Frameworks for Information Security

We live in an era of the existence of numerous information security standards and frameworks—some for many years. This enables information security managers to get a head start on developing controls, policies, and standards instead of starting with a clean slate.

There are several types of frameworks in information security, and sometimes they are confused for one another:

- **Control frameworks**   These include CIS CSC, ISO/IEC 27002, NIST SP 800-53, PCI DSS, NIST CSF, COBIT, ETSI Technical Report (TR) 103 305-1, HITRUST CSF, and others. These frameworks are starting points for organizations that need to implement security controls and do not want to start from scratch.

- **Risk management frameworks**   These include ISO/IEC 27005, ISO/IEC 31000, NIST CSF, and NIST SP 800-37. These frameworks provide the blueprints for a risk management life-cycle program.

- **Architecture frameworks**   These include TOGAF and Zachman.

- **Security program management frameworks**   These include ISO/IEC 27001, NIST CSF, COBIT, and ETSI TR 103 787-1.

Note that some of these standards appear in more than one category. Some are multipurpose in nature. For instance, NIST CSF prescribes a risk management methodology and includes a mapping of controls.

Control Frameworks

Although every organization may have its unique missions, objectives, business models, risk tolerance, and so on, organizations need not invent governance frameworks from scratch to manage their particular IT objectives. In strategy development, some organizations may already have a suitable control framework in place, while others may not. It is not always necessary for an organization to select an industry-standard control framework, but it is advantageous to do so. These frameworks have been used in thousands of companies, and they are regularly updated to reflect changing business practices, emerging threats, and new technologies.

It is often considered a mistake to select or refuse a control framework because of the presence or absence of a small number of specific controls. Usually, a selection is made assuming that control frameworks are rigid and inflexible. Instead, the strategist should select a control framework based on industry alignment and then institute a process for developing additional controls based on the results of risk assessments. Indeed, this is exactly the approach described in ISO/IEC 27001 and NIST CSF: start with a well-known control framework and then create additional controls, if needed, to address risks specific to the organization.

When assessing the use of a specific framework, the strategist may find that a specific control area is not applicable. In such a case, rather than ignoring the section, the strategist should document the business and technical reasons why the organization chose not to use the control area. This will assist if a question is raised in the future as to why the decision was made not to implement the control area. The date and those involved in the decision should also be documented.

Several standard control frameworks are discussed in the remainder of this section:

- COBIT
- IT Infrastructure Library (ITIL) / ISO/IEC 20000
- ISO/IEC 27002
- HIPAA
- NIST SP 800-53
- NIST SP 800-171
- NIST CSF
- CIS CSC
- PCI DSS

 EXAM TIP Control frameworks, risk management frameworks, and security program frameworks are often confused with one another. Keep their differences in mind as you study for the exam.

Information Security Is Older than You

In 1977, the U.S. National Bureau of Standards (the predecessor of NIST) published NBS SP 500-19, "Audit and Evaluation of Computer Security, Proceedings of the NBS Invitational Workshop," a seminal publication in cybersecurity. This publication is attributed with the introduction of the concept of the "confidentiality, integrity and availability of data," known today as the CIA Triad.

(continued)

Numerous other concepts, such as static and dynamic application scanning, are discussed in this document. Selected pages from NBS SP 500-19 (source: U.S. National Institute for Standards and Technology) are shown here.

11. ISSUES FOR THE COMMUNITY 7-35
   11.1 Implications of Future Technology 7-35
   11.2 Adequacy of the Literature 7-36
   11.3 State-of-the-Practice 7-37

REFERENCES 7-39
FIGURES
o Figure 1 Indicators of Application Sensitivity 7-7
o Figure 2 System Levels of Security 7-22

PART VIII: PROGRAM INTEGRITY 8-1
EDITORS' NOTE 8-2

Program Integrity Assessment 8-3

1. WHAT IS PROGRAM INTEGRITY? 8-3

2. A CONTEXT FOR PROGRAM INTEGRITY 8-4
   2.1 Programs Change With Time (Life Cycle) 8-4
   2.2 Visibility of Relationships is Lost Between
       Stages 8-5
   2.3 Program Integrity Assessment is Multi-
       Dimensional Problem 8-6

3. RELEVANT THREATS AND THEIR SEVERITY 8-6

4. METHODS FOR ACHIEVING PROGRAM INTEGRITY 8-7
   4.1 Evidence of Correctness 8-7
      4.1.1 Static Evaluation 8-8
      4.1.2 Dynamic Evaluation 8-9
   4.2 Evidence of Robustness 8-10
      4.2.1 On-Going Testing 8-10
      4.2.2 On-Line Monitoring and Control 8-11
      4.2.3 Redundancy 8-11
      4.2.4 Support Control 8-12
   4.3 Evidence of Trustworthiness 8-12
      4.3.1 People 8-12
      4.3.2 Software Development 8-13
      4.3.3 Tools 8-13

5. PROGRAM INTEGRITY IMPACTS OTHER SESSIONS 8-14

6. RECOMMENDATIONS 8-16
   6.1 Existing Software 8-16
   6.2 Future Software 8-17
   6.3 Organization Actions 8-17

7. BIBLIOGRAPHY 8-18

xii

PART IX: DATA INTEGRITY 9-1
EDITORS' NOTE 9-2

Data Integrity Auditing: A Framework for Standards
Development 9-3

1. INTRODUCTION 9-3

2. DEFINITION OF DATA INTEGRITY 9-4

3. OBJECTIVE OF DATA INTEGRITY AUDIT 9-4

4. SCOPE OF THE DATA INTEGRITY AUDIT 9-4
   o Reliability of the Data Source 9-5
   o Source Data Preparation 9-5
   o Data Entry Control 9-6
   o Data Input Acceptance Control 9-6
   o Data Validation and Error Correction 9-6
   o Processing Specification 9-7
   o Output Controls and Distribution Procedures . . . 9-7
   o Auditability 9-7

5. APPROACH TO A DATA INTEGRITY AUDIT 9-8

6. METHODS FOR DATA INTEGRITY AUDITING 9-9
   o Confirmation 9-9
   o Sampling Techniques 9-9
   o Parallel Processing 9-10
   o Integrated Test Facility (ITF) 9-10
   o System Control Audit Review Files (SCARF) 9-10
   o Tracing 9-10
   o Observation 9-10
   o Analysis by Interrogation of Existing Data 9-10
   o Test Decks or Test Data 9-10
   o Interviews 9-11
   o Program Source Code Review 9-11
   o Questionnaires 9-11
   o Code Analysis and Mapping 9-11
   o Automatic Flowcharting Software 9-11
   o Procedural Walk-throughs 9-11
   o Undercover Observations 9-12
   o Surprise Visits 9-12
   o Analysis of System Activity Logs 9-12
   o Continuous Monitoring and Surveillance Software . . . 9-12

xiii

COBIT

Developed in 1996, Control Objectives for Information and Related Technologies (now known as COBIT) is an IT management framework developed by the IT Governance Institute and ISACA. COBIT has four domains: Plan and Organize, Acquire and Implement, Deliver and Support, and Monitor and Evaluate. As of this writing, COBIT 2019 is the latest version.

COBIT is not primarily a security control framework but an IT process framework that includes security processes interspersed throughout the framework. COBIT contains 37 processes. The security- and risk-related processes are as follows:

- Ensure risk optimization.
- Manage risk.
- Manage security.
- Manage security resources.
- Monitor, evaluate, and assess compliance with external requirements.

A framework of security controls can be derived from these security- and risk-related processes as a starting point.

COBIT is available from www.isaca.org/COBIT/Pages/Product-Family.aspx (registration and payment required).

ITIL / ISO/IEC 20000

ITIL is a framework of IT service delivery and management processes. The U.K. Office of Government Commerce originally developed ITIL to improve its IT management processes. The international standard, ISO/IEC 20000 ("Information technology — Service management — Part 1: Service management system requirements"), is adapted from ITIL.

ITIL is not a security framework but a process framework for IT service management. However, it is often said that an organization will have difficulty building a successful information security program with effective controls in the absence of a service management framework such as ITIL.

One of the pillars of ITIL is security management, which is fully described in the standard ISO/IEC 27001, discussed in Chapter 2.

ITIL is available from www.axelos.com/best-practice-solutions/itil (registration and payment required).

ISO/IEC 27002

ISO/IEC 27002, "Information technology — Security techniques — Code of practice for information security controls," is an international standard controls framework. The controls in ISO/IEC 27002 are fully explained, including implementation guidance. These controls are listed in the appendix of ISO/IEC 27001 but lack any explanation or background.

ISO/IEC 27002 is available from www.iso.org/standard/54533.html (registration and payment required).

 NOTE ISO/IEC 27002 is comparable to NIST SP 800-53 but is not as widely used because of its cost.

HIPAA

The U.S. Health Insurance Portability and Accountability Act established requirements for protecting electronic protected health information (ePHI). These requirements apply to virtually every corporate or government entity (known as a *covered entity*) that stores or processes ePHI. HIPAA requirements fall into three main categories:

- Administrative safeguards
- Physical safeguards
- Technical safeguards

Several controls reside within each of these three categories. Each control is labeled as Required or Addressable. Every covered entity must implement controls that are labeled as Required. Controls labeled as Addressable are considered optional in each covered entity, meaning the organization does not have to implement an Addressable control if it does not apply or if there is negligible risk if the control is not implemented.

A copy of HIPAA is available to view from www.gpo.gov/fdsys/pkg/CRPT-104hrpt736/pdf/CRPT-104hrpt736.pdf.

NIST SP 800-53

Developed by the U.S. National Institute for Standards and Technology, NIST Special Publication (SP) 800-53, "Security and Privacy Controls for Federal Information Systems and Organizations," is one of the most well-known and adopted security control frameworks. NIST SP 800-53 is required for all U.S. government information systems and all information systems in private industry that store or process information on behalf of the federal government.

NIST SP 800-53 controls are organized into 18 categories:

- Access control
- Awareness and training
- Audit and accountability
- Security assessment and authorization
- Configuration management
- Contingency planning
- Identification and authentication
- Incident response
- Maintenance
- Media protection
- Physical and environmental protection
- Planning
- Personnel security
- Risk assessment
- System and services acquisition
- System and communications protection
- System and information integrity
- Program management

Even though the NIST 800-53 control framework is required for federal information systems, many organizations that are not required to employ the framework have used it, primarily because it is a high-quality control framework with in-depth implementation guidance and also because it is available without cost.

NIST SP 800-53 is available from csrc.nist.gov/publications/detail/sp/800-53/rev-5/final.

NIST SP 800-171

NIST SP 800-171, "Protecting Controlled Unclassified Information in Nonfederal Systems and Organizations," is a framework of requirements for the protection of controlled unclassified information (CUI). This framework is required for all information systems in private industry that store or process CUI on behalf of any federal government agency.

NIST SP 800-171 is organized into 13 categories:

- Access control
- Awareness and training
- Audit and accountability
- Configuration management
- Identification and authentication
- Incident response
- Maintenance
- Media protection
- Personnel security
- Physical protection
- Risk assessment
- Security assessment
- System and communications protection

The Cybersecurity Maturity Model Certification (CMMC) is a framework of assessments and assessor certifications used to enforce compliance to NIST SP 800-171 by contractors providing services to the U.S. defense industrial base. More information about CMMC is available from www.acq.osd.mil/cmmc/. More information about CMMC assessments and assessors is available at https://cyberab.org/.

NIST Cybersecurity Framework

The NIST CSF is a risk-based life-cycle methodology for assessing risk, enacting controls, and measuring control effectiveness that is not unlike ISO/IEC 27001. The components of the NIST CSF are as follows:

- **Framework Core**   These are a set of functions—Identify, Protect, Detect, Respond, Recover—that make up the life cycle of high-level functions in an information security program. The Framework Core includes a complete set of controls (known as references) within the four activities.

- **Framework Implementation Tiers**   These are maturity levels, from least mature to most mature: Partial, Risk Informed, Repeatable, Adaptive.

- **Framework Profile**   This aligns elements of the Framework Core (the functions, categories, subcategories, and references) with an organization's business requirements, risk tolerance, and available resources.

Organizations implementing the NIST CSF would first perform an assessment by measuring the maturity (Implementation Tiers) for each activity in the Framework Core. Next, the organization would determine desired maturity levels for each activity in the Framework Core. The identified differences are considered gaps that need to be filled through several means, including the following:

- Hiring additional resources
- Training resources
- Adding or changing business processes or procedures
- Changing system or device configuration
- Acquiring new systems or devices

The NIST CSF can be used as the foundation for a controls framework. Table 2 of Version 1.1 of the CSF maps its Framework Core to CIS CSC, COBIT 2019, ISA 62443, ISO/IEC 27001, and NIST SP 800-53.

The NIST CSF is available from www.nist.gov/cyberframework.

Center for Internet Security Critical Security Controls

The Critical Security Controls framework from the Center for Internet Security (CIS CSC) is a well-known control framework that traces its lineage back to the SANS organization. Despite having 18 sections, the framework is still commonly referred to as the "SANS 20" or "SANS 20 Critical Security Controls."

The CIS CSC control categories are as follows:

- Inventory and Control of Enterprise Assets
- Inventory and Control of Software Assets
- Data Protection
- Secure Configuration of Enterprise Assets and Software
- Account Management
- Access Control Management
- Continuous Vulnerability Management
- Audit Log Management
- Email and Web Browser Protections
- Malware Defenses
- Data Recovery
- Network Infrastructure Management
- Network Monitoring and Defense
- Security Awareness and Skills Training
- Service Provider Management

- Application Software Security
- Incident Response Management
- Penetration Testing

The CIS CSC controls are available from www.cisecurity.org/controls (registration required). The CIS CSC controls are also published by the European Telecommunications Standards Institute (ETSI) as ETSI TR 103 305-1 V4.1.2, available at https://ipr.etsi.org/.

PCI DSS

The Payment Card Industry Data Security Standard is a control framework specifically for protecting credit card numbers and related information when stored, processed, and transmitted on an organization's networks. The PCI DSS was developed in 2004 by the PCI Standards Council, a consortium of the world's dominant credit card brands—namely, Visa, MasterCard, American Express, Discover, and JCB.

The PCI DSS has 12 control objectives:

- Install and maintain a firewall configuration to protect cardholder data.
- Do not use vendor-supplied defaults for system passwords and other security parameters.
- Protect stored cardholder data.
- Encrypt transmission of cardholder data across open, public networks.
- Protect all systems against malware and regularly update antivirus software or programs.
- Develop and maintain secure systems and applications.
- Restrict access to cardholder data by business need to know.
- Identify and authenticate access to system components.
- Restrict physical access to cardholder data.
- Track and monitor all access to network resources and cardholder data.
- Regularly test security systems and processes.
- Maintain a policy that addresses information security for all personnel.

PCI DSS is mandatory for all organizations storing, processing, or transmitting credit card data. Organizations with high volumes of card data are required to undergo annual on-site audits. Many organizations use the controls and the principles in PCI DSS to protect other types of financial, medical, and personal data, such as account numbers, social insurance numbers, and dates of birth.

PCI DSS is available from www.pcisecuritystandards.org/ (registration and license agreement required).

PART III

Information Security Management Frameworks

Information security management frameworks are business process models that include essential processes and activities needed by most organizations. These frameworks are risk-centric because the identification of risk is a key driver for activities in other parts of the framework to reduce risk to acceptable levels.

Following are the four most popular security management frameworks:

- **ISO/IEC 27001:2013**   The well-known international standard ISO/IEC 27001, "Information technology – Security techniques – Information security management systems – Requirements," defines the requirements and steps taken to run an information security management system (ISMS), which is the set of processes used to assess risk, develop policy and controls, and manage all of the typical processes found in information security programs such as vulnerability management and incident management. ISO/IEC 27001 is described fully in Chapter 3.

- **COBIT 2019**   Developed by ISACA, COBIT 2019 is a controls and governance framework for managing an IT organization. COBIT 2019 for Information Security is an additional standard that extends the view of COBIT 2019 and explains each component of the framework from an information security perspective.

- **NIST CSF**   NIST developed the CSF in 2014 to address the rampant occurrence of security breaches and identity theft in the United States. The NIST CSF is an outcomes-based security management and control framework that guides an organization in understanding its maturity levels, assessing risk, identifying gaps, and developing action plans for strategic improvement.

- **ETSI CYBER**   ETSI has developed and published "CYBER; Cybersecurity for SMEs; Part 1: Cybersecurity Standardization Essentials," which describes a top-down approach to developing and managing cybersecurity programs, similar to and partly derived from ISO/IEC 27001 and NIST CSF.

NOTE   Security management frameworks are distinct from control frameworks. Security management frameworks describe the overall activities in an information security program, whereas control frameworks are collections of security controls.

Information Security Architecture

Enterprise architecture (EA) is a business function and a technical model. In terms of a business function, establishing an EA consists of activities that ensure IT systems meet important business needs. The EA may also involve the construction of a model that is used to map business functions into the IT environment and IT systems in increasing levels of detail so that IT professionals can more easily understand the organization's technology architecture at any level.

Information security architecture can be thought of as a subset or special topic within EA that is concerned with the protective characteristics found in many components in an overall EA and specific components in an EA that provide preventive or detective security functions.

The EA and enterprise security architectures serve the following purposes:

- All hardware and software components fulfill a stated specific business purpose.

- All components work well together.

- There is overall structure and consistency in infrastructure throughout the organization.

- Infrastructure resources are used efficiently.

- Infrastructure is scalable and flexible.

- Existing elements can be upgraded as needed.

- Additional elements can be added as needed.

Information security architecture exists in two main layers in an organization:

- **Policy**   At this level, security policy defines the necessary characteristics of the overall environment and some characteristics of individual components. For example, policy will dictate the existence of centralized authentication and endpoint-based web filtering.

- **Standards**   This level includes several types of standards, including vendor standards (that state the makes and models of hardware and software that will be used), protocol standards (that state the network protocols that will be used), algorithm standards (for encryption and message digests), configuration or hardening standards (that define the detailed configuration of different types of systems, devices, and programs), and reference architectures.

Modern information security architecture makes broad use of centralized functions and services that operate more efficiently and effectively than isolated, local instances. Centralized functions and services help amplify the workforce so that a relatively small staff can effectively manage hundreds or even thousands of devices. These functions and services include but are not limited to the following:

- **Authentication**   Organizations make use of centralized identity and access management services such as Microsoft Active Directory (AD) and Lightweight Directory Access Protocol (LDAP) so that users' identities, authentication, access controls, and authorization exist on a single, central service, as opposed to existing on individual systems and devices.

- **Encryption key management**   Organizations can implement centralized certificate authorities (CAs) and key stores for more effective management of encryption keys.

- **Monitoring**   Organizations can implement centralized monitoring for operational and security purposes to observe at a central management console the events occurring on systems and devices at all locations.

- **Device management**   Organizations can implement tools to manage large numbers of similar devices such as servers, workstations, mobile devices, and network devices. Central device management helps make the configuration of systems and devices more consistent.

- **Software development**   Organizations whose mission includes developing and delivering software products often develop a formal architecture describing the end-to-end software development environment, including IDEs, source code structure, software build, security testing, regression testing, and defect management.

This book discusses two frameworks for enterprise architecture: TOGAF and the Zachman Framework. Note that these are EA models, not enterprise security architecture models. TOGAF and Zachman are described fully in Chapter 2.

Information Security Policies, Procedures, and Guidelines

Information security policies, standards, guidelines, and procedures are the written artifacts that define the business and technical rules for information and information systems protection. These artifacts enable intentionality and consistency of approach, representing a higher level of maturity than would exist if safeguards were implemented in an ad hoc fashion.

NOTE   The risk management process is a primary driver for changes to policies, standards, guidelines, and procedures.

Policy Development

Security policy development is foundational of any organization's information security program. Information security policy defines the principles and required actions for the organization to protect its assets and personnel properly.

The audience for security policy is the organization's personnel—not only its full-time and part-time employees, but also its temporary workers, including contractors and consultants. Security policy must be easily accessible by all personnel so that they can never offer ignorance as an excuse for violating policy. To this point, many organizations require all personnel to acknowledge the existence of, and their understanding of, the organization's security policy at the time of hire and periodically (usually annually) thereafter.

Considerations

Security policy cannot be developed in a vacuum. Instead, it needs to align with some internal and external factors. The development of policy needs to incorporate several considerations, including the following:

- Applicable laws, regulations, standards, and other legal obligations
- Risk tolerance
- Controls
- Organizational culture

Alignment with Controls

Security policy and controls need to be in alignment. This is not to say that there must be a control for every policy or a policy for every control, but policies and controls must not contradict each other. For example, suppose a control states that no personally owned mobile devices may connect to internal networks. In that case, the policy cannot state that those devices may be used, provided no corporate information is stored on them. It also makes sense for the structure of policies and controls to resemble one another. This alignment makes it easier for personnel to become familiar with the structure and content of policies and controls.

Alignment with the Audience

Security policy needs to align with the audience. In most organizations, this means that policy statements need to be understood by most workers. A common mistake in developing security policy is the inclusion of highly technical policies such as permitted encryption algorithms or statements about the hardening of servers. Such topics are irrelevant to most workers; the danger of including policies that are irrelevant to most workers is that they are likely to "tune out" and not pay attention to those policies that *do* apply to them. In other words, security policy should have a high signal-to-noise ratio.

In organizations with extensive uses of technology, one avenue is to create a general security policy intended for all workers (technical and nontechnical) and a separate policy for technical workers who design, build, and maintain information systems. Another alternative is to create a general security policy for all workers that states that all controls are mandatory. Either approach would be sufficient by aligning messages about policy with various audiences.

Security Policy Structure

Security policy structure comprises several different topics that may include the following:

- Acceptable use of organization assets
- Mobile devices
- Protection of information and assets
- Access control and passwords

PART III

- Personally owned devices
- Connected devices (such as IoT)
- Vulnerability management
- Security monitoring and incident response
- E-mail and other communications
- Social media
- Ethics and applicable laws
- Workplace safety
- Visitors
- Consequences of noncompliance
- Cloud computing
- Data (and system, facilities, and personnel) classification
- Encryption
- Third-party risk management
- Data exchange with third parties
- Privacy
- Compliance with applicable laws and regulations

Security managers can choose how to package these and other security policies. For example, they may exist in separate documents or together in one document. There is no right or wrong method; instead, a security manager should determine what would work best in the organization by observing how other policies are structured, published, and consumed.

Security policy statements should be general and not cite specific devices, technologies, algorithms, or configurations. Policy statements should state *what* is to be done (or not done) but not *how*. This way, security policies will be durable and will need to be changed infrequently. On the other hand, security standards and procedures may change more frequently as practices, techniques, and technologies change.

Policy Distribution and Acknowledgment

Security policy—indeed, all organization policy—should be well known and easily accessible by all workers. For example, it may be published on a corporate intranet or other online location where workers go to obtain information about internal operations.

All workers need to be informed of the presence of the organization's security policy. The best method in most organizations is for a high-ranking executive to write a memo or an e-mail to all workers stating the importance of information security in the organization and informing them that the information security policy describes required behavior for all workers. Another effective tactic is to have the senior executive record a message outlining the need and importance of security policy. Additionally, the message should state that the executive leadership team has reviewed and fully supports the policies.

Executives need to be mindful that they lead by example. If executives are seen to carve out exceptions for themselves (for example, if an executive insists on using a personal tablet computer for company business when policy forbids it), other workers are apt to notice and take shortcuts wherever they're able. If executives work to comply visibly with security policy, others will too. Organizational culture includes behavior such as compliance with policy or a tendency for workers to skirt policy whenever possible.

Standards

It is said that policy states *what to do,* whereas standards describe *how to do it* or *what to do it with.* Like policies, standards should be written down, periodically examined and updated, approved by management, and published so all personnel can find them.

The topic of standards development is discussed in greater detail in Chapter 2.

Guidelines

Guidelines are nonbinding statements or narratives that provide additional direction to personnel regarding compliance with security policies, standards, and controls. Information security departments often develop guidelines when they receive numerous inquiries for help understanding certain policies or have trouble understanding how to implement them.

Guidelines can be written as separate documents resembling whitepapers or how-to guides, or they may be interspersed within policy or control documents. ISO/IEC 27002 is an excellent example of guidance included with each control in individual sections entitled "guidance."

Requirements

Requirements are formal statements that describe the characteristics of a system that is to be changed, developed, or acquired. Requirements should flow from, and align with, the structure and content of policies and standards. Because of their use in systems and services development and acquisition, requirements should be published in a format that can be easily extracted for use in specific projects.

Organizations should have a standard set of general requirements that apply to all technologies and environments. Then, additional specific requirements should be developed that focus on each specific project or initiative.

Requirements must be specific and verifiable. Any ambiguities should be resolved, so that all parties involved have a clear understanding of each requirement. Further, requirements should become the basis for a *test plan,* a step-by-step procedure for verifying that a system, service, or process complies with all applicable requirements.

It is unlikely that all requirements will be satisfied in large, complex projects. Thus, project managers and subject matter experts should prioritize requirements to distinguish those considered "must-have" versus those that are "nice to have." Further, each bespoke requirement that is not a part of the organization's standard requirements should be traceable to the person or group that requested it be included. If there are questions later in the project about a specific requirement, the project team can easily know who wrote and included the requirement. Those individuals can answer any questions about the requirement to help others better understand it.

Some organizations distinguish *functional requirements* from *nonfunctional requirements*. Functional requirements describe the required actions and functions of a system. Example functional requirements include the following:

- In the password reset function, the system must provide visual information indicating the strength of the proposed new password.
- After five minutes of inactivity, the system must invoke an automatic lock and require the user to reauthenticate to continue work.

On the other hand, a nonfunctional requirement describes the required characteristics of a system, service, or process in terms of its components, structure, or architecture. Example nonfunctional requirements include the following:

- The system must not contain comments, symbol tables, or other human-readable information in its machine-readable state.
- The system must use Microsoft SQL Server as its relational database management system.

Functional and nonfunctional requirements can further be distinguished in this way: nonfunctional requirements define what a system is supposed to *be,* whereas functional requirements define what a system is supposed to *do*. Arguably, some functional versus nonfunctional requirements may be more difficult to distinguish; for instance, requiring that a system include a specific encryption algorithm could be considered a nonfunctional requirement, whereas requiring a system to encrypt data using a specific algorithm could be considered a functional requirement. It matters little whether such requirements are called functional or nonfunctional, however; rather, requirements should be consistent in language and tone to ensure that working with them is not a difficulty in itself.

Processes and Procedures

Processes and procedures are the detailed, sequenced instructions used to complete routine tasks. A *process* is a collection of one or more procedures that together fulfill a higher purpose, while a *procedure* is a written set of instructions for a single task.

Organizations often document processes and procedures to ensure consistency and compliance with individual policies and controls. Written processes and procedures are a cornerstone for audits of policies and controls. Their existence signals higher maturity and (the hope of) greater consistency in routine operations. Auditors generally regard process and procedure documents as outdated and invalid if they have not been reviewed for more than one year.

Policies, standards, and controls are generally developed and maintained by an information security program, whereas processes and procedures are developed and maintained by the business departments that perform them.

Information Security Program Metrics

A *metric* is a measurement of a periodic or ongoing activity intended to help management understand the activity within the context of overall business operations. In short, metrics are the means through which management can measure key processes and know whether their strategies are working. Metrics are used in many operational processes, but this section emphasizes metrics related to security governance. In other words, there is a distinction between tactical IT security metrics and those that reveal the state of the overall security program. The two are often related, however, as discussed in the sidebar "Return on Security Investment," later in this chapter.

Security metrics are often used to observe technical IT security controls and processes and determine whether they are operating properly. This helps management better understand the impact of past decisions and can help drive future decisions. Examples of technical metrics include the following:

- **Firewall metrics**   Number and types of rules triggered
- **Intrusion detection/prevention system (IDPS) metrics**   Number and types of incidents detected or blocked, and targeted systems
- **Antimalware metrics**   Number and types of malware blocked, and targeted systems
- **Other security system metrics**   Measurements from DLP systems, web content filtering systems, CASB systems, and so on

While useful, these metrics do not address the bigger picture of the effectiveness or alignment of an organization's overall security program. They do not answer key questions that boards of directors and executive management often ask, such as the following:

- How much security is enough?
- How should security resources be invested and applied?
- What is the potential impact of a threat event?

These and other business-related questions can be addressed through the appropriate metrics, as addressed in the remainder of this section.

Security strategists sometimes think about metrics in simple categorization, such as the following:

- **Key risk indicators (KRIs)**   Metrics associated with risk measurement
- **Key goal indicators (KGIs)**   Metrics that portray the attainment of strategic goals
- **Key performance indicators (KPIs)**   Metrics that show the efficiency or effectiveness of security-related activities

Monitoring

In the overall information security program, *monitoring* is the continuous or regular evaluation of a system or control to determine its operation or effectiveness. Monitoring generally includes two activities:

- Management's review of certain qualitative aspects of an information security program or the entire program. This may take the form of an executive briefing delivered by the security manager.
- Management's review of key metrics in the information security program to understand its effectiveness, efficiency, and performance.

Effective Metrics

For metrics to be effective, they need to be measurable. A common way to ensure the quality and effectiveness of a metric is to use the SMART method. A SMART metric is

- Specific
- Measurable
- Attainable
- Relevant
- Timely

Additional considerations for good metrics, according to *Risk Metrics That Influence Business Decisions* by Paul Proctor (Gartner, Inc., 2016), include the following:

- **Leading indicator**   Does the metric help management predict future risk?
- **Causal relationship**   Does the metric have a defensible causal relationship to a business impact, where a change in the metric compels someone to act?
- **Influence**   Has the metric influenced decision-making (or will it)?

You can find more information about the development of metrics in NIST SP 800-55 Revision 1, "Performance Measurement Guide for Information Security," available from https://csrc.nist.gov/publications/detail/sp/800-55/rev-1/final.

Strategic Alignment

For a security program to be successful, it must align with the organization's mission, strategy, goals, and objectives. A security program strategy and objectives should contain statements that can be translated into key measurements—the program's key performance and risk metrics.

Consider an example. The fictitious organization CareerSearchCo, which is in the online career search and recruiting business, has the following as its mission statement:

Be the best marketplace for job seekers and recruiters

Here are its most recent strategic objectives:

Integrate with leading business social network LinkedIn
Develop an API to facilitate long-term transformation into a leading career and recruiting platform

To meet these objectives, CareerSearchCo has developed a security strategy that includes the following:

Ensure Internet-facing applications are secure through developer training and application vulnerability testing

Security and metrics would then include these:

Percentage of software developers not yet trained
Number of critical vulnerabilities identified
Time to remediate critical and high vulnerabilities

Based on these criteria, these metrics are all measurable, all align with the security strategy, and are all leading indicators. If the metrics trend in an unfavorable direction, this could indicate that a breach is more likely to occur that would damage CareerSearchCo's reputation and ability to earn new business contracts from large corporations.

Types of Metrics

Many activities and events in an information security program and its controls can be measured. These measurements can be depicted in various ways, depending upon the story being told. When building and improving an information security program, security managers need to understand that no single metrics framework will meet every identified goal.

Compliance

Compliance metrics are measures of key controls related to requirements in regulations, legal contracts, or internal objectives. Compliance metrics depict the level of conformance to these requirements. Organizations need to understand the business context of compliance metrics, including the consequences of noncompliance. Security managers need to consider the tolerance for noncompliance with each metric, including the organization's willingness and ability to initiate corrective action when noncompliant activities occur.

Convergence

Larger organizations with multiple business units, geographic locations, or security functions (which can often result from mergers and acquisitions) may experience issues related to overlapping or underlapping coverage or activities. For instance, an organization that recently acquired another company may have some duplication of effort in the asset management and risk management functions. In another example, local security personnel in a large, distributed organization may be performing security functions that are also being performed on their behalf by other personnel at headquarters.

Metrics in the convergence category will be highly individualized, based on specific circumstances in an organization. Some of the categories of metrics include the following:

- Gaps in asset coverage

- Overlaps in asset coverage

- Consolidation of licenses for security tools

- Gaps or overlaps in skills, responsibilities, or coverage

Value Delivery

Metrics on value delivery focus on the long-term reduction in costs, in proportion to other measures. Examples of value delivery metrics include the following:

- Controls used (seldom used controls may be candidates for removal)

- Percentage of controls that are effective (ineffective controls consume additional resources in audit, analysis, and remediation activities)

- Program costs per asset population or asset value

- Program costs per employee population

- Program costs per revenue

Organizations are cautioned against using only value delivery metrics; doing so will risk the security program spiraling down to nothing, since a program that costs nothing will produce the best possible metric in this case.

Resource Management

Resource management metrics are similar to value delivery metrics; both convey an efficient use of resources in an organization's information security program. But because the emphasis here is program efficiency, these are areas where resource management metrics may be developed:

- Standardization of security-related processes (because consistency drives costs down)

- Security involvement in every procurement and acquisition project

- Percentage of assets protected by security controls

Organizational Awareness

Organizational awareness metrics help management understand the number of workers who understand security policies and requirements. Typical metrics in organizational awareness include the following:

- Percentage of employees who complete security training

- Percentage of employees who acknowledge awareness of, and conformance to, security policies
- Average scores on quizzes and tests of knowledge of security safeguards

Operational Productivity

Operational productivity metrics show how efficiently internal staff is used to perform essential functions. Productivity metrics can help build business cases for the automation of routine tasks. Example productivity metrics include the following:

- Number of hours required to perform a segregation of duties review
- Number of hours required to perform a vulnerability assessment
- Number of hours required to perform a risk assessment

Organizational Support

Organizational support metrics show the degree of support for organizational objectives. Arguably, this is a subjective metric, because it can be difficult to produce meaningful measurements. Though it is possible to show the achievement of key objectives, measuring the degree of support that led to their achievement may be difficult: Was an achievement the result of a determined few or the whole organization?

Often, organizational support metrics take the form of project and program dashboards for projects and programs that support the achievement of organizational objectives. However, failure to complete a project on time is not necessarily an indication of support or the lack thereof but may reflect unanticipated obstacles or changes in project scope.

Risk Management

Effective risk management is the culmination of the highest-order activities in an information security program; these include risk analyses, a risk ledger, formal risk treatment, and adjustments to the suite of security controls.

While it is difficult to measure the success of a risk management program effectively and objectively, it is possible to take indirect measurements—much like measuring the shadow of a tree to gauge its height. Thus, the best indicators of a successful risk management program would be improving trends in metrics involved with the following:

- Reduction in the number of security incidents
- Reduction in the impact of security incidents
- Reduction in the time to remediate security incidents
- Reduction in the time to remediate vulnerabilities
- Reduction in the number of new unmitigated risks

Regarding the previous mention of the reduction of security incidents, a security program improving its maturity from low levels should first expect to see the number of incidents increase. This would be not because of lapses in security controls but because

PART III

of the development of—and improvements in—mechanisms used to detect and report security incidents. Similarly, as a security program is improved and matures over time, the number of new risks will, at first, increase and then later decrease.

Technical Security Architecture

Technical security architecture metrics are typically the numbers of events that occur in automated systems such as firewalls, IDPSs, DLP systems, spam filters, and antimalware systems. This is generally the richest set of metrics data available to a security manager and a category of metrics often presented without proper business context. For example, the number of attacks blocked by a firewall or the number of malware infections blocked by antimalware software may have operational meaning, but these will mean nothing to management. Executives would be right to ask whether an increase in blocked attacks is good, bad, or meaningless.

There are, however, some metrics available that have meaning for business executives. Examples include the following:

- Percentage of employees who responded to (clicked links or opened attachments) e-mail attacks
- Number of attacks that bypassed network controls such as firewalls, IDPSs, and web filters, which resulted in unscheduled downtime
- Number of malware attacks that circumvented antimalware controls and resulted in unscheduled downtime
- Number of brute-force password attacks that were blocked
- Number of records compromised that required disclosure

Operational Performance

Operational performance metrics generally show how well personnel are performing critical security functions. Processes measured by these metrics need to have sufficiently detailed business records so that metrics can be objectively measured. These are some examples of operational performance metrics:

- Elapsed time between the onset of a security incident and incident declaration
- Elapsed time between the declaration of an incident and its containment
- Elapsed time between publication of a critical vulnerability and its discovery in the organization's systems
- Percentage of critical systems not patched with critical patches within the service level agreement (SLA)
- Number of changes made without change control board approval
- Amount of unscheduled downtime of critical systems for security-related reasons

Security Cost Efficiency

Metrics related to security cost efficiency measure the resources required for key controls. Security managers need to be careful with cost efficiency metrics, as demands for improvement (such as reduced costs) over time can increase risk. This is compounded by the fact that it is relatively easy to measure cost, whereas risk measurement is more subjective and qualitative.

Example cost efficiency metrics include the following:

- Cost of antimalware controls per user
- Cost of anti-phishing and antispam controls per user
- Cost of centralized network defenses, such as firewalls, per user

Security managers should consider including staff and tool costs to provide a more complete and accurate picture of the total costs for controls.

Audiences

As mentioned, when building or improving a metrics program, security managers need to consider the purpose of any particular metric and the audience to whom it is sent. A common mistake made by security managers is the publication of metrics to various audiences without first understanding whether any individual metric will have meaning to any particular audience. For example, a metric showing the number of packets dropped by a firewall will probably have no meaning to a member of the organization's board of directors—nor would a trend of this metric have any meaning. Security managers need to determine what metrics are important for various audiences and purposes and then proceed to develop those metrics.

Some metrics will have only operational value, while others can be successfully transformed into a management or strategic metric when portrayed in context. For example, a metric on the number of malware attacks has no business context; however, a metric showing successful malware attacks that result in business disruptions have far more meaning to management. A metric on patch management SLAs by itself has no business context, but if that were transformed into a metric showing that critical systems not patched within SLAs resulted in higher than desired business risk, the metric would have meaning to executive audiences.

Although there may be value in automated systems that keep records that can be examined or measured later, there is often little point in developing metrics with no audience in mind. Such a pursuit would merely take time away from more valuable activities.

Return on Security Investment

An ongoing debate has been raging for years on the return on investment (ROI) of information security safeguards, known as *return on security investment,* also known as *ROSI* (pronounced "rosy"). The problem with investments in information security is that significant events such as highly impactful security attacks are infrequent (occurring far less than once per year for many organizations). Therefore, investments in information security controls may not have a noticeable effect.

(continued)

If there were no break-ins prior to implementing new security systems and no break-ins afterward, an organization's management may well question whether the investment in new security systems was warranted. Could the resources spent on security systems have been better spent in other ways to increase service delivery capacity or production efficiency, resulting in increased revenues or profits? Additionally, if a security investment is made (for example, in security monitoring and vulnerability management solutions), it may uncover new risks previously unknown to the organization. So, the ROI is diminished, but the benefit is that a previously unknown risk was identified.

It is easier to compute ROSI for events that occur more frequently. For example, laptops and mobile devices are frequently lost and stolen in many organizations, so investments in security controls of various types have a more obvious benefit. However, security managers should keep in mind that ROSI is only one of several means that help justify the expenditure of resources on security capabilities. Other means include the following:

- **Fiduciary responsibility**   Many types of security controls are considered part of an organization's fiduciary responsibility to implement, regardless of the organization's actual history of related incidents.

- **Regulation**   Some security controls are required by applicable regulations such as HIPAA, the Canadian Personal Information Protection and Electronic Documents Act (PIPEDA), and PCI DSS.

- **Competitive differentiation**   In many industries, organizations that compete for business include claims of superior security controls as part of their marketing messages.

Security managers, of course, need to employ appropriate means for justifying or explaining security expenditures in various situations.

The Security Balanced Scorecard

The balanced scorecard (BSC) is a management tool used to measure an organization's performance and effectiveness. The BSC is used to determine how well an organization can fulfill its mission and strategic objectives and how well it is aligned with overall organizational objectives. In the BSC, management defines key measurements in each of four perspectives:

- **Financial**   Key financial items measured include the cost of strategic initiatives, support costs of key applications, and capital investment.

- **Customer**   Key measurements include the satisfaction rate with various customer-facing aspects of the organization.

	Financial	Customer	Internal Processes	Innovation and Learning
Awareness and Education	Lower cost of incidents	Increase confidence	Improve processes	Improve awareness
Access Control	Control access	Provide access	Ensure proper access	Improve communication
Vulnerability Management	Reduce vulnerabilities	Protect against vulnerabilities	Manage risks	Learn from incidents
Business Continuity	Ensure continuity	Provide core services	Test continuity	Ensure awareness
Compliance	Comply with regulations	Ensure compliance	Ensure compliance	Review compliance
Program Management	Ensure efficiency	Include customer input	Reduce reactive processes	Continue improvement

Table 5-2   Security Balanced Scorecard Domains

- **Internal processes**   Measurements of key activities include the number of projects and the effectiveness of key internal workings of the organization.
- **Innovation and learning**   Human-oriented measurements include turnover, illness, internal promotions, and training.

Each organization's BSC will represent a unique set of measurements that reflects the organization's type of business, business model, and management style.

The BSC should be used to measure overall organizational effectiveness and progress. A similar scorecard, the security-BSC, can specifically measure security organization performance and results. Like the BSC, the security-BSC has the same four perspectives, mapped to key activities, as depicted in Table 5-2.

The security-BSC should flow directly from the organization's overall security-BSC and its IT-BSC. This will ensure that security will align itself with corporate objectives. While the perspectives between the overall BSC and the security-BSC vary, the approach for each is similar, and the results for the security-BSC can "roll up" to the organization's overall BSC.

Chapter Review

An information security program is a collection of activities used to identify, communicate, and address risks. The security program consists of controls, processes, and practices to increase the resilience of the computing environment and ensure that risks are known and handled effectively.

A charter is a formal, written definition of the objectives of a program, its main timelines, the sources of funding, the names of its principal leaders and managers, and the business executives sponsoring the program.

Information security programs include numerous business processes to fulfill the overall mission of information and information systems protection. These processes fall into three major categories: risk and compliance, architecture, and operations.

Modern information security includes essential business processes such as risk and policy management, but overall it is also heavily involved in IT. After all, information security's mission is the protection of all things IT. To scale with the power and speed of IT, information security has its own portfolio of protective and detective technologies.

Assets are the things of value that an organization protects in an information security program. In a typical organization, assets will consist of information and the information systems that support and protect those information assets.

Asset classification is an activity whereby an organization assigns an asset to a category representing usage or risk. In an information security program, the purpose of asset classification is to determine, for each asset, its level of criticality to the organization.

Information classification is a process whereby different sets and collections of data in an organization are analyzed for various types of value, criticality, integrity, and sensitivity. Most organizations store information that falls into all of these categories, with degrees of importance within them. These levels of information, together with examples of the types of levels that fall into each category and with instructions on handling information at each level, form the heart of a typical information classification program.

Once an organization is satisfied that its information classification is in order, it can embark on system classification. Like various types of information assets, information systems also can be classified according to various security and operational criteria.

In some organizations, additional requirements are imposed on persons who have access to particularly sensitive information. Whether this information consists of trade secrets, government secrets, or other information, organizations may be required to meet specific requirements such as more thorough or frequent background investigations.

A key part of a risk assessment is identifying the value of an asset. Because risk analysis is often qualitative, establishing asset valuation in qualitative terms is common. Instead of assigning a dollar (or other currency) value to an asset, the value of an asset can be assigned to a low-medium-high scale or a numeric scale such as 1 to 5 or 1 to 10.

Many organizations opt to surpass qualitative asset valuation and assign a dollar (or other currency) valuation to their assets. This is common in larger or more mature organizations that want to better understand the actual costs associated with loss events.

There are several types of frameworks in information security, and sometimes they are confused with one another. The types include control frameworks, risk management frameworks, architecture frameworks, and security program management frameworks.

Standard control frameworks include COBIT 2019, ISO/IEC 20000, ISO/IEC 27002, HIPAA, NIST SP 800-53, NIST SP 800-171, NIST CSF, CIS CSC, ETSI TR 103 305-1, and PCI DSS.

Information security management frameworks are business process models that include essential processes and activities needed by most organizations. These frameworks are risk-centric because the identification of risk is a key driver for activities in other parts of the framework to reduce risk to acceptable levels. These frameworks include ISO/IEC 27005, ISO/IEC 31000, COBIT 2019, NIST SP 800-37, and NIST CSF.

Enterprise architecture (EA) is a business function and a technical model. In terms of a business function, establishing an EA consists of activities that ensure that IT systems meet important business needs.

Information security architecture can be thought of as a subset or special topic within EA that is concerned with the protective characteristics found in many components in an overall EA and specific components in an EA that provide preventive or detective security functions.

Information security policies, standards, guidelines, and procedures are the written artifacts that define the business and technical rules for information and information systems protection.

Security policy development is foundational to any organization's information security program. Information security policy defines the principles and required actions for the organization to protect its assets and personnel properly.

Guidelines are nonbinding statements or narratives that provide additional direction to personnel regarding compliance with security policies, standards, and controls. Information security departments often develop guidelines when they receive numerous inquiries for help understanding certain policies or have trouble understanding how to implement them.

Requirements are formal statements describing the characteristics of a system to be changed, developed, or acquired. Requirements should flow from, and align with, the structure and content of policies and standards. Because of their use in systems and services development and acquisition, requirements should be published in a format that can be easily extracted for use in specific projects.

Processes and procedures are the detailed, sequenced instructions to complete routine tasks. A process is a collection of one or more procedures that together fulfill a higher purpose, while a procedure is a written set of instructions for a single task.

A metric is a measurement of a periodic or ongoing activity that intends to help the organization understand the activity within the context of overall business operations. Metrics are the means through which management can measure key processes and know whether their strategies are working.

A formal metrics program provides qualitative and quantitative data on the effectiveness of many elements of an organization's security program and operations. Metrics can be developed via the SMART method: specific, measurable, attainable, relevant, and timely. Metrics must align with the organization's mission, strategy, and objectives. Some metrics can be used to report on results in the recent past, but some metrics should serve as leading indicators or drive a call to action by the leadership team.

A common shortcoming of a metrics program is its failure to provide relevant metrics for various audiences. For instance, reporting the number of packets dropped by a firewall or the number of viruses detected by antivirus to the board of directors provides little or no value for that audience. As an organization develops its metrics program, it must take care to develop metrics that matter for each audience. A security balanced scorecard can also depict the high-level effectiveness of an organization's security program.

Notes

- Whether or not it carries authority in an organization, a charter's usefulness is derived from its descriptions of an organization's vision, objectives, roles and responsibilities, and processes and procedures. A charter can help personnel come to a common understanding of security programs and other programs.

- The three lines of defense model, used often in banking, is a good model for formally separating and defining roles related to control development, operation, and assurance. A similar model can be used for policy development.

- Asset identification is a cornerstone of any risk management and security management program, yet most organizations do a poor job of it. Asset identification is the first control in the Center for Internet Security Critical Security Controls (CIS CSC), and there is a reason for that.

- Qualitative asset valuation is sufficient for qualitative risk assessments. But when it's necessary to calculate figures such as exposure factor or annual loss expectancy, security managers will need to obtain a quantitative valuation for relevant assets. However, precision is challenging because it is difficult to know the probability of threat events.

- Asset inventory is increasingly difficult to manage successfully because of virtualization and the wide use of cloud-based services.

- Enacting a data classification scheme is easy, but implementing the program is difficult. Data classification should be extended to include system classification (the classification of a system should be the same as the highest classified data stored or processed on the system), asset classification, and even facilities (work center) classification.

- Many organizations ruminate over the selection of a control framework. Instead, the organization should select a framework and then adjust its controls to suit the organization.

- A control framework should generally be considered a starting point, not a rigid and unchanging set of controls—except in cases where regulations stipulate that controls may not be changed.

- At present, because there are no well-known frameworks for information security metrics, it is up to every organization to develop meaningful and applicable metrics for various audiences interested in receiving them.

- The methodology for calculating return on security investment is widely discussed but not widely practiced, mainly because it is difficult to calculate the benefit of security controls designed to detect or prevent infrequent incidents.

Questions

1. An organization's board of directors wants to see quarterly metrics on risk reduction. What would be the best metric to present to the board?

    A. Number of firewall rules triggered

    B. Viruses blocked by antivirus programs

    C. Packets dropped by the firewall

    D. Time to patch vulnerabilities on critical servers

2. Which of the following metrics is the best example of a leading indicator?

    A. Average time to mitigate security incidents

    B. Increase in the number of attacks blocked by the intrusion prevention system

    C. Increase in the number of attacks blocked by the firewall

    D. Percentage of critical servers being patched within service level agreements

3. The primary factor related to the selection of a control framework is:

    A. Industry vertical

    B. Current process maturity level

    C. Size of the organization

    D. Compliance level

4. The purpose of a balanced scorecard is to:

    A. Measure the efficiency of a security organization

    B. Evaluate the performance of individual employees

    C. Benchmark a process in the organization against peer organizations

    D. Measure organizational performance and effectiveness against strategic goals

5. In an organization using PCI DSS as its control framework, the conclusion of a recent risk assessment stipulates that additional controls not present in PCI DSS but present in ISO 27001 should be enacted. What is the best course of action in this situation?

    A. Adopt ISO 27001 as the new control framework.

    B. Retain PCI DSS as the control framework and update process documentation.

    C. Add the required controls to the existing control framework.

    D. Adopt NIST 800-53 as the new control framework.

6. A security manager has developed a scheme that prescribes required methods to protect information at rest, in motion, and in transit. This is known as a(n):

    A. Data classification policy

    B. Asset classification policy

    C. Data loss prevention plan

    D. Asset loss prevention plan

7. A security leader has developed a document that describes a program's mission, vision, roles and responsibilities, and processes. This is known as a:

    A. Policy

    B. Charter

    C. Standard

    D. Control

8. Management in an organization has developed and published a policy that directs the workforce to follow specific steps to protect various types of information. This is known as a:

    A. Privacy policy

    B. Data dictionary

    C. Data classification policy

    D. Data governance policy

9. The security leader in an organization is developing a first-ever data classification policy. What is the best first step in this endeavor?

    A. Develop the classification levels.

    B. Perform a data inventory.

    C. Interview end users.

    D. Develop the handling procedures.

10. A security leader wants to develop a scheme whereby the most important assets are protected more rigorously than those deemed less important. What is the best first step in this endeavor?

    A. Map classified data to systems.

    B. Establish a systems inventory.

    C. Interview end users.

    D. Develop the protection guidelines.

11. A retail organization's security leader wants to develop an ISMS. Which standard is the best resource for the leader to use?

    A. ISO/IEC 27001

    B. ISO/IEC 27002

    C. NIST SP 800-53

    D. PCI DSS

12. An IT worker is reading a security-related document that provides suggestions regarding compliance with a particular policy. What kind of a document is the IT worker reading?

    A. Procedure

    B. Policy

    C. Standard

    D. Guideline

13. An IT worker is reading a security-related document that stipulates which algorithms are to be used to encrypt data at rest. What kind of a document is the IT worker reading?

    A. Procedure

    B. Requirements

    C. Standard

    D. Guideline

14. An IT worker is reading a document that describes the essential characteristics of a system to be developed. What kind of a document is the IT worker reading?

    A. Procedure

    B. Requirements

    C. Standard

    D. Guideline

15. The concept of dividing the management of controls into development, operations, and assurance is known as:

    A. Controls framework

    B. Split custody

    C. Separation of duties

    D. Three lines of defense

Answers

1. **D.** The metric on time to patch critical servers will be the most meaningful metric for the board of directors. While potentially interesting at the operational level, the other metrics do not convey business meaning to board members.

2. **D.** The metric of the percentage of critical servers being patched within SLAs is the best leading indicator because it is a rough predictor of the probability of a future security incident. The other metrics are trailing indicators because they report on past incidents.

3. **A.** The most important factor influencing a decision to select a control framework is the industry vertical. For example, a healthcare organization would likely select HIPAA as its primary control framework, whereas a retail organization may select PCI DSS.

4. **D.** The balanced scorecard is a tool used to quantify an organization's performance against strategic objectives. The focuses of a balanced scorecard are financial, customer, internal processes, and innovation/learning.

5. **C.** An organization that needs to implement new controls should do so within its existing control framework. It is unnecessary to adopt an entirely new control framework when a few controls need to be added.

6. **A.** A data classification policy is a statement that defines two or more classification levels for data, together with procedures and standards for the protection of data at each classification for various use cases such as storage in a database, storage on a laptop computer, transmissions via e-mail, and storage on backup media.

7. **B.** A charter document, which describes many facets of a function or program, best fits this description.

8. **C.** Management has created a data classification policy, which defines classification levels and handling procedures for information in various forms at each level.

9. **B.** The best first step in developing a data classification policy is to develop an inventory of data to understand the various types that are stored in use in the organization.

10. **B.** The best first step is the development of an inventory of systems. After that, the best step is the mapping of information (and its classification) stored or processed by each system.

11. **A.** ISO/IEC 27001, "Information technology – Security techniques – Information security management systems – Requirements," defines all of the high-level characteristics of an information security management system (ISMS). The other answers are control frameworks, which are used to develop and organize controls.

12. **D.** The IT worker is reading a guideline, a document that provides nonbinding guidance regarding compliance with a policy, control, or standard.

13. **C.** The IT worker is reading a standard, a document that stipulates the mandatory use of protocols, algorithms, techniques, products, or suppliers.

14. **B.** The IT worker is reading a requirements document, which describes the required characteristics of a system to be developed or acquired.

15. **D.** The three lines of defense model describes the separate roles in control management as development, operations, and assurance (audit).

Information Security Program Management

In this chapter, you will learn about
- Controls and control design
- Managing controls throughout their life cycle
- Assessing controls to determine effectiveness
- Reducing risk by conducting security awareness training
- Identifying and managing third-party service providers
- Communicating and reporting the state of the security program

This chapter covers Certified Information Security Manager (CISM) Domain 3, "Information Security Program," part B, "Information Security Program Management." The entire Information Security Program domain represents 33 percent of the CISM examination.

Supporting Tasks in the CISM job practice that align with the Information Security Program / Information Security Program Development domain include:

15. Establish, promote, and maintain a program for information security awareness and training.

16. Integrate information security requirements into organizational processes to maintain the organization's security strategy.

17. Integrate information security requirements into contracts and activities of external parties.

18. Monitor external parties' adherence to established security requirements.

19. Define and monitor management and operational metrics for the information security program.

Information security program management includes several types of activities intended to ensure that organizational objectives are met. These activities include resource management (staff, professional services, budget, and equipment), decision-making at every level, and coordination of activities through projects, tasks, and routine operations.

Information Security Control Design and Selection

The procedures, mechanisms, systems, and other measures designed to reduce risk through compliance to policies are known as *controls*. An organization develops controls to ensure that its business objectives will be met, risks will be reduced, and errors will be prevented or corrected.

Controls are created to ensure desired outcomes and to avoid unwanted outcomes. They are created for several reasons, including the following:

- **Regulation** A regulation on cybersecurity or privacy may emphasize certain outcomes, some of which may compel an organization to develop controls.
- **Risk assessment** A recent risk assessment or targeted risk analysis may indicate a higher than acceptable risk. The chosen risk treatment may be mitigation in the form of a new control.
- **Audit result** The results of a recent audit may indicate a trouble spot warranting additional attention and care.

Control Classification

Before exploring the steps used to create and manage a control, you should understand the characteristics, or classifications, of controls. Several types, classes, and categories of controls are discussed in this section. Figure 6-1 depicts this control classification.

Figure 6-1
Control classification shows types (along the right side of the box), classes (at the front of the box), and categories (at the top) of controls.

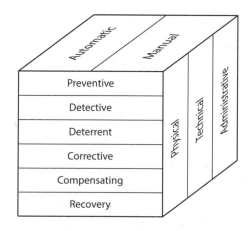

The Multidimensionality of Controls

You can look at controls in many different ways, which can help you better understand them and how they work. In this book, controls are described using the words "types," "classes," and "categories." The use of these three terms is not set in stone, and there is no standard way of modeling controls using these or other terms. In fact, the depiction of controls in this book by type, class, and category is purely arbitrary, but these terms can be useful in helping information security managers, information security auditors, and other security personnel understand controls and how they contribute to the protection of assets.

Types of Controls

The three types of controls are physical, technical, and administrative:

- **Physical**   These types of controls exist in the tangible, physical world. Examples of physical controls are video surveillance, locking doors, bollards, and fences.

- **Technical**   These controls are implemented in the form of information systems and information system components and are usually intangible. Examples of technical controls include encryption, computer access controls, and audit logs. These are sometimes referred to as *logical* controls.

- **Administrative**   These controls are the policies, procedures, and standards that require or forbid certain activities, protocols, and configurations. An example administrative control is a policy that forbids personal use of company-owned information systems. These are sometimes referred to as *managerial* controls.

EXAM TIP   ISACA does not expressly use the terms "type," "class," or "category" in its literature or on the exam to describe and distinguish the variety of controls and their basic characteristics. These terms are used in this book to highlight the multidimensional nature of controls and how they can be understood and classified. Like other constructs, these are models that help you better imagine how controls operate and are used.

Classes of Controls

There are six classes of controls, which speak to their relationship with unwanted outcomes:

- **Preventive**   This type of control is used to prevent the occurrence of an unwanted event. Examples of preventive controls are computer login screens (which prevent unauthorized people from accessing information), keycard systems (which prevent unauthorized people from entering a building or workspace), and encryption (which prevent people lacking an encryption key from reading encrypted data).

NOTE Security professionals generally prefer preventive controls over detective controls, because preventive controls actually block unwanted events. Likewise, security professionals prefer detective controls to deterrent controls, because detective controls record events while deterrent controls do not. However, there are often circumstances where cost, resource, or technical limitations force an organization to accept a detective control when it would prefer a preventive control, or to accept a deterrent control when it would prefer a detective control. For example, there is no practical way to build a control that would prevent criminals from entering a bank, but a detective control (security cameras) would record what they did after they arrived.

- **Detective** This type of control is used to record both wanted and unwanted events. A detective control cannot enforce an activity (whether it is desired or undesired), but it can ensure that the appropriate security personnel are notified of whether, and how, an event occurred. Examples of detective controls include video surveillance and event logs.

- **Deterrent** This type of control exists to convince someone that they should not perform some unwanted activity. Examples of deterrent controls include guard dogs, warning signs, and visible video surveillance cameras and monitors.

NOTE Security managers need to understand one key difference between preventive and deterrent controls: A deterrent control requires knowledge of the control by the potential violator—it can deter their intentions only if they know the control exists. Preventive and detective controls work regardless of whether the violator is aware of them.

- **Corrective** This type of control is activated (manually or automatically) after some unwanted event has occurred. An example of a corrective control is the act of improving a process when it is found to be defective.

- **Compensating** This type of control is enacted because some other direct control cannot be used. For example, a guest sign-in register can be a compensating control when it is implemented to compensate for the lack of a stronger detective control, such as a video surveillance system. A compensating control addresses the risk related to the original control.

- **Recovery** This type of control is used to restore a system or an asset to its pre-incident state. Examples of a recovery control include the use of a tool to remove malware from a computer, and the use of backup software to recover lost or corrupted files.

NOTE Many controls can fit into more than one class. For example, a video surveillance camera can be both a detective control (because it is part of a system that records events) and a deterrent control (because its visibility is designed to discourage persons from committing unwanted acts). Also, an audit log can be both a detective control and a compensating control—detective because it records events, and compensating because it may compensate for a lack of a stronger, preventive control, such as a user IDs and password access control.

Categories of Controls

There are two categories of controls that relate to the nature of their operation:

- **Automatic**   This type of control performs its function with little or no human judgment or decision-making. Examples of automatic controls include a login page on an application that cannot be circumvented, and a security door that automatically locks after someone walks through the doorway.

- **Manual**   This type of control requires a human to operate it. A manual control may be subject to a higher rate of errors than an automatic control. An example of a manual control is a monthly review of computer users.

NOTE Information security and audit professionals generally prefer automatic controls to manual ones, because automatic controls are typically less prone to error. There are often circumstances, however, in which an organization must settle for a manual control because of cost or some other factor, such as the requirement for human decision and intervention, perhaps during an emergency situation or a disaster. Nonetheless, the controls should be documented and artifacts collected to demonstrate that the control is working as designed and documented.

Control Objectives

Control objectives describe the desired states or outcomes of business operations. When building a security program, and preferably prior to selecting a control framework, security professionals must establish high-level control objectives.

Examples of control objective subject matter include the following:

- Protection of IT assets and information
- Accuracy of transactions
- Confidentiality and privacy of sensitive information
- Availability of IT systems
- Controlled changes to IT systems
- Compliance with corporate policies
- Compliance with applicable regulations and other legal obligations

Control objectives are the foundation for controls. For each control objective, one or more controls will exist to ensure the realization of the control objective. For example, the "availability of IT systems" control objective may be implemented via several controls, including the following:

- IT systems will be continuously monitored.
- Interruptions in the availability of IT systems will result in alerts sent to appropriate personnel.
- IT systems will have resource-measuring capabilities.
- IT management will review capacity reports monthly and adjust resources accordingly.
- IT systems will have antimalware controls that are monitored by appropriate staff.

Together, these five (or more) controls contribute to the overall control objective on IT system availability. Similarly, the other control objectives will have one or more controls that will ensure their realization.

After establishing control objectives, the next step is to design controls. This can be a considerable undertaking. A better approach is the selection of one of several high-quality control frameworks that are discussed later in this section.

If an organization elects to adopt a standard control framework, the next step is to perform a risk assessment to determine whether controls in the control framework adequately meet each control objective. Where there are gaps in control coverage, additional controls must be developed and put in place.

General Computing Controls

An IT organization supporting many applications and services will generally have some controls that are specific to each individual application. However, IT will also have a set of controls that apply across all of its applications and services, and these are usually called *general computing controls (GCCs)* or *IT general controls (ITGCs)*.

An organization's GCCs are general in nature and are often implemented in different ways on different information systems, based upon their individual capabilities and limitations, as well as applicability. Examples of GCCs include the following:

- Applications require unique user IDs and strong passwords.
- Passwords are encrypted while stored and transmitted and are not displayed.
- Highly sensitive information, such as bank account numbers, is encrypted when stored and transmitted.
- All administrative actions are logged, and logs are protected from tampering.

If you are familiar with information systems technology, you will quickly realize that these GCCs will be implemented differently across different types of information systems. Specific capabilities and limitations, for example, will result in somewhat different capabilities for password complexity and data encryption. Unless an organization is using really old information systems, the four GCCs shown here can probably be implemented everywhere in an IS environment. *How* they are implemented is the subject of the next section.

Controls: Build Versus Buy

The time-honored phrase "build versus buy" refers to fundamental business decisions that organization leaders make regularly. An organization in need of a new asset, whether tangible or intangible, can build the asset in-house by using whatever raw materials are called for and by following a design and build procedure. Or the organization can buy the finished product—that is, pay another organization to create the asset.

In years past, organizations often custom designed and built their core business applications. Today, however, the majority of organizations buy (or lease) core business applications. And, increasingly, organizations no longer build their own data centers, opting instead to lease data center space from colocation providers or cloud providers.

In part, the build versus buy argument is related to an organization's mission and core competencies. For instance, a new social media company may decide to lease serverless computing platforms rather than buy servers, claiming that the company specializes in social media, not data centers, computer hardware, or operating systems.

Security leaders who need to build a set of controls will have to determine whether to build or buy them. Each approach has pros and cons, as illustrated in Table 6-1.

Organizations generally choose to adopt existing control frameworks that are aligned with their industry. This results in an immediate, complete set of controls that can be implemented over a shorter period of time than would be possible if the organization were to develop a custom set of controls.

Approach	Pros	Cons
• Build a custom control framework	• Aligns precisely to identified risks • Tailored to the company's use case and computing environment	• Considerable time and expertise required to design and implement • Potential for overlooking an important control • End result will resemble standard control frameworks • Control has not been vetted in multiple environments
• Adopt a standard control framework	• Several existing frameworks available • Immediate implementation possible • No risk analysis required to identify common risks • Generally supported and accepted by auditors/assessors	• Potential for overlooking an important risk • Structure may not align with the organization or its security program

Table 6-1   Controls: Build Versus Buy Comparison

Control Frameworks

A *control framework* is a collection of controls, organized into logical categories. Well-known control frameworks such as ISO/IEC 27002, NIST SP 800-53, and CIS CSC are intended to address a broad set of information risks common to most organizations. Such standard control frameworks have been developed to streamline the process of control development and adoption within organizations. If there were no standard control frameworks, organizations would have to assemble their controls using other, inferior methods, such as the following:

- Gut feeling
- Using another organization's experience
- Using a security practitioner from another organization
- Searching the Internet
- Assessing a risk in a deficient or incomplete way

A security manager could perform a comprehensive risk assessment and develop a framework of controls based upon identified risks, and indeed this would not be considered unacceptable. However, with a variety of freely available, high-quality control frameworks (except ISO/IEC 27002, which must be purchased), an organization could start with a standard control framework that requires far less effort.

Selecting a Control Framework

Several high-quality control frameworks are available for organizations that want to start with a standard control framework as opposed to starting from scratch or other means. Table 6-2 lists commonly used control frameworks. Each is discussed in more detail in this section.

There is ongoing debate regarding which control framework is best for an organization. In my assessment, the fact that there is debate on the topic reveals that many do not understand the purpose of a control framework or the risk management life cycle. The common belief is that once an organization selects a control framework, the organization is "stuck" with a set of controls and no changes will be made to the controls used in the organization. Instead, as is discussed throughout this book, selection of a control framework represents a *starting point,* not the perpetual commitment. Once a control framework is selected, the organization can use the risk management life cycle to understand risk in the organization, resulting in changes to the controls used by the organization. In fact, it may be argued that an organization practicing effective risk management will eventually arrive at more or less the same set of controls, regardless of the starting point. This process, however, would likely take many years.

A different and valid approach to control framework selection has more to do with the structure of controls than the controls themselves. Each control framework consists of logical groupings based on categories of controls. For instance, most control frameworks have sections on identity and access management, vulnerability management, incident management, and access management. Some control frameworks' groupings are more sensible in certain organizations based on their operations or industry sector.

Control Framework	Description	Industries Used
ISO/IEC 27002	Broadly adopted international controls	All
NIST SP 800-53	Broadly adopted U.S.-based controls	Government, private industry
CIS Critical Security Controls	Broadly adopted U.S.-based controls	All
ETSI Technical Report (TR) 103 305-1, Critical Security Controls	EU-based controls based on CIS CSC	All
Payment Card Industry Data Security Standard (PCI DSS)	Controls for protection of credit card data	Retail, banking, credit card processing
NIST Cyber Security Framework (CSF)	Emerging U.S.-based controls	All
Health Insurance Portability and Accountability Act (HIPAA) / HITRUST CSF	Controls for the protection of electronic protected health information (ePHI)	Medical services, including delivery, billing, and insurance
COBIT 2019	Broadly adopted international controls	All
Committee of Sponsoring Organizations of the Treadway Commission (COSO)	Controls for preserving the integrity of financial information and financial statement reporting	All U.S. public companies and private companies requiring similar controls
North American Electric Reliability Corporation (NERC) Reliability Standards	Controls for the protection of electric generation and distribution infrastructure	Electric utilities
Cloud Security Alliance (CSA) Cloud Controls Matrix (CCM)	Controls for use by cloud-based service providers	All
(System and Organization Controls Report) SOC 1	Controls for use by financial service providers	All
SOC 2	Controls for use by cloud-based service providers	All

Table 6-2 Commonly Used Control Frameworks

There is also nothing wrong with a security manager selecting a control framework based on his or her familiarity and experience with a specific framework. This is valid to a point, however: for example, selecting the PCI DSS control framework in a healthcare delivery organization might not be the best choice.

 EXAM TIP CISM candidates are not required to memorize the specifics of COBIT or other frameworks, but a familiarity with them will help the candidate better understand how they contribute to effective security governance and control.

Mapping Control Frameworks

Organizations may find that more than one control framework needs to be selected and adopted. The primary factors driving this are as follows:

- Multiple applicable regulatory frameworks
- Multiple operational contexts

For example, suppose a medical clinic delivers healthcare services and accepts payments by credit card. Both the HIPAA and PCI DSS frameworks would be applicable in respective parts of the organization, because neither HIPAA nor PCI DSS fully addresses the security and compliance needs of the business. In another example, a U.S.-based, publicly traded electric utility would need to adopt both COSO and NERC controls. In both examples, the respective organizations may decide to apply each control framework only to relevant parts of the organization. For example, in the medical clinic, HIPAA would apply to systems and processes that process ePHI, and PCI DSS would apply to systems and processes that process credit card data and payments. In the electric utility, NERC controls would apply to the electric generation and distribution infrastructure, while COSO would apply to financial systems. The challenge with this approach, however, is that there will be systems and infrastructure that are in scope for two (or more) frameworks. This can make IT and security operations more complex than they otherwise would be. Nevertheless, applying all frameworks in use across the entire infrastructure would be overly burdensome.

Organizations with multiple control frameworks often crave a simpler organization for their controls. Often, organizations will "map" their control frameworks together, resulting in a single control framework with controls from each framework present. Mapping control frameworks together is time-consuming and tedious, although in some instances the work has already been done. For instance, Appendix H in NIST SP 800-53 contains a forward and reverse mapping between NIST SP 800-53 and ISO/IEC 27001. Other controls mapping references can be found online. A chart that maps two or more control frameworks together is known as a *crosswalk*.

The problem with mapping controls from multiple frameworks together is that, at a control-by-control level, many controls do not neatly map together. For example, NIST SP 800-53 Rev 5 CM-10 is mapped to ISO/IEC 27002:2022 control 5.31. These controls read as follows:

- **NIST SP 800-53 Rev 5 CM-10**   a. Use software and associated documentation in accordance with contract agreements and copyright laws; b. Track the use of software and associated documentation protected by quantity licenses to control copying and distribution; and c. Control and document the use of peer-to-peer file sharing technology to ensure that this capability is not used for the unauthorized distribution, display, performance, or reproduction of copyrighted work.

- **ISO/IEC 27002:2022 5.31**   Legal, statutory, regulatory and contractual requirements relevant to information security and the organization's approach to meet these requirements should be identified, documented and kept up to date.

The control in NIST SP 800-53 Rev 5 is far more specific than the control in ISO/IEC 27002:2022, making this a good example of an imperfect mapping.

In another example, on the topic of audits and audit tools, NIST SP 800-53 Rev 5 AU-9 does not clearly map to any control in ISO/IEC 27002:2022. The closest control in ISO is control 8.34. The text of each control reads as follows:

- **ISO/IEC 27002:2022 8.23** Audit tests and other assurance activities involving assessment of operational systems should be planned and agreed between the tester and appropriate management.
- **NIST SP 800-53 Rev 5 AU-9** The information system protects audit information and audit tools from unauthorized access, modification, and deletion.

These controls do not map together well at all. In the earlier version of ISO/IEC 27002, control 15.3.2 reads, "Access to information systems audit tools should be protected to prevent any possible misuse or compromise." Unfortunately, in the newer revisions of these standards, for this control, the mapping has diverged and is less clear now. Thus, mapping controls requires continual effort.

Working with Control Frameworks

Once an organization selects a control framework and multiple frameworks are mapped together (if the organization has decided to do that), security managers will need to organize its operational activities around the selected/mapped control frameworks, as discussed in the following sections.

Risk Assessment   Before a control can be designed properly, the security manager needs to know the nature of the risk(s) that the control is intended to address. In a running risk management program, when a new risk is identified during a risk assessment, the security manager needs specific information regarding the nature of the risk so that he or she can design a control to handle the identified risk properly.

If a control is implemented without first conducting a risk assessment, the organization may not design and implement the control properly:

- The control may not be rigorous enough to counter a threat.
- The control may be too rigorous and costly (in the case of a moderate or low risk).
- The control may not counter all relevant threats.

In the absence of a risk assessment, the chance of one of these undesirable outcomes occurring is quite high. This is why a risk assessment should precede, and indicate the need for, the creation of a control. If an organization-wide risk assessment is not feasible, then a risk assessment that is focused on the control area should be performed so that the organization will know what risks may exist that need to be mitigated with a control.

Control Design   Before a control can be used, it must be designed. A control framework comprises the control language itself, as well as some degree of guidance. The security manager, together with personnel who are responsible for relevant technologies and business processes, determine what activity is required to implement the control—in other words, they figure out how to operationalize the control.

Suppose, for instance, that an organization wants to comply with NIST SP 800-53 Rev 5, control CM-7 (which reads, "a. Configure the information system to provide only organization-defined mission essential capabilities; and b. Prohibit or restrict the use of the following functions, ports, protocols, and/or services"). This may require that the team develop one or more component hardening standards and implement scanning or monitoring tools to detect nonconformities and configuration drift. Next, one or more people will need to be designated as the responsible parties for designing, implementing, and assessing the control. Also, the control will need to be designed in a way that makes system configuration verifiable.

Proper control design will potentially require one or more of the following:

- New or changed policies
- New or changed business process documents
- New or changed information systems
- New or changed business records

One or more of the following concepts may be included as a part of the design of a control:

- Defense in depth
- Split custody
- Separation of duties

Although it is not necessary to include these control features, they may help improve the effectiveness of a control.

Control Architecture   The term *control architecture* refers to the "big picture" of controls in an organization. In addition to designing and implementing individual controls, information security managers also need to understand how controls work together to protect information and information systems. Risk assessments and other considerations will drive a security manager to develop a *defense-in-depth* architecture for high-risk areas. For instance, a control designed to review staff terminations every week would supplement and detect errors in the staff termination control.

Dealing with Changing Technology   Technologies change more quickly than standard control frameworks can. For this reason, security managers need to keep a close eye on emerging technologies and "plug in" to various business processes in the organization to ensure that they are involved whenever new technologies or practices are introduced into the organization.

Changes in technologies are often, by design, disruptive. This disruption starts in markets where new products, services, and practices are developed, and it continues inside organizations that adopt them. Disruption is the result of innovation—the realization of new ideas that make organizations better in some way. Here are some examples of disruptive technologies:

- **Personal computers** Starting in the early 1980s, IBM and other companies sold PCs to organization departments that grew impatient with centralized IT organizations that were too slow to meet their business needs.

- **Cloud computing** Starting in the early 2000s, many companies developed cloud-based services for data storage and information processing. Organization departments still waiting for corporate IT to help them went to the cloud instead, because it was cheaper and faster. Corporate IT followed, as infrastructure as a service (IaaS) providers made server OSs available at far less cost than before. Disruptive technologies within the realm of cloud computing include virtualization, containers, microsegmentation, software-defined networking, software-defined security, identity-defined security, ransomware, and fileless malware.

- **Smartphones** BlackBerry was the first widely adopted corporate smartphone; it was minimally disruptive but highly liberating for workers who could use it to access e-mail and other functions from anywhere. Sold mainly to consumers, Apple's iPhone proved highly disruptive in the smartphone market, as it provided alternative means for workers to get things done.

- **Bring your own device (BYOD)** Increasingly, company workers bring personal smartphones, tablets, laptops, voice assistants, and other personally owned devices and use them for business operations.

- **Bring your own app (BYOA)** Company workers sometimes use personally owned tools and software on company information systems.

- **Shadow IT** Individuals, groups, departments, and business units bypass corporate IT and procure their own computing services, typically through software as a service (SaaS) and IaaS services, but also through BYOD.

- **Work from home (WFH)** The shift of global workforces to working from home on a part-time or full-time basis changes the risk landscape for individual workers, particularly on the topics of physical security, endpoint management, and LAN management.

- **Artificial intelligence (AI)** As AI is incorporated into devices and commercial applications, organizations will have to determine platform- and practice-specific risks and develop controls to manage and monitor its use.

- **Virtual reality (VR)** VR will find itself in commercial environments, whether for employee or customer use. Security leaders will need to identify specific risks and develop controls and safeguards to protect employees, customers, and sensitive information.

- **Internet of things (IoT)** Internet and/or LAN communications capabilities are being introduced into numerous types of products, such as food storage and cooking appliances, audio/visual equipment (including televisions), medical devices, vehicles, building control systems, manufacturing equipment, laundry equipment, and agriculture machinery. Many of these devices are being introduced into organizational networks, often without considerations for security and privacy.

Security managers understand that they cannot be everywhere at once; neither can they be aware of all relevant activities in the organization. Individual workers, teams, departments, and business units will adopt new services and implement new technologies without informing or consulting with information security. This underscores the need for an annual risk assessment that will reveal emerging technologies and practices so that they may be assessed for risk. While a backward look at technology adoption is not ideal (because risks may be introduced at the onset of use), because security managers are not always involved in changes in the organization, a risk assessment is sometimes the method of last resort to discover risks already present in the business.

ISO/IEC 27002

ISO/IEC 27002, "Information technology—Security techniques—Code of practice for information security controls," is a world-renowned set of controls. The ISO/IEC 27002 control framework consists of 4 control categories and 93 control objectives. Table 6-3 describes these control categories and control objectives for the 2022 version, known as ISO/IEC 27002:2022.

Control	Control Objective
5 Organizational controls	
5.1 Policies for information security	Provides management direction and support for information security per business requirements, relevant laws, and regulations
5.2 Information security roles and responsibilities	Formally establishes security roles and responsibilities
5.3 Segregation of duties	Reduces the risk of fraud, errors, and bypass of controls
5.4 Management responsibilities	Ensures that management is aware of their information security responsibilities
5.5 Contact with authorities	Ensures authorized and proper communication with external agencies
5.6 Contact with special interest groups	Ensures appropriate communications with external professional organizations
5.7 Threat intelligence	Provides awareness of the threat environment
5.8 Information security in project management	Identifies and manages security risks in projects
5.9 Inventory of information and other associated assets	Identifies assets to preserve their security and assign ownership
5.10 Acceptable use of information and other associated assets	Ensures that assets are properly used
5.11 Return of assets	Ensures that assets are returned in changing and terminating employment and contracts

Table 6-3 ISO/IEC 27002:2022 Control Objectives (*continued*)

Control	Control Objective
5.12 Classification of information	Ensures that information receives appropriate protection according to its importance to the organization
5.13 Labelling of information	Uses human and machine-readable labels to ensure proper protection and handling
5.14 Information transfer	Maintains the security of information as it is transferred to/from the organization
5.15 Access control	Ensures authorized access and prevents unauthorized access to assets
5.16 Identity management	Ensures accurate management of people and machine identities
5.17 Authentication information	Ensures proper authentication to systems
5.18 Access rights	Ensures that access to assets is authorized per business requirements
5.19 Information security in supplier relationships	Ensures proper security in supplier relationships
5.20 Addressing information security within supplier agreements	Formally defines security related roles and responsibilities in contracts
5.21 Managing information security in the ICT (information and communication technology) supply chain	Ensures proper security in supplier relationships
5.22 Monitoring, review and change management of supplier services	Ensures proper security in supplier relationships when relationships change
5.23 Information security for use of cloud services	Manages security related to the use of cloud services
5.24 Information security incident management planning and preparation	Ensures effective response to information security incidents
5.25 Assessment and decision on information security events	Ensures categorization and prioritization of security events
5.26 Response to information security incidents	Ensures effective response to information security incidents
5.27 Learning from information security incidents	Improves response to future incidents
5.28 Collection of evidence	Ensures proper collection and management of evidence
5.29 Information security during disruption	Ensures that security remains effective during disruptions
5.30 ICT readiness for business continuity	Ensures the availability of critical systems
5.31 Legal, statutory, regulatory and contractual requirements	Ensures compliance with all legal requirements
5.32 Intellectual property rights	Ensures protection and compliance with intellectual property laws

Table 6-3 ISO/IEC 27002:2022 Control Objectives (*continued*)

PART III

Control	Control Objective
5.33 Protection of records	Ensures that business records are adequately protected
5.34 Privacy and protection of PII	Ensures the proper protection and use of PII
5.35 Independent review of information security	Ensures the integrity of an organization's information security program
5.36 Compliance with policies, rules and standards for information security	Ensures compliance with policies, standards, and requirements
5.37 Documented operating procedures	Ensures correct and secure operations of information-processing facilities
6 People controls	
6.1 Screening	Ensures that personnel understand their responsibilities and are suitable for their roles
6.2 Terms and conditions of employment	Ensures that personnel are aware of and accomplish their information security responsibilities
6.3 Information security awareness, education and training	Ensures that personnel are aware of and can perform their security responsibilities
6.4 Disciplinary process	Ensures that personnel understand the consequences of violating security policy
6.5 Responsibilities after termination or change of employment	Protects the organization as part of changing or terminating employment
6.6 Confidentiality or non-disclosure agreements	Ensures confidentiality of information by personnel and external parties
6.7 Remote working	Ensures protection of information when working remotely
6.8 Information security event reporting	Ensures that personnel can identify and will report security events
7 Physical records	
7.1 Physical security perimeters	Prevents unauthorized access to facilities
7.2 Physical entry	Ensures that only authorized personnel may access facilities
7.3 Securing offices, rooms and facilities	Ensures that only authorized personnel may access offices and rooms in facilities
7.4 Physical security monitoring	Detects physical security events
7.5 Protecting against physical and environmental threats	Identifies and protects against various threats
7.6 Working in secure areas	Protects assets and information in secure areas
7.7 Clear desk and clear screen	Reduces exposure of sensitive information in work spaces
7.8 Equipment siting and protection	Reduces risks associated with the location of work and processing centers

Table 6-3 ISO/IEC 27002:2022 Control Objectives (*continued*)

Control	Control Objective
7.9 Security of assets off-premises	Ensures the protection of assets and information when offsite
7.10 Storage media	Prevents unauthorized misuse of information stored on media
7.11 Supporting utilities	Reduces the impact of disruption of supporting utilities such as electric power and water
7.12 Cabling security	Ensures the protection of communications cabling
7.13 Equipment maintenance	Ensures the proper maintenance of assets
7.14 Secure disposal or re-use of equipment	Prevents leakage of information when disposing or reusing assets
8 Technological controls	
8.1 User endpoint devices	Protects information from risks associated with the use of user endpoints
8.2 Privileged access rights	Ensures that only authorized personnel and services have privileged access
8.3 Information access restriction	Ensures that only authorized personnel and services may access information
8.4 Access to source code	Prevents unauthorized access to, and modification of, source code
8.5 Secure authentication	Ensures the security of authentication events
8.6 Capacity management	Ensures that technological and personnel resources are adequate to perform required business functions
8.7 Protection against malware	Ensures that information systems are protected against malware
8.8 Management of technical vulnerabilities	Prevents exploitation of technical vulnerabilities
8.9 Configuration management	Ensures that information systems have proper security settings
8.10 Information deletion	Ensures that information is retained only as long as required
8.11 Data masking	Masks sensitive information fields as required
8.12 Data leakage prevention	Detects and prevents unauthorized disclosure of information
8.13 Information backup	Protects against accidental or deliberate loss of data
8.14 Redundancy of information processing facilities	Ensures the continuous operation of information systems
8.15 Logging	Covers creation and protection of activities
8.16 Monitoring activities	Monitors for anomalous events and actions taken
8.17 Clock synchronization	Ensures accurate clocks to aid in event troubleshooting

Table 6-3 ISO/IEC 27002:2022 Control Objectives (*continued*)

Control	Control Objective
8.18 Use of privileged utility programs	Ensures that utility programs do not harm systems or information
8.19 Installation of software on operational systems	Ensures the integrity of information systems
8.20 Networks security	Ensures protection of information in networks
8.21 Security of network services	Ensures the security of network services
8.22 Segregation of networks	Develops security boundaries in networks
8.23 Web filtering	Ensures protection from malware and access to unauthorized resources
8.24 Use of cryptography	Ensures use of cryptography to protect the confidentiality, authenticity, and/or integrity of information
8.25 Secure development life cycle	Ensures the inclusion of security in development life-cycle processes
8.26 Application security requirements	Ensures that all security requirements are identified and addressed
8.27 Secure system architecture and engineering principles	Ensures that security is a part of architecture, design, and operations of information systems
8.28 Secure coding	Ensures that coding does not introduce vulnerabilities
8.29 Security testing in development and acceptance	Ensures that security is a part of development and acceptance testing
8.30 Outsourced development	Ensures that security measures are required when outsourcing development
8.31 Separation of development, test and production environments	Ensures that separate development, test, and production systems are used to protect information
8.32 Change management	Ensures that only approved changes are made, and that security is preserved
8.33 Test information	Ensures that information used in testing is protected
8.34 Protection of information systems during audit testing	Ensures that audits and other testing does not impact operations

Table 6-3   ISO/IEC 27002:2022 Control Objectives

ISO/IEC 27002 is available from www.iso.org. This and most other ISO standards are fee-based, meaning that they must be purchased and have licensing and usage restrictions that govern their use in an organization. Generally, these standards are purchased in single quantities and are "single user" in nature, and they are not permitted to be stored on file servers for use by multiple users.

NOTE ISO/IEC 27002 is significantly reorganized with the 2022 version. Appendices in the 2022 version include forward and reverse mapping to the 2005 version.

NIST SP 800-53

NIST SP 800-53 Rev 5, "Security and Privacy Controls for Federal Information Systems and Organizations," is published by the Computer Security Division of the U.S. National Institute for Standards and Technology (NIST). A summary of controls in NIST SP 800-53 appears in Appendix D, "Security Control Baselines," and detailed descriptions of all controls are found in Appendix F, "Security Control Catalog." NIST SP 800-53 Rev 5 is available from http://csrc.nist.gov/publications/PubsSPs.html. The standard is available without cost or registration.

Table 6-4 lists the categories of controls in NIST SP 800-53 Rev 5.

NIST SP 800-53A is a separate standard that provides procedures for assessing controls in NIST SP 800-53.

PART III

Category	Name
AC	Access Control
AT	Awareness and Training
AU	Audit and Accountability
CA	Assessment, Authorization, and Monitoring (renamed in Rev 5)
CM	Configuration Management
CP	Contingency Planning
IA	Identification and Authentication
IR	Incident Response
MA	Maintenance
MP	Media Protection
PE	Physical and Environmental Protection
PL	Planning
PS	Personnel Security
PT	PII Processing and Transparency (new in Rev 5)
RA	Risk Assessment
SA	System and Services Acquisition
SC	System and Communications Protection
SI	System and Information Integrity
SR	Supply Chain Risk Management (new in Rev 5)

Table 6-4 NIST SP 800-53 Rev 5 Control Categories

Center for Internet Security Critical Security Controls

The Center for Internet Security (CIS) maintains a popular and respected control framework called the *CIS Critical Security Controls* (CIS CSC). While CIS CSC currently includes 18 control objectives, it included 20 control objectives for many years and is still commonly known as the "CIS 20" or the "SANS Top 20." Still occasionally referred to as the "SANS 20 Critical Security Controls," this control framework was originally developed by the SANS Institute.

Regarded as a simpler set of security controls, the CIS CSC framework has been widely adopted by organizations seeking a control framework but needing to avoid more burdensome frameworks such as NIST SP 800-53 or ISO/IEC 27001 controls.

Table 6-5 shows the structure of the CIS CSC control framework.

CIS Control	Title	Control Objective
1	Inventory and Control of Enterprise Assets	Actively manage (inventory, track, and correct) all enterprise assets (end-user devices, including portable and mobile; network devices; non-computing/Internet of Things (IoT) devices; and servers) connected to the infrastructure physically, virtually, remotely, and those within cloud environments, to accurately know the totality of assets that need to be monitored and protected within the enterprise. This will also support identifying unauthorized and unmanaged assets to remove or remediate.
2	Inventory and Control of Software Assets	Actively manage (inventory, track, and correct) all software (operating systems and applications) on the network so that only authorized software is installed and can execute, and that unauthorized and unmanaged software is found and prevented from installation or execution.
3	Data Protection	Develop processes and technical controls to identify, classify, securely handle, retain, and dispose of data.
4	Secure Configuration of Enterprise Assets and Software	Establish and maintain the secure configuration of enterprise assets (end-user devices, including portable and mobile; network devices; non-computing/IoT devices; and servers) and software (operating systems and applications).
5	Account Management	Use processes and tools to assign and manage authorization to credentials for user accounts, including administrator accounts, as well as service accounts, to enterprise assets and software.
6	Access Control Management	Use processes and tools to create, assign, manage, and revoke access credentials and privileges for user, administrator, and service accounts for enterprise assets and software.

Table 6-5 CIS CSC Framework (Source: The Center for Internet Security (CIS) www.cisecurity.org) *(continued)*

CIS Control	Title	Control Objective
7	Continuous Vulnerability Management	Develop a plan to continuously assess and track vulnerabilities on all enterprise assets within the enterprise's infrastructure, in order to remediate and minimize the window of opportunity for attackers. Monitor public and private industry sources for new threat and vulnerability information.
8	Audit Log Management	Collect, alert, review, and retain audit logs of events that could help detect, understand, or recover from an attack.
9	E-mail and Web Browser Protections	Improve protections and detections of threats from e-mail and web vectors, as these are opportunities for attackers to manipulate human behavior through direct engagement.
10	Malware Defenses	Prevent or control the installation, spread, and execution of malicious applications, code, or scripts on enterprise assets.
11	Data Recovery	Establish and maintain data recovery practices sufficient to restore in-scope enterprise assets to a pre-incident and trusted state.
12	Network Infrastructure Management	Establish, implement, and actively manage (track, report, correct) network devices, in order to prevent attackers from exploiting vulnerable network services and access points.
13	Network Monitoring and Defense	Operate processes and tooling to establish and maintain comprehensive network monitoring and defense against security threats across the enterprise's network infrastructure and user base.
14	Security Awareness and Skills Training	Establish and maintain a security awareness program to influence behavior among the workforce to be security conscious and properly skilled to reduce cybersecurity risks to the enterprise.
15	Service Provider Management	Develop a process to evaluate service providers who hold sensitive data, or are responsible for an enterprise's critical IT platforms or processes, to ensure these providers are protecting those platforms and data appropriately.
16	Application Software Security	Manage the security life cycle of in-house developed, hosted, or acquired software to prevent, detect, and remediate security weaknesses before they can impact the enterprise.
17	Incident Response Management	Establish a program to develop and maintain an incident response capability (e.g., policies, plans, procedures, defined roles, training, and communications) to prepare, detect, and quickly respond to an attack.
18	Penetration Testing	Test the effectiveness and resiliency of enterprise assets through identifying and exploiting weaknesses in controls (people, processes, and technology), and simulating the objectives and actions of an attacker.

Table 6-5 CIS CSC Framework (Source: The Center for Internet Security (CIS) www.cisecurity.org)

The CIS CSC framework is structured in a way that makes it easy for security practitioners to understand and use. Within each control category is a section entitled "Why Is This Control Critical?" followed by the individual controls. This is followed by a section called "Procedures and Tools" that provides additional guidance. Finally, each control category includes a system entity relationship diagram that depicts the control's implementation in an environment. Many consider the CIS CSC a more pragmatic and less academic framework than NIST SP 800-53 or PCI DSS.

The CIS CSC framework includes one or more controls within each control category. Some controls are flagged as "foundational," meaning they are essential in any organization. The controls not marked as "foundational" may be considered optional.

Some controls include advanced implementation guidelines. For instance, control 8.3 ("Limit use of external devices to those with an approved, documented business need. Monitor for use and attempted use of external devices. Configure laptops, workstations, and servers so that they will not auto-run content from removable media, like USB tokens [thumb drives], USB hard drives, CDs/DVDs, FireWire devices, external serial advanced technology attachment devices, and mounted network shares. Configure systems so that they automatically conduct an anti-malware scan of removable media when inserted....") includes in its advanced guidance, "Actively monitor the use of external devices (in addition to logging)."

The CIS CSC framework is available from www.cisecurity.org/critical-controls.cfm without cost, although registration may be required.

NIST Cyber Security Framework

The NIST Cyber Security Framework (CSF) is a risk management methodology and control framework designed for organizations that want a single standard for identifying risk and implementing controls to protect information assets. Initially released in 2014, the CSF appears to be gaining acceptance in organizations lacking regulations requiring specific control frameworks (such as HIPAA for organizations in the healthcare industry).

The CSF consists of a framework core comprising five key activities in a security management program:

- **Identify** Develop the organizational understanding to manage cybersecurity risk to systems, assets, data, and capabilities.
- **Protect** Develop and implement the appropriate safeguards to ensure delivery of critical infrastructure services.
- **Detect** Develop and implement the appropriate activities to identify the occurrence of a cybersecurity event.
- **Respond** Develop and implement the appropriate activities to take action regarding a detected cybersecurity event.
- **Recover** Develop and implement the appropriate activities to maintain plans for resilience and to restore any capabilities or services that were impaired because of a cybersecurity event.

The CSF contains a "Framework Implementation Tiers" methodology that an organization can use to assess the overall capability of the organization's information security program. The capabilities assessment resembles maturity levels, where the program is determined to be in one of the following tiers:

- **Partial**   Risk management is not formalized but instead is reactive and limited to few in the organization. There are no formal relationships with external entities, and supply chain risk management processes are not formalized.

- **Risk Informed**   Risk management is formalized but not working organization-wide. External relationships are established but not formalized. Supply chain risk management processes occur but are not formalized.

- **Repeatable**   Risk management practices are formal and approved. The risk management program is integrated into the business. External parties are engaged so that the organization can respond to events. Supply chain risk management process is governed.

- **Adaptive**   Risk management practices are monitored and adapted to meet changing threats and business needs. The risk management program is fully integrated into the organization's business and process. The organization shares information with external parties on a methodical basis and receives information to prevent events. The supply chain risk management process provides high-level risk awareness to management.

These implementation tiers are similar to maturity ratings used in the Software Engineering Institute Capability Maturity Model (SEI-CMM) and others.

The CSF contains a methodology for establishing or making improvements to an information security program. The steps in this methodology are similar to the structure used in this book:

- **Step 1: Prioritize and Scope**   The organization determines which business units or business processes are part of the scope of a new or improving program.

- **Step 2: Orient**   The organization identifies assets that are in scope for the program, the risk approach, and applicable laws, regulations, and other legal obligations.

- **Step 3: Create a Current Profile**   The organization identifies the category and subcategory outcomes from the Framework Core (the CSF controls) that are currently in place.

- **Step 4: Conduct a Risk Assessment**   The organization conducts a risk assessment covering the entire scope of the program. This is an ordinary risk assessment like those described throughout this book, where threats (together with their likelihood and impact) are identified for each asset or asset group.

- **Step 5: Create a Target Profile**   The organization determines the desired future states for each of the framework's categories and subcategories (the controls). This includes the desired tier level for each category and subcategory.

- **Step 6: Determine, Analyze, and Prioritize Gaps**   The organization compares the current profile (developed in step 3) and the target profile (step 5) and develops a list of gaps. These gaps are analyzed and prioritized, and the necessary resources to close gaps are identified. A cost-benefit analysis is performed, which also helps with prioritization.

- **Step 7: Implement Action Plan** The organization develops plans to close gaps identified and analyzed in step 6. After action plans have been completed, controls are monitored for compliance.

NIST CSF is available from www.nist.gov/cyberframework.

Payment Card Industry Data Security Standard

The PCI DSS is a control framework whose main objective is the protection of cardholder data. PCI DSS was developed by the PCI Security Standards Council, an organization founded by the major credit card brands in the world including Visa, MasterCard, American Express, Discover, and JCB.

Table 6-6 shows the two-tiered structure of PCI DSS version 4.

Build and Maintain a Secure Network and Systems	
Requirement 1	Install and Maintain Network Security Controls
Requirement 2	Apply Secure Configurations to All System Components
Protect Cardholder Data	
Requirement 3	Protect Stored Account Data
Requirement 4	Protect Cardholder Data with Strong Cryptography During Transmission Over Open, Public Networks
Maintain a Vulnerability Management Program	
Requirement 5	Protect All Systems and Networks from Malicious Software
Requirement 6	Develop and Maintain Secure Systems and Software
Implement Strong Access Control Measures	
Requirement 7	Restrict Access to System Components and Cardholder Data by Business Need to Know
Requirement 8	Identify Users and Authenticate Access to System Components
Requirement 9	Restrict Physical Access to Cardholder Data
Regularly Monitor and Test Networks	
Requirement 10	Log and Monitor All Access to System Components and Cardholder Data
Requirement 11	Test Security of Systems and Networks Regularly
Maintain an Information Security Policy	
Requirement 12	Support Information Security with Organizational Policies and Programs
Appendices	
Appendix A	Additional PCI DSS Requirements
Appendix A1	Additional PCI DSS Requirements for Multi-Tenant Service Providers
Appendix A2	Additional PCI DSS Requirements for Entities Using SSL/Early TLS for Card-Present POS POI Terminal Connections
Appendix A3	Designated Entities Supplemental Validation (DESV)

Table 6-6 PCI DSS version 4.0 Control Framework (Source: PCI Security Standards Council, www.pcisecuritystandards.org)

The PCI Security Standards Council has also defined business rules around the PCI DSS standard. There is a tier structure based on the number of credit card transactions; organizations whose credit card volume exceeds set limits are subject to onsite annual audits, while organizations with lower volumes are permitted to complete annual self-assessments. There is also a distinction between merchants (retail and wholesale establishments that accept credit cards as a form of payment) and service providers (all other organizations that store, process, or transmit credit card data); service providers are required to comply with additional controls.

 NOTE The PCI Security Standards Council release version 4.0 of the PCI DSS standard takes effect in March 2024. The structure of the 4.0 standard is nearly identical with the structure of the 3.2.1 standard.

The PCI Security Standards Council also offers a program of annual training and exams for personnel who can perform PCI audits and for the organizations that employ those people. The certifications are as follows:

- **Payment Card Industry Qualified Security Assessor (PCI QSA)** These are external auditors who perform audits of merchants and service providers that are required to undergo annual audits (as well as organizations that undertake these audits voluntarily).

- **Payment Card Industry Internal Security Assessor (PCI ISA)** These are employees of merchants and service providers required to be compliant with the PCI DSS. The PCI Security Standards Council does not require any employees of merchants or service providers to be certified to PCI ISA; however, the certification does help those so certified to better understand the PCI DSS standard, thereby leading to better compliance. Some of the credit card brands permit an ISA to perform a PCI report on compliance (ROC) in lieu of an external QSA firm.

- **Payment Card Industry Professional (PCIP)** This is an entry-level certification for IT professionals who want to learn more about the PCI DSS standard and earn a certification that designates them as a PCI subject-matter expert.

The PCI Security Standards Council has published additional requirements and standards, including the following:

- **Payment Application Data Security Standard (PA DSS)** A security standard for commercial credit card payment applications

- **PCI Forensic Investigator (PFI)** Requirements for organizations and individuals who will perform forensic investigations of credit card breaches

- **Approved Scanning Vendors (ASV)** Vendors that perform required security external scans of merchants and service providers

PART III

- **Qualified Integrators and Resellers (QIR)**   Vendors that sell and integrate PCI-certified payment applications
- **Point-to-Point Encryption (P2PE)**   A security standard for payment applications that utilize point-to-point encryption of card data
- **Token Service Providers (TSP)**   Physical and logical security requirements and assessment procedures for token service providers that generate and issue EMV (Europay, MasterCard, and Visa) payment tokens
- **PIN Transaction Security (PTS)**   Requirements for the secure management, processing, and transmission of personal identification number (PIN) data during online and offline transactions at ATMs and point-of-sale (POS) terminals

PCI standards and other content are available from www.pcisecuritystandards.org/.

Health Insurance Portability and Accountability Act (HIPAA)

HIPAA was enacted by the U.S. Congress in 2008 to address a number of issues around the processing of healthcare information, including the protection of healthcare information in electronic form, also known as electronic protected healthcare information (ePHI). Organizations that deliver medical care, as well as organizations with access to such information, including medical insurance companies and most employers, are required to comply with HIPAA Security Rule requirements. Table 6-7 shows the structure of the HIPAA Security Rule.

Each requirement in the HIPAA Security Rule is labeled as Required or Addressable. Requirements that are designated as Required must be implemented. For those requirements that are Addressable, organizations are required to undergo analysis to determine whether they must be implemented.

HIPAA is available from www.hhs.gov/hipaa/for-professionals/security/index.html.

Section	Description
164.302	Applicability
164.304	Definitions
164.306	Security standards: General rules
164.308	Administrative safeguards
164.310	Physical safeguards
164.312	Technical safeguards
164.314	Organizational requirements
164.316	Policies and procedures and documentation requirements
164.318	Compliance dates for the initial implementation of the security standards

Table 6-7   Requirement Sections in the HIPAA Security Rule

COBIT 2019

To ensure that a security program is aligned with business objectives, the COBIT 2019 control framework of 5 principles and 37 processes is an industry-wide standard. The five principles are as follows:

- Meeting Stakeholder Needs
- Covering the Enterprise End-to-End
- Applying a Single, Integrated Framework
- Enabling a Holistic Approach
- Separating Governance from Management

COBIT 2019 includes more than 1100 control activities to support these principles. Established in 1996 by ISACA and the IT Governance Institute, COBIT is the result of industry-wide consensus by managers, auditors, and IT users. Today, COBIT 2019 is accepted as a best-practices IT process and control framework. COBIT has absorbed ISACA's Risk IT Framework and Val IT Framework.

COBIT 2019 is available from www.isaca.org/resources/cobit.

COSO

The Committee of Sponsoring Organizations of the Treadway Commission (COSO) is a private-sector organization that provides thought leadership through the development of frameworks and guidance on enterprise risk management, internal control, and fraud deterrence. Its control framework is used by U.S. public companies for management of their financial accounting and reporting systems.

COSO is a joint initiative of the following private-sector associations:

- American Accounting Association (AAA)
- American Institute of Certified Public Accountants (AICPA)
- Financial Executives International (FEI)
- The Association of Accountants and Financial Professionals in Business (IMA)
- The Institute of Internal Auditors (IIA)

The COSO framework is constructed through a set of 17 principles within 5 framework components, shown in Table 6-8. The COSO framework itself is proprietary and can be purchased from www.coso.org.

Figure 6-2 depicts the multifaceted structure of the COSO framework.

NERC Reliability Standards

The North American Electric Reliability Corporation (NERC) develops standards for use by electric utilities throughout most of North America. These standards encompass all aspects of power generation and distribution, including security. Table 6-9 shows the security portion of NERC standards.

Control Environment
1. The organization demonstrates a commitment to integrity and ethical values.
2. The board of directors demonstrates independence from management and exercises oversight of the development and performance of internal control.
3. Management establishes, with board oversight, structures, reporting lines, and appropriate authorities and responsibilities in the pursuit of objectives.
4. The organization demonstrates a commitment to attract, develop, and retain competent individuals in alignment with objectives.
5. The organization holds individuals accountable for their internal control responsibilities in the pursuit of objectives.
Risk Assessment
6. The organization specifies objectives with sufficient clarity to enable the identification and assessment of risks relating to objectives.
7. The organization identifies risks to the achievement of its objectives across the entity and analyzes risks as a basis for determining how the risks should be managed.
8. The organization considers the potential for fraud in assessing risks to the achievement of objectives.
9. The organization identifies and assesses changes that could significantly impact the system of internal control.
Control Activities
10. The organization selects and develops control activities that contribute to the mitigation of risks to the achievement of objectives to acceptable levels.
11. The organization selects and develops general control activities over technology to support the achievement of objectives.
12. The organization deploys control activities through policies that establish what is expected and procedures that put policies into action.
Information and Communication
13. The organization obtains or generates and uses relevant, quality information to support the functioning of internal control.
14. The organization internally communicates information, including objectives and responsibilities for internal control, necessary to support the functioning of internal control.
15. The organization communicates with external parties regarding matters affecting the functioning of internal control.
Monitoring Activities
16. The organization selects, develops, and performs ongoing and/or separate evaluations to ascertain whether the components of internal control are present and functioning.
17. The organization evaluates and communicates internal control deficiencies in a timely manner to those parties responsible for taking corrective action, including senior management and the board of directors, as appropriate.

Table 6-8   COSO Framework and Principles

Figure 6-2
COSO framework
components

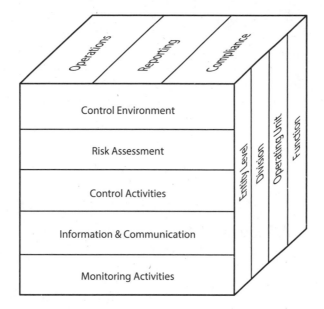

Prior to the Northeast Blackout of 2003, NERC standards were voluntary. The Energy Policy Act of 2005 authorized the Federal Energy Regulatory Commission (FERC) to designate NERC standards as mandatory. NERC has the authority to enforce its standards and does so through audits; it levies fines to public utilities that are noncompliant.

Section	Title
CIP-002-5.1a	Cyber Security – BES (Bulk Electric System) Cyber System Categorization
CIP-003-8	Cyber Security – Security Management Controls
CIP-004-6	Cyber Security – Personnel & Training
CIP-005-6	Cyber Security – Electronic Security Perimeter(s)
CIP-006-6	Cyber Security – Physical Security of BES Cyber Systems
CIP-007-6	Cyber Security – System Security Management
CIP-008-6	Cyber Security – Incident Reporting and Response Planning
CIP-009-6	Cyber Security – Recovery Plans for BES Cyber Systems
CIP-010-3	Cyber Security – Configuration Change Management and Vulnerability Assessments
CIP-011-2	Cyber Security – Information Protection
CIP-013-1	Cyber Security – Supply Chain Risk Management
CIP-014-2	Physical Security

Table 6-9   NERC Critical Infrastructure Protection Framework Cyber Security Controls

PART III

CSA Control Framework

The Cloud Security Alliance (CSA) has developed a control framework known as the Cloud Controls Matrix (CCM) that is designed to provide security principles to cloud vendors and to assist customers with assessments of cloud vendors.

Table 6-10 shows the structure of the CSA CCM version 4.

The CSA has developed an assurance framework known as CSA STAR that includes two assurance levels:

- Self-assessment
- Third-party Audit

More information on CSA and CCM is available at cloudsecurityalliance.org.

Service Organization Controls

The trend of IT outsourcing has continued unabated and is even accelerating, with many organizations shifting to cloud-based applications and infrastructure. Obtaining assurance that IT controls exist and are effective in these third-party organizations can be cost-prohibitive: most organizations' internal IT audit functions do not have sufficient resources to audit even the topmost critical service providers. And most service providers will not permit their customers to audit their controls, because this is also costly for service providers.

Domain	Description
A&A	Audit & Assurance
AIS	Application & Interface Security
BCR	Business Continuity Management & Operational Resilience
CCC	Change Control & Configuration Management
CEK	Cryptography, Encryption & Key Management
DCS	Datacenter Security
DSP	Data Security and Privacy Lifecycle Management
GRC	Governance, Risk and Compliance
HRS	Human Resources
IAM	Identity & Access Management
IPY	Interoperability & Portability
IVS	Infrastructure & Virtualization Security
LOG	Logging and Monitoring
SEF	Security Incident Management, E-Discovery & Cloud Forensics
STA	Supply Chain Management, Transparency, and Accountability
TVM	Threat and Vulnerability Management
UEM	Universal Endpoint Management

Table 6-10 Domains of the Cloud Security Alliance Cloud Controls Matrix

In the early 1990s, the American Institute for Certified Public Accountants (AICPA) developed the Statement on Auditing Standards No. 70 (SAS-70) standard that opened the door for audits that could be performed by public accounting firms on service providers, with audit reports made available to service providers' customers. After the Sarbanes–Oxley Act (SOX) took effect in 2003, SAS-70 audits of service providers satisfied the requirements for U.S. public companies to obtain assurance of control effectiveness for outsourced IT service providers, particularly those that supported financial applications.

The SOC 1, SOC 2, and SOC 3 audit standards are discussed next.

System and Organization Controls 1 In 2010, the SAS-70 standard was superseded by the Statement on Standards for Attestation Engagements No. 16 (SSAE 16) standard in the United States and by International Standards on Assurance Engagements No. 3402 (ISAE 3402) outside the United States. In 2017, SSAE 16 was replaced with SSAE 18. Together, SSAE 16, SSAE 18, and ISAE 3402 are commonly known as System and Organization Controls 1 (SOC 1).

In a SOC 1 audit, the service organization specifies the controls that are to be audited. While a service organization has complete latitude on which controls are in scope for a SOC 1 audit, the service organization must be mindful of which controls its customers and their internal and external auditors will expect to see in a SOC 1 audit report.

There are two basic types of SOC 1 audits:

- **Type I** This is a point-in-time examination of the service organization's controls and their design.
- **Type II** This audit takes place over a period of time (typically three months to one year), where the auditor examines not only the design of in-scope controls (as in Type I) but also business records that reveal whether controls are effective.

SOC 1 audits must be performed by CPA firms in good standing.

System and Organization Controls 2 The SOC 2 audit standard was developed for IT service providers of all types that want to demonstrate assurance in their controls to their customers. A SOC 2 audit of a service provider is based on one or more of the following five trust principles:

- **Security** The system is protected against unauthorized access.
- **Availability** The system is available for operation and use as committed to or agreed upon.
- **Processing integrity** System processing is complete, valid, accurate, timely, and authorized.
- **Confidentiality** Information designated as confidential is protected as committed to or agreed upon.
- **Privacy** Personal information is collected, used, retained, disclosed, and destroyed in accordance with the privacy notice commitments.

Several controls are included within each trust principle. All controls within each selected trust principle are included in a SOC 2 audit.

There are two basic types of SOC 2 audits:

- **Type I**   This is a point-in-time examination of the service organization's controls and their design.

- **Type II**   This is an audit that takes place over a period of time (typically six months to one year), where the auditor examines not only the design of in-scope controls (as in Type I) but also business records that reveal whether controls are effective.

SOC 2 audits must be performed by CPA firms in good standing.

System and Organization Controls 3   A SOC 3 audit is similar to a SOC 2 audit, except that a SOC 3 report lacks a description of control testing or opinion of control effectiveness. Like SOC 2, a SOC 3 audit includes any or all of the five trust principles: security, availability, processing integrity, confidentiality, and privacy.

Information Security Control Implementation and Integrations

After a control has been designed, it needs to be put into service and then managed throughout its life. Depending upon the nature of the control, this could involve operational impact in the form of changes to business processes and/or information systems. Changes with greater impact will require greater care so that business processes are not adversely affected.

For instance, an organization that creates a control related to implementing and managing hardening standards will need to test and implement the new control. If a production environment is affected, it could take quite a bit of time to ensure that the hardening standard configuration items do not adversely affect the performance, integrity, or availability of affected systems.

Controls Development

The development of controls is a foundational part of any security program. To develop controls, a security manager must have an intimate level of knowledge of the organization's mission, goals, and objectives, as well as a good understanding of the organization's degree of risk tolerance. Figure 6-3 illustrates the relationship between an organization and the fundamentals of a security program.

As stated elsewhere in this book, the most common approach to controls development is the selection of an established control framework, such as any of those discussed earlier in this chapter. However, an organization is also free to develop a control framework from scratch. Table 6-1 earlier in this chapter illustrates the pros and cons of each approach.

Figure 6-3
Relationship between an organization's mission, goals, objectives, risk tolerance, risk management, security policies, and security controls

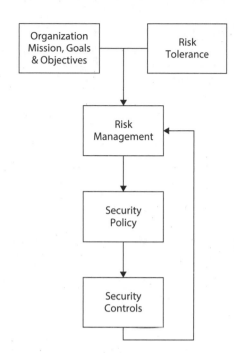

Developing Controls from Scratch

For organizations that elect to develop their controls from scratch, the first step is the development of high-level control objectives. These control objectives could be thought of as overarching principles from which individual controls will be developed. Control objectives are typically similar from organization to organization. However, since each organization is different, some organizations will have one or two unique control objectives that address specific business activities or objectives.

Table 6-11 shows a sample set of control objectives.

Management will approve policies and activities in the security program.
All organization and worker activities will be legal and ethical.
Qualified personnel will periodically assess security and risk and make recommendations for improvement.
Only approved personnel may access organization information and work areas.
Access rules and rights will be periodically reviewed.
All workers and third parties will be vetted prior to being given access to proprietary information and work areas.
Changes to infrastructure, applications, and software will be controlled and managed.
Information will be protected and retained according to its sensitivity and value.
Only approved hardware and software will be used.
A formal incident detection and response function will be established and managed.
Security considerations will be incorporated into all business development and acquisition activities.

Table 6-11   Sample Control Objectives

Developing Control Details

Whether the organization adopts an existing control framework or develops controls from scratch, the security manager must develop several elements for each control. These elements include the following:

- **Control number**   The index number assigned to this control, according to the control numbering scheme adopted by the organization. This could be a simple number (1, 2, 3) or a hierarchical number (10.5, 10.5.1, 10.5.2, 10.6).

- **Mapping**   Any relationships of this control to one or more controls in other control frameworks, whether the other control frameworks are specific to the organization or are industry-standard control frameworks.

- **Title**   The title or name of the control.

- **Control objective**   In a control framework with high-level control objectives, this is a statement of a desired activity.

- **Narrative**   A detailed description of the control. Generally, this should not include implementation details (which could vary from system to system or from place to place), but instead should include details that help a business owner, auditor, or IT worker understand the intent of the control. There should be enough detail so that IT workers and other personnel can properly implement the control.

- **Scope**   The locations, business units, departments, or systems that are affected by the control.

- **Risk**   A description of the risk that this control is intended to address.

- **Owner**   The business owner (or owners) of the control.

- **Affected and related business processes**   The business processes related to the control, as well as the business processes affected by the control.

- **Control frequency**   How often the control is performed, executed, or used.

- **Classification**   Includes whether the control is automatic or manual, preventive or detective, and other classification details.

- **Measurements**   Includes the statistics, metrics, and key performance indicators (KPIs) that are measured as a result of control operation.

- **Testing procedure and frequency**   The steps required to evaluate the control for effectiveness. Like the control narrative, this should be a general description and not specific to any particular technology.

- **Developed by**   The name of the person who developed the control.

- **Approved by**   The name of the person who approved the control.

- **Approval date**   The date of the most recent approval of the control.

- **Version**   The version number of the control, according to whatever version numbering system is used by the organization.

- **Cross references**   Cross references to other controls, control frameworks, systems, documents, departments, processes, risk assessments, or risk treatment. Cross references can help personnel better understand how controls relate to other activities or events in the organization.

- **Modification history**   A list of the changes made to the control, including a description, who made each change, who approved each change, and the date of each change.

While organizations may prefer to document controls in worksheets, a better approach is the development of individual documents for each control. This will lead to better outcomes, because it will be easier to control versions of individual control documents.

 NOTE   Organizations that develop control statements only, without including the metadata described here, will experience problems in the form of ambiguity. Control metadata is essential to ensure that management understands how controls are to be implemented and managed.

Control Implementation

The implementation of a new control should be guided by formal processes, not unlike those that guide systems development: a new control should have a control objective, a design that is reviewed by stakeholders, a test plan that is carried out with results reviewed, a formal authorization to implement the control, and IT and business change management processes to plan its implementation.

Controls must have control owners, who are responsible for proper operation of each control. When an organization implements new controls, control owners should be identified and trained on the operation of the controls they are responsible for. Ideally, control ownership and training is included in the control life cycle to ensure that control owners are identified and trained prior to the control being placed into operation.

New controls should be audited or reviewed more frequently to ensure that they are operating as expected. Measurements of control performance and operation should be established so that management can review actual versus expected performance. In some cases, an organization will also audit or review controls to ensure that they are meeting objectives.

Security and Control Operations

Controls that have been placed into service will transition into routine operations. Control owners will operate their controls and try to be aware of any problems, especially those that appear early on. Whether controls are automatic or manual, preventive or corrective, control owners are responsible for ensuring that their controls operate correctly in every respect.

Modern information security control frameworks comprise a dozen or more categories of operational activities, including these:

- Event monitoring
- Vulnerability management
- Secure engineering and development
- Network protection
- Endpoint protection and management
- Identity and access management
- Security incident management
- Security awareness training
- Managed security services providers
- Data security
- Business continuity planning

Other areas of operational control that are related to business operations, IT, physical security, and privacy are not included here.

Event Monitoring

Event monitoring is the practice of examining the security events that occur on information systems, including applications, operating systems, database management systems, end-user devices, and every type and kind of network device, and then providing information about those events to the appropriate people or systems.

Prior to widespread business use of the Internet, most organizations found it sufficient to review event logs on a daily basis. This comprised a review of the previous day's logged events (or the weekend's events on a Monday) to ensure that no security incidents warranted further investigation. Today, however, most organizations implement *real-time* event monitoring; this means that organizations need to have systems in place that will immediately inform the appropriate parties if any events warrant attention.

Log Reviews   In a *log review,* an event log in an information system is examined to determine whether any security or operational incidents have occurred in the system that warrant action or attention. Typically, a log review involves the examination of activities that occurred on the previous day. Most organizations conduct continuous log reviews by sending log data into a security information and event management system (SIEM).

Centralized Log Management   *Centralized log management* is a practice whereby event logs on various systems are sent over the network to a central collection and storage point, called a *log server.* There are two primary uses for a log server: the first is archival storage of events that may be used at a later date in an investigation, and the second is for the review of events on a daily basis or in real time. Generally, real-time analysis is performed by a SIEM, discussed next.

Security Information and Event Management   A SIEM (pronounced *sim* or *seem*) system collects and analyzes log data from many or all systems in an organization. A SIEM has the ability to correlate events from one or more devices to provide details about an incident. For instance, an attacker performing a brute-force password attack on a web server may be generating alerts on the web server itself and also on the firewall and intrusion detection system. A SIEM would portray the incident using events from these and possibly other devices to provide a rich depiction of the incident.

Threat Intelligence Platform   Modern SIEMs can ingest threat intelligence feeds from various external sources. This enables them to correlate events in an organization's systems with various threats experienced by other organizations. A *threat intelligence platform* (TIP) can be implemented to receive and process threat intelligence information. For example, suppose another organization is attacked by an adversary from a specific IP address in a foreign country. This information is included in a threat intelligence feed that arrives in your organization's SIEM. This helps the SIEM be more aware of activity of the same type or from the same IP address. This can help your organization be prepared should similar incidents occur on your organization's network.

Security Orchestration, Automation, and Response   In the context of SIEM, *orchestration* refers to a scripted response that is automatically or manually triggered when specific events occur. This capability is performed by a security orchestration, automation, and response (SOAR) platform that may be a stand-alone system or may exist as part of the SIEM. Suppose, for example, that an organization has developed "run books," or short procedures for personnel who manage the SIEM, for actions that should be performed when specific types of events occur. The organization, desiring to automate some of these responses, implements a SOAR tool with scripts that can be run automatically when these specific events occur. The orchestration system can be configured to run some scripts immediately, while others can be set up and run when an analyst "approves" them. The advantage of orchestration is twofold: first, repetitive and rote tasks are automated, relieving personnel of boredom and improving accuracy; second, response to some types of events can be performed more quickly, thereby blunting the impact of security incidents.

Vulnerability Management

Vulnerability management is the practice of periodically examining information systems (including but not limited to operating systems, subsystems such as database management systems, applications, network devices, and IoT devices) for the purpose of discovering exploitable vulnerabilities, related analysis, and decisions about remediation. Organizations employ vulnerability management as a primary activity to reduce the likelihood of successful attacks on their IT environments.

Often, one or more scanning tools, such as the following, are used to scan target systems in the search for vulnerabilities:

- Network device identification
- Open port identification

- Software version identification
- Exploitable vulnerability identification
- Web application vulnerability identification
- Source code defect identification

Security managers generally employ several of these tools for routine and nonroutine vulnerability management tasks. Routine tasks include scheduled scans of specific IT assets, while nonroutine tasks include troubleshooting and various types of investigations.

A typical vulnerability management process includes these activities:

- **Periodic scanning**   One or more tools are used to scan assets in the organization to search for vulnerabilities and discover new devices.
- **Analysis of scan results**   A security analyst examines the results of a vulnerability scan, validating the results to make sure there are no false positive results. This analysis often includes a risk analysis to help the analyst understand an identified vulnerability in the context of the asset, its role, and its criticality. Scanning tools generally include a criticality level or criticality score for an identified vulnerability so that personnel can begin to understand the severity of the vulnerability. Most tools utilize the Common Vulnerability Scoring System (CVSS) method for scoring a vulnerability.

  After noting the CVSS score of a specific vulnerability, a security manager analyzes the vulnerability to establish the contextual criticality of the vulnerability. For example, a vulnerability in the Server Message Block (SMB) service on Microsoft Windows servers may be rated as critical. A security manager may downgrade the risk in the organization if SMB services are not accessible over the Internet or if robust safeguards are already in place. In another example, a security manager may raise the severity of a vulnerability if the organization lacks detective controls that would alert the organization that the vulnerable component has been attacked and compromised.

- **Delivery of scan results to asset owners**   The security manager delivers the report to the owners or custodians of affected assets so that those people can begin planning remediation activities.
- **Remediation**   Asset owners make changes to affected assets, typically through the installation of one or more security patches or through the implementation of one or more security configuration changes. Often, risk analysis is performed to determine the risks associated with proposed remediation plans.

Organizations often establish service level agreements (SLAs) for the maximum times required for remediation of identified vulnerabilities. Table 6-12 shows a typical remediation SLA.

Common Vulnerability Scoring System   The CVSS is an open framework that cab be used to provide a common methodology for scoring vulnerabilities. CVSS employs

CVSS Score	Internet-Facing Assets	Internal Assets
8.01 to 10	5 days	10 days
4.01 to 8.0	10 days	15 days
2.01 to 4.0	30 days	45 days
0 to 2.0	90 days	180 days

Table 6-12   Typical Vulnerability Management Remediation SLA

a standard methodology for examining and scoring a vulnerability based on the exploitability of the vulnerability, the impact of exploitation, and the complexity of the vulnerability. The CVSS has made it possible for organizations to adopt a consistent approach for the analysis and remediation of vulnerabilities. Specifically, organizations can develop SLAs that determine the speed by which an organization will remediate vulnerabilities. For more information about CVSS, visit www.first.org/cvss/.

MITRE ATT&CK Framework   The MITRE ATT&CK (adversarial tactics, techniques, and common knowledge) framework is a freely available knowledge base of threats, attack techniques, and attack models. Developed in 2015, the framework has been widely adopted by organizations determined to increase their understanding and prevent cyberattacks. The ATT&CK matrix classifies threats in several areas:

- Reconnaissance
- Resource development
- Initial access
- Execution
- Persistence
- Privilege escalation
- Defense evasion
- Credential access

The ATT&CK framework breaks down these categories into several subtechniques that help security professionals understand how various types of attacks work. The framework can be obtained from https://attack.mitre.org/.

Vulnerability Identification Techniques   Several techniques are used for identifying vulnerabilities in target systems:

- **Security scan**   One or more vulnerability scanning tools are used to help identify easily found vulnerabilities in target systems. A security scan will identify a vulnerability in one or two ways: by confirming the version of a target system or program that is known to be vulnerability, or by making an attempt at proving the existence of a vulnerability by testing a system's response to specific stimulus.

PART III

- **Penetration test**   A security scan, plus additional manual tests that security scanning tools do not employ, are used in a *penetration test*, which is intended to mimic a realistic attack by an attacker who intends to break into a target system. A penetration test of an organization's production environment may fall somewhat short of the techniques used by an actual attacker, however. In a penetration test, a tester is careful not to exploit vulnerabilities that could result in a malfunction of the target system. Often, an actual attacker will not take this precaution unless he or she wants to attack a system without being noticed. For this reason, it is sometimes desirable to conduct a penetration test of nonproduction infrastructure, even though nonproduction environments are often not identical to their production counterparts.

- **Social engineering assessment**   This is an assessment of the judgment of personnel in the organization to determine how well they are able to recognize various ruses used by attackers in an attempt to trick users into performing tasks or providing information. Several means are used, including e-mail, telephone calls, and in-person encounters. Social engineering assessments help organizations identify training and improvement opportunities. Social engineering attacks can have a high impact on an organization. A particular form of social engineering, *BEC (business e-mail compromise)* or *wire transfer fraud,* consists of a ruse by which an attacker sends an e-mail that pretends to originate from a CEO to the chief financial officer (CFO), claiming that a secret merger or acquisition proceeding requires a wire transfer for a significant sum be sent to a specific offshore account. Aggregate losses resulting from CEO fraud over the past few years exceeds $2 billion.

Patch Management   Closely related to vulnerability management, the practice of *patch management* ensures that IT systems, tools, and applications have consistent version and patch levels. In all but the smallest organizations, patch management can be successful only through the use of tools that are used to automate the deployment of patches to target systems. Without automated tools, patch management is labor intensive and prone to errors that are often unnoticed, resulting in systems that remain vulnerable to exploitation even when IT and security staff believe they are protected. Patch management is related to other IT processes including change management and configuration management, which are discussed later in this chapter.

Secure Engineering and Development

Although engineering and software development are not activities performed in an organization's security management program, they are business processes that security managers will typically observe and, occasionally, influence. Most organizations do not adequately include security practices in their IT engineering and development processes, resulting in a higher than necessary number of security defects, inadequate security safeguards, and, occasionally, security breaches.

For decades, IT organizations employed no security personnel, and they did not include security in their design, engineering, or development processes, because security merely involved the assurance that no one could enter the room where the non-networked mainframe computer resided. When networking and the global Internet emerged, many organizations continued to exclude security in their design, engineering, and development departments. Further, in the earlier days of Internet connectivity, security managers were reputed to be inhibitors of innovation, who stopped product development dead in its tracks because of security issues that often were quite solvable. Today, some business executives still believe that security is merely a tactical activity that consists of simple, unobtrusive "overlay" functions such as firewalls and antivirus systems. These historical phenomena largely explain why organizations still fail to include security appropriately in design, engineering, and development phases.

Most current security managers understand the business value of security involvement as early as possible in an organization's business and software development life cycles. Security adds value when security managers understand business processes and understand how to engage in a way that demonstrates value. Security can add value at each stage of the development cycle:

- **Conceptual**   When business executives are discussing new business capabilities, lines of business, or even mergers and acquisitions, security managers can weigh in on these activities with guidance in several topics, including data protection, regulations, compliance, and risk.

- **Requirements**   When requirements are being developed for the development or acquisition of a new business capability, security managers can be sure to add security, compliance, and privacy requirements to improve the likelihood that systems, applications, and other capabilities are more likely to be secure.

- **Design**   With proper input at the requirements stage, product designs are more likely to be secure. Security managers' involvement in design reviews will ensure that initiatives are heading in the right direction.

- **Engineering and development**   With security involvement in requirements and design, it's more likely that engineering and development will create secure results. Still, when engineers and developers are aware of secure engineering and development techniques, results will be improved from a security perspective.

- **Testing**   When requirements are developed in a way that makes them measurable and verifiable, testing can include verification that requirements have been met. This will ensure that security was included properly in the engineering and development phases.

- **Sustainment**   Throughout its operational life cycle, periodic testing and analysis of threat intelligence keeps security managers informed of new vulnerabilities that require configuration changes or patches. Also, scans of an environment after routine changes help ensure that those changes did not introduce new vulnerabilities.

Organizations that fail to include security in each phase of their development cycles are more likely to incur additional rework as security is retrofitted into systems and applications, as opposed to these products being secure by design. Events such as risk assessments and vulnerability assessments can expose the lack of security by design, resulting in rework. Organizations unaware of the principle of security by design are often unaware that they could have performed their engineering and development for less cost overall, when compared to the cost of rework.

Network Protection

Network protection is one of the more mature disciplines in IT and information security. Usenet, the pre-Internet dial-up protocol for transporting e-mail and other information, included user ID and password authentication as early as 1980. The first firewall was developed in 1988 as the primary means for protecting systems and data from attacks originating outside the organization. Firewalls are still considered essential, and other types of devices and design considerations are commonly used to protect organizations' internal networks from many types of unwanted activities.

Networks in organizations often grow organically, with incremental changes over time designed by a succession of network engineers or architects. In all but the most mature organizations, the details of network architecture and the reasons for various architectural features are undocumented and lost to the annals of time. This results in many organizations' networks today consisting of several characteristics and features that are poorly understood, other than knowing that they are essential to the networks' ongoing functionality.

Firewalls   *Firewalls* are network devices that are used to control the passage of network traffic from one network to one or more other networks. Firewalls are typically placed at the boundary of an organization's network and other, external networks. Organizations also use firewalls to logically separate internal networks from each other; examples include the following:

- A data center network is often protected from other internal networks with a firewall.
- Development and testing networks are usually protected by firewalls.
- A special network known as a demilitarized zone (DMZ) is protected by one or more firewalls, as shown in Figure 6-4.

Figure 6-4
A firewall
protects a DMZ
network

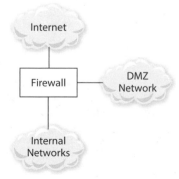

Source IP Address	Source Port	Destination IP Address	Destination Port	Permit or Deny
0.0.0.0 to 255.255.255.255	25	141.204.10.22	25	Permit
0.0.0.0 to 255.255.255.255	53	141.204.10.24	53	Permit
141.204.10.24	53	0.0.0.0 to 255.255.255.255	53	Permit
0.0.0.0 to 255.255.255.255	119	141.204.10.22	119	Permit
141.204.12.1 to 141.204.12.255	80, 443	0.0.0.0 to 255.255.255.255	80, 443	
0.0.0.0 to 255.255.255.255	0 to 65535	141.204.10.1 to 141.204.10.255 + 141.204.12.1 to 141.204.12.255	0–65535	Deny

Table 6-13 Example Firewall Rules

Firewalls are managed through a user interface of some kind. At the heart of a firewall's configuration are its rules, a series of statements that define specific network traffic that is to be permitted or blocked. Table 6-13 shows a set of sample firewall rules.

The rules in Table 6-13 are explained here, in order of appearance:

- Permit e-mail from the entire Internet to reach the e-mail server at 141.204.10.22 only.
- Permit DNS from the entire Internet to reach the DNS server at 141.204.10.24 only.
- Permit NNTP traffic from the entire Internet to reach time server at 141.204.10.22 only.
- Permit all users to access the entire Internet on ports 80 and 443 (HTTP and HTTPS protocols) only.
- Deny all other traffic from the Internet on all ports from reaching any internal system.

Application Firewalls   *Application firewalls* are devices used to examine and control messages being sent to an application server, primarily to block unwanted or malicious content. Most often used to protect web servers, application firewalls block attacks that may represent attempts by an attacker to gain illicit control of an application or steal data that the application server accesses.

Segmentation   *Network segmentation* is the practice of partitioning an organization's network into zones, with protective devices such as firewalls or stateful packet-filtering routers controlling network traffic between the zones. Network segmentation protects

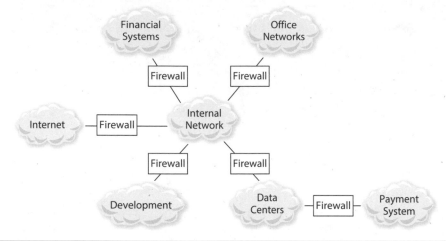

Figure 6-5 Network segmentation creates zones of trust

business functions or asset groups through network-level access control. It is a common technique used to protect high-value assets by permitting network traffic from specific hosts, users, or applications to access certain networks, while denying all others access. Figure 6-5 depicts network segmentation.

Common uses of network segmentation include the following:

- Protection of data center networks from networks containing end-user devices
- Isolation of systems with sensitive data as a means for reducing scope of audits
- Protection of systems on a DMZ network from the Internet, while at the same time protecting internal networks from systems on the DMZ
- Protection of internal networks from activities taking place in a development or testing environment

Intrusion Prevention Systems   *Intrusion prevention systems* (IPSs) detect and block malicious network traffic that may be associated with an intrusion. An IPS differs from a firewall in one important way: an IPS examines the content of network packets to determine whether each packet should be allowed to pass through the network or be blocked. A firewall's decision on whether to block or permit a packet is based strictly upon its origin, destination, and port, regardless of content.

Many IPSs also block traffic from "known-malicious" IP addresses and domains, based upon network "reputation" data that is periodically sent to an IPS. The makers of several IPS products include feeds of reputation data, sometimes with several updates each day. Attackers often frequently switch their attack origins, knowing that most network engineers cannot keep up with the pace of change; however, IPSs with incoming reputation feeds help to automate the update process, resulting in improved security through more effective blocking of traffic from known malicious sites.

Some IPSs can import information from a *threat intel feed,* which is a subscription service about known threats. A threat intel feed often contains IP addresses associated with known malicious sites; an IPS will automatically block traffic being transmitted to or from those IP addresses.

In addition to blocking malicious traffic, an IPS can also permit suspect traffic, log the event, and optionally create an alarm. This falls into the category of network traffic that may or may not be malicious. This would serve to alert personnel who can investigate the event and take necessary action.

IPSs require continuous vigilance. Sometimes an IPS will block traffic that is anomalous but not actually harmful, and this may impede desired business activities. In such cases, a security analyst monitoring and operating an IPS would need to "whitelist" the traffic so that the IPS will not block it in the future. Also, when an IPS sounds an alarm when it has permitted dubious traffic, a security analyst would need to investigate the matter and take needed action.

Like many security systems, IPSs were initially hardware appliances. Most IPSs are now available in the form of virtual machines that can be installed in an organization's public or private cloud.

Intrusion Detection Systems   Intrusion detection systems (IDSs) detect malicious network traffic that may be associated with an intrusion. An IDS is functionally similar to an IPS in its detection capabilities, configurability, and detection rules. The primary difference is that an IDS is strictly a detective control; aside from generating alerts, an IDS does nothing to prevent an attack from progressing.

DDoS Protection   Both appliances as well as cloud-based services are available to absorb the brunt of a distributed denial-of-service (DDoS) attack. This capability recognizes and filters DDoS packets, while permitting legitimate traffic to pass through to the organization. DDoS protection is generally implemented at the Internet boundary in front of firewalls and other devices to prevent the attack from reaching the organization's servers. The advantage of cloud-based DDoS protection is the absence of attack traffic on the organization's Internet connection.

Network Traffic Analysis   *Network traffic analysis* (NTA) is a technique used to identify anomalous network traffic that may be a part of an intrusion or other unwanted event. NTA is a strictly detective tool that does not prevent unwanted traffic. In all cases, when an NTA system identifies potentially unwanted traffic, someone must take action to identify the business nature of the traffic and take steps to block it if needed.

NTA systems work by "learning" about all of the network "conversations" that take place between systems. Over time, the NTA system will easily recognize anomalous traffic, which is network traffic that is novel or unique when compared to all of the traffic that it knows about. There are a number of ways in which an NTA system will identify traffic as anomalous:

- Traffic between two systems that rarely, if ever, have directly communicated before
- Traffic between two systems on a network port that rarely, if ever, has been used before

PART III

- Traffic between two systems at a higher volume than has been observed before

- Traffic between two systems taking place at a different time of day than has been observed before

NTA systems generally do not examine the contents of traffic; instead, they identity the systems, the ports used, and the volume of traffic.

To be effective, NTA systems need to be positioned at locations in a network where large volumes of network traffic pass, such as backbone routers. But more commonly, NTA systems utilize agents on various routers and collect the traffic centrally for analysis. Figure 6-6 shows such an architecture.

There are two main types of NTA systems. The first is a dedicated system (an appliance or virtual machine) that collects network traffic data from various points in the network, as depicted in Figure 6-6. The second method is the use of detailed event logging in core routers and firewalls that are sent to a SIEM, where NTA detection rules are established. These two methods can achieve the same goal: detection of unusual network traffic that may be signs of an intrusion or other unwanted event in the network.

Three standards are used for network behavior anomaly detection:

- **NetFlow**   This protocol, developed by Cisco Systems, is available on Cisco Systems routers.

- **sFlow**   This is an industry-standard protocol for monitoring networks.

- **Remote Monitoring (RMON)**   This earlier protocol permits the remote monitoring of network traffic.

Figure 6-6
NTA systems
collect data from
several sources
for analysis

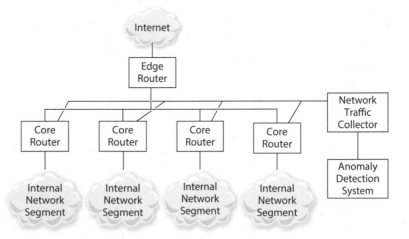

Network Taps, aka Span Ports

Several network-based detective security systems are designed to observe *all* the traffic passing through one or more control points in an organization's network. These systems work by analyzing all of the organization's internal and/or external network traffic and creating alarms when specific conditions are met—generally, signs of intrusions or other unwanted events such as employee misbehavior.

A simple way to make all network traffic available for these detective systems is to place security appliances inline in the network so that they can analyze all network traffic. However, network managers are often reluctant to place inline security tools in the network because they can impact network performance, and they would serve as an additional single point of failure.

A *network tap,* commonly known as a *span port,* is a special connection used on some network routers and switches. A copy of all the network traffic passing through the router or switch will be sent to the network tap. A network tap can be connected to an IPS (which would be running in listen-only mode, since it would not be inline in this case) or an NTA system. An advantage of a network tap is that activities there do not interfere with the network itself.

Packet Sniffers   A *packet sniffer* is a detective tool used by a security engineer or network engineer to analyze traffic on a network. Originally external appliances, packet sniffers today are software tools that can be installed on server and desktop operating systems, as well as network devices. Packet sniffers are typically used when a network engineer is troubleshooting a network issue to understand the precise nature of network traffic flowing between devices on a network. Because even small networks can have large volumes of traffic, packet sniffers employ rules that instruct it to display just the packets of specific interest to the engineer.

Packet sniffers can retain specific types of packets for later analysis. For instance, if a network engineer is troubleshooting a domain name system (DNS) problem, the engineer can capture just the DNS packets so that she can examine the contents of those packets, in hopes that this will lead to a solution to the problem. Because the types of problems that an engineer may be troubleshooting can vary, packet sniffers display packets in different ways, from Ethernet frames, to TCP/IP packets, to application messages.

Figure 6-7 shows the popular Wireshark packet-sniffing tool running on macOS.

Wireless Network Protection   When improperly managed, a wireless network can become an avenue of attack. Older encryption protocols such as Wired Equivalent Privacy (WEP) are highly vulnerable to eavesdropping and intrusion. Employees and intruders may attempt to set up their own wireless network access points. Weak authentication protocols may permit intruders to authenticate to wireless networks successfully. These and other types of attacks compel organizations to undertake a number

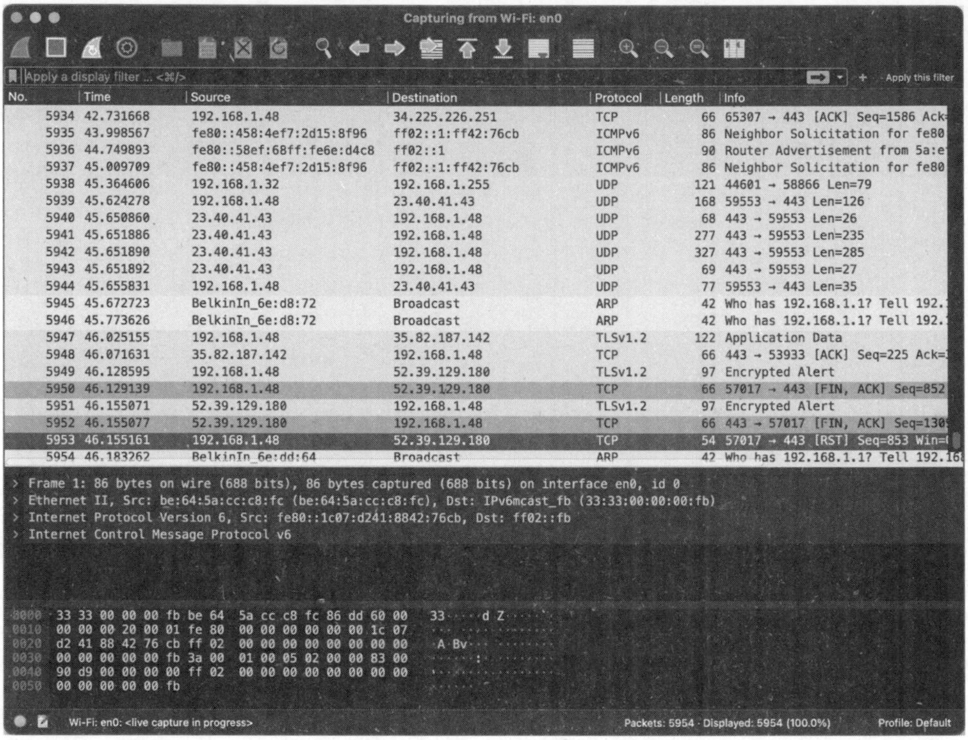

Figure 6-7   Packet-sniffing tool Wireshark capturing packets on a wireless network

of safeguards, including scanning for rogue (unauthorized) access points, penetration testing of wireless networks, and monitoring of wireless access points and controllers for suspicious activity.

Better encryption protocols are now used to protect Wi-Fi network traffic. In commercial use for nearly 20 years, WPA2 (Wi-Fi Protected Access, version 2) is robust and still considered sufficient. WPA3, released in 2018, includes security improvements and is emerging as a new standard.

Most organizations integrate centralized identity and authentication with their Wi-Fi networks, requiring users to provide their network login credentials to use the Wi-Fi network. Many organizations also employ "guest" Wi-Fi access for visitors; generally, guest access is logically separate, permitting devices to communicate only with the Internet and not the internal network. Guest access can be lax, through the use of a network password, or more robust, with each visitor being required to register, with an organization employee required to permit the guest's access for a limited time.

Organizations often encourage (and sometimes require) personnel to utilize virtual private network (VPN) capabilities when connected to any public Wi-Fi network. Such a measure helps to prevent the possibility of an eavesdropping attack, particularly on open networks that do not provide any encryption at all.

Web Content Filters   A *web content filter* is a central network-based system that monitors and, optionally, filters web communications. The primary purpose of a web content filter is to protect the organization from malicious content present on web sites that the organization's users might visit. Figure 6-8 shows an "access denied" window for a user attempting to access http://whitehouse.com/, which was a pornography site for many years.

Web content filters closely monitor the network traffic flowing to and from users' browsers and block traffic containing malicious content as a means for protecting the organization from malware attacks. Being centrally administered by a network engineer or security engineer, web content filters are typically used to block categories of content, making web sites associated with those categories unreachable by the organization's users.

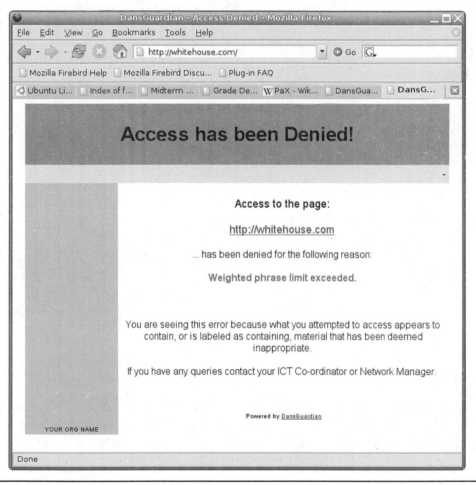

Figure 6-8   End-user "access denied" screen from web content filter (Courtesy of Bluefoxicy at en.wikipidia.org)

For instance, organizations sometimes elect to block traffic not only to sites associated with malware, but also sites that contain specific content categories such as gambling, pornography, weapons, or hate crimes. Sometimes organizations are put in the difficult position of web censorship when employees accuse them of blocking access to sites they want to visit, even if those sites are not business related.

Initial web content filtering products took the form of inline devices located in an organization's data center, thereby protecting all users connected to the internal network. But with more organizations employing remote workers, newer web content filtering products take the form of software agents installed on endpoints so that web content protection takes place regardless of each user's location.

Cloud Access Security Broker   A cloud access security broker (CASB) is a security system that monitors and, optionally, controls users' access to Internet web sites. The purpose of a CASB is to protect sensitive information by observing which service providers can be accessed by users and controlling or blocking access as necessary. For example, suppose an organization has purchased a corporate account with the cloud-based file storage company known as Box. To prevent users from storing sensitive company data with other cloud-based file storage companies, the CASB will be configured to block all users' access to the other cloud-based file storage vendors.

Occasionally, employees will need to retrieve files from another organization that uses a different cloud-based file storage service; most CASB systems permit exceptions where individual users are permitted access to other services. In many cases, CASB systems are aware of and can control individual actions such as file storage versus file retrieval, and exceptions can be made so that individual users can be permitted to store or retrieve files in unsanctioned services.

CASB functionality resembles the capabilities of web content filters. It is my belief that CASB capabilities will be fully integrated into web content filter products, leading to the near disappearance of stand-alone CASB solutions.

DNS Filtering   A *DNS filter* is a content-filtering tool that works through manipulation of DNS queries and replies. Like a web content filter, the purpose of a DNS filter is the protection of an organization from malware and other unwanted content. Essentially, a DNS filter functions much like a web content filter, but its functionality can be extended to other applications and systems in addition to web browsing. For users using web browsers, when a user attempts to view a site that is known by the DNS filter to be malicious (or is part of a blocked category), the response to the DNS query from the user's workstation will direct the user's browser to a page that informs the user that access to the site has been blocked.

On consumer devices, end users can easily change the DNS servers from the network-supplied default to any of several well-known public DNS servers, thereby bypassing any local DNS filters. However, organizations can lock down the network configuration of their devices, preventing employees from changing DNS settings and thereby preserving protections provided by their DNS filters.

E-mail Protection: Spam and Phishing Filters   E-mail has been a preferred method for propagating malware for decades. More than 90 percent of successful network intrusions begin with phishing messages sent to scores of targeted users in the hopes that one or more of them will open a malicious document or visit a compromised web site. The "trendy" schemes include business e-mail compromise (where a fraudster sends e-mails to company executives requesting them to wire large amounts of money in support of a secret merger or acquisition) and ransomware (malware that encrypts users' files and then demands a ransom in exchange for file recovery). To avoid compromise, many organizations employ e-mail protection in the form of spam and phishing filters to keep those unwanted messages from ever reaching end users.

Spam and phishing e-mail filters generally have the following characteristics:

- Built-in rules are used to determine whether any individual e-mail message should be blocked.

- Blocked e-mails are stored in quarantine. End users can typically access their quarantine to view messages and release (to their e-mail inbox) messages that should not have been blocked.

- Whitelists and blacklists are centrally configurable and generally configurable by end users. These specify which e-mail messages, as well as messages from anyone in the domain, should always be blocked or permitted.

In organizations that give users no visibility or control over spam and phishing blocking, end users have no visibility or control regarding blocked messages. In some organizations, users can contact the IT service desk to request that any messages from specific e-mail addresses be released to them. In organizations that give users full visibility and control over the handling of spam and phishing e-mails, end users may view their quarantine, release individual messages, and manage their blacklists and whitelists on their own.

The following terms are used in the context of unwanted e-mail messages:

- **Business e-mail compromise (BEC)** Phishing messages are sent to personnel, claiming to originate from the CEO or other senior executive, in an attempt to trick personnel to take some action, such as performing a wire transfer.

- **Clone phishing** Legitimate e-mail messages are obtained and subtly manipulated for fraudulent use. The attachment or link in the legitimate message is switched for one that is malicious.

- **Phishing** Unwanted e-mails attempt to perpetrate fraud of some kind on the recipient.

- **Smishing** Phishing messages are sent via SMS messages to users' mobile devices and smartphones. Note that enterprise security tools have little visibility or control over SMS content.

- **Spear phishing** Phishing messages are specially crafted for a target group or organization.

- **Spim** Phishing messages are sent to users via instant messaging.

- **Whaling** Phishing messages are sent to key executives.

In connection with their security awareness programs, some organizations acquire or develop a capability to produce test phishing messages to learn which users and user groups are more likely to click links within phishing e-mails. Such messages are usually coded so that security personnel will know which individuals click the links or attachments in test phishing messages. Phishing testing can be used as a metric to determine whether users are improving their skills in identifying fraudulent messages and directives and ignoring them.

Phishing testing is an important activity, even in organizations that use effective phishing filters, because users need to be aware that phishing filters occasionally permit phishing messages to be delivered to their inboxes. Testing helps users better understand fraud of all kinds, including those for which there are no automated filters.

Network Access Control   *Network access control* (NAC) is a network security approach used to determine the conditions wherein a device will be permitted to be attached to a network. NAC is used by organizations that want to enforce specific policies or conditions that control which devices are permitted to connect to a network, such as the following:

- Only company-issued devices
- Only devices with up-to-date security patches
- Only devices with up-to-date antimalware software
- Only devices with specific security settings
- Only devices associated with authorized users

NAC is a valid approach for organizations that want to prevent unauthorized devices, such as personally owned laptops, tablets, or smartphones, from connecting to an internal network. NAC can also be a valuable front line of defense by preventing systems lacking up-to-date patches or malware prevention from connecting to a network and potentially spreading malware. Devices with these attributes are often connected to a "quarantine network" where users are directed to install security patches or other protective measures if they want to connect those devices to the network.

Zero-Trust Network Architecture   *Zero trust* (ZT) is a network and systems design philosophy that focuses on system and data protection, in which trust is not granted implicitly but must be continually evaluated. ZT is not a device, appliance, or configuration, but an architecture where all layers of access are designed to permit only known, verified, and validated devices at acceptable locations, together with known, verified personnel to connect to specific resources.

ZT consists of several techniques, including but not limited to these:

- **Device authentication**   Only known devices are permitted to connect to a network. Additional policies may apply, including:
  - Time of day or day of week
  - Verified and allowed device location
  - Whether the device is believed to already be connected elsewhere (preventing a cloned device attack)

- **Device validation** A known device is examined to ensure the presence of several characteristics, including:
  - Antimalware or antivirus software is up to date and functioning
  - Firewall is in place and complies with configuration standards
  - Operating system is a supported version
  - Security patches and configurations are current and comply with policy
  - Revalidation if a device is connected for long periods
- **User authentication** Only known users are permitted to authenticate to the network. Additional policies may include:
  - Time of day or day of week
  - Multifactor authentication (MFA)
  - Verified and allowed user location
  - Whether the user is believed to already be connected elsewhere (preventing a compromised credentials attack)

  Users may be required to reauthenticate after periods of time to ensure that the named user is still the person using the system.
- **Resource access** Known users are permitted to access only the resources that are specifically allowed. Additional policies may include:
  - Time of day or day of week
  - Such access requires MFA
  - Only specific roles and resources may be accessed
  - Potential limits on transactions or activities based on rules
  - Reauthentication to perform high-value or high-risk tasks
- **Logging** All of the preceding activities are logged to a SIEM and/or user behavior analytics (UBA) system for further analysis that could result in alerts or alarms if business rules are violated. Well-known rules could be tied to a SOAR-TIP platform that would automatically disconnect the user and the device being used if an access violation has occurred.

ZT architecture is defined and described in NIST SP 800-207, "Zero Trust Architecture," available from https://csrc.nist.gov/publications/detail/sp/800-207/final. The United Kingdom's National Cyber Security Centre (NCSC) recommends that all new network deployments utilize ZT principles.

Endpoint Protection and Management

The term *endpoint* now includes smartphones, tablets, laptops, and desktop computers. Endpoints are used to create, process, distribute, and store sensitive information in organizations.

PART III

Endpoints are favorite targets for cybercriminal organizations for several reasons, including the following:

- They frequently contain sensitive information targeted by criminals.

- They are easily lost or stolen.

- Organizations struggle to ensure that antimalware and defensive configurations exist on 100 percent of issued endpoints; therefore, a small percentage of endpoints are more vulnerable to malware attacks.

- They are often permitted to access internal corporate networks where sensitive information resides.

- Some users are more likely to open malicious attachments in phishing messages, resulting in a favorable chance of success for a skilled attacker who targets large numbers of users and their endpoints.

- Many organizations do a marginal job of deploying security patches to all endpoints, meaning that many are vulnerable to exploitable vulnerabilities for extended periods of time.

- Some users have administrative privileges, making them more attractive targets.

- Being quite powerful and often connected to high-speed broadband networks, endpoints make attractive intermediate systems in an attack on other systems, including relaying phishing e-mail and DDoS attacks.

Because endpoints exist in relatively large numbers, cybercriminals are aware of the fact that there will always be a few endpoints that are poorly protected because of one or more of these factors. All of these issues make corporate endpoint management a tiresome, and thankless, job.

Configuration Management   Most organizations manage their endpoint populations using automated tools, which make the management of endpoints more cost effective and the configuration of endpoints far more consistent. Organizations generally employ four main techniques for effective endpoint management:

- **Image management**   An *image* is a binary representation of a fully installed and configured operating system and applications for a computer. A typical computer support department will maintain a collection of images, with one or more images for various classes of users, as well as for various hardware makes, models, and configurations.

- **Configuration management**   A typical computer support department will utilize one or more tools to manage large numbers of endpoint systems through automation. These tools are typically used to deploy patches, change configuration settings, install software programs, remove software programs, and detect configuration drift.

- **Remote control**   A typical computer support team will use a tool that permits them to access running endpoint systems remotely. Some of these tools permit covert remote access to a user's endpoint system without the user's knowledge.

Most of these tools require that the end user initiate a session whereby a computer support person is granted remote access and control of an endpoint for the purpose of assistance and troubleshooting.

- **Remote destruction** If an endpoint is lost or stolen, organizations with a remote destruct capability can direct that a lost or stolen endpoint immediately destroy any locally stored data to keep it out of the hands of a criminal who may have stolen the endpoint. This capability is often employed for laptop computers, tablet computers, and smartphones.

- **Data encryption** Many organizations consider techniques such as *whole-disk encryption* to protect stored information on mobile devices. This helps protect sensitive data stored on mobile devices by making it more difficult for a thief to access stored data on a stolen device.

Organizations often maintain endpoint *configuration standards* that detail the operational and security configuration for its endpoints. Occasionally the security configuration for endpoints will reside in a separate *hardening standard* document.

Malware Prevention The nature of endpoint computing and the designs of modern operating systems mean that malware is a problem that is not going away any time soon. On the contrary, with the advent of *ransomware* and *destructware,* malware is getting more potent and destructive. This does not diminish the impact of older generations of malware that give attackers the ability to access victims' systems remotely (using remote access Trojan, or RAT, software), search for and exfiltrate sensitive data, steal login credentials with keyloggers, relay spam and phishing messages, and participate in DDoS attacks against other organizations.

There are many types of malware. Any individual species of malware may have one or more of the following characteristics:

- **Virus** A fragment of an executable file that is able to attach itself to other executable files. This type of malware exists almost exclusively on Windows operating systems, but with improvements in newer versions of Windows, viruses are less common.

- **Trojan** A stand-alone program that must be executed by the end user to be activated. A Trojan typically claims to be legitimate (such as a game), but actually performs some malicious action.

- **Macro** An executable file that is embedded within another file such as a document or spreadsheet file.

- **Spyware** Malware that records one or more surveillance activities on a target system including web sites visited and keystrokes, reporting back to the spyware owner.

- **Worm** A stand-alone program that is able to propagate itself automatically from one computer to another, typically using network communications.

- **Rootkit** Malware that is designed to evade detection by antimalware and even the operating system itself.

- **Fileless** Malware that exists exclusively in a computer's memory, instead of in the file system. This type of malware is more difficult for traditional antivirus software to detect, as there is no file to examine for matching signatures.

- **Ransomware** Malware that performs some destructive but reversible action such as encrypting files, and that demands a ransom be paid before the destruction can be recovered.

- **Destructware** Malware that performs some permanent destruction, such as irreversible file encryption, on a target system. Also known as a *wiper*.

- **Remote access Trojan** A RAT is malware that provides covert remote access visibility and control of a target system by its attacker.

- **Keylogger** Malware that records an end user's keystrokes on a target system and then sends those keystrokes to the attacker for later analysis.

Formerly known as *antivirus* software, *antimalware* software is designed to detect the presence of malware and neutralize it before it can execute. Antimalware utilizes a number of techniques to detect the presence of malware:

- **Signatures** Time honored but quickly becoming obsolete, signature detection involves the matching of known malware with new files being introduced to the system. A match means malware has been detected.

- **Process observation** Antimalware observes the behavior of processes running in the operating system and generally knows the types of actions that each process will take. When antimalware detects a process performing an action not typical of a given process, it will terminate the process.

- **Sandbox** Antimalware will first install new files in a *sandbox*, a virtual container where the files will be permitted to execute. If the files behave like malware in the sandbox, they will not be permitted to execute in the system. In some products, the sandbox resides in the endpoint, but in other products the sandbox resides in the cloud.

- **Deception** Antimalware will use some technique to scramble the operating system's memory map so that malware will be unable to attack processes' memory images.

Application Whitelisting Organizations can use security tools that employ *application whitelisting,* which permits only registered or recognized programs to execute on a system. This approach can prevent malware from executing on an endpoint, and can also be used to manage policy concerning what software is permitted to be run on systems.

Endpoint Detection and Response   *Endpoint detection and response* (EDR) represents an expansion of protective capabilities employed on endpoints. Going further than anti-malware, EDR solutions employ additional capabilities, such as application whitelisting, intrusion detection, web content filtering, firewall, data loss prevention, and others, all in an integrated solution. EDR provides more comprehensive protection than antimalware alone. An *extended detection and response* (XDR) system is an EDR system with extended capabilities, such as having additional features or being SaaS-based.

The Death of Antivirus Software

Antivirus software works by recognizing the signature of an incoming infection. When a virus spreads to a computer, antivirus software calculates the signature of the incoming file, finds a match, and employs some means to remove it. Initially developed in the mid-1980s, antivirus software initially updated its signatures a couple of times each year because of the slow emergence of computer viruses. But over the years, more and more computer viruses have been discovered, resulting in signature updates multiple times each day.

The creators of malware have won the battle. The techniques used to create malware include a process known as *packing,* whereby the malware program is packaged into an executable (EXE) file. Today, many species of malware repackage themselves prior to attacking each successive endpoint and employ some randomness in the process. The result is that each infected endpoint's virus signature is unique and will never again be seen in the world. Signature-based antivirus software cannot deal with that and has therefore run its course.

Virtual Desktop Infrastructure   Organizations that are highly concerned with malware and other risks associated with endpoint computing can implement virtual desktop infrastructures (VDIs). In a VDI, end-user computing takes place on highly controlled, centralized servers, and end users' computers are essentially functioning as terminals. VDI reduces the risk of malware on endpoints, since endpoints with VDI have a far smaller attack surface than a typical endpoint operating system. Further, no business data is stored or processed on the endpoint or directly accessed by the endpoint; instead, data resides and remains on centralized servers.

Organizations often use enterprise versions of antimalware on endpoints. Unlike consumer-class antimalware programs that act as stand-alone applications, enterprise versions utilize a centralized console that permits an engineer to observe and manage antimalware running on thousands of endpoints. Enterprise consoles can be used to reinstall antimalware when needed, run scans of file systems on demand, and change configurations for any or all endpoints. When malware is detected, consoles can send detailed messages to SIEM systems, alerting personnel in a security operations center (SOC) of the incident so that appropriate action can be taken.

End Users and Local Admin Rights

For decades, a thorny problem with endpoint and end-user management lay in the capability of end users. In earlier versions of Microsoft Windows, end users were automatically given the role of "local administrator." This had two primary implications:

- End users were able to install programs, install drivers, and change system configuration at will, thereby relieving the IT service desk of having to do these actions themselves. While this practice relieving the service desk of drudgery, if an end user botched an install or destroyed the system's registry, service desk personnel had to recover the end user's system, which sometimes required hours of work.

- Malware often executes at the same privilege level as the end user, so when the end user is a local administrator, malware has the run of the machine and can do anything it needs, without restriction. This can make malware attacks far more potent, because the malware can alter any portion of the operating system.

Gradually, IT organizations have taken back administrative privileges from their end users, but not without a fight. In numerous cases, end users would complain and even revolt: they wanted to install their iTunes, personal income tax software, and anything else they wanted. After years of having local admin rights, end users felt entitled to do anything they pleased. Some even went so far as to say that the term *personal computer* meant they could do anything and everything they wanted!

Fortunately, newer versions of Windows have improved the situation by permitting end users without administrative privileges to perform a few "admin-like" tasks. Some users are still not completely happy, but the number of skirmishes has been reduced.

Identity and Access Management

Identity and access management (IAM) represents business processes and technologies used to manage the identities of workers and systems, as well as their access to systems and information. Identity management is the activity of managing the identity and access history of each employee, contractor, temporary worker, supplier worker, and, optionally, customer. These records are then used as the basis for controlling which workplaces, applications, IT systems, and business functions each person is permitted to use.

When organizations had few business applications, organizations provisioned users' access to each separate application. As organizations began to implement additional applications, users had more credentials to use. With the mass migration to cloud-based applications, the numbers of credentials that users had to remember spiraled out of control, leading to unsafe habits, including using the same credentials across many applications and writing down credentials where they could be easily discovered. IT service desks were inundated with password reset requests from users who could not effectively manage their growing portfolio of credentials.

As a result of these developments, organizations began to centralize their IAM systems so that users had to manage fewer sets of credentials. Organizations implemented reduced sign-on and single sign-on to simplify access for users, which also reduced the effort required by IT to manage users' access. Another advantage came in the form of less effort required to manage user credentials. For instance, when an employee left the organization, only the user's single access credential for all applications could be locked or removed, effectively locking the terminated user out of all of the organization's business applications.

Organizations realized that the Achilles heel of reduced sign-on and single sign-on was this: if a user's sole set of credentials were compromised, the attacker would have access to all of the applications that the user had access to. As a result, organizations responded by implementing MFA, whereby a user is required to provide a user ID, a password, and an additional identifier that typically resides in a smart card, mobile phone, or smartphone. Organizations can also implement biometrics, which is a form of MFA. The advantage of MFA is that cases of user ID and password compromise do not permit an attacker to access information unless they also have the user's mobile device in their possession.

The use of userids, passwords, and MFA is giving way to *passwordless authentication,* where authentication consists of an end user providing a userid together with a second factor such as a hardware token or biometric.

Often, access operations are performed by the IT department, while access reviews and recertifications are performed by information security as a form of a check-and-balance system. It would not make sense for IT to perform access reviews because they would be checking their own work, and employees performing these reviews might be tempted to cover up their mistakes.

Access Governance *Access governance* refers to the development of policies, business rules, and controls concerning access to assets and information. These activities ensure that access management operations are managed properly.

Access Operations IAM is an activity-filled discipline that involves everyday activities such as the following:

- Provisioning access to new workers
- Adjusting access rights to workers being transferred
- Assisting workers with access issues such as forgotten passwords
- Assisting workers whose accounts have been locked out for various reasons
- Removing access from departing workers

Less routine events in IAM include these project-related activities:

- Integrating a new business application with a centralized authentication service
- Resetting a user's credentials in response to the loss of a laptop computer or mobile device

PART III

Access Reviews   In an *access review,* management reviews users' access to information and information systems. The purpose of an access review is to confirm that all the workers who have access to information or an information system still require that access. An access review also ensures that any subject no longer requiring access to information or an information system have that access removed. Access reviews take on different forms, including the following:

- Analysis of a single user's access to all information and information systems
- Analysis of all users' access to an information system
- Analysis of all users with a particular set of access rights to one or more information systems

Access reviews are required by various regulations. This requires that personnel who perform access reviews produce a record of the review, including all of the users whose access was examined and specific actions taken as a result of the review.

Accumulation of Privileges

Users who work in an organization for many years may, during their tenure, hold a number of positions in one or more departments. When a user moves from one department to another, the user will require access to new roles or information systems. Over many years, a user may have access to many more information systems and roles than are needed in his or her current role. This phenomenon is known as *accumulation of privileges.*

This is not an easily solved problem. When a user transfers to another department, it makes sense that the user's prior job-related access rights should be terminated right away. However, several factors make this infeasible:

- The user may still have responsibilities in their prior position.
- The user may be training a user who replaced them in their prior position.
- The user may be in the middle of a project that they will complete.

The result of this is that a user's credentials often cannot be removed at the time of their transfer. Methods to remind access administrators of these weeks or months later are error prone. The result is an accumulation of access rights. Access reviews and access recertifications represent a corrective control for this phenomenon.

Segregation of Duties   In the course of managing user access schemes, security managers will recognize that several high-value and high-risk roles in business processes are implemented in information systems and applications. *Segregation of duties* (aka separation of duties) helps ensure that no single individual possesses privileges that could result in unauthorized activities or the manipulation or exposure of sensitive data.

The purpose of segregation of duties is to require that two or more people perform high-value and high-risk activities. This makes it far more difficult for individuals to defraud the organization. For example, segregation of duties is important to avoid a single individual being able to request a user account and provision that user account. It's also important to avoid theft and other malicious activities. For example, an accounting department can allocate roles to individuals so that no single individual has the ability to create a vendor, request a payment to the vendor, and approve a payment to the vendor. If this combination of access rights were granted to a single individual, it could be tempting for the employee to set up a fictitious vendor and then send payments to that vendor.

In a segregation of duties access review, the security manager examines user access rights to various high-risk and high-value roles to determine whether any individuals have access to more than one role within these functions. Any such findings are identified and corrective actions are applied.

In some situations, particularly in smaller organizations, there may not be enough personnel to separate high-value and high-risk activities between two or more persons. In such cases, security managers should recommend that detailed activity reviews be performed periodically to ensure that no fraudulent or erroneous activities are taking place. In high-risk and high-value activities, activity reviews often occur anyway, but when segregation of duties cannot be achieved, these reviews may take place more often or be more thorough.

Privileged and High-Risk Roles Information systems and applications typically have roles for ordinary users, as well as roles that are administrative in nature. These administrative roles are granted a number of high-risk capabilities, including the creation of user accounts, system configuration, and alteration of records. These privileged roles often warrant more frequent and more thorough reviews to ensure that the fewest possible numbers of workers are granted these roles.

Activity Reviews An *activity review* is an examination of an information system to determine which users have been active and which have not been active. The primary purpose of an access review is to identify user accounts that have had no activity for an extended period of time, typically 90 days. The rationale is that if a user has not used an application in more than 90 days, the person probably does not require access to that system. Removing or locking such a user's access helps reduce risk of compromise: if the user's credentials were compromised, they could not be used to access the system. An activity review is a corrective control that helps reduce accumulation of privileges.

Access Recertification *Access recertification* is a periodic review in which information system owners review lists of users and their roles and determine for each user and role whether their access is still required. Like other reviews, personnel often create a business record showing which users and roles were examined and what corrective actions were applied. Access recertification is a corrective control that helps reduce accumulation of privileges.

User Behavior Analytics *User behavior analytics* (UBA), sometimes known as end user behavior analytics (EUBA), represents an emerging technology whereby individual users' behaviors are baselined and anomalous activity triggers events or alarms. UBA systems

PART III

work by observing users' behavior over time and creating events or alarms when user behavior deviates from the norm. UBA is one of several forms of behavior anomaly detection that helps organizations detect unauthorized activities performed by employees or find attackers who have successfully compromised their user accounts.

UBA capabilities can exist in many different contexts. For example, a cloud-based file storage service can establish baselines for each user and report on incidents where individual users are uploading or downloading copious amounts of information. Or an application can baseline each user's behavior and report on anomalies such as unusually large dollar value transactions and other atypical activity. UBA capabilities can counter *insider threats,* a broad category of threats ranging from errors and poor judgment to malice (including information theft and fraud, as well as malware on a user's computer performing actions unknown to the user).

User and entity behavior analytics (UEBA) is functionally similar (if not identical) to EUBA and UBA.

Security Incident Management

Security incident management is the set of activities undertaken by an organization to ensure that it is able to quickly identify a security incident and rapidly and effectively respond and contain the incident. Security incident management is generally divided into two parts:

- **Proactive** The development of policies, procedures, playbooks, and related training
- **Responsive** The actual response to an incident, as well as post-incident activities

Security incident management is covered fully in Chapters 7 and 8.

Managed Security Services Providers

A large number of organizations have centralized logging, a SIEM, vulnerability scanning, and other capabilities, but these organizations are not large enough to warrant staffing a security operations center (SOC) 24/7/365. To ensure full coverage, including coverage for sick days, vacations, holidays, and training, a minimum of 12 personnel may be required to staff a SOC, not counting the SOC manager, along with software licenses and the equipment and space required. For this reason, many organizations outsource the monitoring of their SIEMs and related activities to a *managed security services provider* (MSSP, aka MSS).

Modern MSSPs capabilities include the following:

- Managed SIEM
- Managed vulnerability scanning
- Managed data loss prevention
- Managed endpoint security monitoring
- Managed detection and response (MDR)
- Security incident response and forensics

MSSPs monitor events and incidents in dozens or hundreds of customer organizations and have a large staff to ensure full coverage at peak workloads. Because qualified security personnel can be difficult to attract and retain, many organizations are turning to MSSPs to offload routine tasks and free themselves of the burden of staffing and running a SOC.

Organizations that outsource parts of their security operations to an MSSP need to be mindful of several considerations, including the following:

- **Operational partnership**   An MSSP typically performs a monitoring function but in most cases does not take remedial action. Therefore, when the MSSP identifies an actionable incident, it hands off the incident to someone in the customer organization to take the required action.
- **Service level agreements**   An MSSP typically publishes a schedule of SLAs so that customers understand how responsive the MSSP will be in various scenarios. Organizations should regularly test their MSSP to verify that events are being monitored and comply with the SLAs for alerting and response to events.

Data Governance and Security

Data governance is the collection of management activities and policies that seek to enforce business rules concerning access to and use of data. ISACA defines *data security* as "those controls that seek to maintain confidentiality, integrity, and availability of information." Data security is the heart of everything concerned with information security laws, standards, and practices. Several topics concerning data security are discussed here, including some of the following:

- Access management
- Backup and recovery
- Data classification
- Data loss prevention
- Cloud access security brokers

Cryptography is an important capability often used in support of data governance and security and is covered in the next section.

User behavior analytics is an emerging capability that supports data governance and security. UBA is discussed earlier in this chapter.

Access Management   Access management is part of the broader discipline of IAM. This topic is described in detail earlier in this chapter in the section "Identity and Access Management."

Backup and Recovery   Many types of events can damage information, and some circumstances compel an organization to revert to earlier versions of information. It's essential that copies of stored information exist elsewhere and in a form that enables IT personnel to load this information easily into systems so that processing can resume as quickly as possible.

CAUTION Testing backups is important; testing recoverability is critical. In other words, performing backups is valuable only to the extent that backed-up data can be recovered at a future time.

Backup to Tape and Other Media In organizations still utilizing their own IT infrastructure, tape backup is just about as ubiquitous as power cords. From a disaster recovery perspective, however, the issue probably is not whether the organization has tape backup but whether its current backup capabilities are adequate in the context of disaster recovery. There are times when an organization's backup capability may need to be upgraded:

- If the current backup system is difficult to manage
- If whole-system restoration takes too long
- If the system lacks flexibility with regard to disaster recovery (for instance, a high level of difficulty would be required to recover information onto a different type of system)
- If the technology is old or outdated
- If confidence in the backup technology is low

Many organizations may consider tape backup as a means for restoring files or databases when errors have occurred, and they may have confidence in their backup system for that purpose. However, the organization may have somewhat less confidence in its backup system and its ability to recover all of its critical systems accurately and in a timely manner.

While tape has been the default backup medium since the 1960s, using hard drives and solid-state drives (SSDs) as backup media is growing in popularity: hard disk transfer rates are far higher (and SSDs higher still), and disks/SSD are random-access media, whereas tape is a sequential-access medium. A virtual tape library (VTL) data storage technology sets up a disk-based storage system with the appearance of tape storage, permitting existing backup software to continue to back data up to "tape," which is really just more disk storage.

E-vaulting is another viable option for system backup. E-vaulting permits organizations to back up their systems and data to an offsite location, which could be a storage system in another data center or a third-party service provider. This accomplishes two important objectives: reliable backup and offsite storage of backup data.

 NOTE Backups have always been a critical activity in IT. Ransomware has served to highlight its importance still further.

Backup Schemes   Three main schemes are used for backing up data:

- **Full backup**   A complete copy of a data set
- **Incremental backup**   A copy of all data that has changed since the last full or incremental backup
- **Differential backup**   A copy of all data that has changed since the last full backup

The precise nature of the data to be backed up will determine which combination of backup schemes is appropriate for the organization. Some of the considerations for choosing an overall scheme include the following:

- Criticality of the data set
- Size of the data set
- Frequency of change of the data set
- Performance requirements and the impact of backup jobs
- Recovery requirements

An organization that is creating a backup scheme usually starts with the most common scheme, which is a full backup once per week and an incremental or differential backup every day. However, as stated previously, various factors will influence the design of the final backup scheme. Here are some examples:

- A small data set could be backed up more than once a week, while an especially large data set may be backed up less often.
- A more rapid recovery requirement may induce the organization to perform differential backups instead of incremental backups.
- If a full backup takes a long time to complete, it should probably be performed during times of lower demand or system utilization.

Backup Media Rotation   Organizations will typically want to retain backup media for as long as possible to provide a greater array of choices for data recovery. However, the desire to maintain a large library of backup media will be countered by the high cost of media and the space required to store it. And although legal or statutory requirements may dictate that backup media be kept for some minimum period, the organization may be able to find creative ways to comply with such requirements without retaining several generations of such media. Some example backup media rotation schemes are discussed here.

- **First in, first out**   In this scheme, there is no specific requirement for retaining any backup media for long periods (such as one year or more). The method in the first in, first out (FIFO) rotation scheme specifies that the oldest available backup tape is the next one to be used. The advantage of this scheme is its simplicity.

Day of Cycle

	1	2	3	4	5	6	7	8	9	10	11	12	13	14	15	16	17	18	19	20
Backup Set to Use		A		A		A		A		A		A		A		A		A		A
			B				B				B				B				B	
					C								C							
									D								D			
	E																			

Figure 6-9 Towers of Hanoi backup media rotation scheme

However, there is a significant disadvantage: any corruption of backed-up data needs to be discovered quickly (within the period of media rotation), or else no valid set of data can be recovered. Hence, only low-criticality data without any lengthy retention requirements should be backed up using this scheme.

- **Grandfather-father-son** The most common backup media rotation scheme, grandfather-father-son creates a hierarchical set of backup media that provides for greater retention of backed-up data that is still economically feasible. In the most common form of this scheme, full backups are performed once per week, and incremental or differential backups are performed daily. Daily backup tapes used on Monday are not used again until the following Monday. Backup tapes used on Tuesday, Wednesday, Thursday, Friday, and Saturday are handled in the same way. Full backup tapes created on Sunday are kept longer. Tapes used on the first Sunday of the month are not used again until the first Sunday of the following month. Similarly, tapes used on the second Sunday are not reused until the second Sunday of the following month, and so on, for each week's tapes for Sunday. For even longer retention, for example, tapes created on the first Sunday of the first month of each calendar quarter can be retained until the first Sunday of the first month of the next quarter. Backup media can be kept for even longer if needed.

- **Towers of Hanoi** This backup media retention scheme is complex but results in a more efficient scheme for producing a lengthier retention of some backups. Patterned after the Towers of Hanoi puzzle, the scheme is most easily understood visually, as demonstrated in Figure 6-9, which shows a five-level scheme.

Backup Media Storage Backup media that remains in the same location as backed-up systems is adequate for data recovery purposes but completely inadequate for disaster recovery purposes: any event that physically damages information systems (such as fire, smoke, flood, hazardous chemical spill, and so on) is also likely to damage backup media that is stored nearby. To provide disaster recovery protection, backup media must be stored off site in a secure location. Selection of this storage location is as important as the selection of a primary business location: in the event of a disaster, the survival of the organization may depend upon the protection measures in place at the offsite storage location.

EXAM TIP CISM exam questions relating to offsite backups may include details for safeguarding data during transport and storage, mechanisms for access during restoration procedures, media aging and retention, or other details that may aid you during the exam. Watch for question details involving the type of media, geolocality (distance, shared disaster spectrum such as a shared coastline, and so on) of the offsite storage area and the primary site, or access controls during transport and at the storage site, including environmental controls and security safeguards.

The criteria for selection of an offsite media storage facility are similar to the criteria for selection of a hot/warm/cold recovery site, discussed in Chapter 7. If a media storage location is too close to the primary processing site, it is more likely to be involved in the same regional disaster, which could result in damage to backup media. However, if the media storage location is too far away, it may take too long for a delivery of backup media, which would result in an unacceptably long recovery operation.

Another location consideration is the proximity of the media storage location and the hot/warm/cold recovery site. If a hot site is being used, chances are there is some other near real-time means (such as replication) for data to get to the hot site. But a warm or cold site may be relying on the arrival of backup media from the offsite media storage facility, so it may make sense for the offsite facility to be near the recovery site.

An important factor when considering offsite media storage is the method of delivery to and from the storage location. Chances are that the backup media is being transported by a courier or a shipping company. It is vital that the backup media arrive safely and intact and that the opportunities for interception or loss are reduced as much as possible. Not only can a lost backup tape make recovery more difficult, but it can also cause an embarrassing security incident if knowledge of the loss becomes public. From a confidentiality/integrity perspective, encryption of backup tapes is a good idea, although this digresses somewhat from disaster recovery (concerned primarily with availability).

Backup media that must be kept on site should be stored in locked cabinets or storerooms that are separate from the rooms where backups are performed. This will help to preserve backup media if a minor flood, relatively small fire, or other event occurs in the room containing computers that are backed up.

Protecting Sensitive Backup Media with Encryption

Information security and data privacy laws are expanding data protection requirements by requiring encryption of backup media in many cases. This is a sensible safeguard, especially for organizations that utilize offsite backup media storage. There is a risk of loss of backup media when it is being transported back and forth from an organization's primary data center and the backup media offsite storage facility. If encrypted backup media is misplaced or lost, in some cases this would not be considered a security breach requiring disclosure.

Backup Media Records and Destruction To ensure the ability to restore data from backup media, organizations need to have meticulous records that list all backup volumes in place, where they are located, and which data elements are backed up on them. Without these records, it may prove impossible for an organization to recover data from its backup media library. Laws and regulations may specify minimum and/or maximum periods that specific information may be retained. Organizations need to have good records management that helps them track which business records are on which backup media volumes. When it is time for an organization to stop retaining a specific set of data, those responsible for the backup media library need to identify the backup volumes that can be recycled. If the data on the backup media is sensitive, the backup volume may need to be erased prior to reuse. Any backup media that is being discarded needs to be destroyed so that no other party can possibly recover data on the volume, and records of this destruction should be retained.

Replication During replication, data that is written to a storage system is also copied over a network to another storage system. The result is the presence of up-to-date data that exists on two or more storage systems, each of which could be located in the same room or in different geographic regions. Replication can be handled in several ways and at different levels in the technology stack:

- **Disk storage system** Data-write operations that take place in a disk storage system (such as a SAN or NAS) can be transmitted over a network to another disk storage system, where the same data will be written to the other disk storage system.

- **Operating system** The operating system can control replication so that updates to a particular file system can be transmitted to another server where those updates will be applied locally on that other server.

- **Database management system** The database management system (DBMS) can manage replication by sending transactions to a DBMS on another server.

- **Transaction management system** The transaction management system (TMS) can manage replication by sending transactions to a counterpart TMS located elsewhere.

- **Application** The application can write its transactions to two different storage systems. This method is not often used.

- **Virtualization** Virtual machine images can be replicated to recovery sites to speed the recovery of applications.

Primary-backup replication can take place from one system to another system. This is the typical setup when data on an application server is sent to a distant storage system for data recovery or disaster recovery purposes. *Multiprimary* or *multimaster* replication can also be bidirectional between two or more active servers. This method is more complicated because simultaneous transactions on different servers could conflict with one another (such as two reservation agents trying to book a passenger in the same seat on an airline flight). Some form of concurrent transaction control would be required, such as a distributed lock manager.

In terms of the speed and integrity of replicated information, there are two types of replication:

- **Synchronous replication**   Writing data to a local and to a remote storage system is performed as a single operation, guaranteeing that data on the remote storage system is identical to data on the local storage system. Synchronous replication incurs a performance penalty, as the speed of the entire transaction is slowed to the rate of the remote transaction.

- **Asynchronous replication**   Writing data to the remote storage system is not kept in sync with updates on the local storage system. Instead, there may be a time lag, and you have no guarantee that data on the remote system is identical to that on the local storage system. Performance is improved, however, because transactions are considered complete when they have been written to the local storage system only. Bursts of local updates to data will take a finite period to replicate to the remote server, subject to the available bandwidth of the network connection between the local and remote storage systems.

 NOTE   Organizations need to consider various threat scenarios when selecting data backup and replication methods. Organizations using only replication may find that threats such as software bugs and ransomware may result in damaged data being automatically replicated to other storage systems.

Data Classification   A *data classification* policy defines sensitivity levels and handling procedures for protecting information. Data classification relies partly on human judgment and partly on automation to prevent misuse and compromise of sensitive information. Data classification is discussed fully in Chapter 5.

Data Loss Prevention   *Data loss prevention* (DLP) represents a variety of capabilities by which the movement and/or storage of sensitive data can be detected and, optionally, controlled. DLP technology is considered a content-aware control that some organizations use to detect and even control the storage, transmission, and use of sensitive data. There are two main types of DLP systems:

- **Static DLP**   These tools are used to scan unstructured data storage systems for sensitive information. They can be effective at discovering sensitive data that personnel copy to file servers. Often, users will export sensitive data out of a business application to a spreadsheet and store that data on a file server or cloud-based file storage service. Sometimes this sensitive data is readable by most or all organization personnel and even personnel outside of the organization.

- **Dynamic DLP**   These tools reside in, or communicate with, file storage systems, USB-attached removable storage devices, and e-mail systems, and they are used to detect and even block the movement of sensitive data. Depending on the nature of the data being moved, users may be warned of the activity they are undertaking or their actions may be blocked.

PART III

Implementing DLP systems is a challenging undertaking, mainly because organizations require a thorough understanding of how sensitive and critical data is stored and used. A DLP system can inadvertently block legitimate uses of data while permitting undesired actions.

Digital Rights Management   *Digital rights management* (DRM) represents access control technologies used to control the distribution and use of electronic content. Still considered an emerging technology and practice, DRM exists today in rather narrow usage models and has yet to be widely adopted in general ways. Current capabilities include the following:

- Software license keys
- Copy restriction of music CDs and movie DVDs
- Adobe Acrobat PDF document restriction
- Microsoft Office document restriction

These uses are proprietary and exist as islands of control, as there are no standards that work across multiple technologies or uses.

Cryptography

Cryptography is the practice of hiding information in plain sight, and *encryption* is the application of cryptography that converts data into a code in an attempt to hide the information from unintended viewers. The purpose of encryption is to make it difficult ("impossible" is a word to be avoided here) for someone other than the intended receiver to be able to access the information. Encryption works by scrambling the characters in a message using a method known only to the sender and receiver, which makes the message useless to any unintended party that intercepts the message.

Encryption plays a key role in the protection of sensitive and valuable information. In some situations, it is not practical or feasible to prevent third parties from having logical access to data—for instance, data transmissions over public networks. Encryption is also used as a barrier of last resort—for instance, encryption of data on backup media, to protect the data should that media be lost or stolen.

Encryption can also be used to *authenticate* information that is sent from one party to another. This means that a receiving party can verify that a specific party did, in fact, originate a message and that it is authentic and unchanged. This enables a receiver to know that a message is genuine and that it has not been forged or altered in transit by any third party.

With encryption, best practices call for system designers to use well-known, robust encryption algorithms. Thus, when a third-party intercepts encrypted data, the third party can know which algorithm is being used but still not be able to read the data. What the third party does not know is the *key* that is used to encrypt and decrypt the data. How this works will be further explained in this section.

 NOTE   Encryption can be thought of as another layer of access protection. Like user ID and password controls that restrict access to data to everyone but those with login credentials, encryption restricts access to (plaintext) data to everyone but those with encryption keys.

Terms and Concepts Used in Cryptography   Several terms and concepts often used in cryptography are not used outside of the field. Security managers must be familiar with these terms to be effective in understanding, managing, and auditing IT systems that use cryptography.

- **Plaintext**   An original, unencrypted, message, file, or stream of data that can be read by anyone who has access to it.
- **Ciphertext**   A message, file, or stream of data that has been transformed by an encryption algorithm and rendered unreadable.
- **Encryption**   The process of transforming plaintext into ciphertext, as depicted in Figure 6-10.
- **Hash function**   A cryptographic operation on a block of data that returns a fixed-length string of characters, used to verify the integrity of a message.
- **Message digest**   The output of a cryptographic hash function.

Figure 6-10
Encryption and decryption utilize an encryption algorithm and an encryption key.

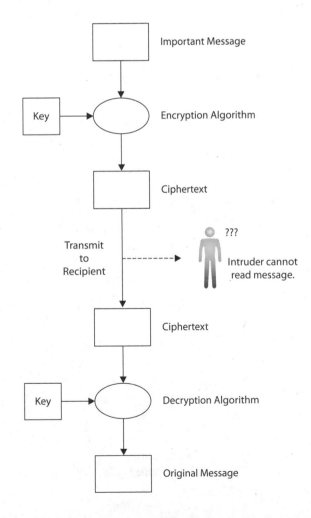

PART III

- **Digital signature**   The result of encrypting the hash of a message with the originator's private encryption key, used to prove the authenticity and integrity of a message. This is depicted in Figure 6-11.

- **Algorithm**   A specific mathematical formula used to perform encryption, decryption, message digests, and digital signatures.

- **Decryption**   The process of transforming ciphertext into plaintext so that a recipient can read it.

- **Cryptanalysis**   An attack on a cryptosystem whereby the attacker is attempting to determine the encryption key that is used to encrypt messages.

- **Encryption key**   A block of characters, along with an encryption algorithm, used to encrypt or decrypt a stream or blocks of data. An encryption key is also used to create and verify a digital signature.

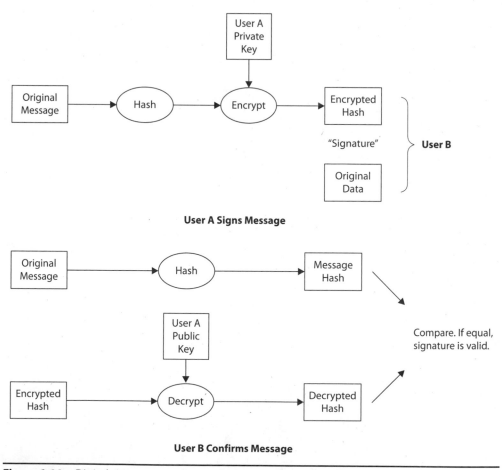

Figure 6-11   Digital signature used to verify the integrity of a message

- **Key-encrypting key**   An encryption key that is used to encrypt another encryption key.

- **Key length**   The size (measured in bits) of an encryption key. Longer encryption keys make it more difficult for an attacker to decrypt the data successfully.

- **Block cipher**   An encryption algorithm that operates on blocks of data.

- **Stream cipher**   A type of encryption algorithm that operates on a continuous stream of data such as a video or audio feed.

- **Initialization vector (IV)**   A random number that is required by some encryption algorithms to begin the encryption process.

- **Symmetric encryption**   A method for encryption and decryption in which both parties must possess a common encryption key.

- **Asymmetric encryption**, or **public key cryptography**   A method for encryption, decryption, and digital signatures that uses pairs of encryption keys: a *public key* and a *private key*.

- **Key exchange**   A technique used by two parties to establish a symmetric encryption key when there is no secure channel available.

- **Nonrepudiation**   The property of encryption and digital signatures that can make it difficult or impossible for a party to deny having sent a digitally signed message, unless the party admits to having lost control of their private encryption key.

Private Key Cryptosystems   A *private key cryptosystem* is based on a symmetric cryptographic algorithm. The primary characteristic of a private key cryptosystem is the necessity for both parties to possess a common encryption key that is used to encrypt and decrypt messages. Following are the two main challenges with private key cryptography:

- **Key exchange**   An *out-of-band* method for exchanging encryption keys is required before any encrypted messages can be transmitted. This key exchange must occur over a separate, secure channel; if the encryption keys were transmitted over the main communications channel, then anyone who intercepted the encryption key would be able to read any intercepted messages, provided they could determine the encryption algorithm used. For instance, if two parties want to exchange encrypted e-mail, they would need to exchange their encryption key first via some other means, such as telephone or fax, provided they are confident that their telephone and fax transmissions are not being intercepted.

- **Scalability**   Private key cryptosystems require that each sender–receiver pair exchange an encryption key. For a group of 4 parties, 6 encryption keys would need to be exchanged; for a group of 10 parties, 45 keys would need to be exchanged. For a large community of 1000 parties, many thousands of keys would need to be exchanged.

Some well-known private key algorithms in use include Advanced Encryption Standard (AES), Blowfish, Data Encryption Standard (DES), Triple DES, Serpent, and Twofish.

PART III

Secure Key Exchange   *Secure key exchange* refers to methods used by two parties to establish a symmetric encryption key securely without actually transmitting the key over a channel. Secure key exchange is needed when two parties, previously unknown to each other, need to establish encrypted communications where no out-of-band channel is available. Two parties can perform a secure key exchange if a third party intercepts their entire conversation. This is because algorithms used for secure key exchange utilize information known by each party but not transmitted between them. The most popular algorithm is the Diffie–Hellman key exchange protocol.

Exchanging Initial Encryption Keys

Think about a private key cryptosystem. In an established cryptosystem, two users exchange messages and encrypt/decrypt them using an encryption key. Before they can begin exchanging encrypted messages, one of the users must first get a copy of the key to the other user. They have to do this prior to the establishment of the cryptosystem, so they cannot use the cryptosystem to transmit the key.

Secure key exchange, such as Diffie–Hellman, is used to transmit the key safely from one party to the other party. Once both parties have the key, they can begin sending encrypted messages to each other. Without secure key exchange, each user would have to use some other safe, out-of-band means for getting the encryption key across to the other user.

Public Key Cryptosystems   Public key cryptosystems are based on *asymmetric,* or *public key,* cryptographic algorithms. These algorithms use two-part encryption keys that are handled differently from encryption keys in symmetric key cryptosystems.

Key Pair   The encryption keys used in public key cryptography are called the *public key* and the *private key*. Each user of public key cryptosystems possesses this key pair. The two keys require different handling and are used together but for different purposes, as explained in the following paragraphs. When a user generates a key pair, the key pair will physically exist as two separate files. The user is free to publish or distribute the public key openly; it could even be posted on a public web site. This is in contrast to the private key, which must be well protected and never published or sent to any other party. Most public key cryptosystems utilize a password mechanism to further protect the private key; without its password, the private key is inaccessible and cannot be used.

Message Security   Public key cryptography is an ideal application for securing messages—e-mail in particular—because users do not need to establish and communicate symmetric encryption keys through a secure channel. With public key cryptography, users who have never contacted each other can immediately send secure messages to each other. Figure 6-12 depicts public key cryptography.

Every user is free to publish a public encryption key so that it is easily retrievable. There are servers on the Internet where public keys can be published and made available to anyone in the world. Public key cryptography is designed so that open disclosure of

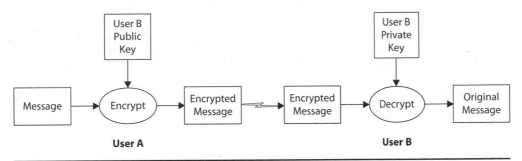

Figure 6-12   Public key cryptography used to transmit a secret message

a user's public key does not compromise the secrecy of the corresponding private key: a user's private key cannot be derived from the public key.

When User A wishes to send an encrypted message to User B, the procedure is as follows:

1. User B publishes his public key to the Internet at a convenient location.
2. User A retrieves User B's public key.
3. User A creates a message and encrypts it with User B's public key and sends the encrypted message to User B.
4. User B decrypts the message with his private key and is able to read the message.

Note that only User B's encryption key is used in this example. This method protects the message from eavesdroppers, but it is not used to verify the authenticity of the message.

Public key cryptography can also be used to verify the authenticity and integrity of a message—to verify that a specific party did, in fact, create the message. The procedure is as follows:

1. User A publishes his public key to the Internet at a convenient location.
2. User B retrieves User A's public key and saves it for later use.
3. User A creates a message and digitally signs it with his private key and then sends the signed message to User B.
4. User B verifies the digital signature using User A's public key. If the message verifies correctly, User B knows that the message originated from User A and has not been altered in transit.

In this example, only the authenticity and integrity of a message are assured. The message is not encrypted, which means that any party that intercepts the message can read it.

Public key cryptography can be used both to encrypt and digitally sign a message, which will guarantee its confidentiality as well as its authenticity. The procedure is as follows:

1. User A and User B publish their public encryption keys to convenient places.
2. User A retrieves User B's public key, and User B retrieves User A's public key.

3. User A creates a message, signs it with his private key and encrypts it with User B's public key, and then sends the message to User B.

4. User B decrypts the message with his private key and verifies the digital signature with User A's public key.

Elliptic Curve Cryptography

A cryptography method called *elliptic curve cryptography* (ECC) is attracting interest for use in public key cryptography applications. ECC requires less computational power and bandwidth than other cryptographic algorithms and is thought to be more secure as well. Because of its low power requirements, it is used extensively in mobile devices.

Public key cryptography also supports encryption of a message with more than one user's public key. This permits a user to send a single encrypted message to several recipients, which can be encrypted with each of their public keys. This method does not compromise the secrecy of any user's private key, since a user's private key cannot be derived from the public key.

Verifying Public Keys   It is possible for a fraudster to claim the identity of another person and even publish a public key that claims the identity of that person. Four methods are available for verifying a user's public key as genuine:

- **Certificate authority (CA)**   A public key that has been obtained from a trusted, reputable CA can be considered genuine.

- **E-mail address**   Public keys used for e-mail will include the user's e-mail address. If the e-mail address is part of a corporate or government domain (for example, *apple.com* or *seattle.gov*), then some level of credence can be attributed to the successful exchange of messages with that e-mail address. However, since e-mail addresses can be spoofed, this should be considered a weak method at best.

- **Directory infrastructure**   A directory services infrastructure such as Microsoft Active Directory, Lightweight Directory Access Protocol (LDAP), or a commercial product can be used to verify a user's public key.

- **Key fingerprint**   Many public key cryptosystems employ a method for verifying a key's identity, known as the key's *fingerprint*. If a user wants to verify a public key, the user retrieves the public key and calculates the key's fingerprint. The user then contacts the claimed owner of the public key, who runs a function against his private key that returns a string of numbers. The user also runs a function against the owner's public key, also returning a string of numbers. If both numbers match, the public key is genuine.

 NOTE   When issuing a public key, it is essential that the requestor of the new public key be authenticated, such as by viewing a government-issued ID or by contacting the owner at a publicly listed telephone number.

Hashing and Message Digests   *Hashing* is the process of applying a cryptographic algorithm on a block of information that results in a compact, fixed-length digest. The purpose of hashing is to provide a unique and compact "fingerprint" for the message or file—even if the file is very large. A message digest can be used to verify the integrity of a large file, thus assuring that the file has not been altered. Properties of message digests that make them ideally suited for verifying integrity include the following:

- Any change made to a file—even a single bit or character—will result in a significant change in the hash.

- It is computationally infeasible to make a change to a file without changing its hash.

- It is computationally infeasible to create a message or file that will result in a given hash.

- It is infeasible to find any two messages that will have the same hash.

One common use of message digests is on software download sites, where the computed hash for a downloadable program is available so that users can verify that the software program has not been altered (provided that the posted hash has not also been compromised).

Digital Signatures   A *digital signature* is a cryptographic operation whereby a sender "seals" a message or file using her identity. The purpose of a digital signature is to authenticate a message and to guarantee its integrity. Digital signatures do not protect the confidentiality of a message, however, as encryption is not one of the operations performed. Digital signatures work by encrypting hashes of messages; recipients verify the integrity and authenticity of messages by decrypting hashes and comparing them to original messages. In detail, a digital signature works like this:

1. The sender publishes his public key to the Internet at a location that is easily accessible to recipients.

2. The recipient retrieves the sender's public key and saves it for later use.

3. The sender creates a message (or file) and computes a message digest (hash) of the message and then encrypts the hash with his private key.

4. The sender sends the original file plus the encrypted hash to the recipient.

5. The recipient receives the original file and the encrypted hash. The recipient computes a message digest (hash) of the original file and sets the result aside. She then decrypts the hash with the sender's public key. The recipient compares the hash of the original file and the decrypted hash.

6. If the two hashes are identical, the recipient knows that (a) the message in her possession is identical to the message that the sender sent, (b) the sender is the originator, and (c) the message has not been altered.

The use of digital signatures was depicted earlier in this chapter in Figure 6-11.

Digital Envelopes   One aspect of symmetric (private key) and asymmetric (public key) cryptography that has not yet been discussed is the performance implications of these two types of cryptosystems. Broadly speaking, public key cryptography requires far more computing power than private key cryptography. The practical implication of this is that public key encryption of large sets of data can be highly compute-intensive and make its use infeasible in some occasions. One solution to this is the use of a so-called *digital envelope* that utilizes the convenience of public key cryptography with the lower overhead of private key cryptography. This practice is known as *hybrid cryptography*. The procedure for using digital envelopes works like this:

1. The sender and recipient agree that the sender will transmit a large message to the recipient.

2. The sender selects or creates a symmetric encryption key, known as the *session key*, and encrypts the session key with the recipient's public key.

3. The sender encrypts the message with the session key.

4. The sender sends the encrypted message (encrypted with the session key) and the encrypted session key (encrypted with the recipient's public key) to the recipient.

5. The recipient decrypts the session key with his private key.

6. The recipient decrypts the message with the session key.

The now-deprecated SET (Secure Electronic Transaction, a predecessor to SSL/TLS) protocol uses digital envelopes. Digital envelopes require less computing overhead than the Diffie–Hellman key exchange, which is why digital envelopes may be preferred in some circumstances.

Public Key Infrastructure   One of the issues related to public key cryptography is the safe storage of public encryption keys. Although individuals are free to publish public keys online, doing so in a secure and controlled manner requires some central organization and control. A *public key infrastructure* (PKI) is designed to fulfill this and other functions. A PKI is a centralized function that is used to store and publish public keys and other information. Some of the services provided by a PKI include the following:

- **Digital certificates**   This digital credential consists of a public key and a block of information that identifies the owner of the certificate. The identification portion of a digital certificate will follow a standard, structured format and include such data as the owner's name, organization name, and other identifying information, such as e-mail address. The public key and the identifying information will reside in a document that is itself digitally signed by a trusted CA.

- **Certificate authority (CA)**   This business entity issues digital certificates and publishes them in the PKI. The CA vouches for the identity of each of the digital certificates in a PKI; the CA undergoes certain safeguards to ensure that each digital certificate is genuine and really does belong to its rightful owner.

- **Registration authority (RA)**   The RA operates within or alongside a CA to accept requests for new digital certificates. The RA vets the request, carefully examines it, and undergoes steps to verify the authenticity of the person making the request. This verification may include viewing government-issued ID cards or passports or taking other steps as needed to make sure that the request is originating from the genuine person and not an imposter. When the RA is satisfied that the requestor is indeed the person making the request, the RA will issue a digital certificate. Part of the certificate issuance will be the delivery of private encryption keys to the requesting party. This may take place in person or over a secured electronic connection.

- **Certificate revocation list (CRL)**   Some circumstances may require that a user's digital certificate be cancelled or revoked. These circumstances include termination of employment (if a person's certificate was issued expressly for employment-related purposes) or loss or compromise of a user's private key. A CRL is an electronic list of digital certificates that have been revoked prior to their expiration date. To be effective, any consumer of digital certificates needs to consult a CRL to be doubly sure that a certificate remains valid.

- **Certification practice statement (CPS)**   This published statement describes the practices used by the CA to issue and manage digital certificates. This helps determine the relative strength and validity of digital certificates that are issued by the CA.

Key Management   *Key management* comprises the various processes and procedures used by an organization to generate, protect, use, and dispose of encryption keys over their lifetimes. Several of the major practices are described in this section.

Key Generation   An encryption key life cycle starts with its generation. While at first glance it would appear that this process should require little scrutiny, further study shows that this is a critical process that requires safeguards. The system on which key generation takes place must be highly protected. If keys are generated on a system that has been compromised or is of questionable integrity, it would be difficult to determine whether a bystander could have electronically observed key generation. For instance, if a keylogger or other process spying tool were active in the system when keys were generated, key generation may have been observable and details about keys captured. This would mean that newly minted keys have already been compromised if an outsider knows their identities.

In many situations, it would be reasonable to require that systems used for key generation be highly protected, isolated, and used by as few people as possible. Regular integrity checks would need to take place to make sure the system continues to be free of any problems. Furthermore, the key generation process needs to include some randomness (or, as some put it, entropy) so that the process cannot be easily duplicated elsewhere. If key generation were not a random event, it could be possible to duplicate the conditions related to a specific key and then regenerate a key with the very same value. This would instantaneously compromise the integrity and uniqueness of the original key.

Key Protection   Private keys used in public key cryptosystems and keys used in symmetric cryptosystems must be continuously and vigorously protected. At all times, they must be accessible only to the parties that are authorized to use them. If protection measures for private encryption keys are compromised (or suspected to be), it will be possible for a key compromise to take place, enabling the attacker to view messages encrypted with these keys and create new encrypted messages in the name of the key's owner. A *key compromise* is any event whereby a private encryption key or symmetric encryption key has been disclosed to any unauthorized third party. When a key compromise occurs, it will be necessary to re-encrypt all materials encrypted by the compromised key with a new encryption key.

TIP   In many applications, an encryption key is protected by a password. The length, complexity, distribution, and expiration of passwords protecting encryption keys must be well designed so that the strength of the cryptosystem (based on its key length and algorithm) is not compromised by a weak password scheme protecting its keys.

Key-Encrypting Keys   Applications that utilize encryption must obtain their encryption keys in some way. In many cases, an intruder may be able to examine the application in an attempt to discover an encryption key in hopes of decrypting communications used by the application. A common remedy for this is the use of encryption to protect the encryption key. This additional encryption requires a key of its own, known as a *key-encrypting key*. Of course, this key also must reside someplace; often, features of the underlying operating system may be used to protect an encryption key as well as a key-encrypting key.

Key Custody   *Key custody* refers to the policies, processes, and procedures regarding the management of keys. This is closely related to key protection but is focused on who manages keys and where they are kept.

Key Rotation   *Key rotation* is the process of issuing a new encryption key and re-encrypting data protected with the new key. Key rotation may occur when any of the following occurs:

- **Key compromise**   When an encryption key has been compromised, a new key must be generated and used.

- **Key expiration**   This happens where encryption keys are rotated on a schedule.

- **Rotation of staff**   In some organizations, if any of the persons associated with the creation or management of encryption keys transfers to another position or leaves the organization, keys must be rotated.

Key Disposal   *Key disposal* refers to the process of decommissioning encryption keys. This may be done upon receipt of an order to destroy a data set that is encrypted with a specific encryption key—destroying an encryption key can be as effective (and a whole lot easier) than destroying the encrypted data itself. Key disposal can present some challenges, however. If an encryption key is backed up to tape, for instance, disposal of the key will require that backup tapes also be destroyed.

Encryption Applications   Several applications utilize encryption algorithms. Many of these are well known and in common use.

Secure Sockets Layer and Transport Layer Security   *Secure Sockets Layer* (SSL) and *Transport Layer Security* (TLS) are the encryption protocols used to encrypt web pages requested with the Hypertext Transfer Protocol/Secure (HTTPS) protocol. Introduced by Netscape Communications for use in its own browser, SSL and its successor, TLS, have become de facto standards for the encryption of web pages.

SSL and TLS provide several cryptographic functions, including public key encryption, private key encryption, and hash functions. These are used for server and client authentication (although in practice, client authentication is seldom used) and session encryption. SSL and TLS support several encryption algorithms, including AES, RC4, IDEA, DES, and Triple DES, and several key lengths, from 40 to 256 bits and beyond. Weaknesses were discovered in all versions of SSL, as well as the first version of TLS. No versions of SSL or TLS 1.0 should be used.

 EXAM TIP   Test-takers need to understand that all versions of SSL and the early version of TLS are now considered deprecated and should no longer be used. The term SSL is still commonly used, however, and it refers to the context but not the algorithm.

Secure Multipurpose Internet Mail Extensions   *Secure Multipurpose Internet Mail Extensions* (S/MIME) is an e-mail security protocol that provides sender and recipient authentication and encryption of message content and attachments. S/MIME is most often used for encryption of e-mail messages.

Secure Shell   *Secure Shell* (SSH) is a multipurpose protocol that is used to create a secure channel between two systems. The most popular use of SSH is the replacement of the Telnet and R series protocols (rsh, rlogin, and so on), but it also supports tunneling of protocols such as X-Windows and File Transfer Protocol (FTP).

Internet Protocol Security   *Internet Protocol Security* (IPsec) is a protocol used to create a secure, authenticated channel between two systems. IPsec operates at the Internet layer in the TCP/IP protocol suite; hence, all IP traffic between two systems protected by IPsec is automatically encrypted. IPsec operates in one of two modes: Encapsulating Security Payload (ESP) and Authentication Header (AH). If ESP is used, all encapsulated traffic is encrypted. If AH is used, only IPsec's authentication feature is used.

Information Security Control Testing and Evaluation

Organizations develop controls to ensure desired outcomes. After implementing a control, organizations need to test and evaluate controls to determine whether they are operating as intended.

Control Monitoring

A control needs to have been designed so that monitoring can take place. In the absence of monitoring, the organization will lack methodical means for observing the control to determine whether it is effective. For example, suppose an organization identified a risk during a risk assessment that indicated that its user accounts were vulnerable to brute-force password guessing. The organization decided to change the login process on affected systems so that incorrect passwords would result in a small delay before the user could re-attempt to log on (to counter machine-driven password guessing) and that user accounts would be temporarily locked out after five unsuccessful attempts within a five-minute period. To facilitate monitoring, the organization also changed the login process to create audit log entries each time a user attempted to log in, regardless of the outcome. This provided the organization with event data that could be examined from time to time to determine whether the control was performing as intended.

Some controls are not so easily monitored. For instance, a control addressing abuse of intellectual property rights includes the enactment of new acceptable use policies (AUPs) that forbid employees from violating intellectual property laws such as copyrights. Many forms of abuse cannot be easily monitored.

Control Reviews and Audits

An essential function in information security management is the use of a set of activities that determine whether security safeguards are in place and working properly. These activities range from informal security reviews to formal and highly structured security audits. Most organizations undergo one or more of these reviews or audits from time to time, either as part of a compliance program or because management realizes that reviews and audits are a necessary part of knowing whether an organization is in fact secure.

In the information security industry, the terms "security review" and "security audit" are used correctly by many professionals but haphazardly by many others. Generally speaking, a *security review* is a less formal and less rigorous examination of one or more controls, processes, or systems to determine their state. A *security audit* is a more formal, methodical, and rigorous examination of one or more controls, processes, or systems. An audit generally requires the presentation of evidence of control design and effectiveness, where a review often does not. Figure 6-13 depicts the relationship between security reviews and security audits.

Figure 6-13
Security reviews
and security
audits

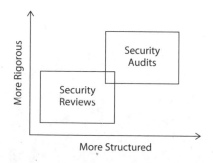

Security Reviews

Sometimes known as a control review, this examination of a process, procedure, system, program, or other object determines the state of security. A security review may be part of an ad hoc request, or it may be part of a repeatable business process. These are some examples of security reviews:

- Review of a firewall configuration to ensure that all expected rules are present and that there are no unwanted rules such as "any-any"

- Review of source code as part of the software development life cycle to ensure that the code in question is free of security defects

- Review of an employee onboarding procedure to make sure that necessary security steps are followed

Organizations sometimes perform security reviews in advance of an audit in an attempt to avoid encountering unexpected audit findings. A security review may also be a *pre-audit,* a sort of "dry run" prior to an audit that helps ensure that personnel are familiar with the subject matter that auditors will be asking them about during the audit.

Security reviews are generally less rigorous than security audits. Security reviews are generally devoid of rules for evidence collection, types of testing, or sampling techniques. For instance, a security review of a firewall configuration may glance at its rules, whereas an audit may examine each individual rule: its purpose and meaning, who approved it, and when it will next be reviewed.

NOTE   A security review is often carried out by the owner of a control, whereas an audit is performed by a separate party.

Audits

An *audit* is a systematic and repeatable process whereby a competent and independent professional evaluates one or more controls, interviews personnel, obtains and analyzes evidence, and develops a written opinion on the effectiveness of a control. In an audit of information systems and the processes that support them, an information systems auditor interviews personnel, gathers and analyzes evidence, and delivers a written opinion on the effectiveness of controls implemented in information systems.

There are generally two parties in an audit: the auditor and the auditee. This is true whether the audit is formal or informal and whether it's internal or external. In terms of the context of an audit, there are two types: internal audit and external audit. These have to do with who performs the audit and why. Otherwise, the methodologies and techniques used in auditing are the same.

NOTE   For a more complete discussion on audits and auditing, see *CISA Certified Information Systems Auditor All-in-One Exam Guide, Fourth Edition* (McGraw Hill, 2020).

Audit Techniques   Like most any business undertaking, an audit is a planned event. Formal planning is required so that the organization successfully achieves the objectives for an audit. The types of planning that are required include the following:

- **Purpose**   The auditor and the auditee must establish why an audit is to be performed. The purpose for a particular audit could be to determine the level of compliance to a particular law, regulation, standard, or contract. Another reason could be to determine whether specific control deficiencies identified in past audits have been remediated. Still another reason is to determine the level of compliance to a new law, standard, or contract that the organization may be subject to in the future.

- **Scope**   The auditor and the auditee must also establish the scope of the audit. Often, the audit's purpose will make the scope evident, but not always. Scope may be multidimensional: it could involve a given period in which the body of evidence includes records spanning from a start date to an end date, or it could involve geography (systems in a particular region or locale), a technology (systems using a specific operating system, a database, application, or other aspect), a business process (systems that support specific processes such as accounting, order entry, or customer support), or a segment of the organization.

- **Risk analysis**   To know which areas require the greatest amount of attention, the auditor needs to be familiar with the levels of risk associated with the domain being audited. Two different perspectives of risk may be needed. First, the auditor needs to know the relative levels of risk among the different aspects of the domain being audited so that audit resources can be allocated accordingly. For example, if the subject of an audit is an enterprise resource planning (ERP) system and the auditor knows that the accounts receivable function has been problematic in the past, the auditor will probably want to devote more resources and time on the accounts receivable function than on others. Second, the auditor needs to know about the absolute level of risk across the entire domain being audited. For example, if this is an audit to determine compliance to new legislation, the overall risk could be very high if the consequences of noncompliance are high. These aspects of risk enable the auditor to plan accordingly.

- **Audit procedures**   The purpose and scope of the audit may help to define the procedures that will be required to perform the audit. For a compliance audit, for example, there may be specific rules on sample sizes and sampling techniques, and auditors may be required to possess specific qualifications. A compliance audit may also specify criteria for determining whether a particular finding constitutes a deficiency. There may also be rules for materiality and additional steps to follow if material weaknesses are identified.

- **Resources**   The auditor must determine what resources are needed and available for the audit. In an external audit, the auditee (a client organization) may have a maximum budget figure available. For an external or internal audit, the auditor needs to determine the number of person-hours that will be required in the audit and the various skills required. Other resources that may be needed include specialized tools to gather or analyze information obtained from information systems—for example, an analysis program to process the roles and permissions in a database management system to identify high-risk areas. To a great degree, the purpose and scope of the audit will determine which resources are required to complete it.

- **Schedule**   The auditor needs to develop an audit schedule that includes enough time for interviews, data collection and analysis, and report generation. Additionally, the schedule could also come in the form of a constraint, meaning the audit must be complete by a certain date. If the auditor is given a deadline, she will need to see how the audit activities can be made to fit within that period. If the date is too aggressive, the auditor will need to discuss the matter with the auditee to make required adjustments in scope, resources, or schedule.

Audit Objectives   The *audit objectives* are the specific goals for an audit. Generally, the objective of an audit is to determine whether controls exist and whether they are effective in some specific aspect of business operations in an organization. An audit is often performed as a requirement of regulations, compliance, or other legal obligations. It may also be performed in the aftermath of a serious incident or event to determine whether any additional weaknesses are found elsewhere in the organization that could also suffer an event. Sometimes, an organization will initiate an internal audit of relevant systems if a competitor or other similar organization has suffered an incident; the purpose here is to determine whether the organization is likely to suffer the same fate.

Depending on the subject and nature of the audit, the auditor may examine the controls and related evidence herself, or the auditor may instead focus on the business content that is processed by the controls. In other words, if the focus of an audit is an organization's accounting system, the auditor may focus on financial transactions in the system to see how they affect financial bookkeeping. Or the auditor could focus on IT processes that support the operation of the financial accounting system. Formal audit objectives should make such a distinction so that the auditor has a sound understanding of the objectives. This tells the auditor where to look and what to look at during the audit. Of course, the type of audit being undertaken helps too.

Types of Audits   The scope, purpose, and objectives of an audit will to a great extent determine the type of audit that will be performed. Auditors need to understand each type of audit, including the procedures that are used for each, so that the correct type will be selected.

- **Operational audit**   An examination of IT controls, security controls, or business controls to determine control existence and effectiveness. The is usually the operation of one or more controls, and it could concentrate on the IT management of a business process or on the business process itself.
- **Financial audit**   An examination of the organization's accounting system, including accounting department processes and procedures. The typical objective is to determine whether business controls are sufficient to ensure the integrity of financial statements.

- **Integrated audit**   Combines an operational audit and a financial audit, offering the auditor a complete understanding of the entire environment's integrity. This audit will closely examine accounting department processes, procedures, and records, as well as the business applications that support the accounting department or other financial function. Virtually every organization uses a computerized accounting system for management of its financial records; the computerized accounting system and all of the supporting infrastructure (database management system, operating system, networks, workstations, and so on) will be examined to see whether the IT department has the entire environment under adequate control.

- **IS audit**   A detailed examination of most or all of an information systems (IS) department's operations. An IS audit looks at IT governance to determine whether IS is aligned with overall organization goals and objectives. The audit also looks closely at all of the major IT processes, including service delivery, change and configuration management, security management, systems development life cycle, business relationship and supplier management, and incident and problem management. It will determine whether each control objective and control is effective and operating properly.

- **Administrative audit**   An examination of operational efficiency within some segment of the organization.

- **Compliance audit**   Performed to determine the level and degree of compliance to a law, regulation, standard, internal control, or legal contract. If a particular law or standard requires an external audit, the compliance audit may have to be performed by approved or licensed external auditors; for example, a U.S. public company's annual financial audit must be performed by a public accounting firm, and a PCI DSS audit must be performed by a licensed qualified security assessor (QSA). If, however, the law or standard does not explicitly require audits, the organization may still want to perform one-time or regular audits to determine the level of compliance to the law or standard. This type of audit may be performed by internal or external auditors and typically is performed so that management has a better understanding of the level of compliance risk.

- **Forensic audit**   Usually performed by an auditor or a forensic specialist in support of an anticipated or active legal proceeding. To withstand cross-examination and to avoid having evidence being ruled inadmissible, strict procedures must be followed in a forensic audit, including the preservation of evidence and a chain of custody of evidence.

- **Service provider audit**   Because many organizations outsource critical activities to third parties, often these third-party service organizations will undergo one or more external audits to increase customer confidence in the integrity and security of the third-party organization's services. In the United States, a Statement on Standards for Attestation Engagements No. 18 (SSAE 18) audit can be performed on a service provider's operations and the audit report transmitted to customers of the service provider. SSAE 18 superseded the similar SSAE 16 standard, which replaced the older Statement of Accounting Standards No. 70 (SAS 70) audit in 2011. The SSAE 18 standard was developed by the AICPA for the purpose of auditing third-party service organizations that perform financial services on behalf of their customers.

NOTE SSAE 18 is closely aligned with the global standard, *International Standard on Assurance Engagements 3402, Assurance Reports on Controls at a Service Organization* (ISAE 3402), from the International Auditing and Assurance Standards Board (IAASB).

- **Pre-audit** Though not technically an audit, a pre-audit is an examination of business processes, information systems, applications, or business records in anticipation of an upcoming audit. Usually, an organization will undergo a pre-audit to get a better idea of its compliance to a law, regulation, standard, or other legal obligation prior to an actual compliance audit. An organization can use the results of a pre-audit to implement corrective measures, thereby improving the outcome of the real audit.

Audit Methodology An *audit methodology* is the set of audit procedures used to accomplish a set of audit objectives. An organization that regularly performs audits should develop formal methodologies so that those audits are performed consistently, even when carried out by different personnel. The phases of a typical audit methodology are described here:

- **Audit subject** Determine the business process, information system, or other domain to be audited. For instance, an auditor might be auditing an IT change control process, an IT service desk ticketing system, or the activities performed by a software development department.

- **Audit objective** Identify the purpose of the audit. For example, the audit may be required by a law, regulation, standard, or business contract, or to determine compliance with internal control objectives to measure control effectiveness.

- **Type of audit** This may be an operational audit, financial audit, integrated audit, administrative audit, compliance audit, forensic audit, or a security provider audit.

- **Audit scope** The business process, department, or application that is the subject of the audit. Usually, a span of time needs to be identified as well so that activities or transactions during that period can be examined.

- **Pre-audit planning** The auditor needs to obtain information about the audit that will enable her to establish the audit plan. Information needed includes locations to visit, a list of the applications to examine, the technologies supporting each application, and the policies, standards, and diagrams that describe the environment.

PART III

This and other information will enable the auditor to determine the skills required to examine and evaluate processes and information systems. The auditor will be able to establish an audit schedule and will have a good idea of the types of evidence that are needed. The IS audit may be able to make advance requests for certain other types of evidence even before the onsite phase of the audit begins.

For an audit with a risk-based approach, the auditor has a couple of options:

- Precede the audit itself with a risk assessment to determine which processes or controls warrant additional audit scrutiny.
- Gather information about the organization and historic events to discover risks that warrant additional audit scrutiny.

Audit Statement of Work   For an external audit, the auditor may need to develop a statement of work or engagement letter that describes the audit purpose, scope, duration, and costs. The auditor may require a written approval from the client before audit work can officially begin.

Establish Audit Procedures   Using information obtained regarding audit objectives and scope, the auditor can now develop procedures for this audit. For each objective and control to be tested, the auditor can specify the following:

- A list of people to interview
- Inquiries to make during each interview
- Documentation (policies, procedures, and other documents) to request during each interview
- Audit tools to use
- Sampling rates and methodologies
- How and where evidence will be archived
- How evidence will be evaluated

Audit Communication Plan   The auditor will develop a communication plan to keep the auditor's management, as well as the auditee's management, informed throughout the audit project. The communication plan may contain one or more of the following:

- A list of evidence requested, usually in the form of a PBC (provided by client) list, which is typically a worksheet that lists specific documents or records and the names of personnel who can provide them (or who provided them in a prior audit)
- Regular written status reports that include activities performed since the last status report, upcoming activities, and any significant findings that may require immediate attention
- Regular status meetings where audit progress, issues, and other matters may be discussed in person or via conference call
- Contact information for both IS auditor and auditee so that both parties can contact each other quickly if needed

Report Preparation The auditor needs to develop a plan that describes how the audit report will be prepared. This will include the format and the content of the report, as well as the manner in which findings will be established and documented. The auditor must ensure that the audit report complies with all applicable audit standards, including ISACA IS audit standards. If the audit report requires internal review, the auditor should identify the parties that will perform the review and make sure they will be available at the time when the auditor expects to complete the final draft of the audit report.

Wrap-up The auditor needs to perform a number of tasks at the conclusion of the audit, including the following:

- Deliver the report to the auditee.
- Schedule a closing meeting so that the results of the audit can be discussed with the auditee and so that the auditor can collect feedback.
- For external audits, send an invoice to the auditee.
- Collect and archive all work papers. Enter their existence in a document management system so that they can be retrieved later if needed and to ensure their destruction when they have reached the end of their retention life.
- Update PBC documents if the auditor anticipates that the audit will be performed again in the future.
- Collect feedback from the auditee and convey to any audit staff as needed.

Post-audit Follow-up

After a given period (which could range from days to months), the auditor should contact the auditee to determine what progress the auditee has made on the remediation of any audit findings. There are several good reasons for doing this:

- It establishes a tone of concern for the auditee organization (and an interest in its success) and demonstrates that the auditee is taking the audit process seriously.
- It helps to establish a dialogue whereby the auditor can help auditee management work through any needed process or technology changes as a result of the audit.
- It helps the auditor better understand management's commitment to the audit process and to continuous improvement.
- For an external auditor, it improves goodwill and the prospect for repeat business.

Audit Evidence *Evidence* is the information collected by the auditor during the audit. The contents and reliability of the evidence obtained are used by the auditor to reach conclusions on the effectiveness of controls and control objectives. The auditor needs to understand how to evaluate various types of evidence and how (and if) it can be used to support audit findings.

The auditor will collect many kinds of evidence during an audit, including observations, written notes, correspondence, independent confirmations from other auditors, internal process and procedure documentation, and business records. When an auditor examines evidence, he needs to consider several characteristics about the evidence, which will contribute to its weight and reliability. These characteristics include the following:

- Independence of the evidence provider
- Qualifications of the evidence provider
- Objectivity
- Timing

Gathering Evidence   The auditor must understand and be experienced in the methods and techniques used to gather evidence during an audit, including the following:

- Organization chart review
- Review of department and project charters
- Review of third-party contracts and SLAs
- Review of IS policies and procedures
- Review of risk register (aka risk ledger)
- Review of incident log
- Review of IS standards
- Review of IS system documentation
- Personnel interviews
- Passive observation

Observing Personnel   It is rarely sufficient for an auditor to obtain and understand process documentation and be able to make judgments about the effectiveness of the process. Usually, the auditor will need to collect evidence in the form of observations to evaluate how consistently a system's process documentation is actually followed. Some of the techniques in observing personnel include the following:

- **Real tasks**   The auditor should request to see some functions actually being carried out.
- **Skills and experience**   The auditor should ask each interviewee about his or her career background to determine the interviewee's level of experience and career maturity.
- **Security awareness**   The auditor should observe personnel to determine whether they are following security policies and procedures.
- **Segregation of duties**   The auditor should observe personnel to determine whether adequate segregation of duties is in place.

An experienced auditor will have a well-developed "sixth sense," an intuition about people that can be helpful in understanding the people who execute procedures.

Sampling   *Sampling* techniques are used when it is not feasible to test an entire population of transactions. The objective of sampling is to select a portion of a population so that the characteristics observed will reflect the characteristics of the entire population. Several methods can be used for sampling:

- **Statistical sampling**   The IS auditor uses a technique of random selection that will statistically reflect the entire population.

- **Judgmental sampling (aka nonstatistical sampling)**   The IS auditor judgmentally and subjectively selects samples based on established criteria such as risk or materiality.

- **Attribute sampling**   This technique is used to study the characteristics of a given population to answer the question of "how many?" After the auditor has selected a statistical sample, she then examines the samples. A specific attribute is chosen, and the samples are examined to see how many items have the characteristic and how many do not. For example, an auditor may test a list of terminated user accounts to see how many were terminated within 24 hours and how many were not. This is used to statistically determine the rate at which terminations are performed within 24 hours among the entire population.

- **Variable sampling**   This technique is used to statistically determine the characteristic of a given population to answer the question "how much?" For example, an auditor who wants to know the total value of an inventory can select a sample and then statistically determine the total value in the entire population based on the total value of the sample.

- **Stop-or-go sampling**   This technique is used to permit sampling to stop at the earliest possible time.

- **Discovery sampling**   The auditor uses this technique to try to identify at least one exception in a population. When he is examining a population where even a single exception would represent a high-risk situation (such as embezzlement or fraud), the auditor will recommend a more intensive investigation to determine whether additional exceptions exist.

- **Stratified sampling**   Here, the event population will be divided into classes, or strata, based upon the value of one of the attributes. Then samples are selected from each class, and results are developed from each class or combined into a single result. An example of where this could be used is a selection of purchase orders (POs), where the auditor wants to make sure that some of the extremely high-value and low-value POs will be selected to determine whether there is any statistical difference in the results in different classes.

 NOTE   Part of the body of evidence in an audit is a description of how a sample was selected and why the particular sampling technique was used.

Reliance upon Third-Party Audit Reports   An organization may choose to rely upon audit reports for an external service provider rather than audit the external service provider directly. A typical example involves an organization that outsources payroll to a payroll services provider that has its own SOC 1 or SOC 2 audit performed by qualified audit firms. The organization's own auditors will likely choose to rely on the payroll service provider's SOC 1 or SOC 2 audit rather than audit the payroll service provider directly. From the service provider's point of view, the costs to commission a SOC 1 or SOC 2 audit and make the audit report available to its clients is less than the cost for even a small percentage of its customers to perform their own audits of the service provider's business. Third-party risk management is described fully later in this chapter.

Reporting Audit Results   The work product of an audit project is the *audit report,* which describes the entire audit project, including audit objectives, scope, controls evaluated, opinions on the effectiveness and integrity of those controls, and recommendations for improvement. While an auditor or audit firm will generally use a standard format for an audit report, some laws and standards require that an audit report regarding those laws or standards contain specific information or be presented in a particular format. Still, there will be some variance in the structure and appearance of audit reports created by different audit organizations. The auditor is typically asked to present findings in a closing meeting, where he can explain the audit and its results and be available to answer questions about the audit. The auditor may include an electronic presentation to guide discussion of the audit.

Structure and Contents   While there are often different styles for presenting audit findings, as well as regulations and standards that require specific content, an audit report will generally include several elements:

- Cover letter
- Introduction
- Summary
- Description of the audit
- Listing of systems and processes examined
- Listing of interviewees
- Listing of evidence obtained
- Explanation of sampling techniques
- Description of findings and recommendations

When the auditor is creating the report, she must make sure that it is balanced, reasonable, and fair. The report should not just be a list of everything that was wrong; it should also include a list of controls that were found to be operating effectively. The auditor also needs to take care when describing recommendations, realizing that any organization is capable of only so much change in a given period. If the audit report contains many findings, the auditor should realize that the organization may not be able to remediate all of them in an elegant manner. Instead, the organization will need to understand which findings should be remediated first—the audit report should provide this guidance.

 NOTE It is typically not the auditor's role to describe how an audit finding should be remediated. Deciding the methods used to apply remediation is the role of auditee management.

Evaluating Control Effectiveness When developing an audit report, the auditor should communicate the effectiveness of controls to the auditee. Often, this reporting is needed at several layers; for instance, the auditor may provide more detailed findings and recommendations to control owners, while the report for senior management may contain only the significant findings. One method that auditors frequently use is the development of a matrix of all audit findings, where each audit finding is scored on a criticality scale. This helps illustrate the audit findings that are the most important and those that are less important, in the auditor's opinion. The auditor can also report on cases where an ineffective control is mitigated (fully or partially) by one or more compensating controls. For example, a system may not have the ability to enforce password complexity (such as requiring upper- and lowercase letters, plus numbers and special characters), but this can be compensated through the use of longer than usual passwords and perhaps even more frequent expiration.

Internal Audit *Internal audits* focus on the organization's controls, processes, or systems and are carried out by personnel who are a part of the organization. Many organizations have one or more people in an internal audit function. Organizations that are serious about their commitment to an effective security program will commit resources to the internal audit function. Recognizing that external resources are far more costly, internal auditors become more familiar with internal processes and systems and can examine them more frequently and provide better feedback to others in the organization.

In U.S. public companies and in many other organizations, internal audit (IA) departments report to the organization's audit committee or board of directors (or a similar "governing entity"). The IA department often has close ties with and a "dotted line" reporting relationship to finance leadership in order to manage day-to-day activities. An internal audit department will launch projects at the request and/or approval of the governing entity and, to a degree, members of executive management.

Some regulations and standards require organizations to conduct internal audits as part of required compliance efforts; examples include Sarbanes–Oxley and ISO/IEC 27001. These regulations and standards play a large role in internal audit work. For example, public companies, banks, and government organizations are all subject to a great deal of regulation, much of which requires regular information systems controls testing. Management, as part of their risk management strategy, also requires this testing. External reporting of the results of internal auditing is sometimes necessary. Similarly, organizations that are ISO/IEC 27001 certified are required to carry out regular internal audit work to ensure that controls continue to be effective.

PART III

A common internal audit cycle consists of several categories of projects:

- Risk assessments and audit planning
- Cyclical controls testing (SOX, ISO/IEC 27001, and OMB Circular A-123, for example)
- Review of existing control structures
- Operational and IS audits

It is common for the IA department to maintain a multiyear plan to maintain a schedule or rotation of audits. The audit plan is shared with the governing entity, which is asked to review and approve the plan. The governing entity may seek to include specific reviews in the audit plan at this point. When an audit plan is approved, the IA department's tasks for the year (and tentative tasks for future years) are determined.

Even if the risk assessment is carried out by other personnel, internal auditors are often included in a formal risk assessment process. Specific skills are needed to communicate with an organization's IT personnel regarding technology risks. Internal auditors will use information from management to identify, evaluate, and rank an organization's main technology risks. The outcome of this process may result in IT-related specific audits within the IA department's audit plan. The governing entity may select areas that are financial or operational and that are heavily supported by information systems. Internal audits may be launched using a project charter, which formalizes and communicates the project to audit sponsors, the auditors, and the managers of the departments subject to the audit.

 TIP The Institute of Internal Auditors (IIA) has excellent guidance for audit planning at www.theiia.org.

Cyclical Controls Testing In *cyclical controls testing,* the organization conducts internal audits on its internal controls. A great deal of effort has recently been expended getting organizations to execute a controls testing life cycle. Most frequently, these practices are supporting the integrity of controls in financially relevant processes. Public corporations are required to comply with SOX Section 404, requirements, and U.S. government organizations have been subject to OMB Circular A-123, compliance with the Federal Information Security Management Act (FISMA), and other similar requirements. Countries outside of the United States have instituted similar controls testing requirements for publicly traded companies and governmental organizations. Many industries, such as banking, insurance, and healthcare, are likewise required to perform control testing because of industry-specific regulations. Organizations that elect to maintain ISO/IEC 27001 certification are required to perform internal control testing.

Organizations often employ GRC tools to assist with tracking controls testing. These systems track the execution and success of control tests performed as part of a testing cycle and can frequently manage archival of supporting evidence.

Establishing Controls Testing Cycles Young or growing organizations may not have established or documented internal controls testing cycles. Internal auditors, working in conjunction with individuals focused on manual controls, will participate in the establishment of controls testing. The auditor produces documentation of controls through a series of meetings with management. During the process, auditors will develop process and controls documentation and confirm their accuracy with control owners through the performance of control walk-throughs.

These engagements are likely to occur when companies prepare to go public. Such companies need to comply with SOX Section 404, requirements, which involve documenting controls and performing a test of existence, also known as a "test set of 1" or a "walk-through," for each identified key control. Private companies will maintain SOX-equivalent documentation to retain the option of seeking public financing or when lenders or private investors require it. Many organizations will find external resources to assist in the documentation and testing of applicable internal controls.

External Audit An *external audit* is performed by auditors who are not employees of the organization. There are three principal reasons that an organization will undergo an external audit versus an internal audit:

- **Legal or regulatory requirement** Various laws and regulations, such as SOX and A-123, require periodic external audit of relevant systems and business processes. Additionally, standards such as PCI DSS, Cybersecurity Maturity Model Certification (CMMC), and ISO/IEC 27001 require organizations to undergo external audits in some circumstances.

- **Lack of internal resources** An organization may not employ internal staff with skills in auditing, or its internal audit staff may not have enough time to conduct all of the organization's internal audits.

- **Objectivity** Organizations sometimes opt to have an objective expert third party perform audits to ensure that audit results are unbiased.

Organizations planning external audits need to understand several aspects of the audit, including the following:

- **Objective** What is the purpose of the audit? This includes whether it is required by regulations, laws, or standards such as SOX, A-123, ISO/IEC 27001, ISO/IEC 27002, CMMC, or PCI DSS.

- **Scope** What business units, departments, systems, processes, and personnel are the subject of the audit?

- **Time** What is the time period for the audit? This generally involves the acquisition of evidence in the form of business records associated with controls that auditors will want to examine.

- **Resources** What resources will be required for the audit? For external audits, this includes office space for one or more auditors, access to workspaces, and access to networks and systems for the acquisition of evidence.

- **Schedule**   When will the audit start? When will specific activities take place during the audit? When is it expected to be completed?
- **Audit firm and auditor qualifications**   Has the firm or auditor conducted the type of audit before? If so, how many audits have they done and in what business segments was the audit conducted? Organizations should assess the quality of the firm and the people conducting the audit when using external audit firms.
- **Audit methodology**   What sampling techniques and other details will be used by the auditors?
- **Personnel**   What internal personnel will be needed for the audit? This includes process and system owners that auditors will want to interview, plus any administrators or coordinators who will manage the scheduling of internal personnel as well as meeting spaces.

Organizations undergoing any particular audit for the first time generally plan much further ahead. In many cases, a pre-audit will get a preliminary idea of the results that will be achieved in the actual audit. Organizations planning a pre-audit need to ensure that the same techniques used in the pre-audit will be used in the audit. This is a common mistake in a pre-audit. If the pre-audit is less rigorous and thorough than the audit, the organization may have a false sense of confidence in a favorable audit outcome; they will be surprised that the audit went poorly while the pre-audit was seemingly successful.

Organizations should ensure that personnel are ready for the audit. In particular, personnel who have never worked with external auditors need to be coached as follows:

- Personnel should answer only questions that auditors ask. Personnel should be trained in the skill of active listening so that they understand what the auditor is asking, prior to giving an answer.
- Personnel should not express their opinions about the subject matter. Determination of the effectiveness of a control is the auditor's job, not that of the control owner or other person providing information.
- Personnel should not volunteer additional information. Doing so will cause confusion and potential delays in completion of the audit.

Seeding Audit Results

Management may spend considerable time and energy making sure that personnel understand one thing when dealing with auditors: they should specifically answer the question that the auditor asked, not the question the auditor should have asked, and they should not volunteer any information.

A useful technique that management (and only management) sometimes uses when working with auditors is "seeding" the audit results. Similar to the technique of seeding rain clouds with substances that cause them to release precipitation, management can use audit seeding as a way of ensuring that auditors are aware of specific situations that they are willing to include in their audit report.

(*continued*)

The purpose of audit seeding is generally the creation of an audit issue that will permit management to prioritize an initiative to improve the business. For example, suppose external auditors are examining access controls, an area where a security manager has had difficulty obtaining funds to make key improvements. While in a discussion with auditors, the security manager may choose to illuminate particular actions, inactions, or other situations in access control processes or technology that the auditor may not have otherwise noticed.

Persons who are considering audit seeding must have a thorough understanding of the subject matter, the controls being tested, the procedures and technologies in play, the auditing methodology in use, and a bit of grit. Audit seeding may be considered a daring move that may have unforeseen results. Finally, people considering audit seeding must not make auditors feel they are being manipulated, because this could have greater consequences. Instead, the technique is used by management simply to make auditors aware of an important aspect of a control being audited.

Control Self-Assessment

The *control self-assessment* (CSA) is a methodology used by an organization to review key business objectives, risks related to achieving these objectives, and the key controls designed to manage those risks. The primary characteristic of a CSA is that the organization takes initiative to self-regulate rather than engage outsiders, who may be experts in auditing but not in the organization's mission, goals, objectives, and culture.

CSA Advantages and Disadvantages   Like almost any business activity, CSAs have a number of advantages and disadvantages that a security manager and others should be familiar with. This will help the organization make the most of this process and avoid some common problems.

The advantages of a CSA include the following:

- Risks can be detected earlier, since subject-matter experts are involved earlier.
- Internal controls can be improved in a timely manner.
- CSA leads to greater ownership of controls through involvement in their assessment and improvement.
- CSA leads to improved employee awareness of controls through involvement in their assessment and improvement.
- CSA may help improve relationships between departments and auditors.

Some of the disadvantages of a CSA include the following:

- CSA could be mistaken by employees or management as a substitute for an internal audit.
- CSA may be considered extra work and dismissed as unnecessary.
- Employees may attempt to cover up shoddy work and misdeeds.

- CSA may be considered an attempt by the auditor to shrug off his or her own responsibilities.
- Lack of employee involvement would translate to little or no process improvement.

The CSA Life Cycle   Like most continuous-improvement processes, the CSA process is an iterative life cycle. The phases in a CSA are as follows:

- **Identify and assess risks**   Operational risks are identified and analyzed.
- **Identify and assess controls**   Controls to manage risks are identified and assessed. If any controls are missing, new controls are designed.
- **Develop questionnaire or conduct workshop**   An interactive session is conducted, if possible, for discussion of risks and controls. If personnel are distributed across several locations, a conference call can be convened or a questionnaire may be developed and sent to them.
- **Analyze completed questionnaires or assess workshop**   If a workshop was held, the workshop results are assessed to see what good ideas for remediation emerged. If a questionnaire was distributed, the results are analyzed to see the deficiencies that were identified and the ideas for risk remediation that were identified.
- **Control remediation**   Using the best ideas from the workshop or questionnaire, controls are designed or altered to improve risk management.
- **Awareness training**   This activity is carried out through every phase of the life cycle to keep personnel informed about the activities in the various phases.

Figure 6-14 illustrates the CSA life cycle.

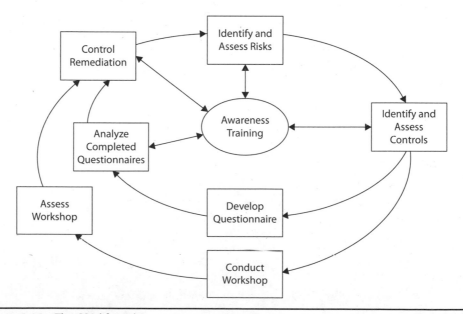

Figure 6-14   The CSA life cycle

Self-Assessment Objectives   The primary objective of a CSA is to transfer some of the responsibility for oversight of control performance and monitoring to the control owners. The roles of the security manager and IS auditor are not diminished, as an internal or external audit still needs to test control effectiveness periodically, but control owners will play a more active role in the audit of their controls.

Another objective of a CSA is a long-term reduction in exceptions. As control owners assume more responsibility for the performance of their controls, they will strive to avoid situations where auditors identify exceptions. The CSA gives control owners an opportunity and a process for cleaning house and improving audit results.

 NOTE   The security manager and internal auditor should be involved in CSAs to ensure that the process is not hijacked by efficiency zealots who try to remove the controls from processes because they do not understand their purpose or significance.

Auditors and Self-Assessment   Auditors should be involved in the CSAs that various departments conduct. The role of an auditor should be that of an objective subject-matter expert who can guide discussions in the right direction so that controls will receive the right kind of development and improvements over time. Auditors should resist having too large a role in CSAs. Responsibility for control development and maturation should lie within the department that owns the CSA. However, if a department is new at conducting a CSA, it may take some time before staff are confident and competent enough to take full ownership and responsibility for the process.

Information Security Awareness and Training

Personnel are the weakest link in information security, mainly because of lapses in judgment, inattentiveness, fatigue, work pressure, or a shortage of skills. Personnel are generally considered the largest and most vulnerable portion of an organization's attack surface. People are sometimes tricked by social engineering attacks such as phishing e-mails that provide attackers with an entry point into an organization's network. In larger organizations, attackers who send phishing messages to hundreds or thousands of personnel are almost assured that at least one of those people will click a link or open an attachment, leading to the potential compromise of the user's workstation—the beachhead that the attacker needs to go farther into the network and reach their ultimate objective.

Many organizations conduct security awareness training so that personnel are aware of these common attacks as well as several other topics that mainly fall into the category known as *Internet hygiene,* which is the safe use of computers and mobile devices while accessing the Internet.

Security Awareness Training Objectives

The primary objective of a security awareness program is the keen awareness, on the part of all personnel, of the different types of attacks they may encounter, together with knowledge of what they are expected to do (and *not* do) in various situations.

Further, personnel are to understand and comply with an organization's acceptable use policy, security policy, privacy policy, and other applicable policies.

Better security awareness training programs include opportunities to practice skills and include a test at the end of training. In computer-based training, users should be required to successfully pass the test with a minimum score—70 percent is a typical minimum score to complete the course. The best security awareness training courses, whether in-person or online, are engaging and relevant. Although some organizations conduct security awareness training for compliance purposes, many organizations do so for security purposes, with a genuine interest in personnel getting the most value out of the training. The point of security awareness training is, after all, the reduction of risk.

Business records should be created to document when each person receives training. Many organizations are subject to information security regulations that require personnel to complete security awareness training; business records provide ample evidence of users' completion of training.

Creating or Selecting Content for Security Awareness Training

Security managers need to develop or acquire security awareness training content for organization personnel. The content that is selected or developed should have the following characteristics:

- **Understandable**   The content should make sense to all personnel. Security managers often create content that is overly technical and difficult for nontechnical personnel to understand.

- **Relevant**   The content should be applicable to the organization and its users. For example, training on the topic of cryptography would be irrelevant to the vast majority of personnel in most organizations. Irrelevant content can cause personnel to disengage from further training.

- **Actionable**   The content should ensure that personnel know what to do (and not to do) in common scenarios.

- **Memorable**   The best content will give personnel opportunities to practice their skills at some of the basic tasks important to information security, including selecting and using passwords, reading and responding to e-mail, and interacting with people inside and outside the organization.

Security Awareness Training Audiences

When planning a security awareness program, security managers need to address the entire worker population and should be familiar with their roles in the organization. Managers are tasked with determining which training materials are relevant and necessary to each group of workers, without overburdening workers with training that is not relevant to their jobs.

Consider, for example, workers in a large retail organization, which fall into five categories:

- **Corporate workers**   All use computers, and most use mobile devices for e-mail and other functions.

- **Retail floor managers**   These people work in retail store locations and use computers daily in their jobs.

- **Retail floor cashiers**   All work in retail store locations and do not use computers, but they do collect payments by cash, check, and credit card.

- **Retail floor workers**   All work in retail store and warehouse locations and do not use computers.

- **Third-party personnel**   Any persons from outside companies that regularly access the organization's networks, systems, or data should be included in portions of security awareness training that are relevant to their tasks and duties.

The security manager of the retail organization should package security awareness training so that each audience receives relevant training. Corporate workers and retail floor managers should probably receive full-spectrum training because they all use computers. Retail floor managers should also receive the same training delivered to retail floor workers and cashiers, because they also work at retail locations and supervise these personnel. Cashiers need training on fraud techniques (counterfeit currency, currency counting fraud, and matters related to credit card payments such as skimming). Retail floor workers probably need no Internet or computer-related security awareness training but can instead receive training on topics related to physical security and workplace safety.

Technical Workers

Technical workers in an organization, typically IT personnel, should be trained in security techniques that are relevant to their positions. Technical workers are responsible for architecture, system and network design, implementation, and administration. Without security training, these workers' lapses in judgment may result in significant vulnerabilities that could lead to compromises.

Software Developers

Software developers typically receive little or no education on secure software development in colleges, universities, and tech schools. The art of secure coding is new to many software developers. Security training for software developers helps them to be more aware of common mistakes, including the following:

- Broken access control
- Cryptographic failures
- Vulnerabilities that permit injection attacks
- Insecure design

- Security misconfiguration
- The use of outdated components
- Broken authentication and session management that can lead to attacks on other user sessions
- Cross-site scripting
- Sensitive data exposure
- Insufficient attack protection
- Cross-site request forgery
- Underprotected APIs

This list is adapted from the "Top 10 Web Application Security Risks," published by the Open Web Application Security Project (OWASP), at https://owasp.org/www-project-top-ten/. This organization is dedicated to helping software developers better understand the techniques needed for secure application development and deployment.

Security training for software developers should also include protection of the software development process itself. Topics in secure software development generally include the following:

- Protection of source code
- Source code reviews
- Care when using open source code
- Testing of source code for vulnerabilities and defects
- Archival of changes to source code
- Protection of systems used to store source code, edit and test source code, build applications, test applications, and deploy applications

Some of these aspects are related to the architecture of development and test environments and may not be needed for all software developers.

Third Parties

Security awareness training needs to be administered to all personnel who have access to an organization's data through any means. Often this includes personnel who are employees of other organizations, so this means that some of those workers need to participate in the organization's security awareness training. In larger organizations, the curriculum for third-party personnel may need to be altered somewhat because portions of the security awareness training content may not be applicable to outsiders.

New Hires

New employees, as well as consultants and contractors, should be required to attend security awareness training as soon as possible. There is a risk that new employees could make mistakes early in their employment and prior to their training, as they would not be familiar with all the security practices in the organization. Better organizations link access control with security awareness training: New employees are not given access to systems until after they have successfully completed their security awareness training. This gives new workers added incentive to complete their training quickly, since they want to be able to access corporate applications and get to work.

Annual Training   Most security awareness programs include annual refresher training for all workers. Required by some regulations, such training is highly recommended, because it helps workers maintain focus on security and Internet safety and helps them avoid common mistakes. Further, because both protective techniques and attack techniques change quickly, annual refresher training keeps workers abreast of these developments.

Training takes time, and people tend to put it off for as long as possible. This is easy to understand, because training takes time away from other important work tasks. Still, the security manager and the organization must ensure that as many workers as possible complete the training. Workers can be offered incentives to complete their training: for example, all workers who complete their training in the first week can be entered into a random drawing for gift cards or other prizes.

Organizations generally choose one of several options for annual training, including:

- **Entire organization**   The organization will develop messaging to the entire organization and conduct annual training at the same time for all workers. The advantage of this is that all-personnel messaging can be utilized in an all-out blitz to get people thinking about this training. One disadvantage is that all workers will be a little less productive at the same time.

- **Hire month anniversary**   The organization enrolls workers in annual training on the month of their original hire date. For example, if a worker's first day was March 4, 2017, that worker (and all others hired in March) will complete security awareness training annually in the month of March. The advantage of this is that disruptions (minor as they are) are spread throughout the year. A key disadvantage is that there would probably not be an opportunity for all-personnel messaging for training.

- **Department**   The organization enrolls workers in various departments for their annual security training. The advantage of department-centric rotation is that training content can be tailored to the audience.

Awareness Training Communications

Security awareness training programs often utilize a variety of means for imparting Internet hygiene and safe computing information to its workers. Communication techniques often include the following:

- **E-mail**   Security managers may occasionally send out advisories to affected personnel to inform them of developments, such as a new phishing attack. Occasionally, a senior executive will send a message to all personnel to impress the point of security being every worker's job and that security is to be taken seriously.

- **Internal web site** Organizations with internal web sites or web portals may from time to time include information security messages.

- **Video monitors, posters, and bulletins** Sometimes a security message on monitors, posters, or bulletins on various security topics keeps people thinking about information security. Typical subjects include using good passwords, being careful with e-mail, and social engineering.

- **Voicemail** Organizations may occasionally send voicemail messages to all personnel or groups of affected personnel to inform them of new developments.

- **Security fairs** Organizations can set up an annual fair or ongoing technology center where users can get answers or view demonstrations of some of the latest threats and exploits to the company. This assists with developing lines of communications between the security team and the users of the computing systems.

  NOTE Security awareness training should not be operated only as a "once per year" event, but rather on a continuous basis to keep the workforce aware of threats and hygienic directives.

Management of External Services

The structures and business models in many organizations have changed dramatically, leading to an increase in the use of external services, or third-party organizations. Organizations rely on goods and services provided by external third parties, and like other cyber risks, third-party cyber risks must be managed. *Third-party risk management* (TPRM) activities are used to discover and manage risks associated with these external third parties.

TPRM extends the techniques used to identify and treat risk within the organization to include risks present in other organizations that provide services. TPRM exists because of the complexities associated with identifying risks in third-party organizations and because of risks inherent in doing business with third parties. At the core, TPRM is similar to other risk management, but the difference lies in the solicitation of information to identify risks outside of the organization's direct control.

Many organizations outsource some of their information processing to third-party organizations, often in the form of cloud-based SaaS and platform as a service (PaaS), for economic reasons: it is less expensive to pay for software in a leasing arrangement as opposed to developing, implementing, and maintaining software internally. TPRM practices have advanced significantly in recent years in response to this wave of outsourcing to cloud-based infrastructure and software services. With so much of corporate IT existing in and being managed by other organizations, TPRM practices have changed so that security and risk managers can continue to identify the risks present in their IT operations, much of which is run by other companies.

NOTE Organizations sometimes fail to understand that although operations can be outsourced, accountability cannot be outsourced. Organizations that outsource operations to third parties are responsible for every outcome, including the success or failure related to the outsourcer.

Benefits of Outsourcing

Organizations that are considering outsourcing operations to third parties need to weigh the benefits and costs carefully to determine whether the effort to outsource will result in measurable improvement in their processing, service delivery, and/or finances.

Outsourcing can offer an organization many benefits:

- **Available skills and experience**   Organizations that have trouble attracting workers with specialized skills often turn to third parties with highly skilled personnel who can benefit a variety of client organizations.
- **Economies of scale**   Specialized third parties can often achieve better economies of scale through discipline and mature practices than organizations are able to achieve.
- **Objectivity**   Some functions are better provided by outsiders. Personnel within an organization may have trouble being objective about some activities, such as process improvement and requirements definitions; in that case, a third-party may offer better solutions. Also, auditors frequently must be from an outside firm to achieve sufficient objectivity and independence.
- **Reduced costs**   When outsourcing involves third parties with offshore personnel, an organization may be able to lower its operating costs and improve its competitive market position through currency exchange rates and differences in standard pay.

When an organization is making an outsourcing decision, it needs to consider these advantages together with risks, as discussed in the next section.

Risks of Outsourcing

In the 1990s, when many organizations rushed to outsource development and support functions to organizations located in other countries, they did so with unrealistic short-term gains in mind and without adequately considering all the real costs and risks of outsourcing. This is not to say that outsourcing to third parties is bad, but many organizations made outsourcing decisions without fully understanding them.

While outsourcing to third parties can bring many tangible and intangible benefits to an organization, it is not without certain risks and disadvantages. Naturally, when an organization employs third parties to perform some of its functions, it relinquishes some control to those third parties.

The risks of outsourcing to third parties include the following:

- **Higher than expected costs**   Reduced costs were the main driver for offshore outsourcing that began in the 1990s. However, many organizations failed to anticipate the actual operational realities and/or the cost savings. For instance, after U.S.-based organizations outsourced to overseas operations, IT personnel had to make many more expensive trips than expected. Also, changes in international currency exchange rates can transform this year's bargain into next year's high cost.

- **Theft of intellectual property**   Outsourcing product manufacturing to certain third-world countries has resulted in systematic theft of intellectual property, made manifest by the presence of nearly identical products. Some countries consider the theft of intellectual property as an entitlement, contrary to the rule of law in other countries.

- **Poor quality**   The work product produced by a third party may be lower than was produced when the function was performed in-house.

- **Poor performance**   The third-party service may not perform as expected. The capacity of networks or IT systems used by third parties may cause processing delays or longer than acceptable response times.

- **Loss of control**   An organization that is accustomed to being in control of its workers may experience a loss of control. Making small adjustments to processes and procedures may be more time-consuming or may increase costs.

- **Employee integrity and background**   It may be decidedly more difficult to determine the integrity of employees in a third-party organization, particularly when the organization is located in another country. Some countries, even where outsourcing is popular, lack nationwide criminal background checks and other means for making a solid determination on an employee's background and integrity.

- **Loss of competitive advantage**   If the services performed by the third party are not flexible enough to meet the organization's needs, this can result in the organization losing some of its competitive advantage. For example, suppose an organization outsources its corporate messaging (e-mail and other messaging) to a third-party service provider. Later, the organization wants to enhance its customer communication by integrating its service application with e-mail. The e-mail service provider may be unable or unwilling to provide the necessary integration, which will result in a loss of competitive advantage.

- **Loss of tribal knowledge**   Development and operations of any portion of IT produces *tribal knowledge*—the knowledge accumulated by the personnel doing the work. While many details of architecture, design, implementation, and operations may be documented in more mature organizations, some portion of the information often goes undocumented, remaining in the memories of the personnel involved. For services that are outsourced, that tribal knowledge is largely absent, as the organization's personnel are not involved in day-to-day details.

- **Errors and omissions**   The third party may make serious errors or fail to perform essential tasks. For instance, a third party may suffer a data security breach that results in the loss or disclosure of sensitive information. This can be a disastrous event when it occurs within an organization's four walls, but when it happens to a third party, the organization may find that the lack of control will make it difficult to take the proper steps to contain and remedy the incident. If a third party experiences a security breach or similar incident, it may be putting its interests first and only secondarily watching out for the interests of its customers.

- **Vendor failure**   The failure of a third party to deliver may result in increased costs and delays in service or product delivery.

- **Differing mission and goals**   An organization's employees are going to be loyal to its mission and objectives. However, employees of a third party may have little or no interest in the hiring organization's interests; instead, they will be loyal to the third party organization's values, which may at times be in direct conflict. For example, a third party may place emphasis on maximizing billable hours, while the hiring organization emphasizes efficiency. These two objectives are in conflict with each other.

- **Difficult recourse**   If an organization is dissatisfied with the performance or quality of the third party, contract provisions may not sufficiently facilitate a remedy. If the third-party operation is in a different country, applying remediation in the court system may also be futile.

- **Lowered employee morale**   If an organization chooses to outsource some operations to a third party, employees who remain may be upset because some of their colleagues may have lost their jobs as a result of the outsourcing. Further, remaining employees may believe that their own jobs may soon be outsourced or eliminated. They may also believe that their organization is more interested in saving money than in taking care of its employees. Personnel who have lost their jobs may vent their anger at the organization through a variety of harmful actions that can threaten assets or other workers.

- **Audit and compliance**   An organization that outsources part of its operation that is in scope for applicable laws and regulation may find it more challenging to perform audits and achieve compliance. Audit costs may rise, as auditors need to visit the third parties' work centers. Requiring the third party to make changes to achieve compliance may be difficult or expensive.

- **Applicable laws**   Laws, regulations, and standards in headquarters and offshore countries may impose requirements on the protection of information that may complicate business operations or enterprise architecture.

- **Cross-border data transfer**   Governments around the world are paying attention to the flow of data, particularly the sensitive data of its citizens. Many countries have passed laws that attempt to exert control over data about their citizens when the data is transferred out of their jurisdiction.

- **Time zone differences**   Communications will suffer when an organization outsources some of its operations to offshore third parties that are several time zones distant. It will be more difficult to schedule telephone conferences when there is very little overlap between workers in each time zone. It will take more time to communicate important issues and to make changes.

- **Language and cultural differences**   When outsourcing crosses language and cultural barriers, it can result in less-than-optimal communication and results. The outsourcing organization will express its needs through its own language and culture, but the third party will hear those needs through its own language and culture. Both sides may be thinking or saying, "They don't understand what we want" and "We don't understand what they want." This can result in unexpected differences in work products produced by the outsourcing firm. Delays in project completion or delivery of goods and services can occur as a result.

CAUTION   Some of the risks associated with outsourcing to third parties are intangible or may be beyond legal remedies. For instance, language and time zone differences may introduce delays in communication, adding friction to the business relationship in a way that may not be easily measurable.

Identifying Third Parties

Because the topic of third-party risk is relatively new, many existing organizations are just getting started with TPRM programs in their organizations—however, metaphorically speaking, the third-party "horse" is already "out of the barn." Many organizations today do not have a firm grasp on the identities of all of the third parties they've partnered with. Indeed, stakeholders from across an organization may be aware of a few third parties critical to their particular focus, but often there is a total lack of central organization with regard to third-party management. An early step in an organization's TPRM may involve conducting an initial inventory of third-party vendors.

There is no single place where information about all third-parties may be found. In part, this is because of the varying nature of third parties and the types of goods or services they provide to the organization. It is suggested, then, that the security manager consult with several stakeholders in the organization to identify subsets of third parties. These stakeholders may include the following:

- **Legal**   One of the most important allies to the security manager, the organization's legal department negotiates purchase and service contracts with third parties. Thus, legal will have a collection of contracts that can identify third parties. Security managers need to understand, however, that legal does not handle contracts for every third party, because some suppliers and vendors do not use contracts. Many online service providers, for example, use simple "click-through" agreements that do not go through the organization's legal department.

- **Procurement**   The procurement function is a critical part of an organization's TPRM program. Larger purchases are frequently negotiated by a procurement function or team. Like the legal team, procurement may have a collection (and perhaps even a list) of third parties it has negotiated business deals with.

- **Accounts payable**   Sometimes the only way to learn about some third parties' involvement is to find out what third parties are being paid for the products or services they provide. Typically, the accounts payable function will remit funds only to organizations that are registered as vendors in the organization's financial accounting system.

- **Information technology (IT)**   The IT department may have established data connections to certain third parties; it may have specific firewall rules associated with system access granted to third parties; and it may have logical connections between its internal identity and access management (IAM) system and some third parties. Finally, information systems including firewalls, intrusion detection/prevention systems, web content filters, and CASB systems can provide a wealth of information, particularly about third-party services that are offered free of charge. Free online services are so numerous that many organizations are challenged to identify them until they utilize a CASB system (even then, a few may go unnoticed).

- **Facilities**   The facilities department may be aware of third parties not discovered by other means, because of its function: maintaining and supplying processing center locations and work locations. The facilities department likely has several third-party relationships with organizations that do not access IT systems. This is one reason why facilities should be involved in the initial search.

- **Department heads and business unit leaders**   An organization's department heads and business unit leaders are certainly going to be aware of key third-party relationships, including key suppliers, service providers, and sources of temporary workers.

- **Location-specific leaders**   The saying goes, "The farther away one is from corporate headquarters, the more that business is conducted by expediency than by policy." In other words, workers in satellite offices are more apt to conduct business with unique, local-to-them third parties that may not be identified otherwise. Security managers may need to tread lightly here so that their quest for information about third parties does not represent a threat to their ongoing internal business relationships and operations.

When conducting an initial inventory, a security manager will, along the way, discover other sources that can identify third-party relationships. Security managers should realize that an initial effort at identifying third parties will probably not identify every one, but most will be identified. Security personnel should be on the lookout for third-party relationships that have not been identified so that they may be brought into the TPRM program.

When building an initial inventory of third parties, the security manager may opt to use a spreadsheet program to track them, adding columns to identify how each third party was identified and those that list criteria used to classify third parties.

PART III

However, managing third parties by spreadsheet may quickly become a burdensome task. Several vendors and service providers have created purpose-built applications that can be used to manage third parties, including the following (in alphabetical order):

- Allgress
- CyberGRX
- Diligent (formerly Galvanize)
- KY3P
- Lockpath
- Prevalent
- RSA Archer
- ServiceNow

 NOTE Because TPRM is a rapidly growing and changing field, the number and types of service vendors providing products that help manage third parties will frequently change.

Cloud Service Providers

Organizations moving to cloud-based environments often assumed that those cloud service providers would take care of many or all information security functions, but often this was not the case. This resulted in innumerable breaches, as each party believed that the other was performing key data protection tasks. Most organizations are unfamiliar with the shared responsibility model that delineates which party is responsible for which operations and security functions. Tables 6-14 and 6-15 depict shared responsibility models in terms of operations and security, respectively.

Component	On-premise	IaaS	PaaS	SaaS
Applications	Org	Org	Org	Provider
Data	Org	Org	Org	Provider
Runtime	Org	Org	Provider	Provider
Middleware	Org	Org	Provider	Provider
Operating system	Org	Org	Provider	Provider
Virtualization	Org	Provider	Provider	Provider
Servers	Org	Provider	Provider	Provider
Storage	Org	Provider	Provider	Provider
Networking	Org	Provider	Provider	Provider
Data center	Org	Provider	Provider	Provider

Table 6-14 Cloud Services Operational Shared Responsibility Model

Activity	On-premise	IaaS	PaaS	SaaS
Human resources	Org	Shared	Shared	Shared
Application security	Org	Org	Shared	Provider
Identity and access management	Org	Org	Shared	Shared
Log management	Org	Org	Shared	Provider
System monitoring	Org	Org	Shared	Provider
Data encryption	Org	Org	Shared	Provider
Host intrusion detection	Org	Org	Shared	Provider
Host hardening	Org	Org	Shared	Provider
Asset management	Org	Org	Shared	Provider
Network intrusion detection	Org	Org	Provider	Provider
Network security	Org	Org	Provider	Provider
Security policy	Org	Shared	Shared	Shared
Physical security	Org	Provider	Provider	Provider

Table 6-15   An Example Cloud Services Security Shared Responsibility Model

Note that the values in Tables 6-14 and 6-15 are not absolutely consistent across different service providers. Instead, these tables serve to illustrate the nature of shared responsibilities between a service organization and its customers. The specific responsibilities for operations and security between an organization and any specific service provider can vary somewhat. It is vital that an organization clearly understand its precise responsibilities for each third-party relationship so that no responsibilities are overlooked or neglected; otherwise, risks may be introduced to the organization's operations and/ or security. The organization is ultimately responsible for ensuring that specific areas are addressed, because if a breach occurs, the organization will be held responsible in the eye of shareholders, board of directors, and customers.

TPRM has been the subject of many standards and regulations that compel organizations to be proactive in discovering risks present in the operations of their critical third-party relationships. Historically, many organizations were not voluntarily assessing their critical third parties. Statistical data about breaches over several years has revealed that more than half of all breaches are caused by inappropriately managed third parties. This statistic illuminates the magnitude of the third-party risk problem and has resulted in the enactment of laws and regulations in many industries that now require organizations to build and operate effective TPRM programs in their organizations. This has also garnered innovation in the form of new tools, platforms, and services that help organizations manage third-party risk more effectively.

TPRM Life Cycle
Managing business relationships with third parties is a life-cycle process that begins when an organization contemplates the use of a third party to augment or support its operations in some way. The life cycle continues during the ongoing relationship with the third party and concludes when the organization no longer requires the third party's services.

Initial Assessment

Prior to the establishment of a business relationship, an organization will assess and evaluate the third party for suitability. Often this evaluation is competitive, involving two or more third parties vying for the formal relationship. The organization will require that each third party provide information describing its services, generally in a structured manner through a request for information (RFI) or a request for proposal (RFP).

In the RFI and RFP, an organization often includes sections on security and privacy to solicit information about how each third party will protect the organization's information. This, together with information about the services themselves, pricing, and other information, reveals details that the organization uses to select the third party that will provide services.

Onboarding

Onboarding is the process by which an organization begins a business relationship with a third party. Before utilizing the products or services from a third party, the organization should perform up-front due diligence to understand the level of risk involved in the relationship. Often, an organization will establish a risk level using criteria discussed earlier in this section and will then perform an assessment utilizing questionnaires and other methods according to the scheme shown in Tables 6-17 and 6-18. These activities will uncover issues that may require remediation and/or specific statements in the initial legal agreement between the organization and the third party.

Legal Agreement

Before services can commence, the organization and the third party will negotiate a legal agreement that describes the services provided, service levels, quality, pricing, and other terms. Based on the details discovered in the assessment phase, the organization can develop a section in the legal agreement that addresses security and privacy, which will typically cover these subjects:

- **Security and/or privacy program**   The third party must have a formal security and/or privacy program including but not limited to governance, compliance, policy, risk management, annual risk assessment, internal audit, vulnerability management, incident management, secure development, security awareness training, data protection, and third-party risk.

- **Security and/or privacy controls**   The third party must have a control framework, including linkages to risk management and internal audit.

- **Vulnerability management**   The third party will have policies and procedures for formally identifying and managing vulnerabilities in their systems and processes.

- **Vulnerability assessments**   The third party will undergo penetration tests or vulnerability assessments of its service infrastructure and applications, performed by a competent security professional services firm of the organization's choosing (or a company that the organization and third party jointly agree upon), with reports made available to the organization upon request.

- **External audits and certifications** The third party is required to undergo annual SOC 1 and/or SOC 2 Type 2 audits, ISO 27001 certifications, HITRUST certifications, PCI DSS reports on compliance (ROCs), CMMC audits, or other industry-recognized and applicable external audits, with reports made available to the organization upon request.

- **Security incident response** The third party must have a formal security incident capability that includes testing and training.

- **Security incident notification** The third party will notify the organization in the event of a suspected and confirmed breach, within a specific time frame, typically 24 hours. The language around "suspected" and "confirmed" needs to be developed carefully so that the third party cannot sidestep this responsibility.

- **Right to audit** The third party will permit the organization to conduct an audit of the third-party organization without cause. If the third party will not permit this, the organization may insist on the right to audit in the event of a suspected or confirmed breach or other circumstances. Further, the contract should include the right for a competent security professional services firm to perform an audit of the third-party security environment on behalf of the organization (useful for several reasons, including geographic location and that the external audit firm will be more objective). The cost of the audit is usually paid for by the organization, and in some cases the organization will provide credits or compensation for the time incurred by the third party's team.

- **Periodic review** The third party will permit an annual onsite review of its operations and security. This can give the organization greater confidence in the third party's security and operations.

- **Annual due diligence** The third party will respond to annual questionnaires and evidence requests as part of the organization's third-party risk program.

- **Cyber insurance** The third party must carry a cyber-insurance policy with minimum coverage levels and will comply with all requirements in the policy to ensure payout in the event of a security event. A great option is to have the organization be a named beneficiary on the policy, in case a widespread breach results in a large payout to many customers.

- **Restrictions on outsourcing** Restrict the third party from outsourcing core functions to other organizations.

Organizations with many third parties may consider developing a standard security clause that includes all of these provisions. Then, when a new contract is being considered, the organization's security team can perform its up-front examination of the third party's security environment and make adjustments to the security clause as needed.

Organizations will often identify one or more shortcomings in the third party's security program that it is unwilling or unable to remediate right away. In this case, the organization can compel the third party to enact improvements in a reasonable period of time after the start of the business relationship. For example, suppose a third-party service provider does not have an external audit, such as a SOC 1 or SOC 2 audit, but agrees to undergo such an audit one year in the future. Or perhaps a third-party service provider that has never had external penetration testing performed could be compelled to begin performing penetration testing at regular intervals. Alternatively, the third party could be required to undergo a penetration test and be required to remediate all issues deemed Critical and High before the organization will begin using the third party's services.

 CAUTION   A legal agreement with a new third party should never be completed until assessments and other due diligence have been completed.

Risk Tiering and Vendor Classification

Most companies have a large number of third-party vendors—so many that they cannot possibly perform all of the due diligence on every vendor. It makes sense, then, to take a risk-based approach to TPRM and apply a level of due diligence to vendors according to the level of risk, by classifying vendors according to risk level and then performing a level of due diligence in proportion to their classification.

To achieve this, an organization needs to establish a few simple criteria, such as the following, by which a vendor can be classified into the appropriate risk level:

- **Volume of sensitive customer data**   The amount of sensitive customer data that the vendor stores on its systems can include contact information, financial information, healthcare information, transaction history, and location. The greater the amount of data or the longer this data resides on a vendor's information systems, the higher the risk. Generally, organizations use a simple numeric scale to reflect their operations. For example, the criteria might be less than 10,000 records, 10,000 to 1 million records, or greater than 1 million records.

- **Volume of sensitive internal data**   The amount of sensitive internal data that the vendor stores on its systems can include employee information, intellectual property, customer lists, marketing plans, and other data. The greater the amount of data or the longer the vendor stores this data on its information systems, the higher the risk.

- **Operational criticality**   The degree to which the organization depends upon the day-by-day, hour-by-hour, minute-by-minute, or even second-by-second readiness and operation of the vendor on the organization's product or services output determines its risk factor. For example, a movies-on-demand service may store its content and serve movies to customers via a third-party IaaS vendor. The service depends upon the IaaS vendor for continuous availability; even a few seconds of downtime would interrupt the movie streaming to all of its customers. Incidentally, in this example, the IaaS vendor would be rated as high risk because of the movie's content stored in its systems.

- **Physical access**   The degree to which a vendor has physical access to the organization's information processing centers or work centers can be rated together or separately. For instance, technical support vendors may have physical access to information systems in a data center, or service vendors may have physical access to work centers, such as freight delivery, janitorial, plant care, office supplies replenishment, or IT service vendors who maintain copiers, scanners, and other office equipment.

- **Access to systems**   Whether the vendor has the ability to access information systems accessed by the organization should be considered. For example, tech support organizations may have occasional or 24/7 access to specific information systems so that they can perform routine maintenance or help troubleshoot problems. Further, risk ratings may vary depending on the type of systems accessed by third parties (those with large amounts of critical or sensitive data, or systems that are operationally critical, as described in prior criteria).

- **Contractual obligations**   Whether the vendor is required to establish and maintain a security program, security controls, vulnerability management, incident response, or other activities should be considered. Third parties may be rated a higher risk if few or no security requirements are imposed upon them in a contract. While effective third-party risk management seeks to add appropriate security clauses to contracts, security managers may occasionally encounter contracts with third parties where no clauses were included.

No matter what criteria are used in contracting with third-party vendors, organizations typically use criteria to identify the most critical vendors and other third parties. Generally, organizations will classify third parties into three levels of criticality. Table 6-16 depicts a typical third-party risk classification scheme. Based on levels of importance, each organization will construct a unique risk tiering scheme.

Organizations can use a system similar to Table 6-16 in a number of ways. First, each third party can be scored based on how many of the low, medium, or high categories are met. Or each third party can be assigned a risk level if any single criterion is met at that level. Organizations are cautioned to refrain from overcomplicating tiering or scoring criteria: the objective is to arrive at no more than three, or perhaps four, tier classifications for each vendor. The reason for this is related to third-party assessments, discussed in the next section.

Criteria	High	Medium	Low
Customer data volume	>10M records	10K to 10M records	<10K records
Internal data volume	HR or product design	None	None
Physical access	24/7	Office hours only	None
System access	High customer data volume	None	None

Table 6-16   Third-Party Risk Tiering Example

In most organizations, a minority of third parties, perhaps 0.5 to 2 percent, will be assigned to the top risk level. A few more will be assigned to the second risk level—perhaps another 5 to 10 percent. The remainder will be assigned to the third risk level.

From time to time, some third parties will need to be reclassified from one risk level to another. For example, suppose a third-party service provider is hired to perform low-risk services, and its initial risk classification is low. However, that third party might earn more business that represents high risk; unless some triggering mechanism (such as the negotiation of an additional legal contract) is in place, the organization would need to analyze the relationship with each of its third parties annually (or more often) to confirm their risk ratings. Similarly, if a third party is originally classified as high risk but later discontinues performing high-risk services, the third party should be reclassified at a lower risk tier; otherwise, the organization is spending too much effort assessing the third party.

Assessing Third Parties

To discover risks to the business, organizations need to assess their third-party service providers, not only at the onset of the business relationship (prior to the legal agreement being signed, as explained earlier) but periodically thereafter, to identify specific risks represented by those vendors. This assessment process should be considered a part of the internal risk assessment process, though the personnel contacted are not internal personnel, but employees of other companies, with a variable degree of cooperation and willingness to respond. As opposed to performing risk assessments of internal processes and systems, the security manager's view of information provided by third-party processes and systems may be obscured. Additional focus and effort are required to learn enough about the practices in a third-party organization to draw conclusions about risk.

Organizations assessing third parties often recognize that IT and security controls are not the only forms of risk that require examination. As a result, organizations generally seek other forms of information about critical third parties, including the following:

- Financial risk, including currency exchange risk
- Geopolitical risk
- Inherent risk
- Recent security breaches
- Lawsuits
- Operational effectiveness/capabilities

These and other factors can influence the overall risk to the organization, which can manifest in various ways, including degradations in overall security, failures to meet production or quality targets, and even business failure.

Once an organization has established its third-party risk classification and has begun to identify its third parties and their respective risk tiering, third parties can be assessed. Before assessments can be performed, however, the organization needs to develop a scheme by which assessments take place. In the preceding section, third parties are classified into three or four risk levels. The manner in which assessments are performed depends upon which risk level any particular third party is assigned. Several techniques can be used to assess third parties, including the following:

- **Questionnaires** Organizations can develop questionnaires to be sent to third parties that include questions about the third party's IT controls and other business activities to assess how effectively its information is being protected.

- **Questionnaire confirmation** After completed questionnaires are received from third parties, organizations can take steps to confirm or validate the answers provided. For example, the organization can request evidence in the form of process documents or samples of business records. This can improve (or reduce) confidence in the vendor's answers and provide a more accurate depiction of control risk.

- **Site visit** If an organization is not satisfied with the use of questionnaires and confirmation, the organization can send security personnel (or, ironically, outsource this activity to a third party) to conduct a site visit of the third party's work locations and information processing centers. Although this is the costliest confirmation method, organizations may improve their confidence in the third party by conducting their own onsite assessment.

- **External attestations** Organizations can compel third parties to undergo external audits or attestations. Established standards such as SOC 1, SOC 2, SSAE 18, ISAE 3402, HITRUST, PCI DSS, CMMC, and ISO/IEC 27001 are examples of control and audit standards that can be used to understand the effectiveness of a third party's IT controls.

- **External business intelligence** Organizations often turn to external business intelligence services such as Dunn & Bradstreet or Lexis Nexus. Such services collect information on the financial health of companies, which can help organizations better understand risk factors related to the health and ongoing viability of its third parties. For example, if an organization learns that a particular vendor is under financial stress (perhaps because of problems with its products or services adversely affecting sales), this will raise concern that a partnership could result in degradations in product or service quality, as well as degradations in information protection efforts and effectiveness.

- **External cyber intelligence** Organizations are beginning to utilize the services of a growing number of companies that gather intelligence on third-party service providers, which sell this information on a subscription basis. These services perform a variety of functions, including security scans and scans of the dark web for signs of an unreported breach. These cyber-intelligence services often perform these services at costs lower than those incurred by organizations that conduct these activities with their own security staff.

- **Security scans and penetration tests**   Organizations can perform security scans or penetration tests on the infrastructure and/or applications of its third parties. Alternatively, organizations can require the third parties to commission these activities from qualified security consulting firms and make the results available to organizations. These activities serve to bolster (or erode) confidence in a third party's ability to manage its infrastructure and applications, including running an effective vulnerability management program.

- **Intrusive monitoring**   Organizations can sometimes compel a third party to permit the organization to view or receive internal controls data in real time. For instance, an organization could provide a security system to the third party to be installed in its network; the system would provide some form of real-time security intelligence to the organization to give it confidence that the third party's environment is free of active threats. Or a third party could make certain internal information available to the organization from its own internal security systems. The types of information that can be made available include security and event log data from operating systems, firewalls, intrusion detection/prevention systems, internal vulnerability scan data, network packet header capture, or network full packet capture. These activities, called intrusive monitoring, represent an intrusion of the organization's visibility into the third party's environment.

As stated earlier, not all third parties are assessed in the same way. Instead, organizations can establish schemes for assessing vendors according to their risk levels. Table 6-17 depicts such a scheme.

Assessment Type	High Risk	Medium Risk	Low Risk
Questionnaire	Longest questionnaire	Medium-sized questionnaire	Shortest questionnaire
Questionnaire confirmation	Highest risk controls	High risk controls	Not performed
Site visits	Yes	Yes	No
External attestations	Required	Nice to have	Nice to have
External business intelligence	Yes	Yes	Yes
External cyber intelligence	Yes	Yes	No
Security scans	Yes	Yes	Yes
Penetration tests	Yes	No	No
Intrusive monitoring	In limited circumstances	No	No

Table 6-17   Assessment Activities at Different Risk Levels

Assessment Type	High Risk	Medium Risk	Low Risk
Questionnaire	Annually	Annually	Annually
Questionnaire confirmation	Annually	Biannually	None
Site visits	Annually	Every three to five years	None
External attestations	Annually	Annual	If available
External business intelligence	Quarterly	Annual	If available
External cyber intelligence	Monthly	Quarterly	None
Security scans	Monthly	Annually	Annually
Penetration tests	Annually	None	None
Intrusive monitoring	Continuous	None	None

Table 6-18 Assessment Frequency

Organizations also need to determine how frequently to perform their assessments of third parties. Table 6-18 shows a sample scheme of assessment frequency.

Some organizations have hundreds to thousands of third-party service providers that require assessments, with the largest organizations having tens of thousands of third parties. Risk tiering is performed precisely because organizations work with so many third parties, and the various types of assessments are time-consuming and expensive to perform. This is why the most thorough assessments are performed only on those that represent the highest risk.

Questionnaires and Evidence

Periodically, a security and/or privacy questionnaire is sent to third-party service providers with a request to answer the questions and return it to the organization in a reasonable amount of time. Often, however, an organization may choose not to rely on the questionnaire answers alone in determining risk. The organization can also request that the third party furnish specific artifacts, such as the following, that serve as evidence to support the responses in the questionnaire:

- Security policy
- Security controls
- Security awareness training records
- New-hire checklists
- Details on employee background checks (not necessarily actual records but a description of the checks performed)
- Nondisclosure and other agreements required to be signed by employees (not necessarily signed copies but blank copies)
- Vulnerability management process
- Secure development process

- Copy of general insurance and cyber-insurance policies
- Incident response plan and evidence of testing

Because a large organization's third-party providers access, store, and process data in a variety of different ways, the organization may choose to send out different versions of questionnaires appropriate to one or more categories of risk or business operation, to ensure that the majority of questions asked are relevant. Otherwise, large portions of a questionnaire may be irrelevant, which could be frustrating to third parties, which would rightfully complain of wasted time and effort.

Organizations often send different questionnaires according to the third party's risk level. For example, third parties deemed to be of the highest risk would be sent extensive questionnaires that include requests for many pieces of evidence, medium-risk third parties would be sent less lengthy questionnaires, and low-risk third parties would be sent short questionnaires. Although this practice avoids overburdening low-risk third parties with extensive questionnaires, it also reduces the burden on the organization, because someone has to review the questionnaires and attached evidence. An organization with hundreds of low-risk third-party contracts should avoid being overburdened with analyzing hundreds of questionnaires, each with hundreds of questions, if possible.

Risk Treatment

Organizations that carefully examine the information provided from the third parties may discover some unacceptable practices or situations. In these cases, the organization can analyze the matter and decide on a course of action. For instance, suppose a highly critical third party indicates that it does not perform annual security awareness training for its employees, and the organization finds this unacceptable. To remedy this, the organization analyzes the risk (in a manner not unlike any risk found internally) and decides on a course of action: it contacts the third party in an attempt to compel them to institute annual training.

Sometimes, a deficiency in a third party is not so easily resolved. For example, suppose a third party that has been providing services for many years indicates in its annual questionnaire that it does not use encryption on the most sensitive data it stores. At the onset of the business relationship, this was not a common practice, but it has since become a common practice in the organization's industry. The service provider, when confronted with this, explains that it is not operationally feasible to implement encryption of stored data in a manner acceptable to the organization, mainly for financial reasons, and because of the significant cost impact on its operations, the third party would have to increase its prices. In this example, the organization and the third party would need to discover the best course of action to ensure that the organization can determine an acceptable level of risk and associated cost.

Proactive Issue Remediation

The only means of exchange between a customer organization and a third party are money, products or services, and reputation. In other words, the only leverage that an organization has against a third party is the withholding of payment and communicating the quality (or lack therein) of the third party to other organizations. This is especially true if the outsourcing crosses national boundaries. Therefore, an organization that is considering outsourcing must carefully consider how it will enforce contract terms so that it receives the quantity and quality goods and services that it is expecting.

Many of the risks of outsourcing to third parties can be remedied through contract provisions such as the following:

- **Service level agreement**   The SLA should provide details on every avenue of work performance and communication, including escalations and problem management.

- **Quality**   Depending upon the product or service, this may translate into an error or defect rate, a customer satisfaction rate, or system performance.

- **Security policy and controls**   Whether the outsourcing firm is safeguarding the organization's intellectual property, keeping business secrets, or protecting information about its employees or customers, the contract should spell out the details of the security controls that it expects the outsourcing firm to perform. The organization should also require periodic third-party audits and the results of those audits. The contract should contain a "right to audit" clause that allows the outsourcing organization to examine the work premises, records, and work papers on demand.

- **Business continuity**   The contract should require the outsourcing firm to have reasonable measures and safeguards in place to ensure resilience of operations and the ability to continue operations with minimum disruption in the event of a disaster.

- **Employee integrity**   The contract should define how the outsourcing firm will vet its employees' backgrounds so that it is not inadvertently hiring individuals with a criminal history and so employees' claimed education and work experience are genuine.

- **Ownership of intellectual property**   If the outsourcing firm is producing software or other designs, the contract must define ownership of those work products and whether the outsourcing firm may reuse any of those work products for other engagements.

- **Roles and responsibilities**   The contract should specify in detail the roles and responsibilities of each party so that each will know what is expected of them.

- **Schedule**   The contract must specify when and how many items of work products should be produced.

- **Regulation**   The contract should require both parties to conform to all applicable laws and regulations, including but not limited to intellectual property, data protection, and workplace safety.

- **Warranty**   The contract should specify terms of warranty for the workmanship and quality of all work products so that there can be no ambiguity regarding the quality of goods or services performed.

- **Dispute and resolution** The contract should contain provisions that define the process for handling and resolving disputes.
- **Payment** The contract should specify how and when the outsourcing provider will be paid. Compensation should be tied not only to the quantity but also to the quality of work performed. The contract should include incentive provisions for additional payment when specific schedule, quantity, or quality targets are exceeded. The contract should also contain financial penalties that are enacted when SLA, quality, security, audit, or schedule targets are missed.

The terms of an outsourcing contract should adequately reward the outsourcing firm for a job well done, which should include the prospect of earning additional contracts as well as referrals that will help it to earn outsourcing contracts from other customers.

Responsive Issue Remediation

Rarely do organizations see perfect answers in returned questionnaires. Often, undesirable situations are identified in questionnaires or during questionnaire confirmation. For example, a third party may specify in a questionnaire that it requires its personnel to change their passwords once per year. But suppose the organization would prefer the third party personnel change their passwords more frequently? What if a third party specifies that it *never* requires its personnel to change their passwords? This is something that an organization would probably find unacceptable. So the organization initiates a discussion with the third party to discover why its personnel are never required to change their passwords, with the hopes that either the organization will find the third party's explanation acceptable (perhaps they use compensating controls such as an effective MFA system) or the parties will agree that the third party will change its systems to require its personnel to update their passwords with some frequency, perhaps quarterly. Such remediation can be costly and time-consuming, so organizations need to be careful about how often and in which situations it will undergo the process.

Security Incidents

If a security incident occurs in a third-party organization, responding to the incident is more complex, mainly because two or more organizations and their respective security teams are involved. A security incident at a third-party organization is also an incident in its customers' organizations, and each needs to respond to it. If a third-party organization's systems are breached, the third-party must respond and perform all of the steps of incident response, such as notifying affecting parties, including its customers.

Customers of third-parties have their own incident response to perform. However, customers are usually not permitted to access detailed event logs or perform forensic analysis on the third-party provider. Often, customers have to wait until the third party's investigation has concluded. Because this can be frustrating to its customers, third parties can keep their customers informed periodically until the event is closed.

This topic is explored in detail in Chapter 8.

Information Security Program Communications and Reporting

Communications are the lifeblood of an effective information security program. Lacking effective communications, the security program will have difficulty interacting with executive management for the exchange of objectives, risk information, and metrics. Ineffective communications will hamper virtually all other security-related activities and processes. This section explores the various internal and external parties with whom security managers communicate and collaborate.

Security Operations

Security operations are associated with much of the action-oriented activities in an information security program, through its monitoring and response processes. Communications and reporting from security operations may include the following:

- **Vulnerability management**   Operations and trends in vulnerability management, including the discovery of new assets, and the time required to correct vulnerabilities

- **Events and incidents**   Security- and privacy-related events and incidents, including the time required to detect and response to events, types of events, impact of events, any effort or cost of recovery, affected data and systems, and external notifications

- **External threat intelligence**   External information, including noteworthy events, intrusions, defensive techniques, new cybercriminal organizations, and trends

- **Use case development**   Improvements in monitoring, including the ability to detect new types of incidents

- **Orchestration and automation**   Improvements and incidents in SOAR capabilities to help improve efficiency and rapid response to events

- **Other operational activities**   Other routine operations that are a part of a security operations center

The highly technical nature of security operations necessitates reporting in layers, with each layer written with the audience in mind. For instance, an internal operational report may contain considerable amounts of technical jargon and statistics, whereas reporting to senior executives would contain the same information, but simplified and in business terms.

Risk Management

Risk management, the risk analysis and risk treatment function that deals with emerging risk, should periodically produce management reports so that executive leaders can stay informed on many aspects of cyber risk in the organization. Risk management reporting consists of a periodic snapshot of the risk register, including changes in overall security posture, new risks, changes in existing risks, and those risks that have been treated. Reporting would also include tracking of risk remediation and whether it is being performed on schedule and within budget.

Trends in risk management reporting could include risk treatment decisions by risk magnitude, indicating whether an organization's risk appetite is increasing, decreasing, or staying the same, and the time taken to complete remediation. Reporting may be misleading if it includes only the numbers of items in the risk register and the number of items being selected for risk treatment.

Internal Partnerships

No security manager can hope to accomplish much if they work alone. Effective information security and information risk is a team sport, and each player on the team can help the security manager in different ways. Further, communication with other corporate departments and business units helps to keep the security manager informed on matters of importance.

An effective way to build those partnerships while increasing the effectiveness of the program is to "deputize" team members from other groups. For example, the security manager can partner with administrative assistants, who will lead the data retention program in their respective departments. Or the security manager may designate a person in another business unit (BU) to serve as the information security liaison to share guidance with the BU and report possible risks or issues that impact information security in the organization. None of this is possible unless proper training is provided to the other team members, and time must be allocated for them to fulfil those added duties.

Legal

In most organizations, the legal department functions as the organization's de facto business risk office, through the negotiation of contract terms with service providers, customers, and other parties. Legal generally always attempts to tip risk in favor of the organization.

Legal and information security can collaborate on the security clauses in almost any contract with customers, suppliers, service providers, and other parties. When other parties send contracts that contain security clauses, the security manager should examine those clauses to ensure that the organization is able to meet all requirements. Similarly, when the organization is considering doing business with another party, the security manager can work with the legal department to make sure that the organization is adequately protected by requiring the other party to take certain steps to protect the organization's information.

Sometimes an organization will enter into a business relationship without informing or consulting with the security manager, who often would want to perform a risk assessment to identify any important risks that should be known. The best arrangement is for legal to inform the security manager of every new contract it receives so that the security manager can attempt to identify risks at this late stage.

Human Resources

As the steward for information and many activities regarding employees and other workers, human resources (HR) is another important ally of information security. HR can bolster the organization's security in many ways, including the following:

- **Recruiting**   As HR recruits new employees, it ensures that potential personnel have the appropriate qualifications and that they are inclined to conform to security policy and other policy. In the candidate screening process, HR will perform background checks to confirm the applicant's education, prior employment, and professional certifications, and to determine criminal history.

- **Onboarding**   HR will ensure that all new employees sign important documents, including nondisclosure agreements, and that they receive their initial training, including security awareness training. In onboarding, new employees will also formally acknowledge receipt of, and pledge conformance to, security policy and other policies. HR will provision human resource information systems (HRISs), which in many organizations are integrated into their identity and access management systems. HR ensures that new employees are assigned to the correct job title and responsibilities, as in some cases this automatically results in new employees receiving "birthright" access to specific information systems and applications.

- **Internal transfers**   HR is responsible for coordinating internal transfers, as employees change from one position or department to another. Internal transfers are somewhat different from promotions; in an internal transfer, an employee may be moving to an entirely different department, where they will need to have access to completely different information systems and applications. Notifying security and IT personnel of internal transfers is important so that employees' former roles in information systems and applications can be discontinued at the appropriate time, avoiding the phenomena known as *accumulation of privileges,* where employees with long tenure accumulate access rights to a growing number of roles in information systems and applications, thereby increasing various risks.

- **Offboarding**   HR is responsible for processing the termination, or offboarding, of employees who are leaving the organization for any reason. HR is responsible for ensuring that security, IT, and other departments are notified of the termination so that all access rights can be terminated at the appropriate time. (This is especially important in a dismissal situation, where the organization must "surgically remove" access at precisely the right moment to avoid the risk of the terminated employee, in the heat of the moment, from exacting revenge on the organization through sabotage and other acts.) HR is also responsible for collecting assets issued to a departing employee such as laptop or tablet computers, mobile devices, and related peripherals. HR may also require departing employees to sign nondisclosure and/or noncompete agreements.

- **Training**   In many organizations, HR is the focal point for most or all training for employees and for keeping records of training. Security awareness training, which may be administered by HR, is vital. HR in many organizations is also the focal point for coordinating various communications to employees on topics including training and security reminders.

- **Investigations**   HR conducts investigations into matters such as employee misconduct. Where such misconduct involves any improper use of information systems or computers, HR will partner with information security, which may conduct a forensic investigation to establish a reliable history of events and establish a chain of custody should the matter develop into legal proceedings such as a lawsuit.

- **Discipline**   HR is the focal point for formal disciplinary actions against employees. From an information security perspective, this includes matters of violations of security policy and other policies. Generally, the security manager will present facts and, if requested, an opinion about such matters, but HR is ultimately responsible for selecting the manner and degree of disciplinary action, whether that includes verbal and written warnings, demotion, time off without pay, reduction in compensation, forfeiture of a bonus, removal of privileges, or dismissal.

Facilities

The facilities function provides stewardship of the workplace to ensure that there is adequate space and support for workers in all office locations. The communication between facilities and information security includes the following subject matter:

- **Workplace access control**   Facilities typically manages workplace access control systems such as badge readers and door lock actuators that control which personnel are permitted to access work centers and zones within them. A well-known principle in information security states that adversaries who obtain physical access to computing assets are able to take them over; this reiterates the need for effective access control that prevents unauthorized personnel from accessing those assets.

- **Workplace surveillance**   Video surveillance is the companion detective control that works with preventive controls such as key card systems. Video cameras at building entrances can help corroborate the identity of personnel who enter and leave. Visible surveillance monitors can add a deterrent aspect to surveillance.

- **Equipment check-in/check-out**   Data centers and other locations with valuable assets can implement equipment check-in and check-out functions, whereby personnel are required to record assets coming and going in a log that resembles a visitor log.

- **Guest processing**   Facilities often assists with the identification and processing of guests and other visitors. Security guards, receptionists, or other personnel can check visitors' government IDs, issue visitor badges, contact the employees being visited, and assist in other ways.

- **Security guards**   Guards represent the human element that provides or supplements access controls and video surveillance. Guards can also assist with equipment check-in/check-out and visitor processing.
- **Asset security**   Through video surveillance, access control, and other means, facilities ensures the protection of assets including data center information-processing systems and office assets, including printers and copiers.
- **Personnel safety**   While not directly in the crosshairs of information security, many security managers are involved in personnel safety, because is closely related to asset security and many of the same protective controls are used.

 NOTE   Although personnel security is cited last in this list, the safety of personnel should be the highest priority in any organization.

Information Technology

Information technology and information security represents perhaps the most strategic partnership that the security manager will establish and develop. Many key functions are performed by IT that have security ramifications, requiring effective collaboration and communication between these two teams. These functions include the following:

- **Access control**   IT typically manages day-to-day access control, including issuing credentials to new employees, removing credentials from terminated employees, processing access requests, and resetting credentials. In some organizations, IT may also perform access reviews and recertifications.
- **Architecture**   IT is responsible for the overall architecture of information systems used in the organization. This includes data architecture, network architecture, and systems architecture. In many organizations, the practice of security architecture affects all other aspects of architecture. Open Security Architecture (www.opensecurityarchitecture.org/) defines IT security architecture as "the design artifacts that describe how the security controls (security countermeasures) are positioned, and how they relate to the overall information technology architecture. These controls serve the purpose to maintain the system's quality attributes: confidentiality, integrity, availability, accountability and assurance services." In other words, security architecture is the big-picture mission of understanding the interplay between all the security controls and configurations that work together to protect information systems and information assets.
- **Configuration and Hardening**   IT owns the configuration of all operating systems for servers and end-user computing; this includes the development and implementation of hardening standards, which are typically developed by IT in accordance to policy and principles developed by information security.

- **Scanning and patching**   Under the guidance of the security manager, IT often operates vulnerability scanning tools and patch management platforms to ensure that IT assets are free of exploitable vulnerabilities. This has proven to be one of the most critical activities to prevent break-ins by external adversaries.

- **Security tools**   In most organizations, IT operates the organization's firewalls, intrusion detection/prevention systems, spam filtering, web filtering, and other security tools. Generally, the security manager establishes policies and principles by which these tools are used, and IT implements, maintains, and operates them according to those policies and principles.

- **System monitoring**   IT typically performs monitoring of its assets to ensure that all are operating normally and to manage alarms that indicate the presence of various operational issues.

- **Security monitoring**   In some organizations, IT performs security monitoring of IT assets to be alerted when security issues occur.

- **Third-party connections**   IT may be involved in the setup of data connections to third-party service providers. As part of an organization's third-party risk program, the security manager needs to be aware of all third-party business relationships as early in the cycle as possible; however, because some vendor relationships escape the scrutiny of security managers early in the process, being informed of new third-party connections may sometimes be the only way a security manager will be aware of new relationships.

Systems Development

Systems development includes software development, systems development, integration, and other activities concerned with the development or acquisition of information systems for use internally or by customers or partners.

Under guidance from the security manager, systems development will manage the entire product development life cycle, with security as an integral part at each stage in the process. Communications and collaboration between systems development and information security include the following topics:

- **Security and privacy by design**   Several activities ensure that all new offerings, components, features, and improvements incorporate security and privacy as part of the design process. This can help the organization avoid issues later in the development process that may be more costly to remediate.

- **Secure development**   Secure coding ensures that all new and changed software is free of exploitable defects that could result in security incidents.

- **Security testing**   Several activities fall under the security testing function, including code-scanning tools used by each developer's integrated development environment (IDE), unit and system testing to confirm the correct implementation of all security requirements, static application security testing (SAST) scanning tools that are run as part of a nightly build process, and dynamic application security testing (DAST) scanning tools that identify security defects in running applications.

- **Code reviews**   Peer reviews of security-related changes to software source code include security-sensitive functions such as authentication, session management, data validation, and data segregation in multitenant environments. Some organizations incorporate code reviews for changes to all software modules.

- **Security review of open source software**   Some organizations perform reviews of various kinds of some or all open source modules to ensure they are not introducing unwanted security defects into the software application.

- **Developer training**   Periodic training for developers includes techniques on secure development, which helps developers avoid common mistakes that result in security defects that must be fixed later.

- **Protection of the development process**   This includes controls to ensure that only authorized developers may access source code (and this may include restrictions on the quantity of source code that a developer can check out at any given time), security scans of source code upon check-in, and protection of all source code.

Procurement

Larger organizations have procurement or purchasing departments that negotiate prices and business terms for new purchases of hardware, software, and services, as well as renewals for subscriptions and services. The security manager should consider a business relationship with procurement departments. The procurement manager can be sure to notify the security manager whenever any new purchase of hardware and software products or related services is being considered. This enables the security manager to begin any needed due diligence related to the product or service being considered and can weigh in with messaging concerning risks and any needed controls or compensating controls to keep risk within accepted tolerances.

Internal Audit

Virtually all U.S. public companies, and many private companies, have an internal audit (IA) function whose main mission is assurance through independent audits of policies and controls. Although IA departments cannot stipulate how controls, policies, and processes should be designed and operated, IA can still be a collaborative partner on controls, policies, and processes by telling IT, information security, and others whether those controls, policies, and processes can be audited as designed.

Business Unit Managers

It has been said that a security manager can protect the organization only to the extent that he understands how it works. Naturally this necessitates that the security manager communicate and develop relationships with business unit and department managers and leaders throughout the organization. These partnerships help the security manager understand how each business unit and department functions, and it helps identify critical personnel, processes, systems, and outside partners. The main purpose of these partnerships is *not* for the security manager to inform business unit managers and leaders how security works, but rather to help the security manager negotiate the best and most transparent ways to respond to management as security matters occur within the organization. As these strategic relationships develop, business unit managers and leaders will begin to trust, share information with, and include the security manager in key conversations and processes. Trust leads to conversations on sensitive security topics, resulting in minor and sometimes significant improvements to the business and its security.

Affiliates and Key Business Partners

As the security manager develops strategic relationships throughout the organization, she should set her sights on affiliates, business partners, and other external entities that are deeply involved in the organization's development and delivery of goods and services. With the extensive information systems integrations that are established between organizations, the security of an organization is dependent upon the security of the organization's information systems ecosystem—the interconnection of information systems, networks, and business processes. Because many security breaches are connected to third parties, the development of strategic relationships is essential.

External Partnerships

Successful information security is possible only when the security manager communicates and has established relationships with key external organizations. Those key organizations can be identified according to the organization's industry sector, relevant regulations, information systems in use, geographic locations, and similar considerations.

Law Enforcement

A roof is best repaired on a sunny day. Similarly, security managers should communicate and cultivate relationships with key law enforcement agencies and relevant personnel in those agencies before there is an urgent matter at hand. Organizations and law enforcement can develop a relationship in which trusted information sharing can take place; then, when an emergency such as a security breach occurs, law enforcement will be familiar with the organization and its key personnel and will be able to respond appropriately.

Organizations may benefit by developing relationships with the following agencies:

- **United States**   The Federal Bureau of Investigation (FBI), Secret Service (for organizations dealing in large volumes of credit card transactions), Cybersecurity and Infrastructure Security Agency (CISA), and city and state police cybercrime units, plus InfraGard (www.infragard.org/), a public–private partnership between the FBI and private organizations
- **Canada**   The Royal Canadian Mounted Police (RCMP) and city and provincial cybercrime units
- **United Kingdom**   Security Service (aka MI5, Military Intelligence, Section 5) and city and county cybercrime units
- **Globally**   International Criminal Police Organization (Interpol)

NOTE Some agencies conduct public and business outreach to inform businesses about local crime trends and methods of asset protection, and many law enforcement agencies conduct a periodic "citizens' academy," which provides an insider look at the agencies and their mission and practices. The FBI Citizens' Academy (www.fbi.gov/about/community-outreach) is noteworthy in this regard.

Regulators and Auditors

To the greatest extent possible, regulators and auditors should be viewed as partners and not adversaries. Communicating and developing relationships with regulators and auditors can help the organization improve their business relationship and the tone of interactions. Security managers should also understand regulators' ethical boundaries. (In some situations, you cannot so much as buy a regulator a cup of coffee to lighten the mood and talk about work or non-work-related matters.)

Standards Organizations

Numerous standards organizations exist in the information security industry, and a multitude of others exist in all other industry sectors. In the information security industry itself, being involved in standards organizations avails the security manager of "insider" information such as "sneak previews" of emerging and updated standards, as well as learning opportunities and even conferences and conventions. These organizations include the following:

- **PCI Security Standards Council**   Involved with protection of credit card data for banks, issuers, processors, and merchants; well-known for PCI DSS and other standards (www.pcisecuritystandards.org)

- **Cloud Security Alliance**   Creates security standards frameworks for cloud-based service providers (https://cloudsecurityalliance.org/)

- **Information Security Forum (ISF)**   Publishes "Standard of Good Practice for Information Security" (www.securityforum.org)

- **International Organization for Standardization (ISO)** and **International Electrotechnical Commission (IEC)**   Development of international standards on numerous topics including security management and IT service management (www.iso.org and www.iec.ch)

- **National Institute for Standards and Technology (NIST)**   Offers a vast library of special publications on cybersecurity (https://csrc.nist.gov/publications/sp)

Professional Organizations

The information security profession is challenging, not only because of the consequences of ineffective security programs but also because of the high rate of innovation that takes place. Professional organizations such as the following help to fill the need for valuable information through training, professional certifications, local chapter organizations, and conferences:

- **ISACA**   The developer of the Certified Information Security Manager (CISM, the topic of this book), Certified Information Systems Auditor (CISA), Certified in Risk and Information Systems Control (CRISC), and other certifications, with conferences and training events worldwide and numerous chapters around the world. (www.isaca/org)

- **Information Systems Security Association (ISSA)**   Offers conferences and supports numerous local chapters worldwide (www.issa.org)

- **International Information Systems Security Certification Consortium (ISC)²**   Developer of the Certified Information Systems Security Professional (CISSP) and other certifications, conducts extensive training and an annual conference (www.isc2.org)

- **Cloud Security Alliance (CSA)**   Developer of the Cloud Controls Matrix (CCM), the CSA Star program, and the Certified in Cloud Security Knowledge (CCSK) certification, conducts conferences worldwide (https://cloudsecurityalliance.org/)

- **International Council of Electronic Commerce Consultants (EC-Council)**   Developer of the well-known Certified Ethical Hacker (CEH) and Certified Chief Information Security Officer (CCISO) certifications, offers worldwide conferences (www.eccouncil.org)

- **SANS**   Developer of the GIAC family of certifications and conducts numerous training events and conferences globally (www.sans.org)

Security Professional Services Vendors

Security managers need to communicate and develop trusted relationships with one or more security professional services vendors. Because there is so much to know in the information security profession and because threats, practices, and frameworks change so often, having one or more trusted advisors can help a security manager to be continually aware of these developments.

Better security professional services vendors have senior advisors on their staff who are available for brief consultations from time to time. Although these advisors may have sales responsibilities, a skilled security manager can seek their expertise now and then to confirm ideas, plans, and strategies.

Some security professional services vendors have virtual CISOs or CISO advisors on their staff (often former CISOs), who help clients develop long-term security strategies. Often these advisors are billable resources who assist their client organizations in understanding their risks and help develop risk-based security strategies that will make the best use of scarce resources to reduce risk. These types of services are especially useful for smaller organizations that are unable to attract and hire full-time security managers of this caliber.

Security professional services vendors can also assist with a strategy for the acquisition, implementation, and operation of security tools. Trusted advisors who are familiar with security tools can often help a security manager identify the better tools that are more likely to work in their environments.

Security Product Vendors

Security managers need to communicate and establish good business relationships with each of the vendors whose security products and services are in use. Through these relationships, security managers will be better informed in a variety of ways, including product or service updates, workshops and seminars, training, and support. Things do not always go smoothly between product vendors and their customers. Establishing strategic relationships will result in faster and more productive interaction and resolution when problems are encountered.

Trusted advisors can help the security manager identify additional vendors for the purpose of relationship building. A new vendor may offer a product that is a competitor of a product already used in the security manager's organization, or the vendor may offer a product or service that the organization does not currently use. These relationships help the security manager understand the capabilities that she could utilize in the future.

Compliance Management

Compliance is the state of conformance to applicable policies, standards, regulations, and other requirements. It is the process by which the security manager determines whether the organization's information systems, processes, and personnel conform to those things. When a security manager develops or adopts a control framework and identifies applicable regulations and legal requirements, he then sees to it that controls and other measures are implemented. Then, as part of the risk management life cycle, he examines those controls, processes, and systems to determine whether they are in compliance with internal and external requirements. As discussed throughout this book, these activities include external audits, internal audits, reviews, and control self-assessments.

As they do with other life cycle processes, security managers need to report on the organization's compliance with policies, standards, regulations, and other cybersecurity related legal obligations. Only then can management understand the organization's compliance posture and be aware of any compliance issues that warrant attention.

Compliance or Security

Security consultants who work with numerous client organizations often observe the ways that organizations treat asset protection. Organizations seem to fall into one of two categories:

- **Compliance based**   These organizations are satisfied to "check the box" on applicable standards or regulations such as PCI DSS and HIPAA. They do the bare minimum possible to pass audits.

(continued)

- **Security and risk based**   These organizations understand that external standards such as PCI DSS and HIPAA are "starting points," and that periodic risk assessments and other activities are needed (in other words, all the activities discussed in this book) to help them determine what other activities and controls they must develop to be secure.

Security professionals often disagree on many topics, but generally they agree on this: being *compliant* is not the same things as being *secure*.

Applicability

Security managers often find that compliance is complicated by multiple, overlapping standards, regulations, and other legal requirements, each of which may be applicable to various portions of the organization. To understand the coverage of these requirements, the security manager can develop a compliance matrix such as the one shown in Table 6-19.

Properly determining applicability helps the security manager better understand what is required of individual information systems and the processes they support. Any organization would be overspending without necessarily reducing risk if it simply applied the requirements from all regulations and other legal obligations to all of its information systems. The result may be a more consistent application of controls but certainly a more expensive application as well. For most organizations, the resources required to develop the means of compliance to applicable regulations is less than the resources required to apply all required controls by all regulations to all systems.

Compliance Risk

As the security manager performs risk assessments and populates the risk register with risk matters requiring discussion and treatment, the security manager should not overlook compliance risk. *Compliance risk* is associated with any general or specific consequences of the failure to be compliant with an applicable law or other legal obligation.

System	HIPAA	PCI	ISO/IEC 27002	SOC 1	SOC 2
Data centers	Yes	Yes	Yes	Yes	Yes
Electronic medical records (EMR) system	Yes	No	Yes	Yes	No
Payment acceptance	No	Yes	Yes	Yes	Yes
Human resources information system (HRIS)	No	No	Yes	No	No
Enterprise resource planning (ERP) system	No	No	Yes	Yes	Yes
Payroll system	No	No	Yes	No	No

Table 6-19   Example Compliance Matrix Depicting Applicability of Regulations and Standards on Systems

Suppose, for example, that during a risk assessment, a security manager observes that the organization stores credit card information in plaintext spreadsheets on internal file servers. The security manager can identify at least two risks in this situation:

- **Sensitive data exposure**   The risk register indicates that such sensitive data could be misused by internal personnel, and it may be discovered by a malicious outsider. The costs associated with a forensic investigation, along with potential mitigation costs such as payment for credit monitoring for victims, would be included in the total cost incurred by the organization should this information be compromised.

- **Fines and sanctions**   The risk register notes that the organization could face fines and other sanctions should the organization's PCI regulators (namely, banks and payment processors) learn of this. The fines and other sanctions are the potential unplanned costs that the organization may incur upon regulators' discovery of this.

Compliance Enforcement

As the security manager reviews the results of internal and external audits, control self-assessments, and other examinations of systems and processes, she will need to weigh not only the direct risks associated with any negative findings but also the compliance risk. The security manager can apply both of these considerations in any discussions and proceedings during which others in the organizations are contemplating their response to these compliance items.

As a part of a metrics program, the security manager will report on the state of compliance to senior management. Matters of compliance will be reflected in metrics as areas of higher risk, whether these are risks of breach and/or risks of compliance to external regulations with potentially public consequences.

Compliance Monitoring

Rules, regulations, and standards are ever-changing. Information security organizations must find a way to stay current with regard to these changes, so that the organization can proactively plan and anticipate changes that must be made to maintain an acceptable compliance posture. Information security departments often collaborate with corporate legal departments that consume subscription services that inform the organization of changes in laws and regulations. Otherwise, organizations would need to spend considerable time researching applicable laws to be aware of important changes.

Security Awareness Training

Covered earlier in this chapter, security awareness training ensures that an organization's workers are aware of security and related policies, as well as expectations of behavior and judgment. Reporting for security awareness training may include

- Training sessions conducted
- Employees trained

- Phishing testing results
- Other social engineering testing results
- Trends in worker-related security incidents

Security managers need to understand that an increase in the number of worker-reported security incidents may not be a sign of an increase in the number of incidents, but may instead indicate improved worker awareness on the nature of security incidents and the need to report them.

Technical Architecture

Monitoring and reporting on technical architecture can help the organization understand the progress being made on the theme of security by design. However, security managers reporting on trends in technical architecture need to understand that some types of measurements may be misunderstood. For instance, one could expect that the number of incidents related to the technical environment should decrease as more of the environment is aligned with better architecture models such as zero trust. However, at the same time, event detection capabilities could also improve, yielding an increase in the number of events. This could be interpreted as the new architecture being more vulnerable, but it could also be an indication of improvements in event visibility, meaning that a greater number of undetected events were occurring in older environments.

Personnel Management

In all but the smallest organizations where the security manager acts alone, personnel management is an important aspect of information security management. In many organizations, information security is staffed with a team ranging from two to dozens of people. The security manager is responsible for all aspects of the security team, starting with identifying and hiring candidates, assigning and supervising work, developing new skills, and developing the security team's "culture within a culture." All of this requires intentional communication and monitoring.

Finding and Retaining Talent

Security personnel are in high demand, and, consequently, those in the profession command good salaries. However, it can be difficult for organizations to find qualified security professionals, because most organizations have trouble finding skilled, qualified persons that can be attracted away from their current employment. Compensation is creeping upward faster than inflation, and as a result, some organizations cannot afford the talent they need. Because security professionals know they are in high demand, they can choose the types of companies they want to work for, and they can live almost anywhere they want. Today, security professionals who want to be remote workers can do so with comparative ease.

Retaining talent is also a challenge in many organizations. Good technologists seem to become bored with routine and repetition, so keeping them engaged with new challenges can itself be a challenge. Security managers need to find the right balance between their security staff wanting to do "cool, new things" and aligning those desires with actual business needs.

Security managers who are looking to grow their security team or fill open positions often need look no further than their own organization: one or more people in the IT department may aspire to join the security team. Many—if not most—IT security professionals "crossed over" from corporate IT to information security, and this is still a common source for new recruits. People transferring over from IT are already familiar with the business and with IT's operations and practices. If they are looking to grow into a security career, they're probably going to be willing to work pretty hard to succeed.

Roles and Responsibilities

As the security manager develops and begins to execute a long-term security strategy, she will identify all the ongoing and occasional tasks that need to be performed by members of the team. Prior to the beginning of this planning, the security manager must understand the difference between roles and responsibilities. A *role* is a designation that denotes an associated set of responsibilities, knowledge, skills, and attitudes. Example roles include security manager, security engineer, and security analyst. A *responsibility* is a stated expectation of activities and performance. Example responsibilities include running weekly security scans, performing vendor risk assessments, and approving access requests.

As a security manager analyzes all the required activities in a security team, she may take the approach of listing all the activities, along with estimates of the number of hours per week or hours per month required to perform them. Next, she will group these activities according to subject matter, skill levels, and other considerations. As the associated workloads are tallied, the number of people required will become evident. Then, these groups of responsibilities can be given roles, followed by job titles.

Most security managers, however, do not have an opportunity to build and staff a program from scratch; instead, they are inheriting an existing program from a previous manager. Still, these activities can serve to delineate all required activities, calculate or observe levels of effort, and confirm that roles and responsibilities are assigned to the right personnel who have the required skills and experience to carry them out properly.

Job Descriptions

A *job description* is a formal description of a position in an organization and usually contains a job title, work experience requirements, knowledge requirements, and responsibilities. Job descriptions are used when an organization is seeking to fill a new or vacant position. The job description will be included in online advertisements to attract potential candidates. In most organizations, HR is the steward of job descriptions. However, when positions become vacant or new positions are opened, HR often will consult with the hiring manager to ensure that the contents of a job description are still accurate and up-to-date.

Job descriptions are also a tool used in professional development. Managers and leadership can develop career paths that represent a person's professional growth through a progression of promotions or transfers into other positions. Job descriptions are a primary means for a worker to understand what another position is like; interviewing people who are already in a desired position is another means for gaining insight into a position that someone aspires to. A small but effective way to drive a culture of security is to add in specific language regarding the responsibilities that each role plays in protecting the organization's data and systems used in storing, processing, and transmitting that data.

Culture

As discussed in Chapter 1, *culture* is the collective set of attitudes, practices, communication, communication styles, ethics, and other behavior in an organization. Culture can be thought of as the collective consciousness of the workers in an organization. It's hard to describe an organization's culture because it has to be experienced to be understood.

Security managers seek to understand an organization's culture so that they may be better and more effective change agents. In organizations that do not regard information security as an important activity, security managers must work to understand the culture and make subtle changes to improve awareness of information security in a form that most workers can understand. Security awareness training, with its attendant messaging from executives, is often regarded as a catalyst for making those subtle changes to the culture.

Security managers and their teams occasionally find they need to develop a "culture within a culture." The rest of an organization with a laissez-faire attitude toward security may have some catching up to do, but the security team already "gets it"—the ever-conscious awareness of day-to-day activities and whether they are handling and protecting data and systems properly.

 NOTE With our codes of ethics from ISACA and other security professional organizations, we are obligated to conduct ourselves according to a higher standard, which is a part of the reason for the culture within a culture.

Professional Development

Dedicated and committed technologists have a built-in thirst for knowledge and for expanding their boundaries. Information security professionals should have this thirst "on steroids," because the velocity of change is higher than that in other aspects of information technology. Cyber-criminal organizations are innovating their malware and other attack techniques, manifested through breaches using increasingly novel methods; security tools vendors are innovating their detective and protective wares; security organizations are continually improving many aspects of security management, including control frameworks, auditing techniques, and security awareness messaging. It's been said that information security professionals must spend four hours each week reading up on these and other new developments just to keep from falling behind. Security managers need to be aware of the present knowledge and skills that each security team member possesses today, what skills are needed in the team in the future, and the professional growth aspirations that drive each team member. Several avenues for professional development are discussed here.

Career Paths   A *career path* is the progression of job responsibilities and job titles that a worker will attain over time. Generally, a worker who is aware of a potential career path within their organization is more likely to remain in the organization. Workers who feel trapped and unable to advance are more likely to consider a position in another organization. With the security employment market as tight as it is, any organization that neglects the topics of professional development and career paths runs the risk of losing good people. Security managers should be aware of any career paths that have been published by their organizations; however, since many organizations don't develop formal career paths, security managers will want to work one-on-one with each security staff member to determine what their individual career paths will look like.

There are many fields of specialty in information security, including the following:

- Risk management
- Risk analysis
- Information systems auditing
- Penetration testing
- Red / blue / purple team
- Malware analysis
- Security engineering
- Security architecture
- Secure development
- Mobile device security
- Telecommunications and network security
- Social engineering
- Security awareness training
- Forensics
- Cryptography
- Business continuity planning and disaster recovery planning
- Identity and access management
- Identity and access governance
- Data governance and classification
- Threat intelligence
- Third-party risk
- Privacy

Certifications   Professional certifications represent skills, knowledge, and experience among security professionals. Certifications are a badge of honor, representing thousands of hours of professional experience as well as the drive to improve oneself. To the extent that team members value the worth of certifications, security managers should encourage their team members to earn additional certifications. Better organizations would not hesitate to reimburse employees' expenses to earn and maintain their certifications, although, practically speaking, there may be reasonable limits on annual spending in this regard. Security managers should invest time in each of their security staff members to understand their career paths and the certifications they may want to earn along the way.

The most popular non-vendor-related security and privacy certifications are, in rough order of increasing seniority, as follows:

- **Entry-Level Cybersecurity Certification**   This relatively new offering by (ISC)² is in its pilot phase as of the writing of this book. Visit www.isc2.org.

- **Security+**   Offered by CompTIA, this is considered a popular entry-level security certification. Visit www.comptia.org.

- **Systems Security Certified Practitioner (SSCP)**   Offered by (ISC)², many believe that SSCP is a "junior CISSP," but this is not the case. SSCP is more technical than the CISSP and is ideal for hands-on security professionals.

- **Global Information Assurance Certification (GIAC)**   Offered by SANS, this family of certifications covers several different topics. Visit www.giac.org.

- **Certified Ethical Hacker (CEH)**   Offered by EC-Council, this certification is ideal for penetration testers and others who want to learn more about the world of vulnerabilities and exploits. Visitwww.eccouncil.org.

- **Certified Cloud Security Professional (CCSP)**   Jointly offered by (ISC)² and the Cloud Security Alliance (CSA), this relatively new certification is sure to become popular. Visit www.isc2.org.

- **Certified Information Systems Security Professional (CISSP)**   Perhaps the most well-known and respected information security certification is popular among strong, established security professionals. It is important for career growth as many organizations require this specific certification for security positions. Visit www.isc2.org.

- **Certified Secure Software Lifecycle Professional (CSSLP)**   Offered by (ISC)², this certification focuses on secure software development. Visit www.isc2.org.

- **Certified Data Privacy Solutions Engineer (CDPSE)**   Offered by ISACA, this is one of ISACA's newest certifications, focusing on data privacy and leaning into the technical side of the profession.

- **Certified Information Security Manager (CISM)**   Offered by ISACA, this certification is the topic of this book. Visit www.isaca.org.

- **Certified Information Systems Auditor (CISA)**   Also offered by ISACA, this is considered the gold-standard certification for IT auditors. Visit www.isaca.org.

- **Certified in Risk and Information Systems Control (CRISC)**   Offered by ISACA, this is an essential certification for security professionals who work in risk assessment, risk management, and the development of controls and control frameworks. Visit www.isaca.org.

NOTE There are many more non-vendor-related security certifications, but they are too numerous to list in this book. You'll find a broad list on Wikipedia at https://en.wikipedia.org/wiki/List_of_computer_security_certifications.

Many IT equipment vendors and IT security tools vendors offer security certifications that represent expertise in various categories of information security. Nearly every major security tools manufacturer has one or more certifications that can be earned. Here is a small sampling:

- Check Point Certified Security Administrator (CCSA)
- Certified Forensic Security Responder (CFSR) from Guidance Software
- Radware Certified Security Specialist (RCSS)
- Metasploit Pro Certified Specialist from Rapid7
- WhiteHat Certified Secure Developer (WCSD)

Training   Another important way to retain talent is to provide training for security staff. Again, because security professionals can be afflicted with boredom, they are happiest when they are learning new things. Security managers may fear that if they provide too much training, personnel might leave for greener pastures—but what may happen if they don't provide enough training? Their personnel would almost certainly feel trapped and be compelled to leave with even more fervor.

Typical organizations provide one week of security training for security professionals. Ideally this means that a security professional is able to attend a one-week conference of her choice. Other companies will pay for web-based training or a number of one-day training courses. One week of training is considered the minimum required for security professionals to stay current in their chosen field. Additional training will be required for security professionals who want to move into a specialty area. Many employers reimburse college and university tuition, often with a yearly cap. This can provide a means for security personnel who want to pursue an undergraduate or graduate degree in information security and related fields.

Personnel-Related Reporting

Reporting that is related to personnel management and development may include the following:

- **Performance management**   As a part of a larger organization's performance management process, security managers can report on staff member and team attendance, engagement, and performance.
- **Staff development**   Security managers can report on staff development by reporting on training, certifications earned, and mentoring sessions.
- **Turnover**   With security professionals in high demand, security managers should keep an eye on staff turnover and take time to understand why any staff members have left the organizations for greener pastures elsewhere.

PART III

- **Compensation**   High demand for security professionals worldwide has resulted in wages and other compensation rising higher than inflation in many cases. An organization's HR department may not be fully attuned to this matter, making it necessary for the security manager to monitor and report on this.

Project and Program Management

The information security field is undergoing constant change. Organizations with mature risk management programs are discovering new actionable risks, attack techniques used by cybercriminals are undergoing constant innovation, security vendors make frequent improvements in their tools, and the practices of managing security are evolving. IT is also undergoing considerable changes, and organizations are reinventing themselves through process development and changes in the organization chart. Mergers and acquisitions in many industries inflict many broad changes in affected organizations.

The result of this phenomenon of continuous change is the fact that most organizations undertake several information security projects each year. In many organizations, information security personnel are spending more time in projects than they are in routine daily operations. For many security managers, *continuous change is the only constant*.

In addition to having a deep understanding of IT, risk management, and most or all of the disciplines within security management, a security manager must also be skilled at both *project management* and *program management*—the management of several concurrent projects—to orchestrate the parade of changes being undertaken to keep the organization out of trouble. Nevertheless, security managers need to keep their eye on the big picture: the strategy and objectives for the security program and alignment with the business. Every program and project in information security should align with these.

 NOTE   The disciplines of project management and program management are outside the scope of this book, but following are some recommended reading: *Engineering Project Management for the Global High Technology Industry,* by Sammy Shina (McGraw Hill, 2014); *The Handbook of Program Management: How to Facilitate Project Success with Optimal Program Management, Second Edition*, by James T. Brown (McGraw Hill, 2014); *A Guide to the Project Management Body of Knowledge* (PMBOK Guide), *Seventh Edition*, by Project Management Institute (PMI, 2021).

Budget

Budgeting is an essential part of long-term planning for information security and arguably a more difficult undertaking than it is for many other departments. Although the development of an information security strategy (in terms of the capabilities needed) is somewhat more straightforward, obtaining management support for the funding required to realize the strategy can be quite difficult. When executive management does not understand the strategic value of information security, the prospect of funding activities that result in existing business capabilities or capacity seems far different from funding information security, which results in no changes in business capabilities or capacity.

The activities that the security manager needs to include in budgets include the following:

- Staff salaries and benefits
- Temporary staff for special projects and initiatives
- Training and tuition reimbursement
- Equipment
- Software tools
- Support for equipment and software
- Space required in data centers
- Travel
- Maintenance of documents and records
- Team building and recognition
- Contingencies

Often, security managers undertake a detailed analysis on the work required for each function in information security. For instance, a security manager may track time spent on routine processes as well as anticipated but unplanned activities such as incident response and investigations.

IT Service Management

IT service management (ITSM) is the set of activities that occur to ensure that the delivery of IT services is efficient and effective, through active management and the continuous improvement of processes. ITSM consists of several distinct activities:

- Service desk
- Incident management
- Problem management
- Change management
- Configuration management
- Release management
- Service-level management
- Financial management
- Capacity management
- Service continuity management
- Availability management

Each of these activities is described in detail in this section.

ITSM is defined in the IT Infrastructure Library (ITIL) process framework, a well-recognized standard. The content of ITIL is managed by AXELOS. ITSM processes can be audited and registered to the international ISO/IEC 20000:2011 standard.

Why ITSM Matters to Security

At first glance, ITSM and information security may not appear to be related. But information security relies a great deal on effective ITSM for the following reasons:

- In the absence of effective change management and configuration management, the configuration of IT systems will be inconsistent, in many cases resulting in exploitable vulnerabilities that could lead to security incidents.

- In the absence of effective release management, security defects may persist in production environments, possibly resulting in vulnerabilities and incidents.

- In the absence of effective capacity management, system and application malfunctions could occur, resulting in unscheduled downtime and data corruption.

- Without effective financial management, IT organizations may have insufficient funds for important security initiatives.

Service Desk

Often known as the help desk, the *IT service desk* handles incidents and service requests on behalf of customers by acting as a single point of contact. The service desk performs end-to-end management of incidents and service requests (at least from the perspective of the customer) and is also responsible for communicating status reports to the customer.

The service desk can also serve as a collection point for other ITSM processes, such as change management, configuration management, service-level management, availability management, and other ITSM functions. A typical service desk function consists of frontline analysts who take calls from users. These analysts perform basic triage and are often trained to perform routine tasks such as password resets, troubleshoot hardware and software issues, and assist users with questions and problems with software programs. When analysts are unable to assist a user, the matter is typically escalated to a subject-matter expert who can provide assistance.

Incident Management

ITIL defines an *incident* as "an unplanned interruption to an IT Service or reduction in the quality of an IT service. Failure of a configuration item that has not yet affected service is also an incident—for example, failure of one disk from a mirror set." ISO/IEC 20000-1:2011 defines an incident as an "unplanned interruption to a service, a reduction in the quality of a service or an event that has not yet impacted the service to the customer." Thus, an incident may be any of the following:

- Service outage
- Service slowdown
- Software bug

IT Infrastructure Library, Not Just for the United Kingdom

While ITIL may have its roots in the United Kingdom, it has very much become an international standard. This is because ITIL was adopted by the International ISO/ IEC, in the ISO/IEC 20000 standard, and because IT management practices are becoming more standardized and mature.

Regardless of the cause, incidents are a result of failures or errors in any component or layer in IT infrastructure. In ITIL terminology, if the incident has been experienced and its root cause is known, it is considered a *known error*. If the service desk is able to access the catalog of known errors, this may result in more rapid resolution of incidents, resulting in less downtime and inconvenience. The change management and configuration management processes are used to make modifications to the system to fix the problem temporarily or permanently. If the root cause of the incident is not known, the incident may be escalated to a *problem,* which is discussed in the next section.

 NOTE Security incident management and response is discussed fully in Chapters 7 and 8.

Problem Management

When several incidents have occurred that appear to have the same or a similar root cause, a *problem* is occurring. ITIL defines a problem as "a cause of one or more incidents." ISO/IEC 20000-1:2011 defines a problem as the "root cause of one or more incidents" and continues by stating, "The root cause is not usually known at the time a problem record is created and the problem management process is responsible for further investigation."

The overall objective of problem management is a reduction in the number and severity of such incidents. Problem management can also include some proactive measures, including system monitoring to measure system health and capacity management, which will help management forestall capacity-related incidents.

Examples of problems include the following:

- A server has exhausted available resources, resulting in similar, multiple errors (known as "incidents" by ITSM).

- A software bug in a service is noticed by and affects many users.

- A chronically congested network causes the communications between many IT components to fail.

Similar to incidents, when the root cause of a problem has been identified, the change management and configuration management processes will be enacted to make temporary and permanent fixes.

Change Management

Change management involves using a set of processes to ensure that all changes performed in an IT environment are controlled and performed consistently. ITIL defines change management as follows: "The goal of the change management process is to ensure that standardized methods and procedures are used for efficient and prompt handling of all changes, in order to minimize the impact of change-related incidents upon service quality, and consequently improve the day-to-day operations of the organization."

The main purpose of change management is to ensure that all proposed changes to an IT environment are vetted for suitability and risk and to ensure that changes will not interfere with one another or with other planned or unplanned activities. To be effective, each stakeholder should review all changes so that every perspective of each change is properly reviewed.

A typical change management process is a formal "waterfall" process that includes the following steps:

1. **Proposal or request** The person or group performing the change issues a change proposal, which contains a description of the change, the change procedure, the IT components that are expected to be affected by the change, a verification procedure to ensure that the change was applied properly, a back-out procedure in the event the change cannot be applied (or failed verification), and the results of tests that were performed in a test environment. The proposal should be distributed to all stakeholders several days prior to its review.

2. **Review** Typically in a meeting or discussion about the proposed change, the personnel who will be performing the change discuss the change and answer any of the stakeholders' questions. Because the change proposal was distributed earlier, each stakeholder should have had an opportunity to read about the proposed change in advance of the review. Stakeholders can discuss any aspect of the change during the review. They may agree to approve the change, or they may request that it be deferred or that some aspect of the proposed change be altered.

3. **Approval** When a change has been formally approved in the review step, the person or group responsible for change management recordkeeping will record the approval, including the names of the individuals who consented to the change. If, however, a change has been deferred or denied, the person or group that proposed the change will need to make alterations to the proposed change so that it will be acceptable, or they can withdraw the change altogether.

4. **Implementation**   The actual change is implemented per the procedure described in the change proposal. Then the personnel identified as the change implementers perform the actual change to the IT systems identified in the approved change procedure.

5. **Verification**   After the implementers have completed the change, they will perform the verification procedure to make sure that the change was implemented correctly and that it produces the desired result. Generally, this will involve one or more steps, including the gathering of evidence (and directions for confirming correct versus incorrect change) that shows the change was performed correctly. This evidence will be filed with other records related to the change and may be useful in the future, especially if the change is suspected to be the root cause of any problems encountered in the system where this change is made.

6. **Post-change review**   Some or all changes in an IT organization will be reviewed after the change is implemented. The personnel who made the change discuss it with other stakeholders to learn more about the change and whether any updates to future changes may be needed.

These activities should be part of a *change control board* (CCB) or *change advisory board* (CAB), a group of stakeholders from IT and every group that is affected by changes in IT applications and supporting infrastructure.

 NOTE   The change management process is similar to the systems development life cycle (SDLC) in that it consists of activities that systematically enact changes to an IT environment.

Change Management Records
Most or all of the activities related to a change should include updates to business records so that all of the facts related to each change are captured for future reference. In even the smallest IT organization, there are too many changes taking place over time to expect that anyone will be able to recall facts about each change later. Records that are related to each change serve as a permanent record.

Emergency Changes
Although most changes can be planned in advance using the change management process described here, there are times when IT systems need to be changed right away. Most change management processes include a process for emergency changes that details most of the steps in the nonemergency change management process, but they are performed in a different order. The steps for emergency changes are as follows:

1. **Emergency approval**   When an emergency situation arises, the staff members attending to the emergency should seek management approval for the proposed change via phone, in person, or in writing (typically, e-mail). If the approval was granted by phone or in person, e-mail or other follow-up is usually performed. Who can approve these emergency changes should be designated in advance.

2. **Implementation**   The staff members perform the change.

3. **Verification**   Staff members verify that the change produced the expected result. This may involve other staff members from other departments or end users.

4. **Review**   The emergency change is formally reviewed, which may be performed alongside nonemergency changes with the change control board, the same group of individuals who discuss nonemergency changes.

As with nonemergency changes, emergency changes should be recorded and available for future reference.

Linkage to Problem and Incident Management

Often, changes are made as a result of an incident or problem. Emergency and nonemergency changes should reference specific incidents or problems so that those incidents and problems may be properly closed once verification of their resolution has been completed.

Configuration Management

Configuration management (CM) is the process of recording and maintaining the configuration of IT systems. Each configuration setting is known in ITSM parlance as a *configuration item* (CI). CIs usually include the following:

- **Hardware complement**   This includes the hardware specifications of each system (such as CPU speed, amount of memory, firmware version, adapters, and peripherals).

- **Hardware configuration**   Settings at the hardware level may include boot settings, adapter configuration, and firmware settings.

- **Operating system version and configuration**   This includes versions, patches, and many operating system configuration items that have an impact on system performance and functionality.

- **Software versions and configuration**   Software components such as database management systems, application servers, and integration interfaces often have many configuration settings of their own.

Organizations with many IT systems may automate the CM function with tools that are used to record and change configuration settings automatically. These tools help to streamline IT operations and make it easier for IT systems to be more consistent with one another. The database of system configurations is called a *configuration management database* (CMDB).

Linkage to Problem and Incident Management

An intelligent problem and incident management system is able to access the CMDB to help IT personnel determine whether incidents and problems are related to specific configurations. This can be an invaluable aid to those who are seeking to determine a problem's root cause.

Linkage to Change Management

Many configuration management tools are able to automatically detect configuration changes that are made to a system, including *configuration drift,* or unintended configuration changes. With some change and configuration management systems, it is possible to correlate changes detected by a configuration management system with changes approved in the change management process. Further, many changes that are approved by the change management process can be performed by configuration management tools, which can be used to push changes out to managed systems.

Release Management

Release management is the ITIL term used to describe the portion of the SDLC where changes in applications are placed into production service. Release management is used to control the changes that are made to software programs, applications, and environments.

The release process is used for several types of changes to a system, including the following:

- **Incidents and problem resolution**   Casually known as bug fixes, these types of changes occur in response to an incident or problem, where it has been determined that a change to application software is the appropriate remedy.

- **Enhancements**   New functions in an application are created and implemented. These enhancements may have been requested by customers, or they may be a part of the long-range vision on the part of the designers of the software program.

- **Subsystem patches and changes**   Changes in lower layers in an application environment may require a level of testing that is similar to what is used when changes are made to the application itself. Examples of changes are patches, service packs, and version upgrades to operating systems, database management systems, application servers, and middleware.

The release process is a sequential process—that is, each change that is proposed to a software program will be taken through each step in the release management process. In many applications, changes are usually assembled into a "package" for process efficiency purposes: it is more effective to discuss and manage groups of changes than it would be to manage individual changes.

The steps in a typical release process are preceded by a typical SDLC process:

1. **Feasibility study**   Activities that seek to determine the expected benefits of a program, project, or change to a system.

2. **Requirements definition**   Each software change is described in terms of a feature description and requirements. The feature description is a high-level explanation of a change to software that may be described using business terms. Requirements are the detailed statements that describe a change in enough detail for a developer to make changes and additions to application code that will provide the desired functionality. Often, end users will be involved in the development of requirements so that they may verify that the proposed software change is really what they desire.

PART III

3. **Design**   After requirements have been developed, a programmer/analyst or application designer will create a formal design. For an existing software application, this will usually involve changes to existing design documents and diagrams, but for new applications, the design will need to be created from scratch or copied from similar designs and modified. Regardless, the design will have a sufficient level of detail to permit a programmer or software engineer to complete development without having to discern the meaning of requirements or design.

4. **Development**   When requirements and design have been completed, reviewed, and approved, programmers or software engineers begin development. This involves actual coding in the chosen computer language with approved development tools, as well as the creation or update to ancillary components, such as a database design or application programming interface (API). Developers will often perform their own unit testing, where they test individual modules and sections of the application code to make sure that it works properly.

5. **Testing**   When the developers have finished coding and unit testing, a more formal and comprehensive test phase is performed. Here, analysts, dedicated software testers, and perhaps end users will test all of the new and changed functionality to confirm that it is performing according to requirements. Depending on the nature of the changes, some amount of *regression testing* is also performed, where functions that were confirmed to be working properly in prior releases are tested again to make sure that they continue to work as expected. Testing is performed according to formal, written test plans that are designed to confirm that every requirement is fulfilled. Formal test scripts are used, and the results of all tests should be recorded and archived. The testing that users perform is usually called *user acceptance testing* (UAT). Often, automated test tools are used, which can make testing more accurate and efficient. After testing is completed, a formal review and approval are required before the process is allowed to continue.

6. **Implementation**   Next, the software is implemented on production systems. Developers hand off the completed software to operations personnel, who install it according to instructions created by developers. This could also involve the use of tools to make changes to data and database design to accommodate changes in the software. When changes are completed and tested, the release itself is prepared and deployed.

   a. **Release preparation**   When UAT and regression testing have been completed, reviewed, and approved, a release management team will begin to prepare the new or changed software for release. Depending upon the complexity of the application and of the change itself, release preparation may involve not only software installation but also the installation or change to database design, and perhaps even changes to customer data. Hence, the software release may involve the development and testing of data conversion tools and other programs that are required so that the new or changed software will operate properly. As with testing and other phases, full records of testing and implementation of release preparation details need to be captured and archived.

b. **Release deployment** When release preparation is completed (and perhaps reviewed and approved), the release is installed on the target systems. Personnel deploying the release will follow the release procedure, which may involve the use of tools that will make changes to the target system at the operating system, database, or other level; any required manipulation or migration of data; and the installation of the actual software. The release procedure will also include verification steps that will be used to confirm the correct installation of all components.

7. **Post-implementation** A post-implementation review examines matters of system adequacy, security, return on investment (ROI), and any issues encountered during implementation.

Utilizing a Gate Process

Many organizations utilize a "gate process" approach in their release management process, in which each step of the process undergoes formal review and approval before the next step is allowed to begin. For example, suppose a formal design review will be performed and attended by end users, personnel who created requirements and feature description documents, developers, and management. If the design is approved, development may begin. But if questions or concerns are raised in the design review, the design may need to be modified and reviewed again before development is allowed to begin.

Agile processes utilize gates as well, although the flow of Agile processes is often parallel rather than sequential. The concept of formal reviews is the same, regardless of the SDLC process in use.

Service-Level Management

Service-level management is composed of the set of activities that confirms whether the IT department is providing adequate service to customers. This is achieved through continuous monitoring and periodic review of IT service delivery.

An IT department often plays two different roles in service-level management: As a provider of service to its own customers, the department will measure and manage the services that it provides directly. Also, many IT departments directly or indirectly manage services that are provided by external service providers. Thus, many IT departments are both service provider and customer, and often the two are interrelated, as depicted in Figure 6-15.

Financial Management

Financial management for IT services consists of several activities, including the following:

- Budgeting
- Capital investment
- Expense management
- Project accounting and project ROI

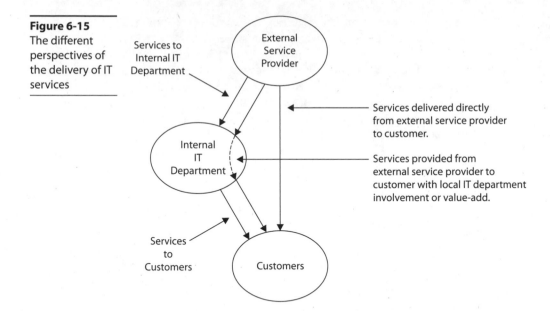

Figure 6-15
The different perspectives of the delivery of IT services

IT financial management is the portion of IT management that takes into account the financial value of IT services that support organizational objectives.

Capacity Management

Capacity management is a set of activities that confirms there is sufficient capacity in IT systems and IT processes to meet service needs. Primarily, an IT system or process has sufficient capacity if its performance falls within an acceptable range, as specified in SLAs. Capacity management is not just a concern for current needs; it must also be concerned about meeting future needs. This is attained through several activities, including the following:

- **Periodic measurements**   Systems and processes need to be regularly measured so that trends in usage can be evaluated to predict future capacity needs.

- **Considering planned changes**   Planned changes to processes and IT systems may impact predicted workload.

- **Understanding long-term strategies**   Changes in the organization, including IT systems, business processes, and organizational objectives, may impact workloads, requiring more (or less) capacity than would be extrapolated through simpler trend analysis.

- **Changes in technology**   Several factors may influence capacity plans, including the expectation that computing and network technologies will deliver better performance in the future and that trends in the usage of technology may influence how end users use technology.

Linkage to Financial Management

One of the work products of capacity management is a projection for the acquisition of additional computer or network hardware to meet future capacity needs. This information needs to be made part of budgeting and spending management processes.

Linkage to Service-Level Management

If there are insufficient resources to handle workloads, capacity issues may result in violations to SLAs. Systems and processes that are overburdened will take longer to respond. In some cases, systems may stop responding altogether.

Linkage to Incident and Problem Management

Systems with severe capacity issues may take excessive time to respond to user requests. In some cases, systems may malfunction or users may give up. Often, users will call the service desk, resulting in the logging of incidents and problems.

Service Continuity Management

Service continuity management is the set of activities that is concerned with the ability of the organization to continue providing services, primarily in the event that a natural or manmade disaster has occurred. Service continuity management is ITIL parlance for the more common terms *business continuity planning* and *disaster recovery planning*.

Business continuity is discussed in Chapter 7.

Availability Management

The goal of availability management is the sustainment of IT service availability in support of organizational objectives and processes. The availability of IT systems is governed by the following:

- **Effective change management** When changes to systems and infrastructure are properly vetted through a change management process, they are less likely to result in unanticipated downtime.

- **Effective application testing** When changes to applications are made according to a set of formal requirements, review, and testing, the application is less likely to fail and become unavailable.

- **Resilient architecture** When the overall architecture of an application environment is designed from the beginning to be highly reliable, it will be more resilient and more tolerant of individual faults and component failures.

- **Serviceable components** When the individual components of an application environment can be effectively serviced by third-party service organizations, those components will be less likely to fail unexpectedly.

NOTE Organizations typically measure availability as a percentage of uptime of an application or service.

Asset Management

Asset management is the collection of activities used to manage the inventory, classification, use, and disposal of assets. It is a foundational activity, without which several other activities could not be effectively managed, including vulnerability management, device hardening, incident management, data security, and some aspects of financial management. Asset management is discussed fully in Chapter 5.

Continuous Improvement

Continuous improvement represents the desire to increase the efficiency and effectiveness of processes and controls over time. It could be said that continuous improvement is a characteristic of an organization's culture. The pursuit of continuous improvement is a roundabout way of pursuing quality.

A requirement in ISO/IEC 27001 certification requires that management promote continual improvement and that security policy include a commitment to the continual improvement of the information security management system (ISMS). ISO/IEC 27001 also requires that management review the ISMS to identify opportunities for continual improvement. The standard also explicitly requires organizations to "continually improve the suitability, adequacy, and effectiveness of its information security management system."

NIST SP 800-53 Rev 5, "Security and Privacy Controls for Federal Information Systems and Organizations," similarly requires that an organization's risk management program incorporate a feedback loop for continuous improvement. Control SA-15 (6) states that the organization must "require the developer of the system, system component, or system service to implement an explicit process to continuously improve the development process."

The NIST Cyber Security Framework cites the requirement for continuous improvement throughout the standard. For instance, in the seven steps for creating an information security program, NIST CSF asserts in section 3.2 that "these steps should be repeated as necessary to continuously improve cybersecurity."

Chapter Review

Controls are the procedures, mechanisms, systems, and other measures designed to reduce risk through compliance to policies. An organization develops controls to ensure that its business objectives will be met, risks will be reduced, and errors will be prevented or corrected.

Controls and control frameworks are used to enforce desired outcomes. Controls need to be carefully considered, as each consumes resources. Security managers need to understand the various types of controls (such as preventive, detective, deterrent, manual, automatic, and so on) so that the correct types of controls can be implemented.

Controls are classified in multiple dimensions so that security professionals can better understand and work with them. Control type descriptors include physical, technical, administrative, preventive, detective, manual, automatic, compensating, and recovery.

An organization's general computing controls (GCCs) are general in nature and often implemented in different ways on different information systems, based upon their individual capabilities and limitations, as well as applicability.

A control framework is a collection of controls that is organized into logical categories. Well-known control frameworks such as ISO/IEC 27002, NIST SP 800-53, and CIS CSC are intended to address a broad set of information risks common to most organizations. A crosswalk maps two or more control frameworks together.

Before a control can be designed, the security manager needs to have some idea of the nature of risks that a control is intended to address. In a running risk management program, a new risk may have been identified during a risk assessment that led to the creation of an additional control.

After a control has been designed, it should be put into service and then managed throughout its life. Depending upon the nature of the control, this could involve operational impact in the form of changes to business processes and/or information systems. Changes with greater impact will require greater care so that business processes are not adversely affected.

Controls should include metadata that describes the purpose, applicability, scope, classification, measurements, testing procedures, cross references, and more.

The implementation of a new control should be guided by formal processes, not unlike that of systems development: a new control should have a control objective, a design that is reviewed by stakeholders, a test plan that is carried out with results reviewed, a formal authorization to implement the control, and IT and business change management processes to plan its implementation.

Controls that have been placed into service will transition into routine operations. Control owners will operate their controls and try to be aware of any problems, especially early on. Whether controls are automatic or manual, preventive or corrective, their owners are responsible for ensuring that their controls operate correctly in every respect.

It is essential for security managers to understand the technology underpinnings of controls to ensure effective design and operation.

Any organization that implements controls to address risks should periodically examine those controls to determine whether they are working as intended and as designed.

SOC 1 and SOC 2 audits provide assurances of effective control design (Type I and Type II) and implementation (Type II only) in third-party service providers.

An essential function in information security management is the set of activities that determines whether security safeguards are in place and working properly. These activities range from informal security reviews to formal and highly structured security audits.

An audit is a systematic and repeatable process whereby a competent and independent professional evaluates one or more controls, interviews personnel, obtains and analyzes evidence, and develops a written opinion on the effectiveness of a control.

A control self-assessment (CSA) methodology is used by an organization to review key business objectives, risks related to achieving these objectives, and the key controls designed to manage those risks.

PART III

Personnel are the primary weak point in information security, mainly because of lapses in judgment, inattentiveness, fatigue, work pressure, or a shortage of skills. Personnel are generally considered the largest and most vulnerable portion of an organization's attack surface.

Third-party risk management is a critical activity that attempts to identify risks in third-party organizations that have access to critical or sensitive data or that perform critical operational functions. Various techniques are needed to identify and manage risks, because many third parties are less than transparent about their internal operations and risks.

Third parties are assessed mainly through the use of questionnaires and requests for evidence that are sent to them by organizations. Most organizations depend on large numbers of third-party services, so they employ a risk tier scheme to identify the third parties that are the most critical to the organization. Third parties at a higher level of risk undergo more frequent and rigorous risk assessments, while those at lower levels undergo less frequent and less rigorous risk assessments.

The management of business relationships with third parties is a life-cycle process. The life cycle begins when an organization contemplates the use of a third party to augment or support the organization's operations in some way. The life cycle continues during the ongoing relationship with the third party and concludes when the organization no longer requires the third party's services.

Communications is the lifeblood of an effective information security program. Lacking effective communications, the security manager will have difficulty interacting with executive management for the exchange of objectives, risk information, and metrics. Ineffective communications will hamper virtually all other security-related activities and processes.

Security programs include a variety of administrative activities that are vital to its success. One important success factor is the development of strategic partnerships with many internal departments within an organization, as well as external organizations and agencies. These partnerships enable the security manager to better influence internal events, learn more about external events, and obtain assistance from outside entities as needed.

IT service management represents a collection of operational activities designed to ensure the quality of IT services and includes several business processes such as service desk, incident management, problem management, change management, configuration management, release management, service-level management, financial management, capacity management, service continuity management, and availability management.

Notes

- The most common approach to controls development is the selection of an already-established control framework, such as those discussed in this chapter. However, an organization is also free to develop a control framework from scratch.

- In a typical security program, the security manager will select a control framework as a starting point and then add, change, or remove controls over time as a result of the risk management process. The initial control framework should be considered only a starting point and not the set of controls that the organization is required to manage permanently.

- Security managers prefer preventive controls but will sometimes need to settle on detective controls.

- The selection of a control framework is less important than the risk management process that will, over time, mold it into the controls that need to exist.

- Many organizations ruminate over the selection of a control framework. Instead, each organization should select a framework and then make adjustments to its controls to suit the business needs. A control framework should generally be considered a starting point, not a rigid and unchanging list of controls—except in cases where regulations stipulate that controls may not be changed.

- Many organizations need to implement multiple control frameworks in response to applicable regulations and other obligations. In such cases, security managers should consider mapping them into a single control framework.

- To the extent than an organization is dependent upon IT for its operations, the organization is equally dependent upon effective cybersecurity to protect its IT.

- Data backup has always been critical, but the rise in ransomware attacks is highlighting the value of backups for business owners.

- Audit planning is multifaceted and includes scope, purpose, methodology, and audience.

- To be effective, security awareness training needs to be relevant and engaging.

- Third-party risk management is best thought of as an extension of an organization's risk management program, with special procedures for conducting risk assessments of third-party organizations that store, process, or transmit sensitive or critical data on behalf of the organization or that perform critical operations.

- Classifying third parties into risk-based tiers helps to allocate scarce resources by focusing rigorous assessments on third parties based on risk.

- The maturity of an information security program will determine the ability for meaningful reporting to be developed.

- Without effective IT service management, no security manager can hope that information security will become truly effective.

- There is always room for improvement.

Questions

1. The most important factor in the selection of a control framework is:

    A. Organization maturity

    B. Industry relevance

    C. Risk tolerance

    D. Risk appetite

2. The life-cycle process that influences controls over time is known as:

   A. Third-party risk management

   B. External audit

   C. Risk management

   D. Internal audit

3. The main reason that preventive controls are preferred over detective controls is:

   A. Preventive controls stop unwanted events from occurring.

   B. Preventive controls are less expensive to implement.

   C. Preventive controls are less expensive to audit.

   D. Detective controls are, by definition, ineffective.

4. An organization wants to protect itself from the effects of a ransomware attack. What is the best data protection approach?

   A. Periodically scan data for malware.

   B. Replicate data to a cloud-based storage provider.

   C. Replicate data to a secondary storage system.

   D. Back up data to offline media.

5. The best definition of general computing controls is:

   A. Controls that are general in nature and implemented across all systems

   B. The basic safeguards required by Sarbanes–Oxley

   C. Policies that apply to all systems and applications

   D. Controls that are required to be audited annually

6. Which of the following is the best reason for adopting a standard control framework?

   A. Controls can be enacted without time-consuming risk assessments.

   B. Audits can begin earlier.

   C. Audit results will be more favorable.

   D. The organization will be considered more progressive.

7. All of the following statements about ISO/IEC 27002 are correct *except:*

   A. ISO/IEC 27002 can be crosswalked to NIST SP 800-53.

   B. ISO/IEC 27002 is a well-known international standard.

   C. ISO/IEC 27002 is available free of charge.

   D. Copies of ISO/IEC 27002 must be purchased.

8. A security manager in a healthcare clinic is planning to implement HIPAA and PCI DSS controls. Which of the following approaches should be taken?

   A. Choose either HIPAA or PCI DSS and use those controls to protect both ePHI and cardholder data.

   B. Enact individual HIPAA and PCI DSS controls per a risk assessment.

   C. Define the applicability of HIPAA and PCI DSS to those portions of the business where ePHI and cardholder data are used.

   D. Apply HIPAA and PCI DSS to the entire organization.

9. Which of the following statements correctly describes the link between risk management and controls?

   A. Risk treatment sometimes calls for the enactment of a new control.

   B. Controls define the scope of risk assessments.

   C. Controls define the scope of risk management.

   D. There is no link between risk management and controls.

10. What organization is the governing body for the PCI DSS standard?

    A. ISO

    B. NIST

    C. PCI Security Standards Council

    D. VISA and MasterCard

11. Which of the following solutions is most suitable for the following control statement: "Safeguards prevent end users from visiting hazardous web sites"?

    A. Cloud access security broker

    B. Web content filter

    C. Virtual private network

    D. Antimalware

12. The philosophy of system and data protection that relies on continual evaluation is known as:

    A. Data loss prevention

    B. Trust but verify

    C. Transitive Trust

    D. Zero Trust

PART III

13. A review of users' access to specific information systems is best known as:

   A. An audit

   B. An activity review

   C. A recertification

   D. A corrective control

14. The information security department has sent a questionnaire and requests for evidence to a control owner. This activity is best known as a(n):

   A. Control self-assessment

   B. Audit

   C. Review

   D. Investigation

15. The most favored practice for security awareness training is:

   A. Training at the time of hire

   B. Training at the time of hire and annually thereafter

   C. Annual training

   D. Reading assignments

Answers

1. **B.** Organizations looking to select a control framework as a starting point for controls should select a framework that aligns with the organization's industry. For instance, a healthcare organization may start with HIPAA, while a global manufacturer would likely select ISO/IEC 27002.

2. **C.** The risk management life cycle, over time, will have the greatest influence on an organization's controls. Newly discovered risks can be managed through the enactment of new controls, for example.

3. **A.** Preventive controls, when available and feasible, are preferred over detective controls, because they prevent unwanted events from occurring. Detective controls, on the other hand, do not prevent events from occurring.

4. **D.** Backing up data to offline media is the best of these choices. For the most part, ransomware targets live data storage. Often, data replication capabilities result in the replication of the encryption to secondary storage systems.

5. **A.** General computing controls, or GCCs, are general in nature and applied across most or all information systems and applications. GCC's are also known as ITGC's, or IT General Controls.

6. **A.** An organization that starts with a standard control framework can enact controls immediately. Without a standard control framework, time-consuming risk assessments would need to be conducted to identify risk areas, followed by control development.

7. **C.** ISO/IEC 27002, as well as other ISO standards, are not available free of charge and must be purchased for individual users or with a site license.

8. **C.** The best approach for enacting controls in a hybrid environment such as this is to define the scope of applicability for HIPAA controls and for PCI DSS controls. HIPAA controls shall apply to systems and processes that process electronic protected healthcare information (ePHI), and PCI DSS controls shall apply to systems and processes that process cardholder data.

9. **A.** In the risk management life cycle, risk assessments are performed and new risks are identified. In risk treatment, sometimes the agreed-upon course of action is the enactment of a new control to mitigate a new risk.

10. **C.** The PCI Security Standards Council, a consortium of the world's leading credit card brands (VISA, MasterCard, American Express, Discover, and JCB), is the governing body for the PCI DSS standard and related standards such as PA DSS.

11. **B.** A web content filter is the best solution for a control that protects users from visiting hazardous web sites.

12. **D.** Zero Trust (ZT) is the philosophy that focuses on system and data protection, where trust is not granted implicitly but must be continually evaluated at all layers.

13. **B.** An activity review is a study of users' access to individual applications or systems to determine whether they access those applications or systems in a given period of time. Users who do not access those applications or systems are candidates for access removal from those systems.

14. **A.** In a control self-assessment (CSA), a control owner is requested to answer questions about a control and provide evidence such as a written procedure and records.

15. **B.** The best practice for security awareness training consists of training at the time of hire and annually thereafter. It is important for new workers to be trained on security protocols and expectations, with periodic reminders to ensure continual awareness and awareness of new protocols and threats.

PART IV

Incident Management

■ **Chapter 7**   Incident Management Readiness
■ **Chapter 8**   Incident Management Operations

Incident Management Readiness

In this chapter, you will learn about

- Similarities and differences between security incident response, business continuity planning, and disaster recovery planning
- Performing a business impact analysis and criticality analysis
- Developing business continuity and disaster recovery plans
- Classifying incidents
- Testing response plans and training personnel

This chapter covers Certified Information Security Manager (CISM) Domain 4, "Incident Management," part A, "Incident Management Readiness." The entire Incident Management domain represents 30 percent of the CISM examination.

Supporting Tasks in the CISM job practice that align with the Incident Management / Incident Management Readiness domain include:

29. Establish and maintain an incident response plan, in alignment with the business continuity plan and disaster recovery plan.
30. Establish and maintain an information security incident classification and categorization process.
31. Develop and implement processes to ensure the timely identification of information security incidents.
32. Establish and maintain processes to investigate and document information security incidents in accordance with legal and regulatory requirements.
33. Establish and maintain incident handling process, including containment, notification, escalation, eradication, and recovery.
34. Organize, train, equip, and assign responsibilities to incident response teams.
35. Establish and maintain incident communication plans and processes for internal and external parties.
36. Evaluate incident management plans through testing and review, including table-top exercises, checklist review, and simulation testing at planned intervals.

Our world is full of surprises, including events that disrupt our plans and activities. In the context of IT and business, several unexpected events can cause significant disruption to business operations, even to the point of threatening the ongoing viability of the organization itself. These events include:

- Natural disasters
- Human-made disasters
- Malicious acts
- Cyberattacks
- Changes with unintended consequences

Organizations cannot, for the most part, *specifically* anticipate these events. Any of these events may inflict damage on information systems, office equipment, and work centers, making it necessary for the organization to act quickly to continue business operations using alternative means. In the case of a cyberattack, it may or may not be possible to reverse the effects of the attack, eradicate whatever harm was caused to information systems, and continue operations on those systems. But in some cases, it may be necessary for the organization to continue information processing on other systems until the primary systems can be expunged of their attacker and the damage that has been inflicted.

Incident management readiness begins with upfront analyses of business processes and their dependence upon business assets, including information systems. This analysis includes a big-picture prioritization of business processes and an up-close examination of business processes and information systems. This is followed by the development of contingency plans, response plans, and restoration plans. A natural by-product of all of this effort is improved resilience of business processes and information systems—even if disruptive events never occur—because overall weaknesses in processes and systems are identified, leading to steps to make tactical improvements.

This chapter explores the available methods and techniques for responding to these disruptive events and returning business operations to their normal, pre-event state. Chapter 8 continues with discussions of incident management tools, techniques, incident containment, recovery, and post-incident activities.

Incident Response Plan

Although security incident response, business continuity planning (BCP), and disaster recovery planning (DRP) are often considered separate disciplines, they share a common objective: the best possible continuity of business operations during and after a disruptive threat event. A wide variety of threat events, if realized, will call upon one or more of these three disciplines in response. Table 7-1 illustrates responses to threat events.

The last entry in Table 7-1 represents an event in which an attacker damages or destroys information or information systems. An incident of this type may necessarily require security incident response, BCP, and DRP. Security incident response is enacted

Event Type	Response
Natural disaster	Business continuity and/or disaster recovery
Human-made disaster	Business continuity and/or disaster recovery
Theft of information	Security incident response
Deliberate corruption or destruction of information or systems	Security incident response and potentially disaster recovery and business continuity

Table 7-1   Event Types and Typical Response

to discover the techniques used by the attacker to compromise systems so that any vulnerabilities can be remediated, thereby preventing similar attacks in the future. Business continuity response is required so that the organization can operate critical business processes without primary processing systems, and disaster recovery planning is needed to recover its systems and resume normal operations as quickly as possible. Figure 7-1 depicts the relationship between incident response, BCP, and DRP.

Life Safety Should Also Be Included in Information Security

The proliferation of connected devices in many industries expands the traditional confidentiality, integrity, and availability (CIA) to become confidentiality, integrity, availability, and safety (CIAS), because many connected devices are directly or indirectly related to life safety. When you consider capabilities such as Bluetooth-equipped pacemakers, IV pumps on the network, self-driving cars, autopilots, GPS navigation, robotic surgery, and other technologies, it is becoming clear that a computer intrusion can have far-ranging effects that go beyond threats to data.

Security incident response, business continuity, and disaster recovery all require advance planning so that the organization will have discussed, documented, and outlined the responses required for various types of incidents in advance of their occurrence.

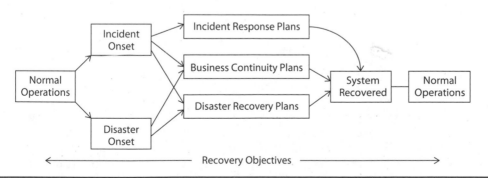

Figure 7-1   Relationship between incident response, business continuity planning, and disaster recovery planning

Risk assessments are the foundation of planning for all three disciplines, because it is necessary for organizations to discover relevant risks and establish priorities during a response. Additionally, by taking this proactive approach, the team will have a framework to lean on for incidents that may not have been considered otherwise.

The improvement of systems and processes is an important byproduct of planning for security incident response, business continuity, and disaster recovery. Primarily, planning efforts reveal improvement opportunities that, when implemented, will result in information systems being more secure and resilient. These improvements generally mean that incidents are either less likely to occur or that they will have less impact on the organization.

> ### Security and BCP: Common Ground
> An analysis of the threats discussed in this section should prompt you to think of natural and human-made disasters that, when they occur, invoke business contingency plans to ensure the continuity of critical services. It is no accident that information security and BCP have a lot in common. Risk assessments are often designed to serve both efforts amply. Indeed, one may argue that BCP is just a branch of information security, because the common objective for both is the protection and availability of critical assets and functions.

Security Incident Response Overview

As a result of a security incident, the confidentiality, integrity, or availability of information (or an information system) has been or is in danger of being compromised. A security incident can also be any event that represents a violation of an organization's security policy. For instance, if an organization's security policy states that it is not permitted for one person to use another person's computer account, then such use that results in the disclosure of information would be considered a security incident. Several types of security incidents can occur:

- **Computer account abuse**   Examples include willful account abuse, such as sharing user account credentials with other insiders or outsiders or one person stealing login credentials from another.
- **Computer or network trespass**   An unauthorized person accesses a computer network. The methods of trespass include malware, using stolen credentials, access bypass, or gaining physical access to the computer or network and connecting to it directly.
- **Information exposure or theft**   Information that is protected by one or more controls may still be exposed to unauthorized people through a weakness in controls or by deliberate or negligent acts or omissions. For instance, an intruder may be able to intercept e-mail messages, client-server communication, file

transfers, login credentials, and network diagnostic information. Or a vulnerability in a system may permit an intruder to compromise the system and obtain information stored or processed there.

- **Malware**   A worm or a virus outbreak may occur in an organization's network. The outbreak may disrupt normal business operations simply through the malware's spread, or the malware may also damage infected systems in other ways, including destroying or altering information. Malware can also eavesdrop on communications and send intercepted sensitive information back to its source.

- **Ransomware and wiperware**   A malware attack may include ransomware, where critical data is encrypted and a ransom is demanded in exchange for a decryption key. Variations of ransomware attacks include exfiltration of critical data with the threat of posting the data publicly and wipers that destroy data instead of encrypting it.

- **Denial-of-service (DoS) attack**   An attacker floods a target computer or network with a volume of traffic that overwhelms the target so that it is unable to carry out its regular functions. For example, an attacker might flood an online banking web site with so much traffic that the bank's depositors are unable to use it. Sending traffic that causes the target to malfunction or cease functioning is another form of a DoS attack. Both types result in the malfunction of the target system.

- **Distributed denial-of-service (DDoS) attack**   Similar to a DoS attack, a DDoS attack emanates simultaneously from hundreds or thousands of computers that comprise a botnet. A DDoS attack can be difficult to withstand because of the volume of incoming messages, as well as the large number of attacking systems.

- **Encryption or destruction of critical information**   A ransomware or wiper attack can result in encrypted or destroyed information.

- **Disclosure of sensitive information**   Any sensitive information may be disclosed to any unauthorized party.

- **Information system theft**   Laptop computers, mobile devices, and other information-processing and storage equipment can be stolen, which may directly or indirectly lead to further compromises. If the stolen device contains retrievable sensitive information or the means to access sensitive information stored elsewhere, then what started out as a theft of a tangible asset may expand to become a compromise of sensitive information as well.

- **Information system damage**   A human intruder or automated malware may cause temporary or irreversible damage to information or an information system. This may result in an interruption in the availability of information, as well as permanent loss of information.

- **Information corruption**   A human intruder or automated malware such as a worm or virus may damage information stored on a system. This damage may or may not be readily noticed.

- **Misconfiguration**   An error made by an IT worker can result in data loss or system malfunction.

- **Sabotage**   A human intruder or automated malware attack may disrupt or damage information, information systems, or facilities in a single organization, several organizations in a market sector, or an entire nation.

These examples should give you an idea of the nature of a security incident. Not all represent cataclysmic events. Other types of incidents may also be considered security incidents in some organizations.

NOTE   A vulnerability that is discovered in an organization is not an incident. However, the severity of the vulnerability may prompt a response similar to that of an actual incident.

The Intrusion Kill Chain

In 2011, scientists at Lockheed-Martin developed a model that depicts a typical computer intrusion. While the model is imperfect and does not portray every type of computer intrusion, information security professionals recognize the kill chain as a valuable way to understand the phases of an attack, which are as follows:

- **Reconnaissance**   The intruder researches and identifies targets and learns still more about the selected target to choose a method of attack.

- **Weaponization**   The intruder creates or obtains malware that will be used to compromise a target system.

- **Delivery**   The intruder creates a means by which the attack will be delivered to the target system, such as e-mail (phishing, pharming, spear phishing, and so on), USB drop, or watering-hole attack.

- **Exploitation**   The malware exploits a weakness identified in the target system during reconnaissance.

- **Installation**   The malware installs itself on the target system.

- **Command and control**   The malware communicates back to an outside server owned or controlled by the intruder so that the intruder may begin his or her actions on the attack objective.

- **Actions on objective**   The intruder proceeds with the attack plan, which may consist of stealing data, damaging or destroying data, or disrupting the operations of one or more systems.

This model makes it easy to imagine an intruder following each of the steps in an attempt to break into a system. The main point of the model is to help security professionals better understand a typical intrusion, as well as develop defenses to stop each phase of an intrusion.

(continued)

Here is how the kill chain is used: For each phase, analysts examine their detective and preventive capabilities that are relevant to the types of activities that an intruder would be performing. This helps an organization better understand ways in which they could detect or prevent an attack in each of its phases.

Incident Response Plan Development

The time to repair the roof is when the sun is shining.

—John F. Kennedy, 1962

As for any emergency, the best time to plan for security incident response is prior to the start of any actual incident. During an incident is a poor time to analyze the situation thoughtfully, conduct research, and work out the sequence of events that should take place to restore normal operations quickly and effectively; emotions may run high, and there may be a heightened sense of urgency, especially if there has been little or no advanced planning.

Effective incident response plans take time to develop. A security manager who is developing an incident response plan must first thoroughly understand the organization's business processes and underlying information systems and then discover resource requirements, dependencies, and failure points. A security manager may first develop a high-level incident response plan, which is usually followed by the development of several *incident response playbooks,* the step-by-step instructions to follow when specific types of security incidents occur.

Executive support is essential in incident response plan development, particularly for escalations and communications. Executives need to be comfortable knowing that low-severity incidents are competently handled without their being notified every time, for instance. Also, executives need to know that they will be notified using established protocols when more serious incidents occur.

Objectives

Similar to any intentional activity, organizations need to establish their objectives prior to undertaking an effort to develop security incident response plans. Otherwise, it may not be clear whether business needs are being met. Following are some objectives that may be applicable to many organizations:

- Minimal or no interruption to customer-facing or revenue-producing business operations
- No loss of critical information
- Recovery of lost or damaged information within DRP and BCP recovery targets, mainly recovery point objective (RPO)
- Least possible disclosure to affected parties
- Least possible disclosure to regulators

- Least possible disclosure to shareholders
- Incident expenses fully covered by cyber insurance and other insurance policies
- Sound internal and external communication protocols and consistent messaging

Organizations may develop additional objectives that are germane to their business model, degree and type of regulation, and risk tolerance.

Maturity

When undertaking any effort to develop or improve business processes, an organization should consider its current and desired levels of maturity. As a quick reminder, the levels of maturity according to the Capability Maturity Model Integration for Development (CMMi-DEV) are as follows:

1. **Initial.** This represents a process that is ad hoc, inconsistent, unmeasured, and unrepeatable.
2. **Repeatable.** This represents a process that is performed consistently and with the same outcome. It may or may not be well documented.
3. **Defined.** This represents a process that is well defined and documented.
4. **Managed.** This represents a quantitatively measured process with one or more metrics.
5. **Optimizing.** This represents a measured process that is under continuous improvement.

In addition to the objectives listed previously, a security manager should seek to understand the organization's existing level of maturity and its desired level. Increasing the maturity level of any process or program takes time, and hastening maturity may be unwise. For example, if an organization's current maturity for incident response is Initial and the long-term desired level is Managed, a number of improvements over one or more years may be required to reach a Managed maturity level.

Resources

Security incident response requires resources; security managers should keep this in mind when developing incident response plans. Each stage of incident response, from detection to closure, requires the involvement of personnel with different skill sets, as well as various tools that enable personnel to detect an incident, analyze it, contain it, and eradicate it. Various types of incidents require various tools and skills.

Personnel   Personnel are the heart of security incident response. Effective security incident response requires personnel with a variety of skills, including the following:

- **Incident detection and analysis**   Security operations center (SOC) analysts and other personnel use a variety of monitoring tools that alert them when actionable events occur. These personnel receive alerts and proceed to analyze an incident by drilling into the details. These same people may also undertake *threat hunting,* proactively searching systems and networks for signs of reconnaissance, malicious command-and-control (C&C) traffic, and intrusion.

This function is often outsourced to managed security service providers (MSSPs) that run large 24/7/365 operations, monitoring hundreds or even thousands of client organizations' networks.

- **Network, system, and application subject matter experts (SMEs)**   With expertise in the network devices, systems, and applications related to alerts, these personnel can help SOC analysts and others better understand the meaning behind incidents and their consequences.

- **Malware analysis and reverse engineering**   These personnel use tools to identify and analyze malware to better understand what it does on a system and how it communicates with other systems. This helps the organization decide how to contain the incident and defend itself against similar attacks in the future.

- **Forensics**   These persons use tools and techniques to collect evidence that helps the organization better understand the nature of the incident. Some evidence may be protected by a chain of custody in anticipation of later legal proceedings.

- **Incident command and control**   These personnel have expertise in overall security incident response and take charge during an incident. Generally, this type of coordination is required only in high-impact incidents involving multiple parties in an organization, as well as external entities such as customers, regulators, and law enforcement.

- **Crisis communications**   These personnel are skilled in internal communications as well as communications with external parties, including regulators, shareholders, customers, and the public.

- **Legal / privacy**   One or more people in an organization's legal department will read and interpret applicable laws and make decisions related to external communications with customers, regulators, law enforcement, shareholders, and other parties.

- **Business unit leaders**   Also referred to as department heads, these personnel will be called to make critical business decisions during an incident. Examples include decisions to take systems offline or transfer work to other processing centers.

- **Executives**   The top leaders in the organization who need to be consistently informed and who will be called upon to ratify or make important decisions.

- **Law enforcement**   Personnel in external agencies may be able to assist in incident investigation.

Most of these responsibilities require training, which is discussed later in this chapter.

Outsourcing Incident Response   Incident response sometimes involves the use of forensic tools and techniques by trained and experienced incident response personnel. Larger organizations may have one or more such personnel on staff, though most organizations cannot justify the expense of hiring them full-time. Many organizations opt to utilize forensic experts on an on-demand or contract basis, typically in the form of incident monitoring and incident response retainers.

PART IV

Incident Response Tools and Techniques   There are many forms of security incident detection, prevention, and alerting tools essential in incident response. These tools and techniques are discussed fully in Chapter 8.

Gap Analysis

Prior to the development of a security incident response plan, the security manager must determine the current state of the organization's incident response capabilities, as well as the desired end state (for example, a completed security incident response plan with specific capabilities and characteristics). A *gap analysis* is the best way for the security manager to understand what capabilities and resources are lacking. Once gaps are known, a strategy for developing security incident response plans will consist of the creation or acquisition of all necessary resources and personnel.

A gap analysis in the context of security incident response program development is the same gap analysis activity described in more detail in Chapter 2.

Plan Development

A *security incident response plan* is a document that defines policies, roles, responsibilities, and actions to be taken in the event of a security incident. Often, a response plan also defines and describes roles, responsibilities, and actions that are related to the detection of a security incident. This portion of an incident response plan is vital, considering the high velocity and high impact of certain types of security incidents.

A security incident response plan typically includes these sections:

- Policy
- Roles and responsibilities
- Incident detection capabilities
- Playbooks
- Communications
- Recordkeeping

Playbooks   Recognizing that there are many types of security incidents, each with its own impacts and issues, many organizations develop a collection of incident response playbooks that provide step-by-step instructions for incidents likely to occur in the organization. A set of playbooks may include procedures for the following incidents:

- Lost or stolen laptop computer
- Lost or stolen mobile device
- Extortion and wire fraud
- Sensitive data exfiltration
- Malware, ransomware, and wipers

- Stolen or compromised user credentials
- Critical vulnerability
- Externally reported vulnerability
- DoS attack
- Unauthorized access
- Violation of information security-related law, regulation, or contract
- Business e-mail compromise

During a serious incident, emotions can run high, and personnel under stress may not be able to remember all of the steps required to handle an incident properly. Playbooks help guide experienced and trained personnel in the steps required to examine, contain, and recover from an incident. They are commonplace in other industries: pilots and astronauts use playbooks to handle various emergency situations, for example, and they practice the steps to help them prepare to respond effectively when needed.

Incidents Involving Third Parties   Organizations outsource many of their critical applications and infrastructure to third-party organizations. The fact that applications and infrastructure supporting critical processes are owned and managed by other parties does not absolve an organization from its responsibilities to detect and respond to security incidents, however, and this makes incident detection and response more complex. As a result, organizations need to develop incident response playbooks that are specific to various incident types at each third party to ensure that the organization will be able to detect and respond to an incident effectively.

Incident response related to a third-party application or infrastructure often requires that the organization and each third party understand their respective roles and responsibilities for incident detection and response. For example, software-as-a-service (SaaS) applications often do not make event and log data available to customers. Instead, organizations must rely on those third parties to develop and manage their incident detection and response capabilities properly, including informing affected customers of an incident in progress. Depending on the architecture of a SaaS solution, both the SaaS provider and the customer may have their own steps to take during incident response, and some of those steps may require coordination or assistance from the other party. Joint exercises between companies and critical SaaS providers help build confidence that their incident response plans will work.

Periodic Updates   All security incident management documents need to be periodically reviewed by all of the responsible parties, SMEs, and management to ensure that all agree on the policies, roles and responsibilities, and steps required to detect, contain, and recover from an incident. Generally, organizations should review and update documents at least once per year, as well as any time a significant change is made in an organization or its supporting systems.

PART IV

Relationship Between Security Incident Management to ITSM Incident Management

Rather than building a separate but similar set of incident management procedures and business records from scratch, most security incident response managers prefer to leverage existing incident management procedures used in IT departments. A well-written ITSM incident management plan will already have record repositories, escalation paths, and communications plans. It is often easier to use this as a foundation for building a security incident response plan.

The IT Infrastructure Library (ITIL) defines an incident as *"any event* which is not part of the standard operation of a service and which causes, or may cause, an interruption to, or a reduction in, the quality of that service. The stated ITIL objective is to restore normal operations as quickly as possible with the least possible impact on either the business or the user, at a cost-effective price." In the context of ITIL, an incident may be any of the following:

- Service outage
- Service slowdown
- Software bug

When IT incidents are combined with security incidents, an organization will be prepared to respond to most any type of IT or security incident.

Communication and Escalation

Because orderly internal communication is critical to effective incident response, incident response plans should include procedures regarding communications during a security incident. Effective communication keeps incident responders and other affected parties informed about the proceedings of the response.

Incident response plans should also include information about how to communicate with regard to *escalations,* which can take two forms:

- *Notifying appropriate levels of upper management when an incident has been detected.* It is good practice to establish triggers or thresholds concerning when appropriate upper management should be notified of the incident based on the incident type and its impact on the organization. Some organizations accomplish this by classifying different types and levels of incidents, with specific escalation plans for each.

- *Notifying appropriate levels of management when incident response service level agreements (SLAs) have not been met.* For example, various tasks performed during an incident response will be expected to require a specific period of time to complete. If a task has not been completed within a reasonable amount of time, appropriate management should be notified. Escalations, in this case, may trigger the use of external resources that can assist with incident response.

Rather than be an ad hoc activity, escalation should be a documented part of the incident response process so that incident responders know how and when to inform executives about issues that occur during incident response and how to proceed when an incident response is not progressing as expected.

Business Impact Analysis

Business impact analysis (BIA) is the study of business processes in an organization to understand their relative criticality, their dependencies upon resources, and how they are affected when interruptions occur. The objective of the BIA is to identify the impact that different business disruption scenarios will have on ongoing business operations. The results of the BIA drive subsequent activities—namely, BCP and DRP. The BIA is one of several steps of critical, detailed analysis that must be carried out before the development of continuity or recovery plans and procedures.

Start with the Big Picture

Organizations that have not undertaken BCP should begin with an executive-level BIA to determine overall business priorities. Business continuity planners should interview company executives to learn their perspectives on the relative importance of the various business units and departments with regard to critical organizational priorities. Executive-level BIAs can provide broad insight to issues with regard to departments and their role in critical business processes. If, instead, BIAs began at the department level, it would be difficult to gauge the relative importance of one department's top-criticality processes compared to another department's top-criticality processes. Only with insight from top executives can each department be analyzed in the context of the organization's overall business priorities.

Inventory of Key Processes and Systems

The first step in a BIA is the identification of key business processes and supporting IT systems. Within the overall scope of a BCP project, the objective is to establish a detailed list of all identifiable processes and systems. The process usually begins with the development of a questionnaire or intake form that is circulated to key personnel in end-user departments and also within IT. Figure 7-2 shows a sample intake form.

NOTE Although the BIA includes an enumeration of information systems, the BIA itself is business- and process-centric. Information systems are not the focus; instead, they are considered supporting assets.

Typically, the information gathered on intake forms is transferred to a multi-columned spreadsheet or a business continuity management system, where date on all of the organization's in-scope processes can be viewed as a whole. This information will become even more useful in subsequent phases of the BCP project, such as the criticality analysis (discussed a bit later in this chapter).

Process or system name	
Interviewee	
Title	
Department	
Contact info	
Date	
Process owner	
Process operator(s)	
Process description	
Customer facing (Y or N)	
IT system(s) used	
Key suppliers	
Communications needed	
Assets needed	
Process dependencies	
Other dependencies	
Documentation location	
Records location	

Figure 7-2   BIA sample intake form for gathering data about key processes

 TIP   Use of an intake form is not the only accepted approach when gathering information about critical processes, dependencies, and systems. It's also acceptable to conduct one-on-one interviews or group interviews with key users and IT personnel to identify critical processes, dependencies, and systems. I recommend the use of an intake form (whether paper-based or electronic), even if the interviewer uses it herself as a framework for note-taking.

Planning Should Precede Action

IT personnel are often eager to get to the fun and meaty part of a project. Developers are anxious to begin coding before design, system administrators are eager to build systems before they are scoped and designed, and BCP personnel fervently desire to begin designing more robust system architectures and to tinker with replication and backup capabilities before key facts are known. In the case of BCP and DRP, completion of the BIA and other analyses is critical, as they help to define the systems and processes most needed before getting to the fun part.

Statements of Impact

When processes and systems are being inventoried and cataloged, it is also vitally important to obtain one or more statements of impact for each process and system. A *statement of impact* is a qualitative or quantitative description of the impact on the business if the process or system were incapacitated for a time.

For IT systems, you might capture the number of users and the departments or functions that are affected by the unavailability of a specific IT system. Include the geography of affected users and functions if that is appropriate. Here are example statements of impact on IT systems:

- *Three thousand users in France and Italy will be unable to access customer records, resulting in degraded customer service.*

- *All users in North America will be unable to read or send e-mail, resulting in productivity slowdowns.*

Statements of impact for business processes might cite the business functions that would be affected. Here are some example statements of impact:

- *Accounts payable and accounts receivable functions will be unable to process, impacting the availability of services and supplies and resulting in reduced revenue.*

- *Legal department will be unable to access contracts and addendums, resulting in lost or delayed revenue.*

Statements of impact for revenue-generating and revenue-supporting business functions could quantify financial impact per unit of time (be sure to use the same units of time for all functions so that they can be easily compared with one another). Here are some examples:

- *Inability to place orders for appliances will cost the rate of $12,000 per hour.*

- *Delays in payments will cost $1,875 per hour in interest charges.*

As statements of impact are gathered, it may make sense to create several columns in the main worksheet so that like units (names of functions, numbers of users, financial figures) can be sorted and ranked later. The statements of impact should be reviewed for relevance. Although business unit leaders are not trying to elevate their importance, some may believe their system is critical to the organization, even though it may make up only a small percentage of the organization's overall revenue. When reviewed, the information in the statements of impact should be considered relative to the totality of impact to the organization.

When the BIA is completed, the following information will be available about each process and system:

- Name of the process
- Who is responsible for its operation
- A description of its function

- Dependencies on systems
- Dependencies on suppliers
- Dependencies on service providers
- Dependencies on key employees
- Quantified statements of impact in terms of revenue, users affected, and/or functions impacted

Criticality Analysis

When all of the BIA information has been collected and charted, a criticality analysis can be performed. *Criticality analysis* is a study of each system and process, a consideration of the impact on the organization if it is incapacitated, the likelihood of incapacitation, and the estimated cost of mitigating the risk or impact of incapacitation. In other words, it's a somewhat special type of a risk analysis that focuses on key processes and systems. The criticality analysis should also include a *vulnerability analysis* (aka vulnerability assessment), an examination of a process or system to identify vulnerabilities that, if exploited, could incapacitate or harm the process or system.

In the context of a BIA, a vulnerability analysis need not be at the level of detail of a security scan to find missing patches or security misconfiguration. Instead, this type of a vulnerability analysis seeks to find characteristics in a process or system, such as the following:

- Single points of failure, such as only one staff member who knows how to perform a key procedure.
- System not backed up.
- System lacks resilient architecture features, such as dual power supplies.
- Procedure uses hard copy records and cannot be performed remotely.
- No training material is available for workers.

The criticality analysis also needs to include, or reference, a *threat analysis,* a risk analysis that identifies every threat that has a reasonable probability of occurrence, plus one or more mitigating controls or compensating controls, and new probabilities of occurrence with those mitigating/compensating controls in place. In case you're having a little trouble imagining what this looks like (I'm writing the book and I'm having trouble seeing this!), take a look at Table 7-2, which is a lightweight example of what I'm talking about.

In Table 7-2, notice the following:

- *Multiple threats are listed for a single asset.* Only nine threats are included, and for all the threats but one, only a single mitigating control is listed. For the extended power outage threat, two mitigating controls are included.

System	Threat	Probability	Mitigating Control	Mitigation Cost	Mitigated Probability
Application Server	Denial of service	0.1%	High-performance filtering router	$60,000	0.01%
	Malware	1%	Antivirus	$200	0.1%
	Storage failure	2%	RAID 5	$30,000	0.01%
	Administrator error	15%	Configuration management tools	$20,000	1%
	Hardware CPU failure	5%	Server cluster	$15,000	1%
	Application software bug	5%	Source code reviews	$10,000	2%
	Extended power outage	10%	UPS Electric generator	$22,000 $70,000	2% 0.5%
	Flood	2%	Relocate data center	$1,800,000	0.1%
	Earthquake	1%	Switch to alternate processing center	$300,000	0.2%

Table 7-2 Example Threat Analysis Identifying Threats and Controls for Critical Systems and Processes

- *Cost of downtime wasn't listed.* For systems or processes with a cost per unit of time for downtime, this should be included, along with some calculations to show the payback for each control.

- *Some mitigating controls can benefit more than one system.* This may not be obvious in this example, but many systems can benefit from a UPS and an electric generator, so the cost for these mitigating controls can be allocated across many systems, thereby lowering the cost for each system. Another similar example, though not included in the analysis example, is a high-availability storage area network (SAN) located in two different geographic areas; though initially expensive, the SAN can be used by many applications storage, and all will benefit from replication to the counterpart storage system.

- *Threat probabilities are arbitrary.* The probabilities are for a single occurrence in an entire year, so, for example, 5 percent means the threat will be realized once every 20 years.

- *The length of the outage was not included.* This should be included, particularly if you are quantifying downtime per hour or other units of time.

Obviously, a vulnerability analysis, threat analysis, and the corresponding criticality analysis can get complicated. The rule here should be this: the complexity of the vulnerability, threat, and criticality analyses should be proportional to the value of the assets (or revenue, or both). For example, in a company at which application downtime is measured in thousands of dollars per minute, it's probably worth taking a few weeks or even months to work out all of the likely scenarios, a variety of mitigating controls,

PART IV

and to work out which ones are the most cost-effective. On the other hand, for a system or business process with a far less costly outage impact, a lot less time may be spent on the supporting analyses.

 EXAM TIP Test-takers should ensure that any question dealing with BIA and criticality analysis places the business impact analysis first. Without this analysis, criticality analysis is impossible to evaluate in terms of likelihood or cost-effectiveness in mitigation strategies. The BIA identifies strategic resources and provides a value to their recovery and operation, which is, in turn, consumed in the criticality analysis phase. If presented with a question identifying BCP at a particular stage, make sure that any answers you select facilitate the BIA and then the CA before moving on toward objectives and strategies.

Determine Maximum Tolerable Downtime

The next step for each critical process is the establishment of a *maximum tolerable downtime* (MTD), aka *acceptable interruption window* (AIW). This theoretical period of time is measured from the onset of a disaster, at which point the organization's very survival is at risk. Establishing MTD for each critical process is an important step that aids in the establishment of key recovery targets, discussed in the next section. It would be a mistake to call MTD a target, but sometimes it is referred to as a target. It would be better to consider MTD as an estimated "point-of-no-return" time value.

Executives should ultimately determine MTD targets for various critical business functions in their organization; there is often no single MTD target for the entire organization, but usually an MTD is established for each major function. For example, an online merchandiser might establish an MTD of 7 days for its online ordering function and 28 days for its payroll function. If the organization's ability to earn revenue is incapacitated for 7 days, in the opinion of its executives, its business will suffer so greatly that the organization itself may fail. However, the organization could tolerate an MTD of four weeks for its payroll system, as enough employees are likely to tolerate a lengthy payroll outage that the organization will survive. After four weeks, enough employees may abandon their jobs that the organization will be unable to continue operations.

MTD is generally used for BCP purposes. However, as some operational and security incidents can become disasters, when severe enough, MTD is also considered in information risk management planning.

Determine Maximum Tolerable Outage

Next, the *maximum tolerable outage* (MTO) metric needs to be determined. MTO is a measure of the maximum time that an organization can tolerate operating in recovery (or alternate processing) mode. This metric comes into play when systems and processes in recovery mode operate at a lower level of throughput, consistency, quality, integrity, or at higher cost. MTO drives the need to reestablish normal production operations within a specific period of time.

Here's an example: Suppose an organization produces online advertising that is specially targeted to individual users based on their known characteristics. This feature makes the organization competitive in the online ad market. In recovery mode, the organization's system lacks several key targeting capabilities; it would not be competitive and could not sustain business operations in the long term in such a state, so it has set its MTO at 48 hours. Running in alternate processing mode for more than 48 hours would result in lost revenue and losses in market share.

 NOTE   Like MTD, MTO is not a target, but when MTO is set, recovery targets such as recovery time objective (RTO), recovery point objective (RPO), service delivery objective (SDO), recovery consistency objective (RCO), and recovery capacity objective (RCapO) can be established.

Establish Key Recovery Targets

When the cost or impact of downtime has been established and the cost and benefit of mitigating controls have been considered, some key targets can be established for each critical process. The two key targets are RTO and RPO, which determine how quickly key systems and processes are made available after the onset of a disaster and the maximum tolerable data loss that results from the disaster. Following are the key recovery targets:

- **Recovery time objective (RTO)**   The maximum period that elapses from the onset of a disaster until the resumption of service

- **Recovery point objective (RPO)**   The maximum data loss from the onset of a disaster

- **Recovery capacity objective (RCapO)**   The minimum acceptable processing or storage capacity of an alternate process or system, as compared to the primary process or system

- **Service delivery objective (SDO)**   The agreed upon level or quality of service at an alternate processing site

- **Recovery consistency objective (RCO)**   The consistency and integrity of processing in a recovery system, as compared to the primary processing system

Once these objectives are known, the business continuity team can develop contingency plans to be followed when a disaster occurs, and the disaster recovery team can begin to build system recovery capabilities and procedures that will help the organization to realize these recovery targets economically.

Recovery Time Objective   The RTO establishes a measurable interval of time during which the necessary activities for recovering or resuming business operations must take place. Various business processes in an organization will have different RTO targets, and some business processes will have RTOs that vary according to business cycles on a daily, weekly, monthly, or annual basis. For instance, point-of-sale terminals may have a short RTO during peak business hours, a longer RTO during less busy hours, and a still longer

RTO when the business is closed. Similarly, financial and payroll systems will have RTOs that are shorter during times of critical processing, such as payroll cycles and financials at the end of the month. RTOs, data classification, and asset classification are all inter-related. Business processes with shorter RTOs are likely to have data and assets that are classified as more operationally critical.

When establishing RTOs, security managers typically interview personnel in middle management as well as senior and executive management. Personnel at different levels of responsibility will have different perspectives on the criticality of business functions. Ultimately, executive management will prioritize business functions across the entire organization. As a result, any particular business function prioritized at one level by a middle manager may be classified as higher or lower by executives. Ultimately, executive prioritization will prevail. For example, a middle manager in the accounting department may assert that accounts payable is the most critical business activity because external service providers will stop providing service if they are not paid. But executives, who have control over the entire organization, stipulate that customer service is the most critical business function since the organization's future revenue depends on the quality of care customers receive every day.

RTOs are established by conducting a BIA, which helps the security manager under-stand the criticality of business processes, their resource dependencies and interdepen-dencies, and the costs associated with interruptions in service. RTOs are a cornerstone objective in BCP. Once RTOs are established for a particular business function, con-tingency plans that support the RTO can be established. While shorter RTOs are most often associated with higher costs, organizations generally seek a break-even point where the cost of recovery is the same as the cost of interruption for the period of time associated with the RTO.

 NOTE For a given organization, it's probably best to use one unit of measure for recovery objectives for all systems. This will help you avoid any errors that would occur during a rank-ordering of systems, so that two days do not appear to be a shorter period than four hours.

Recovery Point Objective   Generally, the RPO equates to the maximum period of time between backups or data replication intervals. It is generally measured in minutes or hours, and like RTO, shorter RPO targets typically are associated with higher costs. The value of a system's RPO is usually a direct result of the frequency of data backup or replication. For example, if an application server is backed up once per day, the RPO is going to be at least 24 hours (or one day, whichever way you like to express it). Maybe it will take three days to rebuild the server, but once data is restored from backup tape, no more than the last 24 hours of transactions are lost. In this case, the RTO is three days, and the RPO is one day.

RPOs represent a different aspect of service quality, as any amount of data loss repre-sents required rework. For example, if an organization receives invoices that are entered into the accounts payable system, an RPO of four hours means that up to four hours of rekeying would be required in the event of an incident or disaster.

RPOs are key objectives in BCP. When RPOs are established, contingency plans can be developed that will help the organization meet its RPO targets.

Recovery Capacity Objective   The RCapO is generally expressed as a percentage. If any incident or disaster results in the organization switching to a temporary or recovery process or system, the capacity of that temporary or recovery process or system may be less than that used during normal business operations. For example, in the event of a communications outage, cashiers in a retail location will hand-write sales receipts, which may take more time than the use of point-of-sale terminals. The manual process may mean cashiers can process 80 percent as much work; this is the RCapO.

For economic reasons, an organization may elect to build a recovery site that has less processing or storage capacity than the primary site. Management may agree that a recovery site with reduced processing capacity is an acceptable trade-off, given the relatively low likelihood that a failover to a recovery site would occur. For instance, an online service may choose to operate its recovery site at 80 percent of the processing capacity of the primary site. In management's opinion, the relatively low decrease in capacity is worth the cost savings.

In an emergency situation, management may determine that a disaster recovery server in another city with, say, 60 percent of the capacity of the original server is adequate. In that case, the organization could establish two RTO targets: one for partial capacity and one for full capacity. In other words, the organization needs to determine how quickly a lower-capacity system should be running and when a full-capacity system should be running.

Service Delivery Objective   Depending on the nature of the business process in question, SDO may be measured in transaction throughput, service quality, response time, available capabilities and features, or something else that is measurable.

Recovery Consistency Objective   Recovery consistency objective (RCO) is a measure of the consistency and integrity of processing at a recovery site, as compared to the primary processing site.

RCO is calculated as 1 – (number of inconsistent objects) / (number of objects). A system that has been recovered in a disaster situation may no longer have 100 percent of its functionality. For instance, an application that lets users view transactions that are more than two years old may, in a recovery situation, contain only 30 days' worth of data. The RCO decision is usually the result of a careful analysis of the cost of recovering different features and functions in an application environment. In a larger, complex environment, some features may be considered critical, while others are less so.

For example, suppose an organization's online application is used to calculate the current and future costs of a household budget. While the primary site uses inputs and performs calculations based upon 12 external data sources, the recovery site performs calculations based on only 8 external data sources. Economic considerations compelled management to accept the fact that the recovery site will calculate results based upon fewer inputs, and that this is an acceptable trade-off between higher licensing fees for the use of some external sources and small variations in the results shown to users of the site.

The RCO comes into play in organizations that decide to scale back the replication of features and functionality at a recovery site versus the primary processing site. For instance, a recovery site may lack detailed reporting capabilities because of the cost of software or service licensing. An organization may have to pay for a second, expensive license for a recovery site that would rarely be used. Instead, management may decide that users or customers can go without those or other functions at a recovery site, instead focusing on core functions.

NOTE SDO, RTO, RPO, and RCapO are related to one another. Organizations are free to construct recovery target models in ways that work for them. One organization may start with SDOs and derive appropriate RTO, RPO, and RCapO targets, while others may start with RTO and RPO and figure out their SDOs.

Business Continuity Plan (BCP)

As mentioned earlier in the chapter, BCP and DRP are interrelated disciplines with a common objective: to keep critical business processes operating throughout a disaster scenario, while recovering/rebuilding damaged assets to restore business operations in their primary locations. Figure 7-3 shows the relationship between a BCP and a DRP.

As mentioned, before business continuity and disaster recovery plans can be developed, a BIA and criticality analysis should be undertaken to define the organization's business processes, the information systems supporting them, and interdependencies. The criticality analysis specifically identifies business processes that are most critical and defines how quickly they need to be recovered during and after any disaster scenario.

The primary by-product of effective BCP and DRP is improved business resilience, not only in disaster situations but on a daily basis. Close examinations of processes and systems often reveal numerous opportunities for improvement that result in better resilience and fewer unplanned outages. Thus, for many organizations, BCP and DRP benefit the organization even if a disaster never strikes.

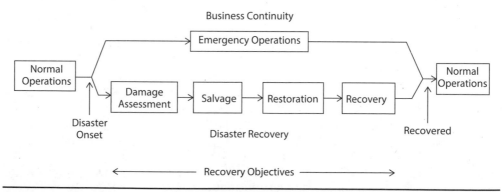

Figure 7-3 The relationship between a BCP and a DRP

NOTE Although CISM candidates are not required to understand the details of BCP and DRP, they are required to understand the relationship between incident response and BCP and DRP. The principles, methodologies, recovery procedures, and testing techniques are so similar between the two disciplines that it is important for information security managers to understand these disciplines and how they relate to each other.

Business Continuity Planning

BCP reduces risks related to the onset of disasters and other disruptive events. BCP activities identify risks and mitigate those risks through changes or enhancements in business processes or technology so that the impact of disasters is reduced and the time to recovery is lessened. The primary objective of BCP is to improve the chances that the organization will survive a disaster without incurring costly or even fatal damage to its most critical activities.

The activities of BCP development scale for any size organization. BCP has the unfortunate reputation of existing only in the stratospheric thin air of the largest and wealthiest organizations. This misunderstanding hurts the majority of organizations that are too timid to begin any kind of BCP efforts, because they believe that these activities are too costly and disruptive. The fact is that any size organization, from a one-person home office to a multinational conglomerate, can successfully undertake BCP projects that will bring about immediate benefits and take some of the sting out of disruptive events that do occur.

Organizations can benefit from BCP projects even if a disaster never occurs. The steps in the BCP development life cycle process bring immediate benefit in the form of process and technology improvements that increase the resilience, integrity, and efficiency of those processes and systems. BCP generally is managed outside of the information security function. Further, BCP is generally external to IT, because BCP is focused on the continuity of business processes, not on the recovery of IT systems.

NOTE Business continuity planning is closely related to disaster recovery planning—both are concerned with the recovery of business operations after a disaster.

Disasters

In a business context, disasters are unexpected and unplanned events that result in the disruption of business operations. A disaster could be a regional event spread over a wide geographic area or an event that occurs within the confines of a single room. The impact of a disaster will also vary, from a complete interruption of all company operations to a mere slowdown. (This question invariably comes up: When is a disaster a disaster? This is somewhat subjective, like asking, "When is a person sick?" Is it when she is too ill to report to work or when she just has a sniffle and a scratchy throat? I'll discuss disaster declaration later in this chapter in the section "Developing Continuity Plans.")

Types of Disasters   BCP professionals broadly classify disasters as natural or human-made, although the origin of a disaster does not figure very much into how we respond to it. Let's examine the types of disasters.

Natural Disasters   Natural disasters occur in the natural world with little or no assistance from humans. They are a result of the natural processes that occur in, on, and above the earth. Here are examples of natural disasters:

- **Earthquakes**   Sudden movements of the earth with the capacity to damage buildings, houses, roads, bridges, and dams; precipitate landslides and avalanches; and induce flooding and other secondary events.

- **Floods**   Standing or moving water spills out of its banks and flows into and through buildings and causes significant damage to roads, buildings, and utilities. Flooding can be a result of locally heavy rains, heavy snow melt, a dam or levee break, tropical cyclone storm surge, or an avalanche or landslide that displaces lake or river water.

- **Volcanoes**   Eruptions of magma, pyroclastic flows, steam, ash, and flying rocks that can cause significant damage over wide geographic regions. Some volcanoes, such as Kilauea in Hawaii, produce a nearly continuous and predictable outpouring of lava in a limited area, whereas the Mount St. Helens eruption in 1980 caused an ash fall over thousands of square miles, brought many metropolitan areas to a standstill for days, and blocked rivers and damaged roads.

- **Landslides**   These sudden downhill movements of the earth, usually down steep slopes, can bury buildings, houses, roads, and public utilities and can cause secondary (although still disastrous) effects such as the rerouting of rivers.

- **Avalanches**   These sudden downward flows of snow, rocks, and debris on a mountainside. In a slab avalanche, a large, stiff layer of compacted snow forcefully moves down the slope. A loose snow avalanche occurs when the accumulated snowpack exceeds its shear strength. A powder snow avalanche is the largest type and can travel in excess of 200 mph and exceed 10 million tons of material. All avalanches can damage buildings, houses, roads, and utilities, resulting in direct or indirect damage affecting businesses.

- **Wildfires**   Fires in forests, chaparral, and grasslands are part of the natural order. However, fires can also damage buildings and equipment and cause injury and death, such as in the 2017 wildfires in California. Figure 7-4 shows a map of Sonoma County and nearby wildfires, as seen from the NASA Aqua satellite that year.

- **Tropical cyclones**   The largest and most violent storms are known in various parts of the world as hurricanes, typhoons, tropical cyclones, tropical storms, and cyclones. Tropical cyclones, such as Hurricane Harvey, consist of strong winds that can reach 190 mph, heavy rains, and storm surges that can raise the level of the ocean by as much as 20 feet, all of which can result in widespread coastal flooding and damage to buildings, houses, roads, and utilities and in significant loss of life.

Figure 7-4
Wildfires in
California
(Source: NASA)

- **Tornadoes**   These violent rotating columns of air can cause catastrophic damage to buildings, houses, roads, and utilities when they reach the ground. Most tornadoes can have wind speeds of 40 to 110 mph and travel along the ground for a few miles. Some tornadoes can exceed 300 mph and travel for dozens of miles.

- **Windstorms**   While generally less intense than hurricanes and tornadoes, windstorms can nonetheless cause widespread damage, including damage to buildings, roads, and utilities. Widespread electric power outages are common when windstorms uproot trees that fall into power lines.

- **Lightning**   These atmospheric discharges of electricity occur during thunderstorms but also during dust storms and volcanic eruptions. Lightning can start fires and also damage buildings and power transmission systems, causing power outages.

- **Ice storms**   When rain falls through a layer of colder air, raindrops freeze onto whatever surface they strike, resulting in widespread power outages after heavy ice coats power lines, causing them to collapse. A notable example is the Great Ice Storm of 1998 in eastern Canada, which resulted in millions being without power for as long as two weeks and in the virtual immobilization of the cities of Montreal and Ottawa.

- **Hail**   This form of precipitation consists of ice chunks ranging from 5 to 150 mm in diameter. An example of a damaging hailstorm is the April 1999 storm in Sydney, Australia, where hailstones up to 9.5 cm in diameter damaged 40,000 vehicles, 20,000 properties, and 25 airplanes and caused one direct fatality. The storm caused $1.5 billion in damage.

- **Tsunamis**   A series of waves that usually result from the sudden vertical displacement of a lake bed or ocean floor can also be caused by landslides, asteroids, or explosions. A tsunami wave can be barely noticeable in open, deep

Figure 7-5
Damage to structures caused by the 2011 Japan tsunami

water, but as it approaches a shoreline, the wave can grow to a height of 50 feet or more. Recent notable examples are the 2004 Indian Ocean tsunami and the 2011 Japan tsunami. Figure 7-5 shows coastline damage from the Japan tsunami.

- **Pandemic**   Infectious diseases may spread over a wide geographic region, even worldwide. Pandemics have regularly occurred throughout history and are likely to continue occurring, despite advances in sanitation and immunology. A pandemic is the rapid spread of any type of disease, including typhoid, tuberculosis, bubonic plague, or influenza. Pandemics include the 1918–1920 Spanish flu, the 1956–1958 Asian flu, the 1968–1969 Hong Kong "swine" flu, the 2009–2010 swine flu, and the COVID-19 pandemic, which began at the end of 2019. Figure 7-6 shows a field hospital during the pandemic.

- **Extraterrestrial impacts**   This category includes meteorites and other objects that fall from the sky from way, way up. Sure, these events are extremely rare, and most organizations don't even include these events in their risk analysis, but I've included them here for the sake of rounding out the types of natural events.

Figure 7-6 A field hospital in Brazil during the 2019 COVID pandemic (Image courtesy of Gustavo Basso)

PART IV

Human-Caused Disasters   Human-caused disasters are directly or indirectly caused by human activity through action or inaction. The results of human-caused disasters are similar to natural disasters: localized or widespread damage to businesses that results in potentially lengthy interruptions in operations. These are some examples of human-caused disasters:

- **Civil disturbances**   These can include protests, demonstrations, riots, strikes, work slowdowns and stoppages, looting, and resulting actions such as curfews, evacuations, or lockdowns.

- **Utility outages**   Failures in electric, natural gas, district heating, water, communications, and other utilities can be caused by equipment failures, sabotage, or natural events such as landslides or flooding.

- **Service outages**   Failures in IT equipment, software programs, and online services can be caused by hardware failures, software bugs, or misconfiguration.

- **Materials shortages**   Interruptions in the supply of food, fuel, supplies, and materials can have a ripple effect on businesses and the services that support them. Readers who are old enough to remember the petroleum shortages of the mid-1970s know what this is all about. Ripple effects from the COVID pandemic lockdown include shortages of baby formula in 2022, shown in Figure 7-7. Shortages can result in spikes in the price of commodities, which is almost as damaging as not having any supply at all.

Figure 7-7 Empty grocery store shelves exhibiting the lack of available baby formula.

- **Fires** These fires originate in or involve buildings, equipment, and materials.
- **Hazardous materials spills** Many created or refined substances can be dangerous if they escape their confines. Examples include petroleum substances, gases, pesticides and herbicides, medical substances, and radioactive substances.
- **Transportation accidents** This broad category includes plane crashes, railroad derailment, bridge collapse, and the like.
- **Terrorism and war** Whether they are actions of a nation, nation-state, or other group, terrorism and war can have devastating but usually localized effects in cities and regions. Often, terrorism and war precipitate secondary effects such as famine, disease, materials shortages, and utility outages.
- **Security events** The actions of a lone hacker or a team of organized cybercriminals can bring down one system or network, or many networks, which may result in a widespread interruption in services. Hackers' activities can directly result in an outage, or an organization can voluntarily (although reluctantly) shut down an affected service or network to contain the incident.

 NOTE It is important to remember that real disasters are usually complex events that involve more than just one type of damaging event. For instance, an earthquake directly damages buildings and equipment, but fires and utility outages can also result. A hurricane also brings flooding, utility outages, and sometimes even hazardous materials events and civil disturbances such as looting.

How Disasters Affect Organizations   Many disasters have direct effects, but sometimes the secondary effects of a disaster event are most significant, from the perspective of ongoing business operations. A risk analysis, which is a part of the BCP process (discussed in the next section in this chapter), will identify the ways in which disasters are likely to affect an organization. During the risk analysis, the primary, secondary, upstream, and downstream effects of likely disaster scenarios are identified and considered. Whoever is performing this analysis will need to have a broad understanding of the interdependencies of business processes and IT systems, as well as the ways in which a disaster will affect ongoing business operations. Similarly, personnel who are developing contingency and recovery plans also need to be familiar with these effects so that those plans will adequately serve the organization's needs.

Disasters, by our definition, interrupt business operations in some measurable way. An event that may be a disaster for one organization would not necessarily be a disaster for another, particularly if it doesn't affect the latter. It would be shortsighted to say that a disaster affects only operations; instead, the longer-term effects created by a disaster can impact the organization's image, brand, reputation, and ongoing financial viability. The factors affecting image, brand, and reputation have as much to do with how the organization communicates to its customers, suppliers, and shareholders, as with how the organization actually handles a disaster in progress.

A disaster can affect an organization's operations in several ways:

- **Direct damage**   Events such as earthquakes, floods, and fires directly damage an organization's buildings, equipment, or records. The damage may be severe enough that no salvageable items remain, or it may be less severe, and some equipment and buildings may be salvageable or repairable.

- **Utility interruption**   Even if an organization's buildings and equipment are undamaged, a disaster may affect utilities such as power, natural gas, or water, which can incapacitate some or all business operations. Significant delays in refuse collection, for example, can result in unsanitary conditions.

- **Transportation**   A disaster may damage or render transportation systems such as roads, railroads, shipping, or air transport unusable for a period, causing interruptions in supply lines and personnel transportation.

- **Services and supplier shortage**   Even if a disaster does not directly affect an organization, critical suppliers affected by a disaster can cause problems for business operations. For instance, a regional baker that cannot produce and ship bread to its corporate customers will soon result in sandwich shops without a critical resource.

- **Staff availability**   A community-wide or regional disaster that affects businesses is likely to affect homes and families as well. Depending upon the nature of a disaster, employees will place a higher priority on the safety and comfort of family members. Also, workers may not be able or willing to travel to work if transportation systems are affected or if there is a significant materials shortage. Employees may also be unwilling to travel to work if they fear for their personal safety or that of their families.

- **Customer availability** Disasters may force or dissuade customers from traveling to business locations to conduct business, as many of the factors that keep employees away may also keep customers away.

 TIP The secondary and tertiary effects a particular organization experiences after a disaster depends entirely upon a unique set of circumstances that constitute the organization's specific critical needs. A risk analysis should be performed to identify these specific factors.

The BCP Process

To plan for disaster preparedness, the organization must start by determining which kinds of disasters are likely and their possible effects on the organization—that is, plan first, act later. The BCP process is a life-cycle process, as shown in Figure 7-8. In other words, BCP (and DRP) is not a one-time event or activity; it's a set of activities that result in the ongoing preparedness for disaster that continually adapts to changing business conditions and that continually improves.

The following are the elements of the BCP process life cycle:

1. Assign ownership of the program.
2. Develop BCP policy.
3. Conduct business impact analysis.
4. Perform criticality analysis.
5. Establish recovery targets.
6. Define KRIs and KPIs.
7. Develop recovery and continuity strategies and plans.
8. Test recovery and continuity plans and procedures.
9. Test integration of business continuity and disaster recovery plans.
10. Train personnel.
11. Maintain strategies, plans, and procedures through periodic reviews and updates.

BCP Policy A formal BCP effort must, like any strategic activity, flow from the existence of a formal policy and be included in the overall governance model discussed throughout this chapter. BCP should be an integral part of the IT control framework, not lie outside of it. Therefore, BCP policy should include or cite specific controls that ensure that key activities in the BCP life cycle are performed appropriately. BCP policy should also define the scope of the BCP strategy, so the specific business processes (or departments or divisions within an organization) that are included in the BCP effort must be defined. Sometimes the scope will include a geographic boundary. In larger organizations, it is possible to "bite off more than you can chew" and define too large a scope for a BCP project, so limiting the scope to a smaller, more manageable portion of the organization can be a good approach.

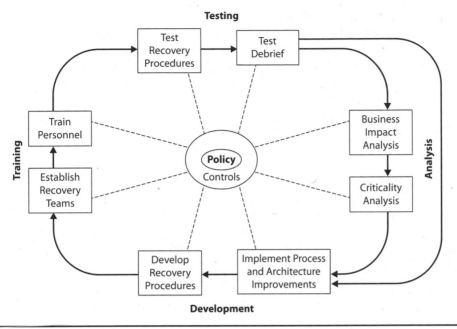

Figure 7-8 The BCP process life cycle

Business Continuity Planning and COBIT Controls

The specific COBIT controls that are involved with BCP are contained within objective DSS04, Managed Continuity. This objective lists eight specific controls that constitute the entire continuity life cycle:

- Define the business continuity policy, objectives, and scope.
- Maintain business resilience.
- Develop and implement a business continuity response.
- Exercise, test, and review the BCP and DRP.
- Review, maintain, and improve the continuity plans.
- Conduct continuity plan training.
- Manage backup arrangements.
- Conduct post-resumption review.

These controls are discussed in this chapter and also appear in COBIT 2019.

Developing Continuity Plans

In the previous section, I discussed the notion of establishing recovery targets and the development of architectures, processes, and procedures. The processes and procedures are related to the normal operation of those new technologies as they will be operated in normal day-to-day operations. When those processes and procedures have been completed, the disaster recovery plans and procedures (actions that will take place during and immediately after a disaster) can be developed.

Suppose, for example, that an organization has established RPO and RTO targets for its critical applications. These targets necessitated the development of server clusters and storage area networks with replication. While implementing those new technologies, the organization developed supporting operations processes and procedures that would be carried out every day during normal business operations. As a separate activity, the organization developed the procedures to be performed when a disaster strikes the primary operations center for those applications; those procedures include all of the steps that must be taken so that the applications can continue operating in an alternate location.

The procedures for operating critical applications during a disaster are a small part of the entire body of procedures that must be developed. Several other sets of procedures must also be developed to prepare the organization, including the following:

- Personnel safety procedures
- Disaster declaration procedures
- Responsibilities
- Contact information
- Recovery procedures
- Continuing operations
- Restoration procedures

Personnel Safety Procedures   When a disaster strikes, measures to ensure the safety of personnel are the first priority. If the disaster has occurred or is about to occur in a building, personnel may need to be evacuated as soon as possible. Arguably, however, in some situations, evacuation is exactly the wrong thing to do; for example, if a hurricane or tornado is bearing down on a facility, the building itself may be the best shelter for personnel, even if it incurs some damage. The point here is that personnel safety procedures need to be carefully developed, and possibly more than one set of procedures will be needed, depending on the event.

NOTE   Remember that the highest priority in any disaster or emergency situation is the safety of human life.

Personnel safety procedures should include the following factors:

- All personnel are familiar with evacuation and sheltering procedures.
- Visitors know how to evacuate the premises and the location of sheltering areas.
- Signs and placards are posted to indicate emergency evacuation routes and gathering areas outside of the building.
- Emergency lighting is available to aid in evacuation or sheltering in place.
- Fire extinguishment equipment (portable fire extinguishers and so on) is readily available.
- Communication with public safety and law enforcement authorities is available at all times, including times when communications and electric power have been cut off and when all personnel are outside of the building.
- Care is available for injured personnel.
- CPR and emergency first-aid training are provided.
- Safety personnel are available to assist in the evacuation of injured and disabled people.
- A process is in place to account for visitors and other nonemployees.
- Emergency shelter is available in extreme weather conditions
- Emergency food and drinking water are available when personnel must shelter in place.
- Periodic tests are conducted to ensure that evacuation procedures will be adequate in the event of a real emergency.

NOTE Local emergency management organizations may provide additional information that can assist an organization with its emergency personnel safety procedures.

Disaster Declaration Procedures   Disaster response procedures are initiated when a disaster is declared. However, a procedure for the declaration itself must be created to ensure that there will be little doubt as to the conditions that must be present to declare a disaster. Why is a disaster declaration procedure required? It's not always clear whether a situation is a "real disaster." Certainly, a 7.5-magnitude earthquake or a major fire is a disaster, but popcorn overcooked in the microwave that sets off a building's fire alarm system might not be. A disaster declaration procedure must provide some basic conditions that will help determine whether a disaster should be declared.

Further, who has the authority to declare a disaster? If senior management personnel frequently travel and are not on site when a disaster occurs, who else can declare a disaster? Finally, what does it mean to declare a disaster—and what happens next? The following points constitute the primary items organizations need to consider for their disaster declaration procedure.

Form a Core Team A core team of personnel needs to be established, all of whom will be familiar with the disaster declaration procedure as well as the actions that must take place once a disaster has been declared. This core team should consist of middle and upper managers who are familiar with business operations, particularly those that are critical. This team must be large enough so that a requisite few of them are on hand when a disaster strikes. In organizations that require second shifts, third shifts, and weekend work, some of the core team members should be supervisory personnel during those times, while others can be personnel who work regular business hours and are not always on site.

Declaration Criteria The declaration procedure must contain some tangible criteria that core team members can consult to guide them down the "Is this a disaster?" decision path. The criteria for declaring a disaster should be related to the availability and viability of ongoing critical business operations. Some example criteria include one or more of the following:

- Forced evacuation of a building containing or supporting critical operations that is likely to last for more than four hours
- Hardware, software, or network failures that result in a critical IT system being incapacitated or unavailable for more than four hours
- Any security incident that results in a critical IT system being incapacitated for more than four hours (such as malware, break-ins, attacks, sabotage, and so on)
- Any event causing employee absenteeism or supplier shortages that, in turn, results in one or more critical business processes being incapacitated for more than eight hours
- Any event causing a communications failure that results in critical IT systems being unreachable for more than four hours

This is a pretty complete list of criteria for many organizations. The periods of downtimes will vary from organization to organization. For instance, a large, pure-online business such as Salesforce.com would probably declare a disaster if its main web sites were unavailable for more than a few minutes. But in an organization whose computers are far less critical, an outage of four hours may not be considered a disaster.

Pulling the Trigger When disaster declaration criteria are met, the disaster should be declared. The procedure for disaster declaration could permit any single core team member to declare the disaster, but it may be better in some organizations to have two or more core team members agree on whether a disaster should be declared. All core team members empowered to declare a disaster should have the procedure on hand at all times. In most cases, the criteria should fit on a small, laminated wallet card that each team member can carry with him or have nearby at all times. For organizations that use the consensus method for declaring a disaster, the wallet card should include the names and contact numbers of other core team members so that each will have a way of contacting others.

Next Steps   Declaring a disaster will trigger the start of one or more other response procedures, but not necessarily all of them. For instance, if a disaster is declared because of a serious computer or software malfunction, there is no need to evacuate the building. While this example may be obvious, not all instances will be this clear. Either the disaster declaration procedure itself or each of the subsequent response procedures should contain criteria that will help determine which response procedures should be enacted.

False Alarms   Probably the most common cause of personnel not declaring a disaster is the fear that an event is not an actual disaster. Core team members empowered with declaring a disaster should not necessarily hesitate, however. Instead, core team members could convene with additional team members to reach a firm decision, provided this can be done quickly. If a disaster has been declared and it later becomes clear that a disaster has been averted (or did not exist in the first place), the disaster can simply be called off and declared to be over. Response personnel can be contacted and told to cease response activities and return to their normal activities.

 TIP   Depending on the level of effort that takes place in the opening minutes and hours of disaster response, the consequences of declaring a disaster when none exists may or may not be significant. In the spirit of continuous improvement, any organization that has had a few false alarms should seek to improve its disaster declaration criteria. Well-trained and experienced personnel can usually avoid frequent false alarms.

Responsibilities   During a disaster, many important tasks must be performed to evacuate or shelter personnel, assess damage, recover critical processes and systems, and carry out many other functions that are critical to the survival of the enterprise. About 20 different responsibilities are described here. In a large organization, each responsibility may be staffed with a team of two, three, or many individuals. In small organizations, a few people may incur many responsibilities each, switching from role to role as the situation warrants.

All roles will be staffed by people who are available; remember that many of the "ideal" people to fill each role may be unavailable during a disaster for several reasons:

- **Injured, ill, or deceased**   Some regional disasters will inflict widespread casualties that will include some proportion of response personnel. Those who are injured, who are ill (in the case of a pandemic, for instance, or who are recovering from a sickness or surgery when the disaster occurs), or who are killed by the disaster are clearly not going to be showing up to help out.

- **Caring for family members**   Some types of disasters may cause widespread injury or require mass evacuation. In some situations, many personnel will be caring for family members whose immediate needs for safety will take priority over the needs of the organization.

- **Unavailable transportation**   Because some disasters result in localized or widespread damage to transportation infrastructure, many people who are willing to be on-site to help with emergency operations will be unable to travel to the site.

- **Out of the area** Some personnel may be away on business travel or on vacation and be unable to respond. However, these situations may provide opportunities in disguise; unaffected by the physical impact of the disaster, these individuals may be able to help out in other ways, such as communicating with suppliers, customers, or other personnel.

- **Communications** Some types of disasters, particularly those that are localized (versus widespread and obvious to an observer), require that disaster response personnel be contacted and asked to help. If a disaster strikes after hours, some personnel may be unreachable if they do not have a mobile phone with them or are out of range.

- **Fear** Some types of disasters (such as a pandemic, terrorist attack, or flood) may instill fear for safety on the part of response personnel who will disregard the call to help and stay away from the site.

 NOTE Response personnel in all disciplines and responsibilities will need to be able to piece together whatever functionality they are called on to do, using whatever resources are available—this is part art form and part science. Although response and contingency plans may make certain assumptions, personnel may find themselves with inadequate resources, requiring them to do the best they can with the resources available.

Each function will be working with personnel in many other functions, including unfamiliar people. An entire response and recovery operation may resemble an entirely new organization in unfamiliar settings and with an entirely new set of rules. Typically, teams work best when members are familiar with and trust one another. In a response and recovery operation, the stress level is very high because the stakes—survival—are higher, and teams may be composed of people who have little experience with one another and these new roles. This additional stress will bring out the best and worst in people, as illustrated in Figure 7-9.

Emergency Response and Command and Control (Emergency Management) The priorities of "first responders" during a disaster include evacuating or sheltering personnel, first aid, triage of injured personnel, and possibly firefighting. During disaster response operations, someone has to be in charge. Resources may be scarce, and many matters will vie for attention. Someone needs to fill the role of decision-maker to keep disaster response activities moving and to handle situations that arise. This role may need to be rotated among various personnel, particularly in smaller organizations, to counteract fatigue.

 TIP Although the first person on the scene may be the person in charge initially, as more personnel show up and the nature of the disaster and response solidifies, qualified assigned personnel will take charge and leadership roles may then be passed among key personnel.

Figure 7-9 Stress is compounded by the pressure of disaster recovery and the formation of new teams in times of chaos.

Scribe It's vital that one or more people document the important events continually during disaster response operations. From decisions, to discussions, to status, to roll call, these events must be recorded so that the details of disaster response can be pieced together afterward. This will help the organization better understand how disaster response unfolded, how decisions were made, and who performed which actions—all of which will help the organization be better prepared for future events.

Internal Communications In many disaster scenarios, personnel may be stripped of many or all of their normal means of communication, such as desk phones, voicemail, e-mail, smartphones, and instant messaging. However, during a disaster, communications are vital, especially when nothing is going according to plan. Good communication ensures that the statuses of various activities can be sent to command and control and priorities and orders can be sent to disaster response personnel. Many organizations establish means for emergency communications, including the following:

- **Broadcast alerts** Sent via text, voice, or mobile app, these help inform large numbers of personnel about events affecting the organization.

- **Emergency radio communications** When wireless and wireline communications are not functioning, emergency communication via radio enables personnel in different locations to pass along important information.

External Communications   People outside of the organization also need to stay informed when a disaster strikes. Many parties may want or need to know the status of business operations during and after a disaster:

- Customers
- Suppliers
- Partners
- Law enforcement and public safety authorities (including first responders)
- Insurance companies
- Shareholders
- Neighbors
- Regulators
- Media

These different audiences need different messages, as well as messages in different forms. For instance, notifications to the public may be sent through media outlets, whereas notifications to customers may be sent through e-mail or surface mail.

Legal and Compliance   Several needs may arise during a disaster that require the attention of inside or outside legal counsel. Disasters present unique situations, such as the following, that may require legal assistance:

- Interpretation of regulations
- Interpretation of contracts with suppliers and customers
- Management of matters of liability to other parties

 TIP   Typical legal matters need to be resolved before the onset of a disaster, and this information should be included in disaster response procedures. Remember that legal staff members may be unavailable during the disaster.

Damage Assessment   After a physically violent event such as an earthquake or volcano, or after an event with no physical manifestation such as a serious security incident, one or more experts are needed to examine affected assets and accurately assess the damage. Because most organizations own many different types of assets (buildings, equipment, and information), qualified experts should assess each asset type; only those whose expertise matches the type of event that has occurred need to be consulted. Some needed expertise may go well beyond the skills present in an organization, such as a structural engineer who can assess potential earthquake damage. In such cases, it may be sensible to retain the services of an outside engineer who will respond and provide an assessment of whether a building is safe to occupy after a disaster. In fact, it may make sense to retain more than one in case they themselves are affected by a disaster.

Salvage Disasters destroy assets that the organization uses to create products or perform services. When a disaster occurs, someone (either a qualified employee or an outside expert) needs to examine assets to determine which are salvageable; then, a salvage team needs to perform the actual salvage operation at a pace that meets the organization's needs. In some cases, salvage may be a critical-path activity, where critical processes are paralyzed until salvage and repairs to critically needed machinery can be performed. Or the salvage operation may be performed on the inventory of finished goods, raw materials, and other items so that business operations can be resumed. Occasionally, when it is obvious that damaged equipment or materials are a total loss, the salvage effort involves selling the damaged items or materials to another organization. Assessment of damage to assets may be a high priority when an organization is filing an insurance claim. Insurance may be a primary source of funding for the organization's recovery effort.

 CAUTION   Salvage operations may be a critical-path activity or may be carried out well after the disaster. To the greatest extent possible, this should be decided in advance. Otherwise, the command-and-control function will need to decide the priority of salvage operations, potentially wasting valuable time.

Physical Security Following a disaster, the organization's usual physical security controls may be compromised. For instance, fencing, walls, and barricades may be damaged, or video surveillance systems may be disabled or have no electric power. These and other failures could lead to an increased risk of loss or damage to assets and personnel until those controls can be repaired. Also, security controls in temporary quarters such as hot/warm/cold sites and temporary work centers may be less effective than those in primary locations.

Supplies During emergency and recovery operations, personnel will require drinking water, writing tablets, writing utensils, smartphones, portable generators, and extension cords, among other items. The supplies function may be responsible for acquiring these items and replacement assets such as servers and network equipment for a cold site.

Transportation When workers are operating from a temporary location, and if regional or local transportation systems have been compromised, many arrangements for all kinds of transportation may be required to support emergency operations. These can include transportation of replacement workers, equipment, or supplies by truck, car, rail, sea, or air. This function could also be responsible for arranging for temporary lodging for personnel.

Work Centers When a disaster event results in business locations being unusable, workers may need to work in temporary locations. These work centers will require a variety of amenities to permit workers to be productive until their primary work locations are again available.

Network   This technology function is responsible for damage assessment to the organization's voice and data networks, building/configuring networks for emergency operations, or both. This function may require extensive coordination with external telecommunications service providers, which, by the way, may be suffering the effects of a local or regional disaster as well.

Network Services   This function is responsible for network-centric services such as the Domain Name System (DNS), Simple Network Management Protocol (SNMP), network routing, and authentication.

Systems   This function is responsible for building, loading, and configuring the servers and systems that support critical services, applications, databases, and other functions. Personnel may have other resources such as virtualization technology to enable additional flexibility.

Database Management Systems   For critical applications that rely upon database management systems (DBMSs), this function is responsible for building databases on recovery systems and for restoring or recovering data from backup media, replication volumes, or e-vaults onto recovery systems. Database personnel will need to work with systems, network, and applications personnel to ensure that databases are operating properly and are available as needed.

Data and Records   This function is responsible for access to and re-creation of electronic and paper business records. This business function supports critical business processes, works with database management personnel, and, if necessary, works with data-entry personnel to rekey lost data.

Applications   This function is responsible for recovering application functionality on application servers. This may include reloading application software, performing configuration, provisioning roles and user accounts, and connecting the application to databases and network services, as well as other application integration issues.

Access Management   This function is responsible for creating and managing user accounts for network, system, and application access. Personnel with this responsibility may be especially susceptible to social engineering and may be tempted to create user accounts without proper authority or approval.

Information Security and Privacy   Personnel in this capacity are responsible for ensuring that proper security controls are being carried out during recovery and emergency operations. They will be expected to identify risks associated with emergency operations and to require remedies to reduce risks. Security personnel will also be responsible for enforcing privacy controls so that employee and customer personal data will not be compromised, even as business operations are affected by the disaster.

Offsite Storage   This function is responsible for managing the effort of retrieving backup media from offsite storage facilities and for protecting that media in transit to the scene of recovery operations. If recovery operations take place over an extended period (more than a couple of days), data at the recovery site will need to be backed up and sent to an offsite media storage facility to protect that information should a disaster occur at the hot/warm/cold site (and what bad luck that would be!).

User Hardware   In many organizations, little productive work is done when employees don't have access to their workstations, printers, scanners, copiers, and other office equipment. Thus, a function is required to provide, configure, and support the variety of office equipment required by end users working in temporary or alternate locations. This function, like most others, will have to work with many other personnel to ensure that workstations and other equipment are able to communicate with applications and services as needed to support critical processes.

Training   During emergency operations, when response personnel and users are working in new locations (and often on new or different equipment and software), some may need to be trained to enable them to restore their productivity as quickly as possible. Training personnel should be familiar with many disaster response and recovery procedures so that they can help people in those roles understand what is expected of them. This function will also need to be able to dispense emergency operations procedures to these personnel.

Restoration   This function comes into play when IT is ready to migrate applications running on hot/warm/cold site systems back to the original (or replacement) processing center.

Contract Information   This function is responsible for understanding and interpreting legal contracts. Most organizations are a party to one or more legal contracts that require them to perform specific activities, provide specific services, and communicate status if service levels have changed. These contracts may or may not have provisions for activities and services during disasters, including communications regarding any changes in service levels. This function is vital not only during the disaster planning stages but also during actual disaster response. Customers, suppliers, regulators, and other parties need to be informed according to specific contract terms.

Recovery Procedures   Recovery procedures are the instructions that key personnel use to bootstrap services (such as IT systems and other business-enabling technologies) that support the critical business functions identified in the BIA and criticality analysis. The recovery procedures should work hand-in-hand with the technologies that may have been added to IT systems to make them more resilient.

An example is useful here. Acme Rocket Boots determines that its order-entry business function is highly critical to the ongoing viability of the business and sets recovery objectives to ensure that order entry would be continued within no more than 48 hours after a disaster. Acme determines that it needs to invest in storage, backup, and replication technologies to make a 48-hour recovery possible. Without these investments, IT systems supporting order entry would be down for at least ten days until they could be rebuilt from scratch. Acme cannot justify the purchase of systems and software to facilitate an auto-failover of the order-entry application to hot-site disaster recovery servers; instead, the recovery procedure would require that the database be rebuilt from replicated data on cloud-based servers. Other tasks, such as installing recent patches, would also be necessary to make recovery servers ready for production use. All of the tasks required to make the systems ready constitute the body of recovery procedures needed to support the business order-entry function.

This example is, of course, an oversimplification. Actual recovery procedures could take dozens of pages of documentation, and procedures would also be necessary for network components, end-user workstations, network services, and other supporting IT services required by the order-entry application. And those are the procedures needed just to get the application running again. More procedures would be needed to keep the applications running properly in the recovery environment.

Continuing Operations Procedures for continuing operations have more to do with business processes than they do with IT systems. However, the two are related, because the procedures for continuing critical business processes have to fit hand in hand with the procedures for operating supporting IT systems that may also (but not necessarily) be operating in a recovery or emergency mode.

Let me clarify that last statement. It is entirely conceivable that a disaster could strike an organization with critical business processes that operate in one city but that are supported by IT systems located in another city. A disaster could strike the city with the critical business function, which means that personnel may have to continue operating that business function in another location, on the original, fully featured IT application. It is also possible that a disaster could strike the city with the IT application, forcing it into an emergency/recovery mode in an alternate location while users of the application are operating in a business-as-usual mode. And, of course, a disaster could strike both locations (or a disaster could strike in one location where both the critical business function and its supporting IT applications reside), throwing both the critical business function and its supporting IT applications into emergency mode. Any organization's reality could be even more complex than this: just add dependencies on external application service providers, applications with custom interfaces, or critical business functions that operate in multiple cities. If you wondered why disaster recovery and business continuity planning were so complicated, perhaps your appreciation has grown just now.

Restoration Procedures When a disaster has occurred, IT operations need to take up residence in an alternate processing site temporarily while repairs are performed on the original processing site. Once those repairs are completed, IT operations would need to be transitioned back to the main (or replacement) processing facility. You should expect that the procedures for this transition will also be documented (and tested—testing is discussed later in this chapter).

NOTE Transitioning applications back to the original processing site is not necessarily just a second iteration of the initial move to the hot/warm/cold site. Far from it. The recovery site may have been a skeleton (in capacity, functionality, or both) of its original self. The objective is not necessarily to move the functionality at the recovery site back to the original site but to restore the original functionality to the original site.

Let's continue the Acme Rocket Boots example. The order-entry application at the disaster recovery site had only basic, not extended, functions. For instance, customers could not look at order history, and they could not place custom orders; they could order only off-the-shelf products. But when the application is moved back to the primary processing facility, the history of orders accumulated on the disaster recovery application needs to be merged back into the main order history database, which was not part of the DRP.

Considerations for Continuity and Recovery Plans A considerable amount of detailed planning and logistics must go into continuity and recovery plans if they are to be effective.

Availability of Key Personnel An organization cannot depend upon every member of its regular expert workforce to be available in a disaster. As discussed earlier, personnel may be unavailable for a number of reasons, including the following:

- Injury, illness, or death
- Caring for family members
- Unavailable transportation
- Damaged transportation infrastructure
- Being out of the area
- Lack of communications
- Fear, related to the disaster and its effects

 TIP An organization must develop thorough and accurate recovery and continuity documentation as well as cross-training and plan testing. When a disaster strikes, an organization has one chance to survive, and this depends upon how well the available personnel are able to follow recovery and continuity procedures and keep critical processes functioning properly.

Emergency Supplies The onset of a disaster may cause personnel to be stranded at a work location, possibly for several days. This can be caused by a number of reasons, including inclement weather that makes travel dangerous or a transportation infrastructure that is damaged or blocked with debris. Emergency supplies should be laid up at a work location and made available to personnel stranded there, regardless of whether they are supporting a recovery effort or not. (It's also possible that severe weather or a natural or human-made event could make transportation dangerous or impossible.)

A disaster can also prompt employees to report to a work location (at the primary location or at an alternate site), where they may remain for days at a time, even around the clock if necessary. A situation like this may make the need for emergency supplies less critical, but it still may be beneficial to the recovery effort to make supplies available to support recovery personnel.

An organization stocking emergency supplies at a work location should consider including the following:

- Drinking water
- Food rations
- First-aid supplies
- Blankets
- Flashlights
- Battery- or crank-powered radio
- Out-of-band communications with internal and external parties (beepers, walkie-talkies, line-of-sight systems, and so on)

Local emergency response authorities may recommend other supplies be kept at a work location as well.

Communications   Communication within organizations, as well as with customers, suppliers, partners, shareholders, regulators, and others, is vital under normal business conditions. During a disaster and subsequent recovery and restoration operations, these communications are more important than ever, while many of the usual means for communications may be impaired.

Identifying Critical Personnel   A successful disaster recovery operation requires available personnel who are located near company operations centers. Although the primary response personnel may consist of the individuals and teams responsible for day-to-day corporate operations, others need to be identified. In a disaster, some personnel will be unavailable for many reasons (discussed earlier in this chapter).

Key personnel, as well as multiple backups, need to be identified. Backup personnel can consist of employees who have familiarity with specific technologies, such as operating system, database, and network administration, and who can cover for primary personnel if needed. Sure, it would be desirable for these backup personnel also to be trained in specific recovery operations, but at the least, if these personnel can access specific detailed recovery procedures, having them on a call list is probably better than having no available personnel during a disaster.

Notifying Critical Suppliers, Customers, and Other Parties   Along with employees, many other parties need to be notified in the event of a disaster. Outside parties need to be aware of the disaster and basic changes in business conditions. During a regional disaster such as a hurricane or earthquake, nearby parties will certainly be aware of the situation. However, they may not be aware of the status of business operations immediately after the disaster: a regional event's effects can range from complete destruction of buildings and equipment to no damage at all and normal conditions. Unless key parties are notified of the status, they may have no other way to know for sure.

The people or teams responsible for communicating with these outside parties will need to have all of the individuals and organizations included in a list of parties to contact.

This information should be included in emergency response procedures. Parties that need to be contacted may include the following:

- **Key suppliers**   This may include electric and gas utilities, fuel delivery, and materials delivery. In a disaster, an organization will often need to impart special instructions to one or more suppliers, requesting delivery of extra supplies or requesting temporary cessation of deliveries.

- **Key customers**   In many organizations, key customer relationships are valued above most others. These customers may depend on a steady delivery of products and services that are critical to their own operations; in a disaster, they may have a dire need to know whether such deliveries will be able to continue or not and under what circumstances.

- **Public safety**   Police, fire, and other public safety authorities may need to be contacted, not only for emergency operations such as firefighting but also for any required inspections or other services. It is important that "business office" telephone numbers for these agencies be included on contact lists, as 911 and other emergency lines may be flooded by calls from others.

- **Insurance adjusters**   Most organizations rely on insurance companies to protect their assets in case of damage or loss in a disaster. Because insurance adjustment funds are often a key part of continuing business operations in an emergency, it's important that appropriate personnel are able to reach insurers as soon as possible after a disaster has occurred.

- **Regulators**   In some industries, organizations are required to notify regulators of certain types of disasters. Though regulators may be aware of noteworthy regional disasters, they may not immediately know an event's specific effects on an organization. Further, some types of disasters are highly localized and may not be newsworthy, even in a local city.

- **Media**   Media outlets such as newspapers and television stations may need to be notified as a means of quickly reaching the community or region with information about the effects of a disaster on organizations.

- **Shareholders**   Organizations are usually obliged to notify their shareholders of any disastrous event that affects business operations. This may be the case whether the organization is publicly or privately held.

- **Stakeholders**   Organizations will need to notify other parties, including employees, competitors, and other tenants, if one or more multitenant facilities is lost.

Setting Up Call Trees   Disaster response procedures need to include a call tree, a method by which the first personnel involved in a disaster begin notifying others in the organization, informing them of the developing disaster, and enlisting their assistance. Just as the branches of a tree originate at the trunk and are repeatedly subdivided, a call tree is most effective when each person in the tree can make just a few phone calls. Not only will the notification of important personnel proceed more quickly, but each person will not be overburdened with many calls. Remember that many personnel may be unavailable or unreachable. Therefore, a call tree should be structured with sufficient

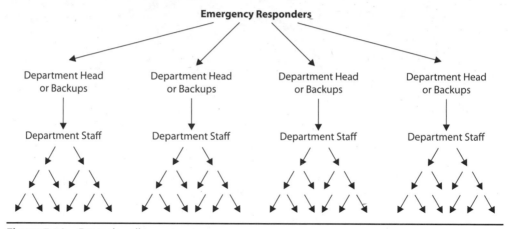

Figure 7-10   Example call tree structure

flexibility as well as assurance that all critical personnel can be contacted. Figure 7-10 shows an example call tree.

An organization can also use an automated outcalling system to notify critical personnel of a disaster. Such a system can play a prerecorded message or request that personnel call an information number to hear a message. Most outcalling systems keep a log of which personnel have been successfully reached. An automated calling system should not be located in the same geographic region, because a regional disaster could damage the system or make it unavailable during a disaster. The system should be Internet-accessible so that response personnel can access it to determine which personnel have been notified and to make any needed changes before or during a disaster.

 NOTE   Consider the use of texting and automated texting platforms or mobile notification apps to inform personnel of disaster situations.

Preparing Wallet Cards   Wallet cards containing emergency contact information should be prepared for core team personnel for the organization, as well as for members in each department who would be actively involved in disaster response. Wallet cards are advantageous because most personnel will have their wallet, pocketbook, or purse nearby at all times, even when away from home, running errands, traveling, or on vacation. Not everyone carries their mobile devices with them every minute of the day. Information on the wallet card should include contact information for fellow team members, a few of the key disaster response personnel, and any conference bridges or emergency call-in numbers that are set up.

 NOTE   A wallet card has no reliance on energy or technology and may still be valuable in extreme disaster scenarios.

Emergency Contacts

Joe Phillips, VP Ops 213-555-1212 h, 415-555-1212 m
Marie Peterson, CFO 206-555-1212 h, 425-555-1212 m
Mark Woodward, IT Ops 360-555-1212 h, 253-555-1212 m
Gary Doan, VP Facilities 509-555-1212 h, 702-555-1212 m
Jeff Patterson, IT Networks 760-555-1212 h, 310-555-1212 m

Documentation at orgname.box.net. Userid=wunderground, password=L0c43Dupt1te
Emergency conference bridge, 1-800-555-1212, host code 443322, PIN 1948
Disaster declaration criteria: 8 hr outage anticipated on critical systems, 2 core members vote, then initiate call tree procedure to notify other response personnel

Off-site media storage vendor 719-555-1212
Telecommunications and network service provider 312-555-1212
Local civil defense authorities 714-555-1212
Local health authorities 702-555-1212
Local law enforcement authorities 512-555-1212
Local hospitals 808-555-1212, 913-555-1212
National weather service hotline 602-555-1212
Regional transportation authority hotline 312-555-1212
Local building inspectors 414-555-1212

Figure 7-11 Example of a wallet card for core team participants with emergency contact information and disaster declaration criteria

Figure 7-11 shows an example wallet card. Organizations may also issue digital versions of wallet cards for people to store on mobile devices.

Electronic Contact Lists   Arguably, most IT personnel and business leaders have smartphones and other mobile devices with onboard storage that is available even when cellular carriers are experiencing outages. Copies of contact lists and even disaster response procedures can be stored in smartphones to keep this information handy during a disaster.

Transportation   Some types of disasters may make certain modes of transportation unavailable or unsafe. Widespread natural disasters, such as earthquakes, volcanoes, hurricanes, and floods, can immobilize virtually every form of transportation, including highways, railroads, boats, and airplanes. Other types of disasters may impede one or more types of transportation, which could result in overwhelming demand for the available modes. High volumes of emergency supplies may be needed during and after a disaster, but damaged transportation infrastructure often makes the delivery of those supplies difficult.

Components of a Business Continuity Plan   The complete set of business continuity plan documents will include the following:

- **Supporting project documents**   These include the documents created at the beginning of the business continuity project, including the project charter, project plan, statement of scope, and statement of support from executives.

- **Analysis documents**   These include the following:
  - BIA
  - Threat assessment and risk assessment
  - Criticality analysis
  - Documents defining recovery targets such as RTO, RPO, RCO, and RCapO
- **Response documents**   These documents describe the required actions of personnel when a disaster strikes, plus documents containing information required by those same personnel. Examples of these documents include the following:
  - **Business recovery (or resumption) plan**   This describes the activities required to recover and resume critical business processes and activities.
  - **Occupant emergency plan**   This describes activities required to care for occupants safely in a business location during a disaster. This will include both evacuation procedures and sheltering procedures, each of which may be required, depending upon the type of disaster that occurs.
  - **Emergency communications plan**   This describes the types of communications imparted to many parties, including emergency response personnel, employees in general, customers, suppliers, regulators, public safety organizations, shareholders, and the public.
  - **Contact lists**   These contain names and contact information for emergency response personnel as well as for critical suppliers, customers, and other parties.
  - **Disaster recovery plan**   This describes the activities required to restore critical IT systems and other critical assets, whether in alternate or primary locations.
  - **Continuity of operations plan**   This describes the activities required to continue critical and strategic business functions at an alternate site.
  - **Security incident response plan**   This describes the steps required to deal with a security incident that could reach disaster-like proportions.
- **Test and review documents**   This is the entire collection of documents related to tests of all of the different types of business continuity plans, as well as reviews and revisions to documents.

Making Plans Available to Personnel when Needed

When a disaster strikes, often one of the effects is no access to even the most critical IT systems. In a 40-hour workweek in an organization with on-site personnel, there is roughly a 25 percent likelihood that critical personnel will be at the business location when a disaster strikes (at least the violent type of disaster that strikes with no warning, such as an earthquake—other types of disasters, such as hurricanes, may afford the organization a little bit of time to anticipate the disaster's impact). The point is that the chances are good that the personnel who are available to respond may be unable to access the procedures and other information that they will need, unless special measures are taken.

CAUTION Complete BCP documentation often contains details of key systems, operating procedures, recovery strategies, and even vendor and model identification of in-place equipment. This information can be misused if available to unauthorized personnel, so the mechanism selected for ensuring availability must include planning to exclude inadvertent disclosure.

Response and recovery procedures can be made available in several ways to personnel during a disaster, including the following:

- **Hard copy**   While many have grown accustomed to the paperless office, disaster recovery and response documentation is one type of information that should be available in hard-copy form. Copies, even multiple copies, should be available for each responder, with a copy at the workplace and another at home, and possibly even a set in the responder's vehicle.

- **Soft copy**   Traditionally, soft-copy documentation is kept on file servers, but as you might expect, those file servers may be unavailable in a disaster. Soft copies should be available on responders' portable devices (laptops, tablets, and smartphones). An organization can also consider issuing documentation on memory sticks and cards. Depending upon the type of disaster, it can be difficult to know what resources will be available to access documentation, so making it available in more than one form will ensure that at least one copy of it will be available to the personnel who need access to it.

- **Alternate work/processing site**   Organizations that utilize a hot/warm/cold site for the recovery of critical operations can maintain hard copies and/or soft copies of recovery documentation there. This makes perfect sense; personnel working at an alternate processing or work site will need to know what to do, and having those procedures on site will facilitate their work.

- **Online**   Soft copies of recovery documentation can be archived on an Internet-based site that includes the ability to store data. Almost any type of online service that includes authentication and the ability to upload documents could be suitable for this purpose.

- **Wallet cards**   It's unreasonable to expect to publish recovery documentation on a laminated wallet card. As described earlier in this chapter, they could be used to store the contact information for core response team members as well as a few other pieces of information, such as conference bridge codes, passwords to online repositories of documentation, and so on. An example wallet card appears in Figure 7-11.

Maintaining Recovery and Continuity Plans

Business processes and technology undergo an almost continuous change in most organizations. A business continuity plan that is developed and tested is liable to be outdated within months and obsolete within a year. If much more than a year passes, a disaster recovery plan in some organizations may approach uselessness. Organizations need to keep disaster recovery plans up-to-date and relevant, and they can do this by establishing a schedule whereby the principal disaster recovery documents will be reviewed. Depending on the rate of change, this could be as frequently as quarterly or as seldom as every two years.

Further, every change, however insignificant, in business processes and information systems should include a step to review, and possibly update, relevant disaster recovery documents. A review/update of relevant documents should be a required step in every business process engineering or information systems change process and a key component of the organization's information systems development life cycle (SDLC). If this is done faithfully, the annual review of documents will likely conclude that only a few (if any) changes are required, although it is still a good practice to perform a periodic review, just to be sure.

Periodic testing of disaster recovery documents and plans is another vital activity. Testing validates the accuracy and relevance of these documents, and any issues or exceptions in the testing process should precipitate updates to appropriate documents.

Sources for Best Practices

It is unnecessary to begin BCP and DRP by inventing a new practice or methodology. These are advanced professions, and several professional associations, certifications, international standards, and publications can provide or lead to sources of practices, processes, and methodologies:

- **National Institute of Standards and Technology (NIST)** This branch of the U.S. Department of Commerce is responsible for developing business and technology standards for the federal government. NIST-created standards are excellent, and as a result, many private organizations all over the world are adopting them. Visit the NIST web site at www.nist.gov.

- **National Incident Management System (NIMS)** As a part of Homeland Security Presidential Directive 5, NIMS is a standard approach to incident management and facilitates coordination between U.S. public agencies' and private organizations' incident response plans and incident responders. Information is available from www.fema.gov/emergency-managers/nims.

- **Business Continuity Institute (BCI)** This membership organization is dedicated to the advancement of business continuity management. BCI has more than 8000 members in almost 100 countries. BCI hosts several events around the world, publishes a professional journal, and has developed a professional certification, the Certificate of the BCI (CBCI). For information, visit www.thebci.org.

- **National Fire Protection Agency (NFPA)** NFPA has developed a pre-incident planning standard, NFPA 1620, which addresses the protection, construction, and features of buildings and other structures in the United States. It also requires the development of pre-incident plans that emergency responders can use to deal with fires and other emergencies. Visit the NFPA web site at www.nfpa.org.

- **Federal Emergency Management Agency (FEMA)** FEMA is part of the U.S. Department of Homeland Security (DHS) and is responsible for emergency disaster relief planning information and services. FEMA's most visible activities are its relief operations in the wake of hurricanes and floods in the United States. For more information, visit www.fema.gov.

- **Disaster Recovery Institute International (DRI International)**   This professional membership organization provides education and professional certifications for disaster recovery planning professionals. Visit www.drii.org. Its certifications include the following:
  - Associate Business Continuity Professional (ABCP)
  - Certified Business Continuity Vendor (CBCV)
  - Certified Functional Continuity Professional (CFCP)
  - Certified Business Continuity Professional (CBCP)
  - Master Business Continuity Professional (MBCP)
- **Business Continuity Management Institute (BCM Institute)**   This professional association specializes in education and professional certification. It is a co-organizer of the World Continuity Congress, an annual conference dedicated to BCP and DRP. Visit www.bcm-institute.org. Certifications offered by BCM Institute include the following:
  - Business Continuity Certified Expert (BCCE)
  - Business Continuity Certified Specialist (BCCS)
  - Business Continuity Certified Planner (BCCP)
  - Disaster Recovery Certified Expert (DRCE)
  - Disaster Recovery Certified Specialist (DRCS)

Disaster Recovery Plan (DRP)

DRP is undertaken to reduce risks related to the onset of disasters and other events. It is mainly an IT function to ensure that key IT systems are available to support critical business processes. DRP is closely related to, but somewhat separate from, BCP: the groundwork for DRP begins in BCP activities such as the business impact analysis, criticality analysis, establishment of recovery objectives, and testing. The outputs from these activities are the key inputs to DRP:

- The BIA and criticality analysis help to prioritize which business processes (and, therefore, which IT systems) are the most important.
- Key recovery targets specify how quickly specific IT applications are to be recovered. This guides DRP personnel as they develop new IT architectures that make IT systems compliant with those objectives.
- Testing of disaster recovery plans can be performed in coordination with tests of business continuity plans to simulate real disasters and disaster response more accurately.

The relationships between BCP and DCP were discussed in detail earlier in this chapter and depicted in Figure 7-3.

Disaster Response Teams' Roles and Responsibilities

Disaster recovery plans need to specify the teams that are required for disaster response, as well as each team's roles and responsibilities. Table 7-3 describes several teams and their roles. Because of variations in organizations' disaster response plans, some of these teams will not be needed in some organizations.

Team	Responsibilities
Emergency management	Coordinates activities of all other response teams
First responders	Usually outside personnel such as police, fire, and rescue who help to extinguish fires, evacuate personnel, and provide emergency medical aid
Communications	Coordinates communication among teams and between teams and outside entities
Damage assessment	Examines equipment, supplies, furnishing, and assets to determine what can be used immediately in support of critical processes and what will need to be handed off to salvage teams
Salvage	Examines equipment, supplies, furnishings, and other assets to determine what can be salvaged for immediate or long-term reuse
Network engineering	Establishes and maintains electronic (voice and data) communications in support of critical services during a disaster
Systems engineering	Establishes and maintains systems as needed to support critical applications and services
Database engineering	Establishes and maintains DBMSs as needed to support critical applications, and performs data recovery using local or remotely stored media as needed
Application support	Establishes and maintains critical applications in support of critical business processes
Application development	Makes changes to critical applications as needed during the recovery effort
End-user computing	Establishes and maintains end-user computing facilities (desktop computers, laptop computers, mobile devices, and so on) as needed in support of critical applications and services
Systems operations	Performs routine and nonroutine tasks such as backups to keep critical applications running
Transportation	Coordinates transportation of personnel to recovery sites
Relocation	Acquires housing and other resources needed by personnel who are working at remote operations centers
Security	Coordinates physical and logical security activities to ensure the continuous protection of staff, assets, and information
Finance	Facilitates the availability of financial resources as needed to commence and continue emergency response operations

Table 7-3   Disaster Response Teams' Roles and Responsibilities

NOTE Some roles in Table 7-3 may overlap with responsibilities defined in the organization's BCP. Disaster recovery and business continuity planners should work together to ensure that the organization's overall response to disaster is appropriate and does not overlook vital functions.

Recovery Objectives

During the BIA and criticality analysis phases of a business continuity and disaster recovery project, the speed with which each business activity (with its underlying IT systems) needs to be restored after a disaster is determined. The primary recovery objectives, as discussed in detail earlier in this chapter, are as follows:

- RTO
- RPO
- RCO
- RCapO

NOTE Senior management should be involved in any discussion related to recovery system specifications in terms of capacity, integrity, or functionality.

Publishing Recovery Targets

If the storage system for an application takes a snapshot every hour, the RPO could be one hour, unless the storage system itself was damaged in a disaster. If the snapshot is replicated to another storage system four times per day, the RPO might be better expressed as six to eight hours. This brings up an interesting point. There may not be one golden RPO figure for a given system. Instead, the severity of a disrupting event or a disaster will dictate the time to get systems running again (RTO) with a certain amount of data loss (RPO). Here are some examples:

- A server's CPU or memory fails and is replaced and restarted in two hours. No data is lost. The RTO is two hours, and the RPO is zero.

- The storage system supporting an application suffers a hardware failure that results in the loss of all data. Data is recovered from a snapshot on another server taken every six hours. The RPO is six hours in this case.

- The database in a transaction application is corrupted and must be recovered. Backups are taken twice per day. The RPO is 12 hours. However, it takes 10 hours to rebuild indexes on the database, so the RTO is closer to 22 to 24 hours since the application cannot be returned to service until indexes are available.

TIP When publishing RTO and RPO figures to customers, it's best to publish the worst-case figures: "If our data center burns to the ground, our RTO is *X* hours and the RPO is *Y* hours." Saying it that way would be simpler than publishing a chart that shows RPO and RTO figures for various types of disasters.

Organizations that publish RCO and RCapO targets will need to include the practical meaning of these targets, whether they represent an exact match of capacity and integrity or some reduction. For example, if an organization's recovery site is engineered to process 80 percent of the transaction volume of the primary site, an organization should consider stating that processing capacity at a recovery site may be reduced.

Pricing RTO and RPO Capabilities

Generally speaking, the shorter the RTO or RPO for a given system, the more expensive it will be to achieve the target. Table 7-4 depicts a range of RTOs along with the technologies needed to achieve them and their relative cost.

The BCP project team needs to understand the relationship between the time required to recover an application and the cost required to recover the application within that time. A shorter recovery time is more expensive, and this relationship is not linear. This means that reducing RPO from three days to six hours may mean that the equipment and software investment could double, or it may increase eightfold. So many factors are involved in the supporting infrastructure for a given application that a BCP project team must knuckle down and develop the cost for a few different RTO and RPO figures.

The business value of the application itself is the primary driver in determining the amount of investment that senior management is willing to make to reach any arbitrary RTO and RPO figures. This business value may be measured in local currency if the application supports revenue, but the loss of an application during a disaster may harm the organization's reputation, which is difficult to monetize. Management must decide how much it is willing to invest in disaster recovery capabilities that bring RTO and RPO figures down to an acceptable level. Figure 7-12 illustrates these relationships.

RTO/RPO	Technologies Needed	Cost
2 weeks	Backup tapes; buy a server when the original server has burned or floated away	$
1 week	Backup tapes; replacement server on hand	$$
2 days	Backup tapes; application software installed on a replacement server	$$
12 hours	Backup tapes or replication; application server installed and running on a replacement server	$$$
1 hour	Server cluster with auto or manual failover; near-real-time replication	$$$$
5 minutes	Load balancing or rapid failover server cluster; real-time replication	$$$$$

Table 7-4 The Lower the RTO, the Higher the Cost to Achieve It

Figure 7-12
Aim for the sweet spot and balance the costs of downtime and recovery.

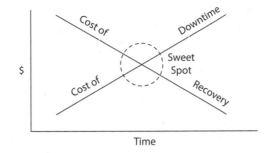

Developing Recovery Strategies

When management has chosen specific RPO and RTO targets for a given system or process, the BCP project team can then roll up its sleeves and devise some ways to meet these targets. This section discusses the technologies and logistics associated with various recovery strategies. This will help the project team decide which types of strategies are best suited for their organization.

NOTE Developing recovery strategies to meet specific recovery targets is an iterative process. The project team will develop a strategy to reach specific targets for a specific cost; senior management could well decide that the cost is too high and may increase RPO and/or RTO targets accordingly. Similarly, the project team could also discover that it is less costly to achieve specific RPO and RTO targets, and management could respond by lowering those targets. This is illustrated in Figure 7-13.

Contingencies for Contingencies

Everyone has a plan until they get punched in the mouth.

—Mike Tyson

When developing contingency plans, disaster recovery planners should keep in mind that contingency plans won't always work out. This is especially true in situations that are more regional in nature. For instance, in a region impacted by a widespread natural disaster, recalling backup tapes by courier may be problematic because transportation infrastructure may be impacted. After the September 11, 2001, attack on the World Trade Center in New York, shipping anything by air was out of the question, because the airspace throughout North America was closed for several days. During the COVID-19 pandemic, shipping was severely hampered at times because of shortages of pilots, drivers, and fuel.

Figure 7-13
Recovery
objective
development
flowchart

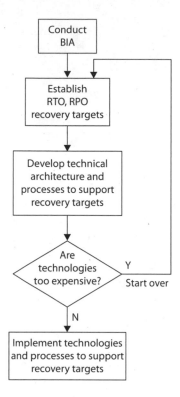

Site Recovery Options   In a worst-case disaster scenario, the site where information systems reside is partially or wholly destroyed. In most cases, the organization cannot afford to wait for the damaged or destroyed facility to be restored, because this could take weeks or months. If an organization can take that long to recover an application, you'd have to wonder whether it is needed. The assumption must be that in a disaster scenario, the organization will recover critical applications at another location. This other location is called a *recovery site.* There are two dimensions to the process of choosing a recovery site: the speed at which the application will be recovered at the recovery site and the location of the recovery site itself.

As you might expect, speed costs: Developing the ability to recover more quickly costs more money and resources. If a system is to be recovered within a few minutes or hours, the costs will be much higher than if the organization can recover the system in five days.

Various types of facilities are available for rapid or not-too-rapid recovery. These facilities are called *hot sites, warm sites, cold sites,* and *cloud sites*. As the names suggest, hot sites permit rapid recovery, while cold sites provide a much slower recovery. The costs associated with these are also somewhat proportional, as illustrated in Table 7-5.

Hot Sites   A *hot site* is an alternate processing center where backup systems are already running and in some state of near-readiness to assume production workload. The systems at a hot site most likely have application software and database management software

Table 7-5
Relative Costs of
Recovery Sites

Site Type	Speed to Recovery	Cost
Hot	0 to 24 hours	$$$$
Warm	24 hours to 7 days	$$$
Cold	More than 7 days	$$
Mobile	2 to 7 days	$$$ to $$$$
Cloud	0 to 7 days	$$
Reciprocal	0 to 7 days	$$ to $$$$

already loaded and running, perhaps even at the same patch levels as the systems in the primary processing center. A hot site is the best choice for systems whose RTO targets range from zero to several hours, perhaps as long as 24 hours.

A hot site may consist of leased rack space (or even a cage for larger installations) at a co-location center. If the organization has its own processing centers, a hot site for a given system would consist of the required rack space to house the recovery systems. Recovery servers will be installed and running, with the same version and patch level for the operating system, DBMS (if used), and application software.

Systems at a hot site require the same level of administration and maintenance as the primary systems. When patches or configuration changes are made to primary systems, they should be made to hot-site systems at the same time or very shortly afterward. Because systems at a hot site need to be at or very near a state of readiness, a strategy needs to be developed regarding a method for keeping the data on hot standby systems current. Systems at a hot site should also have full network connectivity. A method for quickly directing network traffic toward the recovery servers needs to be worked out in advance so that a switchover can be accomplished. All this is discussed in the "Recovery and Resilience Technologies" section later in this chapter.

The organization sends one or more technical staff members to the hot site to set up systems; once the systems are operating, much or all of the system- and database-level administration can be performed remotely. In a disaster scenario, however, the organization may need to send the administrative staff to the site for day-to-day management of the systems. This means that workspace for these personnel needs to be identified so that they can perform their duties during the recovery operation.

 TIP   Hot-site planning needs to consider work (desk) space for on-site personnel. Some co-location centers provide limited work areas that are often shared and offer little privacy for phone discussions. Also, transportation, hotel, and dining accommodations need to be arranged, possibly in advance, particularly if the hot site is in a different city from the primary site.

Warm Sites   A *warm site* is an alternate processing center where recovery systems are present but at a lower state of readiness than recovery systems at a hot site. For example, while the same version of the operating system may be running on the warm site system, it may be a few patch levels behind primary systems. The same could be said about the versions and patch levels of DBMSs (if used) and application software.

A warm site is appropriate for an organization whose RTO figures range from roughly one to seven days. In a disaster scenario, recovery teams would travel to the warm site and work to get the recovery systems to a state of production readiness and to get systems up-to-date with patches and configuration changes to bring the systems into a state of complete readiness. A warm site is also used when the organization is willing to take the time necessary to recover data from tape or other backup media. Depending upon the size of the databases, this recovery task can take several hours to a few days.

The primary advantage of a warm site is that its costs are lower than for a hot site, particularly in the effort required to keep the recovery system up-to-date. The site may not require expensive data replication technology, but instead, data can be recovered from backup media.

Cold Sites   A *cold site* is an alternate processing center where the degree of readiness for recovery systems is low. At the least, a cold site is nothing more than an empty rack or allocated space on a computer room floor. It's just an address in someone's data center or co-location site where computers can be set up and used at some future date. Often, cold sites contain little or no equipment. When a disaster or other highly disruptive event occurs in which the outage is expected to exceed 7 to 14 days, the organization will order computers from a manufacturer or perhaps have computers shipped from some other business location to arrive at the cold site soon after the disaster event has begun. Then personnel would travel to the site and set up the computers, operating systems, databases, network equipment, and so on, and get applications running within several days.

The advantage of a cold site is its low cost. The main disadvantage is the time and effort required to bring it to operational readiness in a short period, which can be costly. But for some organizations, a cold site is exactly what is needed.

Table 7-6 shows a comparison of hot, warm, cold, and cloud-based recovery sites and a few characteristics of each.

	Cold	**Warm**	**Hot**	**Cloud (IaaS)**
Computers	Ship to site	On-site	Running	On-site
Application Software	To be installed	Installed	Running	Any desired state
Data	To be recovered	To be recovered	Continuously updated	To be recovered
Connectivity	To be established	Ready to go	Already connected	Already connected
Support Staff	Travel to site	Travel to site	On-site or remotely managed	Remotely managed
Cost	Lowest	Moderate	Highest	Moderate

Table 7-6   Detailed Comparison of Cold, Warm, Hot, and Cloud Sites

Mobile Site   A *mobile site* is a portable recovery center that can be delivered to almost any location in the world. A viable alternative to a fixed-location recovery site, a mobile site can be transported by semitrailer truck and may even have its own generator, communications, and cooling capabilities. APC and SunGuard provide mobile sites installed in semis. Oracle can provide mobile sites that include a configurable selection of servers and workstations, all housed in shipping containers that can be shipped by truck, rail, ship, or air to any location in the world.

Cloud Sites   Organizations are increasingly using cloud hosting services as their recovery sites. Such sites charge for the utilization of servers and devices in virtual environments. Hence, capital cost for recovery sites is negligible, and operational costs come into play as recovery sites are used. As organizations become accustomed to building recovery sites in the cloud, they are, with increasing frequency, moving their primary processing sites to the cloud as well.

Reciprocal Sites   A *reciprocal recovery site* is a data center that is operated by a separate company. Two or more organizations with similar processing needs will draw up a legal contract that obligates one or more of the organizations to house another party's systems temporarily in the event of a disaster. Often, a reciprocal agreement pledges not only floor space in a data center but also the use of the reciprocal partner's computer system. This type of arrangement is less common but is used by organizations that use mainframe computers and other high-cost systems.

NOTE   With the wide use of Internet co-location centers, reciprocal sites have fallen out of favor. Still, they may be ideal for organizations with mainframe computers that are otherwise too expensive to deploy to a cold or warm site.

Geographic Site Selection   An important factor in the process of recovery site selection is the location of the site. The distance between the main processing site and the recovery site is vital and may figure heavily into the viability and success of a recovery operation. A recovery site should not be located in the same geographic region as the primary site, because the site may be involved in the same regional disaster that affects the primary site and may be unavailable for use. By "geographic region," I mean a location that will likely experience the effects of the same regional disaster that affects the primary site. No arbitrarily chosen distance (such as 100 miles) guarantees sufficient separation. In some locales, 50 miles is plenty of distance; in other places, 300 miles is too close—it all depends on the nature of disasters that are likely to occur. Information on regional disasters should be available from local disaster preparedness authorities or from local disaster recovery experts.

Disaster Recovery for SaaS Services   Many organizations' principal business applications are SaaS-based, so the organization pays a monthly or yearly fee and uses software hosted by a service provider. At first glance, one may believe that DRP for SaaS services is entirely the responsibility of the SaaS provider. For the most part, this is true. There are,

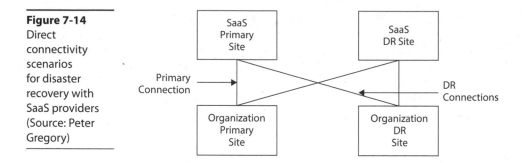

Figure 7-14 Direct connectivity scenarios for disaster recovery with SaaS providers (Source: Peter Gregory)

however, some issues that organizations need to consider as a part of their DRP, including the following:

- **Direct connectivity**   Organizations sometimes employ Multiprotocol Label Switching (MPLS) or virtual private network (VPN) circuitry between their SaaS provider and their core data center. If the SaaS provider experiences a disaster, the provider will host its service from a different location. Or if the organization experiences a disaster, it may be using an alternate processing site for its on-premises systems. In either case, those MPLS/VPN connections will need to change to continue operations. Figure 7-14 depicts this connectivity.

- **Integrations**   In addition to the connectivity issues, other issues regarding integration between the organization and the SaaS provider need to be understood, which can affect disaster response architectures developed for various disaster scenarios in the organization, the SaaS provider, or both. Issues may involve user and machine authentication, license keys, encryption keys, e-mail, and other message routing.

- **Fourth parties**   In addition to the organization and SaaS systems and their various integrations, functionality between the organization and its SaaS provider may involve other parties, such as message processors, security systems (such as event monitoring by an MSSP), customer relationship management (CRM), enterprise resource planning (ERP) integrations, and more.

Considerations When Using Third-Party Disaster Recovery Sites   Because most organizations cannot afford to implement their own secondary processing site, the only other option is to use a disaster recovery site that is owned by a third party, including cloud-based sites. This could be a co-location center, a disaster services center, or a cloud-based infrastructure service provider. An organization considering such a site needs to ensure that its service contract addresses the following:

- **Disaster definition**   The provider's definition of a disaster needs to be broad enough to meet the organization's requirements.

- **Equipment configuration**   IT equipment must be configured as needed to support critical applications during a disaster.

- **Availability of equipment during a disaster**   IT equipment needs to actually be available during a disaster. The organization needs to know how the disaster service provider will allocate equipment if many of its customers suffer a disaster simultaneously.

- **Customer priorities**   The organization needs to know whether any of the disaster services provider's other customers (government or military, for example) have priorities that may exceed their own.

- **Data communications**   The provider must have sufficient bandwidth and capacity for the organization plus other customers who may be operating at the provider's center at the same time.

- **Data sovereignty**   The organization should consider the geographic locations of stored data, particularly when that data involves private citizens. The locations of primary and recovery processing sites, together with the location of data subjects, may be affected by various privacy regulations.

- **Testing**   The organization needs to know what testing it is permitted to perform on the service provider's systems so that the ability to recover from a disaster can be assured prior to a disaster occurring.

- **Right to audit**   The organization should have a "right to audit" clause in its contract to verify the presence and effectiveness of all key controls in place at the recovery facility.

- **Security and environmental controls**   The organization needs to know what security and environmental controls are in place at the disaster recovery facility.

Considerations for a Distributed Workforce   During and after the COVID-19 pandemic, many organizations began hiring out-of-area personnel who worked from their homes most or all of the time. Organizations still operating data centers may find that few IT workers are located near primary or alternate processing centers. This "just-in-time" approach may be suitable for normal business operations, but disaster scenarios may result in few personnel being available for any necessary onsite work. For this reason, it's essential that disaster recovery plans be written for an audience with less familiarity with the organization's operations and practices, because it is possible that outsiders (such as contractors) will be performing some salvage and recovery tasks. For organizations with numerous remote employees, sufficient capacity for remote access (VPN) is essential to support business operations running on an emergency footing.

Acquiring Additional Hardware   Many organizations elect to acquire their own server, storage, and network hardware for disaster recovery purposes. How an organization will go about acquiring hardware will depend on its high-level recovery strategy:

- **Cold site**   An organization must be able to purchase hardware as soon as the disaster occurs.

- **Warm site**   An organization will need to purchase hardware in advance of the disaster, or it may be able to purchase hardware when the disaster occurs. The choice depends on the RTO.

- **Hot site** An organization should purchase its recovery hardware in advance of the disaster.
- **Cloud** An organization will not need to purchase hardware, as this is provided by the cloud infrastructure provider. Infrastructure in the cloud can likewise take on characteristics of being hot, warm, or cold.

Table 7-7 lists the pros and cons of these strategies. Warm-site strategy is not listed because an organization could purchase hardware either in advance of the disaster or when it occurs. Because cold, hot, and cloud sites are deterministic, they are included in the table.

The main reason an organization chooses to employ a cloud hosting provider is to eliminate capital costs. The provider supplies all hardware and charges organizations when the hardware is used. The primary business reason for not choosing a hot site is the high capital cost required to purchase disaster recovery equipment that may never be used. One way around this obstacle is to put those recovery systems to work every day. For example, recovery systems could be used for development or testing of the same applications that are used in production. This way, systems that are purchased for recovery purposes are being well utilized for other purposes, and they'll be ready in case a disaster occurs. When a disaster occurs, the organization will be less concerned about development and testing and more concerned about keeping critical production applications running. It will be a small sacrifice to forgo development or testing (or whatever low-criticality functions are using the recovery hardware) during a disaster.

 NOTE A cloud-based system recovery strategy can also be used in a hot, warm, or cold configuration.

Strategy	Advantages	Disadvantages
Hot	Hardware already purchased and ready for use	Capital tied up in equipment that may never be used Higher cost to continue maintaining recovery systems
Cold	Capital spent only if needed Lower costs (until a disaster occurs)	Suitable equipment may be difficult to find and purchase Difficult to test recovery strategy unless hardware is purchased, leased, or borrowed
Cloud	Zero capital costs Operational costs only as cloud-based infrastructure is used	Physical infrastructure owned and managed by a third party Potential for asset sprawl

Table 7-7 Hardware Acquisition Pros and Cons for Hot/Warm, Cold, and Cloud Recovery Sites

Recovery and Resilience Technologies   Once recovery targets have been established, the next major task is the survey and selection of technologies to enable RTOs and RPOs to be met. The following are important factors when considering each technology:

- Does the technology help the information system achieve the RTO, RPO, and RCapO targets?
- Does the cost of the technology meet or exceed budget constraints?
- Can the technology be used to benefit other information systems (thereby lowering the cost for each system)?
- Does the technology fit well into the organization's current IT operations?
- Will operations staff require specialized training to use the technology for recovery?
- Does the technology contribute to the simplicity of the overall IT architecture, or does it complicate it unnecessarily?

These questions are designed to help determine whether a specific technology is a good fit, from technology, process, and operational perspectives.

RAID   *Redundant Array of Independent Disks* (RAID) is a family of technologies used to improve the reliability, performance, or size of disk-based storage systems. From a disaster recovery or systems resilience perspective, the feature of RAID that is of particular interest is its reliability. RAID is used to create virtual disk volumes over an array (pun intended) of disk storage devices and can be configured so that the failure of any individual disk drive in the array will not affect the availability of data on the disk array.

RAID is usually implemented on a hardware device called a *disk array,* which is a chassis in which several hard disks can be installed and connected to a server. The individual disk drives can usually be "hot-swapped" in the chassis while the array is still operating. When the array is configured with RAID, a failure of a single disk drive will have no effect on the disk array's availability to the server to which it is connected. A system operator can be alerted to the disk's failure, and the defective disk drive can be removed and replaced while the array is still fully operational.

Several options, or levels, of RAID configuration are available:

- **RAID 0**   This is known as a striped volume, in which a disk volume splits data evenly across two or more disks to improve performance.
- **RAID 1**   This creates a mirror, where data written to one disk in the array is also written to a second disk in the array. RAID 1 makes the volume more reliable through the preservation of data, even when one disk in the array fails.
- **RAID 4**   This level employs data striping at the block level by adding a dedicated parity disk, which permits the rebuilding of data in the event one of the other disks fails.
- **RAID 5**   This is similar to RAID 4 block-level striping, except that the parity data is distributed evenly across all of the disks instead of being dedicated on one disk. Like RAID 4, RAID 5 allows for the failure of one disk without losing information.

PART IV

- **RAID 6** This is an extension of RAID 5, in which two parity blocks are used instead of a single parity block. RAID 6 can withstand the failure of any two disk drives in the array instead of a single disk, as is the case with RAID 5.

 NOTE Several nonstandard RAID levels have been developed by various hardware and software companies. Some of these are extensions of RAID standards, while others are entirely different.

Storage systems are hardware devices that are entirely separate from servers—their only purpose is to store a large amount of data. They are highly reliable through the use of redundant components and the use of one or more RAID levels. Storage systems generally come in two forms:

- **Storage area network (SAN)** This stand-alone storage system can be configured to contain several virtual volumes and can be connected to several servers through fiber-optic cables. The servers' operating systems will often consider this storage to be "local," as though it consisted of one or more hard disks present in the server's own chassis.

- **Network-attached storage (NAS)** This stand-alone storage system contains one or more virtual volumes. Servers access these volumes over the network using the Network File System (NFS) or Server Message Block/Common Internet File System (SMB/CIFS) protocols, common on Unix and Windows operating systems, respectively.

Replication During replication, data that is written to a storage system is also copied over a network to another storage system. The result is the presence of up-to-date data that exists on two or more storage systems, each of which could be located in a different geographic region. Replication can be handled in several ways and at different levels in the technology stack:

- **Disk storage system** Data-write operations that take place in a disk storage system (such as a SAN or NAS) can be transmitted over a network to another disk storage system, where the same data will be written to the other disk storage system.

- **Operating system** The operating system can control replication so that updates to a particular file system can be transmitted to another server, where those updates will be applied locally.

- **Database management system** The DBMS can manage replication by sending transactions to a DBMS on another server.

- **Transaction management system** The transaction management system (TMS) can manage replication by sending transactions to a counterpart TMS located elsewhere.

- **Application** The application can write its transactions to two different storage systems. This method is not often used.
- **Virtualization** Virtual machine images can be replicated to recovery sites to speed the recovery of applications.

Replication can take place from one system to another system, called *primary-backup* replication, and this is the typical setup when data on an application server is sent to a distant storage system for data recovery or disaster recovery purposes. Replication can also be bidirectional between two active servers; this is known as *multiprimary* or *multi-master* replication. This method is more complicated, because simultaneous transactions on different servers could conflict with one another (such as two reservation agents trying to book a passenger in the same seat on an airline flight). Some form of concurrent transaction control would be required, such as a *distributed lock manager.*

In terms of the speed and integrity of replicated information, there are two types of replication:

- **Synchronous replication** Writing data to a local and to a remote storage system is performed as a single operation, guaranteeing that data on the remote storage system is identical to data on the local storage system. Synchronous replication incurs a performance penalty, as the speed of the entire transaction is slowed to the rate of the remote transaction.
- **Asynchronous replication** Writing data to the remote storage system is not kept in sync with updates on the local storage system. Instead, there may be a time lag, and you have no guarantee that data on the remote system is identical to that on the local storage system. Performance is improved, however, because transactions are considered complete when they have been written to the local storage system only. Bursts of local updates to data will take a finite period to replicate to the remote server, subject to the available bandwidth of the network connection between the local and remote storage systems.

NOTE Replication is often used for applications where the RTO is smaller than the time necessary to recover data from backup media. For example, if a critical application's RTO is established to be two hours, recovery from backup tape is probably not a viable option unless backups are performed every two hours. While more expensive than recovery from backup media, replication ensures that up-to-date information is present on a remote storage system that can be put online in a short period.

Server Clusters A *cluster* is a collection of two or more servers that appear as a single server resource. Clusters are often the technology of choice for applications that require a high degree of availability and a very small RTO, measured in minutes. When an application is implemented on a cluster, even if one of the servers in the cluster fails, the other server (or servers) in the cluster will continue to run the application, usually with no user awareness that such a failure occurred.

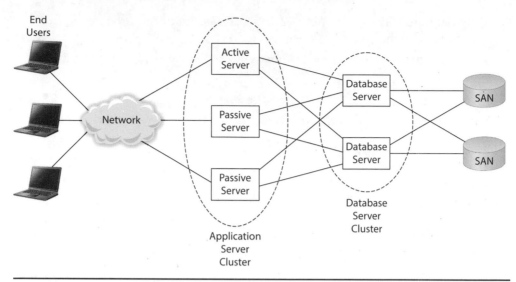

Figure 7-15 Application and database server clusters

There are two typical configurations for clusters, *active/active* and *active/passive*. In active/active mode, all servers in the cluster are running and servicing application requests. This is often used in high-volume applications where many servers are required to service the application workload. In active/passive mode, one or more servers in the cluster are active and servicing application requests, while one or more servers in the cluster are in a "standby" mode; they can service application requests but won't do so unless one of the active servers fails or goes offline for any reason. A *failover* occurs when an active server goes offline and a standby server takes over. Figure 7-15 shows a typical server cluster architecture.

A server cluster is typically implemented in a single physical location, such as a data center. However, in a *geographic cluster*, or geocluster, a cluster can be implemented where great distances separate the servers in the cluster. Servers in a geocluster are connected through a WAN connection. Figure 7-16 shows a typical geographic cluster architecture.

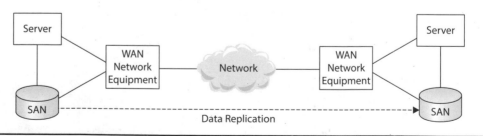

Figure 7-16 Geographic cluster with data replication

Network Connectivity and Services An overall application environment that is required to be resilient and have recoverability must have those characteristics present within the network that supports it. A highly resilient application architecture that includes clustering and replication would be of little value if it had only a single network connection that was a single point of failure.

An application that requires high availability and resilience may require one or more of the following in the supporting network:

- **Redundant network connections** These may include multiple network adapters on a server but also a fully redundant network architecture with multiple switches, routers, load balancers, and firewalls. This could also include physically diverse network provider connections, where network service provider feeds enter the building from two different directions.

- **Redundant network services** Certain network services are vital to the continued operation of applications, such as Domain Name System (DNS; the function of translating server names such as www.mheducation.com into an IP address), Network Time Protocol (NTP; used to synchronize computer time clocks), Simple Mail Transport Protocol (SMTP), Simple Network Management Protocol (SNMP), authentication services, and perhaps others. These services are usually operated on servers, which may require clustering and/or replication of their own, so that the application will be able to continue functioning in the event of a disaster.

Developing Disaster Recovery Plans

A DRP effort starts with the initial phases of the BCP project, the BIA and criticality analysis, which lead to the establishment of recovery objectives that determine how quickly critical business processes need to be back up and running. With this information, the disaster recovery team can determine what additional data processing equipment is needed (if any) and establish a road map for acquiring that equipment. Note that "equipment" may represent physical hardware or virtual assets in public or private cloud environments.

The other major component of the disaster recovery project is the development of recovery plans, the process and procedure documents that will be triggered when a disaster has been declared. These processes and procedures will instruct response personnel on how to establish and operate business processes and IT systems after a disaster has occurred. It's not enough to have all of the technology ready if personnel don't know what to do.

Most disaster recovery plans are going to have common components:

- **Disaster declaration procedure** Includes criteria for how a disaster is determined and who has the authority to declare a disaster

- **Roles and responsibilities** Specify what activities need to be performed and which people or teams are best equipped to perform them

- **Emergency contact lists**   Provide contact information for other personnel so that response personnel can establish and maintain communications as the disaster unfolds and recovery operations begin; lists should contain several different ways of contacting personnel since some disasters have an adverse impact on regional telecommunications infrastructure

- **System recovery procedures**   Detailed steps for getting recovery systems up and running, which describe obtaining data, configuring servers and network devices, testing to confirm that the application and business information is healthy, and starting business applications.

- **System operations procedures**   Detailed steps for operating critical IT systems while they are in recovery mode, because the systems in recovery mode may need to be operated differently than their production counterparts, and they may need to be operated by personnel who have not been doing this before

- **System restoration procedures**   Detailed steps to restore IT operations to the original production systems

 NOTE   Business continuity and disaster recovery plans work together to get critical business functions operating again after a disaster. Because of this, business continuity and disaster recovery teams need to work closely when developing their respective response procedures to ensure that all activities are covered, but without unnecessary overlap.

Disaster recovery plans should consider all the likely disaster scenarios that may occur to an organization. Understanding these scenarios can help the team take a more pragmatic approach when creating response procedures. The added benefit is that not all disasters result in the entire loss of a computing facility. Most are more limited in their scope, although all of them can still result in a complete inability to continue operations. Some of these scenarios are as follows:

- Partial or complete loss of network connectivity

- Sustained electric power outage

- Loss of a key system (such as a server, storage system, or network device)

- Extensive data corruption or data loss

These scenarios are probably more likely to occur than a catastrophe such as a major earthquake or hurricane (depending on where a data center is located).

Data Backup and Recovery

Disasters, cyberattacks (primarily ransomware and destructware), and other disruptive events can damage information and information systems. It's essential that fresh copies of information exist elsewhere and in a form that enables IT personnel to load the information easily into alternative systems so that processing can resume as quickly as possible.

NOTE Testing backups is important; testing recoverability is critical. In other words, performing backups is valuable only to the extent that backed-up data can be recovered at a future time. In addition, it is a good practice to ensure that backups are segmented off the corporate network to prevent an attacker from being able to destroy both production and backup data.

Backup to Tape and Other Media   In organizations still utilizing their own IT infrastructure, tape backup is just about as ubiquitous as power cords. From a disaster recovery perspective, however, the issue probably is not whether the organization has tape backup, but whether its current backup capabilities are adequate in the context of disaster recovery. An organization's backup capability may need to be upgraded if:

- The current backup system is difficult to manage.
- Whole-system restoration takes too long.
- The system lacks flexibility with regard to disaster recovery (for instance, a high degree of difficulty is required to recover information onto a different type of system).
- The technology is old or outdated.
- Confidence in the backup technology is low.

Many organizations may consider tape backup as a means of restoring files or databases when errors have occurred, and they may have confidence in their backup system for that purpose. However, the organization may have somewhat less confidence in its backup system and its ability to recover *all* of its critical systems accurately and in a timely manner.

Although tape has been the default medium since the 1960s, many organizations use hard drives for backup: hard disk transfer rates are far higher, and a disk is a random-access medium, whereas tape is a sequential-access medium. A virtual tape library (VTL) is a type of data storage technology that sets up a disk-based storage system with the appearance of tape storage, permitting existing backup software to continue to back data up to "tape," which is really just more disk storage.

E-vaulting is another viable option for system backup. E-vaulting permits organizations to back up their systems and data to an offsite location, which could be a storage system in another data center or a third-party service provider. This accomplishes two important objectives: reliable backup and offsite storage of backup data.

Backup schemes, backup media rotation methods, and backup media storage are discussed in Chapter 6.

Incident Classification/Categorization

No two security incidents or disasters are alike: some may threaten the very survival of an organization, while others are minor, bordering on insignificant. The degree and type of response must be appropriate for the severity of the incident in terms of mobilization, speed, and communications. Further, an incident may or may not have an

Incident Severity	Incident Impact	Description and Examples
1	Affects a single individual	Policy violation Compromise of a function
2	Affects a workgroup	Compromise or interruption of an important function
3	Affects a department or business unit	Compromise of intellectual property of a critical function
4	Affects the entire organization internally	Significant compromise of intellectual property or interruption of a critical function
5	Affects the entire organization publicly	Significant compromise of personally identifiable information or multiple critical functions

Table 7-8   Example Single-Dimensional Incident Severity Plan

impact on sensitive information, including intellectual property and personally identifiable information (PII).

Organizations generally classify incidents according to severity, typically on a 3-, 4-, or 5-point scale. Organizations that store or process intellectual property, confidential data about their employees, or sensitive information about clients or customers often assign incident severity levels according to the level of impact on this information. Tables 7-8 and 7-9 depict two such schemes for classifying security incidents.

In Table 7-8, incidents are assigned a single numeric value of 1 to 5 based upon the impact as described. In Table 7-9, incidents are assigned a numeric value and an alphabetic value, based on impact on operations and impact on information. For example, an incident involving the loss of an encrypted laptop computer would be classified as 1A, whereas a ransomware incident where some production information has been lost would be classified as 4E or 5E.

Severity Classification	Impact to Operations	Sensitivity Classification	Description
1	No impact to operations	A	No impact on information
2	Minor impact on operations	B	Compromise of a small volume of critical information
3	Critical function impaired	C	Compromise of a moderate volume of critical information
4	Critical function unavailable or significantly impaired	D	Compromise of a large volume of critical information
5	Critical functions unavailable	E	Loss or damage to all critical information

Table 7-9   Example Two-Dimensional Incident Severity Plan

The purpose of classifying incidents by severity level provides guidance on several aspects of response:

- Numbers of personnel assigned to response and recovery
- Utilization of external resources for response and recovery
- Frequency of updates given to executive leadership
- Updates provided to outside parties, including customers, suppliers, shareholders, regulators, and law enforcement
- Emergency spending capabilities and limits
- Notifications to the workforce regarding work assignments

The severity scales discussed here are applicable to security incidents as well as disasters. Both are business-disrupting events that require mobilization, response, communication with key parties, containment, and closure.

Incident Management Training, Testing, and Evaluation

Organizations do not perform incident response plans every day. While low-severity plans may be performed from time to time, high-severity plans may be used rarely, perhaps only once every several years. Organizations that want to have confidence in their incident response plans need to train personnel in their use and test their response plans from time to time to ensure that they will work as expected.

Although security incident response, business continuity plans, and disaster recovery plans are related to one another in some scenarios, it is important to distinguish each from the others. Each has a specific purpose, but in some scenarios, two or all three of these plans may be activated at once.

Security Incident Response Training

Like any procedure, incident response goes far better if responders have been trained prior to an actual incident occurring. Unlike many security procedures, during a security incident, emotions can run high, and those unfamiliar with the procedures and principles of incident response can get tripped up and make mistakes. This is not unlike the emotion and stress that other types of emergency responders, such as firefighters and police officers, may experience.

Incident response training should cover all of the scenarios that the organization is likely to face, ranging from the not-so-dire events such as stolen mobile devices and laptop computers to the truly catastrophic events such as a prolonged DDoS attack, destructive ransomware, or the exfiltration of large amounts of sensitive data.

Incident response personnel should be trained in the use of tools used to detect, examine, and remediate an incident. This includes SOC personnel who use a security information and event management (SIEM) system; security orchestration, automation, and response (SOAR); threat intelligence platform (TIP); and other detection and investigation tools. It also includes forensic specialists who use specialized forensic analysis tools and all personnel who have administrative responsibilities for every type of IT equipment, application, and tool.

Security Incident Response Professional Certifications

Security professionals specializing in incident response should consider one or more of the specialty certifications in incident response, including the following (in alphabetical order):

- **Certified Computer Examiner (CCE)**   www.isfce.com/certification.htm
- **EC-Council Certified Incident Handler (ECIH)**   www.eccouncil.org/programs/ec-council-certified-incident-handler-ecih/
- **GIAC Certified Forensic Analyst (GCFA)**   www.giac.org/certifications/certified-forensic-analyst-gcfa/
- **GIAC Certified Incident Handler (GCIH)**   www.giac.org/certification/certified-incident-handler-gcih
- **GIAC Network Forensic Analyst (GNFA)**   www.giac.org/certifications/network-forensic-analyst-gnfa/
- **GIAC Reverse Engineering Malware (GREM)**   www.giac.org/certifications/reverse-engineering-malware-grem/
- **Professional Certified Investigator (PCI)**   www.asisonline.org/certification/professional-certified-investigator-pci/

A number of vendor-specific certifications are also available, including EnCase Certified Examiner (EnCe) for professionals using the EnCase forensics tool, and AccessData Certified Examiner (ACE) for professionals who use Forensic Toolkit (FTK).

Business Continuity and Disaster Response Training

The value and usefulness of a high-quality set of disaster response and continuity plans and procedures will be greatly diminished if those responsible for carrying out the procedures are unfamiliar with them. A person cannot learn to ride a bicycle by reading even the most detailed instructions on the subject, and it's equally unrealistic to expect personnel to be able to carry out disaster response procedures properly if they are inexperienced in those procedures. Often, the best way to train responders is to participate in testing of business continuity and disaster recovery plans. Learning will be more effective if they understand that these tests are not only about testing the accuracy and effectiveness of the plans, but they also provide an opportunity for responders to become familiar with and be trained on those plans.

Training should not be limited to primary operations personnel and should also include others who may be responding in an actual disaster scenario. Remember that some disasters result in some personnel being unavailable for a variety of reasons.

Several forms of training can be made available for personnel who are expected to be available if a disaster strikes, including the following:

- **Document review** Personnel can carefully read through procedure documents to become familiar with the nature of the recovery procedures. As mentioned, this alone may be insufficient.

- **Participation in walk-throughs** People who are familiar with specific processes and systems should participate in the walk-through processes that deal with those issues. Exposing personnel to the walk-through process will not only help to improve the walk-through and recovery procedures but will also be a learning experience for participants.

- **Participation in simulations** Taking part in simulations will benefit the participants by giving them the experience of thinking through a disaster.

- **Participation in parallel and cutover tests** Other than experiencing an actual disaster and its recovery operations, no experience is quite like participating in parallel and cutover tests. Participants can gain actual hands-on experience with critical business processes and IT environments by performing the same procedures that they would perform in the event of a disaster. When a disaster strikes, those participants can draw upon their experience rather than recalling the information they read in procedure documents.

All of the test levels that need to be performed to verify the quality of response plans are also training opportunities for personnel. The development and testing of disaster-related plans and procedures provide a continuous learning experience for all of the personnel involved.

Testing Security Incident Response Plans

Security incident response plans must be documented and reviewed, but they also need to be periodically tested. Security incident response testing helps to improve the quality of those plans, which will help the organization better respond when an incident occurs. A by-product of security incident plan testing is the growing familiarity of personnel with security incident response procedures. Various types of tests should be carried out:

- **Document review** Individual subject-matter experts (SMEs) carefully read security incident response documentation to understand the procedures and identify any opportunities for improvement.

- **Walk-through** Similar to a document review, this is performed by a group of SMEs who talk through the security incident response plan. Discussing each step helps to stimulate new ideas that could lead to improvements in the plan.

- **Simulation** A facilitator describes a realistic security incident scenario, and participants discuss how they will actually respond. A simulation usually takes half a day or longer. It is suggested that the simulation be "scripted" with new information and updates introduced throughout the scenario. A simulation can be limited to the technical aspects of a security incident, or it can involve corporate communications, public relations, legal, and other externally facing parts of the organization that may play a part in a security incident that is known to the public.

- **Live fire**   During a penetration test, personnel who are monitoring systems and networks jump into action in response to the scans, probes, and intrusions being performed by penetration testers. Note that those personnel could be told in advance about the penetration test; however, it would be more valuable for them to gain experience in responding to a real attack if they were not told in advance. During a test, incident responders need to respond carefully so that their actions do not cause real incidents.

These tests should be performed once each year or even more often. In the walk-through and simulation tests, someone should be appointed as a note-taker so that any improvements will be recorded and the plan can be updated. Tests should include incidents addressed in each playbook and at each classification level so that all procedures will be tested. Regardless of the type of test conducted, an after-action or lessons-learned session should be conducted. Any identified recommendations or remedial actions should be incorporated into incident response plans and supporting documentation.

If the incident response plan contains the names and contact information of response personnel, the plan should be reviewed more frequently to ensure that all contact information is up to date.

Testing Business Continuity and Disaster Recovery Plans

It is amazing how much can be accomplished if no one cares who gets the credit.

—John Wooden

Business continuity and disaster recovery plans may look elegant and even ingenious on paper, but their true business value is unknown until their worth is proven through testing. The process of testing these plans uncovers flaws not only in the plans but also in the systems and processes that they are designed to protect. For example, testing a system recovery procedure might point out the absence of a critically needed hardware component, or a recovery procedure might contain a syntax or grammatical error that misleads the recovery team member and results in recovery delays. Testing is designed to uncover these types of issues.

Testing Recovery and Continuity Plans

Recovery and continuity plans should be tested to prove their viability. Without testing, an organization has no way of really knowing whether its plans are effective. And with ineffective plans, an organization has a far smaller chance of surviving a disaster.

Recovery and continuity plans have built-in obsolescence—not by design but by virtue of the fact that technology and business processes in most organizations are undergoing constant change and improvement. Thus, it is imperative that newly developed or updated plans be tested as soon as possible to ensure their effectiveness.

Types of tests range from lightweight and unobtrusive to intense and disruptive:

- Walk-through
- Simulation
- Parallel test
- Cutover test

 TIP   Usually, an organization should perform the less intensive tests first to identify the most obvious flaws, followed by tests that require more effort.

Test Preparation

Each type of test requires advance preparation and recordkeeping. Preparation will consist of several items:

- **Participants**   The organization will identify personnel who will participate in an upcoming test. It is important to identify all relevant skill groups and department stakeholders so that the test will include a full slate of contributors. This would also include key vendors/partners to support their systems.

- **Schedule**   The availability of each participant needs to be confirmed so that the test will include participation from all stakeholders.

- **Facilities**   For all but the document review test, proper facilities, such as a large conference room or training room, should be identified and set up. If the test takes several hours, one or more meals and refreshments may be needed as well.

- **Scripting**   The simulation test requires some scripting, usually in the form of one or more documents that describe a developing scenario and related circumstances. Scenario scripting can make parallel and cutover tests more interesting and valuable, but this can be considered optional.

- **Recordkeeping**   For all tests except the document review, one or more people should take good notes that can be collected and organized after the test is completed.

- **Contingency plan**   The cutover test involves the cessation of processing on primary systems and the resumption of processing on recovery systems. This is the highest risk plan, and things can go wrong. Develop a contingency plan to get primary systems running again in case something goes wrong during the test.

Table 7-10 shows these preparation activities.

	Document Review	Walk-through	Simulation	Parallel Test	Cutover Test
Participants	Yes	Yes	Yes	Yes	Yes
Schedule	Yes	Yes	Yes	Yes	Yes
Facilities		Yes	Yes	Yes	Yes
Scripting			Yes	Optional	Optional
Recordkeeping	Yes	Yes	Yes	Yes	Yes
Contingency plan					Yes

Table 7-10 Preparation Activities for Disaster Recovery Business Continuity Tests

Document Review   A *document review* test reviews some or all disaster recovery and business continuity plans, procedures, and other documentation. Individuals typically review these documents on their own, at their own pace, but within established time constraints or deadlines. The purpose of this test is to review the accuracy and completeness of document content. Reviewers should read each document with a critical eye, point out any errors, and annotate the document with questions or comments that can be returned to the document's author (or authors), who can make any necessary changes. If significant changes are needed in one or more documents, the project team may want to include a second document review before moving on to more resource-intensive tests.

The owner or document manager for the organization's BCP and DRP project should document which people review which documents and perhaps include the review copies or annotations. This practice will create a complete record of the activities related to the development and testing of important DRP and BCP documents. It will also help to capture the true cost and effort of the development and testing of BCP capabilities in the organization.

Walk-through   A *walk-through* is similar to a document review but includes only the BCP documents. However, where a document review is carried out by individuals working on their own, a walk-through is performed by an entire group of individuals in a live discussion. A walk-through is usually facilitated by a leader who guides the participants page by page through each document. The leader may read sections of the document aloud, describe various scenarios where information in a section may be relevant, and take comments and questions from participants.

A walk-through is likely to take considerably more time than a document review. One participant's question on some minor point in the document could spark a worthwhile and lively discussion that could last from a few minutes to an hour. The group leader or another person should take careful notes to record any deficiencies are discovered in any of the documents, as well as issues to be handled after the walk-through. The leader should be able to control the pace of the review so that the group does not get unnecessarily hung up on minor points. Some discussions may need to be cut short or tabled for a later time or for an offline conversation among interested parties.

Even if major revisions are required in recovery documents, it will probably be infeasible to conduct another walk-through with the updated documents. Follow-up document reviews are probably warranted, however, to ensure that they were updated appropriately, at least in the opinion of the walk-through participants.

TIP Participants in the walk-through should carefully consider that the potential audience for recovery procedures may be people who are not as familiar as they are with the organization's systems and processes. They need to remember that the ideal personnel may not be available during an actual disaster. Participants also need to realize that the skill level of recovery personnel may be a little below that of the experts who operate systems and processes in normal circumstances. Finally, walk-through participants need to remember that systems and processes undergo almost continuous change, which could render some parts of the recovery documentation obsolete or incorrect all too soon.

Simulation   A *simulation* is a test of disaster recovery and business continuity procedures where the participants take part in a "mock disaster" to add some realism to the process of thinking their way through procedures included in emergency response documents. A simulation could be an elaborate and choreographed walk-through test, where a facilitator reads from a script and describes a series of unfolding events in a disaster such as a hurricane or an earthquake. This type of simulation could be viewed as a sort of play-acting, where the script is the emergency response documentation. After stimulating the imagination of simulation participants, participants may find it easier to imagine what disaster recovery and business continuity procedures would be like if an actual disaster occurs. It will help tremendously if the facilitator has actually experienced one or more disaster scenarios to add more realism when describing events.

To make the simulation more credible and valuable, the chosen scenario should have a reasonable chance of actually occurring in the local area. Good choices would include an earthquake in San Francisco or Los Angeles, a volcanic eruption in Seattle, or an avalanche in Switzerland. A poor choice would be a hurricane or tsunami in Central Asia, because these events would never occur there. A simulation can also go a few steps further. For instance, the simulation can take place at an established emergency operations center, the same place where emergency command and control would operate in a real disaster. Also, the facilitator could change some of the participants' roles to simulate the absence of certain key personnel to see how the remaining personnel may conduct themselves in a real emergency.

NOTE   The facilitator of a simulation is limited only by her own imagination when organizing a simulation. One important fact to remember, though, is that a simulation does not actually affect any live or disaster recovery systems—it's all as pretend as the make-believe cardboard television sets and computers in furniture stores.

Parallel Test A *parallel test* is an actual test of disaster recovery and/or business continuity response plans and their supporting IT systems. Its purpose is to evaluate the ability of personnel to follow directives in emergency response plans—to set up the disaster recovery business processing or data processing capability. In a parallel test, personnel are setting up the IT systems that would be used in an actual disaster and operating those IT systems with real business transactions to determine whether the IT systems perform the processing correctly.

The outcome of a parallel test is threefold:

- It evaluates the accuracy of emergency response procedures.
- It evaluates the ability of personnel to follow the emergency response procedures correctly.
- It evaluates the ability of IT systems and other supporting apparatus to process real business transactions properly.

A parallel test is so named because, as live production systems continue to operate, the backup IT systems are processing business transactions in parallel, to test whether both systems process transactions equally well. Setting up a valid parallel test is complicated in many cases. In effect, you need to insert a logical "Y cable" into the business process flow so that the information flow will split and flow both to production systems (without interfering with their operation) and to the backup systems.

Results of transactions are compared. Personnel need to be able to determine whether the backup systems would be able to output correct data without actually having them do so. In many complex environments, you would not want the disaster recovery system to feed information into a live environment, because that may cause duplicate events to occur someplace else in the organization (or with customers, suppliers, or other parties). For instance, in a travel reservations system, you would not want a disaster recovery system to book actual travel, because that would cost real money and consume available space on an airline or other mode of transportation. But it would be important to know whether the disaster recovery system would be *able* to perform those functions. Somewhere along the line, it will be necessary to "unplug" the disaster recovery system from the rest of the environment and manually examine the results.

Organizations that want to see whether their backup/disaster recovery systems can manage a real workload can perform a cutover test, which is discussed next.

Cutover Test A *cutover test,* the most intrusive type of disaster recovery test, also provides the most reliable results in terms of answering the question of whether backup systems have the capacity and correct functionality to shoulder the real workload. The consequences of a failed cutover test, however, may resemble an actual disaster: if any part of the cutover test fails, real, live business processes will be proceeding without the support of IT applications, as though a real outage or disaster were in progress. But even a failure like this would reveal whether the backup systems will or won't work if an actual disaster were to happen.

In some respects, a cutover test is easier to perform than a parallel test. A parallel test is a little trickier, because business information is required to flow to the production system *and* to the backup system, which means that some artificial component has been somehow inserted into the environment. With a cutover test, business processing takes place on the backup systems only, which can often be achieved through a simple configuration someplace in the network or the systems layer of the environment.

When conducting a cutover test, you should determine ahead of time how long the backup platform will be running. Additionally, a cutover test may be a good time to check the security controls of the backup platform.

 NOTE Not all organizations perform cutover tests, because they take a lot of resources to set up and they are risky. Many organizations find that a parallel test is sufficient to determine whether backup systems are accurate, and the risk of an embarrassing incident is almost zero with a parallel test.

Documenting Test Results

Every type and every iteration of disaster recovery plan testing needs to be documented. It's not enough to say, "We did the test on September 10, 2021, and it worked." First of all, no test goes perfectly—opportunities for improvement are always identified. But the most important part of testing is to discover what parts of the plan or the test should be reworked before the next test (or a real disaster) occurs.

As with any well-organized project, success is in the details. The road to success is littered with big and little mistakes, and the things that are identified in every sort of disaster recovery test need to be detailed so that the next iteration of the test will provide better results. Here are some key metrics that can be reported:

- Time required to perform key tasks
- Accuracy of tasks performed (or number of retries needed)
- Amount of data recovered
- Performance against recovery targets, including RTO, RPO, RCO, and RCapO

Recording and comparing detailed test results from one test to the next will also help the organization measure progress. By this, I mean that the quality of disaster response plans should steadily improve from year to year. Simple mistakes of the past will not be repeated, and the only failures in future tests should be in new and novel parts of the environment that weren't well thought out to begin with. And even these should diminish over time.

Improving Recovery and Continuity Plans

Every test of recovery and response plans should include a debriefing or review so that participants can discuss the outcome of the test: what went well, what went wrong, and how things should be done differently next time. This information should be recorded by someone who will be responsible for making changes to relevant documents. The updated documents should be circulated among test participants, who can confirm whether their discussion and ideas are properly reflected in the document.

Evaluating Business Continuity Planning

Audits and evaluations of an organization's business continuity plan are especially difficult, because it is difficult to prove whether the plans will work unless a real disaster is experienced. The lion's share of an evaluation result hinges on the quality of documentation and discussions with key personnel. The evaluation of an organization's business continuity program should begin with a top-down analysis of key business objectives and a review of documentation and interviews to determine whether the business continuity strategy and program details support those key business objectives. This approach is depicted in Figure 7-17.

The objectives of a BCP evaluation should include the following activities:

- *Obtain documentation that describes current business strategies and objectives.* Obtain high-level documentation (such as strategy, charter, and objectives) for the business continuity program and determine whether and how the program aligns with business strategies and objectives.

- *Obtain the most recent BIA and accompanying threat analysis, risk analysis, and criticality analysis.* Determine whether these documents are current and complete, and whether they support the business continuity strategy. Also determine whether the scope of these documents covers those activities considered strategic according to high-level business objectives. Finally, determine whether the methods in these documents represent good practices for these activities.

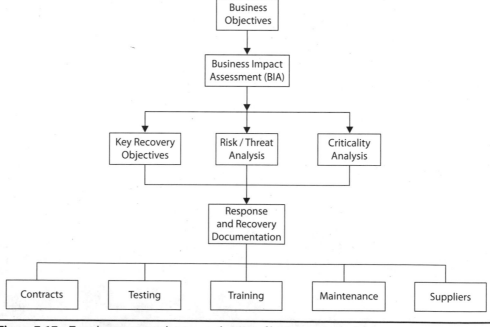

Figure 7-17 Top-down approach to an evaluation of business continuity

- *Determine whether key personnel are ready to respond during a disaster by reviewing test plans and training plans and results.* Learn where emergency procedures are stored and whether key personnel have access to them.

- *Verify whether a process is in place for the regular review and update of business continuity documentation.* Evaluate the process' effectiveness by reviewing records to determine how frequently documents are reviewed.

Examining Business Continuity Documentation

The bulk of an organization's business continuity plan lies in its documentation, so it should be little surprise that the bulk of any evaluation will rest in the examination of this documentation. The following steps will help determine the effectiveness of the organization's business continuity plans:

1. Obtain a copy of business continuity documentation, including response procedures, contact lists, and communication plans.

2. Examine samples of distributed copies of business continuity documentation and determine whether they are up-to-date. These samples can be obtained during interviews of key response personnel, which are covered in this procedure.

3. Determine whether all documents are clear and easy to understand, not just for primary responders, but for alternate personnel who may have specific relevant skills but less familiarity with the organization's critical applications. In some disaster scenarios, primary responders may be unavailable to carry out disaster response activities.

4. Examine documentation related to the declaration of a disaster and the initiation of disaster response. Determine whether the methods for declaration are likely to be effective in a disaster scenario.

5. Obtain emergency contact information, and contact some of the personnel to determine whether the contact information is accurate and up-to-date. Also check to see that all response personnel are still employed in the organization and are in the same or similar roles in support of disaster response efforts.

6. Contact some or all of the response personnel who are listed in emergency contact lists. Interview them to see how well they understand their disaster response responsibilities and whether they are familiar with disaster response procedures. Ask each interviewee whether they have a copy of these procedures, and ask whether their copies are current.

7. Determine whether a process exists for the formal review and update of business continuity documentation. Examine records to see how frequently, and how recently, documents have been reviewed and updated.

8. Determine whether response personnel receive any formal or informal training on response and recovery procedures. Determine whether personnel are required to receive training and whether any records are kept that show which personnel received training and at what time.

9. Determine whether business continuity planners perform tests, walk-throughs, and exercises of plans, and whether retrospectives or after-action reviews of tests are performed to identify opportunities for improvement.

Reviewing Prior Test Results and Action Plans

The effectiveness of business continuity plans relies, to a great degree, on the results and outcomes of tests. Examine these tests carefully to determine their effectiveness and to what degree they are used to improve procedures and train personnel. The following will help determine the effectiveness of business continuity testing:

- Determine whether a strategy exists for testing business continuity procedures. Obtain records for past tests and a plan for future tests. Determine whether prior tests and planned tests are adequate for establishing the effectiveness of response and recovery procedures.

- Examine records for tests that have been performed over the past few years, and determine the types of tests that were performed. Obtain a list of participants for each test. Compare the participants to lists of key recovery personnel. Examine test work papers to determine the level of participation by key recovery personnel.

- Determine whether a formal process exists for recording test results and for using those results to make improvements in plans and procedures. Examine documents and records to determine the types of changes that were recommended in prior tests. Examine business continuity documents to determine whether these changes were made as expected.

- Considering the types of tests that were performed, determine the adequacy of testing as an indicator of the effectiveness of the business continuity program. Were only document reviews and walk-throughs performed, for example, or were parallel or cutover tests conducted?

- If tests have been performed for two years or more, determine whether continuous improvement in response and recovery procedures exists.

- If the organization performs parallel tests, determine whether tests are designed in a way that effectively determines the actual readiness of standby processes and systems. Also determine whether parallel tests measure the capacity of standby systems or merely their ability to process correctly but at a lower level of performance.

Interviewing Key Personnel

The knowledge and experience of key personnel are vital to the success of any business continuity operation. Interviews will help determine whether key personnel are prepared and trained to respond during a disaster. The following will guide discussions:

- Ask the interviewee to summarize his or her professional experience and training and current responsibilities in the organization.

- Ask whether he or she is familiar with the organization's business continuity and disaster recovery programs.

- Determine whether he or she is among the key response personnel expected to respond during a disaster.

- Ask whether the interviewee has been issued a copy of any response or recovery procedures. If so, ask to see those procedures to determine whether they are current versions. Ask if the interviewee has additional sets of procedures in any other locations (residence, for example).

- Ask whether he or she has received any training. Request evidence of this training (certificate, calendar entry, notes, and so on).

- Ask whether the interviewee has participated in any tests or evaluations of recovery and response procedures. Ask whether the tests were effective, whether management takes the tests seriously, and whether any deficiencies in tests resulted in any improvements to test procedures or other documents.

Reviewing Service Provider Contracts

No organization is an island. Every organization has critical suppliers without which it could not carry out its critical functions. The ability to recover from a disaster also frequently requires the support of one or more service providers or suppliers. The examiner or auditor should examine contracts for all critical suppliers and consider the following questions:

- Does the contract support the organization's requirements for delivery of services and supplies, even in the event of a local or regional disaster?

- Does the service provider have its own disaster recovery capabilities that will ensure its ability to deliver critical services during a disaster?

- Is recourse available should the supplier be unable to provide goods or services during a disaster?

Finally, the examiner or auditor should determine whether the organization can continue its own critical business process should a key service provider experience its own disaster. The service provider may elect to activate an alternate processing center; will the organization's systems be able to connect to the service provider's disaster recovery systems easily and continue functioning as expected? Are there instructions for connecting systems to the service provider's disaster recovery systems?

Reviewing Insurance Coverage

The examiner or auditor should examine the organization's insurance policies related to the loss of property and assets supporting critical business processes. Insurance coverage should include the actual cost of recovery or a lesser amount if the organization's executive management has accepted that. Obtain documentation that includes cost estimates for various disaster recovery scenarios, including equipment replacement, business interruption, and the cost of performing business functions and operating IT systems in alternate sites. These cost estimates should be compared with the value of insurance policies.

Evaluating Disaster Recovery Planning

The evaluation of a disaster recovery program and its plans should focus on their alignment with the organization's business continuity plans. To a great extent, DRP should support BCP so that the organization's most critical business processes will have companion disaster recovery plans that may need to be activated when a natural or human-made disaster impairs information systems at the organization's primary processing facility.

The objectives of an examination or audit of DRP should include the following activities:

- Determine the effectiveness of planning and recovery documentation by examining previous test results.

- Evaluate the methods used to store critical information offsite (which may consist of offsite storage, alternate data centers, replication, or e-vaulting).

- Examine environmental and physical security controls in any offsite or alternate sites and determine their effectiveness.

- Note whether offsite or alternate site locations are within the same geographic region, which could mean that both the primary and alternate sites could be involved in common disaster scenarios.

Evaluating Disaster Recovery Plans

The following will help determine the effectiveness of an organization's disaster recovery plans:

- Obtain a copy of the disaster recovery documentation, including response procedures, contact lists, and communication plans.

- Examine samples of distributed copies of the documentation and determine whether they are up-to-date. These samples can be obtained during interviews of key response personnel, which are covered in this procedure.

- Determine whether all documents are clear and easy to understand, not just for primary responders, but for alternate personnel who may have specific relevant skills but less familiarity with the organization's critical applications. Remember that primary responders may be unavailable in some disaster scenarios, and that others may need to carry out disaster recovery plan procedures.

- Obtain contact information for offsite storage providers, hot-site facilities, and critical suppliers. Determine whether these organizations are still providing services to the organization. Call some of the contacts to determine the accuracy of the documented contact information.

- For organizations using third-party recovery sites such as cloud infrastructure providers, obtain contracts and records that define organization and cloud provider obligations, service levels, and security controls.

- Obtain logical and physical architecture diagrams for key IT applications that support critical business processes. Determine whether disaster recovery and business continuity documentation includes recovery procedures for all components that support those IT applications. Determine whether documentation includes recovery for end users and administrators for the applications.

- If the organization uses a hot site, examine one or more systems to determine whether they have the proper versions of software, patches, and configurations. Examine procedures and records related to the tasks in support of keeping standby systems current, and determine whether these procedures are effective.

- If the organization has a warm site, examine the procedures used to bring standby systems into operational readiness. Examine warm-site systems to see whether they are in a state where readiness procedures will likely be successful.

- If the organization has a cold site, examine all documentation related to the acquisition of replacement systems and other components. Determine whether the procedures and documentation are likely to result in systems capable of hosting critical IT applications within the period required to meet key recovery objectives.

- If the organization uses a cloud service provider's service as a recovery site, examine the procedures used to prepare and bring cloud-based systems to operational readiness. Examine procedures and configurations to see whether they are likely to support the organization successfully during a disaster.

- Determine whether any documentation exists regarding the relocation of key personnel to the alternate processing site. Check that the documentation specifies which personnel are to be relocated and what accommodations and supporting logistics are provided. Determine the effectiveness of these relocation plans.

- Determine whether backup and offsite (or replication or e-vaulting) storage procedures are being followed. Examine systems to ensure that critical IT applications are being backed up and that proper media are being stored offsite (or that the proper data is being replicated or e-vaulted). Determine whether data recovery tests are ever performed and, if so, whether the results of those tests are documented and problems are properly dealt with.

- Evaluate procedures for transitioning processing from the alternate processing facility back to the primary processing facility. Determine whether these procedures are complete and effective, and whether they have been tested.

- Determine whether a process exists for the formal review and update of business continuity documentation to ensure continued alignment with DRP. Examine records to see how frequently, and how recently, documents have been reviewed and updated. Determine whether this is sufficient and effective by interviewing key personnel to understand whether significant changes to applications, systems, networks, or processes are reflected in recovery and response documentation.

- Determine whether response personnel receive any formal or informal training on response and recovery procedures. Determine whether personnel are required to receive training, and whether any records are kept that show which personnel received training and at what time.

- Examine the organization's change control process. Determine whether the process includes any steps or procedures that require personnel to decide whether any change has an impact on disaster recovery documentation or procedures.

Reviewing Disaster Recovery Test Results and Action Plans

The effectiveness of disaster recovery plans relies on the results and outcomes of tests. The examiner or auditor needs to examine these plans and activities to determine their effectiveness. The following will help examine disaster recovery testing:

- Determine whether a strategy or policy is in place for testing disaster recovery plans. Obtain records for past tests and a plan for future tests.

- Examine records for tests that have been performed over the past year or two. Determine the types of tests that were performed. Obtain a list of participants for each test, and compare the participants to lists of key recovery personnel. Examine test work papers to determine the level of participation by key recovery personnel.

- Determine whether there is a formal process for recording test results and for using those results to make improvements in plans and procedures. Examine work papers and records to determine the types of changes that were recommended in prior tests. Examine disaster recovery documents to see whether these changes were made as expected.

- Considering the types of tests that were performed, check the adequacy of testing as an indicator of the effectiveness of the disaster recovery program. Did the organization perform only document reviews and walk-throughs, for example, or did the organization also perform parallel or cutover tests?

- If tests have been performed for two years or more, check for continuous improvement in response and recovery procedures.

- If the organization performs parallel tests, determine whether tests are designed in a way that effectively determines the actual readiness of standby systems. Also, determine whether parallel tests measure the capacity of standby systems or merely their ability to process correctly but at a lower level of performance.

- Determine whether any tests included the retrieval of backup data from offsite storage, replication, or e-vaulting facilities. See what disaster scenarios were tested and the types of recovery procedures that were performed.

It is important to keep in mind that a cyberattack may trigger a disaster scenario. Disaster recovery plans must address scenarios such as ransomware and wiper attacks.

Evaluating Offsite Storage

Storage of critical data and other supporting information is a key component in any organization's disaster recovery plan. Because some types of disasters can completely destroy a business location, including its vital records, it is imperative that all critical information is backed up and copies moved to an offsite storage facility. The following will help determine the effectiveness of offsite storage:

- Obtain the location of the offsite storage or e-vaulting facility. Determine whether the facility is located in the same geographic region as the organization's primary processing facility.

- If possible, visit the facility and examine its physical security controls as well as its safeguards to prevent damage to stored information in a disaster. Consider the entire spectrum of physical and logical access controls. Examine procedures and records related to the storage and return of backup media and other information that the organization may store there. If it is not possible to visit the facility, obtain copies of audits or other attestations of controls effectiveness.

- Take an inventory of backup media and other information stored at the facility. Compare this inventory with a list of critical business processes and supporting IT systems to determine whether all relevant information is, in fact, stored at the facility.

- Determine how often the organization performs its own inventory of the facility and whether steps to correct deficiencies are documented and remedied.

- Examine contracts, terms, and conditions for offsite storage providers or e-vaulting facilities, if applicable. Determine whether data can be recovered to the original processing center and to alternate processing centers within a period that will ensure that disaster recovery can be completed within RTOs.

- Determine whether the appropriate personnel have current access codes or license keys for offsite storage or e-vaulting facilities and whether they have the ability to recover data from those facilities.

- Determine what information, in addition to backup data, exists at the facility. Information stored offsite should include architecture diagrams, design documentation, operations procedures, and configuration information for all logical and physical layers of technology and facilities supporting critical IT applications, operations documentation, application source code, and software build systems.

- Obtain information related to the manner in which backup media and copies of records are transported to and from the offsite storage or e-vaulting facility. Determine the adequacy of controls protecting transported information.

- Obtain records supporting the transport of backup media and records to and from the storage facility. Examine samples of records and determine whether they match other records, such as backup logs.

NOTE Organizations need to balance the time practicing backup procedures with procedures used to perform different types of recovery scenarios.

Evaluating Alternate Processing Facilities

The examiner or auditor needs to examine alternate processing facilities to determine whether they are sufficient to support the organization's business continuity and disaster recovery plans. The following will help determine whether an alternate processing facility will be effective:

- Obtain addresses and other location information for alternate processing facilities. These will include hot sites, warm sites, cold sites, cloud-based services, and alternate processing centers owned or operated by the organization. Note that exact locations of cloud services are often unavailable for security reasons.

- Determine whether alternate facilities are located within the same geographic region as the primary processing facility and note whether the alternate facility will also be adversely affected by a disaster that strikes the primary facility.

- Perform a threat analysis on the alternate processing site. Determine which threats and hazards pose a significant risk to the organization and its ability to carry out operations effectively during a disaster.

- Determine the types of natural and human-made events likely to take place at the alternate processing facility. Determine whether there are adequate controls to mitigate the effect of these events.

- Examine all environmental controls and determine their adequacy. This should include environmental controls (HVAC), power supply, uninterruptible power supply (UPS), power distribution units (PDUs), switchgear, and electric generators. Also, examine fire detection and suppression systems, including smoke detectors, pull stations, fire extinguishers, sprinklers, and inert gas suppression systems.

- If the alternate processing facility is a separate organization, obtain the legal contract and all exhibits. Examine these documents and determine whether the contract and exhibits support the organization's recovery and testing requirements.

NOTE Cloud-based service providers often do not permit onsite visits. Instead, they may have one or more external audit reports available through standard audits such as SSAE 18, ISAE 3402, SOC 1, SOC 2, ISO, or PCI. It is vital to determine whether external audit reports are reliable and whether any controls are not covered in external audits.

Evaluating Security Incident Response

Evaluating security incident response plans can be a challenge, because it can be difficult to know whether plans will work, or whether personnel will understand how to follow them, when a real security incident occurs. Evaluation should use the top-down approach, shown in Figure 7-17, by examining business strategies and objectives, high-level documentation, and finally the incident response plans and playbooks themselves.

The steps and details for evaluating security incident response plans are virtually the same as those of evaluations of BCPs and DRPs: plans should be thorough, specific, business aligned, and maintained. Various exercises, from document walk-throughs to live-fire testing, should be performed to ensure that plans are accurate and that personnel use them correctly. After-action reviews should be performed, with follow-through on all action items that were identified.

Evaluations of security incident response plans need to be associated with risk and threat assessments: when new risks and threats are identified, the organization must ensure that detective controls, preventive controls, and response plans address them. Because risks, threats, and detective and preventive capabilities change frequently, reviews and updates to incident response plans and playbooks likewise must be frequent.

Chapter Review

Security incident management, disaster recovery planning, and business continuity planning all support a central objective: resilience and rapid recovery when disruptive events occur.

A security incident occurs when the confidentiality, integrity, or availability of information or information systems has been or is in danger of being compromised. The proliferation of connected devices makes life safety an additional consideration in many organizations.

An organization that is developing security incident response plans needs to determine high-level objectives so that response plans will meet these objectives.

With the proliferation of outsourcing to cloud-based service providers, many security incidents now take place in third-party organizations, which requires additional planning and coordination so that any incident response involving a third party is effective.

BCP and DCP work together to ensure the survival of an organization during and after a cyberattack, natural disaster, or human-made disaster.

The business impact analysis identifies the impact of various disaster scenarios and determines the most critical processes and systems in an organization. The BIA helps an organization focus its BCP and DRP on the most critical business functions. Statements of impact help management better understand the results of disruptive events in business terms. In a criticality analysis, each system and process is studied to consider the impact on the organization if it is incapacitated, the likelihood of incapacitation, and the estimated cost of mitigating the risk or impact of incapacitation.

Maximum tolerable downtime and maximum tolerable outage inform the development of recovery targets, including recovery time objective, recovery point objective, and recovery capacity objective, to help an organization understand how quickly various business processes should be recovered after a disaster. Recovery speed is an important factor as the cost of recovery varies widely.

Business continuity plans define the methods the organization will use to continue critical business operations after a disaster has occurred. Disaster recovery plans define the steps that will be undertaken to salvage and recover systems damaged by a disaster.

Both BCP and DRP activities work toward the restoration of capabilities in their original (or replacement) facilities.

The safety of personnel is the most important consideration in any disaster recovery plan.

DRP is concerned with system resilience matters, including data backup and replication, the establishment of alternate processing sites (hot, warm, cold, cloud, mobile, or reciprocal), and the recovery of applications and data. The complexity of a disaster recovery plan necessitates reviews and testing to ensure that the plan is effective and will be successful during an actual disaster.

Recovery targets established during the BIA directly influence disaster recovery plans through the development of suitable infrastructure and response plans.

Security incident response plans, business continuity plans, and disaster recovery plans all need to be evaluated and tested to ensure their suitability. Organizations need to identify and train incident responders to ensure that they will understand how to respond to incidents properly and effectively.

Notes

- Understanding the computer intrusion kill chain model can help an organization identify opportunities to make their systems more resilient to intruders.

- The development of custom playbooks that address specific types of security incidents will ensure a more rapid and effective response to an incident. High-velocity incidents such as data wipers and ransomware require a rapid, almost-automated, response.

- Organizations must carefully understand all of the terms and exclusions in any cyber-insurance policy to ensure that no exclusions would result in a denial of benefits after an incident.

- With so many organizations using cloud-based services, it's especially important that organizations understand, in detail, their own roles and responsibilities as well as those of each cloud service provider. This will ensure that the organization can build effective incident response should an incident occur at a cloud-based service provider.

- Recovery objectives such as recovery time objective and recovery point objective serve as signposts for the development of risk mitigation plans and business continuity plans. Eventually, plans in support of these objectives must be developed and tested, usually in the context of business continuity planning.

Questions

1. Which of the following recovery objectives is associated with the longest allowable period for a service outage?

    A. Recovery tolerance objective (RTO)

    B. Recovery point objective (RPO)

    C. Recovery capacity objective (RCapO)

    D. Recovery time objective (RTO)

2. A security manager is developing a strategy for making improvements to the organization's incident management process. The security manager has defined the desired future state. Before specific plans can be made to improve the process, the security manager should perform a:

    A. Training session

    B. Penetration test

    C. Vulnerability assessment

    D. Gap analysis

3. A large organization operates hundreds of business applications. How should the security manager prioritize applications for protection from a disaster?

    A. Conduct a business impact analysis.

    B. Conduct a risk assessment.

    C. Conduct a business process analysis.

    D. Rank the applications in order of criticality.

4. The types of incident response plan testing are:

    A. Document review, walk-through, and simulation

    B. Document review and simulation

    C. Document review, walk-through, simulation, parallel test, and cutover test

    D. Document review, walk-through, and cutover test

5. An organization has developed its first-ever business continuity plan. What is the first test of the continuity plan that the business should perform?

    A. Walk-through

    B. Simulation

    C. Parallel test

    D. Cutover test

6. An organization is experiencing a ransomware attack that is damaging critical data. What is the best course of action?

    A. Security incident response

    B. Security incident response followed by business continuity plan

    C. Concurrent security incident response and business continuity plan

    D. Business continuity plan

7. What is the most important consideration when selecting a hot site?

   A. Time zone

   B. Geographic location in relation to the primary site

   C. Proximity to major transportation

   D. Natural hazards

8. An organization has established a recovery point objective of 14 days for its most critical business applications. Which recovery strategy would be the best choice?

   A. Mobile site

   B. Warm site

   C. Hot site

   D. Cold site

9. What technology should an organization use for its application servers to provide continuous service to users?

   A. Dual power supplies

   B. Server clustering

   C. Dual network feeds

   D. Transaction monitoring

10. An organization currently stores its backup media in a cabinet next to the computers being backed up. A consultant told the organization to store backup media at an offsite storage facility instead. What risk did the consultant most likely have in mind when he made this recommendation?

    A. A disaster that damages computer systems can also damage backup media.

    B. Backup media rotation may result in loss of data backed up several weeks in the past.

    C. Corruption of online data will require rapid data recovery from offsite storage.

    D. Physical controls at the data processing site are insufficient.

11. A major earthquake has occurred near an organization's operations center. Which of the following should be the organization's top priority?

    A. Ensuring that an automatic failure to the recovery site will occur because personnel may be slow to respond

    B. Ensuring that visitors know how to evacuate the premises and that they are aware of the locations of sheltering areas

    C. Ensuring that data replication to a recovery site has been working properly

    D. Ensuring that backup media will be available at the recovery site

12. An organization wants to protect its data from the effects of a ransomware attack. What is the best data protection approach?

   A. Periodically scan data for malware.

   B. Replicate data to a cloud-based storage provider.

   C. Replicate data to a secondary storage system.

   D. Back up data to offline media.

13. An auditor is evaluating an organization's disaster recovery plan. Which of the following artifacts should be examined first?

   A. Business impact analysis

   B. After-action reviews

   C. Test results

   D. Training records

14. An organization's top executives are growing tired of receiving reports about minor security incidents. What is the best course of action?

   A. Enact controls to stop the incidents from occurring.

   B. Discontinue informing executives about incidents.

   C. Develop an incident severity schedule.

   D. Review regulatory requirements for incident disclosure.

15. An organization has established a recovery time objective of four hours for its most critical business applications. Which recovery strategy would be the best choice?

   A. Mobile site

   B. Warm site

   C. Hot site

   D. Cold site

Answers

1. **D.** RTO is the maximum period of time from the onset of an outage until the resumption of service.

2. **D.** When the desired end state of a process or system is determined, a gap analysis must be performed so that the current state of the process or system can also be known. Then specific tasks can be performed to reach the desired end state of the process.

3. **A.** A business impact analysis (BIA) is used to identify the business processes to identify the information systems that are most critical for the organization's ongoing operations.

4. **A.** The types of security incident response plan testing are a document review, a walk-through, and a simulation. Parallel and cutover tests are not part of security incident response planning or testing but are used for disaster recovery planning.

5. **A.** The best choice of tests for a first-time business continuity plan is a document review or a walk-through. Since this is a first-time plan, other tests are not the best choices.

6. **C.** If an organization's critical data has been damaged or destroyed by a ransomware incident, the organization should invoke its business continuity plan alongside its security incident response plan. This may help the organization restore services to its customers more quickly.

7. **B.** An important selection criterion for a hot site is the geographic location in relation to the primary site. If they are too close together, a single disaster event may involve both locations.

8. **D.** An organization that has a 14-day recovery time objective (RTO) can use a cold site for its recovery strategy. Fourteen days is enough time for most organizations to acquire hardware and recover applications.

9. **B.** An organization that wants its application servers to be available continuously to its users needs to employ server clustering so that at least one server will always be available to service user requests.

10. **A.** The primary reason for employing offsite backup media storage is to mitigate the effects of a disaster that could otherwise destroy computer systems and their backup media.

11. **B.** The safety of personnel is always the top priority when any disaster event has occurred. While important, the condition of information systems is a secondary concern.

12. **D.** The best approach for protecting data from a high-velocity attack such as ransomware is to back up the data to offline media that cannot be accessed by end users. Replicating data to another storage system may only serve to replicate damaged data to the secondary storage system, making recovery more difficult or expensive.

13. **A.** The auditor should first examine business impact analysis documents, as these define the priority of critical business processes as well as recovery targets.

14. **C.** It is apparent that the security incident response plan does not have severity levels. One property of severity levels is the frequency and level of internal communications. For instance, executives are spared from being informed about minor incidents while they occur. Higher severity incidents include notifications to managers higher in the organization, and more frequent notifications.

15. **C.** An organization that has a four-hour recovery time objective (RTO) should use a hot site for its recovery strategy. Only a hot site would be able to perform primary processing within that period of time.

Incident Management Operations

In this chapter, you will learn about
- The steps of security incident response
- Incident response tools and techniques
- Attorney–client privilege
- Crisis management and communications
- Post incident review and reporting

This chapter covers Certified Information Security Manager (CISM) Domain 4, "Incident Management," part B, "Incident Management Operations." The entire Incident Management domain represents 30 percent of the CISM examination.

One Supporting Task in the CISM job practice aligns with the Incident Management / Incident Management Operations domain:

37. Conduct post-incident reviews to facilitate continuous improvement, including root-cause analysis, lessons learned, corrective actions, and reassessment of risk.

Security incidents cannot be prevented—at least not all of them. In this asymmetric cyber war, attackers have innovation, time, and the element of surprise on their side. It is imperative that every organization using IT develop formal security incident response plans, train their personnel, and continually practice with walk-throughs, drills, and simulations.

Formal, organized security incident response techniques have undergone continuous improvement over many decades and are described in this chapter. These are the phases of incident response:

- Planning
- Detection
- Initiation
- Analysis
- Containment

- Eradication
- Recovery
- Remediation
- Closure
- Post-incident review
- Retention of evidence

Planning

This step involves the development of written response plans, guidelines, and procedures to be followed when an incident occurs. These procedures are created after the organization's practices, processes, and technologies are well understood. This helps to ensure that incident response procedures align with security policy, business operations, the technologies in use, as well as practices regarding organizational architecture, development, management, and operations. The plans, guidelines, and procedures should identify and include key external partners. The planning cannot be conducted in a vacuum, because many organizations rely on partners for key business functions.

Detection

Detection represents the moment in which an organization is initially aware that a security incident is taking place or has taken place. Because a variety of events can characterize a security incident, an organization can become aware of an incident in several ways, including the following:

- Application or network slowdown or malfunction
- Alerts from intrusion detection system (IDS), intrusion prevention system (IPS), data loss prevention (DLP) system, web content filter, cloud access security broker (CASB), extended detection and response (XDR), antivirus, firewalls, and other detective and preventive security systems
- Alerts from a security information and event management (SIEM) system
- Media outlets and their investigators and reports
- Notification from an employee or business partner
- Anonymous tips
- Notification from a regulator
- Notification from a media outlet

Initiation

This is the phase in which response to the incident begins. Typically, it includes declaration of an incident, followed by notifications sent to response team members so that response operations may begin. Depending upon the severity of the incident, notifications may be sent to business executives.

Analysis

In this phase, response team members collect and analyze available data to understand the incident's cause, scope, and impact. This may involve the use of forensic analysis tools to understand activities on individual systems. During this phase, partners or vendors may be engaged to collect information from their systems to determine the extent of the compromise.

Containment

Incident responders perform or direct actions that halt, or contain, the progress or advancement of an incident. The steps required to contain an incident will vary according to the means used by the attacker. Techniques include blocking command and control traffic or taking storage systems offline. Senior leadership is usually involved in approving the containment actions of the team. In some cases, a mature incident response program will already have rules of engagement so the technical teams know which actions are approved and which need input from senior leadership.

Eradication

In this phase of incident response, responders take steps to remove the source of the incident. This could involve removing malware or physically removing an intruder.

Recovery

When the incident has been evaluated and eradicated, there is often a need to recover systems or components to their pre-incident state. This can include restoring data or configurations or replacing damaged or stolen equipment.

Remediation

This activity involves any necessary changes that will reduce or eliminate the possibility of a similar incident occurring in the future. This may take the form of process or technology changes.

Closure

Closure occurs when eradication, recovery, and remediation have been completed. Incident response operations are officially closed.

Post-incident Review

Shortly after the incident closes, incident responders and other personnel meet to discuss the incident: its cause, impact, and the organization's response. Discussion can range from lessons learned to possible improvements in technologies and processes to improve defense and response further.

Retention of Evidence

Incident responders and other personnel direct the retention of evidence and other materials used or collected during the incident. This may include information used in legal proceedings such as prosecution, civil lawsuits, and internal investigations. A chain of custody may be required to ensure the integrity of evidence.

NOTE Several standards guide organizations toward a structured and organized incident response, including NIST SP 800-61, "Computer Security Incident Handling Guide."

Incident Management Tools and Techniques

Security incident management is driven primarily by automation in all but the tiniest organizations. Because a wide variety of security-related events may occur, most organizations rely upon centralized log management and a SIEM system that automatically collects security event log data and generates alerts based on rules, or use cases. Incident response plans, then, consist of the manual and tool-assisted steps taken by personnel when a SIEM generates an alert.

The discovery of security incidents can take on many forms. A SIEM may alert personnel to a security incident, but an organization can become aware of a potential incident in several other ways. The types of detection that may occur are outlined later in this chapter. The framework of security incident response is the main topic of this chapter.

Incident Response Roles and Responsibilities

A security incident response plan contains information about specific roles and responsibilities to ensure that a security incident is handled correctly and promptly. Typical defined roles and responsibilities include the following:

- **Reporting security problems**   Many organizations enact policies that require all personnel to report suspicious issues to security personnel.

- **Incident detection**   This may occur via dedicated security event monitoring personnel (in a security operations center, or SOC) or by people with other responsibilities. In the former case, personnel will periodically examine event logs or be sent messages when security events occur. Also, help desk or service desk personnel need to be trained to recognize security incidents while working with end users and troubleshooting problems.

- **Incident declaration**   Some personnel are granted roles that can formally declare a security incident. They are usually trained to recognize various types of incidents and follow procedures to notify others of an incident. Incident declaration formally triggers the performance of incident response procedures and communications.

- **Incident commander**   Some personnel coordinate various activities as an incident unfolds and is managed. For this role, organizations typically select domain experts and other personnel with technical skills and backgrounds, who can direct other personnel as an incident is examined, contained, and resolved. In severe and prolonged incidents, incident commanders will take shifts.

- **Internal communications** These roles are designated to communicate information about an incident to personnel inside the organization, to keep other internal parties informed on the proceedings of the incident and its response.

- **External communications** These personnel are authorized to communicate with outside parties, including law enforcement, regulators, customers, partners, suppliers, shareholders, and the public. Typically, the matter of external communications is shared, with one or more people who must approve any external communications and those who do the actual communicating.

- **Legal counsel** Inside or outside counselors are generally responsible for interpreting applicable laws, regulations, and legal agreements, and they advise other incident response personnel of steps that should (or should not) be taken. In many cases, incident investigations are protected by attorney–client privilege, which requires that legal counsel be involved in the main proceedings of the incident.

- **Scribe** One or more scribes maintain records of all the proceedings. This includes but is not limited to actions taken by all incident response personnel, decisions, communications, and the location of records such as retained logs and artifacts from forensic analysis.

- **Forensic analysis** Many security events require one or more people with expertise in computer and/or network forensics who seek to determine the cause of an incident and methods that can be used to contain and eradicate it. Because some security incidents may result in subsequent legal proceedings, forensic analysts employ evidence preservation techniques and establish a chain of custody to ensure that evidence is not altered.

- **Containment, eradication, remediation, and recovery** These personnel take measures to halt an incident's progress and recover affected systems to their pre-incident states. While containment, eradication, remediation, and recovery are four distinct steps in incident response, they are often performed by the same personnel.

- **Business continuity and emergency operations** A significant incident may result in considerable downtime or other business disruption, as one or more critical systems may be affected by an incident and taken out of service. An organization may need to invoke business continuity and/or emergency operations to continue critical business operations.

 NOTE Remember that, despite the noise and disruption caused by a serious incident, normal business operations need to continue uninterrupted in the organization.

Incident Response Tools and Techniques

The detection of most security incidents, including malware and intrusions, requires the use of tools. Without these tools, organizations may be unaware of any incident in progress and may not learn of the incident until months or years later, if ever. Some tools are used to examine and analyze an incident that has been identified. They help security personnel understand events in one or more systems and/or networks. Other tools are sometimes used to eradicate and recover from an incident. Finally, tools can be used to chronicle all the events of an incident for later analysis during post-incident review and beyond. Incident response tools include the following:

- **Logging** Events on individual systems and network devices often provide direct or indirect indications of intrusions and other incidents. Logs stored in a central server make this capability more powerful, as events from different systems and devices can appear together, providing a more comprehensive view of events.

- **Log analysis and correlation** A SIEM provides log analysis and correlation to help security personnel realize when unwanted events are occurring or have occurred in the past.

- **Alerting** A SIEM or other log processing system can be configured to produce alerts when specific incidents occur, proactively notifying security personnel that something requires attention.

- **Threat hunting** Specialized tools are available to facilitate proactive threat hunting.

- **Threat intelligence** Many organizations subscribe to one or more cyber-threat intelligence feeds that help make personnel aware of actionable threats, enabling them to confirm that protective and detective measures are in place. Some threat intel feeds are meant to be fed directly into a SIEM, which will correlate threats with identified vulnerabilities to direct personnel to improve defenses. Other threat intel feeds are intended to be human-readable. This functionality is often packaged in a threat intelligence platform (TIP).

- **Malware prevention** Antivirus and advanced antimalware solutions on mobile devices, laptops, and servers detect the presence of malware and can often block or disrupt its activities. Malware detection and prevention capabilities can also be provided by firewalls, IPSs, web filters, and spam/phishing filters.

- **Network intrusion prevention** IPSs analyze the details and contents of network traffic that passes through them, detecting—and often blocking—an initial intrusion or the command-and-control (C&C) traffic generated by malware that has successfully compromised a system. A typical IPS is configured to block specific traffic automatically and produce alerts when this occurs, but it will permit certain traffic. Network intrusion detection will alert personnel of suspected attacks, without doing anything to stop them.

- **Web content filter** Many organizations employ systems that provide protection from the hazards of users browsing malicious and fraudulent web sites. Web content filters can be used to block access to known malicious sites as well as sites associated with various types of inappropriate content. For example, an organization can block users' from accessing sites that focus on pornography, weapons, hate crimes, or online gambling. Some web content filters can examine the contents of traffic and can block malware from reaching end-user devices.

- **File integrity monitoring (FIM)**   FIM systems periodically scan file systems on servers and workstations and report any changes. Although changes may result from periodic maintenance, they can also be indicators of compromise. A typical FIM system sends alerts to a SIEM to notify SOC analysts of a potential intrusion.

- **File activity monitoring (FAM)**   FAM systems monitor directories and files on servers or workstations to detect unusual activities that may indicate compromise. A typical FAM system sends alerts to a SIEM, where SOC analysts will be watching for alerts.

- **Forensic analysis**   These tools are used to study the events that have occurred on a system, examine the contents of file systems and memory, and analyze malware to understand its structure and actions. Their use requires forensic skills and experience, as they usually don't reveal what happened, but instead show detailed information to a forensic examiner, who determines which elements to examine to uncover the relevant chain of events. Forensic analysis is used to examine a malware attack and chronicle the events of an employee accused of misbehavior.

- **Video surveillance**   This is needed for incidents involving human activity— usually the comings and goings of personnel and intruders and any items they are carrying with them.

- **Recordkeeping**   Decisions, steps undertaken, and communications need to be recorded so that incident responders can understand the activities that have taken place during incident response and provide a backward look during post-incident review.

Incident Monitoring by MSSPs

Organizations may outsource security monitoring to a managed security services provider (MSSP). Because security incidents may proceed rapidly, some organizations prefer to have an outside expert organization perform around-the-clock security monitoring of its critical systems to provide expert detection and rapid notification of suspected and confirmed incidents. Some MSSPs may be able to perform additional steps of incident response, including analysis and containment of an incident, on their customers' behalf.

Organizations that choose to outsource security monitoring do so for several reasons, including the following:

- **Domain expertise**   Personnel at an MSSP have security monitoring and incident detection expertise.

- **Dedicated personnel**   The staff at an MSSP have only one job: monitoring customers' systems to identify and respond to security incidents. Unlike an organization's security staff, the personnel at an MSSP are not distracted by other activities or projects, other than the continuous improvement of event monitoring.

- **Staffing shortage**   It is difficult for many organizations to identify, recruit, and retain qualified information security personnel. Outsourcing security monitoring relieves organizations of the burden of staffing their security monitoring function.

- **Cost control**   The fees charged by MSSPs may be less than the salaries, benefits, tools, workspaces, and other costs required for in-house staff, mainly because of economies of scale: MSSP personnel typically perform security monitoring for numerous organizations.

Threat Hunting

The practice of *threat hunting* is used proactively to look for signs of intrusions. Rather than passively monitoring systems, threat hunters use tools to hunt for indicators of compromise (IOCs). The objective of threat hunting is the earliest possible detection of intrusions. When an intrusion is detected early, its impact on the organization may be low, particularly if an attack is detected prior to the intruder achieving her attack objective. Threat hunting is often carried out by organizations with mature event monitoring programs. In other words, organizations considering threat hunting should do so only after achieving a moderate to high level of maturity in their monitoring tools and practices.

Incident Response Retainers

An *incident response retainer* (IRR) is a legal agreement between an organization and a security professional services firm (sometimes the same MSSP used to detect incidents) that contracts to assist the organization in the event of a security incident. The agreement may include a service level agreement (SLA) that commits the security firm to respond quickly to an organization's call for assistance. The IRR agreement may consist of prepaid services, hourly rates for incident response, and other provisions that define roles and responsibilities.

Depending upon the nature of a security incident, the security firm may send forensic experts to the client's location to perform forensics, or, if the incident does not require onsite work, the client organization may send malware samples, incident logs, or other digital information to the security firm, where analysis can be performed remotely. In some cases, the organization experiencing an incident may need a security firm to act as an incident commander who may fulfill the role of managing the organization's activities in response to the incident.

External Legal Counsel

Some organizations retain outside legal counsel through a *retainer agreement*. External legal advisors can provide expertise in the legal aspects of security incident response. Outside counsel can advise an organization on the interpretation of laws regarding cybersecurity and privacy, and it may offer counsel regarding contracts with other organizations as well. An external legal counsel may also be used to assist with legal activities and logistics related to incident response.

Cyber-insurance Companies and Incident Response

Although organizations have been able to purchase cyber-insurance policies for decades, it is only in the last few years that cyber-insurance companies have become intimately involved in organizations' security practices and incident response. This involvement has deepened in recent years following a plague of ransomware attacks and large insurance payouts. As a result, cyber-insurance companies are doing the following:

- Becoming keenly aware of the specific risk factors leading to costly incidents
- Thoroughly vetting organizations' security programs and capabilities, using lengthy questionnaires and requests for specific artifacts such as security policies and even detailed configuration information
- Creating policies with more detailed terms, conditions, and exclusions
- Charging organizations higher premiums with limitations in benefits if an organization is deemed to have substandard security practices and safeguards in place, or denying them coverage at any price
- Becoming deeply involved in security incident response, sometimes by directing one of a short list of security professional services firms to perform computer and network forensics

It is becoming increasingly difficult to obtain cyber-insurance as insurance companies are becoming more stringent on requirements such as multifactor authentication and antimalware. It is imperative that an organization be aware of the fine print of its cyber-security policy; otherwise, the organization may find the policy is worthless when it's time to file a claim.

Incident Investigation and Evaluation

Any response to a security incident consists of several phases, from detection, to closure, to post-incident review. The phases of security incident response are part of a model. As such, security managers realize that certain types of incidents don't require all of the steps included in the model. A stolen laptop computer may require virtually no eradication activities, for example. And a violation of security policy, such as a user sharing login credentials, will pivot into an internal investigation that may result in disciplinary action.

Some incidents may require additional phases. For instance, a security incident involving the theft of a large volume of information will require a series of post-incident proceedings that may represent greater efforts and costs than the initial incident response. Regardless of the seriousness of the incident, successful incident response requires considerable planning, and this involves allocating roles and responsibilities and using multiple tools and techniques.

Incident Detection

The detection phase marks the start of an organization's awareness of a security incident. In many cases, some time elapses between the beginning of an actual incident and the moment that the organization is aware of it; this period is known as *dwell time*. The ability to detect an intrusion or incident requires *event visibility*, which is typically achieved through event log collection and analysis tools (usually a SIEM system), together with other tools that monitor and detect activities in networks, servers, and endpoints.

An organization can be made aware of an incident in a number of ways, including but not limited to the following:

- **Reporting by an employee**   An organization's personnel can be aware of certain types of incidents, especially misbehavior by other employees.

- **Reporting by a MSSP or SOC analyst**   Personnel monitoring the organization's networks and systems are likely to detect suspicious activities and initiate an investigation and response.

- **Reporting by a customer or client**   An organization's customers or clients may have noticed phenomena related to a breach and may report it to the organization.

- **Social media**   Clients, customers, and other parties may report observations about a security incident via social media, particularly if they have no other means of notifying the organization.

- **Notification from law enforcement or regulator**   In the case of information theft, outside organizations and agencies may become aware through higher rates of fraud. Law enforcement investigations reveal the source of the intrusion.

- **Notification from a security researcher**   Security researchers sometimes discover vulnerabilities or signs of intrusion in other organizations' networks.

- **Unknown persons**   Occasionally, someone not associated with the organization will notify the organization of a security problem. For example, a passer-by may notice discarded assets tossed aside by someone who stole them.

- **IT personnel or end users**   A security incident may initially appear as a malfunction or error in a system or application. Only through analysis is the malfunction determined to be caused by an intruder. For this reason, IT service desk personnel need to be trained in the art of detecting security issues when users call for help.

Shortening Dwell Time

According to notable research organizations, dwell time for computer intrusions often exceeds 200 days in many organizations. Realizing this is unacceptable, organizations are implementing better tools that provide earlier warnings of anomalous activities that could be signs of an intrusion. These include SIEM systems that receive the event logs of all servers, endpoints, and network devices, along with tools such as advanced antimalware software, FIM tools, FAM tools, and network and system anomaly detection tools. The velocity of today's cyberattacks demands that organizations become aware of incidents and begin responding within minutes. The consequences of delays can be considerable.

Incident Initiation

When an organization realizes that a security incident has occurred or is occurring, an incident responder will make an incident declaration, signaling the initiation phase. An organization's security incident response plan should include a procedure for initiating an incident. This generally consists of notifying key personnel, including the security manager and the IT manager (whose actual titles may vary), and personnel on the incident response team. Incident response personnel may then initiate and join an emergency communications conference bridge or assemble in a war room. The group will select an incident commander, who will coordinate the use of resources and internal communications to enable the team to work effectively to manage the incident.

False Alarms

Some people are concerned with the prospect of declaring an incident when no incident is taking place—in other words, a false alarm. Organizations need to understand that a false alarm from time to time may be acceptable, especially considering that the opposite problem of not recognizing and declaring an incident may be far more harmful to the organization. It's better to roll the fire trucks and later discover that the alarm was caused by a faulty smoke detector than to use valuable time confirming the presence of a fire, which could result in more property damage and threat to human life.

Incident Analysis

In the analysis phase of security incident response, response team members evaluate and rank available information to reveal the nature and criticality of the incident. This phase may include the use of forensic examination techniques that permit the examiner to determine how an incident was able to occur.

Incident Ranking and Rating

The types and severities of security incidents vary significantly; a relatively minor incident such as the loss of a laptop computer with encrypted contents would be considered far less serious than the theft and exploitation of a large database containing sensitive customer information, for example. Accordingly, an organization's incident response plans should include steps to determine the scope and severity of an incident. This will help the organization determine the amount and types of resources that may be required, and it may determine whether executive management is informed of an incident. Chapter 7 includes a detailed explanation of incident ranking, including the different responses based upon rank.

Forensic Investigations

After a security incident has occurred, the organization may determine that an investigation is needed to determine the incident's cause and effects. A forensic investigator gathers, studies, and retains information that may be needed in a court of law should the incident result in legal proceedings. Because the information collected in an investigation may later be used in a legal proceeding, a forensic investigator must understand the requirements regarding the *chain of custody* and other evidence protection activities that ensure that evidence can be used in court.

Chain of Custody   The key to an effective and successful forensic investigation is the establishment of a sound chain of custody. A chain of custody documents, in precise detail, how and when evidence is protected against tampering through every step of the investigation. Any irregularities in the information acquisition and analysis process will likely be looked at unfavorably in legal proceedings, possibly resulting in the organization failing to convince judicial authorities that the event occurred as described.

Chain of custody is driven primarily by the prospect of future legal proceedings for reasons that could include the following:

- Disciplinary actions against employees, if insiders perpetrated the incident
- Prosecution of perpetrators
- Lawsuits brought by affected parties, particularly employees or customers
- Investigations by regulators

Several major considerations determine the effectiveness of a forensic investigation:

- **Identification**   This includes a description of the evidence acquired and the tools and techniques used to acquire it. Evidence may include digital information acquired from computers, network devices, and mobile devices, as well as interviews of involved people.
- **Preservation**   Several tools and techniques are used to retain evidence. Preservation will include detailed records establishing the chain of custody, which may be presented and tested in legal proceedings.
- **Analysis**   This description of the examination of the evidence gathered may include a reconstruction of events that are the subject of the investigation.
- **Presentation**   This formal document describes the entire investigation, evidence gathered, tools used, and findings that express the examiner's opinion of the events that occurred (or did not occur).

Forensic Techniques and Considerations   Computer and network forensics require several specialized techniques that ensure the integrity of the entire forensic investigation and a sound chain of evidence. Some of these techniques are listed here:

- **Data acquisition**   Data must be acquired for forensic analysis. Subject data may reside on a computer's hard drive, SSD, or RAM; in mobile device memory; in an application's audit log; or on a network device. Several tools are available for forensic data acquisition, including media copiers, which acquire a copy of a computer's hard drive, live memory, USB memory stick, or removable media such as an external hard drive, SSD, or CD/DVD-ROM.

- **Data extraction** If data is being acquired from a running system or a third party, a forensics analyst must use a secure method to acquire the data and demonstrate the integrity of the process used to do so. This shows the data's source and proves that data was not altered during the extraction process.

- **Data protection** Once data is extracted, the forensic investigator must take particular steps to ensure its integrity. Computers used for forensic analysis must be physically locked to prevent unauthorized access, and they must not be connected to any network that would allow for the introduction of malware or other agents that could alter acquired data and influence the investigation's outcome.

- **Analysis and transformation** Often, tools are required to analyze acquired data and search for specific clues. Also, data must frequently be transformed from its native state into a state that is human- or tool-readable; in many cases, computers store information in a binary format that is not easily read and interpreted by humans. For example, the NTUSER.DAT file used in Windows is a binary representation of the HKEY_LOCAL_USER branch of the system's registry. This file cannot be directly read but requires tools to transform it into a human-readable form.

NOTE Decisions on the use of forensic proceedings must be made early during an incident. Employing forensic procedures can consume significant resources that may slow down incident response. Senior executives, including internal or external legal counsel, should make the call on the use of forensic proceedings and should do so as early as possible after an incident is initiated.

Most organizations do not have the luxury of owning computer forensics tools and having expert(s) on staff. Instead, when an incident requiring forensics occurs, a outside forensic investigator is brought in to conduct the forensics portion of the investigation. The forensic investigator will bring her own systems for acquiring live memory and hard drive/SSD images and tools for examining the data she obtains.

Organizations that want to have one or more forensic investigators available can purchase a retainer, an agreement that provides access to a pool of investigators and includes an SLA on their remote or onsite availability. Without a retainer, the costs to hire an investigator may be higher, and the organization may have to wait longer for an investigator to become available.

Some law firms also have in-house or retained forensics experts to assist in investigations. The outside law firm can operate under attorney–client privilege, which would also protect the information obtained by the forensic investigator and her final report.

NOTE Some organizations direct their legal department to conduct incident response so that all correspondence, work papers, reports, and proceedings can be protected under attorney–client privilege. The members of the incident response team, and the incident commander, will be internal personnel in information security, IT, or another department in the organization.

Forensics Certifications

Organizations considering hiring, training, or retaining forensics experts should look for one or more of the following nonvendor forensics certifications:

- **CDFE (Certified Digital Forensics Examiner)** Available from the National Initiative for Cybersecurity Careers and Studies (NICCS); visit https://niccs.cisa.gov/education-training/catalog/mile2/certified-digital-forensics-examiner-cdfe

- **CHFI (Computer Hacking Forensic Investigator)** Available from EC-Council; visit www.eccouncil.org/programs/computer-hacking-forensic-investigator-chfi/

- **CFCE (Certified Forensic Computer Examiner)** Available from the International Association of Computer Investigative Specialists (IACIS); visit www.iacis.com/certification/cfce/

- **GCFE (GIAC Certified Forensic Examiner) and GASF (GIAC Advanced Smartphone Forensics)** Available from SANS GIAC; visit www.giac.org/certifications/

NOTE Discussed in Chapter 6, the MITRE ATT&CK framework can be invaluable to incident responders who need to identify the type of malware involved and the steps needed to contain and eradicate it.

Privacy Breaches

A breach of privacy is a unique type of security incident. In a privacy breach, an attacker may steal or compromise sensitive or private data about employees, customers, or other persons. The steps taken during incident response will be largely the same as those for breaches of other types of information. There are, however, two differences to keep in mind:

- Incident handlers must handle privacy data according to the organization's security and privacy policies.

- The organization may be required to notify affected people during or soon after the incident.

Organizations that store or process information within the scope of privacy laws should include a security incident categorization that covers privacy incidents. Security incident plans or playbooks should include specific information that directs incident responders to perform all necessary steps, including notifications and disclosures.

Incidents Involving a Service Provider

With many organizations outsourcing one or more principal business applications to external service providers, organizations need to develop plans that include the procedure to follow when an incident or breach occurs in a service provider's environment.

An organization that provides software as a service (SaaS) will likely detect an incident such as a malware attack or an intrusion when it occurs. The legal agreement between the organization and the SaaS provider should stipulate the circumstances in which the SaaS provider will notify affected customers. For the most part, the SaaS provider will perform most or all phases of security incident response, but that does not mean that the customer organization has nothing to do. A breach in a SaaS organization is still a breach, and the customer organization must have an incident response plan that considers such circumstances.

Organizations will have to rely mainly on the SaaS provider's incident response to proceed and close the incident. However, the customer organization will need to be informed along the way, as it will need to pursue damage control, including notification of affected parties. Organizations are fully accountable when a breach occurs in a service provider's organization. The organization selected the service provider and is accountable for all outcomes, including breaches. Chapter 6 explores the topic of third-party risk management in detail.

Incident Containment Methods

Incident containment includes the steps taken to prevent the incident from spreading further. Containment requires knowledge of the particulars of the incident and is most successful after the incident is examined and its techniques identified in the assessment phase. Containment is distinct from eradication, which is the removal of threats or threat actors from the environment. When containment has been completed, the threat still exists, but it cannot further proceed because containment measures have been taken.

Many cyberattacks can be contained by curtailing their network communications. If the attacker's communication connections have been severed to prevent reestablishing or resuming communications, often the attack can be considered to be contained. Based upon the nature of the intrusion, containment may involve network changes in a firewall, IPS, or edge router to black-hole communications from the attacker's network. Indeed, one of the main functions of an IPS is to block communications with known domains and IP address ranges known to be malicious. But for an attack originating from a malicious network not yet identified by an IPS, the organization can quickly implement a rule to block the IP address, range, or entire country's range of IP networks, as appropriate.

Many forms of malware, including ransomware, utilize C&C communications from the computer they have attacked, to servers controlled by the malware operator. Well-managed IPS systems block C&C traffic from known adversaries and can recognize new, unclassified commands and proactively block traffic. However, security incident responders also realize that some forms of malware are not completely incapacitated when their C&C traffic is disrupted; they still may be able to operate independently, and may even continue to explore an organization's network and even infect additional systems. This is another reason why isolating affected systems is so important. Similarly, if the malware's C&C is DNS-based, incident responders may be able to block C&C traffic effectively by preventing DNS lookups to the domains identified as malicious.

When an attack has been identified, and once the organization has collected available information about the attack, the attack can be effectively contained by severing most or all network communications from the target system. This may, however, also impair incident responders from carrying out subsequent eradication and restoration steps if they cannot communicate with the system.

 NOTE Incident responders often use the simplest containment method available: the isolation of the affected system by taking it completely off the network.

Other techniques are available in the containment phase. For instance, if the attacker can compromise systems through privilege escalation, locking the affected user or system account may prevent the attacker from successfully compromising additional systems. Also, if ransomware actively encrypts files on a network share, blocks authentication on the network share, or removes the network share altogether, removing affected systems from the network effectively contains the attack.

Containment Activates Disaster Recovery and Business Continuity

Often, the necessary containment steps in security incident response split the response effort into two parts: security incident response and disaster recovery. When the attack has been contained through network curtailment or a similar measure, this often results in the system's isolation from legitimate users. For all practical purposes, the system may have crashed, caught fire, or been stolen; it is no longer operating, which brings about the disruption of a system and, eventually, impacts one or more business processes. More examples of incidents that may require business continuity and/or disaster recovery operations include the following:

- Ransomware makes critical production data unavailable.
- Wiper malware destroys critical production data.
- Denial-of-service attack incapacitates production systems.

If incident responders are required to bring about full containment, eradication, and recovery on the affected system, they may forbid disaster recovery operations from recovering the system in place, instead requiring that the function be resumed from an alternate system so that incident response may continue without the pressure to recover the system quickly, as this could destroy evidence needed later. One valid reason for this is the need to complete forensic work on the affected system.

In such cases, if disaster recovery cannot rapidly recover the system, this will also precipitate the activation of a business continuity plan (BCP), which may include one or more contingency plans for continuing to operate critical business processes without one or more supporting systems in place. For instance, if the attacker compromised a retail store's point-of-sale back office server, and if point-of-sale systems cannot function without that server, the retail store may have to resort to manual methods of completing customer purchase transactions.

Incident Response Communications

Security incident response, in its details, is far from straightforward: while timely communication with specific parties is essential, organizations must take care not to over-communicate the details of an incident. Sometimes, the organization should limit communications about the existence of an incident only to authorized parties, rather than to the entire organization.

The incident response team should also consider using out-of-band communications if normal communications channels are suspected to be compromised. For instance, if the team believes that corporate e-mail and/or instant messaging is compromised, an entirely different system should be used for communication until the incident has been closed.

Crisis Management and Communications

Many organizations employ crisis management and/or crisis communications personnel and procedures. Both exist to improve responses to various business emergencies, including business interruptions of every kind. These capabilities should be incorporated into security incident response plans if they exist.

The *crisis management* process is used by an organization to respond to various business emergencies. One could liken crisis management to a general mobilization plan for business leaders and others to come together to respond quickly and effectively to disruptive events. Given that disasters and security incidents fall into the category of disruptive events, a security incident response plan, business continuity plan, and disaster recovery plan should utilize the capabilities in crisis management.

Why would an organization develop a similar, parallel capability instead of using what it already has? Crisis management does not exist to take over or control business continuity, disaster recovery, or security incident response. Rather, crisis management can provide templates and techniques for communications and escalation. Crisis management should help simplify the overall effort of responding to all kinds of business emergencies.

Crisis communications is a subset of the overall public relations function used to inform internal and external parties of the proceedings of business emergencies. A crisis communications person or team often prepares for a variety of business emergencies through prewritten press releases and prepared remarks that can be tailored for each event.

Crisis communications often establishes relationships with internal and external parties such as investor relations, public safety, and news media. Policy related to crisis management and crisis communications should define the personnel authorized to communicate with external parties. But even then, an organization's top executives may often be required to approve individual external communications.

> ### Attorney–Client Privilege
> Some organizations utilize their legal counsel as a central point of communications during a security incident. When done properly, this may permit an organization to shield communications and other proceedings from discovery in the event of a lawsuit. This practice is known as *attorney–client privilege*. Consult with legal counsel to understand the applicability and procedures for this approach.

Communications in the Incident Response Plan

Communications procedures, including identifying the specific parties to be involved in incident communications, should be sufficiently detailed so that incident responders will know precisely who to inform, what to say (and not say), and how often to communicate. Personnel doing the communicating, as well as personnel receiving communication, need to understand the serious and sensitive nature of incident communications and limit communications to the fewest possible personnel.

Limiting Communications to Few Authorized Persons

Few security incidents should be discussed organization-wide. Rather, communications about an incident should involve the fewest possible numbers of personnel. Each of those persons needs to understand explicitly any obligations regarding the need to keep the lid on news and details about a security incident.

Regulatory Requirements

Internal secrecy must be balanced with regulatory requirements for reporting security incidents to regulators and affected parties. Organizations must have a detailed understanding of regulatory requirements and proceed accordingly. However, security leaders and incident responders must determine how to describe incidents without providing details that could enable other attackers to understand specific weaknesses that could be exploited in further attacks.

Law Enforcement Proceedings

Organizations sometimes choose to involve local, regional, or national law enforcement when an incident occurs. Law enforcement organizations can be outstanding business partners in these situations, sometimes making cyber-incident experts available to help the organization understand what happened. It is a good practice to determine the key points of contact for various agencies with which your organization is most likely to interact during an incident. This helps ensure that lines of communications are already established, which can shorten the time for an agency to engage with the organization.

Often, a law enforcement organization will request that the organization refrain from publicly disclosing details about the incident, sometimes requiring that the organization say nothing to the public. This is understandable, particularly if the law enforcement agency is attempting to identify the perpetrator(s) in the incident to apprehend and charge them with a crime. In these cases, organizations must keep detailed records so that all members of the incident response team know what information is known about the incident, what has been communicated with law enforcement, and what has been communicated publicly.

Security Incident Is a Legal Term

A "security incident" is the legal term that is often defined in privacy and cybersecurity laws, regulations, and legal agreements between organizations. Hence, organizations should use these and other words carefully to avoid being prematurely required to make disclosures. Some organizations avoid using "security incident" altogether, instead referring to an incident as a "security event" and its written procedures as "security event response procedures." The rationale is this: Many regulations and legal agreements require disclosure of a security incident within so many hours of its declaration. Implicitly, if an organization is following a security incident response procedure, it must already know that a security incident is underway. Shifting the nomenclature from "security incident" to "security event" helps protect an organization from prematurely disclosing the matter.

Shaping Public Opinion

Experienced cybersecurity professionals often recognize good and bad examples of organizations' handling security breaches. Better organizations quickly acknowledge a security incident and provide useful information to affected parties and the public. Other organizations handle these matters poorly, either with outright denial, whitewashing, or by minimizing the scope or impact of an incident, disclosing it gradually when forced.

Organizations need to be keenly aware of how their announcements and updates of a security incident will be interpreted. For instance, "There is no evidence of actual data exfiltration," is often code for "We don't have logging turned on, so if the attacker stole data, we have no way of knowing one way or the other." Such a statement can be damning and difficult to undo.

Incident Response Metrics and Reporting

Incident response recordkeeping is critical to the success of the incident response function. Proceedings of individual incidents must be recorded to facilitate activities such as the post-incident review (aka after-action review) and to permit the creation of accurate metrics and reporting. Access to such information must be limited to few authorized personnel.

Recordkeeping

Typical incident response plans often direct that all proceedings of incident response be recorded, so that post-incident activities can be informed by the steps taken during the incident. This recordkeeping should include e-mails, notifications, decisions, artifacts, reports, and virtually everything connected with the incident.

A standard, consistent methodology for recording incidents facilitates future research by making specific types of information easier to find. For instance, if MITRE ATT&CK is used to analyze malware, a folder called "Mitre" containing this information could be created for each incident.

Organizations must identify a secure, reliable data storage system for storing information about each incident. Access should be granted to the fewest numbers of personnel possible, as some of this information is highly sensitive and could help future attackers by revealing the organization's architecture and defenses. The chosen repository should support the chain of custody or a separate storage technique used when a chain of custody is needed.

Organizations that utilize ticketing systems often prefer to record the proceedings of a security incident in the ticketing system. Although this may be a favored solution, many ticketing systems' contents are viewable by numerous personnel. If a ticketing system is used, it should have a way of marking tickets containing incident information as private or restricted, so that only the fewest number of authorized personnel can view notes and artifacts. When access to those tickets cannot be restricted or controlled, a different repository should be selected.

In addition to developing repositories to contain details about each incident, organizations also need to produce and maintain an *incident log*, which serves as a master index that contains all security incidents that have occurred in the past. The log may be a simple worksheet or database containing information such as the following:

- Incident number
- Incident date
- Incident name
- Short description
- Incident context and severity
- URL or other pointer to the repository containing incident details

Access to the incident log should be restricted to few personnel on a need-to-know basis.

Metrics

An organization's security incident response program can be managed and improved only to the extent that key metrics are established to measure the program's performance. Metrics that can be developed and reported include the following:

- Number of incidents of each incident severity and type
- Dwell time (time from the start of the incident to the time the organization became aware of the incident)

- Time required to contain the incident
- Time required to resolve and close each incident
- Number of times incident response SLAs were not met
- Improvements identified and implemented based on tabletop exercises and lessons learned from actual incidents
- Number or percentage of employees receiving security awareness training, as well as any correlation between this and the number of incidents
- Number of records compromised
- Number of external people affected and notified
- Total cost and effort required to resolve each incident

Reporting

Like any management report, the information security manager must identify target audiences and tailor reporting for those audiences based on the types of information of interest to them. Reports may include metrics, key risk indicators (KRIs), and key performance indicators (KPIs) that help management better understand whether the incident response program is effective at detecting and responding to incidents.

For instance, security incident reporting for a board of directors may contain a list of significant incidents (if any), as well as metrics showing the trends of incidents over time. This reporting should inform the audience of basic facts, including:

- Whether the numbers of incidents are increasing or decreasing over time
- Whether the effort and cost of incident response is increasing or decreasing over time
- Whether any significant incidents have occurred, including any requiring regulator or public disclosure
- What measures are planned to improve detection and response

Security leaders need to be able to explain trends to senior executives. For instance, an increase in the number of security incidents does not necessarily mean that defenses are deteriorating; instead, the number of attacks may be increasing or the ability to detect attacks is improving.

Incident Eradication, and Recovery

In security incident response, the threat agent, whatever or whomever it is or was, is contained so that it can advance no further. Next, the incident response team needs to understand what must be done to remove or eradicate the threat, enabling the organization to recover the system to its pre-incident state.

PART IV

Incident Eradication

Eradication is the complete removal of the agent(s) that caused harm in an incident. To remove threat agents successfully, the security incident response team must be confident in the containment steps performed earlier. Depending on the nature of the incident, this may involve the removal of physical subjects from a work center or information processing center or the removal of malware from one or more affected systems.

Modern malware and intrusion techniques can be difficult to identify and even more difficult to remove. Malware can have characteristics or employ techniques that make it more resilient, including the following:

- Hiding within legitimate processes
- Fileless malware
- Antiforensics techniques such as encryption, steganography, file wiping, and trail obfuscation
- Hiding data in memory, slack space, bad blocks, hidden partitions, or the registry
- Hiding "below" the operating system in the master boot record, in a virtual machine hypervisor, or the system's Basic Input/Output System (BIOS) or unified extensible firmware interface (UEFI)

The personnel who examine infected systems must have up-to-date skills and experience to identify and remove malware and other attack artifacts.

 NOTE Certain classes of malware, such as multipartite viruses, contain multiple components that work together to help the malware resist removal.

While targeted eradication can be effective, it is often time-consuming. However, as confidence in complete eradication is not always high, incident responders may take an opposite approach by completely rebuilding the asset from scratch using techniques such as the following:

- Resetting the system or device to its factory-installed state
- Performing a bare-metal restore from a known-clean pre-incident image or backup
- Replacing storage media with factory new media

To succeed, incident responders must be confident and be able to confirm that their eradication results in the complete removal of the malware.

Incident Recovery

The *recovery* phase of security incident response focuses on restoring affected systems and assets to their pre-incident state. Recovery is performed after eradication is completed; this means that any malware or other tools used by the intruder have been removed.

The state of a system entering the recovery phase is described as free of all tools, files, and agents used by the intruder. There are two basic approaches to recovery:

- **Restoration of damaged files**   In this approach, incident responders have a high degree of certainty that all artifacts used by the intruder have been removed from the system. While this is a valid approach, it does come with some risk, as it may be difficult to determine positively that all components used by the intruder are, in fact, removed.

- **Bare-metal restore**   In this approach, all information is removed from the system and recovered from backup. Typically, this involves reformatting main storage. Incident responders need to be aware of advanced techniques attackers use, including persistence in the computer's BIOS, in UEFI, or hidden main storage partitions. Further, if systems being restored are virtual machines, personnel must determine that new virtual machine images are free of infection.

In some situations, a single operation such as bare-metal restore may function as both eradication and recovery. However, incident responders should not necessarily prefer such a measure to save time; instead, eradication and recovery measures should be chosen based on their effectiveness. Malware cannot be permitted to persist in any circumstance.

Incident Remediation

I stated that recovery is the action of returning a system or asset to its pre-incident state, but you must understand a slight, but critical, nuance: we don't want to restore the system to its *exact* pre-incident state, but to a state where the system functions as before the incident, but with one or more immediate safeguards to prevent recurrence of the same or similar attack. This is where recovery leads to remediation. Incident responders understand that the intruder may not be satisfied that he was eradicated from target systems. If any of the same vulnerabilities still exist, the intruder may attempt to re-establish a foothold to resume the intrusion in support of its original objective.

A critical step in incident response is *remediation* of any vulnerabilities exploited during the incident. This includes but is not limited to technical vulnerabilities that may have permitted malware exploits to work; it also includes any supporting technologies, business processes, or personnel training that may have helped to prevent the incident from occurring if they had been in place before the incident. For instance, if an end user's system was successfully attacked with ransomware because that system's endpoint detection and response (EDR) solution was not installed or functioning correctly, remediation of the system will include steps to ensure that the EDR is working correctly.

A key part of the investigation into the security incident must include an identification and detailed analysis of the factors or vulnerabilities that led to the incident's occurrence. The key question that incident responders and investigators should ask is what weakness(es) permitted the attack or intrusion to succeed, and what should be done to the system to prevent the same or similar attack from succeeding in the future? In this context, remediation is more about fixing whatever was broken that permitted the attack or intrusion, rather than re-engineering overall defenses. The latter is generally addressed in a post-incident review that includes recommendations for long-term improvements.

A broader issue of learning from the incident is addressed later, in the section "Post-incident Review."

Post-incident Review Practices

After the affected systems and devices have been eradicated of their attack artifacts and recovered to normal use, incident response moves into a post-incident phase. Incident responders and other key security and IT personnel will close the active portion of incident response and begin discussions that will hopefully lead to the generation of ideas to improve defenses and response.

Closure

After an incident has been identified, its causes eradicated, and any affected systems remediated and recovered, the incident can be closed. Mainly this is a "back to business as usual" declaration. Some activities are necessary for full closure:

- **Archival of forensic evidence**   All information and records obtained through forensic analysis must be archived. The chain of custody must continue, however, should any legal proceedings occur in the future.

- **Archival of communications records**   Copies of internal communications and notifications sent to outside parties need to be preserved.

- **Notification to internal personnel and outside authorities**   All personnel and outside authorities who have been notified of the incident need to be informed that the incident has been closed.

- **Report issuance**   Formal reports are produced for internal and external audiences that describe the incident and all of the steps of detection, response, eradication, remediation, and recovery.

The preceding information should be packaged and stored in a protected system with strict access controls. These technical details require protection because they could be used to exploit the organization in the future.

Post-incident Review

When all incident response proceedings have concluded, the organization should consider reviewing the incident that has taken place. A post-incident review should include a frank, open discussion that identifies what went well during the incident response and what could have been handled or performed better. A typical post-incident review should cover the following:

- **Incident awareness**   Determine whether the organization realized quickly enough that an incident was occurring.

- **Internal communications**   Determine whether internal communications were well organized, the right personnel were involved, and the right information was shared with the appropriate parties.

- **External communications**   Determine whether external communications were well organized, including communications with regulators, law enforcement, customers, insurance companies, and the public.

- **Response procedures**   Determine whether incident response personnel acted quickly, decisively, and correctly.

- **Knowledge and training**   Determine whether incident responders had sufficient experience to perform their tasks effectively.

- **Resilience**   The organization examines its environment, including both technology and business processes, to discover opportunities to improve the organization's resilience. This can help the organization better defend itself in the future through the reduction in incident probability and reduced impact.

Security organizations should always operate with a culture of continuous improvement. In this regard, reviewing every aspect of a recent security incident should seek to identify improvements that will enable the organization to be better prepared when another incident occurs.

Some organizations bring in an expert third party to facilitate post-incident review to minimize emotional response from incident response team members. A third-party facilitator can help the organization avoid any tendency to identify scapegoats, to focus instead on the response itself and potential improvements to detective, preventive, and response controls and procedures.

Chapter Review

Security incident management, disaster recovery planning, and business continuity planning all support a central objective: resilience and rapid recovery when disruptive events occur.

As a result of a security incident event, the confidentiality, integrity, or availability of information or information systems has been or is in danger of being compromised. Although important, the condition of information systems is a secondary concern. Human safety is always the top priority when any disaster event has occurred.

The phases of incident response are planning, detection, initiation, analysis, containment, eradication, recovery, remediation, closure, and post-incident review. Planning consists of the development of incident response policies, roles and responsibilities, procedures, as well as testing and training.

Security incident response requires incident detection capabilities that enable an organization to be aware of an incident as it occurs. Without incident detection capabilities, an organization may not know about an intrusion for many weeks or months, if ever. A primary capability in incident response is event visibility, which is usually provided through a security information and event management (SIEM) system.

Many organizations outsource security event monitoring to a third-party managed security services provider. Organizations also often outsource incident response to security professional services firms by purchasing an incident response retainer, a prepaid arrangement. Remember that outsourcing the activity does not mean that the organization transfers the risk or responsibility of the incident response program or its impact on the business.

With the proliferation of outsourcing to cloud-based service providers, many security incidents now occur on systems managed by a third-party provider. This requires additional planning and coordination on the part of the organization, so that incident response involving a third party is effective. The organization may need to incorporate the third party's incident response plan into its existing plan.

Business continuity planning and disaster recovery planning work together to ensure the survival of an organization during and after a natural or human-made disaster.

Notes

- Developing custom playbooks that address specific types of security incidents will ensure a more rapid and effective response to a security incident. High-velocity incidents such as data wipers and ransomware require a rapid, almost automatic response.

- Organizations must be careful to understand all of the terms and exclusions in any cyber-incident insurance policy to ensure that no exclusions would result in denial of benefits after an incident.

- With so many organizations using cloud-based services, organizations must understand, in detail, their roles and responsibilities and that of each cloud service provider. This is necessary for the organization to build effective incident response should an incident occur at a cloud-based service provider.

- Threat hunting and cyber-threat intelligence can help an organization more effectively anticipate and detect an incident as it unfolds. This helps reduce potentially damaging effects through prevention.

- Many organizations outsource the forensic examination and analysis portion of security incident response, because personnel with these skills are difficult to find and the tools required are expensive.

- When responding to a security incident, organizations should consider establishing attorney–client privilege and chain of custody early on, in case disciplinary or legal proceedings may follow.

Questions

1. The types of incident response plan testing are:

   A. Document review, walk-through, and simulation

   B. Document review and simulation

   C. Document review, walk-through, simulation, parallel test, and cutover test

   D. Document review, walk-through, and cutover test

2. The length of time between incident occurrence and incident detection is known as:

A. Dwell time

B. Lag time

C. Lead time

D. Propagation

3. The purpose of attorney–client privilege during an investigation is:

A. To improve the results of the investigation

B. To obtain better forensic examination services

C. To protect investigation proceedings from a discovery order

D. To improve the integrity of investigation proceedings

4. The purpose of chain of custody procedures is:

A. To prove the ownership of investigation data

B. To determine the cause of an incident

C. To prove the integrity of investigation data

D. To determine who is responsible for an incident

5. An organization has developed its first-ever business continuity plan. Which of the following is the best first choice to test of the continuity plan that the business should perform?

A. Walk-through

B. Simulation

C. Parallel test

D. Cutover test

6. An organization is experiencing a ransomware attack that is damaging critical data. What is the best course of action?

A. Security incident response

B. Security incident response followed by business continuity plan

C. Concurrent security incident response and business continuity plan

D. Business continuity plan

7. An organization has just experienced a major earthquake at its operations center. Which of the following should be the organization's top priority?

A. Ensure that an automatic failure to the recovery site will occur as personnel may be slow to respond.

B. Ensure that visitors and personnel know how to evacuate the premises and are aware of the location of sheltering areas.

C. Ensure that data replication to a recovery site has been working properly.

D. Ensure that backup media will be available at the recovery site.

8. The purpose of a SIEM is:

   A. To centrally log event data

   B. To correlate events and generate alerts

   C. To track remediation of known vulnerabilities

   D. To scan systems and devices for new vulnerabilities

9. An organization lacks personnel and tools to conduct forensic analysis. What is the best way for the organization to acquire this capability?

   A. Purchase advanced antimalware tools.

   B. Purchase a SIEM.

   C. Purchase an incident response retainer.

   D. Hire a full-time computer forensics specialist.

10. An organization wants to protect itself from the effects of a ransomware attack. What is the best data protection approach?

    A. Periodically scan data for malware.

    B. Replicate data to a cloud-based storage provider.

    C. Replicate data to a secondary storage system.

    D. Back up data to offline media.

11. Security personnel are conducting forensic analysis concerning the malicious wrongdoing of a former employee. How should the proceedings of the forensic analysis be protected?

    A. Backup to write-once media

    B. Double locked

    C. Chain of custody

    D. Role-based access control

12. An incident responder has declared a security incident, prompting the mobilization by other incident responders and notification to senior management. Later, the responders determined that no security incident was taking place. What is the best course of action?

    A. Train the incident responder who declared the incident.

    B. Discipline the incident responder who declared the incident.

    C. Stand down and cease incident response activities.

    D. Continue with incident response until its conclusion.

13. An organization has detected a ransomware attack that has destroyed information on several end-user workstations and is now destroying information on a central file server. Incident responders have taken the file server offline. What action should the organization take next?

    A. Inform the organization that the file server is unavailable.

    B. Stop incident response procedures and activate business continuity and disaster recovery plans.

    C. Wait until the security incident is over, and then activate business continuity and disaster recovery plans.

    D. Activate business continuity and disaster recovery plans to be performed concurrently.

14. An organization currently stores its backup media in a cabinet next to the computers being backed up. A consultant advised that the organization should store backup media at an offsite storage facility. What risk did the consultant most likely have in mind when making this recommendation?

    A. A disaster that damages computer systems can also damage backup media.

    B. Backup media rotation may result in loss of data backed up several weeks in the past.

    C. Corruption of online data will require rapid data recovery from off-site storage.

    D. Physical controls at the data processing site are insufficient.

15. An organization with a cyber-insurance policy detected an active ransomware attack. What should be the organization's top priority?

    A. Contain and close the incident, and then notify the cyber-insurance company.

    B. Immediately notify the cyber-insurance company of the attack.

    C. Notify the cyber-insurance company if the organization pays the ransom.

    D. Activate a chain of custody to product the organization from the cyber-insurance company.

Answers

1. **A.** The types of security incident response plan testing are document review, walk-through, and simulation. Parallel and cutover tests are not part of security incident response planning or testing and are used for disaster recovery planning.

2. **A.** Dwell time refers to the period between the occurrence of a security incident and the organization's awareness of the incident.

3. **C.** The purpose of attorney–client privilege is the protection of correspondence and exhibits, including those in an investigation. If an organization that has experienced a security incident believes it may be defending itself in a lawsuit, the organization can choose to protect its investigation (including actions performed by a third-party firm) and its proceedings so that the organization will not be required to turn over that information during the lawsuit.

4. **C.** The purpose of chain of custody procedures is to demonstrate the integrity of the investigation—namely, that no information has been altered, including the contents of any computer memory and hard drives.

5. **A.** The best choice of tests for a first-time business continuity plan is a document review or a walk-through. Because this is a first-time plan, none of the other tests is the best first choice.

6. **C.** If a ransomware incident has damaged an organization's critical data, it should invoke its business continuity plan alongside its security incident response plan. This may help the organization restore services to its customers more quickly.

7. **B.** Human safety is always the top priority when any disaster event has occurred. Although important, the condition of information systems is a secondary concern.

8. **B.** A SIEM is a central event log processing system that correlates events among various devices. It produces alerts that may represent intrusions and other types of security incidents.

9. **C.** An organization lacking personnel and tools to conduct computer forensics should purchase an incident response retainer. With a retainer, forensics experts are available on-call to respond to an incident. Although an organization can consider hiring one or more people with these skills, a job search can take several months, and people with these skills command high salaries.

10. **D.** The best approach for protecting data from a high-velocity attack such as ransomware is to back up the data to offline media that end users cannot access. Replicating data to another storage system may only serve to replicate damaged data to the secondary storage system, making recovery more difficult or expensive.

11. **C.** The results from a forensic investigation, particularly in cases in which legal proceedings are possible, should be protected through a chain of custody. In this example, the organization may believe that the former employee is considering filing a lawsuit.

12. **C.** If a security incident is declared and personnel realize that no incident is actually taking place, incident response activities may cease. An after-action review may be warranted to identify any improvements in declaration procedures to reduce the likelihood of false positives in the future.

13. **D.** The organization should immediately activate business continuity and disaster recovery plans, so that the organization can quickly resume critical business operations and recover the affected server as soon as possible.

14. **A.** The primary reason for employing offsite backup media storage is to mitigate the effects of a disaster that could otherwise destroy computer systems and their backup media.

15. **B.** The organization should notify the cyber-insurance company right away. Often, cyber-insurance companies will assist their policyholders only if they are notified of an attack immediately.

Appendix and Glossary

- **Appendix**   About the Online Content
- **Glossary**

About the Online Content

This book comes complete with TotalTester Online customizable practice exam software with 300 practice exam questions.

System Requirements

The current and previous major versions of the following desktop browsers are recommended and supported: Chrome, Microsoft Edge, Firefox, and Safari. These browsers update frequently, and sometimes an update may cause compatibility issues with the TotalTester Online or other content hosted on the Training Hub. If you run into a problem using one of these browsers, please check your browser's security settings or try using another browser until the problem is resolved.

Your Total Seminars Training Hub Account

To get access to the online content, you will need to create an account on the Total Seminars Training Hub. Registration is free, and you will be able to track all your online content using your account. You may also opt in if you wish to receive marketing information from McGraw Hill or Total Seminars, but this is not required for you to gain access to the online content.

Privacy Notice

McGraw Hill values your privacy. Please be sure to read the Privacy Notice available during registration to see how the information you have provided will be used. You may view our Corporate Customer Privacy Policy by visiting the McGraw Hill Privacy Center. Visit the **mheducation.com** site and click **Privacy** at the bottom of the page.

Single User License Terms and Conditions

Online access to the digital content included with this book is governed by the McGraw Hill License Agreement outlined next. By using this digital content you agree to the terms of that license.

Access   To register and activate your Total Seminars Training Hub account, simply follow these easy steps.

1. Go to this URL: **hub.totalsem.com/mheclaim**

2. To register and create a new Training Hub account, enter your e-mail address, name, and password on the **Register** tab. No further personal information (such as credit card number) is required to create an account.

   If you already have a Total Seminars Training Hub account, enter your e-mail address and password on the **Log in** tab.

3. Enter your Product Key: **p79s-kr6d-4dxt**

4. Click to accept the user license terms.

5. For new users, click the **Register and Claim** button to create your account. For existing users, click the **Log in and Claim** button.

   You will be taken to the Training Hub and have access to the content for this book.

Duration of License   Access to your online content through the Total Seminars Training Hub will expire one year from the date the publisher declares the book out of print.

Your purchase of this McGraw Hill product, including its access code, through a retail store is subject to the refund policy of that store.

The Content is a copyrighted work of McGraw Hill, and McGraw Hill reserves all rights in and to the Content. The Work is © 2023 by McGraw Hill.

Restrictions on Transfer   The user is receiving only a limited right to use the Content for the user's own internal and personal use, dependent on purchase and continued ownership of this book. The user may not reproduce, forward, modify, create derivative works based upon, transmit, distribute, disseminate, sell, publish, or sublicense the Content or in any way commingle the Content with other third-party content without McGraw Hill's consent.

Limited Warranty   The McGraw Hill Content is provided on an "as is" basis. Neither McGraw Hill nor its licensors make any guarantees or warranties of any kind, either express or implied, including, but not limited to, implied warranties of merchantability or fitness for a particular purpose or use as to any McGraw Hill Content or the information therein or any warranties as to the accuracy, completeness, correctness, or results to be obtained from, accessing or using the McGraw Hill Content, or any material referenced in such Content or any information entered into licensee's product by users or other persons and/or any material available on or that can be accessed through the licensee's product (including via any hyperlink or otherwise) or as to non-infringement of third-party rights. Any warranties of any kind, whether express or implied, are disclaimed. Any material or data obtained through use of the McGraw Hill Content is at your own discretion and risk and user understands that it will be solely responsible for any resulting damage to its computer system or loss of data.

Neither McGraw Hill nor its licensors shall be liable to any subscriber or to any user or anyone else for any inaccuracy, delay, interruption in service, error or omission, regardless of cause, or for any damage resulting therefrom.

In no event will McGraw Hill or its licensors be liable for any indirect, special or consequential damages, including but not limited to, lost time, lost money, lost profits or good will, whether in contract, tort, strict liability or otherwise, and whether or not such damages are foreseen or unforeseen with respect to any use of the McGraw Hill Content.

TotalTester Online

TotalTester Online provides you with a simulation of the CISM exam. Exams can be taken in Practice Mode or Exam Mode. Practice Mode provides an assistance window with hints, references to the book, explanations of the correct and incorrect answers, and the option to check your answer as you take the test. Exam Mode provides a simulation of the actual exam. The number of questions, the types of questions, and the time allowed are intended to be an accurate representation of the exam environment. The option to customize your quiz allows you to create custom exams from selected domains or chapters, and you can further customize the number of questions and time allowed.

To take a test, follow the instructions provided in the previous section to register and activate your Total Seminars Training Hub account. When you register, you will be taken to the Total Seminars Training Hub. From the Training Hub Home page, select your certification from the Study drop-down menu at the top of the page to drill down to the TotalTester for your book. You can also scroll to it from the list of Your Topics on the Home page, and then click on the TotalTester link to launch the TotalTester. Once you've launched your TotalTester, you can select the option to customize your quiz and begin testing yourself in Practice Mode or Exam Mode. All exams provide an overall grade and a grade broken down by domain.

Technical Support

For questions regarding the TotalTester or operation of the Training Hub, visit **www.totalsem.com** or e-mail **support@totalsem.com**.

For questions regarding book content, visit **www.mheducation.com/customerservice**.

0-day   *See* zero-day.

A-123   A U.S. Office of Management and Budget (OMB) government circular that defines the management responsibilities for internal controls in federal agencies.

acceptable interruption window (AIW)   *See* maximum tolerable downtime (MTD).

acceptable use policy (AUP)   A security policy that defines the types of activities that are acceptable and those that are unacceptable in an organization, written for general audiences and applying to all personnel.

access bypass   Any attempt by an intruder to bypass access controls to gain entry into a system.

access control   Any means that detects or prevents unauthorized access and that permits authorized access.

access control policy   A statement that defines the policy for granting, reviewing, and revoking access to systems and work areas.

access governance   Policies, procedures, and activities that enforce access policy and management control of access.

access management   A formal business process used to control access to networks and information systems.

access recertification   The process of reconfirming or re-authorizing subjects' access to objects in an organization. *See also* object, subject.

access review   A review by management or system owners of the users, systems, or other subjects permitted to access protected information and information systems to ensure that all subjects should still be authorized to have access.

accumulation of privileges   A situation in which an employee accumulates access rights and privileges over a long period of time after previous access privileges were not removed following internal transfers or other privilege changes.

activity review   An examination of an information system to determine which users have been active and which have not been active. The objective is to identify user accounts that have had no activity for an extended period of time, typically 90 days.

administrative audit   An audit of operational efficiency.

administrative controls   Controls in the form of policies, processes, procedures, and standards.

advanced persistent threat (APT)   A class of threat actor that uses an array of reconnaissance and attack techniques to establish a long-term presence within a target organization.

after-action review (AAR)   *See* post-incident review.

algorithm   In cryptography, a specific mathematical formula used to perform encryption, decryption, message digests, and digital signatures.

allowable interruption window (AIW)   *See* maximum tolerable downtime (MTD).

annualized loss expectancy (ALE)   The expected loss of asset value resulting from threat realization. ALE is defined as single loss expectancy (SLE) × annualized rate of occurrence (ARO).

annualized rate of occurrence (ARO)   An estimate of the number of times that a threat will occur every year.

antiforensics   Any of several techniques whose objective is to make it more difficult for a forensic examiner to identify and understand a computer intrusion.

antimalware   Software that uses various means to detect and block or prevent malware from carrying out its purpose. *See also* antivirus software.

antivirus software   Software that is designed to detect and remove computer viruses.

appliance   A type of computer with preinstalled software that requires little or no maintenance.

application firewall   A device used to control packets being sent to an application server, primarily to block unwanted or malicious content.

application whitelisting   A mechanism that permits only registered or recognized executables to execute on a system. *See also* whitelist.

APT   *See* advanced persistent threat (APT).

architecture standard   A standard that defines current and potentially future technology framework at one or more levels within the enterprise, including database, system, and network.

assessment   An examination of a business process or information system to determine its state and effectiveness.

asset inventory   The process of confirming the existence, location, and condition of assets; also, the results of such a process.

asset management   The processes used to manage the inventory, classification, use, and disposal of assets.

asset value (AV)   The value of an IT asset, which is usually (but not necessarily) the asset's replacement value.

assets   The collection of property of value that is owned by an organization.

asymmetric encryption   A method for encryption, decryption, and digital signatures that uses pairs of encryption keys consisting of a public key and a private key.

asynchronous replication   A type of replication by which writing data to the remote storage system is not kept in sync with updates on the local storage system. There may be a time lag, and there is no guarantee that data on the remote system is identical to that on the local storage system. *See also* replication.

attack surface   A metaphor often used to depict a greater or lesser extent of attackable systems, services, and personnel in an organization; or the attackable programs, services, and features in a running operating system.

attack vector   The path or method used by an attacker to break into an IT system.

attestation of compliance   A written statement that serves as an assertion of compliance to a requirement, standard, or law, often signed by a high-ranking official or executive.

attorney–client privilege   As defined by *Black's Law Dictionary,* "a client's right privilege to refuse to disclose and to prevent any other person from disclosing confidential communications between the client and the attorney." In the context of information security, certain business proceedings can be protected with attorney–client privilege as a means of preventing those proceedings from being made available during legal discovery.

audit   A formal review of one or more processes, controls, or systems to determine their state against a standard.

audit logging   A feature in an application, operating system, or database management system in which events are recorded in a separate log.

audit methodology   A set of audit procedures used to accomplish a set of audit objectives.

audit objective   The purpose or goals of an audit. Generally, the objective of an audit is to determine whether controls exist and are effective in some specific aspect of business operations in an organization.

audit plan   A formal document that guides the control and execution of an audit. An audit plan should align with audit objectives and specify audit procedures to be used.

audit procedures   The step-by-step instructions and checklists required to perform specific audit activities. Procedures may include a list of people to interview and questions to ask, evidence to request, audit tools to use, sampling rates, where and how evidence will be archived, and how evidence will be evaluated.

audit program   The formalized and approved plan for conducting audits over a long period.

audit report   The final, written product of an audit that includes a description of the purpose, scope, and type of audit performed; people interviewed; evidence collected; rates and methods of sampling; and findings on the existence and effectiveness of each control.

audit scope   The business units, departments, processes, procedures, systems, and applications that are the subject of an audit.

authentication   The process of asserting one's identity and providing proof of that identity. Typically, authentication requires a user ID (the assertion) and a password (the proof). However, authentication may also require stronger means of proof, such as a digital certificate, token, smart card, or biometric. *See also* multifactor authentication (MFA).

automatic control   A control that is enacted through some automatic mechanism that requires little or no human intervention.

availability management   The IT function that consists of activities concerned with the availability of IT applications and services. *See also* IT service management (ITSM).

background check   The process of verifying an employment candidate's employment history, education records, professional licenses and certifications, criminal background, and financial background.

background verification   *See* background check.

back-out plan   A procedure used to reverse the effect of a change or procedure that was not successful.

backup   The process of copying important data to another media device to protect the data in the event of a hardware failure, error, or software bug that causes damage to data.

backup media rotation   Any scheme used to determine how backup media is to be reused.

basic input/output system (BIOS)   The firmware on a computer that tests the computer's hardware and initiates the bootup sequence; superseded by unified extensible firmware interface (UEFI). *See also* unified extensible firmware interface (UEFI).

bare-metal restore   The process of recovering a system by reformatting main storage, reinstalling the operating system, and restoring files.

biometrics   Any use of a machine-readable characteristic of a user's physical body that uniquely identifies the user. Biometrics can be used for multifactor authentication. Types of biometrics include voice recognition, fingerprint, hand scan, palm vein scan, iris scan, retina scan, facial scan, and handwriting. *See also* authentication, multifactor authentication (MFA).

block cipher   An encryption algorithm that operates on blocks of data.

board of directors   A body of elected or appointed people who oversee the activities of an organization.

bot   A type of malware in which agents are implanted by other forms of malware and are programmed to obey remotely issued instructions. *See also* botnet.

botnet   A collection of bots that are under the control of an individual. *See also* bot.

bring your own app (BYOA)   A practice whereby workers use personally owned applications for company business.

bring your own bottle (BYOB)   A stipulation in a dinner invitation that implies alcoholic beverages will not be served and that guests are free to bring their own.

bring your own device (BYOD)   A practice whereby workers use personally owned devices (typically laptop computers and mobile devices) to conduct company business.

bring your own software (BYOS)   *See* bring your own app (BYOA).

browser isolation   Any of several techniques of isolating a browser application from the operating system it runs on, as a method of protecting the operating system from attacks.

budget   A plan for allocating resources over a certain time period.

bug   *See* software defect.

business alignment   The effective use of information technology (IT), cybersecurity, and privacy to achieve business objectives.

business case   An explanation of the expected benefits to the business that will be realized as a result of a program or project.

business change management   A formal process by which changes to business processes are planned, tested, and controlled.

business continuity planning (BCP)   The process of developing a formalized set of activities required to ensure the continuation of critical business processes.

business e-mail compromise   A type of fraud where a perpetrator, impersonating an organization's CEO or other executive, sends phishing e-mails to other company executives and directs them to perform some high-value transaction, such as wiring large amounts of money to a bank account, typically in support of a secret merger or acquisition. *See also* phishing, spear phishing, whaling.

business impact analysis (BIA)   A study used to identify the criticality of business processes, dependencies upon resources, and the impact that different disaster scenarios will have on ongoing business operations.

call tree   A method for ensuring the timely notification of key personnel, such as after a disaster.

capability maturity model   A model used to measure the relative maturity of an organization or of its processes.

Capability Maturity Model Integration for Development (CMMI-DEV)   A maturity model used to measure the maturity of a software development process.

capacity management   The IT function that consists of activities that confirm that sufficient capacity is available in IT systems and IT processes to meet service needs. Primarily, an IT system or process has sufficient capacity if its performance falls within an acceptable range, as specified in service level agreements (SLAs). *See also* IT service management (ITSM), service level agreement (SLA).

cardholder data (CHD)   As defined by the PCI Security Standards Council: "At a minimum, cardholder data consists of the full PAN (Primary Account Number, aka credit card number). Cardholder data may also appear in the form of the full PAN plus any of the following: cardholder name, expiration date and/or service code." *See also* Payment Card Industry Data Security Standard (PCI DSS).

career path   The progression of responsibilities and job titles that a worker will attain over time.

catfishing   *See* social engineering.

centralized log management   The practice of aggregating event logs from various systems into a single logical storage location to facilitate automated analysis. *See also* log server, system information and event management system (SIEM).

CEO fraud   *See* business e-mail compromise.

certificate authority (CA)   A trusted party that stores digital certificates and public encryption keys.

certificate revocation list (CRL)   An electronic list of digital certificates that have been revoked prior to their expiration date.

certification practice statement (CPS)   A published statement that describes the practices used by the CA to issue and manage digital certificates.

chain of custody   Documentation that shows the acquisition, storage, control, and analysis of evidence. The chain of custody may be needed if the evidence is to be used in a legal proceeding.

change advisory board (CAB)   *See* change control board (CCB).

change control   *See* change management.

change control board (CCB)   The group of stakeholders from IT and business who propose, discuss, and approve changes to IT systems. Also known as a change advisory board.

change management The IT function used to control changes made to an IT environment. *See also* IT service management (ITSM).

change request A formal request for a change to be made in an environment. *See also* change management.

change review A formal review of a requested change. *See also* change management, change request.

charter *See* program charter.

chief information risk officer (CIRO) The typical job title for the topmost information security executive in an organization. Generally, this represents a change of approach to the CISO position, from protection-based to risk-based. *See also* chief information security officer (CISO).

chief information security officer (CISO) The typical job title for the topmost information security executive in an organization.

chief risk officer (CRO) The typical job title for the topmost risk executive in an organization.

chief security officer (CSO) The typical job title for the topmost security executive in an organization.

ciphertext A message, file, or stream of data that has been transformed by an encryption algorithm and rendered unreadable.

CIS Controls A control framework maintained by the Center for Internet Security (CIS).

clone phishing The practice of obtaining legitimate e-mail messages, exchanging attachments or URLs for those that are malicious, and sending the altered e-mail messages to target users in hopes that messages will trick users on account of their genuine appearance.

cloud Internet-based computing resources.

cloud access security broker (CASB) A system that monitors and, optionally, controls users' access to, or use of, cloud-based resources.

cloud computing A technique of providing a dynamically scalable and usually virtualized computing resource as a service.

cluster A tightly coupled collection of computers used to solve a common task. In a cluster, one or more servers actively perform tasks, while zero or more computers may be in a "standby" state, ready to assume active duty should the need arise.

COBIT A governance framework for managing information systems and security. COBIT is published by ISACA. *See also* ISACA.

code of conduct *See* code of ethics.

code of ethics   A statement that defines acceptable and unacceptable professional conduct.

cold site   An alternate processing center where the degree of readiness for recovery systems is low. At the least, a cold site is nothing more than an empty rack or allocated space on a computer room floor.

command-and-control (C&C)   Network traffic associated with a system compromised with malware. Command-and-control traffic represents communication between the malware and a central controlling entity.

Committee of Sponsoring Organizations of the Treadway Commission (COSO)   A private sector organization that provides thought leadership, control frameworks, and guidance on enterprise risk management.

common vulnerability scoring system (CVSS)   An open framework for communicating the quantitative characteristics and impacts of IT vulnerabilities.

compensating control   A control that is implemented because another control cannot be implemented or is ineffective.

compliance   Activities related to the examination of systems and processes to ensure that they conform to applicable policies, standards, controls, requirements, and regulations; also, the state of conformance to applicable policies, standards, controls, requirements, and regulations.

compliance audit   An audit to determine the level and degree of compliance to a law, regulation, standard, contract provision, or internal control. *See also* audit.

compliance risk   Risk associated with any general or specific consequences of not being compliant with a law, regulation, standard, contract provision, or internal control.

configuration drift   The phenomenon whereby the configuration of a system will slowly diverge from its intended state.

configuration item   A configuration setting in an IT asset. *See also* configuration management.

configuration management   The IT function wherein the configuration of components in an IT environment is independently recorded. Configuration management is usually supported by automated tools used to inventory and control system configurations. *See also* IT service management (ITSM).

configuration management database (CMDB)   A repository for every component in an environment that contains information on every configuration change made on those components.

configuration standard   A standard that defines the detailed configurations that are used in servers, workstations, operating systems, database management systems, applications, network devices, and other systems.

contact list   A list of key personnel and various methods for contacting them, often used in a response document. *See also* response document.

containerization   A form of virtualization whereby an operating system permits the existence of multiple isolated user spaces, called containers. *See also* virtualization.

containment   The act of taking steps to prevent the further spread of an incident.

content delivery network (CDN)   Also known as a content distribution network, a globally distributed network of servers in multiple data centers designed to optimize the speed and cost of delivery of content from centralized servers to end users.

content distribution network   *See* content delivery network (CDN).

continuity of operations plan (COOP)   The activities required to continue critical and strategic business functions at an alternate site. *See also* response document.

continuous improvement   The cultural desire to increase the efficiency and effectiveness of processes and controls over time.

continuous log review   A process whereby the event log for one or more systems is being continuously reviewed in real-time to determine whether a security or operational event warranting attention is taking place. *See also* security information and event management (SIEM).

contract   A binding legal agreement between two or more parties that may be enforceable in a court of law.

control   A safeguard enacted to ensure compliance with a policy, to ensure desired outcomes or to avoid unwanted outcomes.

control architecture   The overall design of a set of controls.

control existence   An audit activity whereby the auditor seeks to determine whether an expected control is in place.

control framework   A collection of controls, organized into logical categories.

control objective   A foundational statement that describes desired states or outcomes from business operations.

control review   A review of the operation and/or design of a control.

control risk   The risk that a significant or material error exists that will not be prevented or detected by a control.

control self-assessment (CSA)   A methodology used by an organization to review key business objectives, risks, and controls. Control self-assessment is a self-regulation activity that may or may not be required by applicable laws or regulations.

controlled unclassified information (CUI) Sensitive information that U.S. laws, regulations, or government policies require government agencies and private organizations to protect.

corrective action An action that is initiated to correct an undesired condition.

corrective control A control that is used after an unwanted event has occurred.

countermeasure Any activity or mechanism that is designed to reduce risk.

covered entity Any organization that stores or processes electronic protected health information (ePHI). *See also* Health Insurance Portability and Accountability Act (HIPAA).

credential harvesting Any of several techniques of covertly obtaining user or administrative logon credentials for the purpose of attacking a system. *See also* keylogger.

crisis communications The subset of an overall public relations function used to inform internal and external parties of the proceedings of business emergencies.

crisis management The process an organization uses to respond to various business emergencies.

criticality analysis A study of each system and process to determine the impact on the organization if it is incapacitated, the likelihood of incapacitation, and the estimated cost of mitigating the risk or impact of incapacitation.

crosswalk A mapping of control frameworks to one another, or a mapping of policies, standards, or controls to one another.

cryptanalysis An attack on a cryptosystem whereby the attacker is attempting to determine the encryption key that is used to encrypt messages.

cryptography The practice of using techniques to hide information from inappropriate viewers.

culture The collective attitudes, practices, communication, communication styles, ethics, and other behaviors in an organization.

custodian A person or group delegated to operate or maintain an asset.

cutover The step in the software development life cycle where an old, replaced system is shut down and a new, replacement system is started.

cutover test A test of disaster recovery and/or business continuity response plans, in which personnel shut down production systems and operate recovery systems to assume actual business workload. *See also* disaster recovery plan.

cyber insurance, cyber-risk insurance An insurance policy designed to compensate an organization for unexpected costs related to a security breach.

cybersecurity framework (CSF)   *See* NIST CSF.

cybersecurity maturity model certification (CMMC)   An assessment framework for meeting the security requirements in NIST SP 800-171 for contractors in the U.S. defense industrial base.

cyclical controls testing   A life-cycle process in which selected controls are examined for effectiveness.

damage assessment   The process of examining assets after a disaster to determine the extent of damage.

data acquisition   The act of obtaining data for later use in a forensic investigation.

data classification   Policy that defines sensitivity levels and handling procedures for information.

data debt   The state of being hampered by data models of older vintages that are no longer business aligned, often resulting in the fracturing of data into an increasing number of silos. *See also* technical debt.

data governance   Management's use of policies, metrics, and monitoring to enforce proper and appropriate access and use of data.

data loss prevention (DLP) system   A hardware or software system that detects and, optionally, blocks the movement or storage of sensitive data.

data protection officer (DPO)   *See* chief privacy officer.

data restore   The process of copying data from backup media to a target system for the purpose of restoring lost or damaged data.

data security   Those controls that seek to maintain confidentiality, integrity, and availability of information.

decryption   The process of transforming ciphertext into plaintext so that a recipient can read it.

denial of service (DoS)   An attack on a computer or network with the intention of causing disruption or malfunction of the target.

desktop computer   A nonportable computer used by an individual end user and located at the user's workspace.

desktop virtualization   Software technology that separates the physical computing environment from the software that runs on an endpoint, effectively transforming an endpoint into a display terminal. *See also* virtualization.

destructware   *See* wiper.

detective control   A control that is designed to detect events.

deterrent control A control that is designed to deter people from performing unwanted activities.

Diffie–Hellman A popular key exchange algorithm. *See also* key exchange.

digital certificate An electronic document that contains an identity that is signed with the public key of a certificate authority (CA).

digital envelope A method that uses two layers of encryption. A symmetric key is used to encrypt a message; then, a public or private key is used to encrypt the symmetric key.

digital rights management (DRM) Any technology used to control the distribution and use of electronic content.

digital signature The result of encrypting the hash of a message with the originator's private encryption key; used to prove the authenticity and integrity of a message.

directory A centralized service that provides information for a particular function.

disaster An unexpected and unplanned event that results in the disruption of business operations.

disaster declaration criteria The conditions that must be present to declare a disaster, triggering response and recovery operations.

disaster declaration procedure Instructions to determine whether to declare a disaster and trigger response and recovery operations. *See also* disaster declaration criteria.

disaster recovery and business continuity requirements Formal statements that describe required recoverability and continuity characteristics that a system or process must support.

disaster recovery plan The activities required to restore critical IT systems and other critical assets, whether in alternate or primary locations, following a disaster event. *See also* response document.

disaster recovery planning (DRP) Activities related to the assessment, salvage, repair, and restoration of facilities and assets after a disaster.

discovery sampling A sampling technique whereby at least one exception is sought in a population. *See also* sampling.

disk array A chassis in which several hard disks can be installed and connected to a server.

distributed denial of service (DDoS) A denial-of-service (DoS) attack that originates from many computers. *See also* denial of service (DoS).

DNS filter A network system or device used to protect systems from malicious content through manipulation of the results of DNS queries. *See also* web content filter.

document review   A review of some or all disaster recovery and business continuity plans, procedures, and other documentation. Individuals typically review these documents on their own, at their own pace, but within established time constraints or deadlines.

documentation   The inclusive term that describes charters, processes, procedures, standards, requirements, and other written documents.

Domain Name System (DNS)   A TCP/IP application layer protocol used to translate domain names (such as www.isecbooks.com) into IP addresses.

drift   *See* configuration drift.

dwell time   The period of time that elapses from the start of a security incident to the organization's awareness of the incident.

dynamic application security testing (DAST)   Tools used to identify security defects in a running software application.

eavesdropping   The act of secretly intercepting and, optionally, recording a voice or data transmission.

elasticity   The property of infrastructure as a service (IaaS) whereby additional virtual assets can be created or withdrawn in response to rising and falling workloads.

electric generator   A system consisting of an internal combustion engine powered by gasoline, diesel fuel, or natural gas that spins an electric generator to supply electricity for as long as several days, depending upon the size of its fuel supply and whether it can be refueled.

electronic protected health information (ePHI)   As initially defined by HIPAA, any information or data in electronic form that concerns the health, health status, and medical treatment of a human patient. *See also* Health Insurance Portability and Accountability Act (HIPAA).

elliptic curve   A public key cryptography algorithm used for encrypting and decrypting information.

e-mail   A network-based service used to transmit messages between individuals and groups.

emergency communications plan   A plan included in a response document that describes the types of communications imparted to many parties, including emergency response personnel, employees in general, customers, suppliers, regulators, public safety organizations, shareholders, and the public. *See also* response document.

emergency response   The urgent activities that immediately follow a disaster, including evacuation of personnel, first aid, triage of injured personnel, and possibly firefighting.

employee handbook   *See* employee policy manual.

PART V

employee policy manual   A formal statement of the terms of employment, facts about the organization, benefits, compensation, conduct, and policies.

employment agreement   A legal contract between an organization and an employee, which may include a description of duties, roles and responsibilities, confidentiality, compliance issues, and reasons and methods for termination.

encryption   The act of hiding sensitive information in plain sight. Encryption works by scrambling the characters in a message using an encryption key known only to the sender and receiver, making the message useless to anyone who intercepts the message.

encryption key   A block of characters used in combination with an encryption algorithm to encrypt or decrypt a stream or block of data.

end-user behavior analytics (EUBA)   *See* user behavior analytics (UBA).

endpoint   A general term used to describe any of the types of devices used by end users, including mobile phones, smartphones, terminals, tablet computers, laptop computers, and desktop computers.

endpoint detection and response (EDR)   The set of capabilities on an endpoint that work together to detect and respond to cyberattacks.

enterprise architecture   Activities that ensure important business needs are met by IT systems; the model that is used to map business functions into the IT environment and IT systems in increasing levels of detail.

enterprise risk management (ERM)   The methods and processes used by an organization to identify and manage broad business risks.

evacuation procedure   Instructions to evacuate a work facility safely in the event of a fire, earthquake, or other disaster.

e-vaulting   The practice of backing up information to an offsite location, often a third-party service provider.

event   An occurrence of relevance to a business or system.

event monitoring   The practice of examining the events that occur in information systems, including operating systems, subsystems such as database management systems, applications, network devices, and end-user devices.

event visibility   A capability that permits an organization to be aware of activities that may signal a security or other type of incident.

evidence   Information gathered by the auditor that provides proof that a control exists and is being operated.

exploitation   The process of exploiting a vulnerability in a target system to take control of the system.

exposure factor (EF)   The financial loss that results from the realization of a threat, expressed as a percentage of the asset's total value.

extended detection and response (XDR)   A term representing a newer generation of endpoint detection and response (EDR) products. *See also* endpoint detection and response (EDR).

facilities classification   A method for assigning classification or risk levels to work centers and processing centers, based on their operational criticality or other risk factors. *See also* data classification, systems classification.

feasibility study   An activity that seeks to determine the expected benefits of a program or project.

fiduciary   A person who has a legal trust relationship with another party.

fiduciary duty   The highest standard of care that a fiduciary renders to a beneficiary.

file   A sequence of zero or more characters that is stored as a whole in a file system. A file may be a document, spreadsheet, image, sound file, computer program, or data that is used by a program. *See also* file system.

file activity monitoring (FAM)   A program that monitors the use of files on a server or an endpoint as a means for detecting indicators of compromise.

file integrity monitoring (FIM)   A program that periodically scans file systems on servers and workstations as a means of detecting changes to file contents or permissions that may be indicators of compromise.

file server   A server used to store files in a central location, usually to make them readily available to many users.

file system   A logical structure that facilitates the storage of data on a digital storage medium such as a hard disk drive (HDD), solid-state drive (SSD), CD/DVD-ROM, or flash memory device.

fileless malware   Malware that resides in a computer's memory instead of in the file system.

financial audit   An audit of an accounting system and accounting department processes and procedures to determine whether business controls are sufficient to ensure the integrity of financial statements. *See also* audit.

financial management   Management for IT services that consists of several activities, including budgeting, capital investment, expense management, project accounting, and project ROI. *See also* IT service management (ITSM), return on investment (ROI).

fingerprint   *See* biometrics, key fingerprint.

firewall A device that controls the flow of network messages between networks. Placed at the boundary between the Internet and an organization's internal network, firewalls enforce security policy by prohibiting all inbound traffic except for the specific few types of traffic that are permitted to a select few systems.

first in, first out (FIFO) A backup media rotation scheme by which the oldest backup volumes are used next. *See also* backup media rotation.

Foreign Corrupt Practices Act of 1977 (FCPA) A U.S. law that forbids persons and organizations from bribing foreign government officials.

forensic audit An audit that is performed in support of an anticipated or active legal proceeding. *See also* audit.

forensics The application of techniques and tools during an investigation of a computer or network-related event.

fraud The intentional deception made for personal gain or to damage another party.

gap analysis An examination of a process or system to determine differences between its existing state and a desired future state.

general computing controls (GCCs) Controls that are general in nature and implemented across most or all information systems and applications.

general data protection regulation (GDPR) The European law that took effect in 2018 that protects the privacy of European Union residents.

geofencing A network-based protective measure whereby an organization blocks incoming network traffic originating from one or more geographic areas.

governance Management's control over policy and processes.

governance, risk, and compliance (GRC) system *See* integrated risk management (IRM) system.

grandfather-father-son A hierarchical backup media rotation scheme that provides for longer retention of some backups. *See also* backup media rotation.

groupthink A human behavior rooted in the desire to conform to group consensus and excluding the consideration of alternate ideas.

guidelines Nonbinding statements or narratives that provide additional information to personnel regarding compliance with security policies and standards.

hacker Someone who interferes with or accesses a computer or system without authorization.

hard disk drive (HDD) A storage device using magnetic storage on rapidly rotating disks. *See also* solid-state drive (SSD).

hardening   The technique of configuring a system so that only its essential services and features are active and all others are deactivated, making it more resilient to attack and compromise. This helps to reduce the attack surface of a system to its essential components only.

hardening standard   A document that describes the security configuration details of a system or class of systems. *See also* configuration standard, hardening.

hardware monitoring   Tools and processes used to continuously observe the health, performance, and capacity of one or more computers.

hash function   A cryptographic operation on a block of data that returns a fixed-length string of characters, used to verify the integrity of a message.

Health Insurance Portability and Accountability Act (HIPAA)   A 1996 U.S. law requiring the enactment of controls to protect electronic protected health information (ePHI).

HITRUST   A healthcare industry control framework and certification that serves as an external attestation of an organization's IT controls.

host-based intrusion detection system (HIDS)   An intrusion detection system installed on a system that watches for anomalies that could be signs of intrusion. *See also* intrusion detection system (IDS).

hot site   An alternate processing center where backup systems are already running and in some state of near-readiness to assume production workload. The systems at a hot site most likely have application software and database management software already loaded and running, perhaps even at the same patch levels as the systems in the primary processing center. *See also* cold site, warm site.

human-made disaster   A disaster that is directly or indirectly caused by human activity, through action or inaction. *See also* disaster.

human resource information system (HRIS)   An information system used to manage information about an organization's workforce.

human resource management (HRM or HR)   Activities regarding the acquisition, onboarding, support, and termination of workers in an organization.

human resources (HR)   The department in most organizations that is responsible for employee onboarding, offboarding, internal transfers, training, and signing important documents such as security policy.

hybrid cryptography   A cryptosystem that employs two or more iterations or types of cryptography.

hybrid virus   *See* multipartite virus.

Hypertext Transfer Protocol (HTTP)   A TCP/IP application layer protocol used to transmit web page contents from web servers to users who are using web browsers.

Hypertext Transfer Protocol Secure (HTTPS)   A TCP/IP application layer protocol that is similar to HTTP in its use for transporting data between web servers and browsers. HTTPS is not a separate protocol but is an extension of HTTP that is encrypted with SSL or TLS. *See also* Hypertext Transfer Protocol (HTTP), Secure Sockets Layer (SSL), Transport Layer Security (TLS).

hypervisor   Virtualization software that facilitates the operation of one or more virtual machines.

identity and access management (IAM)   The activities and supporting systems used to manage workers' identities and their access to information systems and data.

identity management   The activity of managing the identity of each employee, contractor, temporary worker, and, optionally, customer, for use in a single environment or multiple environments.

image   A binary representation of a fully installed and configured operating system and applications for a server or an end user's computer.

impact   The actual or expected result from some action such as a threat or disaster.

impact analysis   The analysis of a threat and the impact it would have if it were realized.

incident   Any event that is not part of the standard operation of a service and that causes, or may cause, interruption to or a reduction in the quality of that service.

incident declaration   The process of determining that a security incident is taking place so that incident responders can begin the task of managing it.

incident log   A business record containing a list of security incidents that have occurred in an organization.

incident management   The IT function that analyzes service outages, service slowdowns, security incidents, and software bugs, and seeks to resolve them to restore normal service. *See also* IT service management (ITSM), security incident management.

incident prevention   Proactive steps taken to reduce the probability or impact of security incidents.

incident responder   A worker in an organization who has responsibility for responding to a security incident.

incident response plan   Written procedures to be followed in response to a security incident.

incident response retainer   A legal agreement between an organization and a security professional services firm that arranges for the security firm to render assistance to the organization in the event of a security incident.

incident response team   Personnel who are trained in incident response techniques.

indicator of compromise (IoC)   An observation on a network or in an operating system that indicates evidence of a network or computer intrusion.

industrial control system (ICS)   A control system used to monitor and manage physical machinery in an industrial environment. *See also* supervisory control and data acquisition (SCADA).

information and communications technology (ICT)   A term signifying information processing and communications systems.

information classification   *See* data classification.

information governance   Governance activities that provide management with visibility and control over the use of information.

information privacy   The right of personal information to be free and safe from unauthorized disclosure, use, and distribution.

information privacy policy   An organization's policy statement that defines how the organization will protect, manage, and handle private information.

information risk   Paraphrased from the ISACA Risk IT Framework, information risk is the business risk associated with the use, ownership, operation, involvement, influence, and adoption of information within an enterprise.

information security management   The aggregation of policies, processes, procedures, and activities to ensure that an organization's security policy is effective.

information security management system (ISMS)   The collection of activities for managing information security in an organization, as defined by ISO/IEC 27001.

information security policy   A statement that defines how an organization will classify and protect its important assets.

infrastructure   The collection of networks, network services, devices, facilities, and system software that facilitates access to, communications with, and protection of business applications.

infrastructure as a service (IaaS)   A cloud computing model in which a service provider makes computers and other infrastructure components available to subscribers. *See also* cloud computing.

inherent risk   The risk that material weaknesses are present in existing business processes with no compensating controls to detect or prevent them.

initialization vector (IV)   A random number that is needed by some encryption algorithms to begin the encryption process.

insider threat   Any scenario whereby an employee or contractor knowingly, or unknowingly, commits acts that result in security incidents or breaches.

integrated audit   An audit that combines an operational audit and a financial audit. *See also* financial audit, operational audit.

integrated development environment (IDE)   A software application that facilitates the writing, updating, testing, and debugging of application source code.

integrated risk management (IRM) system   A software application used to track key aspects of an organization's risk management program. Formerly known as a governance, risk, and compliance (GRC) system.

intellectual property   A class of assets owned by an organization, including the organization's designs, architectures, software source code, processes, and procedures.

internal audit   A formal audit of an organization's controls, processes, or systems, carried out by personnel who are part of the organization. *See also* audit.

internal audit (IA)   The organization's internal department that performs audits of processes and controls.

Internet   The global network that interconnects TCP/IP networks.

Internet hygiene   The practice of security awareness while accessing the Internet with a computer or mobile device to reduce the possibility of attack.

Internet of things (IoT)   Physical objects that are connected to data networks for the purpose of data acquisition and/or control. *See also* industrial control systems (ICS), supervisory control and data acquisition (SCADA).

intrusion detection and prevention system (IDPS)   *See* intrusion prevention system (IPS).

intrusion detection system (IDS)   A hardware or software system that detects anomalies that may be signs of an intrusion.

intrusion kill chain   The computer intrusion model developed by Lockheed-Martin that depicts a typical computer intrusion. The phases of the kill chain are reconnaissance, weaponization, delivery, exploitation, installation, command and control, and actions on objective.

intrusion prevention system (IPS)   A hardware or software system that detects and blocks malicious network traffic that may signal an intrusion.

intrusive monitoring   Any technique used by an organization to actively monitor activities within a third party's IT environment.

IS audit   An audit of an IS department's operations and systems. *See also* audit.

ISACA   The global organization that develops and administers numerous certifications, including Certified Information Security Manager (CISM); Certified Information Systems Auditor (CISA); Certified in Risk, Information Security, and Control (CRISC); Certified Data Privacy Solutions Engineer (CDPSE); and Certified in the Governance of Enterprise IT (CGEIT). Formerly known as the Information Systems Audit and Control Association.

ISACA audit standards   The minimum standards of performance related to security, audits, and the actions that result from audits. The standards are published by ISACA and updated periodically. ISACA audit standards are considered mandatory. *See also* ISACA.

ISAE 3402 (International Standard on Assurance Engagement)   An external audit of a service provider, performed according to rules established by the International Auditing and Assurance Standards Board (IAASB).

ISO/IEC 20000   An ISO/IEC (International Organization for Standardization/International Electrotechnical Commission) standard for IT service management (ITSM). *See also* IT service management (ITSM).

ISO/IEC 27001   An ISO/IEC standard for information security management.

ISO/IEC 27002   An ISO/IEC standard for information security controls.

IT General Controls (ITGCs)   *See* General computing controls.

IT Infrastructure Library (ITIL)   *See* IT service management (ITSM).

IT service management (ITSM)   The set of activities that ensures the delivery of IT services is efficient and effective, through active management and the continuous improvement of processes.

job description   A written description of an employee's job title, work experience requirements, knowledge requirements, and responsibilities.

job title   *See* position title.

judgmental sampling   A sampling technique whereby items are chosen based upon an auditor's judgment, usually based on risk or materiality. *See also* sampling.

key   *See* encryption key.

key compromise   Any unauthorized disclosure of or damage to an encryption key. *See also* key management.

key custody   The policies, processes, and procedures regarding the management of encryption keys. *See also* key management.

key disposal   The process of decommissioning encryption keys. *See also* key management.

key encrypting key   An encryption key that is used to encrypt another encryption key.

key exchange   A technique used by two parties to establish a symmetric encryption key when no secure channel is available.

key fingerprint   A short sequence of characters used to authenticate a public key.

key generation   The initial generation of an encryption key. *See also* key management.

key goal indicator (KGI)   A measure of progress in the attainment of a strategic goal in the organization.

key length   The size (measured in bits) of an encryption key. Longer encryption keys require greater effort to attack a cryptosystem successfully.

key management   The various processes and procedures used by an organization to generate, protect, use, and dispose of encryption keys over their lifetime.

key performance indicator (KPI)   A measure of the performance and quality of a business process, used to reveal trends related to efficiency and effectiveness of key processes in the organization.

key protection   All means used to protect encryption keys from unauthorized disclosure and harm. *See also* key management.

key risk indicator (KRI)   A measure of information risk, used to reveal trends related to levels of risk of security incidents in the organization.

key rotation   The process of issuing a new encryption key and reencrypting data protected with the new key. *See also* key management.

keylogger   A hardware device or a type of malware that records a user's keystrokes and, optionally, mouse movements and clicks, which sends this data to the keylogger's owner.

kill chain   *See* intrusion kill chain.

laptop computer   A portable computer used by an individual user.

learning management system (LMS)   An on-premise or cloud-based system that makes online training and testing facilities available to an organization's personnel. Some LMSs automatically maintain records of training enrollment, test scores, and training completion.

least privilege   The security principle whereby an individual user should have the least access privileges, or authorizations, required to perform necessary work tasks.

Lightweight Directory Access Protocol (LDAP)   A TCP/IP application layer protocol used as a directory service for people and computing resources.

load balancing   Balancing workload or traffic among multiple resources.

Lockheed-Martin kill chain   *See* intrusion kill chain.

log correlation   The process of combining log data from many devices to discern patterns that may be indicators of operational problems or compromise.

log review   An examination of the event log in an information system to determine whether any security events or incidents have occurred. *See also* continuous log review.

log server   A system or device to which event logs from other systems are sent for processing and storage. *See also* centralized log management, security information and event management (SIEM).

macro virus   Malicious software that is embedded within another file, such as a document or spreadsheet.

malware   The broad class of programs designed to inflict harm on computers, networks, or information. Types of malware include viruses, worms, Trojan horses, spyware, and rootkits.

man-made disaster   *See* human-made disaster.

managed security service provider (MSSP)   An organization that provides security monitoring and/or management services for customers.

manual control   A control that requires a human to operate it.

maximum acceptable outage (MAO)   *See* maximum tolerable outage (MTO).

maximum tolerable downtime (MTD)   A theoretical time period, measured from the onset of a disaster, after which the organization's ongoing viability would be at risk.

maximum tolerable outage (MTO)   The maximum period of time that an organization can tolerate operating in recovery (or alternate processing) mode.

message digest   The result of a cryptographic hash function.

methodology standard   A standard that specifies the practices used by the IT organization.

metric   A measurement of a periodic or ongoing activity for the purpose of understanding the activity within the context of overall business operations.

microsegmentation   A design characteristic of a network in which each network node resides on its own segment, resulting in improved network security and efficiency.

mitigating control   *See* compensating control.

MITRE ATT&CK   A framework used for classifying and understanding various types of cyberattacks.

mobile device   A portable computer in the form of a smartphone, tablet computer, or wearable device.

mobile site   A portable recovery center that can be delivered to almost any location in the world.

monitoring   The continuous or regular evaluation of a system or control to determine its operation or effectiveness.

multifactor authentication (MFA)   Any means used to authenticate a user that is stronger than the use of a user ID and password. Examples include digital certificates, tokens, smart cards, or biometrics.

multipartite virus   A computer virus that employs multiple simultaneous attack and/or presence components to aid in a more effective attack and persistence.

natural disaster   A disaster that occurs in the natural world with little or no assistance from humankind. *See also* disaster.

need-to-know   The principle of access management that permits subjects to have access to information or information systems only if they have a specific need to access them.

NetFlow   A network diagnostic tool developed by Cisco Systems that collects all network metadata, which can be used for network diagnostic or security purposes. *See also* network traffic analysis (NTA).

network access control (NAC)   An approach for network authentication and access control that determines whether devices will be permitted to attach to a LAN or wireless LAN.

network attached storage (NAS)   A stand-alone storage system that contains one or more virtual volumes. Servers access these volumes over the network using the Network File System (NFS) or Server Message Block/Common Internet File System (SMB/CIFS) protocols, common on Unix and Windows operating systems, respectively.

network segmentation   The practice of dividing a network into two or more zones, with protective measures such as firewalls between the zones.

network tap   A connection on a network router or network switch. A copy of all of the network traffic passing through the router or switch is also sent to the network tap. Also known as a span port.

network traffic analysis (NTA)   A technique used to identify anomalies in network traffic that may be a part of an intrusion or other unwanted event.

NIST 800 Series   A collection of documents published by the U.S. National Institute for Standards and Technology (NIST).

NIST CSF   A risk management methodology and controls framework developed by the U.S. National Institute for Standards and Technology (NIST).

nonfunctional requirement   Required characteristics of a system, service, or process in terms of its components, structure, or architecture. *See also* functional requirement, requirement.

nonrepudiation   The property of encryption and digital signatures that can make it difficult or impossible for a party to deny having previously sent a digitally signed message—unless they admit to having lost control of their private encryption key.

North American Reliability Corporation (NERC)   The organization that maintains resilience and security controls for use by public utilities.

North American Reliability Council Critical Infrastructure Protection (NERC CIP)   The standards and requirements defined by the North American Reliability Council for the protection of the electric power generation and distribution grid.

object   In the context of access management, a file, database, record, system, or device that a subject may attempt to access. *See also* subject.

occupant emergency plan   Activities required to care for occupants safely in a business location during a disaster. *See also* response document.

offsite media storage   The practice of storing media such as backup tapes at an offsite facility located away from the primary computing facility.

onboarding   The process undertaken when an organization hires a new worker or when it begins a business relationship with a third party.

open source software   Computer software released in a manner in which the owner grants users the right to use, change, and distribute software and its source code.

operational audit   An audit of IS controls, security controls, or business controls to determine control existence and effectiveness. *See also* audit.

operational risk   The risk of loss resulting from failed controls, processes, and systems; internal and external events; and other occurrences that impact business operations and threaten an organization's survival.

Operationally Critical Threat Asset and Vulnerability Evaluation (OCTAVE)   A qualitative risk analysis methodology developed at Carnegie Mellon University.

orchestration   In the context of SIEM, the scripted, automated response that is automatically or manually triggered when specific events occur. *See also* security information and event management (SIEM).

organization chart   A diagram that depicts the manager–subordinate relationships in an organization or in part of an organization.

out of band   Communications that take place separately from the main communications channel.

outsourcing A form of sourcing (obtaining goods or services) whereby an employer uses onsite or offsite contract employees or organizations to perform a function.

owner A person or group responsible for the management and/or operation of an asset.

ownership In the context of information security and privacy, the concept of an individual's or group's accountability for the integrity and effectiveness of policies, procedures, or controls.

packet sniffer A device or program installed on a network-attached system to capture network traffic.

parallel test An actual test of disaster recovery or business continuity response plans intended to evaluate the ability of personnel to follow directives in emergency response plans to set up an actual disaster recovery business processing or data processing capability. In a parallel test, personnel operate recovery systems in parallel with production systems to compare the results between the two to determine the capabilities of recovery systems.

password An identifier that is created by a system manager or a user; a secret combination of letters, numbers, and other symbols that is known only to the person who uses it.

password complexity The characteristics required of user account passwords to ensure their security. For example, a password may not contain dictionary words and must contain uppercase letters, lowercase letters, numbers, and symbols.

password length The minimum and maximum number of characters permitted for a password associated with a computer account.

password reset The process of changing a user account password and unlocking the account so that the user may resume using the account.

password reuse The act of reusing a prior password for a user account. Some information systems can prevent password reuse in case any prior passwords were compromised with or without the user's knowledge.

passwordless authentication An authentication method that uses a public identifier, such as a userid or e-mail address, together with a second factor, such as a hardware token or biometric, for system access.

patch management The process of identifying, analyzing, and applying patches (including security patches) to systems.

Payment Card Industry Data Security Standard (PCI DSS) A security standard whose objective is the protection of credit card numbers in storage, while processed, and while transmitted. The standard was developed by the PCI Security Standards Council, a consortium of credit card companies including Visa, MasterCard, American Express, Discover, and JCB.

personally identifiable information (PII) Information that can be used on its own or combined with other information to identify a specific person.

phishing   A social-engineering attack on unsuspecting individuals whereby e-mail messages that resemble official communications entice victims to visit imposter web sites that contain malware or request credentials to sensitive or valuable assets. *See also* business e-mail compromise, spear phishing, whaling.

physical control   Controls that employ physical means.

plaintext   An original, unencrypted message, file, or stream of data that can be read by anyone who has access to it.

platform as a service (PaaS)   A cloud computing delivery model whereby the service provider supplies the platform on which an organization can build and run software.

playbook   Step-by-step instructions for security incidents likely to affect an organization.

policy   A statement that specifies what must be done (or not done) in an organization. A policy usually defines who is responsible for monitoring and enforcing it.

population   A complete set of entities, transactions, or events that are the subject of an audit.

position title   A label that designates an employee's place or role in an organization.

post-incident review   A formal review of a security incident, disaster recovery, or business continuity event in which all of the proceedings are reviewed to determine whether any improvements need to be made to detection, response, or recovery operations.

pre-audit   An examination of business processes, controls, and records in anticipation of an upcoming audit. *See also* audit.

preventive control   A control intended to prevent unwanted events from happening, such as a computer login screen or a key card system used to control physical access to a computer or facility, respectively.

privacy   *See* information privacy.

privacy policy   *See* information privacy policy.

private cloud   A cloud infrastructure that is dedicated to a single organization.

private key cryptosystem   A cryptosystem based on a symmetric cryptographic algorithm that requires that both parties possess a common encryption key that is used to encrypt and decrypt messages.

privileged access management   Management of administrative access to information, systems, and devices. *See also* access management.

procurement   The process of making a purchase of hardware, software, and services; also, the name of the department that performs this activity.

probability   The chances that an event or incident may occur.

probability analysis   The analysis of a threat and the probability of its realization.

problem   An incident—often multiple incidents—that exhibits common symptoms and whose root cause is not known.

problem management   The IT function that analyzes chronic incidents, seeks to resolve them, and enacts proactive measures in an effort to avoid problems. *See also* IT service management (ITSM).

procedure   A written sequence of instructions used to complete a task.

process   A collection of one or more procedures used to perform a business function. *See also* procedure.

program   An organization of many large, complex activities; it can be thought of as a set of projects that work to fulfill one or more key business objectives or goals.

program charter   A formal definition of the objectives of a program, its main time-lines, its sources of funding, the names of its principal leaders and managers, and the business executives who are sponsoring it.

program management   The management of a group of projects that exist to fulfill a business goal or objective. *See also* program.

project   A coordinated and managed sequence of tasks that results in the realization of an objective or goal.

project management   The process of leading and managing a team to control, measure, and manage the activities in a project.

project plan   The collection of documents that describe the stages and oversight of a project. A project plan outlines the sponsor, stakeholders, goals, milestones, tasks, resources, risks, constraints, and timelines needed to accomplish the stated objective(s).

project planning   The activities related to the development and management of a project.

protocol analyzer   A device connected to a network that views network communications at a detailed level.

public cloud   A cloud infrastructure used by multiple organizations.

public key cryptography   *See* asymmetric encryption.

public key infrastructure (PKI)   A centralized function used to store and publish public encryption keys and other information.

qualitative risk analysis   A risk analysis methodology whereby risks are classified on a nonquantified scale, such as from High to Medium to Low, or a simple numeric scale such as 1 to 5.

quantitative risk analysis A risk analysis methodology whereby risks are estimated in the form of actual costs and/or probabilities of occurrence.

quarantine A holding place for e-mail messages that have been blocked by a spam or phishing filter.

questionnaire A list of questions sent to a party to assess their control effectiveness and risk.

rank A part of a person's position title that denotes seniority or span of control in an organization. *See also* position title.

ransomware Malware that performs some malicious action, requiring payment from the victim to reverse the action. Such actions include data erasure, data encryption, and system damage.

reciprocal site A data center operated by another organization. Two or more organizations with similar processing needs will draw up a legal contract that obligates one or more of the organizations to house another party's systems temporarily in the event of a disaster.

reconnaissance Any activity in which a would-be intruder or researcher explores a potential target system or network, generally to learn of its makeup, to determine a potentially successful attack strategy.

records Documents describing business events such as meeting minutes, contracts, financial transactions, decisions, purchase orders, logs, and reports.

recovery capacity objective (RCapO) The processing and/or storage capacity of an alternate process or system, compared to the normal process or site. RCapO is usually expressed as a percentage.

recovery consistency objective (RCO) A measure of the consistency and integrity of processing at a recovery site, compared to the primary processing site. RCO is calculated as $1 - $ (number of inconsistent objects) / (number of objects).

recovery control A control used following an unwanted event to restore a system or process to its pre-event state.

recovery point objective (RPO) The period of acceptable data loss following an incident or disaster, usually measured in hours or days.

recovery procedure Instructions that key personnel use to bootstrap services that support critical business functions identified in the business impact assessment (BIA).

recovery site An alternate location used for information processing when a primary site is incapacitated.

recovery strategy A high-level plan for resuming business operations after a disaster.

recovery time objective (RTO)　The period from the onset of an outage until the resumption of service, usually measured in hours or days.

Redundant Array of Independent Disks (RAID)　A family of technologies used to improve the reliability, performance, or size of disk-based storage systems.

reference architecture　A template solution developed for a particular purpose, intended to be used repeatedly as needed.

registration authority (RA)　An entity that works within or alongside a certificate authority (CA) to accept requests for new digital certificates.

release management　The IT function that controls the release of software programs, applications, and environments. *See also* IT service management (ITSM).

release process　The IT process whereby changes to software programs, applications, and environments are requested, reviewed, approved, and implemented.

remote access　A service that permits a user to establish a network connection from a remote location to access network resources remotely.

remote access Trojan (RAT)　Malware that permits the attacker to access and control a target system remotely.

remote destruct　The act of commanding a device, such as a laptop computer or mobile device, to destroy stored data. Remote destruct is sometimes used when a device is lost or stolen to prevent anyone from being able to read data stored on the device.

remote monitoring (RMON)　A protocol used to monitor network traffic. Also known as remote network monitoring.

remote work　The practice of an employee working in a location other than the organization's work premises. *See also* work from home (WFH).

reperformance　An audit technique whereby an IS auditor repeats actual tasks performed by auditees to confirm they were performed properly.

replication　An activity whereby data that is written to a storage system is also copied over a network to another storage system and written, resulting in the presence of up-to-date data that exists on two or more storage systems, each of which could be located in a different geographic region.

request for change (RFC)　*See* change request.

request for information (RFI)　A formal process by which an organization solicits information regarding solution proposals from one or more vendors. This is usually used to gather official information about products or services that may be considered in the future.

request for proposal (RFP)   A formal process by which an organization solicits solution proposals from one or more vendors to evaluate vendor proposals and make a selection. The process usually includes formal requirements and desired terms and conditions.

requirements   Formal statements that describe required (and desired) characteristics of a system that is to be developed, changed, or acquired.

residual risk   The risk that remains after being reduced through risk treatment options.

response document   A document that outlines the required actions of personnel after a disaster strikes. It includes the business recovery plan, occupant emergency plan, emergency communication plan, contact lists, disaster recovery plan, continuity of operations plan, and security incident response plan.

Responsible, Accountable, Consulted, Informed (RACI) chart   A tool used to assign roles to individuals and groups according to their responsibilities.

responsibility   A stated expectation of activities and performance.

retainer agreement   A contract in which an organization pays in advance for professional services such as external legal counsel and security incident response.

return on investment (ROI)   The ratio of money gained or lost as compared to an original investment.

return on security investment (ROSI)   The return on investment based on the reduction of security-related losses compared to the cost of related controls.

right to audit   A clause in a contract that grants one party the right to conduct an audit of the other party's operations.

risk   Generally, the fact that undesired events can happen that may damage property or disrupt operations; specifically, an event scenario that can result in property damage or disruption.

risk acceptance   The risk treatment option whereby management chooses to accept the risk as is.

risk analysis   The process of identifying and studying risks in an organization.

risk appetite   The organization's overall acceptable level of risk for a given business venture.

risk assessment   An activity where risks, in the form of threats and vulnerabilities, are identified for each asset.

risk avoidance   The risk treatment option involving a cessation of the activity that introduces an identified risk.

risk awareness   Programmatic activities whose objective is to make business leaders, stakeholders, and other personnel aware of the organization's information risk management program. *See also* security awareness.

risk capacity   The objective amount of loss that an organization can tolerate without its continued existence being called into question.

risk ledger   *See* risk register.

risk management   Management activities used to identify, analyze, treat, and monitor risks.

risk mitigation   The risk treatment option involving the implementation of a solution that will reduce an identified risk.

risk monitoring   Ongoing activities, including control effectiveness assessments and risk assessments to observe changes in risk.

risk owner   A person designated as being responsible for the outcome of a particular risk; typically, the owner of the asset or process that is the subject of a risk.

risk register   A business record containing business risks and information about their origin, potential impacts, affected assets, probabilities of occurrence, and treatments.

risk response   *See* risk treatment.

risk sharing   *See* risk transfer.

risk tolerance   The organization's level of acceptable variation from the risk appetite.

risk transfer   The risk treatment option involving the act of transferring risk to another party, such as an insurance company or service provider.

risk treatment   The decision to manage an identified risk: mitigate the risk, avoid the risk, transfer the risk, or accept the risk.

roadmap   The list of steps required to achieve a strategic objective.

role   A set of user privileges in an application; also, a formal designation assigned to an individual by virtue of a job title or other label.

rollback   A step in the software development life cycle in which system changes need to be reversed, returning the system to its previous state.

root cause analysis   Analysis of a problem to identify the underlying origins, not merely factors or symptoms. *See also* problem management.

sabotage   Deliberate damage of an organization's asset.

salvage   The process of recovering components or assets that still have value after a disaster.

sample   A portion of a population of records that is selected for auditing.

sampled flow (sFlow)   An industry-standard protocol for monitoring networks.

sampling   A technique used to select a portion of a population for auditing when it is not feasible to audit or test an entire population.

sandbox   A security mechanism often used by antimalware programs to separate running programs. *See also* antimalware.

SANS 20 Critical Security Controls, *aka* SANS Top 20 Controls   *See* CIS Controls.

Sarbanes-Oxley Act (SOX)   A 2002 U.S. law requiring public corporations to enact business and technical controls, perform internal audits of those controls, and undergo external audits.

scanning tool   A security tool used to scan files, processes, network addresses, systems, or other objects, often for the purpose of identifying assets or vulnerabilities that may be present in assets.

secure coding   The practice of developing program source code that is free of security defects. *See also* secure development training.

secure development training   Training for software developers on the techniques of writing secure code and avoiding security defects that could be exploited by adversaries.

Secure Multipurpose Internet Mail Extensions (S/MIME)   An e-mail security protocol that provides sender and recipient authentication and encryption of message content and attachments.

Secure Shell (SSH)   A TCP/IP application layer protocol that provides a secure channel between two computers, whereby all communications between them are encrypted. SSH can also be used as a tunnel to encapsulate and thereby protect other protocols.

Secure Sockets Layer (SSL)   An encryption protocol used to encrypt web pages requested with the HTTPS URL. This has been deprecated by Transport Layer Security (TLS). *See also* Hypertext Transfer Protocol Secure (HTTPS), Transport Layer Security (TLS).

security architecture   The overall strategy as well as the details that define the role of technology and asset protection in an organization. *See also* The Open Group Architecture Framework (TOGAF), Zachman Framework.

security audit   A formal review of security controls, processes, or systems to determine their state. *See also* audit.

security awareness   A formal program used to educate employees, users, customers, or constituents on required, acceptable, and unacceptable security-related behaviors. *See also* risk awareness.

security by design   The concept of product and systems development that incorporates security into the design of the system rather than as an afterthought.

security governance   Management's control over an organization's security program.

security incident   An event during which the confidentiality, integrity, or availability of information (or an information system) has been compromised.

security incident log   A business record consisting of security incidents that have occurred.

security incident management   The process by which a framework of programs and activities is created and managed to ensure that an organization is able to detect, respond, and contain a security incident quickly.

security incident response   A formal, planned response enacted when a security incident has occurred. *See also* security incident.

security information and event management (SIEM)   A system that collects logs from hardware devices, operating systems, network devices, and software applications; correlates log data; and produces alerts that require attention.

security operations center (SOC)   An IT function wherein personnel centrally monitor and manage security functions and devices, watch for security anomalies and incidents, and take actions as warranted.

security orchestration and response (SOAR)   A processing platform used to automate routine tasks, usually as a result of a security event that has been detected by a SIEM.

security policy   *See* information security policy.

security review   An examination of a process, procedure, system, program, or other object to determine the state of security.

segregation of duties   The concept of ensuring that no single individual possesses excess privileges that could result in unauthorized activities such as fraud or the manipulation or exposure of sensitive data.

semiquantitative risk analysis   A risk analysis methodology whereby risks are classified on a simple numeric scale, such as 1 to 5.

separation of duties   *See* segregation of duties.

server   A centralized computer used to perform a specific task.

service continuity management   The IT function that consists of activities concerned with the organization's ability to continue providing services, primarily in the event of a natural or human-made disaster. *See also* IT service management (ITSM), business continuity planning (BCP), disaster recovery planning (DRP).

service delivery objective (SDO)   The level or quality of service that is required after an event, compared to normal business operations.

service desk   The IT function that handles incidents and service requests on behalf of customers by acting as a single point of contact. *See also* IT service management (ITSM).

service level agreement (SLA)   An agreement that specifies service levels in terms of the quantity of work, quality, timeliness, and remedies for shortfalls in quality or quantity.

service level management   The IT function that confirms whether IT is providing adequate service to its customers. This is accomplished through continuous monitoring and periodic review of IT service delivery. *See also* IT service management (ITSM).

shadow IT   The phenomenon wherein individuals, groups, departments, and business units bypass corporate IT and procure their own computing services, typically through SaaS and IaaS services. *See also* cloud, infrastructure as a service (IaaS), software as a service (SaaS).

shared responsibility model   A model that depicts responsibilities shared between service providers and customers, typically in a cloud environment.

simulation   A test of disaster recovery, business continuity, or security incident response procedures in which the participants take part in a "mock disaster" or incident to add some realism to the process of thinking their way through emergency response documents.

single loss expectancy (SLE)   The financial loss that results from the realization of a threat. SLE is defined as asset value (AV) × exposure factor (EF). *See also* asset value (AV), exposure factor (EF).

single point of failure   An element or device in a system or network that lacks redundancy; when it fails for any reason, this causes the entire network or system to experience an outage.

skills matrix   A chart that includes names of staff members and their relevant skills as axes, with indicators on which staff members have which skills, and with what levels of proficiency.

smart card   A small, credit-card–sized device that contains electronic memory, used with a smart card reader in two-factor authentication to grant access.

smartphone   A mobile phone equipped with an operating system and software applications.

smishing   Phishing in the context of Short Message Service (SMS) messaging. *See also* phishing.

snapshot   A continuous auditing technique that involves the use of special audit modules embedded in online applications that sample specific transactions. The module copies key database records that can be examined later.

sniffer   *See* packet sniffer.

social engineering   The act of using deception to trick an individual into revealing secrets or performing actions.

software as a service (SaaS)   A software delivery model whereby an organization obtains a software application for use by its employees and the software application is hosted by the software provider, as opposed to the customer organization.

software defect   A defect introduced into a program that results in unexpected behavior. Commonly known as a bug.

Software Engineering Institute Capability Maturity Model (SEI-CMM)   A model used to determine the maturity of security processes. *See also* Capability Maturity Model Integration for Development (CMMI-DEV).

software-defined networking (SDN)   A class of capabilities in which network infra-structure devices such as routers, switches, and firewalls are created, configured, and managed as virtual devices in virtualization environments.

solid-state drive (SSD)   A solid-state device used for persistent data storage, generally a replacement for a hard-disk drive. *See also* hard disk drive (HDD).

SOX   *See* Sarbanes–Oxley Act (SOX).

spam   Unsolicited and unwanted e-mail.

spam filter   A central program or device that examines incoming e-mail and removes all messages identified as spam.

span port   *See* network tap.

spear phishing   Phishing that is specially crafted for a specific target organization or group. *See also* business e-mail compromise, phishing, whaling.

spim   Spam or phishing in the context of instant messaging. *See also* phishing, smish-ing, spam.

spyware   A type of malware in which software performs one or more surveillance-type actions on a computer, reporting back to the spyware owner. *See also* malware.

standard   A statement that defines the technologies, protocols, suppliers, and methods used by an IT organization.

statement of impact   A description of the impact a disaster scenario will have on a business or business process.

Statements on Standards for Attestation Engagements No. 16 (SSAE 16)   An audit standard superseded by SSAE No. 18. *See also* Statements on Standards for Attestation Engagements No. 18 (SSAE 18).

Statements on Standards for Attestation Engagements No. 18 (SSAE 18)   A standard for audits performed on a financial service provider. An SSAE 18 audit is performed according to rules established by the American Institute of Certified Public Accountants (AICPA). *See also* System and Organization Controls 1 (SOC 1).

static application security testing (SAST)   The process of using tools to scan software source code to identify security defects.

statistical sampling   A sampling technique in which items are chosen at random; each item has a statistically equal probability of being chosen. *See also* sampling.

steganography   Any technique that hides data within another data file.

stop-or-go sampling   A sampling technique used to permit sampling to stop at the earliest possible time. This technique is used when the auditor thinks there is low risk or a low rate of exceptions in the population. *See also* sampling.

storage area network (SAN)   A stand-alone storage system that can be configured to contain several virtual volumes and connected to many servers through fiber-optic cables.

strategic objective   A corporate objective that is a part of a high-level strategy.

strategic planning   Activities used to develop and refine long-term plans and objectives.

strategy   The plan required to achieve an objective.

stratified sampling   A sampling technique in which a population is divided into classes, or strata, based upon the value of one of the attributes. Samples are then selected from each class. *See also* sampling.

stream cipher   A type of encryption algorithm that operates on a continuous stream of data, such as a video or audio feed.

strong authentication   *See* multifactor authentication (MFA).

subject   In the context of access management, a user, program, system, or device that may attempt to access an object. *See also* object.

supervisory control and data acquisition (SCADA)   A control system used to monitor and manage physical machinery in an industrial environment. *See also* industrial control system (ICS).

supply chain attack   An indirect attack on an organization that occurs after an attacker infiltrates an organization's trusted supplier. *See also* third-party risk management (TPRM).

symmetric encryption   A method of encryption and decryption that requires both parties to possess a common encryption key.

synchronous replication   A type of replication in which data is written to a local and a remote storage system as a single operation, guaranteeing that data on the remote storage system is identical to data on the local storage system. *See also* replication.

System and Organization Controls 1 (SOC 1)   An external audit of a service provider. A SOC 1 audit is performed according to the SSAE 18 standard established by the American Institute of Certified Public Accountants (AICPA). *See also* Statements on Standards for Attestation Engagements No. 18 (SSAE 18).

System and Organization Controls 2 (SOC 2)   An external audit of a service provider on one or more of the following trust principles: security, availability, processing integrity, confidentiality, and privacy. A SOC 2 audit is performed according to audit standards established by the American Institute of Certified Public Accountants (AICPA).

System and Organization Controls 3 (SOC 3)   An external audit of a service provider on one or more of the following trust principles: security, availability, processing integrity, confidentiality, and privacy.

systems classification   A method for assigning classification or risk levels to information systems, based on their operational criticality, the classification of data they store or process, or other risk factors. *See also* data classification.

tablet   A mobile device with a touchscreen interface. *See also* mobile device.

technical control   A control that is implemented in IT systems and applications.

technical debt   The state of being hampered by information systems of older vintages that are often unsupported, and older or poorer architecture that is no longer business aligned. *See also* data debt.

technology standard   A standard that specifies the software and hardware technologies used by the IT organization.

telework   *See* remote work.

termination   The process of discontinuing the employment of an employee or a contractor.

terrorist   A person or group who perpetrates violence for political, ideological, or religious reasons.

test plan   A step-by-step procedure for verifying that a system, service, or process complies with all applicable requirements. *See also* requirements.

The Open Group Architecture Framework (TOGAF)   A life-cycle enterprise architecture framework used to design, plan, implement, and govern an enterprise security architecture.

third party   An external organization that provides goods or services to an organization.

third-party risk management (TPRM) The practice of identifying risks associated with the use of outsourced organizations to perform business processes.

threat An event that, if realized, would bring harm to an asset.

threat assessment An examination of threats and the likelihood and impact of their occurrence.

threat hunting The proactive search for intrusions, intruders, and indicators of compromise.

threat intel feed A subscription service containing information about known threats. It can be in the form of human-readable or machine-readable information.

threat intelligence Information about security tools, tactics, and trends of intrusions that can help an organization determine how best to protect itself from intrusion.

threat intelligence platform (TIP) A system that receives and processes threat intelligence data sent by various sources.

threat management Activities undertaken by an organization to learn of relevant security threats so that the organization can take appropriate action to counter the threats.

threat modeling Techniques implemented during the software design phase to anticipate potential threats and incorporate design features to mitigate them.

three lines of defense A functional model that defines roles related to the development, operation, and assurance of controls and policies.

Towers of Hanoi A complex backup media rotation scheme, based on the Towers of Hanoi puzzle, that provides for more lengthy retention of some backup media. *See also* backup media rotation.

Towers of Sauron A collection of towers, including Dol Guldur, Orthanc, Cirith Ungol, Minas Tirith, Minas Morgul, and Barad-dûr, all located in Middle-earth.

total cost of ownership (TCO) A financial estimate of all of the costs associated with a process or system.

training The process of educating personnel; also, to impart information or provide an environment where personnel can practice a new skill.

Transport Layer Security (TLS) An encryption protocol used to encrypt web pages requested with the HTTPS URL. This is a replacement for Secure Sockets Layer (SSL). *See also* Hypertext Transfer Protocol Secure (HTTPS), Secure Sockets Layer (SSL).

tribal knowledge Undocumented knowledge of procedures, practices, design, state, and use of information systems.

unified extensible firmware interface (UEFI)   The firmware on a computer that tests the computer's hardware and initiates the bootup sequence. UEFI is considered a successor to BIOS. *See also* basic input/output system (BIOS).

uninterruptible power supply (UPS)   A system that filters incoming power spikes and other noise and supplies power for short periods through a bank of batteries.

user   A business or person that uses an information system.

user activity review   An examination of an information system to determine which users have been active and which have not been active.

user behavior analytics (UBA)   A process whereby user behavior is baselined and anomalous activities trigger events or alarms.

user and entity behavior analytics (UEBA)   *See* user behavior analytics (UBA).

userid, user ID   An identifier created by a system manager and issued to a user for the purpose of identification or authentication.

variable sampling   A sampling technique used to study the characteristics of a population to determine the numeric total of a specific attribute from the entire population. *See also* sampling.

vendor management   *See* third-party risk management (TPRM).

vendor standard   A standard that specifies which suppliers and vendors are used for various types of products and services.

virtual machine   A software implementation of a computer, usually an operating system or another program running within a hypervisor. *See also* hypervisor.

virtual private network (VPN)   A logical network connection that connects systems and devices, often used by a remote worker to access resources in an internal-use-only network.

virtualization   Software technology that separates the physical computing environment from the software that runs on a system, permitting several operating system instances to operate concurrently and independently on a single system.

virus   A type of malware in which fragments of code attach themselves to executable programs and are activated when the program they are attached to is run.

vulnerability   A weakness that may be present in a system and may be exploited by a threat.

vulnerability analysis   *See* vulnerability assessment.

vulnerability assessment   An assessment whose objective is to identify vulnerabilities in target assets.

vulnerability management   A formal business process used to identify and mitigate vulnerabilities in an IT environment.

walk-through   A review of some or all disaster recovery and business continuity plans, procedures, and other documentation, performed by an entire group of individuals in a live discussion.

war room   A meeting room or other place where incident responders gather to coordinate incident response activities.

warm site   An alternate processing center where recovery systems are present but at a lower state of readiness than recovery systems at a hot site. For example, the same version of the operating system may be running on the warm site system, but it may be a few patch levels behind primary systems. *See also* cold site, hot site.

watering hole attack   An attack on one more organizations, performed by an attacker introducing malicious code on a web site that personnel in target organizations are thought to frequent.

weaponization   The process of creating or obtaining malware that is to be delivered to a target as a part of a computer intrusion.

web application firewall (WAF)   A firewall that examines the contents of information in transit between a web server and its users to identify and block malicious content that could represent an attack on the web server.

web-based application   An application design in which the database and all business logic are stored on central servers, and user workstations use only web browsers to access the application.

web content filter   A central program or device that monitors and, optionally, filters web communications, often used to control the sites (or categories of sites) that users are permitted to access from the workplace. Some web content filters can also protect an organization from malware.

web proxy filter   *See* web content filter.

web server   A server that runs specialized software that makes static and dynamic HTML pages available to users.

whaling   Spear phishing that targets executives and other high-value and high-privilege individuals in an organization. *See also* business e-mail compromise, phishing, spear phishing.

whitelist   In a security system, a list of identifiers that should always be permitted, regardless of their other characteristics. *See also* application whitelisting.

whole-disk encryption   The practice of encrypting the main storage on a server, workstation, or mobile device.

Wi-Fi Protected Access version 2 (WPA2)   An encryption protocol that protects Wi-Fi network traffic from attack.

Wi-Fi Protected Access version 3 (WPA3)   An encryption protocol that replaces WPA2.

wiper   Malware designed to wipe the hard drive of a system.

wiperware   *See* wiper.

Wired Equivalent Privacy (WEP)   A now-deprecated encryption protocol used by Wi-Fi networks. *See also* Wi-Fi Protected Access version 2.

work from home (WFH)   An arrangement whereby employees perform work from their places of residence rather than at a business work location. This arrangement can be part-time, full-time, temporary, or permanent. *See also* remote work.

workforce transformation   A major change in the management of a workforce or the work patterns of a workforce.

worm   A type of malware containing stand-alone programs capable of human-assisted and automatic propagation.

Zachman framework   An enterprise architecture framework used to describe an IT architecture in increasing levels of detail.

zero-day   A previously unknown vulnerability in an information system. Also known as 0-day.

zero trust (ZT) security model   A network architecture model in which user and device access must be verified and validated continually.

INDEX

A

acceptable risk, 71–72
acceptable use policies (AUPs), 10, 322
acceptance of risk
    description, 116
    ISO/IEC 27005, 121–123
    residual, 173
    risk assessments, 170–171
access administrators, 27
access governance, 299
access management and control
    business process and business asset
      owners, 20
    data governance, 303
    disasters, 444
    facilities, 366
    identity and access management,
      299–302
    information technology, 367
access recertification, 301
access to resources by boards of directors, 17
accountability
    policies, 43
    RACI charts, 16
    security strategy, 54
accounts payable in TPRM programs, 349
accumulation of privileges, 300–301, 365
accuracy of information classification, 203
acknowledgments in policy development,
    222–223
action plans
    Cybersecurity Framework, 264
    reviewing, 486, 490
actionable content in awareness training, 340
actions phase in intrusion kill chain model, 410
active/active clusters, 470
active/passive clusters, 470
activities in security governance, 7–8
activity reviews, 301

adaptive tier in Cybersecurity Framework,
    87, 263
administrative audits, 326
administrative controls, 243
administrators, access, 27
advanced persistent threats (APTs),
    134–135
advisories
    risk management support, 114, 116
    security strategy, 67
affected and related business processes for
    controls, 274
affected assets in risk register, 177
affiliates, communication with, 370
AI (Artificial intelligence) as disruptive
    technology, 253
AICPA (American Institute for Certified
    Public Accountants), 271–272
ALE (annualized loss expectancy),
    141–142
alerts
    broadcast, 441
    incident detection, 500
    incident response, 504–505
algorithms in cryptography, 312
alignment
    BMIS architecture, 77
    business. *See* business alignment
    business cases, 91
    metrics strategies, 226–227
    policy development, 221
    program development strategy, 193
alternate processing facilities
    evaluating, 492
    IT operations, 446
alternate work sites in business continuity
    plans, 453
American Institute for Certified Public
    Accountants (AICPA), 271–272

analysis
   BIA. *See* business impact analysis (BIA)
   chain of custody, 510
   forensic. *See* forensic investigations
    and analysis
   incident response, 501
   incidents, 509–513
   risk. *See* risk assessment and analysis
   Risk IT framework, 125
   risk management process, 116
   risk register, 177
analysis documents for business continuity
  plans, 452
annual training for awareness, 343
annualized loss expectancy (ALE), 141–142
annualized rate of occurrence (ARO), 141
antimalware
   endpoint protection, 296
   metrics, 225
antivirus software
   death of, 297
   endpoint protection, 296
appearance issues in gap assessment, 59
appetite, risk
   business alignment, 9
   risk management process, 116
   risk response, 174–175
   security strategy, 38, 55, 71–72
applicability in compliance management, 374
application firewalls, 283
application scanning, 151
application servers
   clusters, 470
   continuity plans, 444
   threat analysis, 421
applications
   encryption, 321
   replication, 308, 469
   testing, 393
   whitelisting, 296
approaches in business cases, 91
approvals in change management, 386–387
Approved Scanning Vendors (ASV), 265
approvers for controls, 274
APTs (advanced persistent threats),
  134–135
architectures
   availability management, 393
   BMIS model, 76–77

control frameworks, 252
   information technology, 367
   program development, 218–220
   risk management integration with, 150
   security strategy, 44–45
   zero-trust, 292–293
ARO (annualized rate of occurrence), 141
Artificial intelligence (AI) as disruptive
  technology, 253
assessment
   CSA life cycle, 338
   gap, 56–59
   ISO/IEC 27005, 121–122
   NIST SP 800-30, 119–121
   risk. *See* risk assessment and analysis
   risk register, 148
   third parties, 356–360
   vulnerability. *See* vulnerability assessment
asset identification and classification, 199
   classification, 202–208
   hardware, 199–200
   information, 201
   risk management process, 115
   subsystem and software, 200
   valuation, 209–210
   virtual, 201–202
asset-level risks, 111
asset management
   business process and asset owners, 20
   ITSM, 394
asset value (AV)
   business alignment, 8
   identification, 136
   quantitative risk analysis, 141
   risk management process, 115
assets
   facilities, 367
   risk register, 177
   security strategy, 47
assistants, 14
assurance process integration
   program development, 194
   security strategy, 38
ASV (Approved Scanning Vendors), 265
asymmetric encryption, 313
asynchronous replication, 309, 469
attestations for third parties, 357
attorney–client privilege, 516
attribute sampling for audit evidence, 331

audiences
    awareness training, 340–343
    metrics, 231
    policy development, 221
audit rights in TPRM, 353
auditors
    partnerships, 371
    self-assessment, 339
audits
    controls, 322–323
    disaster recovery sites, 465
    evidence, 329–331
    external, 335–336
    gap assessment, 57
    internal, 333–335, 369
    methodology, 327–329
    monitoring, 29
    objectives, 325
    outsourcing, 347
    results, controls, 242
    rcsults, reporting, 332–333
    results, seeding, 336–337
    risk register, 148
    security strategy, 53
    statements of work, 328
    techniques, 324–325
    third-party reports, 332
    TPRM, 353
    types, 325–327
AUPs (acceptable use policies), 10, 322
authentication
    encryption, 310
    identity and access management, 299
    Information security architecture, 219
    multifactor, 174, 299
    zero-trust architecture, 292–293
authorized persons in incident response
    plans, 516
automatic controls, 245
automation
    BMIS model, 77
    security operations, 363
AV. See asset value (AV)
availability management in ITSM, 393–394
availability principle in SOC 2, 271
avalanches, 428
avoidance, risk
    description, 117
    ISO/IEC 27005, 123
    risk response, 169–170

awareness
    audit evidence, 330
    risk management programs, 107
    risk response, 181–182
    security strategy, 54, 65–66
awareness training
    audiences, 340–343
    communications, 343–344
    content filters, 340
    CSA life cycle, 338
    gap assessment, 58
    objectives, 339–340
    reporting, 375–376

B

background checks in human resource
    management, 156
backups, 303–304. See also recovery
    disaster recovery plans,
        472–473
    encryption, 307
    media storage, 306–307
    records, 308
    replication, 308–309
    rotation, 305–306
    schemes, 305
    tape, 304
balanced scorecards (BSCs), 232–233
bare-metal restores, 521
Bayesian analysis, 143
BCDR (business continuity and disaster
    recovery) programs, 50
BCI (Business Continuity Institute), 454
BCM Institute (Business Continuity
    Management Institute), 455
BCPs. See business continuity plans (BCPs)
BEC (business e-mail compromise),
    280, 291
behavioral skills, 46
BIA. See business impact analysis (BIA)
bias, normalcy, 68–69
big data architects, 24
biometric recognition in BMIS model, 79
blacklists for e-mail, 291
block ciphers, 313
BMIS (Business Model for Information
    Security), 73
    elements and dynamic interconnections,
        74–79
    working with, 79–81

boards of directors
    roles, 16–18
    security strategy, 39
    security strategy meetings, 67
book value in asset valuation, 209
books for risk management, 114
bow-tie analyses, 143
breaches
    privacy, 512
    third-party, 49
breadth of coverage policies in security
  strategy, 42
bring your own app (BYOA)
    as disruptive technology, 253
    security strategy, 50
bring your own device (BYOD)
    as disruptive technology, 253
    security strategy, 50
broadcast alerts, 441
BSCs (balanced scorecards), 232–233
budgets
    program management, 382–383
    security strategy, 70
build vs. buy control decisions, 247
bulletins for awareness training
  communication, 344
business alignment
    criticality, 39
    gap assessment, 56
    information security governance, 8–9
    security strategy, 38
business analysts, 29
business cases, developing, 89–91
business continuity
    containment methods, 514–515
    responsibilities, 503
    security governance, 7
    third-party remediation, 361
    training, 476–477
business continuity and disaster recovery
  (BCDR) programs, 50
Business Continuity Institute (BCI), 454
Business Continuity Management Institute
  (BCM Institute), 455
business continuity plans (BCPs)
    availability to personnel, 452–453
    best practices, 454–455
    COBIT controls, 435
    components, 451–452

considerations, 447–451
development overview, 436
disaster declaration procedures,
  437–439
disasters, 427–434
evaluating, 484–487
gap assessment, 58
maintaining, 453–454
overview, 406–408, 426–427
personnel safety procedures, 436–437
policies, 434–435
process, 434
risk management, 145
roles, 27
testing, 478–483
business e-mail compromise (BEC),
  280, 291
business experience of boards of directors, 17
business impact analysis (BIA)
    big picture, 417
    criticality analysis, 420–422
    executive level, 417
    key processes and systems inventory,
      417–418
    key recovery targets, 423–426
    maximum tolerable downtime, 422
    maximum tolerable outage, 422–423
    security strategy, 50
    statements of impact, 419–420
business intelligence in third parties, 357
business leaders in security strategy, 40
Business Model for Information Security
  (BMIS), 73
    elements and dynamic interconnections,
      74–79
    working with, 79–81
business operations as asset, 201
business partners, communication with, 370
business prevention, security as, 9
business processes
    detection techniques, 128
    owner responsibilities, 20–21
business recovery plans, 452
business resilience roles, 27
business terms in business cases, 91
business unit leaders
    communication with, 369–370
    incident response plans, 413
    TPRM programs, 349

buy vs. build control decisions, 247
BYOA (bring your own app)
    as disruptive technology, 253
    security strategy, 50
BYOD (bring your own device)
    as disruptive technology, 253
    security strategy, 50

C

CABs (change advisory boards), 387
call trees for disaster communication, 449–450
Canada, law enforcement agencies in, 370
Capability Maturity Model Integration for Development (CMMi-DEV)
    incident response plans, 412
    security strategy, 60–61
capacity, risk, 174–175
capacity management in ITSM, 392–393
career paths in professional development, 379
CAs (certificate authorities), 316, 318
CASBs (cloud access security brokers), 290
cashiers, awareness training for, 341
categories
    CIS CSC controls, 216
    controls, 84, 245
    CSF functions, 86
    HIPAA requirements, 213
    incidents, 473–475
    information security processes, 195
    ISO/IEC 27002, 254–256
    NIST SP 800-53, 214, 259–260
    NIST SP 800-171, 214–215
    operational activities, 276
    retail workers, 341
    risk management, 104–105
    strategic objectives, 55
causal relationships in metrics, 226
CCBs (change control boards), 387
CCEs (Certified Computer Examiners), 476
CCM (Cloud Controls Matrix), 249, 270
CCOs (chief compliance officers), 23
CCSP (Certified Cloud Security Professional), 380
CDFEs (Certified Digital Forensics Examiners), 512
CDPSEs (Certified Data Privacy Solutions Engineers), 380
CEHs (Certified Ethical Hackers), 380

Center for Internet Security (CIS)
    Critical Security Controls framework, 216–217, 249, 260–262
    standards, 43
centralized log management, 276
certificate authorities (CAs), 316, 318
certificate revocation lists (CRLs), 319
certificates in public key infrastructure, 318
certification practice statements (CPSs), 319
certifications
    forensics, 512
    incident response, 476
    PCI Security Standards Council, 265
    professional development, 379–381
    professional organizations, 372
Certified Cloud Security Professional (CCSP), 380
Certified Computer Examiners (CCEs), 476
Certified Data Privacy Solutions Engineers (CDPSEs), 380
Certified Digital Forensics Examiners (CDFEs), 512
Certified Ethical Hackers (CEHs), 380
Certified Forensic Computer Examiners (CFCEs), 512
Certified in Risk and Information Systems Control (CRISC) certification, 4, 380
Certified in the Governance of Enterprise IT (CGEIT), 4
Certified Information Security Managers (CISMs), 380
Certified Information Systems Auditors (CISAs), 380
Certified Information Systems Security Professionals (CISSPs), 380
Certified Secure Software Lifecycle Professionals (CSSLPs), 380
CFCEs (Certified Forensic Computer Examiners), 512
CGEIT (Certified in the Governance of Enterprise IT), 4
chain of custody in forensic investigations, 510
change advisory boards (CABs), 387
change and change management
    availability management, 393
    capacity management, 392
    configuration management link, 389
    controls, 63
    ITSM, 386–388

change and change management (*cont.*)
  organizational inertia, 72
  project and program management, 382
  resistance to, 68, 72
  risk management integration with, 152
  risk ownership, 178–179
change control boards (CCBs), 387
changing technologies in control frameworks, 252–253
charters in program development, 194
charts, RACI, 15–16
CHFIs (Computer Hacking Forensic Investigators), 512
chief compliance officers (CCOs), 23
chief information officers (CIOs), 18
chief information risk officers (CIROs), 21–22
chief information security officers (CISOs), 18, 21–22
chief privacy officers (CPOs), 23
chief risk officers (CROs), 21–22
chief security officers (CSOs), 21–22
chief technical officers (CTOs), 18
CIAS (confidentiality, integrity, availability, and safety), 407
CIOs (chief information officers), 18
ciphers, 313
ciphertext, 311
CIROs (chief information risk officers), 21–22
CIS (Center for Internet Security)
  Critical Security Controls framework, 216–217, 249, 260–262
  standards, 43
CIs (configuration items) in ITSM, 388
CISAs (Certified Information Systems Auditors), 380
CISMs (Certified Information Security Managers), 380
CISOs (chief information security officers), 18, 21–22
CISSPs (Certified Information Systems Security Professionals), 380
civil disturbances, 431
classification
  assets, 202–208
  controls, 242–245, 274
  facilities, 207
  hardware assets, 200
  incidents, 473–475
  information, 203–205
  personnel, 207–208

system, 206–207
vendor, 354–356
clients for incident reporting, 508
clone phishing, 291
closure
  activities, 522
  incident response, 501
cloud
  business titles, 26
  cloud-based information assets, 201
  as disruptive technology, 253
  service providers, 350–351
cloud access security brokers (CASBs), 290
Cloud Controls Matrix (CCM), 249, 270
Cloud Security Alliance (CSA)
  Cloud Controls Matrix, 249, 270
  description, 371–372
cloud sites
  disaster recovery plans, 463
  hardware, 466
clusters in disaster recovery plans, 469–470
CM (configuration management)
  endpoint protection, 294–295
  ITSM, 388–389
  risk management integration with, 152–153
CMDBs (configuration management databases), 388
CMMC (Cybersecurity Maturity Model Certification) framework, 215
CMMi-DEV (Capability Maturity Model Integration for Development)
  incident response plans, 412
  security strategy, 60–61
COBIT 2019. *See* Control Objectives for Information and Related Technology (COBIT 2019) framework
Code of Professional Ethics, 10–11
coding
  reviews, 151, 369
  scanning, 151
  standards, 151
cold sites
  backup storage, 307
  disaster recovery plans, 462
  hardware, 465–466
command and control
  disasters, 440–441
  incident response plans, 413
  intrusion kill chain model, 410

commanders incident responsibilities, 502
Committee of Sponsoring Organizations of the Treadway Commission (COSO)
   control framework, 249
   private-sector associations, 267–269
Common Vulnerability Scoring System (CVSS), 278–279
communication and reporting
   affiliates and key business partners, 370
   audits, 328–329, 332, 369
   awareness training, 343–344, 375–376
   budgets, 382–383
   business continuity plans, 452
   business unit managers, 369–370
   compliance management, 373–375
   crisis management, 515–516
   disaster recovery sites, 465
   disasters, 440–442, 448
   external partnerships, 370–373
   facilities, 366–367
   incident response, 515–519
   incident response plans, 416–417, 516–517
   incident responsibilities, 502–503
   information technology, 367–368
   internal partnerships, 364–370
   ISO/IEC 27005, 123
   monitoring, 30
   NIST SP 800-30, 120–121
   personnel management, 376–382
   policies, 42
   post-incident reviews, 522–523
   procurement, 369
   project and program management, 382
   risk management, 107, 363–364
   risk management support, 114
   risks, 117, 180–182
   security governance, 6
   security operations, 363
   security strategy, 66–67
   systems development, 368–369
   technical architecture, 376
   third-party audits, 332
compensating controls, 244
compensation in project and program management, 382
competitive advantage in outsourcing, 346
competitive differentiation in resource expenditures, 232

compliance and compliance management
   applicability, 374
   audits, 326
   disasters, 442
   insurance, 48
   metrics, 227
   monitoring, 375
   outsourcing, 347
   overview, 373–374
   policies, 43
   risk, 176–177, 374–375
   vs. security, 373–374
components in risk management frameworks, 108–109
compromised keys, 320
computer account abuse, 408
Computer Hacking Forensic Investigators (CHFIs), 512
conceptual stage in security involvement, 281
conduct assessment in NIST SP 800-30, 119
conferences for risk management support, 114
confidential information classification, 203–205
confidentiality, integrity, availability, and safety (CIAS), 407
confidentiality principle in SOC 2, 271
configuration
   faults, 127
   standards, 64
configuration items (CIs) in ITSM, 388
configuration management (CM)
   endpoint protection, 294–295
   ITSM, 388–389
   risk management integration with, 152–153
configuration management databases (CMDBs), 388
conflicts of interest in RACI charts, 16
consequences identification in ISO/IEC 27005, 122
consequences of policies in security strategy, 43
consequential financial cost in asset valuation, 209
consistency in BMIS architecture, 77, 79
constraints in security strategy, 68–72
consultants
   RACI charts, 16
   risk management programs, 107–108
   risk management support, 112
   risk register, 148

contact lists
    business continuity plans, 452
    disaster communications, 451
    disaster recovery plans, 472
containerization for cloud services, 202
containment
    incident response, 501
    incident responsibilities, 503
    methods, 513–515
content
    audit reports, 332–333
    awareness training, 340
content filters
    incident response tools, 505
    web, 289–290
context
    ISO/IEC 27005, 121
    risk management programs, 109–110
contingencies
    BCP and DRP plans tests, 479–480
    disaster recovery plans, 459
continuing operations
    business continuity plans, 452
    disasters, 446
continuous improvement, 394
contract information for disasters, 445
contractors
    employee benefits, 156
    in workforce, 29
contractual obligations
    enterprise governance, 11–12
    vendor classification, 355
control assurance in three lines of defense
  model, 196
control deficiency analysis, 127–129
control frameworks, 210–212
    Center for Internet Security, 260–262
    changing technologies, 252–253
    COBIT, 212–213, 267
    COSO, 267
    Critical Security Controls, 216–217
    CSA, 270
    HIPAA, 213–214, 266
    ISO/IEC 27002, 213, 254–259
    ISO/IEC 27005, 122
    ITIL / ISO/IEC 20000, 213
    mapping, 250–251
    NERC, 267–269
    NIST CSF. *See* Cybersecurity
      Framework (CSF)

    NIST SP 800-53, 214, 259
    NIST SP 800-171, 215
    overview, 248
    PCI DSS, 217, 264–266
    risk mitigation, 168
    security strategy, 63
    selecting, 248–249
    service organization, 270–272
    standards, 64
    working with, 251–252
Control Objectives for Information and
  Related Technology (COBIT 2019)
  framework
    business continuity plans, 435
    control framework, 249
    management framework, 218
    overview, 212–213
    principles, 267
    risk management frameworks, 108
control self-assessment (CSA), 337–338
control testing and evaluation, 321
    audits. *See* audits
    monitoring, 322
    reviews, 322–323
controls
    alignment in policy development, 221
    BMIS model, 77
    build vs. buy decisions, 247
    categories, 245
    classes, 243–245
    classification, 242–243
    developing, 272–275
    disaster recovery sites, 465
    effectiveness evaluation, 333
    event monitoring, 276–277
    frameworks. *See* control frameworks
    gap assessment, 57
    general computing, 246–247
    implementation, 275
    monitoring activities, 29
    network protection. *See* network protection
    objectives, 245–246
    operations, 196, 275–276
    outsourcing issues, 346
    overview, 145
    ownership in risk response, 179–180
    purpose, 242
    risk assessment for third parties, 52
    secure engineering, 280–282
    security governance, 6

security strategy, 45, 62–63
self-assessment, 337–339
standards, 72–88
third-party remediation, 361
three lines of defense model, 196
TPRM, 352
types, 243
vulnerability management, 277–282
controls analysts, 25
controls managers, 26
convergence in metrics, 227–228
core of NIST Cybersecurity Framework, 215
core teams in disaster declaration, 438
corporate workers, awareness training for, 341
corrective actions, risk implications associated
with, 154
corrective controls, 244
corruption of data incidents, 409
COSO (Committee of Sponsoring
Organizations of the Treadway Commission)
control framework, 249
private-sector associations, 267–269
costs
asset valuation, 209
BMIS architecture, 77
efficiency metrics, 230–231
MSSP control of, 506
outsourcing, 345–346
quantitative risk analysis, 141
risk response, 172–173
security strategy, 70
covered entities in HIPAA, 213
CPOs (chief privacy officers), 23
CPSs (certification practice statements), 319
creation cost in asset valuation, 209
CRISC (Certified in Risk and Information
Systems Control) certification, 4, 380
crisis communications
incident response plans, 413
management, 515–516
role, 27
criteria
disaster declaration, 438
risk evaluation, 121
risk measurement, 142
success, 91
vendor classification, 354–355
critical data in security strategy, 49–50
critical personnel for disasters, 448

Critical Security Controls framework (CSC),
216–217
criticality
business alignment, 39
business impact analysis, 420–422
CRLs (certificate revocation lists), 319
CROs (chief risk officers), 21–22
cross-border data transfer in outsourcing, 347
cross references to controls, 275
crosswalks, 250
cryptography
key management, 319–321
overview, 310
private key cryptosystems, 313–314
public key cryptosystems, 314–318
public key infrastructure, 318–319
terms and concepts, 311–313
CSA (Cloud Security Alliance)
Cloud Controls Matrix, 249, 270
description, 371–372
CSA (control self-assessment), 337–338
CSC (Critical Security Controls framework),
216–217
CSF. See Cybersecurity Framework (CSF)
CSOs (chief security officers), 21–22
CSSLPs (Certified Secure Software Lifecycle
Professionals), 380
CTOs (chief technical officers), 18
cultural differences in outsourcing, 348
culture
acceptable use policies, 10
BMIS model, 75–76
business alignment, 8
constraints, 69
organizational, 9–11
personnel management, 378
security strategy, 53–54
current state in business cases, 91
custodial responsibilities, 21
custodians of hardware assets, 200
custody of keys, 320
customer availability in disasters, 434
customer data in vendor classification, 354
customer information as asset, 201
customer metrics in balanced scorecards, 232
customer notifications in disasters, 448–449
customer priorities in disaster recovery sites, 465
customer requirements in insurance, 48
customers, incident reporting by, 508

cutover tests
    BCP and DRP, 482–483
    training, 477
CVSS (Common Vulnerability Scoring
    System), 278–279
Cyber Incident Reporting for Critical
    Infrastructure Act, 192
cyber insurance
    MSSPs, 506
    security strategy, 48–49
    TPRM, 353
cyber intelligence in third parties, 357
"Cyber-Risk Oversight 2020," 18
Cybersecurity Canon, 114
Cybersecurity Framework (CSF)
    activities, 262–264
    components, 215–216
    control framework, 249
    highlights, 86–87
    overview, 85–86
    purpose, 218
    steps, 87–88
Cybersecurity Maturity Model Certification
    (CMMC) framework, 215
cyclical controls, testing, 334–335
cyclone damage, 428

D

damage assessment in disasters, 442
damaged files, recovering, 521
data acquisition
    forensic investigations, 510
    Risk IT framework, 125
data communications for disaster recovery
    sites, 465
data debt, 45
data encryption in endpoint protection, 295
data entry in BMIS model, 79
data extraction in forensic investigations, 511
data flow diagrams (DFDs), 81–82
data governance
    access management, 303
    backup and recovery, 303–309
    cryptography, 311–321
    data classification, 309
    data loss prevention, 309–310
data issues in disasters, 444
data loss prevention (DLP), 309–310

data management roles, 24
data managers, 24
data protection in forensic investigations, 511
data scientists, 24
data sovereignty in disaster recovery sites, 465
database administrators (DBAs), 24
database analysts, 24
database architects, 24
database management servers, 206
database management systems (DBMSs)
    disasters, 444
    replication, 308, 468
    vulnerability detection techniques, 128
dates in controls development, 274
DBAs (database administrators), 24
DDoS (distributed denial-of-service) attacks
    incidents, 409
    protection against, 285
deception in antimalware, 296
declaration of incidents
    business continuity plans, 437–439
    disaster recovery plans, 471
    responsibilities, 502
decryption, 312
dedicated personnel in MSSPs, 505
defense-in-depth architecture, 252
Defense Information Systems Agency Security
    Technical Implementation Guides
    (DISA STIG), 43
delivery phase in intrusion kill chain model, 410
Delphi method, 143
demilitarized zones (DMZs), 206, 282–284
denial-of-service (DoS) attacks, 409
department heads in TPRM programs, 349
departments in awareness training, 343
deployment in release management, 391
descriptions in risk register, 177
design
    architecture issues, 44
    control frameworks, 251–252
    faults in, 127
    release management, 390
    security involvement, 281
desired state in business cases, 91
destruction
    backups, 308
    of data in incidents, 409
destructware, 295–296
details in controls development, 274–275

detection
  Cybersecurity Framework, 86, 262
  incident phase, 507–508
  incident response, 500
  incident responsibilities, 502
detective controls, 244
deterrent controls, 244
developer controls, 274
development step in release management, 390
device authentication in zero-trust
  architecture, 292
device management in information security
  architecture, 220
device validation in zero-trust architecture, 293
DFDs (data flow diagrams), 81–82
differential backups, 305
digital certificates and envelopes in public key
  infrastructure, 318
digital rights management (DRM), 310
digital signatures, 312, 317
direct connectivity in SaaS services, 464
direct damage from disasters, 433
directory infrastructure in public key
  cryptosystems, 316
DIs (dynamic interconnections) in BMIS
  model, 74–79
DISA STIG (Defense Information Systems
  Agency Security Technical Implementation
  Guides), 43
disaster declaration procedures
  business continuity plans, 437–439
  disaster recovery plans, 471
  incident responsibilities, 502
Disaster Recovery Institute International (DRI
  International), 455
disaster recovery plans (DRPs)
  alternate processing facilities, 492
  business continuity plans, 452
  data backup and recovery, 472–473
  developing, 471–472
  distributed workforce, 465
  evaluating, 488–492
  gap assessment, 58
  hardware, 465–466
  inputs, 455
  offsite storage, 491–492
  overview, 406–408
  recovery and resilience technologies, 467–471
  recovery objectives, 457

results, 490
roles, 27
RTO and RPO, 457–459
SaaS services, 463–464
security governance, 7
site recovery options, 460–465
strategies, 459–460
team roles and responsibilities, 456–457
testing, 478–483
disasters
  business continuity plans, 427–434
  communication in, 440–442
  containment methods, 514–515
  continuing operations, 446
  effects, 433–434
  human-caused, 431–432
  natural, 428–431
  recovery procedures, 445–447
  responsibilities, 439–445
  training for, 476–477
discipline in human resources, 366
disciplines in security strategy skills, 46
disclosure of sensitive information, 409
discovery sampling for audit evidence, 331
disk storage systems for replication, 308, 468
display in BMIS model, 79
disposal of keys, 320–321
disputes in third-party remediation, 362
distributed denial-of-service (DDoS) attacks
  incidents, 409
  protection against, 285
distributed lock managers, 469
distributed workforce in disaster recovery
  plans, 465
distribution of policy development, 222–223
DLP (data loss prevention), 309–310
DMZs (demilitarized zones), 206, 282–284
DNS (domain name system) filtering, 290
document reviews
  BCP and DRP tests, 480
  incident response plans, 477
  training, 477
documentation
  BCP and DRP tests, 483
  business continuity plans, 451–453,
    485–486
  chain of custody, 510
  risk, 182
  risk ownership, 178

domain expertise of MSSPs, 505
domain name system (DNS) filtering, 290
DoS (denial-of-service) attacks, 409
DRI International (Disaster Recovery Institute International), 455
DRM (digital rights management), 310
DRPs. *See* disaster recovery plans (DRPs)
due diligence
    onboarding, 352
    outsourced services, 51–52
    TPRM, 353–354
duties
    RACI charts, 16
    segregation of, 300–301
dwell time
    incident detection, 507
    reducing, 508
dynamic data loss prevention, 309
dynamic interconnections (DIs) in BMIS model, 74–79

E

e-mail
    awareness training communication, 343
    protecting, 290–292
    public key cryptosystems, 316
e-vaulting for backups, 304
EA (enterprise architecture), 218–220
earthquake damage, 428
EC-Council Certified Incident Handlers (ECIHs), 476
EC-Council (International Council of Electronic Commerce Consultants), 372
ECC (elliptic curve cryptography), 316
economies of scale for outsourcing, 345
EDR (endpoint detection and response), 297
EF (exposure factor) in quantitative risk analysis, 141
effective metrics, 226
effective processes in BMIS model, 75
effective risk management, 38
effectiveness evaluation for controls, 333
efficiency in BMIS architecture, 77
elasticity in cloud services, 202
electronic contact lists for disasters, 451
electronic protected health information (ePHI), 213
elements in BMIS model, 74–75

elliptic curve cryptography (ECC), 316
emergence in BMIS model, 77–78
emergency changes, 387–388
emergency communications plans in BCPs, 452
emergency contact lists, 472
emergency management, 440–441
emergency operations responsibilities, 503
emergency radio communications, 441
emergency supplies, 447–448
emerging threats, identifying, 135–136
employee integrity factor in third-party remediation, 361
employees, incident reporting by, 508
empowerment in security strategy, 54
enabling and support DI in BMIS model, 78
encryption
    applications, 321
    backups, 307
    cryptography. *See* cryptography
    endpoint protection, 295
    incidents, 409
    key management, 219
end user behavior analytics (EUBA), 301–302
end users, incident reporting by, 508
endpoint detection and response (EDR), 297
endpoint protection and management, 293
    configuration management, 294–295
    EDR, 297
    local administrators, 298
    malware, 295–296
    targets, 294
    VDIs, 297
    whitelisting, 296
engineering stage in security involvement, 281
enhancements in release management, 389
ENISA (European Union Agency for Cybersecurity), 43
enterprise architecture (EA), 218–220
enterprise governance, 3
    legal, regulatory, and contractual requirements, 11–12
    notes, 31–32
    organizational culture, 9–11
    organizational roles. *See* organizational roles
    questions, 32–35
    review, 30–31
    security, 4–9

enterprise-level risks, 111

enterprise risk management (ERM)
    description, 111
    risk management integration with, 155

Entry-Level Cybersecurity Certification, 380

envelopes in public key cryptosystems, 318

environment
    BMIS model, 79
    risk management programs, 110

environmental controls in disaster recovery
   sites, 465

ePHI (electronic protected health
   information), 213

equipment
    disaster recovery sites, 464–465
    facilities, 366

eradication
    incident response, 501
    incident responsibilities, 503
    process, 519–520

ergonomics in BMIS model, 79

ERM (enterprise risk management)
    description, 111
    risk management integration with, 155

error recovery in BMIS model, 79

errors and omissions in outsourcing, 347

escalation in incident response plans,
   416–417

ETA (event-tree analysis), 143

ethics in organizational culture, 10–11

EUBA (end user behavior analytics), 301–302

European Telecommunications Standards
   Institute (ETSI)
    CYBER standard, 218
    Technical Report control framework, 249

European Union Agency for Cybersecurity
   (ENISA), 43

evaluation
    alternate processing facilities, 492
    business continuity plans, 484–487
    control effectiveness, 333
    disaster recovery plans, 488–492
    incident response, 492–493
    ISO/IEC 27005, 121–122
    offsite storage, 491–492
    risk, 144

event-tree analysis (ETA), 143

events
    cost in quantitative risk analysis, 141
    identification in security governance, 7

monitoring, 276–277
    probability in quantitative risk analysis, 140
    security operations, 363
    visibility in incident detection, 507

evidence
    audits, 329–331
    gap assessment, 58
    retaining in incident response, 501
    third parties, 359–361

executive management
    incident response plans, 413
    responsibilities, 18–19
    security strategy, 39

existing strategy in gap assessment, 56

experience in outsourcing, 345

expiration of keys, 320

exploitation phase in intrusion kill chain
   model, 410

exposure factor (EF) in quantitative risk
   analysis, 141

extended detection and response (XDR)
   systems, 297

external attestations for third parties, 357

external audits
    compliance, 326, 375
    reasons, 335–336
    reports, 57
    statements of work, 328
    TPRM, 353

external communications
    disasters, 442
    incident responsibilities, 503
    post-incident reviews, 523

external environments in risk management
   programs, 110

external legal counsel, 506

external partnerships
    law enforcement, 370–371
    professional organizations, 371–372
    regulators and auditors, 371
    security product vendors, 373
    security professional services vendors,
     372–373
    standards organizations, 371

external services
    cloud providers, 350–351
    outsourcing, 345–348
    overview, 344–345
    third parties. *See* third parties
    TPRM life cycle, 351–354

external support in risk management, 112–113
external threat intelligence in security
    operations, 363
external threats, identifying, 132–134
extraterrestrial impacts, 430

F

facilities
    alternate processing, 402
    as asset, 199
    for BCP and DRP tests, 479–480
    classification, 207
    communication with, 366–367
    TPRM programs, 349
Factor Analysis of Information Risk (FAIR),
    124–125
failover in server clusters, 470
fairs for awareness training communication, 344
false alarms
    disaster declaration, 439
    incident initiation, 509
FAM (file activity monitoring), 505
fault-tree analysis (FTA), 143
FCPA (Foreign Corrupt Practices Act of
    1977), 11
fear culture, 69
feasibility studies for release management, 389
Federal Emergency Management Agency
    (FEMA), 454
fiduciary responsibility
    boards of directors, 17
    resource expenditures, 232
FIFO (first in, first out) backup strategy, 305
file activity monitoring (FAM), 505
file integrity monitoring (FIM), 505
fileless malware, 296
filters
    DNS, 290
    phishing, 290–292
    web content, 289–290, 504
FIM (file integrity monitoring), 505
finance managers, 29
financial audits, 325
financial management, 391–393
financial metrics in balanced scorecards, 232
finding talent, 376–377
fines, risk of, 375

fingerprints, 316
fire disasters, 432
firewalls
    metrics, 225
    network protection, 282–284
first in, first out (FIFO) backup strategy, 305
flexibility in BMIS architecture, 77
flood damage, 428
floor managers, awareness training for, 341
follow-ups for audits, 329
forecasting data for threats, 136
Foreign Corrupt Practices Act of 1977
    (FCPA), 11
forensic investigations and analysis
    audits, 326
    certifications, 512
    chain of custody, 510
    incident ranking and rating, 509
    incident response, 505
    incident response plans, 413
    incident responsibilities, 503
    techniques and considerations,
        510–511
forensics analysts, 27
fourth parties in SaaS services, 464
frameworks
    Business Model for Information Security,
        73–81
    control. See control frameworks
    information governance, 72–88
    ISO/IEC 27001, 83–85
    management, 218
    mitigation, 168
    NIST CSF. See Cybersecurity Framework
        (CSF)
    Open Group Architecture Framework,
        83–84
    policy development, 62
    risk management programs, 108–109
    standards, 64
    Zachman, 81–82
frequency of control use, 274
FTA (fault-tree analysis), 143
full backups, 305
function definitions by asset owners, 20
functional requirements in program
    development, 224

G

GAISPs (generally accepted information security principles), 173
gap analysis and assessment
  Cybersecurity Framework, 263
  incident response plans, 414
  risk management, 112
  security strategy, 56–59
GASF (GIAC Advanced Smartphone Forensics) certification, 512
GASSPs (generally accepted security systems principles), 173
gate processes in release management, 391
GCCs (general computing controls), 246–247
GCFAs (GIAC Certified Forensic Analysts), 476
GCFEs (GIAC Certified Forensic Examiners), 512
GCIHs (GIAC Certified Incident Handlers), 476
general computing controls (GCCs), 246–247
generally accepted information security principles (GAISPs), 173
generally accepted security systems principles (GASSPs), 173
generation of keys, 319
geographic clusters in disaster recovery plans, 470
geographic site selection in SaaS services, 463
GIAC Advanced Smartphone Forensics (GASF) certification, 512
GIAC Certified Forensic Analysts (GCFAs), 476
GIAC Certified Forensic Examiners (GCFEs), 512
GIAC Certified Incident Handlers (GCIHs), 476
GIAC (Global Information Assurance Certification), 380
GIAC Network Forensic Analysts (GNFAs), 476
GIAC Reverse Engineering Malware (GREM), 476
GLBA (Gramm-Leach-Bliley Act), 176
Global Information Assurance Certification (GIAC), 380
GNFAs (GIAC Network Forensic Analysts), 476
goals
  business alignment, 8–9
  outsourcing, 347

governance
  activities and results, 7–8
  BMIS model, 76
  business alignment, 8–9
  data. *See* data governance
  defined, 3
  enterprise. *See* enterprise governance
  frameworks and standards, 72–88
  information security strategy.
    See security strategy
  introduction, 4–6
  reasons, 6–7
governance meetings for security strategy, 67
governance, risk, and compliance (GRC)
  risk registers, 178
  roles, 26
Gramm-Leach-Bliley Act (GLBA), 176
grandfather-father-son backup strategy, 306
GRC (governance, risk, and compliance)
  risk registers, 178
  roles, 26
GREM (GIAC Reverse Engineering Malware), 476
groups for hardware assets, 200
guards for facilities, 367
guest processing for facilities, 366
guidelines
  gap assessment, 57
  program development, 223
  security strategy, 43–44

H

hail damage, 429
hard copies for business continuity plans, 453
hard disk drives
  backups, 304
  encryption, 295
hardening
  information technology, 367
  standard documents in endpoint protection, 295
hardware
  assets, 199–200
  configuration items, 388
  disaster recovery plans, 465–466
  disasters, 445
hash functions, 311, 317
hazardous materials spills, 432

HCI (human–computer interaction)
in BMIS model, 78
Health Insurance Portability and
Accountability Act (HIPAA)
control framework, 213–214, 249
sections, 266
healthy cultures, importance of, 69
high risk roles in identity and access
management, 301
HITRUST CSF control framework, 249
hot sites
backup storage, 307
disaster recovery plans, 460–461
hardware, 466
HR (human resources), 365–366
HRM (human resource management), 155–156
human-caused disasters, 431–432
human resource information system
(HRIS), 156
human resource management (HRM),
155–156
human resources (HR), 365–366
human–computer interaction (HCI)
in BMIS model, 78
hybrid cryptography, 318
hygiene in risk likelihood, 137

I

IAM. *See* identity and access management
(IAM)
ice storms, 429
identification
chain of custody, 510
Cybersecurity Framework, 86, 262
hardware assets, 200
NIST SP 800-30, 119
risk, 116, 136–137
risk register, 177
third parties, 348–350
vulnerability management, 279–280
identity and access management (IAM)
access governance, 299
access operations, 299–300
access recertification, 301
accumulation of privilege, 300
activity reviews, 301
high risk roles, 301
overview, 300–301
segregation of duties, 300–301
user behavior analytics, 301–302

IDPS (intrusion detection/prevention system)
metrics, 225
IDSs (intrusion detection systems), 285
IEC (International Electrotechnical
Commission), 371
IG (information governance), 87–88
ignoring risk, 171
image management in endpoint protection, 294
impact
business impact analysis, 419–420
identifying, 137
ISO/IEC 27005 criteria, 121
NIST SP 800-30 determination, 120
risk, 138–139
risk management process, 116
risk response, 172
implementation
change management, 387–388
controls, 275
Cybersecurity Framework tiers, 215
release management, 390–391
improvements from security governance, 7
Improving Critical Infrastructure
Cybersecurity executive order, 85
incident management
capacity management link, 393
change management link, 388
configuration management link, 388
ITSM, 384–385, 416
parts, 302
risk management integration with,
153–154
incident management operations
communications, 515–517
containment methods, 513–515
incident analysis, 509–513
incident detection, 507–508
incident eradication, 519–520
incident initiation, 509
metrics and reporting, 517–519
notes, 524
overview, 499
phases, 499–502
post-incident review practices, 522–523
questions, 524–528
recovery, 520–521
remediation, 521–522
review, 523–524
roles and responsibilities, 502–503
tools and techniques, 503–507

incident management readiness
    business continuity plans. *See* business
      continuity plans (BCPs)
    business impact analysis, 417–426
    disaster recovery plans. *See* disaster recovery
      plans (DRPs)
    incident classification and categorization,
      473–475
    incident response, 492–493
    incident response plans, 406–417
    notes, 494
    overview, 405–406
    questions, 494–498
    review, 493–494
    training, 475–477
incident response
    evaluating, 492–493
    overview, 408–410
    playbooks, 411
    release management, 389
    security governance, 7
    TPRM, 353
    training, 475–477
incident response plans
    communications, 416–417, 516–517
    developing, 411–417
    escalation, 416–417
    gap analysis, 414
    maturity, 412
    objectives, 411–412
    overview, 406–410
    playbooks, 414–415
    resources, 412–414
    testing, 477–483
    third-party incidents, 415
    updates, 415
incident response retainers (IRRs), 506
incidents
    analysis, 509–513
    classification and categorization, 473–475
    closure, 522
    detection, 507–508
    forensic investigations, 509–512
    gap assessment, 57–58
    initiation, 509
    insurance company notifications, 49
    logs in security strategy, 50–51
    managing. *See* incident management;
      incident management operations;
      incident management readiness

monitoring by MSSPs, 505–507
ranking and rating, 509
remediation, 521–522
response. *See* incident response; incident
    response plans
risk register, 148
security operations, 363
security steering committees
    responsibilities, 20
security strategy, 67
third parties, 362
increased trust in security governance, 8
incremental backups, 305
indicators of compromise (IOCs), 506
industry development in risk register, 148
inertia, organizational, 72
infinite regress, 52
influence, metrics for, 226
information assets, 201
information classification, 203–205
information exposure and theft, 408–409
information gathering in risk assessment and
    analysis, 139–140
information governance (IG), 87–88
information governance position, 26
information security and privacy, 444
Information security architecture, 218–220
Information Security Forum (ISF), 371
information security governance. *See* governance
information security program management.
    See program management
information security risk assessment.
    See risk assessment and analysis
information security risk response.
    See risk response
information security strategy.
    See security strategy
information sources for risk register, 148
information system theft and damage from
    incidents, 409
information systems (IS) audits, 326
Information Systems Security Association
    (ISSA), 372
information systems view in
    NIST SP 800-39, 118
information technology (IT)
    communication, 367–368
    gap assessment, 58
    operations roles, 25
    TPRM programs, 349

information technology (IT) personnel,
   incident reporting by, 508
informed people in RACI charts, 16
Inherent risk assessment for third parties, 52
initial assessment in TPRM life cycle, 352
initialization vectors (IVs) in cryptography, 313
initiation, incident
      response, 500
      steps, 509
innovation and learning in balanced
   scorecards, 233
insider threats in user behavior analytics, 302
installation phase in intrusion kill chain
   model, 410
institutional knowledge in gap assessment, 59
insurance
      coverage reviews, 487
      security strategy, 48–49
      TPRM, 353
insurance adjusters for disasters, 449
insurance companies for incident response, 506
integrated audits, 326
integration
      assurance process, 38, 194
      controls, 272
      risk management programs, 109, 150–157
      SaaS services, 464
integrity
      information classification, 203
      outsourcing issue, 346
      third-party remediation, 361
intellectual property
      as asset, 201
      outsourcing theft, 346
      third-party remediation, 361
intelligence
      AI, 253
      risk management support, 115
      third parties, 357
      threat, 148, 277, 363, 504
internal audits
      monitoring, 29
      overview, 333–335
      reports, 57
      risk register, 148
internal communications
      disasters, 441
      incident responsibilities, 503
      post-incident reviews, 522

internal data in vendor classification, 354
internal environments in risk management
   programs, 110
internal partnerships
      human resources, 364–365
      legal issues, 364
      overview, 364
internal processes in balanced scorecards, 233
internal threats, identifying, 130–132
internal transfers in human resources, 365
internal web sites for awareness training
   communication, 344
International Council of Electronic
   Commerce Consultants (EC-Council), 372
International Electrotechnical Commission
   (IEC), 371
International Information Systems Security
   Certification Consortium (ISC)^2, 372
International Organization for
   Standardization (ISO), 371
Internet hygiene, 339
Internet of things (IoT) as disruptive
   technology, 253
Internet Protocol Security (IPsec), 321
Internet time servers, 206
interviews
      of personnel for business continuity plans,
         486–487
      risk analysis information gathering, 139
intrusion detection/prevention system (IDPS)
   metrics, 225
intrusion detection systems (IDSs), 285
intrusion kill chain model, 410–411
intrusion prevention systems (IPSs), 284–285
intrusive monitoring by third parties, 358
inventory of key processes and systems
   inventory in business impact analysis,
   417–418
investigations for human resources, 366
investor representation on boards of
   directors, 17
IOCs (indicators of compromise), 506
IoT (Internet of things) as disruptive
   technology, 253
IPsec (Internet Protocol Security), 321
IPSs (intrusion prevention systems),
   284–285
IRRs (incident response retainers), 506
IS (information systems) audits, 326

ISACA
    BMIS, 73–74
    certifications, 372
    COBIT 2019, 218
    Code of Professional Ethics, 10–11
    data security definition, 303
    governance description, 76
    risk appetite description, 9, 174
    Risk IT framework, 75, 125–126
ISC² (International Information Systems
    Security Certification Consortium), 372
ISF (Information Security Forum), 371
ISO (International Organization for
    Standardization), 371
ISO/IEC 20000 standard, 213
ISO/IEC 27001 standard
    risk management frameworks, 108
    sections, 83–85
    security management framework, 218
ISO/IEC 27002 standard
    control framework, 249–251
    description, 213
    objectives, 254–259
ISO/IEC 27005 standard
    methodologies, 121–124
    risk management frameworks, 108
ISO/IEC 31010 standard, 108
ISSA (Information Systems Security
    Association), 372
IT. See information technology (IT)
IT general controls (ITGCs), 246–247
IT Infrastructure Library (ITIL) process
    framework, 213, 384
IT service management (ITSM)
    activities, 383–384
    asset management, 394
    availability management, 393–394
    capacity management, 392–393
    change management, 386–388
    configuration management, 388–389
    financial management, 391–392
    importance, 384
    incident management, 384–385
    incident management link, 416
    problem management, 385–386
    release management, 389–391
    service continuity management, 393
    service desk, 384
    service-level management, 391–392

iterative risk treatment, 173–174
ITGCs (IT general controls), 246–247
ITIL (IT Infrastructure Library) process
    framework, 213, 384
ITSM. See IT service management (ITSM)
IVs (initialization vectors) in cryptography, 313

J

job descriptions, 377–378
job titles, 13
judgmental sampling in audit evidence, 331

K

key business partners, communication with, 370
key goal indicators (KGIs), 225
key performance indicators (KPIs), 225
key personnel
    availability in disasters, 447
    interviewing, 486–487
key processes inventory in business impact
    analysis, 417–418
key recovery targets in business impact
    analysis, 423–426
key risk indicators (KRIs)
    metrics, 225
    overview, 180–181
keyloggers, 296
keys in cryptography, 312–313
    encryption applications, 321
    exchanging, 313–314
    generating, 319
    information security architecture, 219
    key-encrypting keys, 320
    key pairs, 314
    managing, 319–321
    protecting, 320
KGIs (key goal indicators), 225
knowledge reviews, post-incident, 523
known risks, 166
known unpatched weaknesses, 127
KPIs (key performance indicators), 225
KRIs (key risk indicators)
    metrics, 225
    overview, 180–181

L

landslide damage, 428
language differences in outsourcing, 348
last management reviews, security policy for, 43

law enforcement
  communication with, 370–371
  incident reporting by, 508
  incident response plan communications,
    516–517
  incident response plans, 413
laws
  outsourcing issues, 347
  risk register, 148
  security steering committees
    responsibilities, 19
leadership
  executive management responsibilities, 19
  security strategy, 40, 53
leading indicators
  KRIs, 181
  metrics, 226
learning curves in organizational inertia, 72
legal agreements
  human resource management, 156
  TPRM life cycle, 352–353
legal counsel
  attorney–client privilege, 516
  external, 506
  incident responsibilities, 503
legal departments
  incident response, 511
  incident response plans, 413
  internal partnerships, 364
  third parties relation, 348
legal issues
  disasters, 442
  risk response, 175–176
legal requirements
  business alignment, 8
  enterprise governance, 11–12
  external audits, 335
  security strategy, 71
levels in risk management, 111–112
life cycles
  BCP, 434–435
  BMIS, 81
  CSA, 337–338
  governance, 88
  human resources, 155–156
  risk management, 115–126
  TPRM programs, 351–354
  vulnerability management programs, 47
life safety, 407
lightning damage, 429

likelihood of risk
  considerations, 137–138
  NIST SP 800-30, 120
live exercises for training and awareness, 66
live fire tests for incident response plans, 478
local administrators for endpoint protection
  and management, 298
location of hardware assets, 200
location-specific leaders in TPRM
  programs, 349
log servers, 276
logical controls, 243
logistical plans in ISO/IEC 27005, 121
logs
  analysis and correlation in incident
    response, 504
  reviews for controls, 276
  security strategy, 50–51
  zero-trust architecture, 293
long-term strategies in capacity
  management, 392
losses in Factor Analysis of Information
  Risk, 124

M
macros in endpoint protection, 295
maintaining business continuity plans,
  453–454
malware
  description, 409
  endpoint protection, 295–296
  incident response plans, 413
  incident response tools, 504
managed security services providers (MSSPs)
  incident management, 302–303
  incident monitoring, 505–507
management
  commitment in security strategy, 67–68
  frameworks, 218
  security strategy reviews, 43
managerial controls, 243
managing, meaning of, 14
mandatory protective measures in risk
  response, 175
mandatory risk assessments in risk
  response, 176
manual controls, 245
mapping controls, 250–251, 274
market conditions in business alignment, 8
materials shortages, 431

maturity
    incident response plans, 412
    security strategy, 54
maximum tolerable downtime (MTD), 422
maximum tolerable outage (MTO),
  422–423
media managers, 25
media notification for disasters, 449
mediation in CSA life cycle, 338
memorable content for awareness training, 340
message digests, 311, 317
message security, 314–316
methodologies
    audits, 53, 327–329
    CSA, 337
    CVSS, 278–279
    Cybersecurity Framework, 263–264
    external audits, 336
    FAIR, 124–125
    OCTAVE, 143
    risk analysis, 143
    risk management, 117–119
    standards, 64
metrics
    audiences for, 231
    balanced scorecards, 232–233
    controls, 274
    gap assessment, 57
    incident response, 517–519
    monitoring, 30
    program development, 225–233
    security governance, 6–7
    security strategy, 46, 67
    types, 227–231
MFA (multifactor authentication)
    identity and access management, 299
    requiring, 174
misconfiguration, incidents from, 410
mission/business process view in
  NIST SP 800-39, 118
missions
    business alignment, 8
    outsourcing, 347
mitigation
    cost-benefit considerations, 172–173
    ISO/IEC 27005, 123
    OCTAVE, 142
    risk analysis, 116
    risk response, 167–168

MITRE ATT&CK framework, 279
mobile sites in disaster recovery plans, 463
modification history for controls, 275
monetary value in information
  classification, 203
monitoring
    audits, 29
    compliance management, 375
    controls, 276–277, 322
    incidents, 505–507
    information security architecture, 220
    information technology, 368
    ISO/IEC 27005, 124
    metrics, 226
    NIST SP 800-39, 118
    responsibilities, 29–30
    risks, 180–182
    third parties, 358
monitors for awareness training
  communication, 344
Monte Carlo analysis, 144
morale issues in outsourcing, 347
motivation in risk likelihood, 137
MSS analysts, incident reporting by, 508
MSSPs (managed security services providers)
    incident management, 302–303
    incident monitoring, 505–507
MTD (maximum tolerable downtime), 422
MTO (maximum tolerable outage), 422–423
multifactor authentication (MFA)
    identity and access management, 299
    requiring, 174
multimaster replication, 308
multimedia content for training and
  awareness, 66
multiprimary replication, 308, 469

N

NAC (network access control), 292
NACD (National Association of Corporate
  Directors), 18
narratives for controls, 274
NAS (network-attached storage) in disaster
  recovery plans, 468
National Association of Corporate Directors
  (NACD), 18
National Bureau of Standards, 211–212
National Cyber Security Centre (NCSC), 293
National Fire Protection Agency (NFPA), 454

National Incident Management System
(NIMS), 454
National Institute for Standards and
Technology (NIST) standards, 43, 118
BCP practices, 454
CSF activities, 262–264
CSF components, 215–216
CSF control framework, 249
CSF highlights, 86–87
CSF overview, 85–86
CSF purpose, 218
CSF steps, 87–88
publications, 371
Risk Management Framework, 85
SP 800-30, 119
SP 800-37, 108
SP 800-39, 108, 118
SP 800-53, 214, 249–251, 259
SP 800-171, 215
SP 800-207, 293
natural disasters, 428–431
NCSC (National Cyber Security Centre), 293
NERC (North American Electric Reliability
Corporation) Standards
control framework, 249
infrastructure, 267–269
net present value (NPV) in asset valuation, 209
NetFlow standard, 286
network access control (NAC), 292
network administrators, 25
network architects, 24
network-attached storage (NAS) in disaster
recovery plans, 468
network engineers, 24
network management roles, 24–25
network protection
CASB, 290
DDoS, 285
DNS filtering, 290
e-mail, 290–292
firewalls, 282–284
IDSs, 285
IPSs, 284–285
NAC, 292
NTA, 285–286
overview, 282
packet sniffers, 287
segmentation, 283–284
span ports, 287

web content filters, 289–290
wireless, 287–288
zero-trust architecture, 292–293
network segmentation, 207
network traffic analysis (NTA), 285–286
networks
connectivity and services in disaster
recovery plans, 471
device vulnerabilities, 128
disasters, 444
intrusion prevention, 504
new hires, awareness training for, 342–343
NFPA (National Fire Protection Agency), 454
NIMS (National Incident Management
System), 454
NIST. *See* National Institute for Standards and
Technology (NIST) standards
nonfunctional requirements in program
development, 224
nonrepudiation in cryptography, 313
nonstatistical sampling of audit evidence, 331
normalcy bias, 68–69
North American Electric Reliability
Corporation (NERC) Standards
control framework, 249
infrastructure, 267–269
notifications for disasters, 448–449
NPV (net present value) in asset valuation, 209
NTA (network traffic analysis), 285–286
numbering controls, 274

O

objectives
audits, 325, 327
awareness training, 339–340
business alignment, 8–9
controls, 245–246, 274
controls self-assessment, 339
disaster recovery plans, 457
incident response plans, 411–412
security governance, 5
security strategy, 38–39
objectivity
audits, 53, 335
outsourcing, 345
occupant emergency plans in business
continuity plans, 452
OCTAVE (Operationally Critical Threat,
Asset, and Vulnerability Evaluation), 142–143

offboarding in human resources, 365
offsite storage
    disasters, 444–445
    evaluating, 491–492
onboarding
    purpose, 365
    TPRM life cycle, 352
ongoing due diligence for outsourced
    services, 52
online documents for business continuity
    plans, 453
The Open Group Architecture Framework
    (TOGAF), 83–84
open source software for systems
    development, 369
operating systems
    configuration management, 388
    replication, 308, 468
    vulnerability detection techniques, 128
operational audits, 325
operational criticality
    information classification, 203
    vendor classification, 354
operational efficiency changes in risk
    response, 172
operational maturity in vulnerability
    assessments, 48
operational partnerships, 303
operational performance metrics, 230
operational productivity metrics, 229
Operationally Critical Threat, Asset, and
    Vulnerability Evaluation (OCTAVE),
    142–143
operations
    controls, 275–276
    disaster recovery plans, 472
    incident management. See incident
        management operations
operations analysts, 25
operations managers, 25
opportunities
    SWOT analysis, 60
    training and awareness, 66
optional protective measures in risk
    response, 175
orchestration
    security operations, 363
    SOAR, 277

organization chapters for risk management
    support, 113
organization element in BMIS model, 74
organization view in NIST SP 800-39, 118
organizational awareness metrics, 228–229
organizational controls in ISO/IEC 27002,
    254–256
organizational culture, 9–10
    acceptable use policies, 10
    ethics, 10–11
organizational inertia in security strategy, 72
organizational roles
    boards of directors, 16–18
    business process and business asset owners,
        20–21
    business resilience, 27
    chief compliance officers, 23
    chief information officers, 21–22
    chief privacy officers, 23
    custodial responsibilities, 21
    data management, 24
    executive management, 18–19
    general staff, 29
    governance, risk, and compliance, 26
    IT operations, 25
    miscellaneous, 28
    monitoring responsibilities, 29–30
    network management, 24–25
    overview, 12–14
    quality assurance, 28
    RACI charts, 15–16
    security audit, 28
    security operations, 27
    security steering committees, 19–20
    service desk, 28
    software development, 23–24
    systems management, 25
organizational structure in security strategy, 69
organizational support metrics, 229
out-of-band key exchange method, 313
outages, 431
outcomes in program development, 193–194
outdated components in architecture, 45
outside experts in security strategy, 40
outsourcing
    benefits, 345
    incident response, 413–414
    risks, 345–346
    security strategy services, 51–52

ownership
    controls, 274
    hardware assets, 200
    risk, 144–145, 178–180
    risk response, 179–180
    risk treatments, 167

P

P2PE (Point-to-Point Encryption), 266
PA DSS (Payment Application Data Security
    Standard), 265
packet sniffers, 287–288
packing malware, 297
pandemics, 430–431
parallel tests
    BCP and DRP, 482
    training, 477
partial tier in Cyber Security Framework,
    86, 263
participants in BCP and DRP tests,
    479–480
partnerships
    external, 370–373
    internal, 364–370
    operational, 303
    security product vendors, 373
passwordless authentication, 299
patch management
    information technology, 368
    vulnerability management, 280
Payment Application Data Security Standard
    (PA DSS), 265
Payment Card Industry Data Security
    Standard (PCI DSS)
    description, 249
    objectives, 217
    structure, 264–266
Payment Card Industry Forensic Investigator
    (PFI), 265
Payment Card Industry Internal Security
    Assessor (PCI ISA), 265
Payment Card Industry (PCI) Security
    Standards Council, 371
Payment Card Industry Professional
    (PCIP), 265
Payment Card Industry Qualified Security
    Assessor (PCI QSA), 265
payments in third-party remediation, 362

PCI DSS (Payment Card Industry Data
    Security Standard)
    description, 249
    objectives, 217
    structure, 264–266
PCI Forensic Investigator (PFI), 265
PCI ISA (Payment Card Industry Internal
    Security Assessor), 265
PCI QSA (Payment Card Industry Qualified
    Security Assessor), 265
PCI Security Standards Council, 371
PCIP (Payment Card Industry
    Professional), 265
PCIs (Professional Certified Investigators), 476
peer pressure in security tooling, 198–199
penetration testers, 27
penetration tests
    software development, 151
    third parties, 358
    vulnerability detection, 280
people controls in ISO/IEC 27002, 256
people element in BMIS model, 74
performance
    monitoring, 30
    outsourcing issues, 346
    personnel management, 381
    program development, 193
    security strategy, 38
periodic measurements in capacity
    management, 392
periodic reviews in TPRM, 353
periodic scanning in vulnerability
    management, 278
permanent records for training and
    awareness, 66
personal computers as disruptive
    technology, 253
personnel
    as asset, 199
    business continuity plans availability to,
        452–453
    changes in, 179
    classification, 207–208
    critical, in disasters, 448
    external audits, 336
    facility safety for, 367
    incident reporting by, 508
    incident response plans, 412–413
    interviewing, 486–487

MSSPs, 505
safety procedures in business continuity
plans, 436–437
vulnerability detection techniques, 128
personnel management, 376
culture, 378
job descriptions, 377–378
professional development, 378–381
reporting in, 381–382
roles and responsibilities, 377
talent finding and retaining, 376–377
personnel observations for audit evidence, 330
phishing filters, 290–292
physical access in vendor classification, 355
physical controls, 243
physical location of assets, 20
physical records controls in ISO/IEC 27002,
256–257
physical security
disasters, 443
risk management integration with,
154–155
vulnerability detection techniques, 128
PIN Transaction Security (PTS), 266
PKI (public key infrastructure), 318–319
plaintext, 311
planned changes in capacity management, 392
plans
audit communication, 328
audits, 327
business cases, 91
business continuity. See business continuity
plans (BCPs)
disaster recovery. See disaster recovery
plans (DRPs)
incident response. See incident response
plans
playbooks for incident response plans, 414–415
Point-to-Point Encryption (P2PE), 266
policies
business continuity plans, 434–435
executive management responsibilities, 19
gap assessment, 56
Information security architecture, 219
program development, 220–223
security governance, 5
security strategy, 42–43, 61–62
third-party remediation, 361
training and awareness, 66

policy managers, 26
ports, span, 287
position benchmarking, 30
position titles, 13–14, 22
post-audit follow-ups, 329
post-change reviews, 387
post-implementation in release
management, 391
post-incident reviews
incident response, 501
practices, 522–523
posters for awareness training
communication, 344
pre-audits, 327
predisposing conditions in NIST SP 800-30,
119–121
presentation in chain of custody, 510
preservation in chain of custody, 510
preventive controls, 243–244
previous strategy in gap assessment, 56
primary-backup replication, 308, 469
principle of proportionality in total cost of
ownership, 173
principles
business alignment, 8
COBIT, 267
COSO, 267–268
importance of information security, 18
risk identification, 111
SOC 2, 271
prior incidents, insurance costs related to, 49
prior results in business continuity plans, 486
priorities in security governance, 5
privacy
breaches, 512
business continuity plans, 444
CPOs, 23
incident response plans, 413
SOC 2 principle, 271
TPRM programs, 352
privacy by design, 368
private key cryptosystems, 313
privilege accumulation
description, 300
from internal transfers, 365
privileged roles, 301
proactive incident management, 302
proactive issue remediation for third parties,
360–362

proactive support from insurance
  companies, 49
probability
    quantitative risk analysis, 140
    risk analysis, 140–141, 149, 421
    risk likelihood, 137–139
    risk management process, 116
    threat changes, 172
    threat forecasting, 136
problem management
    capacity management link, 393
    change management link, 388
    configuration management link, 388
    ITSM, 385–386
    risk management integration with,
      153–154
problem resolution in release management, 389
problem statements in business cases, 89
procedures
    audits, 324, 328
    gap assessment, 57
    program development, 224–225
    security strategy, 44, 65
process-level risks, 111
processes
    antimalware observation of, 296
    balanced scorecards, 233
    BMIS model, 74–75, 77
    business process and business asset
      owners, 20
    program development, 195–196, 224–225
    security governance, 6–7
    security strategy, 44, 65
    systems development, 369
processing integrity principle in SOC 2, 271
Proctor, Paul, 226
procurement
    communication for, 369
    TPRM programs, 349
Professional Certified Investigators (PCIs), 476
professional development, 378
    career paths, 379
    certifications, 379–381
    training, 381
professional organizations for partnerships,
    371–372
profiles in CSF, 215, 263
program charters in gap assessment, 56

program development, 191–192
    architectures, 218–220
    asset identification and classification,
      199–210
    charters, 194
    control frameworks, 210–217
    guidelines, 223
    management frameworks, 218
    metrics, 225–233
    notes, 236
    outcomes, 193–194
    policy development, 220–223
    processes and procedures, 224–225
    questions, 237–240
    requirements, 223–224
    resources, 192–199
    review, 233–235
    scope, 195
    security governance, 6
    security processes, 195–196
    standards, 223
    technologies, 196–198
    trends, 192–193
program management
    awareness training, 339–344
    communication and reporting.
      See communication and reporting
    continuous improvement, 394
    control testing and evaluation. See control
      testing and evaluation
    controls. See controls
    data governance. See data governance
    endpoint protection and management,
      293–298
    external services. See external services
    identity and access management,
      298–302
    incident management, 302
    introduction, 241–242
    ITSM. See IT service management (ITSM)
    MSSPs, 302–303
    network protection. See network protection
    notes, 396–397
    questions, 397–401
    review, 394–396
programming language standards, 64
project documents in business continuity
  plans, 451

project management
communications in, 382
human resources, 157
security governance, 6
project managers, 29
proportionality principle in total cost of
ownership, 173
proposals in change management, 386
protect activity in CSF, 262
protection function in NIST CSF, 86
protection of private keys, 320
protective measures in risk response, 175
protocol standards, 64
PTS (PIN Transaction Security), 266
public information classification, 203–205
public key cryptosystems, 313
digital envelopes, 318
digital signatures, 317
elliptic curve cryptography, 316
hashing and message digests, 317
key pairs, 314
key verification, 316
public key infrastructure (PKI), 318–319
public opinion issues in incident response plan
communications, 517
public safety issues in disasters, 449
published information in risk management
practices, 113

Q

QA managers, 28
QC managers, 28
qualifications of auditors, 53, 336
Qualified Integrators and Resellers (QIR), 266
qualitative asset valuation, 209
qualitative risk analysis, 140
quality assurance roles, 28
quality issues
outsourcing, 346
third-party remediation, 361
quantitative asset valuation, 209–210
quantitative risk analysis, 140–141
quarantines, e-mail, 291
questionnaires
CSA life cycle, 338
key processes inventory, 417–418
onboarding, 352
risk analysis, 143
third parties, 357–360
quizzes for training and awareness, 66

R

RACI (Responsible, Accountable, Consulted,
Informed) charts, 15–16
radio communications for disasters, 441
RAID (Redundant Array of Independent
Disks), 467–468
rank and file individuals for security
strategy, 40
ranks
incidents, 509
position titles, 14, 22
risk, 144
ransomware
endpoint protection, 295
incidents, 409
insurance, 49
RAs (registration authorities), 319
rating incidents, 509
RATs (remote access Trojans), 296
RCapO (recovery capacity objective) in
business impact analysis, 423, 425
RCO (recovery consistency objective), 423–426
reacquisition cost in asset valuation, 209
readability in BMIS model, 79
recertification of access in IAM, 301
reciprocal sites in disaster recovery plans, 463
recommendations for risk management
process, 116
reconnaissance in intrusion kill chain
model, 410
recordkeeping
BCP and DRP tests, 479–480
incident response, 505, 518
records
backing up, 308
change management, 387
disaster plans, 444
recovery. See also backups
approaches, 520–521
business impact analysis targets, 423–426
Cybersecurity Framework, 262
disaster procedures, 445–446
DRPs. See disaster recovery plans (DRPs)
incident response, 501
incident responsibilities, 503
maintaining plans, 453–454
recovery capacity objective (RCapO) in
business impact analysis, 423, 425
recovery consistency objective (RCO), 423–426

recovery controls, 244
recovery function in NIST CSF, 86
recovery point objective (RPO)
    disaster recovery plans, 457–458
    overview, 423–425
    pricing, 458
recovery time objective (RTO)
    disaster recovery plans, 457–458
    overview, 423–424
    pricing, 458
recruitment in human resources, 365
redeployment cost in asset valuation, 209
Redundant Array of Independent Disks
    (RAID), 467–468
redundant network connections, 471
registration authorities (RAs), 319
regulations and regulatory requirements
    controls, 242
    enterprise governance, 11–12
    external audits, 335
    gap assessment, 59
    incident response plan communications, 516
    resource expenditures, 232
    risk register, 148
    risk response considerations, 175–176
    security steering committees
        responsibilities, 19
    security strategy, 71
    third-party remediation, 361
regulators
    disaster notifications for, 449
    partnerships with, 371
relationship risk assessment for third parties, 51
release management, 389–391
relevant content in awareness training, 340
relevant policies in security strategy, 42
remediation
    incident response, 501
    incident responsibilities, 503
    incidents, 521–522
    third parties, 360–362
    vulnerability management, 278
remote access Trojans (RATs), 296
remote control, endpoint protection for,
    294–295
remote destruction, endpoint protection for, 295
Remote Monitoring (RMON), 286
repeatability tier in CSF, 87, 263
replacement cost in asset valuation, 209

replication
    backups, 308–309
    disaster recovery plans, 468–469
reports. See communication and reporting
reputation concerns in security governance, 8
reputational value in information
    classification, 203
requests in change management, 386
requirements
    business cases, 91
    program development, 223–224
    regulatory. See regulations and regulatory
        requirements
    release management, 389
    security involvement stage, 281
    security steering committees
        responsibilities, 19
research organization reports for risk
    management support, 114
researchers, incident reporting by, 508
residual risk
    risk registers, 150
    risk response, 173
resilience
    BMIS architecture, 77
    business, 27
    disaster recovery plan technologies, 467–471
    post-incident reviews, 523
resistance to change, 68, 72
resolution in third-party remediation, 362
resource access
    boards of directors, 17
    zero-trust architecture, 293
resource optimization in security strategy, 38
resources and resource management
    audits, 324–325, 335
    incident response plans, 412–414
    metrics, 228
    program development, 192–199
    security governance, 7
response documents in business continuity
    plans, 452
response function in CSF, 86, 262
response reviews, post-incident, 523
responsibilities
    disaster recovery plans, 471
    disasters, 439–446
    DRP teams, 456–457
    executive management, 19

incident response, 502–503
meaning, 14
monitoring, 29–30
personnel management, 377
RACI charts, 16
security steering committees, 19
security strategy, 65
third-party remediation, 361
Responsible, Accountable, Consulted,
Informed (RACI) charts, 15–16
responsive issue remediation with third
parties, 362
responsive security incident management, 302
restoration. *See* recovery
restore service actions, risk implications
associated with, 154
restricted information classification, 203–205
results
audits, 332–333, 336–337
disaster recovery plans, 490
security governance, 7–8
resumption plans in business continuity
plans, 452
retail floor cashiers, awareness training for, 341
retail floor managers, awareness training for, 341
retaining talent, 376–377
retention of evidence, 501
return on security investment (ROSI), 231–232
reverse engineering in incident response
plans, 413
RIMS Risk Maturity Model, 108
risk
compliance management, 374–375
controls, 274
CSA life cycle, 338
evaluation and ranking, 144
impact, 138–139
likelihood, 137–138
outsourcing, 345–346
ownership, 144–145
security steering committees
responsibilities, 19
risk appetite
business alignment, 9
risk management process, 116
security strategy, 38, 55, 71–72
risk assessment and analysis, 101–102
audits, 324
business continuity plans, 145
control frameworks, 251

controls, 242
external support, 112–115
gap analysis, 112
gap assessment, 57
importance, 102–103
integration into other processes, 150–157
levels, 111–112
mandatory, 176
NIST SP 800-39, 118
notes, 159–160
objectives, 103
outcomes, 103
questions, 160–164
review, 157–158
risk identification, 136–137
risk impact, 138–139
risk likelihood, 137–138
risk management life cycle, 115–126
risk management programs, 103–110
risk register, 146–150
security strategy, 41
techniques and considerations, 139–145
technologies, 104–105
threat identification, 129–136
vulnerability and control deficiency
analysis, 127–129
risk determination in NIST SP 800-30, 120
risk framing step in NIST SP 800-39, 118
risk identification, 136–137
risk informed tier in CSF, 86, 263
Risk IT framework, 125–126
risk management
business continuity planning, 145
communications and reporting, 363–364
integration into other processes,
150–157
metrics, 229–230
program development, 193
security governance, 7
technologies, 104–105
Risk Management Framework (RMF), 85
risk management life cycle, 115
methodologies, 117–126
process, 115–117
risk management methodologies, 117
Factor Analysis of Information Risk,
124–125
ISACA Risk IT framework, 125–126
ISO/IEC 27005, 121–124
NIST, 118–121

risk management programs
    context, 109–110
    frameworks, 108–109
    implementing, 105–106
    outcomes, 103
    strategies, 106–108
risk managers, 26
Risk Metrics That Influence Business Decisions
    (Proctor), 226
risk monitoring step in NIST SP 800-39, 118
risk profiles in Risk IT framework, 126
risk registers
    analysis contributions, 149
    elements, 177–178
    gap assessment, 57
    information sources, 148
    residual risk, 150
    security strategy, 47–48
    strategic vs. tactical risks, 148–149
    structure, 146–147
risk response, 165–166
    acceptance, 170–171
    avoidance, 169–170
    cost and benefits, 172–173
    ignoring, 171
    iterative risk treatment, 173–174
    legal and regulatory considerations, 175–176
    mitigation, 167–168
    monitoring and reporting, 180–182
    NIST SP 800-39, 118
    notes, 183
    options evaluation, 171–172
    options overview, 166–167
    questions, 184–188
    residual risk, 173
    review, 182–183
    risk and control ownership, 178–180
    risk appetite, capacity, and tolerance,
        174–175
    risk register, 177–178
    transfer, 168–169
risk tiering
    outsourced services, 52
    TPRM programs, 354–356
risk tolerance in business alignment, 8–9
risk treatment
    actions, 166–167
    insurance, 49
    ISO/IEC 27005, 122

iterative, 173–174
    options evaluation, 116–117
    risk register, 177
    third parties, 360
risk treatment records in gap assessment, 57
RMF (Risk Management Framework), 85
RMON (Remote Monitoring), 286
roadmap development in strategic planning, 89
roles
    disaster recovery plans, 471
    disasters, 439–446
    DRP teams, 456–457
    human resource management, 156
    incident response, 502–503
    organizational. *See* organizational roles
    personnel management, 377
    security strategy, 65
    third-party remediation, 361
root-cause analysis, 154
rootkits, 296
ROSI (return on security investment),
    231–232
rotation
    backup media, 305–306
    keys, 320
round tables for risk management support, 113
RPO (recovery point objective)
    disaster recovery plans, 457–458
    overview, 423–425
    pricing, 458
RTO (recovery time objective)
    disaster recovery plans, 457–458
    overview, 423–424
    pricing, 458
rules
    e-mail, 291
    firewalls, 283

S

S/MIME (Secure Multipurpose Internet Mail
    Extensions), 321
SaaS services, 463–464
sabotage incidents, 410
salvage operations, 443
sampling audit evidence, 331
sanctions, risk, 375
sandboxes for antimalware, 296
SANS organization, 372
SANs (storage area networks), 468

Sarbanes-Oxley Act, 17
SAS-70 (Statement on Auditing Standards No. 70), 271–272
scalability
    BMIS architecture, 77
    private key cryptosystems, 313
scans
    information technology, 368
    third parties, 358
    vulnerability management, 278–280
schedules
    audits, 325, 336
    BCP and DRP tests, 479–480
    third-party remediation, 361
scope
    audits, 53, 324, 327, 335
    controls, 63, 274
    program development, 195
    risk management process, 115
scribes
    disaster documentation, 441
    incident responsibilities, 503
scripting in BCP and DRP tests, 479–480
SDN (software-defined networking), 202
SDO (service delivery objective), 423, 425
secret information classification, 203–205
secure engineering for controls, 280–282
secure key exchange, 314
Secure Multipurpose Internet Mail Extensions (S/MIME), 321
Secure Shell (SSH), 321
Secure Sockets Layer (SSL), 321
security
    BMIS architecture, 77
    as business prevention, 9
    vs. compliance, 373–374
security analysts, 27
security and privacy with disasters, 444
security architects, 27
security audit managers, 28
security auditors, 28
security awareness buy-in, 54
security awareness training
    gap assessment, 58
    trainers, 26
security by design in software development, 151
security cost efficiency metrics, 230–231
security directors, executive management opinion of, 22

security engineers, 27
security events, 432
security governance
    activities and results, 7–8
    BMIS model, 76
    business alignment, 8–9
    data. See data governance
    defined, 3
    enterprise. See enterprise governance
    frameworks and standards, 72–88
    information security strategy.
        See security strategy
    introduction, 4–6
    reasons, 6–7
security guards, 367
security incident, legal term, 517
security incidents. See incidents
security industry news sources for risk management support, 113
security information and event management (SIEM)
    controls, 277
    incident logs, 51
security leaders in security strategy, 40
security managers
    executive management opinion of, 22
    risk treatment involvement, 167
security maturity, vulnerability detection assessments for, 48
security operations
    communications and reporting, 363
    roles, 27
security orchestration, automation, and response (SOAR) platform, 277
security policies
    gap assessment, 56
    structure, 221–222
security principle in SOC 2, 271
security processes in program development, 195–196
security professional services vendors, partnerships with, 372–373
security program charters in gap assessment, 56
security projects, security steering committees responsibilities for, 19
security risk assessment. See risk assessment and analysis
security round tables for risk management support, 113

security scans
  third parties, 358
  vulnerability management, 279–280
security steering committees responsibilities,
  19–20, 167
security strategy
  architecture, 44–45
  assets, 47
  audits, 53
  business impact analysis, 50
  capability maturity models, 60–61
  communications and reporting, 66–67
  constraints, 68–72
  controls, 45
  controls development, 62–63
  critical data, 49–50
  culture, 53–54
  developing, 55–68
  gap assessment, 56–59
  governance frameworks, 72–88
  guidelines, 43–44
  insurance, 48–49
  introduction, 37
  management commitment, 67–68
  maturity, 54
  metrics, 46
  notes, 93–94
  objectives, 38–39
  outsourced services, 51–52
  participants, 39–40
  policies, 42–43
  policy development, 61–62
  processes and procedures, 44, 65
  questions, 94–98
  resources, 40–55
  review, 91–93
  risk appetite, 55
  risk assessments, 41
  risk registers, 47–48
  roles and responsibilities, 65
  security incident logs, 50–51
  skills, 46
  standards, 43
  standards development, 64–65
  strategic planning, 88–91
  SWOT analysis, 59–60
  threat assessments, 42
  training and awareness, 65–66
  vulnerability assessments, 48

security teams, 40
Security+ certification, 380
seeding audit results, 336–337
segmentation, network, 207, 283–284
segregation of duties
  audit evidence, 330
  identity and access management,
    300–301
  RACI charts, 16
SEI (Software Engineering Institute), 60
self-assessment
  auditors, 339
  controls, 337–339
semiquantitative risk analysis, 140
sensitive customer data in vendor
  classification, 354
sensitive data exposure risk, 375
sensitive internal data in vendor
  classification, 354
sensitivity in information classification, 203
server clusters in disaster recovery plans,
  469–470
Server Message Block (SMB) service, 278
service continuity management in ITSM, 393
service delivery objective (SDO),
  423, 425
service desk, 384
service desk analysts, 28
service desk managers, 28
service level agreements (SLAs)
  incident response, 416
  managed security services providers, 303
  third-party remediation, 361
service-level management
  capacity management link, 393
  ITSM, 391–392
service organization controls, 270–272
service outages, 431
service providers
  audits, 326–327
  contract reviews, 487
  incidents involving, 513
service shortages in disasters, 433
serviceable components in availability
  management, 393
sFlow standard, 286
shadow ITs
  description, 9
  as disruptive technology, 253

shareholder notification for disasters, 449
SIEM (security information and event
    management)
        controls, 277
        incident logs, 51
signature-based antivirus software,
    death of, 297
signatures
        antimalware, 296
        cryptography, 312–317
simulations
        BCP and DRP tests, 481
        incident response plans, 477–480
        training, 477
single loss expectancy (SLE), 141
site recovery options
        cloud sites, 463
        cold sites, 462
        disaster recovery plans, 460
        geographic site selection, 463
        hot sites, 460–461
        mobile sites, 463
        reciprocal sites, 463
        third-party sites, 464–465
        warm sites, 461–462
site visits to third parties, 52, 357
skills
        for attacks, 138
        audit interviews, 330
        outsourcing, 345
        RACI charts, 16
        staff, in security strategy, 46
SLAs (service level agreements)
        incident response, 416
        managed security services providers, 303
        third-party remediation, 361
SLE (single loss expectancy), 141
SMART metrics, 226
smartphones as disruptive technology, 253
SMB (Server Message Block) service, 278
SMEs (subject matter experts) in incident
    response plans, 413
smishing, 291
sniffers, 287–288
SOAR (security orchestration, automation,
    and response) platform, 277
SOC. See System and Organization Controls
    (SOC)
SOC analysts, incident reporting by, 508

social engineering assessments, 280
soft copies for business continuity plans, 453
software
        as asset, 199–200
        configuration items, 388
        vulnerability detection techniques, 128
software-defined networking (SDN), 202
software developers, awareness training for,
    341–342
software development
        Information security architecture, 220
        risk management integration with, 150–151
        roles, 23–24
Software Engineering Institute (SEI), 60
software engineers/developers, 23
software testers, 23
solid-state drives (SSDs) for backups, 304
sound considerations in BMIS model, 79
spam protection, 290–292
span ports, 287
spear phishing, 291
spim, 291
spyware, 295
SSCP (Systems Security Certified
    Practitioner), 380
SSDs (solid-state drives) for backups, 304
SSH (Secure Shell), 321
SSL (Secure Sockets Layer), 321
staff availability in disasters, 433
staff capabilities in security strategy, 69–70
staff development, 381
staffing shortages, MSSPs for, 505
stakeholder notification for disasters, 449
standards, 43
        coding, 151
        configuration, 64
        controls, 64, 72–88
        gap assessment, 57
        information governance, 72–88
        Information security architecture, 219
        NIST. See National Institute for Standards
            and Technology (NIST) standards
        policy development, 62
        program development, 223
        security governance, 6
        security strategy, 43, 64–65
standards organizations, partnerships with, 371
Statement on Auditing Standards No. 70
    (SAS-70), 271–272

statements of impact in business impact analysis, 419–420
static data loss prevention, 309
statistical sampling for audit evidence, 331
steering committees
    responsibilities, 19–20
    risk treatment responsibilities, 167
    security strategy meetings, 67
stop-or-go sampling for audit evidence, 331
storage
    backups. *See* backups
    disasters, 444–445
    evaluating, 491–492
storage area networks (SANs), 468
storage engineers, 25
strategic alignment
    metrics, 226–227
    program development, 193
strategic planning
    business cases, 89–91
    roadmap development, 89
    security strategy, 88–91
strategic risks, 148–149
strategies
    business alignment, 8
    disaster recovery plans, 459–460
    information security. *See* security strategy
    risk management programs, 106–108
    security governance, 5
stratified sampling in audit evidence, 331
stream ciphers, 313
strengths, weaknesses, opportunities, and threats (SWOT) analysis, 59–60
strictness of policies, 42
strong culture, 69
structure
    audit reports, 332–333
    PCI DSS, 264–266
    risk register, 146–147
    security policy, 221–222
subject matter experts (SMEs) in incident response plans, 413
subjects for audits, 327
subsystem assets, 200
subsystem patches and changes in release management, 389
success criteria in business cases, 91
supplier notifications for disasters, 448–449

supplier shortages in disasters, 433
supplies in disasters, 443
surveillance of facilities, 366
sustainment stage in security involvement, 281
SWOT (strengths, weaknesses, opportunities, and threats) analysis, 59–60
symmetric encryption, 313
synchronous replication, 309, 469
System and Organization Controls (SOC)
    audit reports, 332
    audit standards, 271–272
    compliance risk, 374
    description, 249
system classification, 206–207
system monitoring in information technology, 368
system operations procedures in disaster recovery plans, 472
system recovery procedures in disaster recovery plans, 472
systems access in vendor classification, 355
systems administrators, 25
systems analysts, 23
systems architects, 23, 25
systems development, communication with, 368–369
systems engineers, 25
systems function in disasters, 444
systems hardware as asset, 199
systems inventory in business impact analysis, 417–418
systems management roles, 25
systems operators, 25
Systems Security Certified Practitioner (SSCP), 380

T

tactical risks, 148–149
talent, finding and retaining, 376–377
tape backups
    disaster recovery plans, 473
    overview, 304
taps, network, 287
tasks for audit evidence, 330
TCO (total cost of ownership), 172–173
teams
    disaster recovery plans, 456–457
    security strategy, 40

technical architecture
  for communications and reporting, 376
  metrics, 230
technical controls, 243
technical debt in architecture, 44
technical support analysts, 28
technical workers, awareness training
  for, 341
technologies
  BMIS model, 75
  disaster recovery plans, 467–471
  ISO/IEC 27002 controls,
    257–258
  program development, 196–198
  risk management, 104–105
  skills for, 46
technology change issues in capacity
  management, 392
telecom engineers, 25
temps, 29
tenure in skills, 46
terrorism, 432
test and review documents in business
  continuity plans, 452
testing
  backups, 304
  controls, 63, 274
  cyclical controls, 334–335
  disaster recovery sites, 465
  incident response plans, 477–483
  release management, 390
  security involvement, 281
  systems development, 368
text in BMIS model, 79
theft of intellectual property, 346
third parties
  assessing, 356–360
  audit reports by, 332
  awareness training for, 341–342
  disaster recovery sites, 464–465
  identifying, 348–350
  incidents involving, 362, 415
  information technology, 368
  issue remediation, 360–362
  questionnaires and evidence,
    359–360
  risk treatments, 360

TPRM programs. *See* third-party risk
  management (TPRM) programs
  vulnerability identification by, 129
third-party breaches, insurance coverage for, 49
third-party risk
  gap assessment, 58
  security strategy, 51
third-party risk management (TPRM)
  programs, 26, 344
  cloud service providers, 350–351
  life cycle, 351–354
  risk tiering and vendor classification,
    354–356
  third-party identification, 348–350
threat advisories, 116
threat agents in FAIR, 124–125
threat hunting
  incident response plans, 412
  incident response tools, 504
  MSSPs, 506
threat identification
  actors, 136
  advanced persistent threats, 134–135
  emerging, 135–136
  external, 132–134
  forecasting data, 136
  internal, 130–132
  ISO/IEC 27005, 121
  overview, 129–130
threat intelligence
  incident response tools, 504
  IPSs, 285
  risk register, 148
  security operations, 363
threat intelligence platforms (TIPs), 277
threat modeling for software development, 151
threat probability changes in risk response, 172
threats
  assessments, 42
  business impact analysis, 420–421
  SWOT analysis, 60
360 feedback, 30
three lines of defense model, 196
time issues in security strategy, 70–71
time periods for external audits, 335
time servers, 206
time zone differences in outsourcing, 348

TIPs (threat intelligence platforms), 277
titles
    cloud, 26
    controls, 274
    position, 13–14
    ranks, 22
TLS (Transport Layer Security), 321
TMSs (transaction management systems) for
  replication, 308, 468
TOGAF (The Open Group Architecture
  Framework), 83–84
Token Service Providers (TSP), 266
tolerance, risk, 174–175
tornado damage, 429
total cost of ownership (TCO), 172–173
Towers of Hanoi backup strategy, 306
TPRM. *See* third-party risk management
  (TPRM) programs
training
    awareness. *See* awareness training
    disasters, 445
    gap assessment, 58
    human resource management, 156
    human resources, 366
    incident logs, 51
    incident management, 475–477
    post-incident reviews about, 523
    professional development, 381
    risk management support, 114
    risk response, 181–182
    security strategy, 65–66
    systems development, 369
transaction management systems (TMSs)
  for replication, 308, 468
transfer, risk
    description, 117
    ISO/IEC 27005, 123
    risk response, 168–169
transfers, internal, 365
transformation of data in forensic
  investigations, 511
Transport Layer Security (TLS), 321
transportation accidents, 432
transportation issues in disasters, 433,
  443, 451
treatment. *See* risk treatment
trends in program development, 192–193
tribal knowledge
  gap assessment, 59
  outsourcing, 346

Trojans, 295–296
tropical cyclones, 428
trust improvements in security governance, 8
TSP (Token Service Providers), 266
tsunamis, 429–430
turnover in personnel management, 381

U

UAT (user acceptance testing) in release
  management, 390
UBA (user behavior analytics), 301–302
UEBA (user and entity behavior analytics), 302
UIs (user interfaces) in BMIS model, 78
undefined responsibilities in risk treatments, 167
understandable content for awareness
  training, 340
undisclosed unpatched weaknesses, 127
undiscovered weaknesses, 128
United Kingdom, law enforcement agencies
  in, 370
United Kingdom Bribery Act, 11
unknown risks, 166
unpatched weaknesses, 127
unsupported components in architecture, 45
up-front due diligence for third-party
  risk, 51
updates for incident response plans, 415
use case development, 363
user acceptance testing (UAT) in release
  management, 390
user and entity behavior analytics (UEBA), 302
user authentication in zero-trust
  architecture, 293
user behavior analytics (UBA), 301–302
user hardware requirements in disasters, 445
user interfaces (UIs) in BMIS model, 78
utility interruptions and outages, 431, 433

V

validation in zero-trust architecture, 293
valuation of assets, 200, 209–210
value delivery
  metrics, 228
  program development, 193
  security strategy, 38
variable sampling for audit evidence, 331
VDIs (virtual desktop infrastructures), 297
velocity factor in risk likelihood, 137
vendor managers, 28

vendors
    failures, 347
    security products, 373
    standards, 64
    TPRM classification of, 354–356
verification
    change management, 387–388
    public keys, 316
versions of controls, 274
vice presidents, executive management
    opinion of, 22
video monitors for awareness training
    communication, 344
video surveillance in incident response, 505
virtual assets, 199, 201–202
virtual desktop infrastructures (VDIs), 297
virtual reality (VR) as disruptive
    technology, 253
virtual sprawl, 202
virtualization in replication, 308, 469
viruses
    antivirus software, 296
    endpoint protection, 295
visibility consideration in risk likelihood, 137
voice recognition in BMIS model, 79
voicemail for awareness training
    communication, 344
volcanos, 428
VR (virtual reality) as disruptive
    technology, 253
vulnerabilities
    business impact analysis, 420
    forms, 127–128
    identification, 122, 136
    ISO/IEC 27005, 122
    third-party, 129
vulnerability assessment
    NIST SP 800-30, 119
    risk management process, 116
    risk register, 148
    security strategy, 48
    TPRM, 352
vulnerability management
    controls, 277–282
    security operations, 363
    TPRM, 352

W

walk-throughs
    BCP and DRP tests, 480–481
    training, 477
wallet cards
    business continuity plans, 453
    disasters, 450–451
war damage, 432
warm sites
    backup storage, 307
    disaster recovery plans, 461–462
    hardware, 465
warranties in third-party remediation, 361
weak culture, 69
weaknesses
    SWOT analysis, 59
    undiscovered, 128
weaponization in intrusion kill chain
    model, 410
web content filters
    incident response tools, 504
    overview, 289–290
web sites for awareness training
    communication, 344
WFH (work from home) as disruptive
    technology, 253
whaling, 291
whitelists
    applications, 296
    e-mail, 291
whole-disk encryption, 295
wildfires, 428–429
windstorms, 429
wiperware, 409
wire transfer fraud, 280
wireless network protection,
    287–288
Wireshark packet-sniffing tool,
    287–288
work centers for disasters, 443
work from home (WFH) as disruptive
    technology, 253
work measurement, monitoring, 30
work sites in business continuity
    plans, 453

workforce in disaster recovery plans, 465
workforce transformation policies in security
  strategy, 42
workplace access control, 366
workshops in CSA life cycle, 338
worms, endpoint protection for, 295
wrap-up for audits, 329

X

XDR (extended detection and response)
  systems, 297

Z

Zachman Framework, 81–82
zero-trust (ZT) network architecture, 292–293